Beverly Morrow, Photo Stylist, and Charles E. Walton, Senior Foods Photographer

Margaret Chason, Associate Foods Editor, and Lynn Lloyd, Test Kitchens Director

Jean Wickstrom Liles, Foods Editor

Introducing the *Southern Living* Foods Staff

On these pages we show the Foods Staff (left to right in each photograph) at work as they compile, test, taste, and photograph the recipes that appear each month in *Southern Living.*

Center right: *Susan M. McIntosh and Deborah Garrison, Assistant Foods Editors*

Center far right: *Carroll Sessions, Fran Tyler, and Diane Hogan, Test Kitchens Staff*

Right: *Catherine B. Garrison, Wanda Butler, and Cathy Chumney, Editorial Assistants*

Connie Shedd, Test Kitchens Staff; Susan M. McIntosh, Assistant Foods Editor; Betsy Fannin, Assistant Foods Editor; Carroll Sessions, Test Kitchens Staff; Diane Hogan, Test Kitchens Staff; Margaret Chason, Associate Foods Editor; Gary E. McCalla, Editor; Jean Wickstrom Liles, Foods Editor; Deborah Garrison, Assistant Foods Editor; Fran Tyler, Test Kitchens Staff; Peggy Smith, Test Kitchens Staff; Susan Payne, Assistant Foods Editor; and Lynn Lloyd, Test Kitchens Director

Susan Payne and Betsy Fannin, Assistant Foods Editors

Peggy Smith and Connie Shedd, Test Kitchens Staff

Southern Living®
1983 ANNUAL RECIPES

Oxmoor House, Inc., Birmingham

Copyright 1983 by Oxmoor House, Inc.
Book Division of the Southern Progress Corporation
P.O. Box 2463, Birmingham, Alabama 35201

Southern Living® 1983 Annual Recipes

Southern Living® is a federally registered trademark of Southern
Living, Inc. *Breakfasts & Brunches™*, *Summer Suppers®*,
Holiday Dinners™, and *Holiday Desserts™* are trademarks of
Southern Living, Inc.

Library of Congress Catalog Number: 79-88364
ISBN: 0-8487-0548-3

Manufactured in the United States of America
First Printing 1983

Southern Living®:
    Foods Editor: Jean Wickstrom Liles
    Associate Foods Editor: Margaret Chason
    Assistant Foods Editors: Betsy Fannin, Deborah Garrison,
        Susan M. McIntosh, Susan Payne
    Test Kitchens Director: Lynn Lloyd
    Test Kitchens Staff: Diane Hogan, Carroll Sessions, Connie
        Shedd, Peggy Smith, Fran Tyler
    Photo Stylist: Beverly Morrow
    Editorial Assistants: Wanda Butler, Cathy Chumney,
        Catherine Garrison
    Production Manager: Clay Nordan
    Photographers: Charles Walton: cover, i, ii, iii, iv, 27, 28, 62
        top left, 64, 98, 131, 132, 165, 166, 167, 168, 201, 235,
        236, 237, 238, 271, 272 bottom right, 273, 274, 308, 309,
        310; John O'Hagan: 62 top and bottom right, 63, 97, 272
        top right and bottom left, 307; Jim Bathie: pages 61, 202;
        Jean Wickstrom Liles: ii top left

Oxmoor House, Inc.:
    Manager, Editorial Projects: Ann H. Harvey
    Editor: Annette Thompson
    Editorial Assistant: Patty E. Howdon
    Production: Jerry Higdon

    Designer: Carol Middleton
    Illustrator: Cindia Pickering

Cover: *The rich traditions of Christmas offer a variety of festive
breads. Front to back: Holiday Braid (page 295), Saffron Rolls
(page 296), Portuguese Round Bread (page 295), and Eggnog Bread
(page 294).*

Page i: *You won't miss the meat in filling main dishes like our
Vegetable Fettuccine (page 312), Cheesy Zucchini Quiche (page 312),
and Bean Chalupas (page 313).*

Page iv: *Citrus brings delightful flavor to Fresh Orange Cake (page
300) and Lemon Gold Cake (page 301).*

Table of Contents

Country-Style Coleslaw (page 59)

Fruit-Stuffed Goose (page 320)

Créme de Menthe Brownies (page 244)

Our Year at Southern Living®

One of the greatest joys of a foods editor is receiving a positive response from readers. Overwhelmed by your happy response to our annual cookbook series, our Foods Staff is pleased to present our *1983 Annual Recipes.* Your letters tell us you've been delighted to have a permanent record of the year's favorite recipes all in one volume. You have enjoyed the convenience of not having to clip each month's recipes, enabling you to keep each issue of *Southern Living* intact.

Since we introduced our first *Annual Recipes* cookbook in 1979, the series has proved to be one of your favorite cookbook collections. Already a Southern tradition, our fifth *Southern Living®️ Annual Recipes* gives you the pick of the South's most cherished recipes.

We're sure you'll make *1983 Annual Recipes* our most successful volume yet. Every recipe that appeared on the pages of *Southern Living* in 1983 has been collected in this cookbook—and this year's volume is our biggest and best ever.

The recipes in *1983 Annual Recipes* come from cooks who are well known for the delicious food they serve their family and friends. Each recipe chosen for this volume is a time-honored treasure that has first been perfected in the contributor's home and then re-tested in our test kitchens by our staff of home economists. Here contributor recipes undergo the most rigorous scrutiny in terms of taste,

appearance, cost, originality, and ease of preparation to assure you of perfect results every time.

1983 Annual Recipes is organized into monthly chapters, and within each chapter the recipes spotlight seasonal foods: avocados in January, asparagus in March, stuffed summer vegetables in June, eggplant in August, pecans and peanuts in October, and gift food ideas throughout December.

Since Southerners enjoy entertaining in their homes, we feature in *Southern Living* special entertaining sections in addition to our regular monthly food sections. In March we share a Mexican brunch plus other exciting new ways to entertain your family and friends in our *Breakfasts & Brunches.* Our July *Summer Suppers* offers old-fashioned fun with a catfish fry along with a variety of dishes perfect for hot summer days.

Our holiday gift to you is our November *Holiday Dinners* and our December *Holiday Desserts.* In *Holiday Dinners* you'll find a wealth of recipes and ideas—an elegant dinner with all the trimmings, a quick-and-easy company menu, plus wonderful desserts appropriate for any occasion. Desserts are favorites among our readers, and many of you are "famous" in your hometown for your holiday specialties. Choosing from your favorite recipes for *Holiday Desserts* was a great challenge because there were so many dazzling desserts to select. We

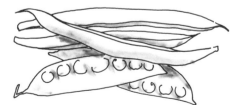

think our holiday pages offer much to help you celebrate the season.

During the past few years we introduced several new monthly features in the magazine. We've incorporated your ideas in our feature "From Our Kitchen to Yours." Prepared by our test kitchens director, this column is designed to answer the many questions you are asking about food preparation. This year you'll find a brief description of each "From Our Kitchen to Yours" in the Month-by-Month Index.

Each year more and more of you are using microwave ovens on a daily basis,

so our "Microwave Cookery" feature has been very popular with those of you who are both time and energy conscious. To aid you in locating these recipes in the indexes, we have preceded all microwave recipe page numbers with an "M."

Your favorable response to our "Cooking Light" feature convinced us you wanted and needed more low-calorie and low-sodium recipes for the South's favorite foods. Look for the "Cooking Light" category in the General Recipe Index for a complete listing of all "Cooking Light" recipes.

Enjoy your *1983 Annual Recipes.* It represents both a busy year at *Southern Living* and the best recipes of 1983. We believe you'll find this cookbook a welcome and helpful addition to your kitchen library.

Jean Wickstrom Liles

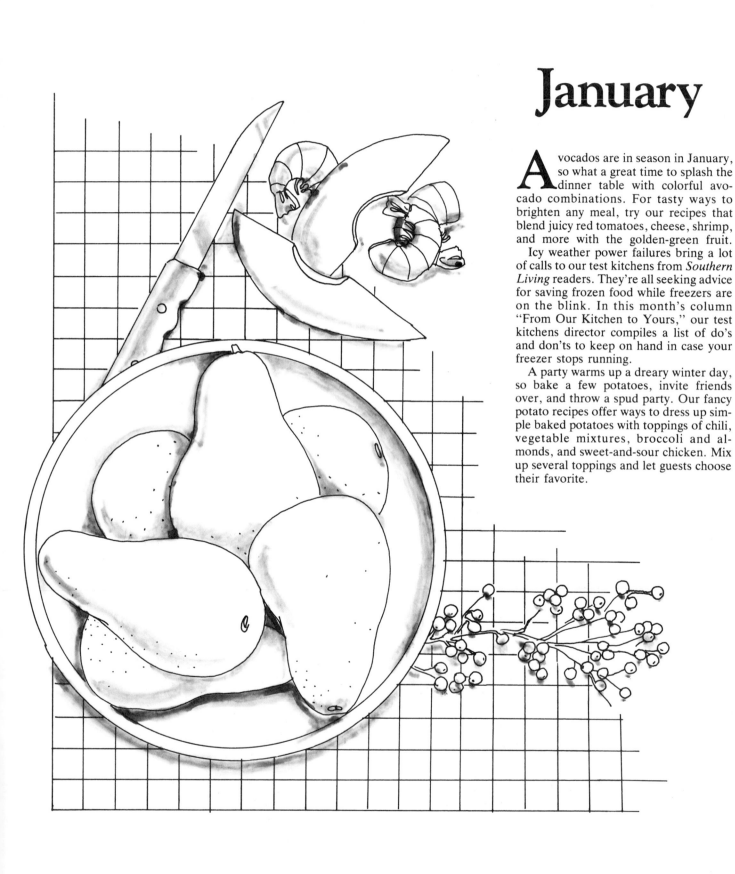

January

Avocados are in season in January, so what a great time to splash the dinner table with colorful avocado combinations. For tasty ways to brighten any meal, try our recipes that blend juicy red tomatoes, cheese, shrimp, and more with the golden-green fruit.

Icy weather power failures bring a lot of calls to our test kitchens from *Southern Living* readers. They're all seeking advice for saving frozen food while freezers are on the blink. In this month's column "From Our Kitchen to Yours," our test kitchens director compiles a list of do's and don'ts to keep on hand in case your freezer stops running.

A party warms up a dreary winter day, so bake a few potatoes, invite friends over, and throw a spud party. Our fancy potato recipes offer ways to dress up simple baked potatoes with toppings of chili, vegetable mixtures, broccoli and almonds, and sweet-and-sour chicken. Mix up several toppings and let guests choose their favorite.

Accent The Meal With Avocados

The nutty-tasting avocado has been winning its way into the favor and onto the tables of Southerners. This green- and golden-fleshed fruit has brought with it a wealth of tasty ideas and uses for its versatile flavor.

You'll want to prepare avocados as close to serving time as possible; like bananas, they turn brown when exposed to air. Rubbing lemon or lime juice on cut surfaces helps preserve the color.

If you must store already cut half shells, put the seed back in place to keep the avocado from darkening. Then fit the shells together, wrap tightly in plastic wrap or foil, and refrigerate.

Be certain to purchase avocados several days before you plan to use them; they'll need to sit at room temperature to soften. To check for ripeness, cradle an avocado in both palms and squeeze gently. Ripe fruit will yield to gentle pressure. If necessary, you can speed the ripening process. Place firm avocados in a closed paper bag, and put in a warm place. After ripening, avocados can be stored in the refrigerator up to one week.

CRISPY TOSTADAS

½ pound ground beef
¼ teaspoon salt
⅛ teaspoon pepper
1 (16-ounce) can refried beans
6 (6-inch) flour tortillas
Vegetable oil
2 medium tomatoes, chopped
2 cups shredded lettuce
2 ripe avocados, peeled, seeded, and sliced
3 cups (12 ounces) shredded Cheddar
  cheese
Commercial picante sauce (optional)

Combine ground beef, salt, and pepper in a skillet; cook until beef is browned, stirring to crumble meat. Drain off pan drippings; set beef aside.

Heat beans in a small saucepan over medium heat. Set aside.

Fry tortillas, one at a time, in ¼ inch hot oil (375°) 20 to 30 seconds on each side or until crisp and golden brown. Drain on paper towels.

Spread beans over warm tortillas. Spoon meat, tomatoes, lettuce, avocados, and cheese on tortillas. Serve with picante sauce, if desired. Yield: 6 servings. *Carolyn Look, El Paso, Texas.*

CHICKEN-AVOCADO SALAD PLATTER

1 (8-ounce) jar commercial spicy-sweet
  French dressing
4 slices bacon, cooked and crumbled
½ cup crumbled blue cheese
½ head lettuce, shredded
2 cups chopped tomatoes
2 cups diced cooked chicken
2 hard-cooked eggs, chopped
1 ripe avocado, peeled, seeded, and sliced

Combine first 3 ingredients; mix well. Arrange shredded lettuce on a serving platter. Layer remaining ingredients over lettuce. Serve with dressing. Yield: 4 to 6 servings. *Mrs. H. G. Drawdy, Spindale, North Carolina.*

AVOCADO-CRABMEAT SANDWICHES

2 (6-ounce) cans crabmeat, drained and
  flaked
¼ cup mayonnaise
2 tablespoons lemon juice
1 teaspoon dried whole dillweed
¼ teaspoon white pepper
6 slices rye bread
Softened butter
3 ripe avocados, peeled, seeded, and sliced
3 slices bacon, cooked and crumbled

Combine first 5 ingredients in a small bowl; mix well, and chill thoroughly.

Toast bread on both sides; lightly butter one side of each slice. Spread crab mixture evenly over toast; top sandwiches with avocado slices and crumbled bacon. Yield: 6 servings.

SHRIMP-FILLED AVOCADOS

½ cup vegetable oil
½ cup lime or lemon juice
2 tablespoons vinegar
2 teaspoons capers
1½ teaspoons salt
½ teaspoon dillseeds
½ teaspoon dry mustard
Dash of ground red pepper
1 pound fresh medium shrimp, cooked,
  peeled, and deveined
3 or 4 ripe avocados

Combine first 8 ingredients in a large bowl; stir in shrimp. Cover and marinate overnight in the refrigerator.

Drain shrimp, reserving marinade. Cut avocados in half lengthwise; remove seed, and peel. Brush avocados with reserved marinade, and fill with shrimp mixture. Yield: 6 to 8 servings.

AVOCADO ACAPULCO

2 large tomatoes, cut into wedges
1 (14-ounce) can artichoke hearts, drained
½ cup chopped ripe olives
1 cup commercial Italian dressing
¼ cup tarragon vinegar
1 clove garlic, minced
2 ripe avocados
¼ cup lemon juice
Lettuce leaves

Arrange tomatoes, artichokes, and olives in a single layer in a shallow container. Combine next 3 ingredients in a jar. Cover tightly, and shake vigorously. Pour over vegetables. Cover and chill overnight.

Peel avocados; remove seeds, and thinly slice. Sprinkle avocados with lemon juice. Arrange avocado slices on lettuce leaves. Spoon salad over avocados using a slotted spoon. Yield: 6 to 8 servings. *Sylvia Pettit, Austin, Texas.*

Fancy Potatoes? Spoon On A Topping

Baked potatoes are usually served as a side dish, but when covered with these flavorful toppings they're hearty enough to be served as the entrée.

When selecting potatoes for baking, choose fairly large ones that have a uniform oval or oblong shape. Avoid potatoes that have wrinkled skin, deep-set eyes, cut surfaces, or a green appearance (caused by sunburn).

It's best to store baking potatoes in a cool, dark, well-ventilated place. At a temperature of about 45°F. they will keep for several weeks; at room temperature, only one week. Never store potatoes in the refrigerator, or they'll develop a sweet taste, the result of potato starch turning to sugar.

Most medium or large potatoes bake in 45 minutes to 1 hour at 400°F. However, it's possible to bake them along with whatever else you have in the oven, as long as the baking temperature is at least 325°F. and no higher than 450°F. Wrapping in foil is not recommended, as this steams, rather than bakes, the potatoes.

Baked potatoes are done if they feel soft when mashed with mitted hands or tested with a fork. For a softer skin on the baked potato, rub the outside with vegetable oil before baking.

If versatility isn't reason enough to enjoy baked potatoes, then consider their nutritional value. The potato is an excellent source of vitamin C and is low in fat, cholesterol, and sodium. Calorie counters need not shy away from potatoes; one 5-ounce baked potato "weighs in" at only about 100 calories. Just remember that a tablespoon of butter will double the number of calories in a baked potato. So if you're watching the scales, select a low-calorie topping.

CHILI-TOPPED POTATOES

4 large baking potatoes
Vegetable oil
½ pound ground beef
⅓ cup finely chopped onion
1 clove garlic, minced
1 (8-ounce) can tomato sauce
½ cup water
1 to 1½ tablespoons chili powder
¼ teaspoon salt
¼ teaspoon pepper
Shredded Cheddar cheese
Chopped green onion

Wash potatoes, and rub with oil. Bake at 400° for 1 hour or until soft when pierced with a fork.

Cook ground beef, onion, and garlic in a large skillet until beef is browned, stirring to crumble. Drain well. Add next 5 ingredients; reduce heat and simmer 30 minutes or until thickened.

Split tops of potatoes lengthwise, and fluff pulp with a fork. Spoon topping over potatoes. Sprinkle with cheese and green onion. Yield: 4 servings.

MEXICAN-TOPPED POTATOES

6 large baking potatoes
Vegetable oil
½ pound hot bulk pork sausage
1 pound process American cheese, cubed
¼ cup milk
1 (10-ounce) can tomatoes and green chiles, undrained and chopped
Shredded lettuce
Chopped tomato

Wash potatoes, and rub with oil. Bake at 400° for 1 hour or until soft when pierced with a fork.

Cook sausage until browned, stirring to crumble; drain well. Combine cheese and milk in top of a double boiler; bring water to a boil. Reduce heat to low; cook until cheese melts. Stir in sausage and tomatoes and green chiles.

Split tops of potatoes lengthwise, and fluff pulp with a fork. Spoon topping over potatoes. Sprinkle with lettuce and tomato. Yield: 6 servings.

CHEESY FRANK-TOPPED POTATOES

4 large baking potatoes
Vegetable oil
¼ cup finely chopped onion
¼ cup chopped green pepper
2 tablespoons butter or margarine
2 tablespoons all-purpose flour
1¾ cups milk
1 cup (4 ounces) shredded Cheddar cheese
2 tablespoons chopped pimiento
½ teaspoon salt
¼ teaspoon pepper
4 frankfurters, cut in ¼-inch slices
½ cup (2 ounces) shredded Cheddar cheese

Wash potatoes, and rub with oil. Bake at 400° for 1 hour or until soft when pierced with a fork.

Sauté onion and green pepper in butter in a medium saucepan until tender. Add flour, stirring until smooth. Cook 1 minute, stirring constantly. Gradually add milk; cook over medium heat, stirring constantly, until thickened and bubbly. Stir in next 5 ingredients; stir until cheese melts.

Split tops of potatoes lengthwise, and fluff pulp with a fork. Spoon topping over potatoes; top each with 2 tablespoons cheese. Yield: 4 servings.

CRABMEAT-TOPPED POTATOES

4 large baking potatoes
Vegetable oil
¼ cup chopped pecans
1 tablespoon butter or margarine
¼ cup chopped green onion
¼ cup chopped green pepper
1 (8-ounce) package cream cheese, softened
¼ cup milk
1 (6-ounce) can crabmeat, drained and flaked
½ cup commercial sour cream
½ teaspoon white pepper
¼ teaspoon garlic powder
Fresh parsley sprigs

Wash potatoes, and rub with oil. Bake at 400° for 1 hour or until soft when pierced with a fork.

Sauté pecans in butter 1 minute. Add onion and green pepper; sauté 2 additional minutes. Add cream cheese, milk, and crabmeat; cook over low heat, stirring constantly, until smooth. Remove from heat, and stir in next 3 ingredients.

Split tops of potatoes lengthwise, and fluff pulp with a fork. Spoon topping over potatoes. Garnish with parsley sprigs. Yield: 4 servings.

AVOCADO-TOPPED POTATOES

4 large baking potatoes
Vegetable oil
2 (3-ounce) packages cream cheese, softened
1 ripe avocado, peeled and mashed
2 tablespoons milk
1 tablespoon lemon juice
1 tablespoon grated onion
¼ teaspoon salt
4 slices bacon, cooked and crumbled
2 small tomatoes, cut into wedges

Wash potatoes, and rub with oil. Bake at 400° for 1 hour or until soft when pierced with a fork.

Beat cream cheese with electric mixer until smooth. Add avocado and milk, beating until smooth. Stir in lemon juice, onion, and salt.

Split tops of potatoes lengthwise, and fluff pulp with a fork. Spoon topping over potatoes. Sprinkle with bacon, and top with tomato. Yield: 4 servings.

BROCCOLI-AND-ALMOND-TOPPED POTATOES

4 large baking potatoes
Vegetable oil
1 medium onion, chopped
1 clove garlic, crushed
2 tablespoons vegetable oil
1 (10-ounce) package frozen broccoli spears
1½ cups chicken broth
1 teaspoon vinegar
1 tablespoon cornstarch
1 tablespoon soy sauce
⅓ cup slivered almonds, toasted
¼ cup diced pimiento

Wash potatoes, and rub with oil. Bake at 400° for 1 hour or until soft when pierced with a fork.

Sauté onion and garlic in 2 tablespoons oil in a large skillet until onion is tender. Add broccoli, chicken broth, and vinegar, stirring gently.

Combine cornstarch and soy sauce, stirring well; add to broccoli mixture. Cook, stirring constantly, until thickened. Stir in almonds and pimiento.

Split tops of potatoes lengthwise, and fluff pulp with a fork. Spoon topping over potatoes. Yield: 4 servings.

GARDEN-TOPPED POTATOES

4 large baking potatoes
Vegetable oil
1 large green pepper, coarsely chopped
1 cup sliced green onion
1 clove garlic, crushed
3 tablespoons butter or margarine
1 cup sliced zucchini
**2 medium tomatoes, unpeeled and
  chopped**
¾ cup whipping cream
¼ cup grated Parmesan cheese
¼ teaspoon salt
Dash of pepper

Wash potatoes, and rub with oil. Bake at 400° for 1 hour or until soft when pierced with a fork.

Sauté green pepper, onion, and garlic in butter in a large skillet 2 to 3 minutes. Stir in zucchini; sauté 1 to 2 minutes. Add tomatoes; cook 2 minutes. Stir in next 4 ingredients; cook until thoroughly heated.

Split tops of potatoes lengthwise, and fluff pulp with a fork. Spoon topping over potatoes. Yield: 4 servings.

SWEET-AND-SOUR-TOPPED POTATOES

4 large baking potatoes
Vegetable oil
2 small onions, thinly sliced
1 large green pepper, cut into thin strips
3 tablespoons butter or margarine
2 cups pineapple juice, divided
¼ cup firmly packed dark brown sugar
¼ cup vinegar
3 tablespoons soy sauce
⅛ teaspoon hot sauce
3 tablespoons cornstarch
2 cups diced cooked chicken
¼ cup sliced cooked carrots

Wash potatoes, and rub with oil. Bake at 400° for 1 hour or until soft when pierced with a fork.

Sauté onion and green pepper in butter in a large skillet 5 minutes. Add 1¾ cups pineapple juice; bring to a boil. Stir in sugar, vinegar, soy sauce, and hot sauce. Combine remaining pineapple juice and cornstarch, stirring well; gradually add to vegetable mixture. Bring to a boil, reduce heat, and simmer 3 minutes. Add chicken and carrots; cook until thoroughly heated.

Split tops of potatoes lengthwise, and fluff pulp with a fork. Spoon topping over potatoes. Yield: 4 servings.

They All Enjoy His Cooking

Practically everyone around Whiteville, North Carolina, has heard of Frank Gault. Throughout the years, his cooking has satisfied the hearty appetites of thousands.

When entertaining, he finds Curried Beef Dinner gets a lot of attention. Featuring 18 condiments ranging from fresh vegetables to raisins and nuts, the dish gets everyone involved in the action.

Frank also cooks a special Chili Meat Sauce, which he serves over spaghetti. "I like it because it's not heavy with tomatoes," he says. Seasoned with garlic powder, oregano, curry powder, and chili powder, the sauce is good over hot dogs, too.

Frank's Shrimp Stew is a tasty and unusual dish that begins by cooking the shrimp in a covered pan without adding water. "In 10 or 15 minutes, the shrimp will turn pink and will be sitting in their own juices," says Frank. Served over rice, Shrimp Stew is flavored with onion, green pepper, and Sauterne.

Following Frank's specialties are favorite recipes from other men who also enjoy cooking.

CURRIED BEEF DINNER

¼ pound fresh mushrooms, sliced
½ cup chopped onion
2 tablespoons butter or margarine
2 tablespoons all-purpose flour
2 cups beef broth
**3 pounds boneless lean beef, cut into
  ½-inch cubes**
2 tablespoons bacon drippings
½ teaspoon curry powder
1 teaspoon salt
¼ teaspoon pepper
Hot cooked rice
Condiments

Sauté mushrooms and onion in butter in a large skillet until tender; add flour, stirring until smooth. Cook 1 minute, stirring constantly. Gradually add broth; cook over medium heat, stirring constantly, until gravy is thickened and bubbly. Set aside.

Brown beef in bacon drippings in a heavy Dutch oven. Cover and simmer 10 minutes, stirring occasionally. Add gravy mixture, curry powder, salt, and pepper; cover and simmer 20 minutes or until beef is tender.

Serve beef and gravy over rice with several of the following condiments: (about 1 cup each) chow mein noodles,

chopped tomato, chopped celery, chopped green pepper, chopped onion, shredded carrot, chopped hard-cooked egg, sweet pickle relish, bean sprouts, bamboo shoots, sliced water chestnuts, unpeeled chopped apple, cooked crumbled bacon, raisins, flaked coconut, salted peanuts, toasted slivered almonds, and chutney. Yield: 8 servings.

CHILI MEAT SAUCE

3 pounds ground beef
1 large onion, chopped
1 large green pepper, chopped
6 medium tomatoes, peeled and chopped
1 pound fresh mushrooms, sliced
**1 (10¾-ounce) can cream of mushroom
  soup, undiluted**
1 (10¾-ounce) can tomato soup, undiluted
3 tablespoons Worcestershire sauce
1 to 2 tablespoons chili powder
1 teaspoon salt
1 teaspoon garlic powder
1 teaspoon ground oregano
1 teaspoon curry powder
½ teaspoon pepper
Hot cooked spaghetti

Brown ground beef in a large Dutch oven, stirring to crumble; drain and remove beef, reserving 2 tablespoons drippings. Add onion and green pepper to drippings; sauté until tender. Add beef and remaining ingredients except spaghetti; stir well. Reduce heat and simmer, uncovered, 4 hours, stirring occasionally. Serve over spaghetti. Yield: 12 servings.

SHRIMP STEW

**5 pounds fresh shrimp, peeled and
  deveined**
¼ cup plus 2 tablespoons bacon drippings
½ cup all-purpose flour
1 large onion, chopped
1 large green pepper, chopped
3 cups water
2 teaspoons Old Bay Seasoning
1 teaspoon salt
¼ to ½ teaspoon pepper
½ cup Sauterne or other dry white wine
Hot cooked rice

Place shrimp in a heavy skillet. Cover tightly, and simmer over medium-low heat in own juices 15 to 20 minutes. Remove from heat, and set aside.

Heat bacon drippings in a heavy Dutch oven; stir in flour. Cook over medium heat 10 minutes or until roux is the color of a copper penny, stirring often. Add onion and green pepper; cook until tender. Gradually add water, stirring constantly; bring to a boil. Reduce heat; simmer 10 to 15 minutes.

Add shrimp with its cooking liquid and seasonings; simmer, uncovered, 20 minutes. Stir in wine. Serve over rice. Yield: about 1 quart.

SPICY FRIED CHICKEN

1¼ cups all-purpose flour
¾ cup finely crushed potato chips
1 teaspoon chili powder
½ teaspoon paprika
⅛ teaspoon garlic powder
Pepper to taste
2 eggs
1 tablespoon water
8 chicken breast halves, boned and skinned
½ cup butter or margarine
1 medium onion, chopped
2 tablespoons butter or margarine
1½ cups milk

Combine first 6 ingredients; mix well, and set aside. Combine eggs and water in a shallow dish; beat until blended. Dip chicken in egg mixture, and dredge in flour mixture. Reserve remaining flour mixture.

Melt ½ cup butter in a large skillet over medium-low heat. Add chicken, and cook about 10 minutes on each side or until golden brown. Drain chicken on paper towels, and keep warm.

Add onion and 2 tablespoons butter to skillet; sauté until tender. Stir in 3 tablespoons reserved flour mixture; cook 1 minute, stirring constantly. Gradually add milk. Cook over medium heat, stirring constantly, until thickened and bubbly. Serve with chicken. Yield: 8 servings.
Greg Sisserson,
Garland, Texas.

DILLY CHEESE BREAD

3 cups biscuit mix
1½ cups (6 ounces) shredded sharp Cheddar cheese
1 tablespoon sugar
½ teaspoon dried whole dillweed
½ teaspoon dry mustard
1¼ cups milk
1 egg, beaten
1 tablespoon vegetable oil

Combine first 5 ingredients in a large mixing bowl; mix well. Add remaining ingredients; stir just until dry ingredients are moistened.

Spoon batter into a greased 9- x 5- x 3-inch loafpan. Bake at 350° for 50 minutes or until loaf is golden brown. Yield: 1 loaf.
George Barr,
Birmingham, Alabama.

TANGY CRAB DIP

¼ cup mayonnaise
1 tablespoon prepared mustard
1 tablespoon Worcestershire sauce
1 teaspoon lemon juice
Dash of seasoned salt
Dash of hot sauce
½ pound fresh crabmeat, drained and flaked

Combine first 6 ingredients; mix well. Stir in crabmeat. Serve with assorted crackers. Yield: 1½ cups.
Tom W. Justice,
Gulf Breeze, Florida.

New Ideas For Frozen Vegetables

Versatile as well as convenient, frozen vegetables lend themselves nicely to being deep fried, simmered, and served in a sweet-and-sour sauce or baked in a cheesy casserole. Consider these time-saving recipes.

CHEESY ITALIAN BROCCOLI BAKE

1 (12-ounce) package wide egg noodles
1 tablespoon vegetable oil
2 (10-ounce) packages frozen broccoli spears
1 (16-ounce) carton cream-style cottage cheese
¼ cup commercial sour cream
2 (15½-ounce) jars commercial spaghetti sauce
3 cups (12 ounces) shredded mozzarella cheese

Cook noodles according to package directions; drain. Stir in vegetable oil, and set aside.

Cook broccoli according to package directions; drain and set aside. Combine cottage cheese and sour cream; mix well, and set aside.

Layer one-third of noodles, half of broccoli, one-third of spaghetti sauce, and one-third of mozzarella in a lightly greased 13- x 9- x 2-inch baking dish; repeat layers once.

Spoon cottage cheese mixture over mozzarella; top with remaining noodles and remaining sauce. Bake, uncovered, at 350° for 25 minutes; sprinkle with remaining mozzarella. Bake an additional 5 minutes or until cheese melts. Yield: 8 servings.
Gloria Fields,
Johnson City, Tennessee.

SCALLOPED MIXED VEGETABLES

1 (10-ounce) package frozen mixed vegetables
1 tablespoon butter or margarine
1 tablespoon all-purpose flour
½ teaspoon dry mustard
½ cup milk
½ cup (2 ounces) shredded Cheddar cheese
¾ teaspoon Worcestershire sauce
¼ teaspoon salt
Dash of red pepper
Dash of black pepper
¼ cup chopped onion
¼ cup soft breadcrumbs
1 tablespoon butter or margarine, melted

Cook frozen mixed vegetables in a medium saucepan according to package directions; drain well, and set aside.

Melt 1 tablespoon butter in a heavy saucepan over low heat; add flour and mustard, stirring until smooth. Cook 1 minute, stirring constantly. Gradually add milk; cook over medium heat, stirring constantly, until thickened and bubbly. Add cheese, Worcestershire sauce, salt, and pepper; stir until cheese melts. Stir cheese sauce and onion into vegetables; mix well. Spoon mixture into a greased 1-quart casserole. Combine breadcrumbs and melted butter; sprinkle over vegetable mixture. Bake, uncovered, at 375° for 20 minutes or until bubbly. Yield: 4 servings.
Janet G. Comegys,
Doraville, Georgia.

FRIED CAULIFLOWER

1 cup all-purpose flour
1 teaspoon salt
Pinch of baking powder
1 teaspoon paprika
1 cup beer
1 egg, beaten
2 tablespoons vegetable oil
2 (10-ounce) packages frozen cauliflower, thawed
Additional vegetable oil
Grated Parmesan cheese (optional)

Combine first 4 ingredients; mix well. Add beer, egg, and 2 tablespoons oil; stir until smooth. Dip cauliflower into batter; fry in deep hot oil (375°) until golden. Drain well. Sprinkle with Parmesan cheese, if desired. Yield: 4 to 6 servings.
Mrs. John H. Kolek,
Lakeland, Florida.

SWEET-AND-SOUR GREEN BEANS AND CARROTS

1 cup chopped carrots
¾ cup water
1 (9-ounce) package frozen cut green beans
2 slices bacon
1 medium onion, coarsely chopped
1 medium apple, peeled, cored, and cut into wedges
2 tablespoons vinegar
1 tablespoon sugar
¼ teaspoon salt

Combine carrots and water in a saucepan; bring to a boil. Cover, reduce heat, and simmer 5 minutes. Add green beans; return to a boil. Cover, reduce heat, and simmer 5 minutes or until vegetables are tender. Drain.

Cook bacon in a large skillet until crisp; remove bacon, reserving drippings in skillet. Crumble bacon, and set aside. Sauté onion in drippings until tender. Stir in apple, vinegar, sugar, and salt; cover and cook 3 to 4 minutes or until apple is tender. Stir in green bean mixture, and cook until thoroughly heated. Place in a serving dish, and sprinkle with bacon. Yield: 4 to 6 servings.

Carol Bowen,
Tifton, Georgia.

MICROWAVE COOKERY

Mastering Microwaved Pasta

Microwaved pasta is often a controversial subject because it takes about the same amount of time to microwave as it does to cook conventionally. Advocates of microwaved pasta insist their end product combines the desired *al dente* texture with better flavor. Others prefer to cook the pasta conventionally because this leaves the microwave oven free to cook a sauce to accompany the pasta.

As in all microwave cooking, you need to be alert and test your pasta as it cooks. If you cook a very thin and delicate type of noodle, such as vermicelli or thin spaghetti, it will cook faster than a thicker pasta, such as lasagna noodles or manicotti shells. We found it to be more effective to bring the water to a boil before adding the delicate pastas;

adding olive oil to the water also helped prevent delicate noodles from sticking.

One word of caution for microwaving pasta: If it microwaves too long, it becomes gummy and soft. To prevent overcooking, always check for doneness at the lower end of the microwaving time range. Also, be sure to stop and stir the pasta as directed in the recipes.

LASAGNA

1 pound lean ground beef
½ cup chopped onion
½ (16-ounce) package lasagna noodles
½ teaspoon salt
1 tablespoon vegetable oil
2 (8-ounce) cans tomato sauce
1 (6-ounce) can tomato paste
2 teaspoons dried whole oregano
2 teaspoons dried whole basil
½ teaspoon garlic powder
1 (12-ounce) carton small-curd cottage cheese
1 egg
½ teaspoon salt
2 (6-ounce) packages sliced mozzarella cheese
½ cup grated Parmesan cheese

Crumble beef into a 2-quart baking dish, and stir in onion. Cover with waxed paper. Microwave at HIGH for 5 to 7 minutes, stirring twice. Drain well.

Place lasagna noodles in a 12- x 8- x 2-inch baking dish; cover with water, and add ½ teaspoon salt. Cover with heavy-duty plastic wrap. Microwave at HIGH for 14 minutes, rearranging noodles after 7 minutes. Drain well.

Stir next 6 ingredients into beef mixture, mixing well.

Combine cottage cheese, egg, and ½ teaspoon salt; stir mixture well.

Spread half of meat sauce over bottom of a 12- x 8- x 2-inch baking dish. Top with half of lasagna noodles, half of cottage cheese mixture, and half of mozzarella cheese. Cover with half of remaining meat sauce. Repeat layers of noodles, cottage cheese, and mozzarella cheese; top with remaining meat sauce, and sprinkle with Parmesan cheese.

Cover and microwave at HIGH for 13 to 18 minutes, rotating dish at 5-minute intervals. Let stand 10 minutes. Yield: 6 servings.

STUFFED MANICOTTI

8 manicotti shells
Vegetable oil
1 (6-ounce) package sliced mozzarella cheese, diced
2 cups ricotta cheese
½ cup grated Romano cheese
1 (7¾-ounce) can spinach, drained well
½ teaspoon garlic powder
½ teaspoon salt
¼ teaspoon pepper
1 (15-ounce) can tomato sauce
⅛ teaspoon dried whole marjoram

Brush manicotti shells with vegetable oil; place in a 12- x 8- x 2-inch baking dish and cover with water. Cover with heavy-duty plastic wrap, and microwave at HIGH for 18 to 20 minutes; drain.

Set aside ⅓ cup diced mozzarella cheese for topping. Combine remaining mozzarella with next 6 ingredients, stirring well. Stuff manicotti shells with cheese filling. Return the filled shells to the 12- x 8- x 2-inch baking dish.

Pour tomato sauce over manicotti; sprinkle with reserved mozzarella cheese and marjoram. Cover and microwave at HIGH for 12 to 16 minutes, rotating the baking dish after 6 minutes. Yield: 8 servings.

A mixture of spinach and three kinds of cheese fills these manicotti shells. Then they're topped with tomato sauce, mozzarella cheese, and marjoram before microwaving.

When microwaving lasagna noodles, place them in a baking dish and add water to cover. A covering of heavy-duty plastic wrap holds in the steam while the noodles are cooking.

CHEESY PARMESAN NOODLES

6 cups water
½ teaspoon salt
1 tablespoon olive oil
1 (8-ounce) package thin spaghetti
½ cup butter or margarine
¾ cup grated Parmesan cheese
2 tablespoons half-and-half
3 tablespoons chopped fresh parsley
Freshly ground black pepper

Combine water, salt, and olive oil in a 12- x 8- x 2-inch baking dish. Cover with heavy-duty plastic wrap, and microwave at HIGH for 10 minutes. Add spaghetti; cover and microwave at HIGH for 8 minutes, stirring after 4 minutes. Let stand from 1 to 3 minutes; drain well.

Place butter in a 1-cup glass measure; microwave at HIGH for 1 minute or until melted. Pour over noodles, tossing well. Add remaining ingredients; toss until well mixed. Serve immediately. Yield: 6 servings.

MACARONI AND CHEESE

1 (8-ounce) package elbow macaroni
3 cups water
1 teaspoon salt
¼ cup butter or margarine
¼ cup plus 2 tablespoons all-purpose flour
1 teaspoon salt
2 cups milk
2 cups (8 ounces) shredded Cheddar cheese
Paprika

Combine macaroni, water, and 1 teaspoon salt in a 2-quart baking dish; cover with heavy-duty plastic wrap. Microwave at HIGH for 10 to 12 minutes, stirring after 5 minutes. Drain well.

Place butter in a 1-quart glass measure; microwave at HIGH for 55 seconds or until melted. Blend in flour and 1 teaspoon salt; stir until smooth. Gradually stir in milk; microwave at HIGH for 5½ to 7 minutes or until thickened, stirring at 1-minute intervals. Add cheese, and stir until melted.

Stir cheese sauce into macaroni, mixing well. Cover and microwave at MEDIUM HIGH (70% power) for 7 to 8 minutes, stirring after 4 minutes. Sprinkle with paprika. Let stand 2 minutes before serving. Yield: 6 to 8 servings.

Tip: Plastic bags that have been used to wrap dry foods, vegetables, and fruits can often be washed and reused.

A New Twist For Pot Roast

Pot roast doesn't have to be predictable. Our readers have combined a basic chuck roast with a variety of cooking liquids and a sometimes surprising choice of seasonings and vegetables.

To tenderize a roast, brown the meat to seal in the juices, then simmer slowly in liquid. Add herbs, spices, and vegetables during the simmering.

AUTUMN GOLD POT ROAST

¼ cup all-purpose flour
1 teaspoon salt
¼ teaspoon pepper
1 (3- to 4-pound) boneless chuck or arm roast
2 tablespoons vegetable oil
¾ cup water
½ teaspoon dried whole oregano
¼ teaspoon celery seeds
1¼ cups water
1 (6-ounce) can frozen orange juice concentrate, thawed, undiluted, and divided
4 medium-size sweet potatoes, peeled and halved lengthwise
8 small onions, peeled
1 tablespoon brown sugar

Combine first 3 ingredients; dredge roast in flour mixture. Set aside remaining flour mixture.

Brown roast on all sides in hot oil in a Dutch oven. Pour off drippings into a medium saucepan, and set aside. Combine ¾ cup water, oregano, and celery seeds; pour over roast. Cover and cook over low heat 2 hours.

Combine 1¼ cups water and ½ cup orange juice concentrate; mix well, and pour over roast. Add sweet potatoes and onions. Cover and cook over low heat 1 hour or until roast and vegetables are tender. Remove roast and vegetables to serving platter; keep warm.

Combine reserved flour mixture, remaining orange juice concentrate, and brown sugar; mix well. Stir orange juice mixture into pan drippings; cook over medium heat, stirring constantly, until thickened. Serve gravy with roast. Yield: 4 to 6 servings. *Tammy Smith, Talbott, Tennessee.*

PERFECT POT ROAST

1 (4-pound) boneless chuck roast
2 tablespoons vegetable oil
2 tablespoons butter or margarine, melted
1 small onion, sliced
1 teaspoon ground thyme
1 teaspoon ground marjoram
1 bay leaf, crushed
8 whole peppercorns
1 teaspoon salt
1 (10½-ounce) can consommé, undiluted
1 pound carrots, scraped and cut into 2-inch pieces
3 medium onions, quartered
3 tablespoons all-purpose flour
¼ cup water

Brown roast on all sides in hot oil and butter in a large Dutch oven over medium heat for 30 minutes. Add next 7 ingredients. Cover, reduce heat, and simmer 2 hours. Add carrot and onion; cover and simmer 1 hour.

Remove roast and vegetables to serving platter; strain pan drippings. Pour 2 cups strained drippings back into Dutch oven. Combine flour and water; stir until smooth. Pour flour mixture into drippings; cook, stirring constantly, until thickened. Serve gravy with roast. Yield: 8 servings. *Mrs. R. P. Hotaling, Martinez, Georgia.*

SPICY APPLE POT ROAST

2 cups apple juice
1 teaspoon salt
1 teaspoon ground cinnamon
¼ teaspoon ground ginger
¼ teaspoon ground cloves
¼ teaspoon pepper
1 (5-pound) boneless chuck roast
¼ cup all-purpose flour
2 tablespoons vegetable oil
3 tablespoons all-purpose flour

Combine first 6 ingredients in a large shallow container; add roast, turning to coat. Cover and marinate overnight in refrigerator.

Remove roast, reserving marinade. Dredge roast in ¼ cup flour. Brown roast on all sides in hot oil in a Dutch oven. Add reserved marinade; bring to a boil. Cover, reduce heat, and simmer 2½ hours or until roast is tender.

Remove roast to serving platter, reserving pan drippings. Combine 3 tablespoons flour and ½ cup pan drippings; stir until smooth. Pour flour mixture into remaining pan drippings; cook, stirring constantly, until thickened and bubbly. Serve gravy with roast. Yield: about 8 to 10 servings. *Marge Killmon, Annandale, Virginia.*

ROAST BEEF SUPREME

¼ pound salt pork, cubed
1 (3- to 3½-pound) boneless chuck roast
2 medium onions, chopped
1 cup chopped green pepper
1 (16-ounce) can whole tomatoes, undrained and coarsely chopped
1 cup commercial French salad dressing
1 quart water
2 carrots, scraped and thinly sliced
2 medium potatoes, peeled and cubed
½ cup chopped fresh mushrooms
½ cup chopped pimiento
¼ teaspoon pepper
3 cups frozen English peas, thawed

Place salt pork in a large ovenproof Dutch oven; cook over medium heat, stirring constantly, until browned. Push pork to side of pan; add roast, and brown on all sides. Remove pork and discard. Add next 5 ingredients to roast; cover and bake at 325° for 2 hours. Add carrots, potatoes, mushrooms, pimiento, and pepper; cover and bake 45 additional minutes. Add peas; cover and bake 15 additional minutes. Remove roast and vegetables to serving platter; serve with pan drippings. Yield: 6 servings.
Mrs. J. A. Satterfield,
Fort Worth, Texas.

SWEET-AND-SOUR POT ROAST

¼ cup all-purpose flour
1 teaspoon salt
⅛ teaspoon pepper
½ teaspoon celery seeds
1 (3- to 4-pound) boneless chuck roast
2 tablespoons vegetable oil
⅓ cup vinegar
2 tablespoons brown sugar
¼ cup water
¼ teaspoon ground nutmeg
6 small onions, peeled
½ cup sliced celery

Combine first 4 ingredients; dredge roast in flour mixture. Brown roast on all sides in hot oil in a large ovenproof Dutch oven.
Combine vinegar, brown sugar, water, and nutmeg; pour over roast. Cover and bake at 325° for 2 hours. Add onions and celery; cook 30 additional minutes or until roast and vegetables are tender. Yield: 6 to 8 servings.
Frances Jean Neely,
Jackson, Mississippi.

Tip: Freeze small portions of leftover meat or fowl until you have enough for a pot pie, curry, or rice casserole.

COOKING LIGHT

A Light Approach To Dinner For Two

Light the candles, turn on some music, and treat someone special to an elegant dinner. While this generally brings to mind fancy dishes high in calories, that need not be the case. Our "Cooking Light" dinner lets you take a diet-conscious approach to a special evening. Recipes are scaled for two, and calories total about 500 per person.

Knowing how much to buy and cook for two is the best way we know to avoid the temptation for second helpings. If you're cooking boned or ground meat or poultry, purchase about ½ pound for two servings; you'll need about ¾ pound if the meat contains some bone, such as with pork chops and steaks. Count on 1 to 2 pounds for very bony pieces of meat, such as ribs (but remember that ribs are very high in fat and should be avoided by dieters).

Plan on one whole chicken breast or one-half of a small broiler-fryer for two servings. Here's what you'll need for two servings of seafood: 1⅓ pounds of whole fish, ½ to ⅔ pound of fish fillets, and ½ to 1 pound of shucked or shelled crab, lobsters, scallops, oysters, and shrimp.

When buying fresh vegetables, such as mushrooms, green beans, eggplant, carrots, and potatoes, plan on ½ to ¾ pound for two servings. A 10-ounce package of frozen vegetables makes two or three servings. Although ½ pound of apples, peaches, bananas, and pears usually yields enough for two, you'll need 1 pound of grapefruit, oranges, strawberries, and other bulky fruit.

Tomato Bouillon
Chicken in Orange Sauce
or
Veal Scallopini
Herbed New Potatoes
Ginger Carrots
Lettuce Wedges   Tangy Dressing
Spiced Peach Dessert

TOMATO BOUILLON

2 cups tomato juice
1 medium onion, sliced
1 stalk celery, chopped
2 bay leaves
4 whole peppercorns
2 lemon wedges

Combine first 5 ingredients in a medium saucepan; cover and let stand for 1 hour.
Bring mixture to a boil; cover, reduce heat, and simmer 10 minutes. Strain mixture; discard vegetables. Serve hot or chilled; garnish with lemon wedges. Yield: 2 cups (about 46 calories per 1-cup serving).
Mrs. C. M. Florio,
Orlando, Florida.

CHICKEN IN ORANGE SAUCE

1 (1-pound) whole chicken breast, split and skinned
1 small onion, sliced and separated into rings
⅔ cup unsweetened orange juice
2 tablespoons dry sherry
1 tablespoon minced fresh parsley
½ tablespoon all-purpose flour
¾ teaspoon grated orange rind
Paprika
Orange slices

Place chicken breast halves in a shallow 1-quart casserole; arrange onion rings over each piece. Combine next 5 ingredients in a small saucepan; bring to a boil, stirring constantly.
Pour sauce over chicken; cover and bake at 350° for 30 minutes. Uncover and bake 25 to 30 additional minutes or until chicken is tender, basting occasionally with sauce. Sprinkle chicken with paprika, and garnish with orange slices. Yield: 2 servings (about 207 calories per serving).
Mrs. Delbert R. Snyder,
Williamsburg, Virginia.

VEAL SCALLOPINI

½ pound (¼-inch-thick) veal cutlets, trimmed
1½ tablespoons all-purpose flour
¼ teaspoon salt
¼ teaspoon freshly ground pepper
Vegetable cooking spray
2 teaspoons vegetable oil
⅓ cup Chablis or other dry white wine
2 tablespoons lemon juice
Lemon twists (optional)

Flatten veal to ⅛-inch thickness, using a meat mallet or rolling pin; cut into 2-inch pieces. Combine flour, salt, and pepper; dredge veal in flour mixture. Coat a large skillet with cooking spray; add oil to skillet, and place over medium-high heat until hot. Add veal, and cook 1 minute on each side or until lightly browned. Remove veal from skillet, and set aside.

Pour wine and lemon juice into skillet; bring to a boil. Return veal to skillet, turning to coat well; reduce heat and simmer 1 to 2 minutes or until sauce is slightly thickened, and the veal is thoroughly heated. Garnish with lemon twists, if desired. Yield: 2 servings (about 225 calories per serving).
Mrs. H. G. Drawdy,
Spindale, North Carolina.

HERBED NEW POTATOES

4 small new potatoes (about ½ pound)
2 teaspoons minced fresh parsley
2 teaspoons minced chives
2 teaspoons reduced-calorie margarine

Peel a ½-inch strip around center of each potato. Cook, covered, in boiling water 20 minutes or until tender. Drain potatoes; add remaining ingredients, tossing to coat. Yield: 2 servings (about 88 calories per serving).

GINGER CARROTS

3 medium carrots, cut into 3- x ¼-inch strips (about 1½ cups)
1 teaspoon reduced-calorie margarine
1 teaspoon brown sugar
⅛ teaspoon ground ginger

Cook carrots in a small amount of boiling water until crisp-tender; drain and set aside.

Melt margarine in saucepan; stir in sugar and ginger. Cook over medium-low heat, stirring constantly, until sugar is dissolved. Add carrots; cook, stirring gently, until carrots are well coated and thoroughly heated. Yield: 2 servings (about 48 calories per serving).

TANGY DRESSING

½ cup reduced-calorie mayonnaise
2 tablespoons lemon juice
2 tablespoons white wine vinegar
1 tablespoon Dijon mustard
2 tablespoons minced fresh parsley
2 tablespoons minced green olives
1 tablespoon minced onion
1 tablespoon minced celery
1 tablespoon minced capers
½ teaspoon freshly ground pepper

Combine first 4 ingredients; mix well. Stir in remaining ingredients; cover and chill 1 hour. Serve dressing over lettuce wedges. Yield: 1 cup (about 26 calories per tablespoon).

SPICED PEACH DESSERT

1 (16-ounce) can peach halves in unsweetened juice, undrained
½ teaspoon cornstarch
¼ teaspoon whole cloves
⅛ teaspoon ground cinnamon
Dash of ground nutmeg
Dash of ground cloves
⅛ teaspoon grated orange rind

Drain peaches, reserving juice; set aside. Combine cornstarch, spices, and orange rind in a medium saucepan; stir in reserved peach juice, mixing well. Add peaches; bring to a boil, stirring constantly. Reduce heat and simmer 2 minutes. Remove whole cloves, and serve warm. Yield: 2 servings (about 52 calories per serving).

Basic Breads To Bake In No Time

Supper's almost ready, and you have only a few minutes to think about the bread. For times like these, we compiled some basic bread recipes you can mix up quickly.

QUICK CHEESE BREAD

2 eggs
¾ cup water
1⅓ cups biscuit mix
1½ cups (6 ounces) shredded Cheddar cheese, divided
2 teaspoons dry mustard
2 tablespoons chopped fresh parsley
1 tablespoon butter or margarine

Beat eggs; stir in water. Add biscuit mix, mixing until smooth. Stir in 1 cup cheese, mustard, and parsley.

Spoon batter into a lightly greased 8-inch square pan. Sprinkle with remaining cheese, and dot with butter. Bake at 350° for 35 minutes. Cut into squares to serve. Yield: 9 servings.
Shirley Hodge,
Delray Beach, Florida.

ONE-EGG MUFFINS

2 cups all-purpose flour
2 teaspoons baking powder
½ teaspoon salt
1 tablespoon sugar
¾ cup milk
1 egg, beaten
⅓ cup shortening, melted

Combine first 4 ingredients; make a well in center of mixture. Combine milk, egg, and shortening; add to dry ingredients, stirring just until moistened. Spoon into greased muffin pans, filling two-thirds full. Bake at 425° for 20 minutes. Yield: 12 muffins.
Marian Cox,
Deming, New Mexico.

SESAME STICKS

2 cups all-purpose flour
2 teaspoons baking powder
½ teaspoon salt
¼ cup plus 1 tablespoon shortening
⅔ cup milk
2 tablespoons butter or margarine, melted
Sesame seeds

Combine first 3 ingredients, mixing well; cut in shortening with a pastry blender until mixture resembles coarse meal. Add milk, stirring until dry ingredients are moistened. Turn dough out onto a lightly floured surface; knead lightly 3 or 4 times.

Roll dough into a ¼-inch-thick rectangle; cut into 3- x 1-inch strips. Place on a lightly greased baking sheet. Brush tops with melted butter, and sprinkle with sesame seeds. Bake at 425° for 10 to 12 minutes or until golden brown. Yield: about 2½ dozen.

QUICK-AND-EASY CORNBREAD

1 cup self-rising flour
1 cup self-rising cornmeal
1 cup milk
¼ cup vegetable oil
1 egg, beaten

Combine all ingredients; mix well. Pour batter into a well-greased 8-inch cakepan. Bake at 450° for 25 minutes. Yield: 6 to 8 servings. *Marie Elrod,*
Warner Robins, Georgia.

Tip: Bread stays fresher longer at room temperature or frozen. Do not store bread in the refrigerator.

Squeeze In Some Citrus

Cakes, sauces, and even biscuits can benefit from a squeeze of fresh lemon juice or grated rind from an orange.

If your recipe calls for grated rind as well as juice, it's easier to grate it before squeezing. Leftover grated rind and juice can be frozen for as long as four months.

When buying fresh citrus, look for fruit with smooth, blemish-free skin. The juiciest fruit will feel firm and heavy for its size. Store citrus fruit in the refrigerator.

MIXED FRUIT AMBROSIA

1 (20-ounce) can pineapple chunks, undrained
2 teaspoons sugar
1 teaspoon grated orange rind
1 large pink grapefruit, peeled, seeded, and sectioned
3 medium oranges, peeled, seeded, and sectioned
2 bananas, sliced
½ cup flaked coconut

Drain pineapple, reserving ½ cup juice in a medium bowl. Add sugar and orange rind to juice, stirring well. Add pineapple, grapefruit, oranges, and bananas, tossing well. Cover and refrigerate several hours. Sprinkle with coconut to serve. Yield: 6 servings.
Mrs. Thomas Lee Adams,
Kingsport, Tennessee.

GRAPEFRUIT JUICE BISCUITS

2 cups all-purpose flour
1 tablespoon sugar
1 teaspoon baking soda
½ teaspoon salt
¼ cup shortening
½ cup plus 1 tablespoon fresh grapefruit juice

Combine first 4 ingredients; cut in shortening with pastry blender until mixture resembles coarse meal. Add grapefruit juice, stirring until dry ingredients are moistened. Turn dough out on a lightly floured surface; knead lightly 4 or 5 times. Roll dough to ½-inch thickness; cut with a 2-inch biscuit cutter. Place biscuits on a lightly greased baking sheet. Bake at 425° for 10 minutes or until golden brown. Yield: 1 dozen. *Emily Hardwick,*
Pinellas Park, Florida.

ORANGE-PECAN CRUNCH CAKE

½ cup finely chopped pecans
⅔ cup butter or margarine, softened
1½ cups sugar
3 eggs, separated
¾ cup milk
1 teaspoon grated orange rind
2 tablespoons orange juice
2⅓ cups all-purpose flour
2 teaspoons baking powder
¾ teaspoon salt
¼ teaspoon baking soda
1 teaspoon vanilla extract
½ teaspoon cream of tartar
Glaze (recipe follows)

Grease and flour a 10-inch Bundt pan; sprinkle pecans in pan. Set aside.

Cream butter; gradually add sugar, beating well. Add egg yolks, one at a time, beating well after each addition.

Combine milk, orange rind, and juice. Combine flour, baking powder, salt, and soda; add to creamed mixture alternately with milk mixture, beginning and ending with flour mixture. Stir in vanilla. Combine egg whites (at room temperature) and cream of tartar; beat until stiff peaks form. Fold into batter.

Pour batter into prepared pan; bake at 350° for 50 to 55 minutes or until a wooden pick inserted in center comes out clean. Cool in pan 10 minutes; remove from pan, and cool completely. Spoon glaze over cake. Yield: one 10-inch cake.

Glaze:

½ teaspoon grated orange rind
½ cup orange juice
¼ cup sugar
1 tablespoon butter or margarine

Combine all ingredients in a small saucepan; cook over medium heat, stirring constantly, until sugar dissolves and mixture is hot. Yield: about ¾ cup.
Mrs. Paul Raper,
Burgaw, North Carolina.

LEMON SPONGE CUPS

2 tablespoons butter or margarine, softened
¾ to 1 cup sugar
¼ cup all-purpose flour
1¾ teaspoons grated lemon rind
¼ cup plus 1 tablespoon lemon juice
1½ cups milk
3 eggs, separated
Powdered sugar (optional)

Cream butter; gradually add sugar, beating well. Add flour, lemon rind, and juice; beat until smooth. Combine milk and egg yolks; mix well. Add to creamed mixture, mixing well.

Beat egg whites (at room temperature) until stiff peaks form; gently fold into lemon mixture. Pour into six 6-ounce greased custard cups. Place cups in pan of hot water, and bake at 350° for 20 to 30 minutes or until browned.

Let stand 15 minutes. Sprinkle with powdered sugar, if desired. Yield: 6 servings. *Mrs. Paul Ritter,*
Lake Charles, Louisiana.

ORANGE SAUCE

1 (8-ounce) package cream cheese, softened
⅓ cup sugar
1 teaspoon vanilla extract
2 tablespoons grated orange rind
¼ cup orange juice

Combine cream cheese and sugar, beating until smooth. Add remaining ingredients, beating well. Serve over fruit. Yield: 1½ cups. *Susan Friesen,*
Montgomery, Alabama.

Barbecue Comes Indoors

Too cold for an outdoor barbecue? Then have one inside and barbecue the meat in your oven.

Bring smoky barbecue flavor indoors by dousing beef brisket with liquid smoke. Pour on commercial barbecue sauce during baking to give Barbecued Beef Brisket a sweet and spicy flavor.

SAUCY OVEN-BARBECUED STEAK

2 pounds boneless round steak
1 tablespoon vegetable oil
¾ cup catsup
½ cup water
½ cup cider vinegar
1 tablespoon brown sugar
1 tablespoon prepared mustard
1 tablespoon Worcestershire sauce
½ teaspoon salt
⅛ teaspoon pepper

Trim excess fat from steak, and cut into serving-size pieces. Heat oil in a large skillet; add steak, and brown on both sides. Transfer steak to a 2-quart shallow baking dish.

Combine remaining ingredients, stirring well; pour over steak. Cover and bake at 325° for 1½ hours or until tender. Yield: 6 to 8 servings.

Mrs. Joe D. Wilson,
Pulaski, Virginia.

BARBECUED BEEF BRISKET

1 (4- to 5-pound) beef brisket
½ teaspoon onion salt
½ teaspoon celery salt
¼ teaspoon garlic powder
2 tablespoons liquid smoke
¼ cup plus 2 tablespoons Worcestershire sauce
¾ cup commercial barbecue sauce

Sprinkle beef with salt and garlic powder; place in a shallow baking dish. Pour liquid smoke and Worcestershire sauce over meat, and cover with foil. Refrigerate several hours or overnight, turning once.

Bake, covered, at 300° for 4 to 4½ hours or until tender. Pour commercial barbecue sauce over beef and bake, uncovered, an additional 30 minutes. Yield: 8 to 10 servings.   *Rene Ralph,*
Newkirk, Oklahoma.

SPARERIBS WITH ORANGE BARBECUE SAUCE

4 pounds spareribs
1½ tablespoons lemon-pepper seasoning
1 (6-ounce) can frozen orange juice concentrate, undiluted
½ cup catsup
½ cup commercial hot barbecue sauce
¼ cup butter or margarine
2 tablespoons brown sugar
1 tablespoon soy sauce
2 teaspoons prepared mustard
4 to 5 green onions, finely chopped

Sprinkle both sides of ribs with lemon-pepper; cut into serving-size pieces. Place ribs in a single layer in a large, shallow roasting dish. Cover and bake at 350° for 45 minutes.

Combine remaining ingredients in a saucepan; simmer 10 minutes, stirring occasionally. Brush sauce over ribs; cover and bake an additional 45 minutes, basting and turning occasionally. Yield: 4 servings.   *H. W. Asbell,*
Leesburg, Florida.

Tip: Lower oven temperature 25° when using heat-proof glass dishes to ensure even baking.

SAUCY BARBECUED CHICKEN

⅔ cup catsup
⅓ cup red currant jelly
2 tablespoons Worcestershire sauce
¼ teaspoon hot sauce
1 (2½- to 3-pound) broiler-fryer, quartered

Combine first 4 ingredients in a small saucepan; mix well. Simmer mixture 10 minutes, stirring occasionally.

Place chicken in a lightly greased 13- x 9- x 2-inch baking dish; brush with half of sauce. Cover and bake at 350° for 45 minutes. Baste with remaining sauce; bake, uncovered, 15 minutes or until chicken is tender. Yield: 4 servings.   *Kay Castleman Cooper,*
Burke, Virginia.

OVEN-BARBECUED FRANKFURTERS

1 pound frankfurters
1 tablespoon all-purpose flour
2 tablespoons water
½ cup catsup
¼ cup finely chopped onion
2 tablespoons vinegar
1 tablespoon brown sugar
1½ tablespoons Worcestershire sauce
1 teaspoon paprika
1 teaspoon chili powder
¼ teaspoon salt
½ teaspoon pepper
Hot dog buns

Pierce each frankfurter several times with a fork, and place in a 10- x 6- x 2-inch baking dish. Combine flour and water in a small bowl, stirring until smooth. Add next 9 ingredients, stirring well; pour over frankfurters. Cover and bake at 350° for 40 minutes. Serve in warm buns. Yield: 4 to 5 servings.

Mrs. Herbert W. Rutherford,
Baltimore, Maryland.

Let Sausage Spice The Dish

Elsie Schmetzer is a two-time winner of the Kentucky Chicken Cooking Contest, but chicken's not her only specialty. Her recipe for Italian Sausage and Pepper Loaves made an instant hit with us. "It has most everything on it that a pizza has," she says, "but it's all served on a loaf."

SAUSAGE AND KRAUT

2 pounds Polish sausage, cut into 1-inch slices
3 tablespoons vegetable oil
1 (16-ounce) can sauerkraut, drained
1 (16-ounce) can tomatoes, undrained
1 cup sliced celery
1 large onion, coarsely chopped
1 large green pepper, coarsely chopped
1 bay leaf
1 teaspoon dried whole oregano
3 tablespoons firmly packed brown sugar
¼ teaspoon salt
½ teaspoon pepper
Hot cooked rice

Cook sausage in oil in a large Dutch oven until browned; drain well. Add remaining ingredients, except rice, stirring well. Cover, reduce heat, and simmer 20 to 25 minutes. Serve over rice. Yield: 8 to 10 servings. *Betty J. Moore,*
Belton, Texas.

ITALIAN SAUSAGE AND PEPPER LOAVES

1½ pounds Italian sausage links
1 medium onion, chopped
3 to 4 medium-size green peppers, chopped
1 (4-ounce) can sliced mushrooms, drained
2 (16-ounce) jars Italian cooking sauce
2 (10-ounce) packages French bread
2 cups (8 ounces) shredded mozzarella cheese
Paprika (optional)

Cut sausage links into 1-inch pieces; cut each piece in half. Brown sausage over medium heat; remove from skillet and drain, reserving 1 tablespoon drippings. Sauté onion, green pepper, and mushrooms in pan drippings. Add sausage and cooking sauce; reduce heat and simmer 45 minutes.

Split loaves of French bread; spoon meat mixture on each half, and sprinkle with cheese. Place sandwiches on a baking sheet; broil until the cheese melts. Sprinkle with paprika, if desired. Yield: 8 servings.   *Ann Elsie Schmetzer,*
Madisonville, Kentucky.

FRIED RICE WITH SAUSAGE

1½ pounds Italian sausage
3 tablespoons peanut oil, divided
2 eggs, slightly beaten
8 scallions or small green onions, minced
½ cup frozen English peas
3 cups cooked regular rice
2 tablespoons soy sauce

Cover sausage with water in a saucepan; cook over medium heat 45 minutes. Drain and thinly slice. Set aside.

Pour 2 tablespoons oil around top of preheated wok, coating sides; allow to heat at medium high (325°) for 1 minute. Add eggs and scallions; cook, stirring constantly, until eggs are set. Remove from wok, and set aside.

Add peas to wok, stir-fry 2 to 3 minutes. Remove and set aside.

Add remaining oil around top of wok, coating sides. Add sausage, and stir-fry 3 to 4 minutes. Drain well.

Add rice to wok; stir-fry 2 to 3 minutes. Stir in soy sauce. Add egg mixture, peas, and sausage; stir well. Yield: 6 servings. *Margaret Drew, Gore, Oklahoma.*

MEXICAN-STYLE SKILLET

1 pound bulk pork sausage
¼ cup chopped onion
½ cup chopped green pepper
1 cup uncooked elbow macaroni
1 (8-ounce) can tomato sauce
1 (16-ounce) can whole tomatoes, undrained
2 tablespoons sugar
1 teaspoon salt
1 teaspoon chili powder
½ cup commercial sour cream
Grated Parmesan cheese

Combine sausage, onion, and green pepper in a heavy skillet; cook until sausage is browned, stirring to crumble. Drain well.

Stir in next 6 ingredients. Cover, reduce heat, and simmer 20 to 25 minutes, stirring occasionally. Stir in sour cream; cook until thoroughly heated. Sprinkle with cheese. Yield: 6 servings. *Mrs. Ronny Bumpus, Lampasas, Texas.*

Tip: To use a griddle or frying pan, preheat on medium or medium-high heat before adding the food. It is properly preheated when a few drops of water spatter when they hit the surface. Add food and reduce heat so that it cooks without spattering and smoking.

A Menu For New Year's

A meal of ham, black-eyed peas, turnip greens, and cornbread has become a New Year's Day tradition. Here is a complete menu that includes all these favorites.

**Baked Ham Slice
Saucy Turnip Greens
Black-Eyed Peas With Rice
Southern Cornbread
Chocolate Pecan Pie**

BAKED HAM SLICE

1 (3½- to 4-pound) ham slice, about 2 inches thick
½ cup apple juice or cider
¼ cup maple-flavored syrup
¼ teaspoon ground nutmeg
¼ teaspoon dry mustard
Dash of ground cloves

Place ham slice in a 12- x 8- x 2-inch baking dish. Combine remaining ingredients, and pour over ham slice. Cover and bake at 350° for 45 to 50 minutes or until tender. Serve with drippings, if desired. Yield: 8 servings. *Agnes Kolk, Arlington, Texas.*

SAUCY TURNIP GREENS

2 pounds fresh turnip greens with roots
3 cups water
½ teaspoon salt
3 slices bacon
½ cup chopped onion
1 tablespoon all-purpose flour
¾ teaspoon sugar
2 tablespoons vinegar

Pick and wash turnip greens. Peel turnip roots; cut in half.

Combine greens, roots, water, and salt in a large Dutch oven; bring to a boil. Reduce heat, cover, and simmer 1 hour or until greens and roots are tender. Drain greens, reserving 1 cup liquid. Set aside.

Cook bacon in a skillet until crisp; remove bacon, reserving drippings in skillet. Crumble bacon, and set aside. Sauté onion in drippings. Add to greens in Dutch oven.

Dissolve flour and sugar in vinegar; stir in reserved cooking liquid. Add mixture to greens; cook over medium heat, stirring occasionally, until thickened. Stir in the reserved bacon. Yield: 6 servings. *Sarah Watson, Knoxville, Tennessee.*

BLACK-EYED PEAS WITH RICE

2 slices bacon
1 medium onion, chopped
1 (15-ounce) can black-eyed peas, drained
1 (14½-ounce) can stewed tomatoes, undrained
1 cup cooked regular rice
¼ teaspoon salt
¼ teaspoon pepper

Cook bacon in a large skillet until crisp; remove bacon, reserving 2 tablespoons drippings in skillet. Crumble bacon, and set aside. Sauté onion in drippings until tender. Add remaining ingredients, stirring well. Spoon mixture into a 1½-quart casserole. Bake at 350° for 30 minutes. Garnish with reserved bacon. Yield: 6 servings. *Rublelene Singleton, Scotts Hill, Tennessee.*

SOUTHERN CORNBREAD

2 cups self-rising cornmeal
1 egg, beaten
¼ cup shortening, melted
1½ cups buttermilk

Combine all ingredients; stir well.

Grease an 8-inch square baking pan; heat in a 450° oven for 3 to 5 minutes or until very hot. Immediately fill with cornmeal mixture; bake at 450° for 25 to 30 minutes. Yield: 9 servings. *Mary Chambers, Luttrell, Tennessee.*

CHOCOLATE PECAN PIE

2 (1-ounce) squares unsweetened chocolate
¼ cup coffee
2 tablespoons butter or margarine
4 eggs
1 cup light corn syrup
½ cup sugar
1½ cups chopped pecans
1 unbaked 9-inch pastry shell
6 to 8 pecan halves

Combine chocolate and coffee in a medium saucepan; cook over low heat, stirring constantly, until chocolate melts. Remove from heat; add butter. Stir until butter melts; cool.

Combine eggs, syrup, and sugar; beat until light and fluffy. Gradually stir into chocolate; stir in pecans. Pour into pastry shell; garnish with pecan halves. Bake at 375° for 40 to 45 minutes or until filling is set. Yield: one 9-inch pie.
Pam Snellgrove,
LaGrange, Georgia.

Mushrooms Are Popping Up All Over

Fresh mushrooms can do more than top a green salad or round out a pizza. Our readers enjoy serving them in entrées, side dishes, and appetizers.

When shopping, choose only off-white or cream-colored mushrooms with a smooth surface. Store them in the refrigerator in a container that will let them breathe. Don't soak or wash mushrooms prior to storage; before using, wipe them with a damp cloth or paper towel.

COQUILLES ST. JACQUES CREPES

1 pound scallops
1 pound sliced fresh mushrooms
2 tablespoons Sauterne
¼ cup plus 2 tablespoons butter or margarine, divided
¼ cup all-purpose flour
1⅔ cups milk
⅓ cup Sauterne
½ cup (2 ounces) shredded Swiss cheese
¼ cup grated Parmesan cheese
¼ teaspoon salt
⅛ teaspoon pepper
⅛ teaspoon paprika
Crêpes (recipe follows)

Rinse scallops; place in a medium skillet, and add water to cover. Bring to a boil; cover, reduce heat, and simmer 5 minutes. Drain scallops; cut into bite-size pieces, and set aside.

Sauté mushrooms and 2 tablespoons Sauterne in 2 tablespoons butter in a medium skillet over low heat until mushrooms are tender; set aside.

Melt ¼ cup butter in a heavy saucepan over low heat; add flour, and stir until smooth. Cook 1 minute, stirring constantly. Gradually add milk and ⅓ cup Sauterne; cook over medium heat, stirring constantly, until mixture is thickened and bubbly. Add Swiss and Parmesan cheese, stirring until melted.

Season with salt, pepper, and paprika. Stir in mushrooms; reserve 1 cup mushroom sauce, and set aside. Stir scallops into remaining mushroom sauce.

Spread 3 tablespoons of mushroom-scallop filling in center of each crepe; roll up and place, seam side down, in a greased 13- x 9- x 2-inch baking dish. Spread reserved mushroom sauce evenly over crêpes. Bake at 350° for 15 minutes. Yield: 6 servings.

Crêpes:

3 eggs
1½ cups milk
1⅓ cups all-purpose flour
½ teaspoon salt
1½ tablespoons vegetable oil
Additional vegetable oil

Combine first 5 ingredients in container of an electric blender; process 1 minute. Scrape down sides of blender with rubber spatula; process an additional 15 seconds. Refrigerate 1 hour. (This allows flour particles to swell and soften so crepes are light in texture.)

Brush the bottom of an 8-inch crêpe pan or nonstick skillet with vegetable oil; place pan over medium heat until oil is just hot, not smoking.

Pour 2½ to 3 tablespoons batter into pan; quickly tilt the pan in all directions so batter covers the pan in a thin film. Cook crêpe about 1 minute.

Lift edge of crêpe to test for doneness; crêpe is ready for flipping when it can be shaken loose from the pan. Flip the crêpe, and cook about 30 seconds on the other side. (This side is rarely more than spotty brown and is the side on which filling is placed.)

When crêpes are done, place on a towel and allow to cool. Stack between layers of waxed paper to prevent sticking. Yield: 12 crêpes. *Dee Buchfink,*
Oologah, Oklahoma.

STUFFED MUSHROOMS

About 18 large fresh mushrooms
½ pound ground beef
2 tablespoons finely chopped onion
⅓ cup fine, dry breadcrumbs
¼ cup chopped walnuts
¼ cup beef broth
2 eggs, beaten
2 tablespoons chopped fresh parsley
¼ teaspoon pepper
⅛ teaspoon salt
1 to 2 tablespoons butter or margarine

Clean mushrooms with damp paper towels. Remove mushroom stems, and reserve for other uses.

Combine ground beef and onion in a medium skillet; cook over medium heat until meat is browned, stirring to crumble. Drain well. Add next 7 ingredients, and mix well.

Spoon ground beef mixture into mushroom caps; dot each with butter. Place in a shallow baking pan. Bake at 375° for 20 minutes. Yield: about 1½ dozen.
Marie Greiner,
Baltimore, Maryland.

SPECIAL MARINATED MUSHROOMS

1 (2-ounce) can anchovies, drained
1 clove garlic, minced
1 (2-ounce) jar sliced pimiento, drained
⅔ cup vegetable oil
½ cup lemon juice
¼ teaspoon dried whole tarragon
¼ teaspoon dried whole basil
⅛ teaspoon dried whole oregano
⅛ teaspoon pepper
2 pounds small fresh mushrooms
Lettuce leaves (optional)

Mash anchovies in a large bowl. Add next 8 ingredients; stir well. Add mushrooms, and toss gently to coat. Cover and refrigerate overnight. Drain well, and serve on lettuce leaves, if desired. Yield: 8 servings.   *K. L. Soudrette,*
Memphis, Tennessee.

SHERRIED MUSHROOMS

1 teaspoon chicken-flavored bouillon granules
¼ cup dry white wine
1 pound fresh mushrooms
3 tablespoons butter
1 tablespoon all-purpose flour
1 bay leaf
Dash of ground nutmeg
2 tablespoons dry sherry

Dissolve bouillon granules in wine; set aside. Clean mushrooms with damp paper towels; remove stems, and reserve for use in another recipe.

Sauté mushroom caps in butter about 1 minute. Stir in flour; cook over low heat 1 minute, stirring constantly. Add bouillon mixture, bay leaf, and nutmeg; cook, uncovered, 6 minutes, stirring occasionally. Stir in sherry, and remove bay leaf; serve immediately. Yield: 4 servings.
Sandy Preston,
Biloxi, Mississippi.

MUSHROOM-EGG DELIGHT

1 pound fresh mushrooms, sliced
½ cup finely chopped onion
¼ cup butter or margarine
1 (10¾-ounce) can cream of mushroom soup, undiluted
¼ cup chopped fresh parsley
¼ teaspoon pepper
6 hard-cooked eggs, coarsely chopped
6 baked patty shells

Sauté mushrooms and onion in butter in a large skillet 5 minutes. Stir in soup, parsley, and pepper; bring to a boil. Reduce heat to low; gently stir in eggs, and cook until thoroughly heated. Serve in patty shells. Yield: 6 servings.

Cindi Rawlins,
Dunwoody, Georgia.

Entrées For Your Chafing Dish

If you're planning a buffet for your next dinner party, use your chafing dish. Not only will the food stay warm, but a chafing dish can be an attractive centerpiece, as well.

BEEF MARENGO

1 (4-pound) boneless chuck roast
½ cup vegetable oil
1 cup chopped onion
1 cup chopped celery
1 clove garlic, crushed
1 cup Chablis or other dry white wine, divided
2 (8-ounce) cans tomato sauce
2 bay leaves
1 teaspoon dried whole oregano
½ teaspoon dried whole rosemary
½ teaspoon salt
½ teaspoon pepper
1 tablespoon chopped fresh parsley
1 pound fresh mushrooms, sliced
2 tablespoons lemon juice
¼ cup butter or margarine
1 tablespoon all-purpose flour
2 tablespoons water
Chopped fresh parsley (optional)
Hot cooked noodles

Trim excess fat from roast; cut into 1-inch cubes.
Brown meat in hot oil in a large Dutch oven; remove meat. Add onion, celery, and garlic to pan drippings; sauté until tender. Return meat to Dutch oven, and add ½ cup wine and next 7 ingredients; bring to a boil. Cover, reduce heat, and simmer 1 hour or until meat is tender, stirring occasionally. Discard bay leaves.

Combine mushrooms and lemon juice, tossing gently. Sauté mushrooms in butter in a large skillet until tender.

Combine flour and water; stir until smooth. Stir flour mixture, sautéed mushrooms, and remaining ½ cup wine into meat mixture. Cover and cook over medium heat 15 minutes. Transfer mixture to a chafing dish; sprinkle with chopped parsley, if desired. Serve over noodles. Yield: 8 to 10 servings.

Carolyn Brantley,
Greenville, Mississippi.

TANGY ROUND STEAK

2 pounds boneless round steak
½ cup commercial spicy-sweet French dressing, divided
½ cup chopped onion
1½ cups water
1 (1.25-ounce) package sour cream sauce mix
1 teaspoon Worcestershire sauce
½ cup chopped celery
1 (3-ounce) can sliced mushrooms, drained
Hot cooked noodles

Trim excess fat from steak; cut steak into 2- x ¼-inch strips.
Heat ¼ cup dressing in a Dutch oven; add steak and onion. Cook until steak is brown and onion is tender, stirring often.

Stir in next 5 ingredients and remaining dressing; bring to a boil. Cover, reduce heat, and simmer 1 hour, stirring occasionally. Transfer steak mixture to a chafing dish. Serve over noodles. Yield: 6 servings.

Charlene Keebler,
Savannah, Georgia.

CREAMED CHICKEN

1 (3- to 3½-pound) broiler-fryer
1 (10-ounce) package frozen English peas
3 tablespoons butter or margarine
3 tablespoons all-purpose flour
3 cups milk
¾ teaspoon salt
¾ teaspoon white pepper
1 (3-ounce) can sliced mushrooms, drained
1 (2-ounce) jar diced pimiento, drained
⅓ cup slivered almonds, toasted
Commercial patty shells, baked

Place chicken in a Dutch oven, and cover with water; bring to a boil. Cover, reduce heat, and simmer 1 hour or until tender. Remove chicken from broth; let cool. (Reserve broth for another use.) Bone chicken; cut into bite-size pieces. Set aside.

Cook peas according to package directions; drain and set aside.

Melt butter in a large saucepan over low heat; add flour, stirring until smooth. Cook 1 minute, stirring constantly. Gradually add milk; cook over medium heat, stirring constantly, until thickened and bubbly. Add next 5 ingredients; mix well. Stir in chicken and peas. Cook over low heat until thoroughly heated, stirring frequently. Transfer creamed chicken to a chafing dish. Serve over patty shells. Yield: 6 servings.

Kathryn Ryan,
Noblesville, Indiana.

From Our Kitchen To Yours

Has your freezer ever stopped running due to a power failure or mechanical problem? If it has, then you know the panicky feeling caused by the thought of losing a freezer full of food.

If Your Freezer Goes Off

The most important thing is not to open the freezer door. If kept closed, a full freezer will keep foods frozen for two days; a partially filled freezer will keep food frozen about a day.

If the freezer motor is running but there is no refrigeration, call a serviceman. If the motor is not running, check to see that it is plugged in properly. If it is, test the outlet by plugging in a small appliance; if it doesn't work, check the fuse box or circuit breakers. If these check out, then the problem may be in the unit itself and will require servicing.

If your power goes off, find out how soon it will be restored. If the power will be off for several days, or if your freezer can't be repaired quickly, take some of the following measures.

What to do—You may want to check with neighbors first to see if they have spare room in their freezer. If not, contact a food locker plant in your area to see if your food can be stored there.

If neither of these options is available, use dry ice as soon as possible. About 25 pounds will keep the temperature below freezing for three to four days in a full 10-cubic-foot freezer and about two to three days in a half-full freezer of the same size.

Dry ice must be handled carefully; always wear gloves. Wrap the ice block in several thicknesses of heavy paper, and place wrapped block on heavy cardboard or small boards over the food packages but not directly on them. Also, don't let the ice touch the sides of the freezer coils.

Once dry ice has been placed in the freezer, don't open the door except to add more dry ice or until the freezer has been operating several hours. Cover the freezer with heavy blankets or quilts to help insulate. Avoid covering the condenser or air vents.

Thawing time—Remember that a fully loaded freezer will stay cold longer than one only partially full. The kind of food also affects how long it will stay cold; a freezer filled with meats will remain cold longer than one with baked goods. The larger the freezer, the longer the food will stay frozen.

If food thaws—Once the power is restored or your freezer is repaired, check your foods carefully to determine the extent of thawing. Get rid of any food that is off-color or has a strange odor. Never taste any food in question. The old saying "if in doubt, throw it out" is definitely the rule to follow.

You may safely refreeze food if it still has ice crystals or if the freezer temperature is below 40°F. and has not been at that temperature longer than one or two days. Foods warmed to 40°F. or higher are unfit for refreezing.

You can refreeze thawed fruit that still smells and tastes good. Or, use it immediately for cooking and making jam, jellies, and preserves.

Meats and poultry should be examined carefully. If they still have ice crystals, they may be safe to refreeze. Look carefully at the color and check the odor. Discard if there is any question.

Shellfish, vegetables, ice cream, and cooked foods such as TV dinners and leftovers spoil quickly. Once thawed, don't refreeze—throw them away.

Refreezing food—Refreeze food as quickly as possible. Turn the freezer temperature control to the coldest setting. Place the warmer packages against the refrigerated surfaces, leaving space for cold air to circulate. If you have quite a bit to refreeze, you may want to place the coldest items in the refrigerator while others refreeze. Gradually return these refrigerated items to the freezer.

When all foods are frozen (0°F.), turn the temperature control back to its normal setting. Also, be sure to label those packages that have been refrozen so that you can use them first.

A Bounty Of Winter Squash

Hidden within the shells of acorn, butternut, and other winter squash is a sweet, delicious pulp that inspires a bounty of cold-weather dishes.

The pulp of either hubbard or butternut squash may be used to prepare Tasty Whipped Squash. Laced with nutmeg and golden raisins, the dish is lightly sweetened and topped with a delicate brown sugar and pecan glaze.

STUFFED ACORN SQUASH

3 large acorn squash
¾ pound ground beef
¼ pound bulk pork sausage
⅓ cup chopped onion
1 (10¾-ounce) can cream of mushroom soup, undiluted
½ cup chopped celery
1 cup soft breadcrumbs
2 tablespoons butter or margarine, melted

Cut squash in half lengthwise; remove seeds. Place cut side down in shallow baking pans; add 1 inch water. Bake, uncovered, at 400° for 30 minutes.

Cook ground beef, sausage, and onion in a large skillet over medium heat until meat is browned and onion is tender, stirring to crumble. Remove from heat; drain. Stir in soup and celery. Spoon evenly into squash halves. Combine breadcrumbs and butter; sprinkle over squash. Bake, uncovered, at 400° for 20 minutes. Yield: 6 servings.
Mrs. H. G. Drawdy, Spindale, North Carolina.

TASTY WHIPPED SQUASH

5 pounds butternut or hubbard squash
2 tablespoons butter or margarine, softened
2 tablespoons brown sugar
⅓ cup golden raisins
½ teaspoon salt
¼ teaspoon ground nutmeg
⅛ teaspoon pepper
1 tablespoon butter or margarine
1 tablespoon brown sugar
1 tablespoon light corn syrup
2 tablespoons finely chopped pecans

Cut squash in half lengthwise; remove seeds. Place cut side down in shallow baking pans; add ½ inch water. Cover and bake at 400° for 40 minutes or until tender. Drain. Scoop out pulp, and discard shell.

Combine squash pulp, 2 tablespoons butter, and 2 tablespoons brown sugar in a large bowl; beat with an electric mixer until smooth. Spoon squash mixture into a large saucepan; cook over medium heat 5 minutes, stirring often. Stir in raisins, salt, nutmeg, and pepper; cook 10 minutes, stirring often. Transfer squash mixture to a serving dish, and keep warm.

Combine remaining ingredients in a small saucepan; cook over medium heat until sugar dissolves, stirring constantly. Pour over squash. Yield: 6 to 8 servings.
Alice McNamara, Eucha, Oklahoma.

SQUASH PUDDING

5 medium butternut squash
¼ cup butter or margarine, softened
2 eggs
1 tablespoon milk
1 teaspoon vanilla extract
½ teaspoon grated lemon rind
½ teaspoon ground nutmeg
½ teaspoon ground cinnamon
1 teaspoon ground mace
½ cup sugar
½ cup firmly packed brown sugar
½ cup chopped pecans, divided

Cut squash in half lengthwise, and remove seeds. Place cut side down in shallow baking pans; add ½ inch water. Cover and bake at 400° for 40 minutes or until tender. Drain. Scoop out pulp, and discard shell.

Combine squash pulp and next 10 ingredients in a large bowl; beat with an electric mixer until smooth. Stir in ¼ cup pecans. Spoon mixture into a greased 2-quart baking dish. Bake, uncovered, at 350° for 45 minutes. Sprinkle with remaining pecans; bake an additional 5 minutes. Yield: 6 to 8 servings.
Cheryl Corriveau, DeLand, Florida.

Tip: Store spices in a cool place and away from any direct source of heat as the heat will destroy their flavor. Red spices (chili powder, paprika, and red pepper) will maintain flavor and retain color longer if refrigerated.

Spotlighting Corned Beef

As our readers will attest, there are many ways to enjoy canned corned beef. Ethel Jernegan of Savannah suggests Corned Beef Soup. It's simmered with chunks of cabbage, potato, onion, and mixed vegetables.

CORNED BEEF AND CABBAGE AU GRATIN

1 medium cabbage, coarsely shredded
1 small onion, thinly sliced
2 cups milk
2 tablespoons butter or margarine
½ teaspoon salt
1 cup mashed potato mix
1 egg, beaten
2 cups (8 ounces) shredded Swiss cheese, divided
¼ teaspoon dried whole tarragon
¼ teaspoon dried whole thyme
Freshly ground pepper to taste
1 (12-ounce) can corned beef, flaked
1 tablespoon butter or margarine, melted
¼ cup Italian-style breadcrumbs

Cook cabbage and onion in a small amount of boiling salted water 5 minutes or until crisp-tender. Drain well.

Combine milk, 2 tablespoons butter, and salt in a large saucepan; bring to a boil. Remove from heat, and stir in potato mix. Let mixture stand about 30 seconds or until liquid is absorbed. Whip with a fork. Add egg, ½ cup Swiss cheese, tarragon, thyme, and pepper; mix well.

Layer half each of potato mixture, corned beef, cabbage mixture, and remaining cheese in a lightly greased 2-quart casserole; repeat layers. Combine melted butter and breadcrumbs; sprinkle over casserole. Bake, uncovered, at 350° for 20 minutes. Yield: 4 to 6 servings. *Fred T. Marshall,*
Hollywood, Maryland.

CORNED BEEF SOUP

2 (16-ounce) cans mixed vegetables, undrained
2 (12-ounce) cans corned beef, cubed
2 (10¾-ounce) cans tomato soup, undiluted
4 cups water
1 small cabbage, coarsely chopped
4 medium potatoes, peeled and cubed
3 medium onions, chopped
½ teaspoon pepper

Drain mixed vegetables, reserving liquid. Set vegetables aside.

Combine reserved liquid and next 7 ingredients in a large Dutch oven; bring to a boil. Cover, reduce heat, and simmer 35 minutes, stirring occasionally. Stir in mixed vegetables; cover and cook an additional 10 minutes. Yield: 5 quarts. *Ethel Jernegan,*
Savannah, Georgia.

CORNED BEEF-CAULIFLOWER SALAD

1 (12-ounce) can corned beef, cubed
3 stalks celery, cut into ¼-inch slices
1 cup cauliflower flowerets
1 (15¼-ounce) can pineapple chunks, drained
½ cup commercial sour cream
½ teaspoon prepared horseradish
Lettuce leaves (optional)

Combine first 4 ingredients; mix well. Chill. Combine sour cream and horseradish, mixing well; chill. Spoon corned beef mixture on lettuce leaves, if desired. Top with sour cream dressing. Yield: about 6 servings.
Mrs. Thomas Lee Adams,
Kingsport, Tennessee.

Homemade Rolls Highlight Dinner

The only thing better than the aroma of freshly baked yeast rolls is biting into one. If you take the time to prepare any of these rolls, you'll discover that their flavor and aroma are worth the effort.

SHREDDED WHEAT FEATHER ROLLS

2 packages dry yeast
½ cup warm water (105° to 115°)
⅔ cup milk, scalded
½ cup butter or margarine
2 tablespoons sugar
1½ teaspoons salt
2 eggs, beaten
4 cups all-purpose flour
4 shredded whole wheat cereal biscuits, crumbled (1½ cups)

Dissolve yeast in ½ cup warm water, and set aside.

Combine milk, butter, sugar, and salt in a large mixing bowl; stir until sugar and salt are dissolved. Cool mixture to 105° to 115°.

Add yeast mixture and eggs to milk mixture; mix well. Stir in 2 cups flour. Add remaining flour and shredded wheat; beat at medium speed of electric mixer 1 minute, scraping sides of bowl with a spatula. Cover and let rise in a warm place (85°), free from drafts, 1 hour or until doubled in bulk.

Punch dough down. Shape into ¾-inch balls; place 3 balls in each cup of well-greased muffin pans. Cover and let rise in a warm place (85°), free from drafts, 45 minutes or until doubled in bulk. Bake at 375° for 18 to 20 minutes. Yield: 1½ dozen. *Judy Cunningham,*
Roanoke, Virginia.

DEEP SOUTH CRESCENT ROLLS

1 package dry yeast
½ cup warm water (105° to 115°)
½ cup sugar
½ cup shortening
2 cups milk
7 cups all-purpose flour, divided
1½ teaspoons salt
½ teaspoon baking soda
½ teaspoon baking powder

Dissolve yeast in ½ cup warm water, and set aside.

Combine sugar, shortening, and milk in a medium saucepan; place over medium heat, stirring until shortening melts. Cool to 105° to 115°.

Combine milk mixture and yeast mixture in a large mixing bowl; mix well. Add 5 cups flour; stir well. Cover and let rise in a warm place (85°), free from drafts, 2 hours or until doubled in bulk.

Combine remaining 2 cups flour, salt, baking soda, and baking powder; mix well. Punch dough down; stir in flour mixture. Knead dough 8 to 10 minutes or until smooth and elastic. Place in a well-greased bowl, turning to grease top. Cover. Refrigerate until needed.

Punch dough down, and divide into fourths. Roll each fourth into a circle about 12 inches in diameter and ¼-inch thick; cut into 10 wedges. Roll each wedge tightly, beginning at wide end.

Place rolls on greased baking sheets, point side down; curve into crescent shape. Cover and let rise in a warm place (85°), free from drafts, about 1½ hours or until doubled in bulk. Bake at 400° for 10 minutes or until lightly browned. Yield: about 3 dozen.
Elizabeth M. Haney,
Dublin, Virginia.

Tip: Use baking soda on a damp cloth to shine up your kitchen appliances.

PARKER HOUSE REFRIGERATOR ROLLS

2 packages dry yeast
1 cup warm water (105° to 115°)
½ cup sugar
1½ teaspoons salt
⅔ cup shortening
1 cup water
2 eggs, beaten
6 cups all-purpose flour
Melted butter or margarine

Dissolve yeast in 1 cup warm water, and set aside.

Combine sugar, salt, shortening, and 1 cup water in a small saucepan; heat, stirring often, until shortening melts. Cool mixture to 105° to 115°. Combine yeast mixture, shortening mixture, and eggs in a large mixing bowl. Gradually stir in flour.

Turn dough out onto a floured surface, and knead 5 to 8 minutes or until smooth and elastic. Place in a well-greased bowl, turning to grease top; cover and refrigerate 1½ hours.

Punch dough down; turn out onto a floured surface. Roll out to ¼-inch thickness. Cut into 2½-inch circles, and brush with melted butter. Make a crease across each circle, and fold one half over. Gently press edges to seal. Place on greased cookie sheets, and let rise in a warm place (85°), free from drafts, 1 hour or until doubled in bulk. Bake at 400° for 15 minutes or until golden brown. Brush rolls with melted butter. Yield: about 3 dozen.
Mrs. Michael A. Cohen,
Havre de Grace, Maryland.

SPEEDY YEAST ROLLS

4½ cups all-purpose flour, divided
3 tablespoons sugar
½ teaspoon baking soda
1 teaspoon salt
2 packages dry yeast
1¼ cups buttermilk
½ cup water
½ cup butter or margarine
Melted butter or margarine

Combine 1½ cups flour, sugar, baking soda, salt, and yeast in a large mixing bowl; set aside. Combine buttermilk, water, and ½ cup butter in a small saucepan; heat to 120° to 130°. Stir well, and add to flour mixture. Beat at medium speed of electric mixer 4 minutes. Gradually add remaining flour, mixing well.

Turn dough out onto a floured surface, and knead 5 to 8 minutes or until smooth and elastic. Place in a greased

bowl, turning to grease top. Cover and let rise in a warm place (85°), free from drafts, about 30 minutes or until doubled in bulk.

Punch dough down, and shape into 1½-inch balls. Place on greased cookie sheets; cover and let rise in a warm place (85°), free from drafts, 30 minutes or until doubled in bulk. Bake at 400° for 15 to 20 minutes. Brush with melted butter. Yield: about 2 dozen.
Carol Forcum,
Marion, Illinois.

REFRIGERATOR YEAST ROLLS

1 package dry yeast
¼ cup warm water (105° to 115°)
¼ cup shortening
¼ cup sugar
1 egg, slightly beaten
1 cup warm water (105° to 115°)
1 to 1½ teaspoons salt
4 cups all-purpose flour

Dissolve yeast in ¼ cup warm water, and set aside.

Cream shortening; gradually add sugar, beating until light and fluffy. Stir in egg, 1 cup warm water, and yeast mixture; beat until smooth. Stir in salt and flour to make a soft dough.

Place dough in a well-greased bowl, turning to grease top. Cover and chill for 24 hours.

Lightly grease muffin pans. Shape dough into ¾-inch balls; place 3 balls in each muffin cup. Cover and let rise in a warm place (85°), free from drafts, 1 hour or until doubled in bulk. Bake at 400° for 12 to 15 minutes or until rolls are golden brown. Yield: about 1½ dozen.
Rena C. Nixon,
Mount Airy, North Carolina.

Make The Bread Whole Wheat

Biscuits and loaf breads have a delightful nutty flavor when they're made with whole wheat flour. Since the flour is ground with the entire wheat kernel, it's more nutritious.

Whole wheat breads may be heavier, denser in texture, and have a lower volume than breads made with all-purpose flour. This is especially true of stone-ground whole wheat flour products since the flour is more coarse.

When preparing a whole wheat recipe, be sure not to sift the flour. Instead, stir it lightly before measuring, then spoon it into the measuring cup.

Because the oil-rich wheat germ in whole wheat flour increases the possibility of spoilage, store the flour in an airtight container in the refrigerator or freezer. It should keep about three months when properly stored.

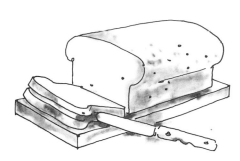

WHOLE WHEAT BREAD

7 to 8 cups whole wheat flour, divided
2 packages dry yeast
1 tablespoon plus 1 teaspoon salt
1½ cups milk
1½ cups water
¼ cup plus 2 tablespoons butter or margarine
¼ cup honey
Melted butter or margarine

Combine 3 cups flour, yeast, and salt in a large bowl. Stir well; set aside.

Combine milk, water, butter, and honey in a medium saucepan; place over low heat, stirring constantly, until mixture reaches 120° to 130°. (Butter does not need to melt.) Stir milk mixture into flour mixture; beat at medium speed of electric mixer 2 minutes or until smooth. Stir in remaining 4 to 5 cups flour to make a stiff dough.

Turn dough out onto a lightly floured surface; let dough rest 10 minutes. Knead dough 3 minutes or until smooth and elastic; place in a well-greased bowl, turning to grease top.

Cover and let rise in a warm place (85°), free from drafts, 50 minutes or until doubled in bulk. Punch dough down, and divide in half; shape each half into a loaf. Place in 2 greased 9- x 5- x 3-inch loafpans. Cover and let rise in a warm place (85°), free from drafts, 50 minutes or until doubled in bulk.

Bake at 375° for 35 to 45 minutes or until loaves sound hollow when tapped. (Cover the loaves with aluminum foil when crusts are golden brown.) Brush loaves with melted butter; remove from pans, and cool on wire racks. Yield: 2 loaves.
Linda E. Whitt,
Missouri City, Texas.

WHOLE WHEAT PANCAKES

½ cup all-purpose flour
½ cup whole wheat flour
1 teaspoon baking soda
½ teaspoon salt
1 cup buttermilk
1 egg, beaten
1 tablespoon vegetable oil
2 tablespoons molasses
Maple syrup (optional)

Combine first 4 ingredients; mix well. Combine buttermilk, egg, oil, and molasses; mix well. Add buttermilk mixture to dry ingredients, stirring just until moistened (batter will be slightly lumpy). For each pancake, pour about ¼ cup batter onto a hot, lightly greased griddle or skillet. Turn pancakes over when the tops are covered with bubbles and edges appear slightly dry. Serve with maple syrup, if desired. Yield: twelve 4-inch pancakes.   *Karen Pass,*
Glenmont, New York.

WHOLE WHEAT BISCUITS

1 cup whole wheat flour
1 cup all-purpose flour
1 tablespoon baking powder
½ teaspoon baking soda
½ teaspoon salt
½ cup shortening
¾ cup buttermilk

Combine first 5 ingredients, mixing well; cut in shortening with a pastry blender until mixture resembles coarse meal. Add buttermilk to dry ingredients, stirring until moistened. Turn dough out onto a lightly floured surface, and knead lightly 4 to 5 times.

Roll dough to ½-inch thickness; cut with a 2¾-inch biscuit cutter. Place biscuits on an ungreased baking sheet. Bake at 450° for 10 minutes or until browned. Yield: 1 dozen.

Leatha Cantaloupe,
Horseheads, New York.

Fry Your Own Eggrolls

If you've never made eggrolls, now's the time to start. Shrimp and Pork Eggrolls are loaded with crunch and fried to crispy perfection, and—best of all—they're easy to make. That's because you make them with commercial eggroll wrappers. Although Chinese cooks say it's best to chop the vegetables by hand, you may want to try chopping them in the food processor to save time.

SHRIMP AND PORK EGGROLLS

1½ teaspoons cornstarch
1 tablespoon soy sauce
½ pound lean boneless pork, cut into
    ¼-inch cubes
1 (6-ounce) package frozen cooked shrimp,
    thawed and drained
1 teaspoon dry sherry
3 tablespoons peanut or vegetable oil,
    divided
3 cups shredded cabbage
2½ cups fresh bean sprouts, chopped
½ pound fresh mushrooms, thinly sliced
½ cup finely chopped celery
1 (8-ounce) can bamboo shoots, drained
    and finely chopped
½ teaspoon salt
¼ teaspoon pepper
1 egg, beaten
1½ teaspoons water
2 (1-pound) packages fresh or frozen
    eggroll wrappers
Peanut oil
Commercial sweet-and-sour sauce
    (optional)
Commercial mustard sauce (optional)

Combine cornstarch and soy sauce in a small bowl; mix well. Stir in pork, and let stand 20 minutes. Combine shrimp and sherry in another small bowl; stir well. Let stand 20 minutes.

Heat 2 tablespoons oil in a preheated wok, coating sides; allow to heat at medium high (325°) for 2 minutes. Add pork and shrimp mixtures; stir-fry 2 minutes or until pork is lightly browned. Remove from wok and drain.

Heat remaining oil in wok. Add cabbage, bean sprouts, mushrooms, and celery; stir-fry 2 minutes or until vegetables are crisp-tender. Add bamboo shoots, pork, and shrimp; sprinkle with salt and pepper. Cook 1 minute, stirring constantly. Remove mixture from wok, and chill.

Combine egg and water in a custard cup; mix well, and set aside.

Mound ⅓ cup of chilled filling in center of each eggroll wrapper. Fold top corner of wrapper over filling; then fold left and right corners over filling. Lightly brush exposed corner of wrapper with egg mixture. Tightly roll the filled end of the wrapper toward the exposed corner; gently press to seal.

Heat 1½ inches peanut oil to 375° in wok. Place 2 eggrolls in hot oil, and fry for 35 to 45 seconds on each side, or until golden brown; drain on paper towels. Repeat with remaining eggrolls. Serve with sweet-and-sour sauce and mustard sauce, if desired. Yield: about 20 eggrolls.

Note: Remaining eggroll wrappers may be frozen and reserved for later use.   *Cherry Tyree,*
Pelham, Alabama.

Pretzels Worth A Party

If your friends are gathering for an informal evening, chances are they'll enjoy nibbling on these pretzels as much as our foods staff did. Mrs. Harlan J. Stone of Ocala, Florida, boils her pretzels before baking, and they come out of the oven thick and chewy like a hot pretzel should be.

SOFT PRETZELS

1 package dry yeast
½ cup plus 2 tablespoons warm water
    (105° to 115°)
2 cups all-purpose flour
½ teaspoon salt
1 egg yolk, beaten
Kosher salt (rock or table salt may be
    substituted)

Dissolve yeast in warm water. Combine flour and ½ teaspoon salt; add yeast mixture, and mix until blended. Turn out onto a very lightly floured surface, and knead dough 3 minutes or until smooth and elastic.

Cover and let rise in a warm place (85°), free from drafts, 1 hour or until doubled in bulk.

Using kitchen shears dipped in flour, cut dough into 10 pieces; roll each into a ball. With floured hands, roll each ball between hands to form a rope 14 to 16 inches long; twist each into a pretzel shape, and drop into boiling water. Cook pretzels 3 minutes. Remove pretzels to a wire rack (mesh type); allow to dry 8 to 10 minutes.

Brush each pretzel with egg yolk; sprinkle with Kosher salt. Place pretzels on a greased wire rack (mesh type), and bake at 400° for 30 minutes or until golden. Serve warm. Yield: 10 pretzels.

Mrs. Harlan J. Stone,
Ocala, Florida.

February

Warm up February with a steaming bowl of chowder. Thick and rich with seafood, cheese, and vegetables, our chowder recipes inspire cozy fireside meals on days when you wouldn't dream of going outside.

When company comes, today's working homemakers face the dilemma of whipping up a fabulous meal on a workday schedule. Knowing what this is like, our staff devised an entire menu from appetizer to dessert suited for company and a tight schedule as well. After the menu appeared in *Southern Living*, our readers wrote and called to say that they tried the whole menu and were delighted to find that it solved their after-work entertaining problems.

When you do have more time to entertain, you'll enjoy a unique party like the one we found in Birmingham, Alabama. A Chinese party theme lets your guests join in the fun of preparation. Try recipes for Crispy Fried Wontons, Cashew Chicken, Almond Cookies, and more on the pages to follow.

Sit Down To A Steaming Bowl Of Chowder

When you're coming in from a nippy day outdoors, few foods are as inviting as a hot and hearty chowder. Thick with vegetables as well as meat, seafood, or cheese, chowders offer the variety of a whole meal in one dish.

Chowder got its name from the *chaudière*, a large kettle early French settlers in America used to cook soups and stews. Settlers often contributed part of their daily catch of fish to a community *chaudière*, along with vegetables such as potatoes and corn. Today, our chowders are more varied than ever.

SAUSAGE-BEAN CHOWDER

2 pounds bulk pork sausage
4 cups water
2 (16-ounce) cans kidney beans, undrained
2 (16-ounce) cans whole tomatoes, undrained and chopped
2 medium onions, chopped
2 medium potatoes, peeled and cubed
½ cup chopped green pepper
1 large bay leaf
½ teaspoon salt
½ teaspoon dried whole thyme
¼ teaspoon garlic powder
¼ teaspoon pepper

Brown sausage in a Dutch oven, stirring to crumble; drain off drippings. Stir in remaining ingredients; bring to a boil. Cover, reduce heat, and simmer 1 hour. Remove bay leaf before serving. Yield: 3 quarts.
Cindy Winburn, Butler, Missouri.

CORN CHOWDER

6 slices bacon
1 medium onion, coarsely chopped
2 medium potatoes, peeled and cubed
½ cup water
2 cups milk
1 (17-ounce) can cream-style corn
½ teaspoon salt
Dash of pepper

Fry bacon in a Dutch oven until crisp; remove bacon, reserving 2 tablespoons drippings in Dutch oven. Crumble bacon, and set aside.

Sauté onion in reserved drippings until tender; add potatoes and water. Cover and simmer 15 to 20 minutes or until potatoes are tender. Stir in milk, corn, salt, and pepper; cook over medium heat, stirring frequently, until thoroughly heated. Sprinkle each serving with bacon. Yield: about 5 cups.
Ann Elsie Schmetzer, Madisonville, Kentucky.

CHICKEN CHOWDER

4 chicken breast halves, skinned
4 cups water
½ teaspoon salt
2 medium potatoes, peeled and cubed
2 medium carrots, coarsely chopped
1 (17-ounce) can cream-style corn
1 (15-ounce) can tomato sauce with tomato bits
¼ teaspoon pepper

Combine first 3 ingredients in a Dutch oven; bring to a boil. Cover, reduce heat, and simmer 30 to 45 minutes or until chicken is tender. Remove chicken from broth, reserving 3 cups broth in Dutch oven. Remove the meat from bones, and cut into bite-size pieces; set aside.

Add potatoes and carrots to broth; bring to a boil. Cover, reduce heat, and simmer 10 to 12 minutes. Add chicken, corn, tomato sauce, and pepper; cover and simmer 15 minutes or until vegetables are tender, stirring occasionally. Yield: 2 quarts.
Linda Peek, Birmingham, Alabama.

SOUTHERN SEAFOOD CHOWDER

2 (6½-ounce) cans minced clams, undrained
1 (28-ounce) can whole tomatoes, undrained and chopped
2 cups water
1 large potato, peeled and cubed
2 medium onions, thinly sliced
1 medium-size green pepper, coarsely chopped
2 cloves garlic, minced
1 bay leaf
1 teaspoon salt
½ teaspoon dried whole basil
⅛ teaspoon pepper
1 (10-ounce) package frozen cut okra
1 pound flounder or sole fillets, cut into bite-size pieces

Drain clams, reserving liquid; set clams aside. Combine clam liquid and next 10 ingredients in a Dutch oven; bring to a boil. Cover, reduce heat, and simmer for 15 to 20 minutes or until the potatoes are tender.

Stir in okra, flounder, and clams; bring to a boil. Reduce heat and simmer, uncovered, 8 minutes or until fish flakes easily; remove bay leaf before serving. Yield: about 3 quarts.
Mrs. Carlton James, New Orleans, Louisiana.

CHEESY VEGETABLE CHOWDER

½ cup chopped onion
1 clove garlic, minced
1 cup sliced celery
¾ cup sliced carrots
1 cup cubed potatoes
3½ cups chicken broth
1 (17-ounce) can whole kernel corn, drained
¼ cup butter or margarine
¼ cup all-purpose flour
2 cups milk
1 tablespoon prepared mustard
¼ teaspoon white pepper
⅛ teaspoon paprika
2 tablespoons diced pimiento
2 cups (8 ounces) shredded Cheddar cheese

Combine first 6 ingredients in a large Dutch oven; bring to a boil. Cover, reduce heat, and simmer 15 to 20 minutes or until potatoes are tender. Stir in corn; remove from heat.

Melt butter in a heavy saucepan over low heat; add flour, stirring until smooth. Cook 1 minute, stirring constantly. Gradually add milk; cook over medium heat, stirring constantly, until thickened and bubbly. Stir in remaining ingredients. Cook just until cheese melts, stirring constantly. Gradually stir cheese mixture into vegetable mixture. Cook over medium heat, stirring constantly, until thoroughly heated. Serve immediately. Yield: 2 quarts.

Stir Up A Chinese Party

Cooks across the South have experimented with Chinese cuisine for years because Oriental cooking techniques retain the color, juiciness, and nutrients of foods. But Marty Lloyd of Birmingham, Alabama, cooks in the Chinese style for another reason.

"Chinese cooking makes a great way to have a party," explains Marty. "I do some advance preparation, and as guests arrive I turn them loose folding and frying wontons, chopping fresh vegetables, and even stir-frying in the woks. The evening's entertainment takes care of itself—in the kitchen!"

The group nibbles on appetizers of Crispy Fried Wontons and Sweet-and-Sour Spareribs in the den before beginning preparation for the main meal. Marty serves green tea and plum wine with the entire menu.

Then it's into the kitchen and out with the cleaver as Marty assigns the final chopping of meat and vegetables for the stir-fries. She does much tedious measuring and assembling ahead of time, however. It's the fun, novel assignments she saves for her guests, like cutting grooves down the length of a carrot so that slicing magically produces petaled flowers.

Marty tends to the Stir-Fry Beef and Snow Peas in a wok on the cook surface and supervises the Cashew Chicken in an electric wok across the room.

At the last minute, Marty reheats the Shrimp Egg Foo Yong and Egg Drop Soup made earlier, dramatically drizzling egg into the soup before serving.

The Chinese usually don't plan a dessert course, but the Southern sweet tooth demands one. Marty offers Almond Cookies, as well as Chinese Fruit Medley highlighted by sweet-smelling lychee fruit, a Chinese favorite.

Sweet-and-Sour Spareribs
Crispy Fried Wontons
Egg Drop Soup
Cashew Chicken
Shrimp Egg Foo Yong
Stir-Fry Beef and Snow Peas
Almond Cookies
Chinese Fruit Medley
Green Tea   Plum Wine

SWEET-AND-SOUR SPARERIBS

1½ pounds spareribs
⅓ cup sugar
⅓ cup soy sauce
¼ cup rice wine
¼ cup red wine vinegar
4 cloves garlic, minced
2 slices gingerroot, minced
1 tablespoon sesame seeds
Fresh parsley sprigs
Radish roses

Have butcher cut rib section lengthwise into individual ribs, and crosswise, through the bone, into 2- to 2½-inch rib pieces.

Combine next 7 ingredients in a 13- x 9- x 2-inch baking dish. Add ribs; cover and marinate overnight in refrigerator. Drain marinade, and discard. Bake ribs at 375° for 1 hour. Arrange on platter, and garnish with parsley and radish roses. Yield: 6 to 8 appetizer servings.

CRISPY FRIED WONTONS

½ pound ground pork
2 tablespoons sesame oil
2 tablespoons chopped green onion
1½ teaspoons salt
1 (1-pound) package frozen wonton wrappers, thawed
1 tablespoon cornstarch
2 tablespoons water
Peanut or vegetable oil
Commercial duck sauce
Mustard Sauce

Combine first 4 ingredients, mixing well. Working one at a time, spoon ¾ teaspoon pork mixture in center of wonton wrapper. Combine cornstarch and water; stir until smooth. Brush edges of wonton wrapper lightly with cornstarch mixture. Fold wrapper once to form a triangle, pressing edges together to seal.

On long side of triangle, fold opposite ends together, overlapping them; brush ends with cornstarch mixture, and press to seal. Fold point of triangle backwards, away from overlapping edges. Repeat procedure with remaining wrappers. Keep wrappers covered to prevent drying out.

Drop wontons into small amount of oil heated to 375°; cook until golden, turning once. Drain on paper towels. Serve with commercial duck sauce or Mustard Sauce. Yield: about 5 dozen.

Mustard Sauce:

2 tablespoons dry mustard
2 tablespoons water
1 teaspoon sesame oil

Combine all ingredients, and mix well. Yield: about ¼ cup.

EGG DROP SOUP

2 (10¾-ounce) cans chicken broth, diluted
1 (3-ounce) can sliced mushrooms, undrained
2 cloves garlic
1 teaspoon soy sauce
¼ pound medium shrimp, peeled and deveined
⅛ teaspoon white pepper
1 egg, slightly beaten
1 teaspoon sesame oil
2 green onions, chopped

Combine chicken broth, mushrooms, garlic, and soy sauce in a Dutch oven; bring to a boil. Cover, reduce heat, and simmer 30 minutes.

Add shrimp and pepper; cook 3 minutes. Remove from heat. Combine egg and oil, stirring well. Slowly pour beaten egg mixture into soup, stirring constantly. (The egg forms lacy strands as it cooks.) Remove garlic.

Ladle soup into individual bowls, and sprinkle with onion. Serve immediately. Yield: about 5 cups.

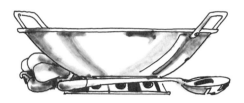

CASHEW CHICKEN

3 chicken breast halves, skinned and boned
1 egg white, slightly beaten
1 tablespoon rice wine
1 teaspoon cornstarch
1 tablespoon peanut or vegetable oil
½ cup cashews
2 tablespoons peanut or vegetable oil
½ teaspoon salt
1 (8-ounce) can sliced water chestnuts, drained
1 (8-ounce) can sliced bamboo shoots, drained
4 green onions, cut into 1-inch pieces
3 stalks celery, thinly sliced
2 red or green peppers, cut into 1-inch squares
⅓ cup chicken broth
1 tablespoon cornstarch
1 tablespoon rice wine
1 tablespoon soy sauce
1 teaspoon sesame oil
Green onion fans

Cut chicken into 1-inch pieces. Combine chicken and next 3 ingredients; mix well, and let stand in refrigerator 1 hour or overnight.

Pour 1 tablespoon oil around top of preheated wok, coating sides. Add cashews; stir-fry 30 seconds and remove. Pour 2 tablespoons oil around top of wok; add chicken, and stir-fry until lightly browned. Sprinkle chicken with salt. Add next 5 ingredients; stir-fry 5 minutes or until vegetables are crisp-tender. Combine next 5 ingredients, mixing well. Pour over chicken mixture; cook, stirring constantly, until thickened. Spoon onto platter, and sprinkle with cashews; garnish with green onion fans. Yield: 6 to 8 servings.

SHRIMP EGG FOO YONG

2 cups water
½ pound medium shrimp
3 eggs, beaten
¾ cup bean sprouts
½ cup chopped fresh mushrooms
¼ cup chopped green onion
Peanut or vegetable oil
Green Pea Sauce

Bring water to a boil; add shrimp, and return to a boil. Lower heat and simmer 3 to 5 minutes. Drain well; rinse with cold water. Peel, devein, and dice.

Combine shrimp, eggs, and vegetables. Let stand 10 minutes; mix well.

Heat small amount of oil in a large skillet. Spoon ¼ cup egg mixture into hot oil, shaping into a 3-inch circle with a spatula. Cook until browned on one side; turn and brown other side. Repeat with remaining egg mixture, adding oil to skillet as necessary. Serve with Green Pea Sauce. Yield: 8 patties.

Green Pea Sauce:
¾ cup chicken broth
1 tablespoon cornstarch
1 tablespoon soy sauce
1 teaspoon sugar
½ cup frozen English peas

Combine chicken broth, cornstarch, soy sauce, and sugar in a saucepan; stir until smooth. Cook over low heat until thickened, stirring constantly. Add peas, and cook until thoroughly heated. Yield: 1 cup.

STIR-FRY BEEF AND SNOW PEAS

1 pound boneless sirloin steak
1 tablespoon soy sauce
2 teaspoons cornstarch
½ teaspoon sugar
2 carrots, scraped
¼ cup peanut or vegetable oil
1 (2-ounce) package cellophane noodles
1 (6-ounce) package Chinese pea pods, thawed and drained
2 tablespoons peanut or vegetable oil
2 slices gingerroot
1 tablespoon peanut or vegetable oil
1 (10-ounce) can baby corn cobs, drained
1 (15-ounce) can straw mushrooms, drained
2 tablespoons soy sauce
2 tablespoons rice wine
2 teaspoons sugar
1 teaspoon cornstarch

Partially freeze steak; slice diagonally across grain into 2- x ¼-inch strips. Combine next 3 ingredients; pour over steak. Marinate 1 hour at room temperature or overnight in refrigerator.

Cut 4 or 5 lengthwise triangular grooves ⅛-inch deep at even intervals down length of carrots. Slice carrots ⅛-inch thick. Set aside.

Pour ¼ cup oil into preheated wok; heat to 325°. Add noodles, a few at a time; fry 2 to 3 seconds or until noodles expand and turn white. Remove from wok; drain. Arrange around border of serving platter.

Drain oil from wok. Add pea pods to wok; stir-fry 1 to 2 minutes. Remove from wok, and arrange around inside border of cellophane noodles. Pour 2 tablespoons oil around top of wok, coating sides. Add gingerroot and steak; stir-fry 4 to 5 minutes. Remove from wok. Pour 1 tablespoon oil around top of wok, coating sides. Add carrots, corn, and mushrooms; stir-fry 2 to 3 minutes. Combine next 4 ingredients, mixing well; add to carrot mixture, and cook until thickened, stirring constantly. Stir in steak. Pour steak mixture into center of platter. Yield: 6 to 8 servings.

ALMOND COOKIES

2 cups all-purpose flour
1 teaspoon baking powder
1 teaspoon baking soda
1 cup shortening
1 cup sugar
1 teaspoon vanilla extract
½ teaspoon almond extract
1 egg
1 egg yolk
1 tablespoon water
4 dozen whole almonds (about ½ cup)

Combine first 3 ingredients; set aside.

Cream shortening; gradually add sugar, beating until light and fluffy. Stir in vanilla and almond extract. Add whole egg, beating well. Add dry ingredients, and mix well.

Combine egg yolk and water; mix well. Shape dough into ¾-inch balls. Press an almond into center of each cookie; brush with egg yolk mixture. Bake on ungreased cookie sheets at 350° for 10 to 12 minutes. Cool on wire racks. Yield: about 4 dozen.

CHINESE FRUIT MEDLEY

1 (20-ounce) can lychee fruit, undrained
1 (15¼-ounce) can pineapple chunks, drained
1 (11-ounce) can mandarin oranges, drained
¼ cup maraschino cherries

Combine all ingredients; stir gently. Cover and chill. Yield: 6 to 8 servings.

Put Some Sizzle In Your Salad

Although warm weather and salads seem to go hand in hand, chilly days can also be salad days—especially if the salads are heated like the ones we offer.

BAKED SHRIMP-RICE SALAD

1½ cups cooked regular rice
1 (4¼-ounce) can shrimp, drained
¾ cup diced fresh cauliflower
¼ cup chopped green pepper
1 tablespoon chopped green onion
1 tablespoon chopped ripe olives
½ teaspoon salt
⅓ cup mayonnaise
2 tablespoons commercial French salad dressing
2 tablespoons lemon juice
Green onion fans (optional)

Combine first 7 ingredients in a mixing bowl; mix well. Combine next 3 ingredients; stir well, and pour over shrimp mixture, tossing gently. Spoon into a lightly greased 1-quart shallow baking dish. Bake at 350° for 20 minutes. Garnish with green onion, if desired. Yield: 4 servings.

Azine G. Rush,
Monroe, Louisiana.

HOT CHICKEN-AND-RICE SALAD

1 (10¾-ounce) can cream of chicken soup, undiluted
½ cup mayonnaise
¼ cup milk
1 tablespoon lemon juice
¼ teaspoon salt
3 hard-cooked eggs, chopped
2 cups chopped, cooked chicken
1 cup cooked regular rice
1 (8-ounce) can sliced water chestnuts, drained
1 (2-ounce) jar diced pimiento, drained
½ cup chopped celery
1 tablespoon finely chopped onion
⅓ cup crushed corn flake cereal
¼ cup slivered almonds
1 tablespoon butter or margarine, melted

Combine first 5 ingredients; stir until blended. Add next 7 ingredients; stir well. Spoon mixture into a lightly greased 12- x 8- x 2-inch baking dish. Combine crushed cereal, almonds, and butter; sprinkle over casserole. Bake at 375° for 20 to 25 minutes or until bubbly. Yield: 6 to 8 servings.

Rachel Youree,
Murfreesboro, Tennessee.

HOT INDIAN CURRY SALAD

2 cups chopped, cooked chicken
3 hard-cooked eggs, chopped
1 cup finely chopped celery
½ cup raisins
1 (10¾-ounce) can cream of chicken soup, undiluted
½ cup mayonnaise
1 tablespoon lemon juice
1 to 1½ teaspoons curry powder
¼ teaspoon pepper
2 tablespoons flaked coconut
¼ cup chopped walnuts

Combine first 9 ingredients, stirring well. Spoon into a lightly greased 1½-quart casserole. Sprinkle with coconut, and top with walnuts. Bake at 400° for 30 minutes. Yield: 6 servings.

Arlene Kummer,
Arlington, Texas.

CRUNCHY BAKED HAM SALAD

3 cups cubed, cooked ham
1 cup chopped celery
⅔ cup mayonnaise
½ cup chopped pimiento-stuffed olives
2 hard-cooked eggs, chopped
¼ cup chopped onion
1 tablespoon lemon juice
1½ teaspoons prepared mustard
Dash of pepper
1 cup crushed potato chips

Combine first 9 ingredients; stir well. Spoon mixture into a greased 8-inch square baking dish; top with potato chips. Bake at 400° for 20 to 25 minutes. Yield: 6 servings.

Cyndi Copenhaver,
Virginia Beach, Virginia.

GERMAN-STYLE POTATO SALAD

6 medium potatoes, peeled and cut into ¼-inch slices
1 medium onion, chopped
6 slices bacon, cooked and crumbled
½ cup vinegar
½ cup water
½ cup sugar
2 tablespoons cornstarch
¼ teaspoon salt
¼ teaspoon pepper
3 hard-cooked eggs, chopped

Cook potatoes in boiling water 15 to 20 minutes or until tender. Drain well. Combine remaining ingredients, except eggs, in a saucepan; cook 20 minutes, stirring frequently. Pour vinegar mixture over potatoes; add egg, and toss. Serve immediately. Yield: 6 servings.

Bettye Cortner,
Cerulean, Kentucky.

Look What You Can Do With A Cake Mix

If you need a luscious dessert in a matter of minutes, start with a cake mix and embellish it with your favorite ingredients. Caramels, marshmallows, peanuts, pecans, chocolate chips, and mandarin oranges are just a few tasty morsels we've stirred into basic cake mixes for cakes with that "made from scratch" flavor.

For an impressive cake, don't forget that even simple garnishes transform a pretty cake into a spectacular dessert. You can get some ideas for garnishing from the ingredients in the cake. For example, sprinkle lemon rind atop a lemon cake, or decorate the platter with lemon roses.

ICE CREAM ANGEL CAKE

1 (14.5-ounce) package white angel food cake mix
1 quart strawberry ice cream, softened
1 pint chocolate ice cream, softened
2 cups whipping cream
¼ cup sifted powdered sugar
¼ teaspoon almond extract
¼ cup slivered almonds, toasted
Chocolate leaves (optional)

Prepare and bake cake mix according to package directions, using a 10-inch tube pan. Invert pan on funnel or bottle about 2 hours or until cake is completely cooled.

Loosen cake from sides of tube pan using a small metal spatula. Remove from pan; split the cake horizontally into 4 layers.

Place bottom layer of cake on a cake plate, and spread with half of strawberry ice cream; freeze. Add second cake layer, and spread with chocolate ice cream; freeze. Repeat with third layer and remaining strawberry ice cream. Place remaining layer, cut side down, on top of cake. Cover and freeze cake several hours or overnight.

Beat whipping cream until foamy; gradually add powdered sugar and almond extract, beating until stiff peaks form. Frost sides and top of cake with whipped cream. Sprinkle with almonds. Garnish with chocolate leaves, if desired. Yield: one 10-inch cake.

CHOCOLATE-COCONUT CAKE

1 (18.5-ounce) package devils food cake mix without pudding
1 cup sugar
1 cup evaporated milk
15 large marshmallows
2 cups flaked coconut
1 teaspoon vanilla extract
½ cup butter or margarine, softened
1 (16-ounce) package powdered sugar, sifted
½ cup cocoa
½ cup evaporated milk

Prepare cake mix according to package directions; pour batter into 3 greased and floured 9-inch round cake-pans. Bake at 350° for 20 to 25 minutes or until a wooden pick inserted in center comes out clean. Cool in pans 10 minutes; remove layers from pans, and let cool completely.

Combine 1 cup sugar, 1 cup evaporated milk, and marshmallows in a heavy saucepan; bring to a boil, and cook 5 minutes, stirring constantly. Remove from heat; stir in coconut and vanilla. Let cool 10 minutes or until mixture reaches spreading consistency. Spread evenly between cake layers.

Combine remaining ingredients; beat on high speed of electric mixer until smooth and creamy. Spread frosting on top and sides of cake. Yield: one 9-inch cake.

Beverly Gwynn,
Chesapeake, Virginia.

CHOCOLATE-CARAMEL-NUT CAKE

1 (18.5-ounce) package German chocolate cake mix with pudding
1 (14-ounce) bag caramels
½ cup butter or margarine
⅓ cup milk
1 cup chopped dry-roasted peanuts
¾ cup milk chocolate morsels

Prepare cake mix according to package directions; spoon half of batter into a greased and floured 13- x 9- x 2-inch baking pan. Bake at 350° for 10 minutes. (Cake will not test done.) Cool cake for 10 minutes.

Combine caramels, butter, and milk in a saucepan; cook over low heat, stirring constantly, until caramels melt. Spread over cake.

Sprinkle peanuts and chocolate morsels over caramel mixture. Spread remaining cake batter evenly over top. Bake at 350° for 20 to 25 minutes. Cut cake into squares to serve. Yield: 15 to 18 servings.

Grace Anne Siekman,
Broken Bow, Nebraska.

CARROT PUDDING CAKE

1 (18.5-ounce) package yellow cake mix
    without pudding
1 (3¾-ounce) package vanilla instant
    pudding mix
½ teaspoon salt
2 teaspoons ground cinnamon
4 eggs
⅓ cup water
¼ cup vegetable oil
3 cups shredded carrots
½ cup raisins, finely chopped
½ cup chopped pecans
Creamy Orange Frosting
Pecan halves

Combine first 7 ingredients; beat 2 minutes at medium speed of electric mixer. Stir in carrots, raisins, and chopped pecans. Pour into 3 greased and floured 9-inch round cakepans.

Bake at 350° for 20 to 25 minutes or until a wooden pick inserted in center comes out clean. Cool in pans 10 minutes; remove from pans, and let cool completely. Spread Creamy Orange Frosting between layers and on top and sides of cake. Garnish top of cake with pecan halves. Yield: one 3-layer cake.

Creamy Orange Frosting:

3 tablespoons butter or margarine,
    softened
1 (8-ounce) package cream cheese,
    softened
1 (16-ounce) package powdered sugar,
    sifted
1 tablespoon grated orange rind

Combine butter and cream cheese, beating until light and fluffy. Add powdered sugar and grated orange rind; beat until smooth. Yield: enough for one 3-layer cake.

EASY LEMON CAKE

2 tablespoons butter or margarine, melted
½ cup chopped pecans
½ cup flaked coconut
1 (18.5-ounce) package lemon cake mix
    without pudding
1 (8-ounce) carton commercial sour cream
4 eggs
¼ cup water
2 tablespoons vegetable oil
1 tablespoon grated lemon rind
1 teaspoon lemon extract
1 cup sifted powdered sugar
2 tablespoons lemon juice

Grease and flour a 10-inch Bundt pan. Combine first 3 ingredients; spread evenly in bottom of pan. Set aside.

Combine next 7 ingredients in a large mixing bowl; beat 2 minutes on medium speed of electric mixer. Spoon batter into prepared pan; bake at 350° for 45 to 50 minutes or until a wooden pick inserted in center comes out clean. Cool in pan 10 minutes; remove from pan, and invert onto cake platter.

Combine sugar and lemon juice, mixing well. Drizzle over warm cake. Yield: one 10-inch cake. *Beulah Smith, Bay Saint Louis, Mississippi.*

MANDARIN ORANGE CAKE

1 (18.5-ounce) package yellow cake mix
    without pudding
1 (11-ounce) can mandarin oranges,
    undrained
4 eggs
½ cup vegetable oil
1 (15¼-ounce) can crushed pineapple,
    undrained
1 (9-ounce) carton frozen whipped
    topping, thawed
1 (3¾-ounce) package vanilla instant
    pudding mix

Combine cake mix, mandarin oranges, eggs, and oil; beat 2 minutes at high speed of electric mixer. Reduce speed to low; beat 1 minute.

Pour batter into 3 greased and floured 9-inch round cakepans. Bake at 350° for 20 to 25 minutes or until a wooden pick inserted in center comes out clean. Cool in pans 10 minutes; remove from pans, and cool completely.

Combine 3 remaining ingredients; beat 2 minutes at medium speed of electric mixer; let stand 5 minutes or until mixture reaches spreading consistency. Spread mixture between layers and on top and sides of cake. Chill at least 2 hours before serving. Store in refrigerator. Yield: one 3-layer cake.

June Bostick, Greenwood, Delaware.

After-Work Entertaining Made Easy

Entertaining on a week night isn't easy, especially if you work outside the home. Compiled for working hosts and hostesses, we offer a company menu that will fit into an after-work schedule and please guests as well.

Any advance preparation will save time on the day of the party. With this menu, you can make the appetizer and salad the day before; they'll be ready to serve when guests arrive.

Creamy Baked Chicken Breasts and the rice casserole can bake at the same temperature about an hour.

Herb-Cream Cheese Spread
Crackers
Creamy Baked Chicken Breasts
French Rice
Crunchy Broccoli and Cauliflower Toss
Sunshine Carrots
Commercial Hard Rolls
Vanilla Ice Cream   Praline Sauce
Iced Tea   Coffee

HERB-CREAM CHEESE SPREAD

2 (8-ounce) packages cream cheese,
    softened
1 tablespoon commercial sour cream
2 tablespoons chopped chives
2 tablespoons chopped fresh parsley
2 teaspoons dried whole dillweed

Combine all ingredients; beat on medium speed of electric mixer until smooth. Serve with crackers or rye bread. Yield: 2 cups. *Tammy Mayo, Lucama, North Carolina.*

CREAMY BAKED CHICKEN BREASTS

8 chicken breasts halves, skinned and
    boned
8 (4-inch) slices Swiss cheese
1 (10¾-ounce) can cream of chicken soup,
    undiluted
¼ cup dry white wine
1 cup herb-seasoned stuffing mix, crushed
¼ cup butter or margarine, melted

Arrange chicken in a lightly greased 13- x 9- x 2-inch baking dish. Top with cheese slices.

Combine soup and wine; stir well. Spoon evenly over chicken; sprinkle with stuffing mix. Drizzle butter over crumbs; bake at 350° for 45 to 55 minutes. Yield: 8 servings. *Thelma Betz, Commerce, Texas.*

FRENCH RICE

1 (10½-ounce) can onion soup, undiluted
½ cup butter or margarine, melted
1 (4½-ounce) jar sliced mushrooms,
    undrained
1 (8-ounce) can sliced water chestnuts,
    undrained
1 cup uncooked regular rice

Combine soup and butter; stir well. Drain mushrooms and water chestnuts, reserving liquid. Add enough water to reserved liquid to equal 1⅓ cups.

Add mushrooms, water chestnuts, liquid, and rice to soup mixture; stir well. Pour into a lightly greased 10- x 6- x 2-inch baking dish. Cover and bake at 350° for 1 hour. Yield: 6 servings.
Mildred Sheppard,
Crawfordville, Florida.

CRUNCHY BROCCOLI AND CAULIFLOWER TOSS

1 small head cauliflower, broken into flowerets
½ pound fresh broccoli, broken into flowerets
½ pint cherry tomatoes, halved
½ cup Italian reduced-calorie dressing

Combine vegetables in a medium bowl. Add dressing; toss lightly. Cover and chill overnight. Yield: 6 servings.
Judy Wilson,
Jupiter, Florida.

SUNSHINE CARROTS

¼ cup plus 2 tablespoons orange juice
¼ cup maple-flavored syrup
2 tablespoons orange marmalade
2 (16-ounce) cans small whole carrots, drained

Combine first 3 ingredients in a medium saucepan; bring to a boil, stirring constantly. Add carrots; return to a boil. Reduce heat to low; cook 5 minutes. Yield: 6 servings.
Mrs. Lloyd E. Reynolds,
York, Pennsylvania.

PRALINE SAUCE

3 tablespoons butter or margarine
1 cup firmly packed brown sugar
½ cup half-and-half
1 cup chopped pecans
1 teaspoon vanilla extract
Ice cream

Melt butter in a heavy saucepan over low heat; add sugar. Cook 5 to 8 minutes, stirring constantly. Remove from heat, and gradually stir in half-and-half. Cook 1 minute, and remove from heat. Stir in pecans and vanilla. Serve over ice cream. Yield: about 1½ cups.

Tip: For a great dessert, pour cream sherry over a chilled grapefruit.

Side Dishes Designed For Two

If you are cooking for two and don't care to store leftovers, try our Green Beans Vinaigrette or Glazed Carrots and Onions; they're colorful, nutritious, and just right for two.

GREEN BEANS VINAIGRETTE

1 (10-ounce) package frozen cut green beans
½ teaspoon prepared mustard
2 tablespoons white wine vinegar
2½ tablespoons olive oil
1 teaspoon diced pimiento
1 teaspoon chopped chives
1 teaspoon minced fresh parsley
¼ teaspoon salt
Dash of ground pepper

Cook beans according to package directions, omitting salt; drain and cool.
Stir mustard into vinegar; add remaining ingredients, mixing well. Pour dressing over beans, and toss. Cover and refrigerate 2 to 3 hours. Yield: 2 servings.
Jolene Christian,
Harrison, Tennessee.

SPANISH-STYLE LIMA BEANS

½ cup dried lima beans
1⅔ cups water
¼ teaspoon salt
1 medium onion, chopped
2 tablespoons vegetable oil
1 cup canned whole tomatoes, undrained and quartered
1 small bay leaf
⅛ to ¼ teaspoon salt
Dash of pepper

Sort and wash beans; place in a saucepan. Cover with water; let sit 8 hours or overnight. Drain.
Combine beans, water, and ¼ teaspoon salt; bring to a boil. Reduce heat, cover, and simmer 30 minutes. Drain, reserving ½ cup liquid in saucepan.
Sauté onion in oil in a heavy skillet until tender. Add onion and remaining ingredients to beans; cover and simmer 1 hour or until beans are tender. Remove bay leaf before serving. Yield: 2 servings.
Margaret Warren,
Crofton, Kentucky.

GLAZED CARROTS AND ONIONS

4 small carrots, scraped and cut into strips
2 tablespoons sugar
⅛ teaspoon ground ginger
½ (16-ounce) jar onions, drained
1½ tablespoons butter or margarine

Cook carrots in a small amount of boiling water 12 to 15 minutes or until tender; drain. Combine sugar and ginger. Roll carrots and onions in sugar mixture until evenly coated.
Sauté carrots and onions in butter in a medium skillet 3 to 5 minutes. Yield: 2 servings.
Irene Harding,
Beckley, West Virginia.

CREAMED POTATOES

2 medium potatoes, peeled and cut into ½-inch slices
¼ cup commercial sour cream
2 tablespoons mayonnaise
½ teaspoon prepared mustard
¼ teaspoon salt
2 tablespoons sliced pitted ripe olives
Chopped fresh parsley

Cook potatoes in boiling water to cover 15 minutes or until tender; drain and keep warm.
Combine sour cream, mayonnaise, mustard, and salt in a medium bowl; stir well. Add potatoes and olives; toss gently to mix. Spoon into serving dish; sprinkle parsley over top. Yield: 2 servings.
Ruth E. Horomanski,
Satellite Beach, Florida.

SWEET POTATO-APPLE BAKE

2 small sweet potatoes
2 small apples, cored and cut into ½-inch slices
1½ tablespoons butter or margarine
¼ cup maple-flavored syrup
1½ tablespoons butter or margarine, melted
½ teaspoon salt

Cook potatoes in boiling water to cover 15 minutes or until fork-tender. Cool. Peel and cut into ½-inch slices.
Sauté apple slices in 1½ tablespoons butter in a large skillet 5 minutes or until apples are slightly tender.
Alternate potatoes and apples, slightly overlapping, in a greased 1-quart baking dish. Combine remaining ingredients; pour over potatoes and apples. Bake, uncovered, at 350° for 25 to 30 minutes. Yield: 2 servings.
Lyn Riggan,
Graham, North Carolina.

Dried Beans Mean Flavor, Economy

It's hard to believe there's a food that's easy on the budget, full of flavor, and rich in nutrients. But that's just what you'll find in dried beans like pintos, navy, or Great Northern beans.

Dried beans are a good source of protein, iron, and several B-complex vitamins, which makes them an excellent choice for meatless main dishes. They add extra flavor to meat dishes as well.

Before cooking, the beans should be soaked in water to replace the moisture lost in drying. It's easiest to soak them overnight, but if you're pressed for time, you can use the quick-soak method. Simply boil the beans in water for 2 minutes. Remove them from the heat; cover and let soak for 1 hour.

TEX-MEX CHILI

½ pound dried pinto beans
1 tablespoon bacon drippings
3 tablespoons chili powder
2 pounds ground beef
2 large green peppers, chopped
2 medium onions, chopped
2 cloves garlic, minced
⅓ cup chili powder
1 tablespoon salt
1 teaspoon sugar
1 teaspoon cumin seeds
1 (16-ounce) can whole tomatoes, undrained
1 dried hot red pepper

Sort and wash pinto beans; place in a large Dutch oven. Cover with water 2 inches above beans; cover and let soak overnight.

Add bacon drippings and 3 tablespoons chili powder to beans. Cover and simmer 1 hour or until tender, adding more water if necessary.

Combine ground beef, green peppers, onion, and garlic in a Dutch oven. Cook over medium heat until ground beef is browned, stirring to crumble; drain. Stir in next 5 ingredients. Cover, reduce heat, and simmer 1 hour and 15 minutes. Add beans and hot red pepper; continue to cook for 15 minutes. Remove hot red pepper before serving. Yield: 2½ quarts. *Marilyn Salinas, Fort Worth, Texas.*

Tip: If soups, stews, or other foods are too salty, add 1 teaspoon of vinegar, 1 teaspoon of sugar, and reheat.

CAJUN RED BEANS AND RICE

1 pound dried kidney beans
½ pound salt pork
3 cups chopped onion
1 cup chopped green onion
1 cup chopped fresh parsley
1 tablespoon garlic salt
¼ teaspoon dried whole oregano
1 teaspoon red pepper
1 tablespoon Worcestershire sauce
1 teaspoon pepper
1½ teaspoons hot sauce
1 (8-ounce) can tomato sauce
1 pound smoked sausage, cut into ¼-inch slices
Hot cooked rice

Sort and wash beans; place in a large Dutch oven. Cover with water 2 inches above beans; let soak overnight. Add salt pork to beans; cover and simmer 45 minutes. Stir in next 10 ingredients; continue to cook 1 hour.

Brown sausage and drain; add to bean mixture. Cover and simmer 45 minutes, adding more water if necessary. Serve over rice. Yield: 6 to 8 servings. *Sallie Speights, Lafayette, Louisiana.*

BEAN AND BACON SOUP

1 pound dried navy beans
6 cups water
2 teaspoons salt
¼ teaspoon pepper
2 cloves garlic, minced
1 bay leaf
4 slices bacon
2 medium onions, finely chopped
1 small green pepper, finely chopped
½ cup finely chopped carrots
1 (8-ounce) can tomato sauce
1 teaspoon minced fresh parsley

Sort and wash beans; place in a large Dutch oven. Cover with water 2 inches above beans; let soak overnight.

Drain beans; cover with 6 cups water. Add salt, pepper, garlic, and bay leaf.

Cook bacon until crisp; remove bacon, reserving drippings. Crumble bacon, and set aside. Add onion and green pepper to drippings; sauté until tender. Add onion, green pepper, and carrots to beans. Bring to a boil; cover, reduce heat, and simmer 1 hour.

Add tomato sauce and parsley to soup; cover and simmer an additional 30 minutes. Remove bay leaf. Ladle into serving bowls, and sprinkle with reserved bacon. Yield: about 3 quarts. *Gwen Tant, Senatobia, Mississippi.*

SPICY HOT PINTOS

1 pound dried pinto beans
¼ pound salt pork, cubed
1 clove garlic, minced
3 to 6 jalapeño peppers, seeded and chopped
3 green onions, chopped
2 medium tomatoes, peeled and chopped
1 teaspoon dried whole coriander
½ teaspoon salt

Sort and wash beans; place in a large Dutch oven. Cover with water 2 inches above beans, and bring to a boil; cook 2 minutes. Remove pinto beans from heat; cover and let soak about 1 hour.

Add salt pork and garlic to beans; cover and simmer 30 minutes. Stir in remaining ingredients; cover and simmer an additional 30 minutes or until beans are tender. Yield: 8 to 10 servings. *Henry D. Medina, San Antonio, Texas.*

GENUINE BAKED BEANS

1 pound dried Great Northern beans
1 (16-ounce) can tomatoes, undrained and cut into eighths
3 medium onions, chopped
½ pound salt pork, cubed
1 cup sugar
1 tablespoon vinegar
1 teaspoon prepared mustard
1 teaspoon salt
⅛ teaspoon pepper

Sort and wash beans; place in a large Dutch oven. Cover with water 2 inches above beans, and bring to a boil; cook 2 minutes. Remove from heat; cover and let soak 1 hour. Drain, reserving ½ cup liquid.

Add liquid and remaining ingredients to beans; spoon bean mixture into a 4-quart casserole. Cover and bake at 350° for 4 to 4½ hours or until tender, adding more water if necessary. Yield: 8 to 10 servings. *Frances C. Hoge, Rogers, Arkansas.*

Right: *Top Crispy Tostadas with avocado wedges and cheese, or spoon a tasty filling into avocado shells for Shrimp-Filled Avocados (recipes on page 2). Just a squirt of lime or lemon juice on cut surfaces will preserve the avocado's fresh color.*

Above: *As varied as the ingredients that go into them, chowders offer something for everyone. Clockwise from the front: Cheesy Vegetable Chowder, Southern Seafood Chowder, and Sausage-Bean Chowder are a few tasty suggestions (recipes on page 20).*

Right: *Our Chili-Topped Potato (page 3) is garnished with cheese and green onion, while the Mexican-Topped Potato (page 3) is crowned with hot cheese sauce, lettuce, and tomato. In the background are two more baked potato variations: a Sweet-and-Sour-Topped Potato (page 4) and Broccoli-and-Almond-Topped Potato (page 3).*

Entrées From The Skillet

Skillet entrées are a good idea for family dinners. They take little time to prepare, and cleanup is a breeze.

SKILLET ROUND STEAK

1 pound boneless round steak, ½-inch thick
¼ cup all-purpose flour
1 teaspoon salt
¼ teaspoon pepper
2 tablespoons butter or margarine
1½ tablespoons Dijon mustard
1 teaspoon Worcestershire sauce
2 cups thinly sliced mushrooms
1 small onion, thinly sliced
3 tablespoons butter or margarine
2 beef-flavored bouillon cubes
½ cup boiling water
¼ cup brandy
1 teaspoon Worcestershire sauce
Chopped fresh parsley (optional)

Trim excess fat from steak. Cut steak into 4 serving pieces; pound to ¼-inch thickness. Combine flour, salt, and pepper; mix well. Dredge steak in flour mixture. Melt 2 tablespoons butter in a large skillet; add steak, and brown on both sides. Remove steak from skillet. Combine mustard and 1 teaspoon Worcestershire sauce, mixing well; spread on both sides of steak. Set aside.

Sauté mushrooms and onion in 3 tablespoons butter until tender. Dissolve bouillon cubes in boiling water; stir into mushroom mixture. Add brandy, 1 teaspoon Worcestershire sauce, and steak. Cover, reduce heat, and simmer 20 minutes. Sprinkle with parsley, if desired. Yield: 4 servings.
Mrs. W. P. Mayes,
Shelby, North Carolina.

TASTY LIVER

1½ pounds thinly sliced beef liver
½ cup all-purpose flour
1 teaspoon chili powder
⅛ teaspoon salt
3 tablespoons shortening
2 cups thinly sliced onion
½ cup chopped green pepper
1 (16-ounce) can whole tomatoes, undrained and coarsely chopped

Cut liver into 2- x ½-inch strips. Combine flour, chili powder, and salt; dredge liver strips in flour mixture.

Melt shortening in a large skillet; add liver, and cook until browned. Remove liver from skillet, reserving pan drippings. Sauté onion and green pepper in reserved drippings. Add liver and tomatoes. Cover, reduce heat, and simmer 25 to 30 minutes, stirring occasionally. Yield: 6 servings. *Ruby Vineyard,*
Rutledge, Tennessee.

PORK CHOPS WITH PEANUT SAUCE

2 tablespoons vegetable oil
6 (½-inch-thick) pork chops
¼ cup chopped onion
¼ cup butter or margarine
1½ cups water
2 chicken-flavored bouillon cubes
3 tablespoons chopped fresh parsley
⅛ teaspoon garlic powder
⅛ teaspoon pepper
⅛ teaspoon ground cloves
⅛ teaspoon ground cinnamon
1 small bay leaf
1 to 2 drops hot sauce
2 tablespoons all-purpose flour
½ cup water
Hot cooked rice
½ cup chopped roasted peanuts

Heat vegetable oil in a large skillet; add pork chops, and brown on both sides. Remove chops from skillet; drain.

Sauté onion in butter in skillet until tender. Stir in next 9 ingredients; add chops. Cover and simmer 45 minutes or until tender. Remove chops from skillet, and discard bay leaf.

Combine flour and ½ cup water, stirring until smooth. Gradually stir flour mixture into skillet mixture; cook over medium heat, stirring constantly, until thickened and bubbly.

Arrange rice on a platter; top with pork chops. Pour sauce over chops; sprinkle with peanuts. Yield: 6 servings.
Linda H. Sutton,
Winston-Salem, North Carolina.

SAUSAGE SKILLET DINNER

1 pound smoked sausage, cut into ¼-inch slices
1 medium onion, chopped
½ cup chopped green pepper
½ cup sliced celery
2 tablespoons butter or margarine
4 cups cooked elbow macaroni
2 (8-ounce) cans tomato sauce
1 teaspoon chili powder
¼ teaspoon pepper
½ cup (2 ounces) shredded Cheddar cheese

Sauté sausage, onion, green pepper, and celery in butter in a large skillet until vegetables are tender. Stir in remaining ingredients, except cheese. Cook over low heat, stirring frequently, until thoroughly heated. Sprinkle with cheese, and cook until cheese melts. Yield: 6 servings. *Kathryn Stade,*
Rosenberg, Texas.

Serve A Savory Shrimp Dish

Shrimp is always a favorite, and with a dish of Cashew Shrimp Supreme, you can enjoy this delicacy in a colorful one-dish meal. The shrimp are halved lengthwise for a pretty shape, sautéed, then tossed with a mixture of cooked rice, chopped zucchini, sweet red pepper, and cashews.

CASHEW SHRIMP SUPREME

1 pound medium shrimp, peeled and deveined
1 tablespoon plus 1 teaspoon cornstarch
¼ teaspoon sugar
¼ teaspoon baking soda
¼ teaspoon salt
⅛ teaspoon pepper
½ cup vegetable oil
½ cup chopped onion
¼ cup chopped sweet red pepper
1 small clove garlic, minced
1 cup chopped, unpeeled zucchini
3½ cups cooked rice
¾ cup cashews
Sweet red pepper rings

Cut shrimp in half lengthwise. Combine next 5 ingredients; mix well. Add shrimp, and toss gently to coat. Let stand 15 minutes.

Heat oil in a large skillet over medium-high heat, and add shrimp. Cook, stirring constantly, 3 to 5 minutes. Remove shrimp; set aside. Drain off drippings, reserving 2 tablespoons in skillet.

Sauté onion, chopped red pepper, and garlic in skillet until tender. Add zucchini, and sauté 2 minutes. Stir in shrimp, rice, and cashews; cook over low heat, stirring constantly, until thoroughly heated. Spoon into serving dish. Garnish with red pepper rings. Yield: 4 servings. *Mrs. R. L. Bradley,*
Sparta, Tennessee.

Warm Up With Chili

A bowl of spicy chili is one of the best warm-ups on a cold winter day. Many chili lovers like to individualize the basic recipe—making it as fiery as they choose. A generous amount of chili powder goes into Texas-Style Chili, while Company Chili gets extra hotness from smoked sausage and mustard.

CHILI CON CARNE

1½ pounds boneless round steak, cut into
½-inch cubes
2 tablespoons vegetable oil
1 (15-ounce) can tomato sauce
1½ cups water
1 beef-flavored bouillon cube
2 tablespoons chili powder
2 teaspoons dried whole oregano
1 teaspoon salt
1 teaspoon ground cumin
1 teaspoon minced garlic
½ teaspoon hot sauce
2 tablespoons cornmeal
2 (16-ounce) cans kidney beans, undrained

Brown meat in oil in a Dutch oven. Add tomato sauce, water, and bouillon cube; cover and simmer 30 minutes. Add next 6 ingredients; cover and simmer 40 minutes, stirring occasionally. Stir in cornmeal and beans. Cover and simmer 30 minutes, adding additional water if necessary. Yield: about 2 quarts. *Charlie R. Hester,*
Austin, Texas.

Sausage, beef, and beans make Company Chili a hearty main dish that's rich in protein.

EASY CHILI

1 pound ground beef
1 onion, chopped
1 (8-ounce) can tomato sauce
1 cup water
½ cup chopped green pepper
1½ to 2 tablespoons chili powder
½ teaspoon salt
¼ teaspoon pepper
Dash of ground oregano
2 (16-ounce) cans kidney beans, undrained

Combine ground beef and onion in a Dutch oven; cook until beef is browned, stirring to crumble meat. Drain off pan drippings. Add remaining ingredients, except beans; cover and simmer 20 minutes. Stir in beans; continue to cook, covered, 45 minutes. Remove cover, and cook an additional 15 minutes. Yield: 2 quarts. *Virginia M. Mathews,*
Jacksonville, Florida.

COMPANY CHILI

1 pound ground beef
1 pound hot smoked sausage, sliced
1 cup chopped onion
1 (28-ounce) can pinto beans, undrained
1 (28-ounce) can whole tomatoes,
undrained and chopped
½ cup catsup
1 tablespoon chili powder
2 teaspoons brown sugar
1 teaspoon spicy brown mustard
½ teaspoon salt

Combine ground beef, sausage, and onion in a Dutch oven; cook until beef is browned, stirring to crumble. Drain.

Drain pinto beans, reserving liquid. Add liquid to Dutch oven; stir in remaining ingredients except beans. Cover and simmer 45 minutes. Stir in beans. Cook an additional 15 minutes. Yield: about 3 quarts. *Mary H. Gilliam,*
Cartersville, Virginia.

TEXAS-STYLE CHILI

3 pounds ground chuck
1 pound hot bulk sausage
3 medium onions, chopped
4 cloves garlic, minced
¼ cup chili powder
2 tablespoons all-purpose flour
1 tablespoon sugar
1 tablespoon ground oregano
1 teaspoon salt
2 (28-ounce) cans whole tomatoes,
undrained and chopped
3 (16-ounce) cans kidney beans, drained

Combine ground chuck, sausage, onion, and garlic in a Dutch oven; cook until meat is browned, stirring to crumble. Drain. Stir in next 6 ingredients. Cover and simmer 1 hour, stirring occasionally. Add beans, and simmer an additional 20 minutes. Yield: about 5 quarts. *Faye Beard,*
Lipscomb, Alabama.

A Pocket Full Of Flavor

If sandwiches are a favorite at your house, you've probably already discovered the advantages of pita bread. Each bread round, when cut in half, becomes two ideal sandwich pockets. Since the edges of the pockets are sealed, even the juiciest of sandwich fillings aren't messy to eat.

TACO PITAS

1 pound ground beef
1 (1¼-ounce) package taco seasoning mix
¾ cup water
1 (10-ounce) can tomatoes and green chiles, drained
1 (8¾-ounce) can whole kernel corn, drained
5 (6-inch) pocket bread rounds
1 cup shredded lettuce
¾ cup (3 ounces) shredded Cheddar cheese

Cook ground beef until browned, stirring to crumble meat; drain off drippings. Add next 4 ingredients; bring to a boil. Reduce heat and simmer, uncovered, 15 to 20 minutes.

Cut bread rounds in half; place on a baking sheet. Bake at 250° for 10 minutes or until warm.

Fill each pocket half full with meat mixture; top with lettuce and cheese. Yield: 10 sandwiches. *Susan Bellows, Birmingham, Alabama.*

BAVARIAN PITA SANDWICHES

1 pound ground beef
½ cup chopped onion
¼ cup chopped green pepper
1 (0.87-ounce) package beef gravy mix
1¼ cups water
2 cups shredded cabbage
4 (6-inch) pocket bread rounds
1 cup (4 ounces) shredded Cheddar cheese

Combine first 3 ingredients in a large skillet; cook over medium heat until meat is browned, stirring to crumble. Drain. Add gravy mix, water, and shredded cabbage; cook over medium heat 5 minutes or until thickened.

Cut bread rounds in half; place on a baking sheet. Bake at 250° for 10 minutes or until warm.

Fill each pocket about three-fourths full with ground beef mixture. Top with cheese. Yield: 8 sandwiches.
Mrs. Robert W. Pierce, Germantown, Tennessee.

HAM AND SWISS IN THE POCKET

1 (6¾-ounce) can chunk ham, drained
2 teaspoons prepared mustard
¼ teaspoon onion powder
2 (6-inch) pocket bread rounds
4 (3½-inch) slices Swiss cheese, cut in half diagonally

Combine first 3 ingredients; mix well. Cut bread rounds in half. Place 2 cheese triangles in each pocket. Fill each pocket with one-fourth of ham mixture, and place on a baking sheet. Cover and bake at 350° for 15 to 20 minutes or until thoroughly heated. Yield: 4 sandwiches. *Aida N. Moultrie, Birmingham, Alabama.*

Green Chiles Are Spicy But Mild

In a family known for being fiery, green chiles enjoy the reputation of being delightfully mild, but with a pungent flavor. Unlike hot jalapeño chile peppers (also green), mild green chiles are large and long. They can be purchased fresh or in cans.

GREEN CHILE QUICHE

Pastry for 9-inch pie
½ pound ground beef
¼ cup chopped onion
1 (4-ounce) can chopped green chiles, drained
2 cups (8 ounces) shredded Monterey Jack cheese
3 eggs, beaten
1 cup milk
¼ teaspoon salt
Dash of garlic powder

Line a 9-inch quiche dish with pastry; trim excess pastry around edges. Prick bottom and sides of quiche shell with a fork; bake at 375° for 10 minutes. Let cool on a rack.

Cook beef and onion until beef is browned and onion is tender, stirring to crumble; drain.

Sprinkle ground beef mixture into pastry shell; top with green chiles and cheese. Combine last 4 ingredients, mixing well. Pour into pastry shell. Bake at 375° for 35 minutes or until set. Yield: one 9-inch quiche. *Patricia Burch, Wichita Falls, Texas.*

MEXICAN RICE CASSEROLE

1 cup uncooked regular rice
1 (16-ounce) carton commercial sour cream
2 cups (8 ounces) shredded Monterey Jack cheese
2 (4-ounce) cans chopped green chiles, drained
2 cups cooked, chopped turkey
¼ teaspoon salt

Cook rice according to package directions, omitting salt. Stir remaining ingredients into rice, and spoon mixture into a 2-quart casserole. Bake, uncovered, at 350° for 30 minutes. Yield: 8 servings. *Mrs. William C. DeLee, Dallas, Texas.*

MEXICAN SQUASH

5 medium zucchini, unpeeled and cut into ¼-inch slices
1 large onion, chopped
2 tablespoons vegetable oil
1 (16-ounce) can whole tomatoes, undrained
1 (4-ounce) can chopped green chiles, undrained
½ cup grated Parmesan cheese

Cook zucchini in boiling salted water to cover 10 minutes or until tender. Drain well, and set aside.

Sauté onion in oil until tender; stir in tomatoes and green chiles, and cook 15 minutes or until thick.

Place zucchini in a 12- x 8- x 2-inch baking dish; top with tomato mixture. Sprinkle casserole with Parmesan cheese. Bake at 350° for 20 minutes. Yield: 6 to 8 servings. *Bobbye Crane, Dallas, Texas.*

CHEESE-AND-CHILE DIP

1 (8-ounce) package cream cheese, softened
1½ cups (6 ounces) shredded mild Cheddar cheese
1 tablespoon lemon juice
1 tablespoon chicken-flavored bouillon granules
Dash of hot sauce
1 medium tomato, chopped
1 (4-ounce) can chopped green chiles, drained
1 tablespoon finely chopped onion
Green chile strip

Combine first 5 ingredients in a mixing bowl; beat at medium speed of electric mixer until smooth. Stir in next three ingredients. Chill. Garnish with green chile strip. Yield: about 2 cups.
Cynthia Shipley, Dallas, Texas.

Vegetable Casseroles In 30 Minutes

When time is running short, you'll appreciate the convenience of these delicious vegetable casseroles. Made with canned or frozen vegetables, they take only 30 minutes to bake.

CHEESY ASPARAGUS CASSEROLE

2 tablespoons butter or margarine
1 tablespoon all-purpose flour
1 (10¾-ounce) can cream of mushroom soup, undiluted
2 cups (8 ounces) shredded Cheddar cheese
2 hard-cooked eggs, sliced
2 (15-ounce) cans asparagus spears, drained
½ cup soft breadcrumbs

Melt butter in a heavy saucepan over low heat; add flour, stirring until smooth. Add soup and Cheddar cheese; cook until cheese melts and mixture is smooth, stirring constantly.

Layer half each of egg slices, asparagus spears, and cheese sauce in a lightly greased 10- x 6- x 2-inch baking dish; repeat the layers. Sprinkle with breadcrumbs. Bake at 325° for 30 minutes. Yield: 8 servings. *Margaret Smith, Lauderdale-by-the-Sea, Florida.*

PEA CASSEROLE SUPREME

⅓ cup finely chopped green pepper
1 small onion, grated
2 cups finely chopped celery
3 tablespoons butter or margarine
2 (17-ounce) cans tiny English peas, drained
2 tablespoons diced pimiento
1 (8-ounce) can whole water chestnuts, drained and thinly sliced
1 (10¾-ounce) can cream of mushroom soup, undiluted
2 tablespoons milk
¾ cup soft breadcrumbs

Sauté green pepper, onion, and celery in butter in a large saucepan until tender. Remove from heat. Add next 5 ingredients; mix well. Spoon mixture into a greased 10- x 6- x 2-inch baking dish; sprinkle with breadcrumbs. Bake, uncovered, at 350° for 30 minutes. Yield: 8 servings. *Mrs. Windsor Pipes, Baton Rouge, Louisiana.*

ITALIAN BROCCOLI CASSEROLE

2 (10-ounce) packages frozen chopped broccoli
2 eggs, beaten
1 (11-ounce) can condensed Cheddar cheese soup, undiluted
½ teaspoon dried whole oregano
1 (8-ounce) can stewed tomatoes, drained
3 tablespoons grated Parmesan cheese

Cook broccoli according to package directions, omitting salt; drain well.

Combine next 3 ingredients in a large bowl; mix well. Stir in broccoli and tomatoes. Spoon mixture into a greased 10- x 6- x 2-inch baking dish; sprinkle with Parmesan cheese. Bake, uncovered, at 350° for 30 minutes. Yield: 8 servings. *Barbara Schildgen, Dothan, Alabama.*

SPINACH-PARMESAN CASSEROLE

2 (10-ounce) packages frozen chopped spinach
½ cup chopped onion
1 tablespoon butter or margarine
1 (8-ounce) carton commercial sour cream
½ cup grated Parmesan cheese
2 tablespoons lemon juice
¼ teaspoon garlic salt
½ cup soft breadcrumbs

Cook spinach according to package directions; drain well, and set aside.

Sauté onion in butter in a large saucepan until tender; remove from heat. Add spinach and remaining ingredients except breadcrumbs; mix well. Spoon mixture into a greased 1-quart casserole; sprinkle with breadcrumbs. Bake, uncovered, at 350° for 30 minutes. Yield: about 6 servings.
Brett Van Dorsten, Arcadia, California.

Rolls Baked With Sugar And Spice

A whiff of warm, spicy sweet rolls brings memories of favorite flavors. Try Orange Butter Rolls, crescent-shaped yeast rolls enriched with sour cream and spread with a coconut and orange rind filling. They're coated with a mixture of orange juice, butter, sour cream, and sugar while warm, then sprinkled with toasted coconut.

RAISIN CINNAMON PULL-APARTS

1 package dry yeast
½ cup warm water (105° to 115°)
3 tablespoons sugar
½ teaspoon salt
2 tablespoons butter or margarine, softened
1 egg
About 2½ cups all-purpose flour, divided
2 tablespoons butter or margarine, melted
⅓ cup sugar
1 teaspoon ground cinnamon
⅓ cup raisins
1 cup sifted powdered sugar
2 tablespoons water

Dissolve yeast in warm water. Add sugar, salt, butter, egg, and 1 cup flour; beat well. Gradually stir in enough remaining flour to make a soft dough. Turn out onto a lightly floured surface; knead 5 minutes. Roll into an 18- x 9-inch rectangle.

Brush dough with melted butter; sprinkle with ⅓ cup sugar, cinnamon, and raisins. Roll dough up jellyroll fashion, beginning at long side; moisten edges with water to seal. Cut roll into 1½-inch slices; place slices cut side down in a lightly greased 8-inch round cakepan. Cover; let rise in a warm place (85°), free from drafts, 1 hour or until doubled in bulk.

Bake at 375° for 30 to 35 minutes. Combine powdered sugar and 2 tablespoons water, mixing well. Drizzle glaze over warm rolls. Yield: 1 dozen.
Judy Cunningham, Roanoke, Virginia.

SPIRAL CINNAMON ROLLS

¼ cup milk, scalded
¼ cup sugar
½ teaspoon salt
3 tablespoons butter or margarine
1 package dry yeast
¼ cup warm water (105° to 115°)
2¼ cups all-purpose flour, divided
1 egg
2 tablespoons butter or margarine, softened
¼ cup firmly packed brown sugar
½ teaspoon ground cinnamon
1 tablespoon butter or margarine, melted
1 cup sifted powdered sugar
2 tablespoons milk

Combine first 4 ingredients; stir until butter melts. Cool mixture to lukewarm (105° to 115°).

Dissolve yeast in warm water in a large mixing bowl. Stir in milk mixture, 1½ cups flour, and egg; beat at medium speed of electric mixer until smooth.

Stir in the ¾ cup remaining flour to make a stiff dough.

Turn dough out onto a lightly floured surface; knead 8 minutes or until smooth and elastic. Place dough in a greased bowl, turning to grease top. Cover and let rise in a warm place (85°), free from drafts, about 1 hour (dough will not double in bulk).

Turn dough out onto a lightly floured surface; roll into a 12- x 8-inch rectangle, and spread with 2 tablespoons butter. Combine brown sugar and cinnamon; sprinkle mixture over rectangle. Roll up jellyroll fashion, beginning at long side; moisten edges with water to seal. Cut rolls into 1-inch slices; place slices cut side down in greased muffin pans. Brush tops with 1 tablespoon melted butter. Using a fork, gently lift center of rolls to form a peak.

Cover and let rise in a warm place (85°), free from drafts, about 40 minutes (rolls will not double in bulk). Bake at 350° for 20 minutes. Combine powdered sugar and 2 tablespoons milk, beating well. Drizzle over warm rolls. Yield: 1 dozen. *Mrs. Larry Edlefson, Houma, Louisiana.*

ORANGE BUTTER ROLLS

1 package dry yeast
¼ cup warm water (105° to 115°)
¼ cup plus 2 tablespoons butter, melted
½ cup commercial sour cream
¼ cup sugar
2 eggs
1 teaspoon salt
About 3¼ cups all-purpose flour
¾ cup sugar
1 cup flaked coconut, toasted and divided
2 tablespoons grated orange rind
2 tablespoons butter, melted
Orange glaze (recipe follows)

Dissolve yeast in warm water in a large mixing bowl. Add next 5 ingredients, mixing well. Gradually stir in enough flour to make a soft dough; mix well. Place in a well-greased bowl, turning to grease top. Cover and let rise in a warm place (85°), free from drafts, 1½ to 2 hours or until doubled in bulk.

Combine ¾ cup sugar, ¾ cup coconut, and orange rind; set aside.

Punch dough down. Turn dough out onto a floured surface, and knead 7 minutes or until smooth and elastic. Divide dough in half. Roll each half into a circle about 12 inches in diameter; brush each circle with 1 tablespoon butter. Sprinkle each with half the coconut mixture; cut into 12 wedges. Roll each wedge tightly, beginning at wide end.

Place rolls on greased baking sheets, point side down. Curve into crescent shape. Cover and let rise 45 minutes or until doubled in bulk. Bake at 350° for 25 to 30 minutes or until lightly browned. While rolls are warm, drizzle with glaze. Sprinkle with remaining ¼ cup coconut. Yield: 2 dozen.

Orange Glaze:

¾ cup sugar
½ cup commercial sour cream
¼ cup butter or margarine
2 tablespoons orange juice

Combine all ingredients in a saucepan. Cook over low heat, stirring frequently, until heated. (Do not boil.) Yield: about ½ cup. *Betty Rabe, Plano, Texas.*

Warm Up To A Hot Punch

When you need a hot, nutritious beverage, we suggest steaming-hot mugs of Spiced Pineapple Punch. It's four kinds of fruit juice simmered with cinnamon sticks, cardamom, and cloves.

Grape juice, orange juice, whole cloves, and cinnamon sticks combine for another spicy brew called Hot Fruit Punch.

HOT FRUIT PUNCH

4 cups water
½ cup sugar
10 whole cloves
2 (3-inch) sticks cinnamon
4 cups grape juice
2 cups orange juice
Orange slices (optional)

Combine first 4 ingredients in a large saucepan; bring to a boil, stirring until sugar is dissolved. Reduce heat, and simmer 5 minutes. Strain mixture, discarding the spices. Gradually add juice to hot mixture; heat thoroughly. Garnish with orange slices, if desired. Yield: 10 cups. *Mrs. Edward E. Gnau, Pine Bluff, Arkansas.*

SPICED PINEAPPLE PUNCH

4 cups unsweetened pineapple juice
2 cups apple cider
1 (12-ounce) can apricot nectar
1 cup orange juice
2 (3-inch) sticks cinnamon, broken
1 teaspoon whole cloves
4 cardamom seeds or 1 teaspoon ground cardamom

Combine all ingredients in a 4-quart saucepan; bring to a boil. Reduce heat and simmer, uncovered, 15 minutes. Strain punch, discarding spices. Yield: about 8½ cups. *Dorothy Burgess, Huntsville, Texas.*

Hot Sandwiches For Chilly Days

Lighten up lunch or liven up supper with one of these hot and saucy sandwiches. Add a serving of coleslaw, potato salad, or a choice of relishes, and enjoy an easy but nourishing meal.

OPEN-FACE CHILI BURGERS

1½ pounds ground beef
½ cup chopped onion
1 (8-ounce) can tomato sauce
1 (1¼-ounce) package taco seasoning mix
6 hamburger buns
12 slices tomato
1 cup (4 ounces) shredded Cheddar cheese
¾ cup shredded lettuce
¼ cup chopped stuffed olives
1 small onion, cut into rings and separated
1½ tablespoons chopped red and green chiles

Brown beef and onion in a large skillet, stirring to crumble; drain. Stir in tomato sauce and taco seasoning; simmer 5 minutes. Split and toast hamburger buns; spread with meat mixture. Place tomato slice on each sandwich, and sprinkle with cheese; bake at 400° for 4 minutes or until cheese melts. Top with lettuce, olives, onion, and chiles. Yield: 12 servings. *Dorothy Cox, Snyder, Texas.*

Tip: Always turn saucepan and skillet handles toward the back of the range to prevent accidents.

EASY SLOPPY JOES

1 pound ground beef
1 medium onion, chopped
1 teaspoon salt
¼ teaspoon pepper
1 (10¾-ounce) can chicken gumbo soup, undiluted
1½ tablespoons catsup
1 tablespoon prepared mustard
6 to 8 hamburger buns

Combine beef, onion, salt, and pepper in a large skillet; cook until meat is lightly browned, stirring to crumble. Drain. Stir in soup, catsup, and mustard; simmer 15 minutes. Serve on buns. Yield: 6 to 8 servings.
Gayle Hurdle,
Carthage, Mississippi.

BARBECUED BEEF SANDWICHES

1½ pounds ground beef
¾ cup finely chopped celery
¾ cup finely chopped onion
½ cup finely chopped green pepper
1 (8-ounce) can tomato sauce
¼ cup catsup
2 tablespoons brown sugar
2 tablespoons barbecue sauce
2 tablespoons vinegar
1 tablespoon prepared mustard
1 tablespoon Worcestershire sauce
1½ teaspoons salt
¼ teaspoon pepper
8 to 10 hamburger buns

Brown beef in a large skillet, stirring to crumble; drain. Add celery, onion, and green pepper; cook 5 minutes or until onion is tender. Add next 9 ingredients; cover and simmer 1 hour. Serve on buns. Yield: 8 to 10 servings.
Sherry Smith,
Afton, Tennessee.

SAUCY CHICK-WICHES

4 slices cooked chicken
4 slices bread, toasted and buttered
8 slices tomato
4 slices process American cheese
1 (10½-ounce) can chicken gravy

Arrange chicken on toast; top with tomato slices. Broil 4 inches from heat for 3 minutes or until hot. Top with cheese, and broil until melted. Heat gravy, and spoon over sandwiches. Yield: 4 servings. *Melody Fowler,*
Devine, Texas.

Bake Oysters In A Casserole

Many oyster fans like to eat this delicately flavored shellfish raw—right out of the shell. But if you prefer yours cooked, try combining them with spinach, corn, or wild rice for a casserole.

OYSTER AND WILD RICE CASSEROLE

1 (6-ounce) package long grain and wild rice
½ cup cream of chicken soup, undiluted
½ cup half-and-half
1 tablespoon finely chopped onion
1 teaspoon curry powder
½ teaspoon dried whole thyme
Dash of Worcestershire sauce
¼ cup dry sherry
1 pint oysters, drained
8 mushroom caps
1 tablespoon lemon juice
Fresh parsley sprigs (optional)

Prepare rice according to package directions; set aside.
Combine next 6 ingredients in a small bowl; mix well.
Pour sherry in a lightly greased 10- x 6- x 2-inch baking dish; top with half of rice. Pour one-third soup mixture over rice. Arrange oysters and mushroom caps over soup mixture. Sprinkle with lemon juice. Top with remaining rice and soup mixture. Bake at 350° for 45 minutes. Garnish with parsley, if desired. Yield: 6 to 8 servings.
Fred T. Marshall,
Hollywood, Maryland.

OYSTER AND CORN BAKE

¼ cup butter or margarine, melted
1½ cups fine cracker crumbs
2 tablespoons chopped fresh parsley
⅓ cup chopped onion
⅓ cup chopped celery
2 tablespoons butter or margarine
1 pint oysters, undrained
1 (8¾-ounce) can whole kernel corn, drained
1 (2-ounce) jar diced pimiento, drained
1 teaspoon Worcestershire sauce
½ teaspoon salt
Pinch of pepper

Combine ¼ cup butter, crumbs, and parsley; mix well. Set aside.
Sauté onion and celery in 2 tablespoons butter in a skillet until tender. Drain oysters, reserving ¼ cup liquid.

Stir reserved oyster liquid, corn, pimiento, Worcestershire sauce, salt, and pepper into sautéed vegetables.
Place 1 cup crumb mixture in a lightly greased 10- x 6- x 2-inch baking dish. Arrange oysters over crumbs; spoon vegetable mixture on top. Cover with remaining crumb mixture; bake at 375° for 30 minutes or until golden brown. Yield: 6 servings. *Kathryn Bibelhauser,*
Louisville, Kentucky.

OYSTER AND SPINACH CASSEROLE

1 (10-ounce) package frozen chopped spinach
½ pint oysters, drained
¼ cup grated Parmesan cheese
⅛ teaspoon garlic powder
⅛ teaspoon pepper
3 slices bacon, cooked and crumbled
2 tablespoons butter or margarine, melted
1 tablespoon lemon juice

Cook spinach according to package directions, omitting salt; drain well.
Place spinach in a lightly greased 1-quart casserole; arrange oysters over spinach. Sprinkle with cheese, garlic powder, and pepper; top with bacon. Combine butter and lemon juice; pour over oyster mixture. Bake at 450° for 5 to 7 minutes. Yield: 4 servings.
David L. Nickel,
Irvington, Virginia.

COOKING LIGHT

Discover Entrées Without Salt

Nutrition experts tell us we'd be better off eating less salt. For many people, that's tough advice to follow. But cutting back on salt can open up a whole new world of flavors. You suddenly learn to appreciate the real taste of food instead of the salt-covered taste.
Since most marinades for meat have a reputation for saltiness, we developed a low-sodium marinade that tenderizes flank steak, and adds only a minimal amount of sodium. When adapting your own marinades, be careful about using ingredients that contain sodium, such as

soy sauce, steak sauce, chili sauce, Worcestershire sauce, salted meat tenderizers, MSG (monosodium glutamate), catsup, and prepared mustard.

Feel free to use wine in marinades and other meat, fish, and poultry dishes. Experiment with a variety of table wines in your recipes, but avoid using cooking wines.

Look for hidden sources of salt and sodium by reading food labels. Most natural cheeses are high in sodium, as are canned fish and cured or processed meats such as bacon, ham, sausage, and luncheon meats.

MARINATED FLANK STEAK

¼ cup vinegar
¼ cup vegetable oil
1 onion, finely chopped
2 cloves garlic, crushed
½ teaspoon dried whole basil
½ teaspoon dry mustard
¼ teaspoon Tabasco pepper sauce
2 (1-pound) flank steaks

Combine first 7 ingredients in a large baking dish, blending well. Place steaks in dish; spoon marinade over steaks. Cover and refrigerate overnight.

Remove steak from marinade. Place on grill 5 inches from hot coals, or broil 5 inches from heat. Cook about 4 minutes on each side or to desired doneness; baste frequently with marinade. To serve, slice steak across the grain into thin slices. Yield: 8 servings (about 90 milligrams sodium per serving).

PARSLEYED MEAT LOAF

2 pounds lean ground beef
2 cups chopped fresh parsley
1¼ cups soft, low-sodium breadcrumbs
1 medium onion, chopped
1 large clove garlic, crushed
2 eggs, beaten
2 tablespoons chopped green pepper
1 teaspoon freshly ground pepper
½ teaspoon dried whole thyme
¼ teaspoon ground allspice
⅛ teaspoon ground nutmeg
⅛ teaspoon red pepper
3 bay leaves

Combine all ingredients except bay leaves in a large mixing bowl; mix lightly. Spread mixture in a shallow 2-quart casserole, and arrange bay leaves on top. Bake meat loaf at 350° for 1 hour or until done. Drain off drippings. Yield: 8 servings (about 101 milligrams sodium per serving). *Janet MacHardy, Maitland, Florida.*

CHICKEN PICCATA

4 (½-pound) chicken breast halves, boned and skinned
3 tablespoons all-purpose flour
2 tablespoons unsalted margarine
1 tablespoon vegetable oil
1 tablespoon unsalted margarine
½ cup chopped onion
1 cup water
1 teaspoon low-sodium chicken-flavored bouillon granules
1 lemon, thinly sliced
2 tablespoons chopped fresh parsley

Place each chicken breast half on a sheet of waxed paper. Flatten chicken to ¼-inch thickness using a meat mallet or rolling pin; dredge with flour. Heat 2 tablespoons margarine and oil in a large skillet over medium-high heat; add chicken, and cook 2 to 3 minutes on each side or until golden brown. Remove chicken, and set aside.

Melt 1 tablespoon margarine in skillet; add onion, and sauté until tender. Stir in water, bouillon granules, and lemon; bring to a boil, scraping skillet to loosen clinging particles. Return chicken to skillet, reduce heat, and simmer 3 to 4 minutes or until bouillon dissolves and sauce is slightly thickened.

To serve, arrange chicken on a platter. Pour sauce over chicken, and garnish with parsley. Yield: 4 servings (about 65 milligrams sodium per serving). *Helen Cohrs, Lexington, Missouri.*

CHICKEN-TOMATO BAKE

¼ cup unsalted margarine
1 (3½-pound) broiler-fryer, cut up and skinned
1 large onion, finely chopped
3 cloves garlic, minced
8 large mushrooms, sliced
3 large tomatoes, peeled and chopped
½ cup minced fresh parsley
1 teaspoon dried whole rosemary
¼ teaspoon freshly ground pepper
6 ounces uncooked spaghetti

Melt margarine in a large, heavy skillet over medium-high heat; add chicken pieces, and brown on all sides. Transfer chicken to a 13- x 9- x 2-inch baking dish, reserving 2 tablespoons drippings in skillet.

Add onion, garlic, and mushrooms to skillet; sauté until vegetables are tender. Stir in next 4 ingredients; cover and simmer 5 minutes.

Spoon vegetable mixture over chicken; cover and bake at 350° for 35 to 40 minutes or until chicken is tender.

Cook spaghetti according to package directions, omitting the salt. Serve spaghetti with chicken and sauce. Yield: 6 servings (about 164 milligrams sodium per serving). *Mary M. Kruse, Mesa, Arizona.*

ORANGE LAMB CHOPS

1 tablespoon grated orange rind
½ cup unsweetened orange juice
½ teaspoon dried whole thyme
⅛ teaspoon freshly ground pepper
4 (½-inch-thick) lamb chops (about 1¼ pounds)
Vegetable cooking spray
1 tablespoon unsalted margarine
1 cup sliced fresh mushrooms
½ cup Chablis or other dry white wine

Combine first 4 ingredients in a shallow baking dish, mixing well. Trim excess fat from lamb chops. Place chops in dish; spoon orange juice mixture over chops. Cover and refrigerate 3 hours.

Coat a large skillet with cooking spray. Remove lamb chops from marinade, reserving liquid; arrange in skillet. Place skillet over medium-high heat, and brown lamb chops on both sides. Remove chops from skillet.

Melt margarine in skillet over medium heat; add mushrooms, and sauté just until tender. Stir in reserved marinade and wine; bring to a boil. Return lamb chops to skillet. Cover, reduce heat, and simmer 10 minutes. Uncover and simmer for 10 minutes or until sauce reduces to about ½ cup. Yield: 4 servings (about 74 milligrams sodium per serving). *Mrs. J. R. Currie, Huntsville, Alabama.*

POACHED SALMON

1½ cups Chablis or other dry white wine
½ cup water
1 onion, sliced
1 lemon, sliced
4 sprigs fresh parsley
1 teaspoon dried whole dillweed
¼ teaspoon pepper
4 (1-inch-thick) salmon steaks (about 1½ pounds)
Lemon slices

Combine first 7 ingredients in a large skillet, and bring to a boil. Cover, reduce heat, and simmer 10 minutes. Add salmon steaks; cover and simmer 8 minutes or until fish flakes easily. Garnish with lemon slices. Yield: 4 servings (about 84 milligrams sodium per serving). *Mrs. Joseph T. Brown, Towson, Maryland.*

SPECIAL BOILED SHRIMP

4 large bay leaves
20 whole peppercorns
12 whole cloves
1 teaspoon mustard seeds
1 teaspoon crushed red pepper
1 teaspoon dried whole marjoram
½ teaspoon dried whole basil
¼ teaspoon dried whole thyme
⅛ teaspoon caraway seeds
⅛ teaspoon cumin seeds
⅛ teaspoon fennel seeds
⅛ teaspoon celery seeds
2 quarts water
1 lemon, quartered
4 cloves garlic
2½ pounds unpeeled medium or large
  shrimp
Green onion strips (optional)
Seafood Sauce or Green Herb Sauce

Combine first 12 ingredients in a doubled cheesecloth bag, and tie securely with string.

Combine water, lemon, garlic, and herb bag in a Dutch oven. Bring to a boil, reduce heat, and simmer 2 minutes. Stir in shrimp; return to a boil, and cook 3 to 5 minutes. Drain well; chill. Garnish with green onion strips, if desired; serve with Seafood Sauce or Green Herb Sauce. Yield: 6 servings (about 191 milligrams sodium per serving).

Seafood Sauce:

1½ cups low-sodium catsup
2 tablespoons lemon juice
1 to 2 teaspoons prepared horseradish
½ teaspoon garlic powder
½ teaspoon ground celery seeds
¼ teaspoon Tabasco pepper sauce

Combine all ingredients; mix well, and chill. Serve with boiled shrimp. Yield: 1⅔ cups sauce (about 5 milligrams sodium per tablespoon).

Green Herb Sauce:

¾ cup vegetable oil, divided
¼ cup tarragon vinegar
1 egg
½ cup packed fresh parsley sprigs
4 green onions, sliced
1 teaspoon dried whole thyme
1 teaspoon dry mustard
½ teaspoon dried whole marjoram
½ teaspoon dried whole oregano
½ teaspoon dried whole savory
¼ teaspoon Tabasco pepper sauce

Combine ¼ cup oil and remaining ingredients in container of electric blender; process at medium speed until smooth, scraping sides of container often. Remove cover; continue to process, adding remaining ½ cup oil in a thin, steady stream. Chill; serve with boiled shrimp. Yield: 1¾ cups (about 3 milligrams sodium per tablespoon).

Swiss Chard Gets Special Attention

A bumper crop of Swiss chard means lots of leafy greens to enjoy.

Swiss chard leaves can be cooked alone, combined with other vegetables, or substituted in recipes calling for spinach or turnip greens.

The stalks of Swiss chard, which are sometimes called ribs, can also be cooked. When the chard is young, the stalks are similar to celery or asparagus stalks, but older stalks are tough, with a woody texture.

BUTTERED CHARD

2 pounds Swiss chard
1 cup chopped green onion
¼ cup butter or margarine
1 medium-size green pepper, chopped
¼ cup plus 1 tablespoon lemon juice
¼ teaspoon salt
⅛ teaspoon pepper
Pinch of ground nutmeg
Shredded Cheddar cheese (optional)

Trim roots; wash chard thoroughly. Drain. Remove leaves from stalks. Tear leaves into small pieces, and set aside; cut stalks into 2-inch pieces.

Sauté onion in butter in a large skillet until tender. Add chard stalks; cook, stirring constantly, 1 minute. Add chard leaves, green pepper, lemon juice, salt, pepper, and nutmeg. Reduce heat, cover, and simmer 15 minutes, stirring occasionally. Spoon into serving dish; sprinkle with cheese, if desired. Yield: 4 servings.
Ella C. Stivers,
Abilene, Texas.

SWISS CHARD WITH TOMATOES

2 pounds Swiss chard
2 cloves garlic, minced
¼ cup olive oil
1½ cups peeled and chopped tomatoes
¼ teaspoon celery salt
⅛ teaspoon coarsely ground black pepper
1 tablespoon capers

Trim roots; wash chard thoroughly. Drain. Remove leaves from stalks. Tear leaves into small pieces; cut stalks into 1-inch pieces. Cover and cook in 1 inch boiling water 3 to 5 minutes or until leaves are tender. Drain.

Sauté garlic in oil in a large skillet until golden. Remove and discard garlic. Add tomatoes, salt, and pepper to skillet; cover and simmer 8 to 10 minutes. Add chard and cook, uncovered, 10 minutes, stirring frequently. Stir in capers. Yield: 4 servings.

MICROWAVE COOKERY

Speed Up Yeast Bread In The Microwave

If you don't bake yeast bread because it takes too long to rise, then let your microwave oven turn you into a breadmaker. Yeast bread will rise in as little as one-third of the time required when making it conventionally; baking time is significantly reduced as well.

Baking bread in the microwave oven yields the same tender crumb you get in the conventional oven, but there are differences in the end product that you should keep in mind. Bread will not brown in a microwave oven, so either bake with naturally colored ingredients or sprinkle a dark topping over the bread before baking. One of our breads includes whole wheat or rye flour, which color the bread naturally. Another recipe depends on a syrup-and-nut topping for color.

Other toppings you can use to color the crust include crushed dried herbs, toasted sesame seeds, poppy seeds, or dark cracker crumbs.

Bread baked in a microwave oven does not develop a hard crust like conventionally baked bread. For a crunchy crust, sprinkle on cornmeal, poppy seeds, toasted sesame seeds, dark cracker crumbs, or a brown sugar topping before baking.

Whether you add toppings for color or crunch, brush the dough lightly with butter before sprinkling on the topping to make it adhere.

To let our dough recipes rise in the microwave oven, place dough in a greased bowl, turning to grease all sides. Set the bowl in a larger, shallow dish, and pour about 1 inch of water into the bottom dish. Cover dough loosely with waxed paper, and place in oven. Microwave at MEDIUM-LOW (30% power) for 2 minutes; let stand in oven 5 minutes. Repeat microwaving and standing 2 to 4 times or until dough has doubled in bulk. Remove water and waxed paper before baking.

If surface of dough appears to be drying out during rising, turn dough over in bowl. Discontinue microwaving if dough begins to cook, and let dough rise conventionally. When rising is complete, punch dough down, and proceed as directed in recipe.

Here are other tips to make your microwave bread baking successful:

—When baking bread in the microwave oven, place baking container of dough on an inverted custard cup or saucer to promote even doneness.

—Bake microwave bread at MEDIUM (50% power) for even cooking. This slower speed still bakes bread as much as two times faster than in a conventional oven.

—To encourage even doneness, rotate the baking container several times during baking.

—To check for doneness, lightly touch bread with finger; bread will spring back when done.

—Most microwave bread continues cooking after it is removed from the oven. Place baking container of bread on aluminum foil during standing time if your recipe calls for standing.

—Invert large, dense loaves of microwave bread on a wire rack to cool; this will prevent the bottom crust from becoming soggy.

—Bread baked in the microwave oven sometimes dries out faster than conventionally baked bread, so be sure to wrap it tightly for storage.

SUGARPLUM COFFEE RING

½ cup milk
⅓ cup shortening
⅓ cup sugar
1 teaspoon salt
2 packages dry yeast
¼ cup warm water (105° to 115°)
2 eggs
4 cups all-purpose flour, divided
¼ cup butter or margarine
½ cup firmly packed brown sugar
3 tablespoons light corn syrup
½ cup pecan halves
¼ cup halved candied red cherries

Place milk in a glass bowl; microwave at HIGH for 1½ minutes or until hot. Stir shortening, ⅓ cup sugar, and salt into milk; stir until shortening is partially melted. Cool to lukewarm.

Combine yeast and water; let stand 5 minutes. Add to milk mixture; stir in eggs and 1 cup flour, beating well. Add enough flour to make a soft dough.

Place dough in a lightly greased bowl, turning to grease top. Set bowl in a larger, shallow dish; pour 1 inch hot water into bottom dish. Cover dough loosely with waxed paper. Microwave at MEDIUM-LOW (30% power) for 2 minutes; let stand in oven 5 minutes. Repeat microwaving and standing 2 times or until doubled in bulk. Carefully turn dough over in bowl if surface appears to be drying out during rising period. Punch dough down.

Divide dough into 20 pieces; shape each piece into a ball, and set aside.

Place butter in a glass bowl. Microwave at HIGH for 55 seconds or until melted; stir in brown sugar and corn syrup. Pour half of butter mixture into a lightly buttered 9-inch microwave tube pan. Arrange pecan halves and candied cherries in butter mixture; arrange 8 balls of dough over mixture in pan, squeezing to fit if necessary. Spoon remaining butter mixture over dough, and top with remaining balls of dough.

Place pan in microwave on an inverted custard cup or saucer. Microwave at MEDIUM (50% power) for 7 to 10 minutes or until surface springs back when touched lightly with finger, giving dish a quarter turn at 3-minute intervals. Invert bread onto serving platter, and let stand 10 minutes before serving. Yield: one 9-inch ring.

WHOLE WHEAT-RYE BREAD

3 cups whole wheat flour
2 cups rye flour
1½ cups all-purpose flour
1 tablespoon sugar
1 tablespoon salt
2 packages dry yeast
2¼ cups water
¾ cup yellow cornmeal
⅓ cup molasses
3 tablespoons butter or margarine
1 tablespoon caraway seeds
1 tablespoon butter or margarine
1 tablespoon yellow cornmeal

Combine all flour, stirring well. Combine sugar, salt, yeast, and 1½ cups flour mixture in a large bowl; stir well, and set aside.

Combine next 5 ingredients in a large bowl; microwave at HIGH for 3 to 4 minutes or until butter melts, stirring after 2 minutes. Cool liquid mixture to 120° to 130°.

Gradually add liquid mixture to yeast mixture, beating well at high speed of electric mixer. Beat 2 additional minutes at medium speed. Gradually add enough of remaining flour to form a moderately stiff dough.

Turn dough out onto a lightly floured surface, and knead 10 minutes or until smooth and elastic. Shape into a ball, and place in well-greased bowl, turning to grease top. Set bowl in a larger, shallow dish; pour 1 inch hot water in bottom dish. Cover dough loosely with waxed paper. Microwave at MEDIUM-LOW (30% power) for 2 minutes; let stand in oven 5 minutes. Repeat microwaving and standing 3 times or until doubled in bulk. Carefully turn dough over in bowl if surface appears to be drying out during rising period. Punch dough down.

Roll dough into a 16- x 9-inch rectangle. Starting at long end, roll up dough jellyroll fashion; pinch seam and ends to seal. Place loaf, seam side down, on a greased glass pizza plate, and shape loaf into a ring. Invert a greased custard cup in center of ring. Set plate over a 13- x 9- x 2-inch baking dish containing 1 inch hot water. Cover dough loosely with waxed paper. Microwave at MEDIUM-LOW for 2 minutes; let stand 5 minutes. Repeat microwaving and standing 2 times or until doubled in bulk.

Remove plate and dish from oven. Place 1 tablespoon butter in a custard cup. Microwave at HIGH for 35 seconds or until melted. Brush butter over top of loaf, and sprinkle with 1 tablespoon cornmeal.

Place plate with loaf in microwave oven on an inverted custard cup or saucer. Microwave at MEDIUM (50% power) 14 to 16 minutes or until surface springs back when lightly touched with finger, giving dish a quarter turn at 3-minute intervals. Place plate on a sheet of foil, and let stand 10 minutes. Invert loaf onto a wire rack, and cool completely. Yield: one 10½-inch ring.

Tip: Microwave one or two slices of bread quickly for crumbs or toppings. Place bread on a paper towel and microwave at HIGH for 1½ minutes. Turn slices over after half the cooking time. After standing, the bread slices will become crisp and dry and can be easily crushed.

From Our Kitchen To Yours

Whether it's a pot roast for Sunday dinner or a juicy steak still sizzling from the grill, Southerners enjoy eating beef.

About Beef

To determine the best way to cook a cut of beef, it's important to know whether the cut is a "tender" one.

Tenderness is determined by the location of the cut on the carcass. The tender cuts come mainly from the rib, loin, and short loin sections, the areas along the backbone. These include rib roasts, rib-eye steaks, and sirloin steaks. When preparing them, you'll want to roast, broil, pan broil, or fry.

The less tender cuts include the chuck, fore shank, brisket, short plate, tip, and round. These are taken from the shoulder, legs, breast, and flanks, or areas with heavy muscle development. But by using the proper cooking method you can make them fork-tender. Braising and cooking in liquid are two methods that make tough cuts such as round steak and corned beef tender as a fine steak.

Here are some specifics on the various cooking methods.

Roasting: To roast means to cook by dry heat in an oven without liquid. This is best for large tender cuts of beef such as rib roast, rolled rump roast, and a top-quality beef tip roast.

Place the roast, fat side up, on a rack in a shallow roasting pan. The fat self-bastes the roast during cooking. Insert a meat thermometer so the bulb sits in muscle tissue, not in fat or against bone. Do not cover. Cook at 275° to 325° until it reaches the desired degree of doneness. These internal temperatures are a guide for most beef roasts: 140°F. (rare), 160°F. (medium), and 170°F. (well done).

Broiling: To broil means to cook by direct heat in an oven or over hot coals. This method is ideal for tender steaks like rib eye, porterhouse, or sirloin, and, ground beef patties.

Set the oven on broil. Depending on the thickness of the cut, place the beef 2 to 5 inches from the broiler element (steaks and patties that are ¾ to 1 inch thick need to be 2 to 3 inches from the element—larger cuts from 1 to 2 inches thick should cook 3 to 5 inches from the heat source). Broil until the top browns; the meat should be about half cooked at this point. Season with salt now. (Don't salt before cooking because salt draws out the moisture and inhibits browning.) Turn and brown the other side.

Pan Broiling: To pan broil is to cook by direct heat in a pan. This method is used for cooking the same cuts as "broiling" but the cooking is done in a frying pan or griddle, not the oven.

When pan broiling, don't add fat or water to the skillet unless the cut is extremely lean and a bit of fat is needed to prevent sticking. Cook slowly over medium low heat, turning occasionally, making sure the meat browns evenly. Don't overcook. Also, don't let fat accumulate as you cook, or you'll be frying, not pan broiling.

Frying: Fried meats are cooked in oil over medium heat. For pan frying, you use a small amount of oil; for deep fat frying, enough oil to completely cover the meat. Pan frying is best for tender meat such as cubed beef steaks about ¼ to 1 inch thick or round steak, tenderized by pounding.

To fry, heat oil over medium heat. When hot, add the meat and brown. Don't cover the skillet because you'll lose the crispness. Continue to cook on medium heat until done, turning occasionally. Remove from pan and serve. During cooking if the fat begins smoking, lower the heat immediately.

Braising: Braised meats are cooked slowly in a small amount of liquid. The slow cooking and moisture are vital for tenderizing tough cuts of beef. Top and bottom round steak, flank steak, arm pot roasts, and blade roasts are all good choices for braising.

To braise, first brown the meat in a small amount of fat; then pour off the pan drippings. The browning adds flavor and improves the appearance. Season the beef; add a small amount of liquid such as water, tomato juice, or soup. Cover tightly, and simmer until tender. Depending on the size of the cut, braising could take 1 to 4 hours. Make gravy with the pan drippings.

Cooking in Liquid: To cook in liquid, cover the beef completely with water. Corned beef, beef brisket, and stew meat are best prepared this way.

First, brown the beef; cover with water, and add seasonings. Cover with a lid, and simmer gently until tender. Boiling tends to dry out the meat and increases shrinkage. If vegetables are to be cooked with the beef, add them near the end of the cooking time.

Some Other Tips

Browning Beef: When browning a large amount of beef, add only a small amount to the skillet at a time. Brown some of the beef; remove and then add more. If you add too much at once, the large amount of beef juices produced tends to slow down browning, and gives the beef a gray tone.

Buying Beef: Always consider the cost per serving instead of the cost per pound of the beef cut you're selecting. Bone and fat may reduce the actual amount of servings you'll get.

Tenderizing Beef: Try marinating or pounding less tender cuts of beef. Use an acid such as wine, vinegar, tomato, or citrus juices as a marinade; they "soften" the connective tissue of the beef. Let the beef marinate in the refrigerator several hours or overnight before cooking. If you don't have time to marinate, pound the beef with a meat mallet. This process breaks down the connective tissue and gives you a more tender product.

Making Gravy From Pan Drippings: Making delicious gravy is easy. Spoon off fat from pan drippings. Add 1 to 2 cups of water. Combine about 1 or 2 tablespoons of flour or cornstarch with ¼ cup water; mix well. Stir into pan drippings, and cook over medium high heat, stirring constantly, until thickened and bubbly.

Crisp Ideas For Celery

Celery is most often thought of as a good low-calorie snack or appetizer, but it can be spotlighted in a side dish or salad, as well.

Select celery with crisp, fresh leaves and stalks. Wash each bunch, and store it in the crisper section of your refrigerator. If kept cold and moist, celery should stay fresh about two weeks.

When preparing celery, separate the stalks and scrub them with a brush. Be sure to trim off the roots and blemishes.

CELERY AU GRATIN

5 cups (1-inch-thick) sliced celery
2 cups water
½ teaspoon salt
¼ cup butter or margarine
¼ cup all-purpose flour
2 cups milk
½ teaspoon salt
¼ teaspoon pepper
¼ teaspoon ground nutmeg
2 tablespoons shredded Swiss cheese
¼ cup grated Parmesan cheese, divided

Combine first 3 ingredients in a saucepan; bring to a boil. Cover, reduce heat, and simmer 5 minutes or until crisp-tender. Drain well.

Melt butter in a heavy saucepan over low heat; add flour, stirring until smooth. Cook 1 minute, stirring constantly. Gradually add milk; cook over medium heat, stirring constantly, until thickened and bubbly. Stir in ½ teaspoon salt, pepper, and nutmeg. Stir in Swiss cheese, 2 tablespoons Parmesan cheese, and celery; spoon mixture into a lightly greased 1½-quart casserole. Sprinkle with remaining Parmesan cheese. Broil 4 inches from heat until golden brown. Yield: about 6 to 8 servings. *Mrs. Bernard W. Reiben, Orlando, Florida.*

SAUCY CELERY

4½ cups thinly sliced celery
¼ cup butter or margarine
2 tablespoons all-purpose flour
¼ teaspoon salt
1 cup milk
1 cup (4 ounces) shredded Cheddar cheese, divided
1 (3-ounce) can mushroom stems and pieces, drained
3 tablespoons chopped green pepper

Sauté celery in butter in a large skillet 15 minutes or until tender. Stir in flour and salt; cook 1 minute, stirring constantly. Gradually add milk; cook over medium heat, stirring constantly, until thickened and bubbly. Add ¾ cup cheese, and stir until melted. Stir in mushrooms and green pepper, mixing well. Pour into a greased 1-quart shallow casserole. Bake at 350° for 15 minutes. Sprinkle with remaining ¼ cup cheese, and bake an additional 5 minutes. Yield: 4 to 6 servings.
Cecilia Breithaupt, Boerne, Texas.

CRUNCHY BROCCOLI SALAD

2 (10-ounce) packages frozen broccoli spears
6 hard-cooked eggs
1½ cups sliced celery
3 green onions, chopped
½ cup mayonnaise
¾ teaspoon celery salt
¼ teaspoon pepper
Lettuce leaves

Cook broccoli according to the package directions; drain and cool. Cut into 1-inch pieces.

Coarsely chop eggs, reserving one yolk. Combine broccoli, chopped eggs, celery, and onion; toss. Add mayonnaise, celery salt, and pepper; toss gently, and chill.

Spoon mixture into a lettuce-lined bowl. Sieve reserved egg yolk; sprinkle over salad. Yield: 6 to 8 servings.
Adell Whitfield, El Dorado, Arkansas.

CELERY-AND-CAULIFLOWER SALAD

1 large head cauliflower
5 stalks celery, sliced
4 radishes, sliced
4 green onions, chopped
1 (8-ounce) carton commercial sour cream
½ cup mayonnaise
Dash of garlic salt
Dash of pepper

Remove outer leaves of cauliflower. Break cauliflower into flowerets, and wash thoroughly. Combine vegetables in a large bowl; toss well.

Combine the remaining ingredients, mixing well; pour over vegetables, and toss. Chill. Yield: 10 to 12 servings.
Kris Ragan, Midlothian, Virginia.

Pork Chops Make Meaty Meals

Everybody knows how good pork chops taste. And they can taste even better by enhancing their flavor with the addition of sauces and seasonings.

APPLE-CRUMB STUFFED PORK CHOPS

4 (1-inch-thick) pork chops, cut with pockets
Apple-Crumb Stuffing
Salt and pepper to taste
1 tablespoon butter or margarine
3 tablespoons water

Stuff pockets of pork chops with Apple-Crumb Stuffing, and secure with wooden picks. Sprinkle pork chops with salt and pepper. Melt butter in a large, heavy skillet; brown pork chops on both sides. Add water. Cover, reduce heat, and simmer 50 minutes or until pork chops are tender. Yield: 4 servings.

Apple-Crumb Stuffing:
1 cup soft breadcrumbs
½ cup diced apple
3 tablespoons minced onion
3 tablespoons raisins, chopped
½ teaspoon salt
½ teaspoon sugar
Pinch of pepper
Pinch of ground sage
1½ tablespoons butter or margarine, melted

Combine all ingredients; mix well. Yield: about 1¾ cups.
Mrs. Sidney I. McGrath, Hopkinsville, Kentucky.

ORANGE-GLAZED PORK CHOPS

4 (¾-inch-thick) pork chops
Salt and pepper to taste
All-purpose flour
1 tablespoon vegetable oil
½ cup orange juice
2 tablespoons orange marmalade
2 tablespoons brown sugar
1 tablespoon vinegar

Sprinkle pork chops lightly with salt and pepper; dredge in flour.

Heat oil in a heavy skillet; brown pork chops on both sides. Combine remaining ingredients, mixing well; pour over pork chops. Cover, reduce heat, and simmer 40 to 45 minutes. Yield: 4 servings. *Mrs. Russell Spear, Hilliard, Florida.*

PEPPERED PORK CHOP CASSEROLE

6 (½-inch-thick) pork chops
Salt and pepper to taste
2 medium-size green peppers, cut into ¼-inch rings
1½ cups uncooked regular rice
2 (8-ounce) cans tomato sauce
1 cup water
½ cup chopped onion
1 teaspoon salt
¼ teaspoon pepper

Sprinkle pork chops with salt and pepper, and arrange in a lightly greased 13- x 9- x 2-inch baking dish. Top each pork chop with one green pepper ring; spoon uncooked rice into and around pepper rings.

Chop remaining green pepper rings; stir in remaining ingredients, and pour mixture over rice. Cover and bake at 350° for 55 to 60 minutes or until done. Yield: 6 servings. *Cindy Murphy, Cleveland, Tennessee.*

OVEN-BARBECUED PORK CHOPS

2 cups soy sauce
1 cup water
½ cup firmly packed brown sugar
1 tablespoon molasses
1 teaspoon salt
6 (¾- to 1-inch-thick) pork chops
1 tablespoon dry mustard
½ cup firmly packed brown sugar
⅓ cup water
1 (14-ounce) bottle catsup
1 (12-ounce) bottle chili sauce

Combine soy sauce, 1 cup water, ½ cup brown sugar, molasses, and salt in a large shallow container; mix well. Add pork chops, and turn once to coat; cover and marinate overnight.

Remove pork chops from marinade, reserving marinade for use with other meat recipes. Place pork chops in a 13- x 9- x 2-inch baking pan. Cover and bake at 350° for 1½ hours.

Combine remaining ingredients in a heavy saucepan; bring to a boil, stirring constantly. Pour over pork chops; bake, uncovered, an additional 20 to 25 minutes. Yield: 6 servings.

Note: The remaining sauce may be stored in the refrigerator and used to prepare either barbecued chicken or beef.   Mina DeKraker,
Holland, Michigan.

A chocolate greeting card makes a thoughtful and delicious way to honor a special occasion.

Mold A Chocolate Greeting Card

Plastic molds available in many kitchen shops make it easy to personalize a chocolate greeting card. And we think you'll agree, chocolate cards taste much better than those made from cardboard! Here are some tips on the materials you'll need and how to go about molding a chocolate card.

On Molds and Chocolate

The molds for this type of candymaking are usually flat and are fashioned from transparent plastic that allows you to peek underneath while molding to check for unwanted air bubbles.

Semisweet or milk chocolate in the chunk, block, or chip forms are most often used for these projects. For contrasting color, mold with white chocolate; this is available at candy counters in many large department stores.

If your mold needs a red heart or a green leaf, melt white chocolate, and stir in paste food coloring. Don't use liquid coloring; it will cause the chocolate to thicken and lump.

Chocolate-flavored compounds made specifically for molding projects are also available in some areas. These compounds, often called summer coatings, make candymaking easy. They harden quickly after molding, are not hard to melt, and are more resistant to heat and humidity than real chocolate.

Summer coatings are available in a rainbow of colors in either the chunk or wafer form. The advantage to the wafer form is that you don't have to chop it before melting. If you use large chunks of chocolate, chop or grate them before beginning your molding project.

Making a Chocolate Mold

Because chocolate can scorch easily, always heat it in top of a double boiler over hot, not boiling, water until almost melted. Then remove top part of double boiler from water, and stir until melted.

When melting small amounts of many different colors, use small jars (one for each color) set in an electric skillet filled with water to simulate a double boiler. Let the jars stand in warm water while painting designs. If candy hardens too much, reheat slowly.

Be careful not to let any steam or water droplets get into the chocolate or summer coating or it will thicken and be hard to work with. All cooking utensils should be absolutely dry.

If you're molding with only one color per mold, simply spoon in the melted chocolate. Greasing molds is not necessary, and would harm the finished appearance. Underfill molds so the finished candy won't have a base larger than the design. Tap molds on the table to level them and to bring any bubbles to the surface. Let chocolate harden (refrigerate or freeze to hasten the process); invert the mold, and tap it gently to release chocolate.

If you want to make a multicolored card, use a small paintbrush to paint details directly onto the mold. Freeze mold a few minutes after painting each color to harden candy so that the first color won't run while painting the next. Use good quality brushes that won't lose their bristles, and use a separate brush for each color.

After the colors are painted into the mold, spoon in melted chocolate to fill the mold; freeze.

When frozen, invert the mold and gently tap it to release candy. Store in a

Paint details directly onto mold using desired color of melted candy; fill remainder of mold with chocolate.

cool dry place, away from extremes in temperature. If chocolate becomes soft at room temperature, refrigerate it until ready to serve.

Cards made with real chocolate can develop "bloom" if exposed to extremes in temperature; bloom is a gray discoloration on the surface of the chocolate, but it only affects the appearance of the chocolate, not the flavor.

Flavor Breads With Herbs And Spices

Ever tasted a well-seasoned bread that makes you ask, "What *is* that flavor?" If so, you've likely detected an herb or spice that has been used correctly—the seasoning whispers, but not loud enough for you to identify it. We think you'll find that's the case with these delectable herb and spice breads.

ITALIAN-STYLE FLAT BREAD

1 (13¾-ounce) package hot roll mix
¾ cup warm water (115° to 125°)
1 egg
½ teaspoon dried whole rosemary
2 tablespoons olive oil
¼ teaspoon salt (optional)
⅛ teaspoon red pepper

Dissolve contents of yeast packet (included in roll mix) in warm water. Combine yeast mixture, egg, flour packet, and rosemary; stir well to form a soft dough. Place in a greased bowl, turning to grease top. Cover and let rise in a warm place (85°), free from drafts, 45 minutes or until doubled in bulk.

Punch dough down, and turn out on a lightly floured surface. Knead 1 to 2 minutes or until smooth and elastic. Shape dough into a round, flat loaf; place on a greased cookie sheet. Cover and let rise in a warm place (85°), free from drafts, about 45 minutes. Score top of loaf. Combine remaining ingredients, and brush lightly over surface of loaf. Bake at 350° for 40 minutes or until bread sounds hollow when tapped. Cut in wedges to serve. Yield: 1 loaf.

Susan Bellows,
Birmingham, Alabama.

PARMESAN HERB BREAD

1½ cups biscuit mix
1 tablespoon sugar
1 tablespoon instant minced onion
1 egg, beaten
¼ cup milk
¼ cup white wine or apple juice
½ teaspoon dried whole oregano
¼ cup grated Parmesan cheese

Combine first 7 ingredients; stir well. Spread dough into a greased 8-inch round cakepan. Sprinkle cheese over dough. Bake at 400° for 20 minutes or until wooden pick inserted in center comes out clean. Cut in wedges to serve. Yield: 6 to 8 servings.

Kathryn Bibelhauser,
Louisville, Kentucky.

CARDAMOM WHITE BREAD

2 cups milk, scalded
3 tablespoons sugar
1 tablespoon salt
1 teaspoon ground cardamom
¼ cup plus 1 tablespoon margarine
3 tablespoons sugar
2 packages dry yeast
2 cups warm water (105° to 115°)
10 cups bread flour, divided
1½ tablespoons margarine, melted

Combine first 5 ingredients; stir until margarine melts. Cool to lukewarm (105° to 115°).

Dissolve 3 tablespoons sugar and yeast in warm water in a large bowl; stir well. Add 2 cups bread flour, mixing well (mixture will be very thin). Cover and let rise in a warm place (85°), free from drafts, about 20 minutes. Stir in milk mixture and remaining 8 cups bread flour; beat at medium speed of electric mixer until smooth.

Turn dough out onto a lightly floured surface; knead 8 to 10 minutes or until smooth and elastic. Place dough in a greased bowl, turning to grease top. Cover and let rise in a warm place (85°), free from drafts, 1 hour and 15 minutes or until doubled in bulk. Punch dough down, and turn out onto a lightly floured surface. Let rest for 10 minutes.

Divide dough in thirds, and shape each into a loaf. Place the loaves in 3 greased 9- x 5- x 3-inch loafpans. Cover and let rise in a warm place (85°), free from drafts, 1 hour or until doubled in bulk. Brush each loaf with melted margarine. Bake at 400° for 30 minutes or until golden brown. Remove loaves from pans, and cool on wire racks. Yield: 3 loaves.

Mae Harkey,
Mount Pleasant, North Carolina.

Sprouts Add Crunch, Taste Green

More people are eating bean sprouts and alfalfa sprouts than ever before.

When buying fresh sprouts, remember that they spoil after a day or two, losing their bright-white color and crispness. Sprouts that are brownish or coated with a slippery film have already begun to spoil. Store fresh sprouts in the refrigerator, and always wash them thoroughly before using.

ALFALFA POCKET BREAD SANDWICHES

1 (3-ounce) package cream cheese, softened
1 tablespoon mayonnaise
4 (6-inch) pocket bread rounds
4 lettuce leaves
8 tomato slices
2 (5-ounce) cans chunk chicken, drained
1 (4½-ounce) package fresh alfalfa sprouts, washed and drained

Combine cream cheese and mayonnaise; mix well. Cut slit halfway around edge of each bread round; spread cream cheese mixture on inside of each. Divide lettuce, tomato, chicken, and alfalfa sprouts among sandwiches. Yield: 4 servings.

Sara A. McCullough,
Broaddus, Texas.

BEEF AND BEAN SPROUTS

½ pound boneless round steak
3 tablespoons vegetable oil
½ cup chopped green onion
½ teaspoon seasoned salt
½ teaspoon garlic powder
1 pound fresh bean sprouts, washed and
  drained
½ cup sliced fresh mushrooms
1 small green pepper, cut into ¼-inch
  strips
¼ cup water
3 to 4 tablespoons soy sauce
1 tablespoon vinegar
1 tablespoon cornstarch
Hot cooked rice

Partially freeze steak; slice across grain into 3- x ½-inch strips.

Heat oil in large skillet over medium heat; add green onion, and stir-fry 1 minute. Add steak, seasoned salt, and garlic powder; stir-fry 4 minutes. Add bean sprouts, mushrooms, and green pepper; stir-fry 3 minutes.

Combine next 4 ingredients, mixing well; add to bean sprout mixture. Cook, stirring constantly, for 3 minutes or until thickened. Serve over rice. Yield: about 4 servings.   *Dianna Woody,*
Bunnell, Florida.

RISING SUN OMELET

¾ cup fresh bean sprouts, washed and
  drained
1 tablespoon butter or margarine
4 eggs
2 tablespoons water
¼ teaspoon salt
¼ teaspoon pepper
1 tablespoon butter or margarine
⅓ cup sliced water chestnuts
Parmesan cheese
Fresh parsley sprigs (optional)

Sauté bean sprouts in 1 tablespoon butter until tender; set aside.

Combine eggs, water, salt, and pepper; mix just until blended. Heat 1 tablespoon butter in a 10-inch omelet pan or heavy skillet over medium heat until slightly golden at edges.

Pour egg mixture into skillet. As mixture starts to cook, gently lift edges of omelet with a spatula, and tilt pan so uncooked portion flows underneath.

When egg mixture is set, spoon bean sprouts in center; top with water chestnuts. Fold 2 outer edges of omelet toward center to cover filling; slide onto a warm platter, and sprinkle with Parmesan cheese. Garnish with parsley, if desired. Yield: 2 servings.
          Mrs. George P. Robinson,
          High Point, North Carolina.

FRESH SPINACH-SPROUT SALAD

1½ pounds fresh spinach, torn into
  bite-size pieces
1 cup fresh alfalfa sprouts or bean
  sprouts, washed and drained
1 small onion, thinly sliced and separated
  into rings
1 (8-ounce) can sliced water chestnuts,
  drained
8 slices bacon, cooked and crumbled
2 hard-cooked eggs, sliced
Dressing (recipe follows)

Combine vegetables, bacon, and eggs in a large bowl; toss well. Serve with dressing. Yield: 10 servings.

Dressing:

½ cup sugar
½ cup vegetable oil
½ cup red wine vinegar
⅓ cup catsup
Dash of salt

Combine all ingredients in a jar. Cover jar tightly, and shake vigorously. Yield: 1⅔ cups.   *Virginia Cavender,*
Memphis, Tennessee.

Spice Cakes–Rich With Tradition

Everyone remembers old-fashioned spice cakes—rich with molasses and warm with a fragrant blend of cinnamon, allspice, cloves, and nutmeg. We found these versions of this classic dessert among our readers' recipes. In Spice Cake With Caramel Frosting, molasses was substituted for some of the sugar and white wine added for flavor.

APPLESAUCE-SPICE CAKE

½ cup shortening
1 cup sugar
1 egg
1¾ cups all-purpose flour, divided
¾ cup raisins
½ cup chopped pecans
1 teaspoon baking soda
½ teaspoon salt
½ teaspoon ground cinnamon
½ teaspoon ground allspice
½ teaspoon ground ginger
¼ teaspoon ground cloves
1 cup applesauce

Cream shortening; gradually add sugar, beating well. Add the egg, and beat well. Combine 2 tablespoons flour,

raisins, and pecans; set aside. Combine remaining flour, baking soda, salt, and spices; add to creamed mixture alternately with applesauce, beginning and ending with flour mixture. Stir in raisins and pecans.

Pour batter into a greased and floured 10-inch tube pan. Bake at 350° for 40 to 45 minutes or until a wooden pick inserted in cake comes out clean. Cool in pan 10 minutes; remove from pan, and cool completely. Yield: one 10-inch cake.

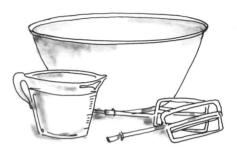

SPICE CAKE WITH CARAMEL FROSTING

2¼ cups all-purpose flour
1 cup sugar
1 tablespoon baking powder
1 teaspoon salt
1 teaspoon ground cinnamon
½ teaspoon ground nutmeg
¼ teaspoon ground allspice
¼ teaspoon ground cloves
½ cup shortening
1 tablespoon molasses
¾ cup dry white wine
1½ teaspoons vanilla extract
¼ cup milk
2 eggs
Caramel Frosting
½ cup finely chopped pecans

Combine first 8 ingredients in a large mixing bowl; mix well. Add shortening, molasses, wine, and vanilla; beat on medium speed of electric mixer until ingredients are well blended. Add milk and eggs, one at a time, beating well after each addition. Beat mixture 2 minutes on medium speed of electric mixer.

Pour batter into 2 greased and floured 9-inch round cakepans. Bake at 325° for 25 minutes or until a wooden pick inserted in center comes out clean. Cool in pans 10 minutes; remove layers from pans, and cool completely. Spread Caramel Frosting between layers and on sides of cake; add pecans to remaining frosting, and spread on top of cake. Yield: one 2-layer cake.

Caramel Frosting:
½ cup butter or margarine
1 cup firmly packed brown sugar
3 to 4 tablespoons milk
3 cups sifted powdered sugar
1 teaspoon vanilla extract

Melt butter in a medium saucepan. Add brown sugar, and cook 1 minute over low heat. Stir in remaining ingredients; beat until smooth, adding more milk if necessary for proper spreading consistency. (Frosting will be thin.) Yield: enough for one 2-layer cake.
Cheryll Tuthill,
Virginia Beach, Virginia.

DARK SPICE CAKE

1 cup butter or margarine, softened
1 cup sugar
6 eggs, separated
1 cup molasses
4 cups all-purpose flour
1 teaspoon salt
1 teaspoon ground allspice
1 teaspoon ground cinnamon
1 teaspoon ground cloves
1 teaspoon ground nutmeg
1 (8-ounce) carton commercial sour cream
1 teaspoon baking soda
Powdered sugar

Cream butter; gradually add sugar, beating until light and fluffy. Add egg yolks and molasses, beating well.

Combine flour, salt, and spices; mix well. Combine sour cream and baking soda; mix well. Add flour mixture to creamed mixture alternately with sour cream mixture, beginning and ending with flour mixture.

Beat egg whites (at room temperature) until stiff peaks form; gently fold into batter.

Pour batter into a greased and floured 10-inch tube pan. Bake at 300° for 1 hour and 40 minutes or until cake tests done. Cool in pan 10 minutes; remove from pan, and cool completely. Sprinkle with powdered sugar. Yield: one 10-inch cake.
Mrs. E. Lamar McMath,
Jacksonville, Florida.

Tip: Always measure accurately. Level dry ingredients in a cup with a knife edge or a spoon handle. Measure liquids in a cup so that the fluid is level with the top of the measuring line. Measure solid shortening by packing it firmly in a graduated measuring cup.

There's Zucchini In The Pie

Try this new idea for zucchini. Sauté it with onion; then bake it in a pastry shell in a quiche-like filling. Italian-Style Zucchini Pie is a meatless dish you are sure to enjoy.

ITALIAN-STYLE ZUCCHINI PIE

Pastry for a 9-inch pie
2 medium zucchini, thinly sliced
1 medium onion, chopped
3 tablespoons vegetable oil
¼ teaspoon garlic salt
Pepper to taste
3 tablespoons Italian-style breadcrumbs
3 tablespoons grated Parmesan cheese
3 eggs
½ cup milk
Zucchini slices (optional)
Fresh parsley sprigs (optional)

Line a 9-inch pieplate with pastry; trim excess pastry around edges and flute. Prick bottom and sides of pastry shell with a fork. Bake at 400° for 3 minutes; remove from oven, and gently prick with a fork. Bake 5 minutes longer. Let cool on rack.

Sauté zucchini and onion in oil until onion is tender. Add garlic salt and pepper; cover and cook over low heat 3 to 4 minutes. Drain well, and spoon into prepared pastry shell.

Combine breadcrumbs and cheese; sprinkle over zucchini. Combine eggs and milk, beating well; pour into shell, being careful to moisten all breadcrumbs. Bake at 375° for 25 minutes or until set. Garnish with zucchini slices and parsley, if desired. Yield: one 9-inch pie.
Barbara Sgueglia,
Deltona, Florida.

Canned Tuna And Salmon Are Always Ready

Nutritious, versatile, and convenient, canned tuna and salmon are always ready when you need a new luncheon or dinner idea. Try our Tuna Lasagna, for example; like it's traditional counterpart made with meat, it's layered with spicy tomato sauce, mozzarella, and ricotta cheese.

SALMON FLORENTINE

2 (10-ounce) packages frozen chopped spinach
1 (15½-ounce) can salmon
2 tablespoons minced onion
¼ cup butter or margarine
¼ cup all-purpose flour
½ teaspoon dry mustard
2 cups milk
1½ cups (6 ounces) shredded sharp Cheddar cheese, divided
Dash of red pepper
2 cups cooked rice

Cook spinach according to package directions, omitting salt; drain well.

Drain salmon, reserving liquid; flake salmon into small chunks, and set aside.

Sauté onion in butter in a heavy saucepan until tender. Add flour and mustard, stirring until smooth. Cook 1 minute, stirring constantly. Gradually add milk and salmon liquid; cook over medium heat, stirring constantly, until thickened and bubbly. Add 1 cup cheese and pepper, stirring until cheese melts.

Spread spinach in a greased 13- x 9- x 2-inch baking dish. Layer with salmon and rice. Top with cheese sauce. Bake, uncovered, at 400° for 15 minutes. Sprinkle with remaining cheese, and bake an additional 5 minutes. Yield: 8 servings.
Janet M. Filer,
Arlington, Virginia.

SALMON CARBONARA

1 (7¾-ounce) can salmon
1 (8-ounce) package spaghetti
2 eggs, beaten
1 cup grated Parmesan cheese
¼ cup butter or margarine, melted
½ cup chopped fresh parsley
⅛ teaspoon coarsely ground black pepper
Additional grated Parmesan cheese

Drain salmon; flake into small chunks, and set aside.

Cook spaghetti according to package directions; drain well. Combine spaghetti and next 5 ingredients, tossing to coat. Add salmon, and toss gently. Spoon spaghetti into a serving dish, and sprinkle with Parmesan cheese. Yield: 4 servings.

SALMON-SPINACH TURNOVERS

1 (10-ounce) package frozen chopped
    spinach
1 (7¾-ounce) can salmon, drained and
    flaked
1 (3-ounce) package cream cheese,
    softened
¼ cup minced onion
½ teaspoon lemon juice
1 (10-ounce) package frozen patty shells,
    thawed
1 egg, beaten

Cook spinach according to package
directions; drain well. Place spinach on
paper towels, and squeeze until barely
moist. Combine spinach, salmon, cream
cheese, minced onion, and lemon juice,
mixing well.

Roll each patty shell into a 6-inch
circle. Place ¼ cup salmon mixture off
center of each circle. Moisten edges of
circles, and fold pastry in half, making
sure edges are even. Press with a fork
to seal. Place turnovers on a lightly
greased baking sheet. Prick tops with
fork, and brush with egg. Bake at 400°
for 18 to 20 minutes or until golden
brown. Yield: 6 servings.
Mrs. H. J. Grogaard,
Baltimore, Maryland.

TUNA LASAGNA

1 (15½-ounce) jar spaghetti sauce with
    mushrooms
2 (8-ounce) cans tomato sauce
1 teaspoon dried whole oregano
¼ cup minced onion
1 clove garlic, minced
2 (6½-ounce) cans tuna, drained and
    flaked
1 (8-ounce) package lasagna noodles
1 cup ricotta cheese
1 (8-ounce) package sliced mozzarella
    cheese
½ cup grated Parmesan cheese

Combine first 6 ingredients in a medium saucepan, stirring well; bring to a
boil. Cover, reduce heat, and simmer 15
minutes, stirring occasionally.

Cook lasagna noodles according to
package directions; drain.

Spoon one-third of tuna mixture into
a lightly greased 12- x 8- x 2-inch baking
dish. Layer half each of noodles, ricotta
cheese, and mozzarella cheese; top with
one-third of tuna mixture. Repeat layers
with remaining noodles, ricotta, mozzarella, and tuna mixture; sprinkle with
Parmesan. Bake, uncovered, at 350° for
40 minutes. Yield: 6 to 8 servings.
Mrs. Charles W. Kelly,
Somerville, New Jersey.

TUNA JAMBALAYA

4 slices bacon, diced
¼ cup chopped onion
¼ cup chopped celery
¼ cup chopped green pepper
2 (6½-ounce) cans water-packed tuna
2 (16-ounce) cans whole tomatoes,
    undrained and coarsely chopped
1 (10-ounce) package frozen cut okra,
    thawed
¼ cup chopped fresh parsley
1 cup uncooked regular rice
1 bay leaf
1 chicken-flavored bouillon cube
1 tablespoon Worcestershire sauce

Place bacon in a Dutch oven; fry until
just crisp. Add next 3 ingredients, and
sauté until vegetables are tender. Drain.

Drain tuna, reserving liquid; flake
tuna, and set aside. Add enough water
to reserved liquid to make 1 cup; stir
into bacon mixture. Add tomatoes and
next 6 ingredients, mixing well; bring to
a boil. Cover, reduce heat, and simmer
20 to 25 minutes. Remove bay leaf and
stir in tuna. Yield: 6 servings.
Peggy Dowdy,
Roanoke, Virginia.

TUNA MACARONI SALAD

1 cup (4 ounces) uncooked elbow
    macaroni
3 hard-cooked eggs, chopped
1 cup chopped sweet pickle
1 (6½-ounce) can tuna, drained and
    flaked
½ cup chopped celery
½ cup chopped onion
½ cup mayonnaise
1 tablespoon prepared mustard
2 tablespoons sweet pickle juice
Leaf lettuce (optional)
Tomato wedges (optional)
Fresh parsley sprigs (optional)

Cook macaroni according to package
directions; drain. Rinse macaroni with
cold water; drain.

Combine macaroni and next 5 ingredients; toss gently. Combine mayonnaise, mustard, and pickle juice; mix
well. Pour over macaroni mixture; toss
gently. Cover; chill at least 1 hour.
Serve salad on lettuce, and garnish with
tomato wedges and parsley, if desired.
Yield: 4 to 6 servings. *Kathy Chaney,*
Charleston, West Virginia.

Ladle Up A Bowl Of Soup

Plan a luncheon menu around one of
these hot and hearty soups. Either can
be mixed up in minutes with ingredients
you'll likely have on hand. Just add a
sandwich or salad to complete the meal.

HOT BROCCOLI SOUP

1 (10-ounce) package frozen chopped
    broccoli
1 (10¾-ounce) can cream of mushroom
    soup, undiluted
1½ cups milk
2 tablespoons butter or margarine
¼ teaspoon dried whole tarragon, crushed
Dash of pepper

Cook broccoli according to package
directions; drain well. Add remaining
ingredients. Cook over medium heat,
stirring constantly, until thoroughly
heated. Yield: about 1 quart.

TOMATO SOUP

1 tablespoon butter or margarine
¼ cup finely chopped celery
2 tablespoons chopped onion
1 (8-ounce) can stewed tomatoes,
    undrained
1 cup water
¼ cup dry white wine
1 chicken-flavored bouillon cube
2 slices bacon, cooked, drained, and
    crumbled

Melt butter in a 1-quart saucepan;
add celery and onion. Sauté over low
heat until onion is tender. Add tomatoes, water, wine, and bouillon cube,
stirring well; bring mixture to a boil.
Reduce heat, and simmer 15 minutes,
stirring occasionally.

Spoon soup into serving bowls; top
with bacon. Yield: about 2 cups.
Alice McNamara,
Eucha, Oklahoma.

Tip: Burned food can be removed
from an enamel saucepan by using the
following procedure: Fill the pan with
cold water containing 2 to 3 table-
spoons salt, and let stand overnight.
The next day, cover and bring water to
a boil.

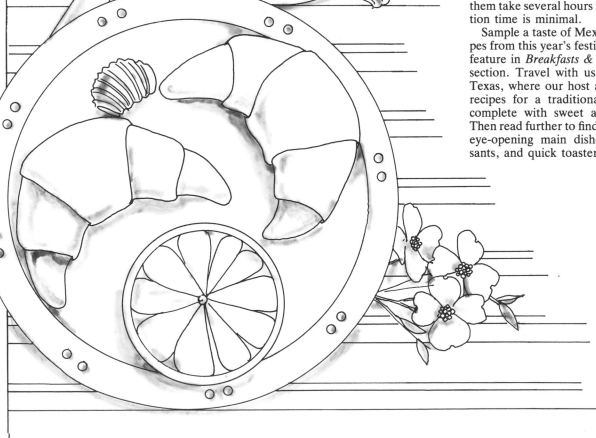

March

A fresh breath of spring rushes over the South during March to bring tender, green asparagus. In this chapter, you'll find tips for cooking the short-seasoned vegetable to enjoy its flavor to the fullest while available. The foods staff loved taste-testing recipes such as Asparagus With Orange Sauce and Pickled Asparagus.

Like our readers, we are always looking for quick-to-fix recipes that look like we spent all day in the kitchen. That's just what we found with our splendid entrées such as Shrimp Élégante and Mandarin Pork Roast. Although some of them take several hours to cook, preparation time is minimal.

Sample a taste of Mexico with the recipes from this year's festive entertainment feature in *Breakfasts & Brunches* special section. Travel with us to San Marcos, Texas, where our host and hostess offer recipes for a traditional Mexican feast complete with sweet and hot tamales. Then read further to find more recipes for eye-opening main dishes, classic croissants, and quick toaster oven treats.

Fresh Ideas For Asparagus

Put the frozen or canned asparagus aside when asparagus is fresh.

Fresh asparagus offers more flavor, better texture, and lower prices than its prepackaged counterparts. In addition, the bright-green vegetable is loaded with nutrients—vitamins A, B, C, and iron. To preserve these nutrients and yield a crisp-tender end product, cook asparagus by boiling the stalks and steaming the tips.

To cook the vegetable, tie the stalks with string into either one large bundle or several serving-size bundles. Stand the asparagus upright in a deep saucepan, and cover just the stalks with boiling water. Invert another saucepan over the asparagus, and cook until crisp-tender. A double boiler works well for this cooking method. Boiling water cooks the tougher stalks and steaming cooks the more delicate tips, yielding an evenly tender vegetable.

If you need to store fresh asparagus a few days before cooking, cut a thin slice from the base of each stalk, and stand stalks upright in a vase-like container holding about 1 inch of water. Cover the exposed asparagus loosely with plastic wrap, and refrigerate. The vegetable will stay fresh up to three days.

ASPARAGUS WITH TOMATO SAUCE

2 pounds fresh asparagus spears
2 tablespoons butter or margarine
½ cup sliced fresh mushrooms
2 (8-ounce) cans tomato sauce
2 tablespoons frozen chopped chives
¼ teaspoon dried whole basil
½ cup grated Parmesan cheese

Snap off tough ends of asparagus. Remove the scales from stalks with a knife or vegetable peeler, if desired. Cook asparagus, covered, in boiling water 6 to 8 minutes or until crisp-tender; drain. Arrange asparagus in a lightly greased 2-quart casserole.

Melt butter in a saucepan; add mushrooms, and sauté 2 to 3 minutes. Stir in next 3 ingredients, and simmer about 10 minutes.

Spoon sauce over asparagus; top with Parmesan cheese. Broil 2 to 3 inches from heat for 3 minutes or just until cheese is lightly browned. Yield: 8 servings.
Linda Keeton,
Memphis, Tennessee.

ASPARAGUS WITH ORANGE SAUCE

1½ pounds fresh asparagus spears
⅓ cup butter or margarine
2 tablespoons grated orange rind
¼ cup orange juice
¼ teaspoon salt
¼ teaspoon white pepper
1 orange

Snap off tough ends of asparagus. Remove the scales from stalks with a knife or vegetable peeler, if desired. Cook asparagus, covered, in boiling water 6 to 8 minutes or until crisp-tender. Drain. Arrange on serving platter, and keep warm.

Combine butter, orange rind, orange juice, salt, and pepper in a small saucepan. Bring to a boil; boil 6 minutes or until mixture thickens slightly.

Cut a 12-inch strip of rind from orange using a citrus zester. Carefully tie strip into a bow, and set aside. Slice remaining rind from orange, and cut 2 orange slices. Reserve remaining part of orange for other uses.

Pour sauce down center of asparagus; garnish with orange slices and bow. Yield: 6 servings.
Mina DeKraker,
Holland, Michigan.

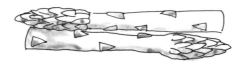

FRENCH-FRIED ASPARAGUS

1 pound fresh asparagus spears
2 tablespoons butter or margarine
3 tablespoons all-purpose flour
1 cup milk
½ teaspoon salt
1 cup grated Parmesan cheese
3 eggs, beaten
1½ cups fine, dry breadcrumbs
Vegetable oil

Snap off tough ends of asparagus. Remove the scales from stalks with a knife or vegetable peeler, if desired. Cook asparagus, covered, in boiling water 6 to 8 minutes or until crisp-tender; drain.

Melt butter in a heavy saucepan over low heat; add flour, stirring until smooth. Cook 1 minute, stirring constantly. Gradually add milk; cook over medium heat, stirring constantly, until thickened and bubbly. Stir in salt.

Dip each asparagus spear in white sauce, dredge in Parmesan cheese, dip in egg, and coat with breadcrumbs.

Fry in hot oil (375°) until golden brown. Drain on paper towels. Yield: 4 to 6 servings.
John L. Wood,
Memphis, Tennessee.

ASPARAGUS WITH SOUR CREAM

1½ pounds fresh asparagus spears
½ cup commercial sour cream
½ cup grated Parmesan cheese
2 tablespoons mayonnaise

Snap off tough ends of asparagus. Remove the scales from stalks with a knife or vegetable peeler, if desired. Cook asparagus, covered, in boiling salted water 8 to 10 minutes or until tender; drain. Arrange asparagus in a serving dish, and keep warm.

Combine sour cream, Parmesan cheese, and mayonnaise in top of a double boiler. Place mixture over boiling water, and heat thoroughly; stir frequently. Pour sauce over warm asparagus, and serve immediately. Yield: 6 servings.
Karen Davage,
Spring, Texas.

MARINATED ASPARAGUS

1 pound fresh asparagus spears
3 tablespoons vinegar
¼ cup vegetable oil
½ teaspoon salt
¼ teaspoon white pepper
2 tablespoons diced pimiento
1 tablespoon dried parsley flakes
Shredded lettuce

Snap off tough ends of asparagus. Remove the scales from stalks with a knife or vegetable peeler, if desired. Cook asparagus, covered, in boiling water 6 to 8 minutes or until crisp-tender; drain.

Combine next 6 ingredients; pour over asparagus. Marinate overnight. Serve over shredded lettuce. Yield: 4 servings.
Mrs. John A. Wyatt,
Palmyra, Tennessee.

PICKLED ASPARAGUS

4½ pounds fresh asparagus spears
3 cloves garlic
1 teaspoon pickling spice
3 cups water
2 cups vinegar (5% acidity)
1 tablespoon pickling salt

Snap off tough ends of asparagus. Pack asparagus tightly into hot sterilized widemouthed jars. Leave ¼-inch headspace. Place a garlic clove in each jar.

Remove whole cloves from pickling spice; reserve cloves for other uses. Combine pickling spice and remaining ingredients in a medium saucepan; bring to a boil. Pour vinegar mixture over asparagus, leaving ¼-inch headspace.

Cover at once with metal lids, and screw bands tight. Process in boiling-water bath 15 minutes. Yield: 3 pints.
Dorothy Milne,
Prosser, Washington.

ASPARAGUS WITH TARRAGON MARINADE

1 pound fresh asparagus spears
½ cup vegetable oil
¼ cup plus 2 tablespoons tarragon vinegar
1 teaspoon salt
1 teaspoon dry mustard
¼ teaspoon white pepper
1 (7-ounce) jar artichoke hearts, rinsed, drained, and quartered
¾ cup sliced ripe olives
1 (2-ounce) jar sliced pimiento, drained
3 tablespoons chopped onion
Bibb lettuce leaves
2 hard-cooked eggs, sliced

Snap off tough ends of asparagus. Remove the scales from stalks with a knife or vegetable peeler, if desired. Cook asparagus, covered, in boiling salted water 6 to 8 minutes or until crisp-tender; drain.

Combine next 5 ingredients in a small jar; cover tightly, and shake vigorously.

Layer asparagus spears, artichoke hearts, olives, pimiento, and onion in a shallow dish; pour dressing over vegetables. Cover and chill several hours or overnight. Drain well. Arrange salad on lettuce leaves, and garnish with egg slices. Yield: 6 servings.
Mrs. John W. Stevens,
Lexington, Kentucky.

ASPARAGUS SALAD CUPS

1 pound fresh asparagus spears
1 head iceburg lettuce
6 slices bacon, cooked and crumbled
⅓ cup sliced ripe olives
1 (8-ounce) bottle creamy cucumber dressing

Snap off tough ends of asparagus. Remove the scales from stalks with a knife or vegetable peeler, if desired. Cook asparagus, covered, in boiling salted water 6 to 8 minutes or until crisp-tender; drain. Chill asparagus.

Remove 6 to 8 outer leaves from lettuce, and place on individual serving plates. Shred remaining lettuce; fill lettuce cups with shredded lettuce.

Arrange asparagus spears over lettuce. Sprinkle with bacon and olives. Drizzle dressing over each. Yield: 6 to 8 servings.
Pauline Russelburg,
Mayfield, Kentucky.

Serve An Elegant Entrée With Ease

Not every dramatic entrée requires you to spend all day in the kitchen. If you'll read our selection of recipes closely, you'll see that many dishes bake or cook several hours, but time spent in preparation is short.

You can save time with any recipe by preparing as much as possible in advance. Chop vegetables, grate cheese, prepare breadcrumbs, or mix up a sauce the day before. Read the recipe carefully to determine how best to budget your time.

STEAK DIANNE

1½ teaspoons Worcestershire sauce
2 (6-ounce) Delmonico steaks
½ teaspoon salt
½ teaspoon garlic powder
½ teaspoon instant minced onion
½ teaspoon pepper
1 tablespoon butter or margarine
½ cup dry white wine
1 cup water
1 (3-ounce) can sliced mushrooms, drained

Spoon Worcestershire sauce over both sides of steaks; sprinkle meat with next 4 ingredients. Refrigerate 1 hour.

Melt butter in a large skillet; add steaks. Cook over medium heat until browned. Pour wine over meat; cover. Reduce heat, and simmer 15 minutes.

Remove steaks to serving plate; keep warm. Add 1 cup water and mushrooms to pan drippings; boil, uncovered, stirring frequently, about 10 minutes or until gravy is reduced to about ½ cup. Pour over steaks. Yield: 2 servings.
Thomas Lewis Ellis, Jr.,
Green Cove Springs, Florida.

BEEF ROULADES

1 (3-pound) boneless sirloin tip roast
Salt and pepper
½ cup butter or margarine, divided
2 cups soft breadcrumbs
1 clove garlic, minced
2 hard-cooked eggs, grated
3 tablespoons chopped fresh parsley
¼ cup grated Parmesan cheese
1 (10½-ounce) can onion soup, undiluted
1 cup Burgundy or other dry red wine
½ cup sliced mushrooms
Hot cooked rice

Have butcher slice roast into six ¼-inch slices. Sprinkle beef with salt and pepper; set aside.

Melt ¼ cup butter in a large Dutch oven. Add breadcrumbs and garlic; sauté 2 minutes, stirring constantly. Stir in next 3 ingredients. Spoon ⅓ cup breadcrumb mixture on each beef slice. Roll each piece jellyroll fashion; secure with wooden picks.

Melt remaining butter in Dutch oven; brown beef rolls over medium heat. Combine soup, wine, and mushrooms; pour over beef. Cover, reduce heat, and simmer 1 hour or until tender. Remove wooden picks; serve rolls over rice. Yield: 6 servings.
Marian Lloyd,
Huntsville, Alabama.

MANDARIN PORK ROAST

1 (4-pound) boneless pork loin
1 teaspoon salt
¼ teaspoon pepper
½ teaspoon garlic powder
2 tablespoons Dijon mustard
1 (11-ounce) can mandarin oranges
¼ cup light brown sugar
¼ cup vinegar
1 chicken-flavored bouillon cube
1 tablespoon soy sauce
2 tablespoons cornstarch
½ cup water
1 medium onion, chopped
⅓ cup chopped green pepper

Trim excess fat from roast. Sprinkle roast with salt, pepper, and garlic powder. Spread mustard over roast; place in a large Dutch oven. Cover and bake at 325° about 2½ hours or until meat thermometer registers 170°.

Drain mandarin oranges, reserving liquid. Set oranges aside. Combine liquid and next 6 ingredients in a saucepan; cook over medium heat, stirring constantly, until smooth and thickened. Remove from heat; stir in onion, green pepper, and oranges.

Spoon sauce over roast. Bake, uncovered, at 400° for 30 minutes, basting occasionally. Slice pork, and serve with warm pan drippings. Yield: 12 to 14 servings.
Thomas Farmer,
Richmond, Virginia.

SHRIMP ELEGANTE

3 pounds large shrimp, unpeeled
½ cup butter
¾ cup olive oil
2 cups coarsely chopped onion
3 cloves garlic, crushed
¼ cup chopped fresh parsley
1 teaspoon dried whole oregano
½ cup Sauterne or other dry white wine
⅓ cup Italian salad dressing
¼ cup water
1 tablespoon plus 1 teaspoon
 chicken-flavored bouillon granules
Freshly ground pepper to taste
1 (8-ounce) package fettuccine

Peel shrimp, leaving tails on; devein and butterfly. Place shrimp in boiling salted water 30 seconds. Drain and place in a shallow broiling pan.

Combine butter and olive oil in a large saucepan; place over medium heat until butter melts. Add onion, garlic, parsley, and oregano; cook, stirring occasionally, until onion is transparent. Add next 5 ingredients. Stir until bouillon is dissolved; reduce heat to low, and cook 5 minutes. Pour mixture over shrimp. Cover; refrigerate 2 hours.

Cook fettuccine according to package directions; drain. Uncover shrimp; broil 4 inches from heat for 5 minutes on each side or until done. Serve over fettuccine. Yield: 6 servings.

Ben P. Gocheski,
Columbus, Georgia.

Bananas, Always In Season

While many fruits and vegetables are in season for only a few short months, bananas are available any time of the year. Southerners have found a variety of ways to enjoy them, and you'll find some of their favorite recipes below.

Bananas are at the peak of flavor when the skins are yellow flecked with brown. If you can't use bananas as soon as they ripen, store uncovered in the refrigerator to prevent them from becoming mushy and overripe. The skins will turn brown, but the fruit inside the peel will remain unblemished.

GLAZED FRUIT SALAD

2 (20-ounce) cans pineapple chunks,
 undrained
1 (11-ounce) can mandarin orange
 sections, drained
1 cup maraschino cherries, drained
3 large bananas, sliced
1 cup coarsely chopped pecans
1 (3¾-ounce) package vanilla instant
 pudding mix

Drain pineapple, reserving 1 cup juice. Combine pineapple, remaining fruit, and pecans in a large bowl; toss gently. Combine pudding and reserved pineapple juice in a mixing bowl. Beat on high speed of electric mixer 1 minute. Pour pudding mixture over fruit and pecans; toss gently. Yield: 10 to 12 servings.
Mrs. Kenneth Corley,
Indianola, Mississippi.

BANANA BRAN MUFFINS

1 cup 100% wheat bran cereal
1 cup mashed bananas
⅔ cup milk
¼ cup firmly packed brown sugar
¼ cup vegetable oil
1 egg, beaten
1½ cups all-purpose flour
1 tablespoon baking powder
1 teaspoon ground cinnamon
½ teaspoon salt

Combine first 3 ingredients in a large bowl, stirring well; let stand 5 minutes. Add sugar, oil, and egg; mix well.

Combine next 4 ingredients; stir into bran mixture just until combined. Spoon into greased muffin pans, filling half full. Bake at 375° for 20 to 25 minutes. Yield: 1½ dozen. *Betty R. Butts,*
Kensington, Maryland.

BANANA-PINEAPPLE SAUCE

2 cups mashed bananas
1 (20-ounce) can crushed pineapple,
 drained
4 cups sugar
2 (3-ounce) packages liquid fruit pectin

Combine bananas, pineapple, and sugar in a Dutch oven; bring to a rolling boil. Cook 1 minute, stirring frequently; remove from heat. Stir in fruit pectin; skim off foam with a metal spoon.

Quickly ladle sauce into hot sterilized jars, leaving ¼-inch headspace; cover at once with metal lids, and screw bands tight. Process in boiling-water bath 10 minutes. Serve with ice cream, toast, pound cake, or pancakes. Yield: 6 half pints.
Mrs. A. Howard Elam II,
Albuquerque, New Mexico.

Chocolate, Kahlúa, And Cheesecake

Ursula Bambrey of Springfield, Virginia, loves luscious cheesecake and rich coffee flavor, so she combined them into one fine dessert—Heavenly Kahlúa Cheesecake. The cocoa in the recipe offers chocolate lovers a special treat.

HEAVENLY KAHLUA CHEESECAKE

1¼ cups graham cracker crumbs
¼ cup sugar
¼ cup cocoa
⅓ cup butter or margarine, melted
2 (8-ounce) packages cream cheese,
 softened
¾ cup sugar
½ cup cocoa
2 eggs
¼ cup strong coffee
¼ cup Kahlúa or other coffee-flavored
 liqueur
1 teaspoon vanilla extract
1 (8-ounce) carton commercial sour cream
2 tablespoons sugar
1 teaspoon vanilla extract
6 to 8 chocolate curls (optional)

Combine first 4 ingredients; mix well. Firmly press mixture into bottom of a 9-inch springform pan. Bake at 325° for 5 minutes; cool.

Beat cream cheese with electric mixer until light and fluffy; gradually add ¾ cup sugar, mixing well. Beat in ½ cup cocoa. Add eggs, one at a time, beating well after each addition. Stir in next 3 ingredients. Pour into prepared pan. Bake at 375° for 25 minutes. (Filling will be soft but will firm up as the cake stands.)

Combine sour cream, 2 tablespoons sugar, and 1 teaspoon vanilla; spread over hot cheesecake. Bake at 425° for 5 to 7 minutes. Let cool to room temperature on a wire rack; chill 8 hours or overnight.

Remove sides of springform pan. To garnish, place 3 chocolate curls in center of cheesecake; gently break remaining chocolate curls, and sprinkle over cheesecake, if desired. Yield: 10 to 12 servings.
Ursula Brambrey,
Springfield, Virginia.

Tip: Bent or dented measuring utensils give inaccurate measures. Use only standard measuring cups and spoons that are in good condition.

BREAKFASTS&BRUNCHES™

Depend On Eggs For The Entrée

How do you start your morning? With a leisurely breakfast in bed, a substantial meal of bacon and eggs, or a hasty slice of toast eaten on the run? Or maybe your preference is to sleep late and then collect friends to share a casual brunch.

In this special section, you'll find a wide range of recipes suitable for any of these occasions. We've included fresh suggestions to "spruce up" traditional favorites and a surprise or two that may become a regular part of your morning.

Whether they are scrambled or hard-cooked, baked in a quiche, or stirred into waffle batter, eggs are basic to morning meals in the South. Here are some creative ways to make your egg entrées a little different.

EGG-MUSHROOM CASSEROLE

8 eggs, beaten
1 cup milk
¼ teaspoon salt
⅛ teaspoon pepper
2 cups cooked rice
1 (4½-ounce) jar sliced mushrooms, drained
Cheese sauce (recipe follows)

Combine first 4 ingredients; mix well. Stir in rice and mushrooms; pour into a buttered 12- x 8- x 2-inch baking dish. Bake at 350° for 30 to 35 minutes or until set. Cut into squares, and serve immediately with cheese sauce. Yield: 8 servings.

Cheese Sauce:

2 tablespoons butter or margarine
2 tablespoons all-purpose flour
1⅓ cups milk
1 cup (4 ounces) shredded Cheddar cheese
½ teaspoon salt
⅛ teaspoon pepper

Melt butter in a heavy saucepan over low heat; add flour, and stir until smooth. Cook 1 minute, stirring constantly. Gradually add milk; cook over medium heat, stirring constantly, until thickened and bubbly. Add cheese, salt, and pepper; stir until cheese melts. Yield: about 1½ cups.

Mrs. Bob Nester,
Charleston, West Virginia.

SHERRIED MUSHROOM EGGS

1 (10-ounce) package frozen patty shells
¼ pound fresh mushrooms, sliced
1 tablespoon finely chopped onion
¼ cup plus 2 tablespoons butter or margarine, divided
3 tablespoons all-purpose flour
1½ cups milk
¾ teaspoon salt
Pinch of ground red pepper
6 hard-cooked eggs
1 tablespoon plus 1 teaspoon dry sherry
Fresh parsley sprigs

Bake patty shells according to package directions; set aside.

Sauté mushrooms and onion in 2 tablespoons butter in a heavy skillet until tender. Set aside.

Melt remaining ¼ cup butter in a heavy saucepan over low heat; add flour, stirring until smooth. Cook 1 minute, stirring constantly. Gradually add milk; cook over medium heat, stirring constantly, until thickened and bubbly. Stir in salt and pepper.

Finely chop 5 eggs. Stir chopped eggs, sautéed vegetables, and sherry into sauce; cook, stirring constantly, just until thoroughly heated. Spoon into patty shells. Cut remaining egg into 6 wedges. Garnish each serving with an egg wedge and a sprig of parsley. Yield: 6 servings.

Debby Sharpe,
Dallas, Texas.

SPANISH SCRAMBLED EGGS

½ pound bacon
1 dozen eggs, beaten
1 (4-ounce) can chopped green chiles, drained
1 (4-ounce) jar diced pimiento, drained
1 bunch green onions, finely chopped
1 large tomato, chopped
1 (4½-ounce) jar sliced mushrooms, drained
¼ cup butter or margarine
Tomato roses

Cook bacon in a large skillet until crisp. Remove bacon; crumble and set aside. Discard drippings.

Combine eggs, chiles, and pimiento; set aside. Sauté onion, tomato, and mushrooms in butter in skillet until tender. Add egg mixture; cook over medium heat, stirring often, until eggs are firm but still moist. Spoon onto serving platter; garnish with crumbled bacon and tomato roses. Yield: 6 servings.

Marian K. Davis,
Jasper, Alabama.

CRUSTLESS POTATO QUICHE

5 eggs, beaten
1 (12-ounce) package frozen hash browns, thawed
1 cup (4 ounces) shredded Swiss cheese
1 large green onion, chopped
½ cup cream-style cottage cheese
¼ teaspoon salt
⅛ teaspoon pepper
Dash of hot sauce
Paprika
6 slices bacon, cooked and crumbled

Combine first 8 ingredients; stir well. Pour mixture into a lightly greased 9-inch pieplate; sprinkle with paprika. Bake at 350° for 25 minutes or until set. Sprinkle bacon evenly on top; bake an additional 5 minutes. Let stand 5 minutes before serving. Yield: one 9-inch quiche.

Chris Bruggman,
Columbia, South Carolina.

SAUSAGE WAFFLES

½ pound mild bulk pork sausage
2 eggs, beaten
1 cup milk
1 tablespoon butter or margarine, melted
1¾ cups all-purpose flour
1 tablespoon baking powder
½ teaspoon salt

Crumble sausage into a medium skillet; cook over medium heat until sausage is browned. Drain well on paper towels, and set aside.

Combine eggs, milk, and butter in a medium-size bowl; mix well. Combine dry ingredients; add to the liquid mixture, mixing well.

Pour half of batter into a hot, lightly oiled waffle iron. Sprinkle half of sausage evenly over batter. Cook about 5 minutes or until done. Repeat procedure with remaining batter and sausage. Yield: eight 4-inch waffles.

Mary Lou Vaughn,
Dallas, Texas.

Get Started With Something Different

For Bill and Eleanor Crook of San Marcos, Texas, brunch is the ideal time for entertaining. They find brunches more relaxed than formal dinners, and their friends seem to find morning a good time to attend a party. And, friends look forward to this event because they can count on sampling some authentic Mexican food.

"I became involved with Mexican cooking 15 years ago when Esperanza Valdez became our family cook," explains Eleanor.

Their knowledge of south-of-the-border cuisine becomes evident when Eleanor and Esperanza set up the colorful buffet. Fruit is an important part of most Mexican menus, and several platters of attractively arranged avocado, mango, and watermelon are included.

At one end of the table, Esperanza heats a small portable burner and begins to shape and fry one of her specialties—Mushroom Panuchos. Guests

dip the tiny fried pies into green or red hot sauce. Accompanying the panuchos are two types of tamales—hot or sweet.

A quiche, filled to the brim with shrimp, and a large container of black beans complete the buffet. The traditional bean recipe is served as a dip with sour cream and tortilla chips. Add a glass of refreshing Fruit Punch, and guests are set to enjoy the meal. For dessert, there are Dark Pralines.

Hot Beef Spread
Avocado, Mango, and
Watermelon Fruit Plates
Black Bean Appetizer
Shrimp Quiche
Mushroom Panuchos
Commercial Red and Green Hot Sauces
Hot Tamales   Sweet Tamales
Dark Pralines
Fruit Punch

HOT BEEF SPREAD

½ cup chopped onion
1 tablespoon butter or margarine
2 tablespoons dry white wine
1 (8-ounce) package cream cheese, softened
½ cup commercial sour cream
½ cup mayonnaise
1 (2½-ounce) jar dried beef, finely chopped
½ cup chopped pecans

Sauté onion in butter in a skillet until tender. Stir in wine; simmer 2 minutes. Add next 4 ingredients; mix well.

Spoon mixture into an 8-inch square baking dish; sprinkle with pecans. Bake at 350° for 15 to 20 minutes. Serve with assorted crackers. Yield: 4 cups.

BLACK BEAN APPETIZER

1 pound dried black beans
2 quarts water
½ cup chopped onion
2 to 3 cloves garlic, minced
1 teaspoon salt
¼ cup chopped fresh cilantro or parsley
Tortilla chips
Commercial sour cream

Sort beans, and rinse thoroughly. Combine beans and water in a Dutch oven; let sit overnight. Bring bean mixture to a boil; reduce heat, and simmer, covered, 1 hour. Add onion, garlic, and salt to bean mixture; stir well. Cook an additional 2 hours or until thick.

Sprinkle cilantro over beans; serve with tortilla. chips and sour cream. Yield: about 5 cups.

SHRIMP QUICHE

Pastry for 9-inch quiche dish
8 fresh green poblano chiles
4 cups water
1½ pounds fresh shrimp, peeled and deveined
1 slice lemon
½ cup chopped onion
¼ cup butter or margarine
2 tablespoons butter or margarine
2 tablespoons dry white wine
1 tablespoon dry sherry
1 teaspoon chicken-flavored bouillon granules
1 clove garlic, crushed
⅛ teaspoon ground thyme
⅛ teaspoon ground marjoram
3 eggs, beaten
2 cups (8 ounces) shredded Muenster cheese
1 cup chopped unpeeled tomato
2 tablespoons mayonnaise
2 tablespoons commercial sour cream

Line a 9-inch quiche dish with pastry; trim excess pastry around edges. Prick bottom and sides of pastry with a fork. Bake at 400° for 3 minutes; remove from oven, and gently prick with a fork. Bake 5 minutes longer. Cool on rack.

Place chiles on a baking sheet; broil 5 to 6 inches from heat, turning often with tongs, until blistered on all sides. Immediately place chiles in a plastic bag. Fasten securely; wrap in a towel, and let steam 30 minutes. Remove and discard stems and peels. Cut a small slit in side of each chile, and rinse under cold water to remove seeds; chop.

Bring water to a boil. Add shrimp and lemon; return to a boil. Reduce heat, and simmer 1 minute. Drain well; discard lemon, and chop shrimp.

Sauté onion in ¼ cup butter in a large skillet until tender. Stir in chiles;

sauté 3 to 5 minutes. Add 2 tablespoons butter and next 6 ingredients. Stir over low heat 2 to 3 minutes. Add shrimp; cook, stirring often, 3 minutes.

Combine shrimp mixture and remaining ingredients; mix well. Pour into pastry shell. Bake at 350° for 1 hour or until set. Yield: one 9-inch quiche.

MUSHROOM PANUCHOS

1½ cups instant corn masa
1 cup water
2 teaspoons salt
3 cups mashed potatoes (about 6 medium potatoes)
1 egg, slightly beaten
½ cup all-purpose flour
Mushroom filling (recipe follows)
1 cup (4 ounces) shredded Muenster cheese
Vegetable oil
1 (7-ounce) can commercial Mexican red picante sauce
1 (7-ounce) can commercial Mexican green hot sauce

Combine masa and water; mix well. Add salt, potatoes, and egg; mix well. Add flour; knead until mixture is blended and smooth.

Divide pastry into 4 portions. Place each portion between 2 sheets of heavy-duty plastic wrap, and roll into 9-inch squares. Cut each square into four 4-inch circles. Place about 1 tablespoon filling and 1 tablespoon cheese on each pastry circle. Moisten edges of circles; fold pastry in half over filling, making sure edges are even.

Using a fork dipped in flour, press and seal edges of pastry together. Heat ½ inch oil to 375°. Cook panuchos until golden brown, turning once. Drain well. Serve with red and green sauces. Yield: 16 panuchos.

Mushroom Filling:

2 or 3 poblano chiles
1 tablespoon vegetable oil
1 teaspoon chicken-flavored bouillon granules
1½ cups sliced fresh mushrooms
½ cup chopped onion
½ cup finely chopped fresh cilantro or parsley

Place chiles on a baking sheet; broil 5 to 6 inches from heat, turning often with tongs, until blistered on all sides. Immediately place chiles in a plastic bag. Fasten securely; wrap in a towel, and let steam 30 minutes. Remove and discard stem and peel of each chile. Cut a small slit in the side of each chile, and rinse under cold water to remove seeds; chop chiles, and set aside.

Heat oil in a heavy skillet; add bouillon granules, and stir until dissolved. Add chiles and remaining ingredients. Sauté until vegetables are tender. Yield: about 1 cup.

HOT TAMALES

1 (4-pound) pork roast
1 medium onion, quartered
3 cloves garlic, crushed
1 teaspoon salt
4 to 5 dozen cornhusks
5 fresh green serrano chiles
8 tomatoes, peeled and quartered
1 medium onion, quartered
3 cloves garlic
1 tablespoon chicken-flavored bouillon granules
2 cups shortening
1 teaspoon baking powder
1 teaspoon baking soda
5 cups instant corn masa
2 tablespoons vegetable oil

Combine first 4 ingredients in a Dutch oven. Add water to cover; bring to a boil. Cover, reduce heat, and simmer 1 to 1½ hours or until meat is tender. Drain; reserve 1 cup broth. Shred meat with a fork. Set aside.

Cover dried cornhusks with hot water; let stand 1 hour or until softened. Drain well, and pat with paper towels to remove excess water. (If husks are too narrow, overlap 2 husks to make a wide one. If husks are too wide, tear off one side.)

Place chiles on a baking sheet; broil 3 to 4 inches from heat, turning often with tongs, until blistered on all sides.

Immediately place chiles in a plastic bag. Fasten securely; wrap in a towel, and let steam 15 minutes. Remove and discard stem and peel of each chile. Cut a small slit in side of each chile, and rinse under cold water to remove seeds; coarsely chop chiles.

Combine chiles, half of tomatoes, onion, garlic, and bouillon in container of electric blender; process until smooth, and pour into a large mixing bowl. Add remaining tomatoes to the blender, and process until smooth; stir into tomato mixture, and set aside.

Cream shortening in a large bowl; add baking powder, soda, and reserved broth, mixing well. Gradually add corn masa, mixing well; beat 10 minutes on medium speed of heavy-duty electric mixer until mixture is light and fluffy.

Sauté reserved meat in oil until browned; stir in tomato mixture. Cook, uncovered, over low heat 15 to 20 minutes, stirring occasionally.

Place 1 tablespoon of masa dough in the center of each husk, spreading to within ½ inch of edge. Place 2 tablespoons meat mixture on dough, spreading evenly. Fold short ends of husks to center. Fold one long side of husk to center, enclosing filling completely; roll up from same side. Tie with string or narrow strip of softened cornhusk.

Place a cup in center of a steaming rack or metal colander in a large pot. Add just enough water to fill pot below rack level to keep tamales above water. Stand tamales on folded ends around the cup. Bring water to a boil. Cover and steam 1 hour or until tamale dough pulls away from husk; add more water as necessary. Yield: 4 dozen.

Note: Steamed tamales may be frozen. Allow to cool, place in a plastic bag or wrap securely in aluminum foil, and put in freezer. To reheat, follow above steaming procedure until tamales are thoroughly heated.

Tip: Use the store's comparative pricing information for good buys. The unit-price data allows you to compare the cost of similar products of different sizes by weight, measure, or count.

SWEET TAMALES

3 to 4 dozen cornhusks
8 large dried red chiles
½ cup water
2½ cups shortening
5 cups instant corn masa
2¾ cups sugar
1 tablespoon baking powder
2 teaspoons baking soda
¼ teaspoon salt
1 cup water
1½ cups (6 ounces) shredded Muenster
   cheese

Cover dried cornhusks with hot water; let stand 1 hour or until softened. Drain well, and pat with paper towels to remove excess water. (If husks are too narrow, overlap 2 husks to make a wide one. If husks are too wide, tear off one side.)

Place chiles and water to cover in a saucepan; bring to a boil. Reduce heat and cook 30 minutes or until chiles are soft and the stems fall off. Discard stems. Cut a slit in side of each chili, and rinse pulp under cold water to remove seeds. Combine chiles and ½ cup water in container of electric blender; process until smooth.

Cream shortening in a large bowl. Combine next 5 ingredients. Add dry ingredients, 1 cup water, and chile puree to shortening. Beat 10 minutes on medium speed of electric mixer until light and fluffy. Fold in cheese.

Place about ¼ cup masa mixture in center of each husk, spreading to within ½ inch of edge. Fold short ends of husk to center. Fold one long side of husk to center, enclosing filling completely; roll up from same side. Tie with string or narrow strips of softened cornhusk.

Place a cup in center of a steaming rack or metal colander in a large pot. Add just enough water to fill pot below rack level to keep tamales above water. Stand tamales on folded ends around the cup. Bring water to a boil. Cover and steam 1 hour or until tamale dough pulls away from husk; add more water as necessary. Yield: 3 dozen.

Note: Steamed tamales may be frozen. Allow to cool, place in a plastic bag or wrap securely in aluminum foil, and put in freezer. To reheat, follow above steaming procedure until tamales are thoroughly heated.

DARK PRALINES

2 cups sugar
1 cup buttermilk
1 teaspoon baking soda
2 cups pecan halves
2 tablespoons butter or margarine

Combine first 3 ingredients in a large heavy saucepan; bring to a boil, and cook 5 minutes.

Stir in pecans and butter; cook over medium heat, stirring occasionally, until mixture reaches soft ball stage (234°). Remove from heat; beat with a wooden spoon 2 to 3 minutes or until mixture is creamy and begins to thicken. Working rapidly, drop mixture by rounded tablespoonfuls onto waxed paper; let cool. Yield: 1½ dozen.

FRUIT PUNCH

4 cups orange juice, chilled
2 cups lime juice, chilled
3 cups cubed fresh pineapple
2 pints fresh strawberries
3 apples, peeled, cored, and coarsely
   chopped
3 bananas, peeled and sliced
1 cup sugar
1 bottle dry white wine, chilled
1 (67.6-ounce) bottle ginger ale, chilled
½ cup Cognac

Combine fruit juice; set aside.

Combine all fruit with 1 cup fruit juice in container of electric blender; process until smooth. Pour mixture into a large bowl; stir in remaining fruit juice. Add the remaining ingredients. Serve punch over ice, if desired. Yield: about 2 gallons.

Side Dishes For Morning Menus

When you read our recipes for colorful morning side dishes, you may have trouble deciding which one to try first. We hope you'll add one or two to your next special breakfast or brunch menu.

GRITS PATTIES

⅓ cup uncooked regular grits
2 tablespoons self-rising flour
¼ teaspoon salt
⅛ teaspoon pepper
1 egg, slightly beaten
Hot vegetable oil

Cook grits according to package directions. Stir in flour, salt, pepper, and egg; mix well.

Drop mixture by tablespoonfuls into hot oil. Gently flatten with spatula. Brown on both sides; drain on paper towels. Serve patties immediately. Yield: 8 servings.   *Thelma Brooks, Winter Haven, Florida.*

GOLD COAST HOMINY

3 tablespoons butter or margarine
½ cup chopped green pepper
¼ cup finely chopped onion
3 tablespoons all-purpose flour
1½ cups milk
1 cup (4 ounces) shredded Cheddar cheese
½ teaspoon salt
½ teaspoon dry mustard
1 teaspoon hot sauce
1 (15½-ounce) can hominy, drained
½ cup chopped ripe olives
½ cup soft breadcrumbs
1 tablespoon butter or margarine, melted

Melt 3 tablespoons butter in a heavy saucepan over low heat. Add green pepper and onion; sauté until tender. Add flour and cook 1 minute, stirring constantly. Gradually add milk; cook over medium heat, stirring constantly, until thickened and bubbly. Add cheese, salt, mustard, and hot sauce; stir until cheese melts. Stir in hominy and olives.

Spoon mixture into a lightly greased 1½-quart casserole. Combine breadcrumbs and melted butter; sprinkle over hominy mixture. Bake, uncovered, at 375° for 20 minutes or until mixture is bubbly. Yield: 6 servings.
Mrs. John W. Stevens, Lexington, Kentucky.

CHEESY POTATO CASSEROLE

4 cups peeled, cubed potatoes
1 (8-ounce) carton cream-style cottage
 cheese
1 (8-ounce) carton commercial sour cream
½ cup chopped green onion
1 tablespoon chopped fresh parsley
1 clove garlic, minced
½ teaspoon salt
½ cup (2 ounces) shredded Cheddar
 cheese
Paprika
1 green onion with top (optional)

Cook potatoes in boiling salted water 15 minutes or until tender; drain well.

Combine next 6 ingredients in a large bowl; mix well. Stir in potatoes. Spoon mixture into a lightly greased 1½-quart casserole; bake at 350° for 25 minutes. Top with cheese; sprinkle with paprika. Bake an additional 5 minutes or until cheese melts. Garnish with green onion, if desired. Yield: 6 servings.
Brenda Blalock,
Lawrenceville, Georgia.

BAKED TOMATOES

4 medium tomatoes, cut in half crosswise
¼ teaspoon salt
⅛ teaspoon pepper
½ cup soft breadcrumbs, toasted
3 tablespoons chopped fresh parsley
2 cloves garlic, minced
¼ teaspoon dried whole thyme
¼ teaspoon dried whole oregano
2 tablespoons vegetable oil
Fresh parsley sprigs (optional)

Place tomato halves in a lightly greased 12- x 8- x 2-inch baking dish. Sprinkle salt and pepper over cut surface of each tomato half.

Combine next 6 ingredients; mix well, and spoon over cut surface of each tomato. Bake at 350° for 12 to 15 minutes or until tomato is thoroughly heated. Garnish with parsley sprigs, if desired. Yield: 8 servings. *Janine Kuykendall,*
Cedar Park, Texas.

Tip: When making coffee for a crowd, allow 1 pound of coffee plus 2 gallons water for 40 servings.

HOT FRUIT COMPOTE

1 (15¼-ounce) can pineapple chunks,
 drained
1 (16-ounce) can sliced peaches, drained
1 (15-ounce) jar spiced apple rings,
 drained
1 (16-ounce) can pear halves, drained
1 (16-ounce) can apricot halves, drained
½ cup butter or margarine
2 tablespoons all-purpose flour
½ cup sugar
1 cup sherry
12 red maraschino cherries

Layer first 5 ingredients in a 13- x 9- x 2-inch baking dish.

Melt butter in top of a double boiler. Add flour, sugar, and sherry; mix well. Cook 15 minutes or until mixture is slightly thickened. Pour sauce over fruit; arrange cherries on top. Bake at 350° for 20 minutes. Serve immediately. Yield: 10 servings. *Sue Garrison,*
Kingsport, Tennessee.

PEACH AMBROSIA

1 (15¼-ounce) can pineapple tidbits,
 drained
½ cup seedless green grapes
½ cup orange sections
½ cup miniature marshmallows
½ cup flaked coconut
½ cup commercial sour cream
14 peach halves, drained
½ cup slivered almonds, toasted

Combine first 5 ingredients, tossing gently; chill. Before serving, add sour cream to fruit mixture; mix well. Spoon ¼ cup fruit mixture into each peach half; top with almonds. Yield: 14 servings. *Kay Castleman Cooper,*
Burke, Virginia.

Classic Morning Breads

You don't have to go to New Orleans to enjoy freshly baked croissants. With our recipe, you can serve them hot and flaky from your own oven. That goes for our other classic breads as well, like our Orange Muffins and Cinnamon Twists; they're all perfect choices for breakfast or brunch.

Croissants get their flakiness from repeatedly rolling, folding, and refrigerating the dough the day before they're served. In the morning, they're just shaped and baked.

CINNAMON TWISTS

1 (8-ounce) carton commercial sour cream
3 tablespoons sugar
2 tablespoons shortening
1 package dry yeast
1 teaspoon salt
⅛ teaspoon baking soda
3 cups all-purpose flour, divided
1 egg
2 tablespoons butter or margarine,
 softened
⅓ cup firmly packed brown sugar
1 teaspoon ground cinnamon
Glaze (recipe follows)

Place sour cream in a small saucepan; cook over low heat until warm (105° to 115°). Remove from heat. Add next 5 ingredients; stir until shortening melts.

Combine yeast mixture, 2 cups flour, and egg in a large mixing bowl; beat at medium speed of electric mixer until smooth. Stir in remaining 1 cup flour.

Turn dough out onto a floured surface, and knead about 5 minutes until smooth and elastic. Roll dough into a 24- x 8-inch rectangle; brush with softened butter. Combine brown sugar and cinnamon; sprinkle evenly over dough.

Fold dough in half lengthwise; cut into 4- x 1-inch strips. Twist each strip once. Place 2 inches apart on greased baking sheets; press ends down.

Cover and let rise in a warm place (85°), free from drafts, 1 hour. Bake at 375° for 15 to 17 minutes or until golden brown. Drizzle glaze over warm twists. Yield: 2 dozen.

Glaze:

1 cup sifted powdered sugar
1 to 2 tablespoons milk

Combine sugar and milk, stirring until smooth. Yield: about ½ cup.
Marylou Coffin,
Albuquerque, New Mexico.

LEMON-PECAN BREAD

¾ cup butter or margarine, softened
1½ cups sugar
3 eggs
2¼ cups all-purpose flour
¼ teaspoon baking soda
¼ teaspoon salt
¾ cup buttermilk
¾ cup chopped pecans
1 teaspoon grated lemon rind

Cream butter; gradually add sugar, beating well. Add eggs, one at a time, beating well after each addition.

Combine flour, soda, and salt; add to creamed mixture alternately with buttermilk, beginning and ending with flour mixture. Stir in pecans and lemon rind.

Pour batter into a greased and floured 9- x 5- x 3-inch loafpan. Bake at 350° for 1 hour and 15 to 20 minutes or until a wooden pick inserted in center comes out clean. Cool 10 minutes; remove loaf from pan, and cool completely. Yield: 1 loaf. *Debra Leckie, Shreveport, Louisiana.*

CROISSANTS

1 cup butter, softened
⅔ cup milk
2 packages dry yeast
½ cup warm water (105° to 115°)
4 to 4½ cups all-purpose flour, divided
¼ cup vegetable oil
3 tablespoons sugar
2 teaspoons salt
2 eggs
1 egg yolk
1 tablespoon milk

Stir butter with a wooden spoon until smooth; spread on waxed paper into a 10- x 8-inch rectangle. Chill until needed.

Scald ⅔ cup milk; cool to 105° to 115°. Dissolve yeast in warm water in a large bowl. Stir in scalded milk, 2 cups flour, and next 4 ingredients; beat at medium speed of an electric mixer until smooth. Gradually stir in enough remaining flour to make a soft dough.

Turn dough out onto a floured surface; knead 8 to 10 minutes until smooth and elastic. Place in a well-greased bowl, turning to grease top. Cover and let rise in a warm place (85°), free from drafts, 1 hour or until doubled in bulk.

Punch dough down. Cover and refrigerate 1 hour.

Punch dough down, and place on a lightly floured surface; roll into a 24- x 10-inch rectangle. Place butter on half of dough. Fold other half of dough over butter to form a 12- x 10-inch rectangle; pinch edges to seal.

Roll dough into an 18- x 10-inch rectangle. Fold into thirds, beginning with short side. Cover and chill 1 hour.

Repeat rolling and folding process (roll into an 18- x 10-inch rectangle and fold into thirds) 2 additional times, covering and chilling dough 30 minutes between procedures. Wrap dough in aluminum foil, and chill overnight.

Divide dough into 4 equal portions; chill 3 portions. Roll 1 portion into a 12-inch circle on a lightly floured surface; cut into 6 wedges. Roll up each wedge tightly, beginning at wide end. Seal points, and place point side down on greased baking sheets; curve into crescent shapes. Repeat with remaining dough. Refrigerate 30 minutes.

Combine egg yolk and 1 tablespoon milk; brush over croissants. Bake at 425° for 14 to 16 minutes or until golden brown. Yield: 2 dozen.

ORANGE MUFFINS

1½ cups all-purpose flour
½ cup sugar
2 teaspoons baking powder
½ teaspoon salt
1 egg, slightly beaten
½ cup milk
1 teaspoon grated orange rind
¼ cup orange juice
¼ cup vegetable oil
½ cup golden raisins

Combine first 4 ingredients in a large bowl; make a well in center of mixture. Combine egg, milk, orange rind, orange juice, and oil, mixing well; add to dry ingredients, stirring just until moistened. Stir in raisins. Spoon batter into greased muffin pans, filling two-thirds full. Bake at 400° for 20 minutes. Yield: 1 dozen. *Janet Benton, Monroe, Georgia.*

Get A Headstart On Brunch

Everyone enjoys a brunch, but the event should be fun for the host or hostess as well as for the guests. Too many last-minute preparations mean little time for fun. Here are a few make-ahead recipes that will be ready and waiting in the refrigerator the night before your brunch.

COUNTRY GRITS AND SAUSAGE

2 cups water
½ teaspoon salt
½ cup uncooked quick grits
4 cups (16 ounces) shredded extra-sharp Cheddar cheese
4 eggs, beaten
1 cup milk
½ teaspoon dried whole thyme
⅛ teaspoon garlic salt
2 pounds mild bulk pork sausage, cooked, crumbled, and drained
Tomato roses
Fresh parsley sprigs

Bring water and salt to a boil; stir in grits. Return to a boil, and reduce heat. Cook 4 minutes, stirring the mixture occasionally.

Combine grits and cheese in a large mixing bowl; stir until cheese is melted. Combine eggs, milk, thyme, and garlic salt; mix well. Add a small amount of hot grits mixture to egg mixture, stirring well. Stir egg mixture into grits mixture. Add sausage, stirring well. Pour into a 12- x 8- x 2-inch baking dish. Cover and refrigerate overnight.

Remove from refrigerator; let stand 15 minutes. Bake at 350° for 50 to 55 minutes. Garnish with tomato roses and parsley sprigs. Yield: 8 servings.

Note: Recipe may be halved; bake at 350° in a 10- x 6- x 2-inch baking dish for 45 minutes. *Mrs. Robert L. Spence, Baton Rouge, Louisiana.*

EGG SOUFFLE CASSEROLE

1½ pounds pork sausage links
4 eggs, beaten
2½ cups milk
¼ teaspoon dry mustard
3 cups plain croutons
2½ cups (10 ounces) shredded Cheddar
    cheese
1 (10¾-ounce) can cream of mushroom
    soup, undiluted
1 (2½-ounce) jar sliced mushrooms,
    drained
⅔ cup milk

Cut each sausage link into 4 pieces. Cook in a large skillet until browned; drain and set aside.

Combine eggs, 2½ cups milk, and mustard.

Layer croutons, cheese, sausage, and egg mixture in a buttered 13- x 9- x 2-inch baking dish. Cover and chill overnight.

Combine remaining ingredients; stir well, and spread over top of casserole. Bake, uncovered, at 300° for 1½ hours. Yield: 8 to 10 servings.   *Marti Lee, Overland Park, Kansas.*

FRUIT CUP WITH RUM

1 (17-ounce) can apricot halves, drained
1 (16-ounce) can sliced peaches, drained
1 (16-ounce) can sliced pears, drained
1 (16-ounce) can seedless grapes, drained
1 (15¼-ounce) can pineapple chunks,
    drained
1 (11-ounce) can mandarin oranges,
    drained
1 (6-ounce) jar maraschino cherries,
    drained
½ cup rum
Lemon rind twists
Mint leaves

Combine the fruit; add rum, and toss gently. Cover and refrigerate overnight. Garnish with a lemon rind twist and mint leaves. Yield: 12 servings.
Mrs. Bob Nester, Charleston, West Virginia.

Tip: Make ice cubes for a party ahead of time and store them in plastic bags in the freezer. Count on 350 cubes for 50 people or 7 cubes per person.

EASY BRAN MUFFINS

3 cups shreds of wheat bran cereal
1 cup raisins
1 cup boiling water
2⅓ cups all-purpose flour
1½ cups sugar
2½ teaspoons baking soda
½ teaspoon salt
2 cups buttermilk
½ cup vegetable oil
2 eggs, beaten
1 cup chopped pecans

Combine cereal and raisins in a large bowl; pour boiling water over cereal mixture, and mix well. Cool.

Combine next 4 ingredients; make a well in center of flour mixture. Add buttermilk, oil, eggs, pecans, and bran mixture; stir just enough to moisten dry ingredients. Cover and store in refrigerator up to one week.

When ready to bake, spoon batter into greased muffin pans, filling two-thirds full. Bake at 400° for 15 to 18 minutes. Yield: about 2½ dozen.
Zee H. Pohler, Virginia Beach, Virginia.

Beverages To Please Morning Taste Buds

Whether you prefer waking up to a hot cup of coffee or a cool fruit slush, there's a beverage here to please you. Our home economists tested this group of recipes first thing one morning, and enjoyed sipping on the leftovers during the rest of the day.

FAVORITE HOT CHOCOLATE

1½ cups sugar
½ cup cocoa
¾ teaspoon salt
5 cups water
1 (13-ounce) can evaporated milk
2 cups milk
Marshmallows (optional)

Combine sugar, cocoa, and salt in a large Dutch oven; mix well. Slowly stir in water; bring to a boil. Add milk; cook until thoroughly heated.

Place marshmallows in individual cups, if desired; fill cups with hot chocolate. Yield: 2½ quarts.
Mrs. Walter Perdue, Collinsville, Virginia.

COCOA-COFFEE

1 cup instant cocoa mix
⅓ cup instant coffee granules
4 cups boiling water
Whipped cream

Combine cocoa mix, instant coffee, and boiling water; stir until coffee granules dissolve.

Garnish each serving with whipped cream. Yield: 1 quart.   *Pat Boschen, Ashland, Virginia.*

SPICED TEA COOLER

½ cup water
3 whole cloves
1 (2-inch) stick cinnamon
3 tablespoons honey
½ cup orange juice
2 regular tea bags

Combine water, cloves, and cinnamon in a saucepan. Cover and simmer over low heat 10 minutes. Stir in honey and orange juice; bring to a boil. Remove from heat, and add tea bags; cover and steep 5 minutes. Discard tea bags, cloves, and cinnamon; cool slightly, and refrigerate until ready to serve. Serve chilled. Yield: 1 cup. *Alice McNamara, Eucha, Oklahoma.*

BANANA SLUSH

4 cups sugar
6 cups water
1 (46-ounce) can pineapple juice
1 (46-ounce) can orange juice
5 bananas, mashed
½ cup lemon juice
5 quarts ginger ale, chilled

Combine sugar and water in a saucepan; bring to a boil, stirring until sugar dissolves. Cool. Pour sugar mixture into a 5-quart freezer container. Stir in next 4 ingredients, and freeze until firm.

Remove mixture from freezer several hours before serving (mixture should be slushy); pour into punch bowl, and stir in ginger ale. Yield: about 2½ gallons.
Carol Bowen,
Tifton, Georgia.

GOLDEN FRUIT PUNCH

2 (12-ounce) cans apricot nectar, chilled
1½ cups orange juice, chilled
¾ cup lemon juice
1½ quarts apple cider, chilled
Maraschino cherries

Combine first 4 ingredients, mixing well. Pour into pitcher or punch bowl. Serve punch over ice, and garnish with cherries. Yield: about 3 quarts.
Carla C. Hunter,
Norcross, Georgia.

COOKING LIGHT

Take A Light Look At Brunch

Who would consider serving a classic dish like Eggs Florentine to a dieter? You will, if you've stripped away excess calories by "Cooking Light." We have done just that and made this gourmet entrée the center of a light brunch menu. It's accompanied by a flavorful carrot side dish and followed by a refreshing fruit dessert. Even with an appetizer, the calorie count is less than 440 for the complete meal.

Trimming away calories for this delicious menu starts by using skim milk, plain low-fat yogurt, and unsweetened strawberries for an appetizer beverage. You'll need only 2 tablespoons of sugar to sweeten Strawberry Cooler, with vanilla extract added for extra flavor.

Poaching is an ideal way to keep the calories down when cooking eggs. Place poached eggs atop toasted English muffin halves, spinach, and sliced tomatoes for Eggs Florentine. Tarragon Sauce made with reduced-calorie mayonnaise keeps the dish light.

Cook sliced carrots in a mixture of Marsala wine and reduced-calorie margarine for Carrots Marsala. The alcohol in the wine evaporates during cooking, leaving behind lots of flavor but few calories; that's why wine is often recommended for light cooking.

Strawberry Cooler
Eggs Florentine
Carrots Marsala
Brunch Ambrosia

STRAWBERRY COOLER

1 cup skim milk
1 cup plain low-fat yogurt
2 tablespoons sugar
2 teaspoons vanilla extract
2 cups frozen whole strawberries

Combine first 4 ingredients in container of an electric blender; process until smooth. Gradually add strawberries; process until smooth and thickened. Yield: 3¾ cups (about 73 calories per ⅝-cup serving).
Candy Gardner,
Shalimar, Florida.

EGGS FLORENTINE

1 (10-ounce) package frozen leaf spinach
6 tomato slices
3 whole wheat English muffins, split and toasted
6 poached eggs
Tarragon Sauce
Paprika

Cook spinach according to package directions, omitting salt; drain well. Place a tomato slice on each muffin half. Spoon an equal amount of spinach over each slice; top with a poached egg. Spoon 2 tablespoons Tarragon Sauce over each egg; sprinkle with paprika. Yield: 6 servings (about 222 calories per serving).

Tarragon Sauce:

½ cup reduced-calorie mayonnaise
3 tablespoons water
2 to 3 teaspoons lemon juice
1 teaspoon prepared mustard
¼ teaspoon dried whole tarragon
⅛ teaspoon white pepper

Combine all ingredients in a saucepan; stir until smooth. Cook over low heat, stirring constantly, 3 to 4 minutes until thoroughly heated. Yield: ¾ cup.

CARROTS MARSALA

1½ pounds carrots, scraped and diagonally sliced
¼ cup plus 2 tablespoons Marsala wine
¼ cup plus 2 tablespoons water
1½ tablespoons reduced-calorie margarine
½ teaspoon salt
⅛ teaspoon pepper
1½ tablespoons chopped fresh parsley

Combine first 6 ingredients in a large saucepan. Bring to a boil. Cover, reduce heat, and simmer 10 minutes or until most of liquid evaporates, tossing carrots occasionally. Sprinkle with parsley. Yield: 6 servings (about 54 calories per serving).
Thelma Olson,
Lexington, Oklahoma.

Tip: Remove the tops of carrots before refrigerating. Tops drain the carrots of moisture, making them limp and dry.

BRUNCH AMBROSIA

2 small apples, sliced
2 medium grapefruit, peeled and sectioned
2 medium oranges, peeled and sectioned
½ cup unsweetened orange juice
2 tablespoons flaked coconut
Mint sprigs (optional)

Combine first 4 ingredients; cover and chill 1 hour. Arrange fruit in individual serving dishes; sprinkle with coconut and garnish with mint, if desired. Yield: 6 servings (about 88 calories per serving).   *Jan Hughes,*
Batesville, Arkansas.

Breakfast From The Toaster Oven

In households of all sizes, cooks find the tabletop toaster oven to be a convenient, energy-saving appliance. The oven heats up quickly for baking, and since the space to be heated is so much smaller than a conventional oven, it conserves energy as well.

Originally designed to offer the option of toasting bread on both sides or just on top, toaster ovens now feature thermostatic controls for baking and broiling.

You'll need to adjust baking times for some foods. Because of the oven size, the food is closer to the heating elements and may brown before it's completely cooked. If you notice the food browning too quickly, cover it with foil. This will increase the cooking time slightly but will allow the food to cook without burning on top. Be sure the foil doesn't touch the heating elements.

Any piece of bakeware is suitable for the toaster oven as long as it doesn't interfere with the door closing; all parts of the container (including lids and handles) should be at least 1 inch from the heating elements. For a regular-size toaster oven, you'll find the following equipment useful: 6-ounce and 10-ounce custard cups, a 6-cup muffin pan, an 8-inch square baking pan, 16-ounce square casseroles, and a round or rectangular 1-quart casserole.

Not all standard baking equipment will fit in every toaster oven. Check the owner's manual to see what types of bakeware the manufacturer recommends for use with your oven.

BAKED EGG CRISPS

6 slices bread
1 tablespoon butter or margarine, softened
1½ teaspoons grated Parmesan cheese
¼ teaspoon salt
¼ teaspoon pepper
6 eggs
6 slices bacon, cooked and crumbled

Remove crust from bread, and spread butter evenly over one side. Using a 2½-inch biscuit cutter, cut a circle from center of each bread slice; then cut each remaining square into 4 triangles (cut through center of each side).

Place each bread circle, buttered side up, in a buttered 6-ounce custard cup. Place triangles around edges of custard cup with points facing upward. Bake at 350° for 7 minutes.

Combine cheese, salt, and pepper; mix well, and set aside.

Gently break 1 egg into each toast cup; sprinkle eggs with cheese mixture. Bake 12 to 15 minutes. Sprinkle bacon evenly over eggs. Yield: 6 servings.
Mrs. Werner A. Senff,
Longboat Key, Florida.

UPSIDE-DOWN ORANGE PUFFS

2 tablespoons butter or margarine, melted
¼ cup sugar
1 teaspoon grated orange rind
3 tablespoons orange juice
1 (4.5-ounce) can refrigerated biscuits

Combine butter, sugar, orange rind, and orange juice, mixing well.

Pour about 1 tablespoon orange mixture in each cup of a 6-cup muffin pan. Place 1 biscuit in each cup. Bake at 400° about 10 minutes. Invert pan on serving plate; serve warm. Yield: 6 servings.
Mrs. Ward Kirkpatrick,
Waynesville, North Carolina.

LITTLE EGG SOUFFLES

2 eggs, beaten
1 tablespoon commercial sour cream
1 teaspoon water
½ teaspoon baking powder
Dash of fines herbes
4 to 5 drops of hot sauce
½ cup (2 ounces) shredded Cheddar cheese

Combine all ingredients except cheese; mix well. Stir in cheese. Pour into two greased 6-ounce custard cups or individual soufflé dishes. Bake at 350° for 12 to 14 minutes or until set. Yield: 2 servings.

Mrs. Peter Rosato III,
Memphis, Tennessee.

MAYONNAISE MUFFINS

1 cup self-rising flour
2 tablespoons mayonnaise
½ cup milk

Combine all ingredients; stir until smooth. Spoon batter into greased 6-cup muffin pans, filling two-thirds full. Bake at 425° for 10 to 12 minutes. Yield: ½ dozen.   *Debra Leckie,*
Shreveport, Louisiana.

Tip: Reheat frozen pancakes for a quick breakfast by popping them into the toaster. Or, thaw and heat them in sauce, butter, or margarine in a frying pan over moderate heat.

Microwave Menu Just For Two

Dinner for two can be ready in about 30 minutes with this easy microwave menu. It's dressy enough to serve for a special guest but casual enough for a regular evening meal.

In order to streamline the cooking time, we suggest microwaving the Parsleyed Rice first. While it's cooking and standing the required 10 minutes, you can slice and microwave the carrots.

To save even more time, flatten the chicken breasts for Chicken Alla Romano as soon as you buy them. Stir together the ice cream sauce, slice the celery for the soup, and you'll be ready to start microwaving.

Tomato-Celery Soup
Chicken Alla Romano
Parsleyed Rice   Spice-Glazed Carrots
Cocoa-Kahlúa Sundaes

TOMATO-CELERY SOUP

2 tablespoons butter or margarine
⅓ cup thinly sliced celery
¼ cup chopped onion
1 (10¾-ounce) can condensed tomato soup, undiluted
1¼ cups water
1 to 2 tablespoons lemon juice
2 tablespoons chopped fresh parsley
1 teaspoon sugar
¼ teaspoon coarsely ground black pepper
Sliced lemon (optional)

Place butter in a deep 1½-quart casserole. Microwave at HIGH for 40 seconds or until melted; stir in celery and onion. Cover with heavy-duty plastic wrap. Microwave at HIGH for 2 minutes or until onion is tender.

Stir next 6 ingredients into celery mixture. Cover and microwave at HIGH for 5 minutes, stirring after 3 minutes. Spoon into serving bowls, and top with slices of lemon, if desired. Yield: 2 servings.

CHICKEN ALLA ROMANO

2 chicken breast halves, skinned and boned
1 (1-ounce) slice Swiss cheese, halved
1 thin slice prosciutto or smoked ham, halved
3 tablespoons fine, dry breadcrumbs
1 tablespoon grated Parmesan cheese
1 teaspoon paprika
⅛ teaspoon garlic salt
Pinch of dried whole tarragon
2 tablespoons butter or margarine

Place each chicken breast half on a sheet of waxed paper; flatten to ¼-inch thickness, using a meat mallet or rolling pin. Place a piece of Swiss cheese and prosciutto in center of each piece of chicken. Roll up lengthwise, and secure with a wooden pick.

Combine next 5 ingredients, stirring well. Place butter in a 1-cup glass measure; microwave at HIGH for 40 seconds or until melted.

Dip each chicken breast half in butter; roll each piece in crumb mixture. Place rolls, seam side down, in a 1-quart shallow casserole. Cover with waxed paper, and microwave at HIGH for 4 minutes or until chicken is fork tender, rotating dish after 2 minutes. Yield: 2 servings.

PARSLEYED RICE

½ cup uncooked regular rice
1 cup plus 2 tablespoons hot water
2 tablespoons chopped fresh parsley
2 teaspoons butter or margarine
¼ teaspoon salt

Place all ingredients in a 1-quart casserole; cover with heavy-duty plastic wrap. Microwave at HIGH for 3 minutes. Reduce heat, and microwave at MEDIUM (50% power) for 7 to 9 minutes. Let stand, covered, for 10 minutes before serving. Yield: 2 servings.

SPICE-GLAZED CARROTS

½ pound carrots, scraped and sliced into thin strips
3 tablespoons orange juice
1 tablespoon butter or margarine
1 tablespoon brown sugar
⅛ teaspoon ground cinnamon
⅛ teaspoon ground cloves
⅛ teaspoon salt

Combine carrots and orange juice in a 1-quart casserole. Cover with heavy-duty plastic wrap. Microwave at HIGH for 5 to 6 minutes. Let stand, covered, for 3 minutes.

Place butter in a 1-cup glass measure; microwave at HIGH for 35 seconds. Stir in next 4 ingredients. Drain carrots. Pour glaze over carrots, and stir well. Microwave at HIGH for 20 seconds or until the sugar is melted. Stir well. Yield: 2 servings.

COCOA-KAHLUA SUNDAES

2 tablespoons plus 1 teaspoon sugar
2 tablespoons plus 1 teaspoon brown sugar
1 tablespoon cocoa
2¼ teaspoons all-purpose flour
¼ cup Kahlúa or other coffee-flavored liqueur
1 tablespoon butter or margarine
1 teaspoon corn syrup
1 pint vanilla ice cream
¼ cup chopped pecans

Combine sugar, cocoa, and flour in a 2-cup glass measure. Stir in next 3 ingredients. Microwave at HIGH for 1½ to 2 minutes or until thick and smooth, stirring after 1 minute.

Scoop ice cream into 2 individual serving dishes. Spoon sauce over ice cream, and sprinkle with pecans. Serve immediately. Yield: 2 servings.

Try These Coleslaw Variations

Most Southerners would agree that crispy fried fish or a plateful of barbecue just wouldn't taste the same without a side dish of coleslaw. But they probably wouldn't agree on which coleslaw recipe is the best.

BACON COLESLAW

6 slices bacon
⅓ cup vinegar
⅓ cup sugar
¼ cup water
½ teaspoon salt
¼ teaspoon pepper
1 medium head cabbage, shredded
4 medium carrots, shredded

Cook bacon in a large skillet until crisp; remove bacon, reserving 3 tablespoons drippings in skillet. Crumble bacon, and set aside.

Stir vinegar, sugar, water, salt, and pepper into drippings. Cook, stirring constantly, until sugar dissolves; cool.

Combine cabbage and carrots in a large bowl. Pour vinegar mixture over cabbage mixture, stirring gently to coat. Chill 1 to 2 hours; sprinkle bacon over top just before serving. Yield: 8 servings.
Jeanne H. Minetree,
Dinwiddie, Virginia.

POLKA DOT SLAW

1 medium head cabbage, shredded
1 (8-ounce) can crushed pineapple, drained
1 cup (4 ounces) shredded sharp Cheddar cheese
¾ cup raisins
1 cup mayonnaise

Combine all ingredients in a large mixing bowl; stir gently to mix. Chill 1 to 2 hours before serving. Yield: 8 servings.
Linda H. Sutton,
Winston-Salem, North Carolina.

COUNTRY-STYLE COLESLAW

1 large cabbage, coarsely chopped
1½ cups shredded carrots
1 cup chopped green pepper
¼ cup chopped green onion
1 cup mayonnaise
3 tablespoons sugar
3 tablespoons vinegar
1½ teaspoons salt
¾ teaspoon dry mustard
¼ teaspoon celery seeds
Leaf lettuce
1 small green pepper, sliced into rings

Combine first 4 ingredients; set aside.
Combine mayonnaise, sugar, vinegar, salt, mustard, and celery seeds; stir well. Pour dressing over cabbage mixture, and toss well. Chill. Serve in a lettuce-lined bowl; garnish with green pepper rings. Yield: 12 servings.
Betty Ellis,
Havana, Arkansas.

TANGY COLESLAW

5 cups shredded cabbage
2 cups shredded carrots
1 cup raisins
½ teaspoon celery seeds
½ cup buttermilk
⅓ cup vegetable oil
2 tablespoons vinegar
1 tablespoon sugar
1½ teaspoons Dijon mustard
¼ teaspoon salt
1 egg

Combine cabbage, carrots, raisins, and celery seeds; set aside.

Combine remaining ingredients in container of an electric blender; process until smooth. Pour over cabbage mixture; toss and chill thoroughly. Yield: 8 servings.
Nina Woodson,
Paris, Texas.

COLESLAW WITH GRAPES AND ALMONDS

1 medium head cabbage
2 cups seedless green grapes, halved
1 cup slivered almonds, toasted
2 tablespoons cider vinegar
1 tablespoon minced onion
1 teaspoon sugar
1 teaspoon dry mustard
½ teaspoon salt
1 cup mayonnaise

Combine cabbage, grapes, and almonds in a large bowl; set aside.
Combine next 5 ingredients; mix well. Gradually stir in mayonnaise. Pour over cabbage mixture; stir gently to coat. Chill at least 1 to 2 hours before serving. Yield: 8 servings.
Mrs. John R. Armstrong,
Farwell, Texas.

Raisins Are More Than A Snack

Raisins are for more than munching—their sweetness and chewy texture are welcome additions to a variety of foods. What's more, raisins are low in fat, cholesterol, and sodium.

Interestingly, dark seedless raisins and golden seedless raisins are both made from the same grape; the difference lies in their drying. Dark raisins are sun dried, while golden raisins are dried indoors under special conditions that help the grape retain its light color. Golden raisins have a more tangy flavor than dark raisins and, if preferred, may be substituted for dark raisins in many recipes.

RAISIN SAUCE

1 cup firmly packed brown sugar
1 tablespoon all-purpose flour
1 tablespoon butter or margarine
½ teaspoon salt
1 cup water
2 tablespoons orange juice
¾ cup raisins

Combine sugar and flour in a small saucepan, mixing well; add remaining ingredients. Cook, uncovered, over low heat 15 minutes, stirring often. Serve warm with ham. Yield: 1¾ cups.
Betty Hornsby,
Columbia, Maryland.

OATMEAL-RAISIN BREAD

½ cup whole wheat flour
½ cup firmly packed dark brown sugar
1 teaspoon salt
½ cup butter or margarine, softened
1 cup quick-cooking oats, uncooked
1 cup raisins
2 cups boiling water
1 package dry yeast
½ cup warm water (105° to 115°)
5 to 6 cups all-purpose flour
½ cup sugar
1 tablespoon ground cinnamon
Melted butter or margarine

Combine first 6 ingredients in a large bowl; mix well. Add boiling water, stirring to melt butter; cool mixture to 105° to 115°.
Dissolve yeast in warm water; let stand 5 minutes. Add to oats mixture, and mix well. Gradually stir in enough flour to make a soft dough.
Turn dough out on a floured surface, and knead 8 to 10 minutes until smooth and elastic. Place in a well-greased bowl, turning to grease top. Cover and let rise in a warm place (85°), free from drafts, 1 hour or until doubled in bulk.
Punch dough down; turn out on a floured surface, and knead 2 minutes. Divide dough in half, and let rest for 10 minutes. Roll each half into an 18- x 9-inch rectangle.
Combine sugar and cinnamon. Sprinkle half the sugar mixture evenly over each rectangle. Roll up, jellyroll fashion, beginning at short end. Fold under ends, and place in two greased 9- x 5- x 3-inch loafpans. Brush with melted butter. Cover and let rise in a warm place (85°), free from drafts, 40 to 50 minutes, or until doubled in bulk. Bake at 375° for 40 to 45 minutes or until loaves sound hollow when tapped. Remove loaves from pans, and cool on wire racks. Yield: 2 loaves.
Mrs. J. Russell Buchanan,
Monroe, Louisiana.

RAISIN-NUT PARTY MIX

2 (6-ounce) cans whole almonds
1 (7-ounce) jar dry roasted cashews
1 (8-ounce) jar dry roasted peanuts
1 (5-ounce) can chow mein noodles
¼ cup plus 2 tablespoons butter or
    margarine, melted
1½ tablespoons soy sauce
1½ tablespoons Worcestershire sauce
3 dashes of hot sauce
1 (15-ounce) package raisins

Combine first 4 ingredients in a large bowl, mixing well. Combine butter, soy sauce, Worcestershire sauce, and hot sauce; pour over nut mixture, tossing to coat. Spread half of mixture in a 15- x 10- x 1-inch jellyroll pan. Bake at 325° for 15 minutes; cool and place in a large bowl. Repeat with remaining mixture. Add raisins, and mix well. Store in an airtight container. Yield: 8 cups.

Enjoy Spinach At Its Best

You don't need a garden to enjoy fresh spinach, because it's available at the supermarket year-round.

Spinach will keep from 3 to 4 days when stored, unwashed, in the crisper section of your refrigerator. And it's a good idea to cook spinach in nonaluminum cookware; aluminum gives it an acidic flavor and grayish appearance.

CREAMY SPINACH SALAD

1½ pounds fresh spinach
3 hard-cooked eggs, chopped
¾ cup (3 ounces) shredded sharp Cheddar
    cheese
½ cup chopped celery
½ cup chopped green onion with tops
¾ cup mayonnaise
1 teaspoon vinegar
Dash of hot sauce

Remove stems from spinach; wash the leaves thoroughly, and pat dry. Tear the spinach into bite-size pieces.

Combine spinach and next 4 ingredients in a large bowl. Combine mayonnaise, vinegar, and hot sauce; stir well. Add the dressing to spinach mixture, and toss gently. Serve spinach salad immediately. Yield: about 6 servings.

Priscilla Petsick,
Oakwood, Texas.

FRESH SPINACH FETTUCCINE

1 pound fresh spinach
1 cup fresh parsley sprigs
½ cup olive oil
1 cup grated Parmesan cheese
½ cup walnut pieces
2 cloves garlic
½ teaspoon salt
¼ teaspoon pepper
1 (12-ounce) package fettuccine
Additional grated Parmesan cheese
    (optional)

Remove stems from spinach; wash leaves thoroughly, and pat dry.

Position knife blade in food processor bowl. Gradually add spinach; process until evenly chopped. Add parsley to spinach, and process until evenly chopped. Add olive oil to the spinach-parsley mixture, and process well. Add next 5 ingredients, and process until mixture is smooth.

Cook fettuccine according to package directions; drain well. Combine fettuccine and spinach mixture; toss gently. Place mixture in a serving dish. Sprinkle with additional Parmesan cheese, if desired. Yield: 8 to 10 servings.

Patricia Pashby,
Memphis, Tennessee.

Freeze A Banana Pop

The next time your family wants something sweet, offer fruit treats that are good for them—frozen Banana Pops. They're quick to make and convenient to keep on hand.

BANANA POPS

3 bananas
2 tablespoons orange juice
1 (6-ounce) package semisweet chocolate
    morsels
1 tablespoon shortening
¾ cup finely chopped pecans or flaked
    coconut

Peel bananas, and slice in half crosswise; brush bananas with orange juice. Insert wooden skewers in cut end of bananas, and place on a waxed paper-lined cookie sheet. Freeze until firm.

Combine chocolate and shortening in top of double boiler; bring water to a boil. Reduce heat to low; cook until chocolate melts. Cool slightly. Spoon chocolate evenly over frozen bananas; roll coated bananas in pecans or coconut. Serve immediately, or wrap in plastic and freeze. Yield: 6 servings.

Bake Enchiladas With Spinach

This recipe for Spinach Enchiladas is one of the best Mexican dishes we've ever tasted. Fill tortillas with chopped onion and Monterey Jack cheese, then spoon on a spicy spinach sauce.

SPINACH ENCHILADAS

1 (10-ounce) package frozen chopped
    spinach, thawed and pressed dry
1 (10¾-ounce) can cream of chicken soup,
    undiluted
1 (8-ounce) carton commercial sour cream
1 (4-ounce) can chopped green chiles,
    drained
2 tablespoons minced green onion
12 (4½-inch) corn tortillas
Vegetable oil
4 cups (16 ounces) shredded Monterey
    Jack cheese, divided
¾ cup minced onion

Combine first 5 ingredients in container of an electric blender or food processor; process until smooth.

Fry tortillas, one at a time, in ¼ inch of hot oil 5 seconds on each side or until softened. Drain tortillas well on paper towels.

Spoon 1 tablespoon each of cheese and onion on each tortilla; roll up tightly and place tortillas, seam side down, in a lightly greased 12- x 8- x 2-inch baking dish. Spoon spinach mixture over tortillas. Sprinkle with remaining cheese. Bake at 325°, uncovered, for 30 minutes. Serve immediately. Yield: 6 servings.

Virginia Atkinson,
Omaha, Texas.

Right: *Large, butterflied shrimp are marinated and broiled in a spicy wine and butter sauce for a special entrée of Shrimp Élégante (page 48).*

Page 64: *In Asparagus With Orange Sauce (page 46), citrus flavors the sauce and provides the garnish for this attractive and flavorful dish.*

Above: *Serve Banana Slush (page 56) with breakfast or as a midmorning refresher; ginger ale binds this icy blend of juices.*

Above right: *Croissants (page 54) take time to prepare, but their buttery flavor and light flaky texture make every minute worthwhile.*

Right: *Stir eggs in a skillet with green onion, mushrooms, tomato, green chiles, and pimiento for Spanish Scrambled Eggs (page 49). Garnish with bacon and tomato roses.*

Far right: *A serving of crisp Sausage Waffles (page 50), accompanied by a side dish of fresh fruit adds up to a breakfast that's irresistible.*

From Our Kitchen To Yours

If you need to know the shelf life of pasta or how long cornmeal is likely to keep, then check this handy chart. Readers are constantly asking how long certain food products will keep their freshness, flavor, and particular cooking qualities. We consulted various food industry sources and found the following information on safe lengths of food storage in your pantry.

See April, page 94, for a chart on safe food storage in the refrigerator.

PANTRY

Food Item	Length of Storage
STAPLES	
Baking powder	1 year
Baking soda	1 year
Breakfast cereal, ready to eat	Check date on package
—uncooked	1 year
Catsup (opened)	1 month
Coffee (opened)	6 to 8 weeks
(Refrigerate after opening)	
Cornmeal, regular and self-rising	10 months
Dried beans and peas	18 months
Flour, all-purpose	10 to 15 months
—whole wheat (refrigerated)	3 months
Grits, regular	10 months
—instant, flavored	9 months
Milk, evaporated and sweetened condensed	1 year
Pasta	10 to 15 months
Peanut butter	6 months
Salt and pepper	18 months
Shortening	8 months
Spices, ground	6 months
—whole	1 year
(Discard spices if aroma fades)	
Sugar	18 months
Tea bags	1 year
Vegetable oil	3 months
Worcestershire sauce	2 years
CANNED FOODS	
Fruit	1 year
Vegetables	1 year
Soups	1 year
Meat, fish, and poultry	1 year
PACKAGED MIXES	
Cake mix	1 year
Casserole mix	18 months
Frosting mix	8 months
Pancake mix	6 months

Tips for Pantry Storage: Store food in the coolest area of your kitchen, away from the oven and range. Hot, humid air decreases the storage life of most products. Keep all dry foods in their original containers or in airtight ones. Date your purchases and always use the oldest items first. When selecting canned foods, watch for dents, bulges, or stickiness; these could be signs of contamination.

Soups To Start A Meal

What better way to start a dinner party than with soup. Whether served at the table or offered in mugs on a tray in the den, soup will spark both appetites and your party.

SWEDISH FRUIT SOUP

1¾ cups mixed dried fruit
½ cup golden raisins
1 (3-inch) stick cinnamon
4 cups water
2¼ cups unsweetened pineapple juice
½ cup red currant jelly
¼ cup sugar
2 tablespoons quick-cooking tapioca
¼ teaspoon salt
1 medium orange, unpeeled, sliced, and seeded

Slice dried fruit in half. Combine dried fruit, raisins, cinnamon, and water in a Dutch oven; stir well. Bring to a boil. Reduce heat; simmer, uncovered, 30 minutes or until fruit is tender.

Stir in remaining ingredients, and bring to a boil. Reduce heat; cover and simmer 15 minutes, stirring occasionally. Cover soup, and chill 3 to 4 hours. Yield: 7 cups.   *Doris Garton,*
Shenandoah, Virginia.

EGG FLOWER SOUP

1½ tablespoons cornstarch
⅓ cup water
6 cups chicken broth
1 cup (8 ounces) cubed tofu (soy bean curd)
1 (2- x 1- x ⅛-inch) slice gingerroot
½ teaspoon sugar
⅛ teaspoon pepper
3 eggs, beaten
1 teaspoon sesame seed oil
1 green onion, minced

Combine cornstarch and water; stir well, and set aside.

Bring broth to a boil in a large saucepan; add tofu, gingerroot, sugar, and pepper, and boil 1 minute. Stir in cornstarch mixture; boil 1 minute. Remove from heat.

Slowly pour beaten egg into soup, stirring constantly. The egg forms lacy strands as it cooks. Remove gingerroot.

Stir in sesame seed oil, and sprinkle with onion. Serve immediately. Yield: about 7 cups.   *Sue-Sue Hartstern,*
Louisville, Kentucky.

CREAM OF BROCCOLI SOUP

2 (10-ounce) packages frozen chopped
   broccoli
2 (10¾-ounce) cans cream of mushroom
   soup, undiluted
2⅔ cups milk
3 tablespoons butter or margarine
¼ to ½ teaspoon dried whole tarragon
Dash of pepper

Cook broccoli according to package directions; drain well. Add remaining ingredients; cook over low heat until thoroughly heated. Yield: about 8 cups.

Mary Pappas,
Richmond, Virginia.

CHEESY ANYTIME SOUP

¼ cup butter or margarine
¼ cup plus 2 tablespoons all-purpose flour
2 (10¾-ounce) cans chicken broth,
   undiluted
2 cups milk
¼ teaspoon white pepper
2 tablespoons chopped pimiento
¼ cup plus 2 tablespoons dry white wine
½ teaspoon Worcestershire sauce
¼ teaspoon hot sauce
2 cups (8 ounces) shredded sharp Cheddar
   cheese

Melt butter in a heavy saucepan over low heat; add flour, stirring until smooth. Cook 1 minute, stirring constantly. Gradually add the broth and milk; cook over medium heat, stirring constantly, until thickened and bubbly. Stir in pepper.

Add next 4 ingredients. Heat to boiling, stirring frequently. Remove from heat; add Cheddar cheese, and stir until melted. Serve immediately. Yield: about 5 cups.

Jodie McCoy,
Tulsa, Oklahoma.

SHRIMP-VEGETABLE BISQUE

1 pound zucchini, thinly sliced
1 cup thinly sliced carrots
½ cup chopped celery
½ cup sliced green onion
½ cup chicken broth
1¾ cups skim milk
½ cup water
1 (10¾-ounce) can cream of mushroom
   soup, undiluted
½ cup plain yogurt
1 (4½-ounce) can small shrimp, drained
   and rinsed
1 tablespoon dry white wine

Combine vegetables and chicken broth in a Dutch oven; cover and simmer 15 to 20 minutes or until vegetables are tender.

Spoon half of vegetable mixture into container of electric blender, and process until smooth. Repeat procedure with remaining mixture.

Return vegetable mixture to Dutch oven; stir in remaining ingredients. Cook over low heat, stirring constantly, until thoroughly heated. Yield: 10 cups.

Marie Hayman,
Lake Worth, Florida.

Look What's Gotten Into Vegetables

Mushrooms, green peppers, and acorn squash are natural containers for a variety of stuffings. After tasting these stuffed vegetables, you'll agree that flavor is what's gotten into them.

STUFFED MUSHROOMS

1 pound fresh medium mushrooms
¼ cup chopped onion
¼ cup chopped celery
¼ cup butter or margarine
1 teaspoon Worcestershire sauce
½ teaspoon salt
⅛ teaspoon pepper
Melted butter or margarine
¼ cup (1 ounce) shredded process
   American cheese

Clean mushrooms with damp paper towels. Remove stems and chop, reserving caps.

Sauté onion, celery, and mushroom stems in ¼ cup butter in a skillet until celery is tender. Stir in Worcestershire sauce, salt, and pepper.

Brush mushroom caps with melted butter; fill with vegetable mixture. Arrange mushrooms in a greased shallow baking dish; sprinkle with cheese. Bake at 350° for 15 minutes or until cheese is melted. Yield: 4 to 5 servings.

Mrs. W. P. Chambers,
Louisville, Kentucky.

HAM-STUFFED ACORN SQUASH

2 medium acorn squash
2 tablespoons butter or margarine
½ cup chopped celery
⅓ cup chopped onion
1½ cups chopped cooked ham
2 tablespoons light brown sugar
⅛ teaspoon ground allspice

Cut squash in half lengthwise, and remove seeds. Place cut side down in a greased baking dish; add ½ inch water to dish. Cover squash, and bake at 350° for 30 minutes.

Melt butter in a small saucepan. Add celery and onion; cook until tender. Add ham, sugar, and allspice; stir well. Cook over medium heat until mixture is thoroughly heated. Stuff squash with ham mixture. Cover and bake at 350° for 15 minutes. Remove cover, and bake an additional 15 minutes. Yield: 4 servings.

Mrs. James Barden,
Suffolk, Virginia.

STUFFED PEPPERS

6 large green peppers
1 pound ground beef
1 large onion, minced
1 clove garlic, minced
3 tomatoes, peeled and chopped
1 teaspoon Worcestershire sauce
½ teaspoon ground allspice
1 teaspoon salt
¼ teaspoon pepper
1 cup bread cubes or cooked regular rice
½ cup buttered breadcrumbs

Cut off tops of green peppers; remove seeds. Cover peppers with boiling salted water. Cook 5 minutes; drain.

Cook beef, onion, and garlic in skillet over medium heat, stirring to crumble meat. Add tomatoes; simmer 10 minutes. Add remaining ingredients except breadcrumbs, and stir well.

Stuff peppers with beef mixture; place in a shallow baking dish. Top with breadcrumbs. Bake at 350° for 25 minutes. Yield: 6 servings.

Mrs. Carlton James,
New Orleans, Louisiana.

This Texan Shares His Specialties

As a pilot in the Air Force, Ed Tarbutton of San Marcos, Texas, flew all over the world. Now, Ed enjoys spending time in the kitchen preparing the delicacies he sampled during his travels.

"Ed loves to cook," says his wife Myrtle. They once owned a steak and seafood restaurant near San Marcos, and Ed was the chef. His appreciation for fine cuisine began as a young boy in France, where his mother attended the Cordon Bleu Cooking School.

Ed turns to his collection of 150 cookbooks whenever he wants to experiment. One of his favorite discoveries for small dinner parties is Shrimp in Lemon Garlic Sauce. He uses the food processor to whirl up a tangy garlic mixture; the shrimp and sauce are served in individual baking dishes. "Add a loaf of French bread and a tossed salad with vinaigrette dressing, and you have a sumptuous meal," says Ed.

For dessert, try Kahlúa Delight. Served in cordial glasses, it's topped with dollops of whipped cream and chopped toasted almonds.

Along with Ed Tarbutton's specialties, we've listed recipes from other men who enjoy cooking.

SHRIMP IN LEMON GARLIC SAUCE

1 pound large shrimp, peeled and
    deveined
About 1½ cups milk
2 egg yolks
1½ tablespoons lemon juice
1 tablespoon finely chopped fresh parsley
2 to 3 cloves garlic, crushed
2 teaspoons chopped chives
½ teaspoon salt
½ teaspoon dry mustard
⅛ teaspoon ground red pepper
½ cup butter, melted
1 cup vegetable oil
1 cup all-purpose flour
¼ teaspoon salt
⅛ teaspoon pepper

Place shrimp in a shallow pan; cover with milk. Let stand in refrigerator for 20 minutes.

Position knife blade in food processor bowl; add next 8 ingredients to bowl, and top with cover. Process 30 seconds or until well mixed.

With processor running, add butter through food chute; process 1 minute or until sauce is thickened. Set aside.

Heat oil in a large skillet to 375°. Combine flour, salt, and pepper. Drain shrimp, and dredge in flour mixture. Fry shrimp in hot oil until golden brown, turning once; drain.

Arrange shrimp in 4 or 5 individual baking dishes, and top with the sauce. Broil shrimp 30 to 45 seconds. Yield: 4 to 5 servings.

SEAFOOD MORNAY

½ pound scallops
1¼ pounds shrimp, peeled and deveined
½ cup dry white wine
2 dozen oysters
½ cup dry vermouth
¼ cup plus 2 tablespoons butter
1 tablespoon finely chopped onion
¼ cup plus 2 tablespoons all-purpose flour
3 cups milk
½ cup (2 ounces) shredded Gruyère cheese
½ cup (2 ounces) shredded Swiss cheese
⅔ cup grated Parmesan cheese
¼ teaspoon salt
¼ teaspoon pepper
⅛ teaspoon ground nutmeg
¾ cup cracker crumbs
¼ cup butter or margarine, melted
⅛ teaspoon paprika

Poach scallops and shrimp in wine 3 to 4 minutes; drain well. Repeat procedure with the oysters in vermouth. Combine seafood, and spoon into six individual baking dishes.

Melt ¼ cup plus 2 tablespoons butter in a heavy saucepan; add onion, and sauté until tender. Add flour, stirring until smooth. Cook 1 minute, stirring constantly. Gradually add milk; cook over medium heat, stirring constantly, until thickened and bubbly. Add cheese, stirring until melted. Stir in salt, pepper, and nutmeg.

Spoon sauce over seafood, and sprinkle with cracker crumbs. Drizzle ¼ cup melted butter over cracker crumbs; sprinkle with paprika. Bake at 350° for 20 to 30 minutes. Yield: 6 servings.

KAHLUA DELIGHT

1 (6-ounce) package semisweet chocolate morsels
½ cup sugar
¼ cup water
2 eggs
2 tablespoons Kahlúa or other coffee-flavored liqueur
½ teaspoon instant coffee granules
1 cup whipping cream, whipped
Additional whipped cream
Chopped toasted almonds

Melt chocolate over hot water in top of double boiler; set aside to cool.

Combine sugar and water in a small saucepan; bring to a boil. Cook, stirring constantly, until sugar dissolves.

Beat eggs on medium speed of an electric mixer. Gradually stir melted chocolate into eggs; stir in the liqueur and coffee granules.

While beating at medium speed of electric mixer, slowly pour hot sugar syrup in a thin stream over egg mixture.

Continue beating until well blended. Fold in the whipped cream. Spoon into small cordial glasses. Refrigerate. Garnish with additional whipped cream and almonds. Yield: 6 servings.

CHICKEN PASQUALE

8 pitted dates
1½ tablespoons Triple Sec or other orange-flavored liqueur
1 (3-pound) broiler-fryer, cut up and skinned
¼ cup vegetable oil
½ teaspoon salt
¼ teaspoon pepper
Rind of 1 orange, cut into thin strips
1½ cups orange juice
¼ cup Chablis or other dry white wine
1½ teaspoons lemon juice
3 tablespoons brown sugar
1 tablespoon prepared mustard
¼ cup chicken broth
1 tablespoon cornstarch
2 tablespoons cold water

Combine dates and Triple Sec; set aside. Brush chicken with oil; sprinkle with salt and pepper. Place in a lightly greased 13- x 9- x 2-inch baking dish.

Combine next 6 ingredients; pour over chicken. Cover and bake at 350° for 45 minutes. Remove cover; bake 30 minutes, basting occasionally. Drain dates, reserving Triple Sec. Add dates to chicken; bake 15 additional minutes.

Remove chicken to serving platter, and keep warm. Stir reserved Triple Sec and chicken broth into pan drippings. Pour mixture into a small saucepan. Combine cornstarch and water, stirring well; stir into broth mixture. Cook over medium-high heat, stirring constantly, until thickened and bubbly. Pour gravy over chicken. Yield: 4 servings.

Pasquale Anthony Santarone,
Phoenix, Maryland.

BEAN BUNDLES

2 (16-ounce) cans whole green beans, drained
1 cup commercial Italian dressing
8 to 10 slices bacon, cut in half

Combine beans and dressing, tossing gently; cover and chill overnight.

Drain beans; arrange in bunches of 10 to 12. Wrap a half slice of bacon around each bunch, and secure with a toothpick. Broil bundles 5 inches from heat about 7 minutes until bacon is cooked. Yield: 8 to 10 servings.

H. Webb Cowan,
Kerrville, Texas.

HOT-AND-SOUR SOUP

2 teaspoons cornstarch
2 teaspoons vegetable oil
1 teaspoon soy sauce
1 teaspoon dry sherry
¼ pound boneless pork
2 tablespoons vegetable oil
2 medium onions, chopped
5 cups chicken broth
1 (16-ounce) can bean sprouts, drained
1 (8-ounce) can water chestnuts, drained
  and chopped
1 cup (8 ounces) cubed tofu (soy
  bean curd)
4 fresh mushrooms, sliced
2 tablespoons red wine vinegar
1½ to 2 tablespoons soy sauce
1 tablespoon lemon juice
½ to 1 teaspoon pepper
½ teaspoon hot sauce
1 egg, beaten
1 teaspoon sesame seed oil
3 tablespoons water
2 tablespoons cornstarch
1 green onion, minced

Combine first 4 ingredients; stir well. Partially freeze pork; slice across grain into 3- x ¼-inch strips. Stack strips, and slice as finely as possible. Stir pork into soy mixture, and set aside.

Heat 2 tablespoons oil in a Dutch oven; add onion, and sauté until tender. Stir in pork and next 10 ingredients. Bring soup to a boil. Cover; reduce heat, and simmer 1 hour.

Combine egg and sesame seed oil; stir well, and set aside. Combine water and 2 tablespoons cornstarch, stirring well. Add cornstarch mixture to soup; boil 1 minute, stirring constantly. Remove from heat. Slowly pour beaten egg mixture into soup, stirring constantly. (The egg forms lacy strands as it cooks.)

Sprinkle with onion, and serve immediately. Yield: about 9 cups.

Bill Clarke,
Georgetown, Tennessee.

CHEESY BREAD PUDDING

½ cup butter or margarine
10 slices white bread, cut into 1-inch
  cubes
3 cups (12 ounces) shredded Cheddar
  cheese
2 cups milk
3 eggs, separated
½ teaspoon salt
½ teaspoon dry mustard
½ teaspoon red pepper

Melt butter; add bread cubes, stirring until coated. Add cheese, and stir well. Combine milk, egg yolks, salt, mustard, and pepper; beat well. Pour over bread cubes. Beat egg whites (at room temperature) until stiff but not dry; fold into the bread mixture. Spoon into a lightly greased 12- x 8- x 2-inch baking dish. Cover, and chill overnight.

Bake, uncovered, at 325° for 30 minutes or until set. Yield: 8 servings.

James E. Boggess,
Miami, Florida.

Avocados With
A Flair

These recipes prove that our readers know how to make the most of a favorite fruit—the avocado.

Fresh avocados in supermarkets are generally too firm for eating right away and should be allowed to soften several days at room temperature on a countertop or in a fruit bowl. To test for softness, cradle the avocado between the palms of your hands, and press gently. If it yields to gentle pressure, it's ready to eat and will be easy to cut.

You can hurry the ripening process a little by putting avocados in a brown paper bag. This facilitates softening by confining and concentrating the gases the fruit gives off. Once ripe, store in the refrigerator up to 10 days.

MEXICAN SALAD SUPPER

1 pound ground beef
1 (15½-ounce) can kidney beans, drained
1 medium head lettuce, shredded
2 medium avocados, peeled and chopped
2 large tomatoes, chopped
1 small onion, chopped
1 medium-size green pepper, chopped
1 cup sliced fresh mushrooms
1 cup chopped celery
1 carrot, thinly sliced
4 cups (16 ounces) shredded Cheddar
  cheese
1 (8-ounce) bottle commercial French or
  Catalina dressing
1 (8-ounce) package tortilla chips,
  crumbled

Cook ground beef until brown, stirring to crumble; drain and cool slightly. Combine meat with remaining ingredients, except tortilla chips, tossing well. Add tortilla chips, and serve immediately. Yield: 12 to 15 servings.

Jan Dreasher,
Lubbock, Texas.

CHILI-TAMALE PIE

1 (25-ounce) can chili with beans
1 (14½-ounce) can tamales, cut into thirds
1 medium onion, chopped
1 or 2 jalapeño peppers, seeded and finely
  chopped
1 cup crushed corn chips
1 cup (4 ounces) shredded Cheddar cheese
1 avocado, peeled and sliced

Combine first 4 ingredients in a lightly greased 1¾-quart casserole. Bake at 400° for 25 minutes or until bubbly. Combine corn chips and cheese; sprinkle over top of casserole. Bake 5 additional minutes or until cheese melts. Top with avocado. Yield: 6 servings.

Mrs. W. C. Olsen,
Bastrop, Texas.

CHICKEN-AVOCADO KABOBS

2 slices bacon, cut in half
¾ cup all-purpose flour
¼ teaspoon salt
⅛ teaspoon pepper
1 pound skinned and boned chicken
  breasts, cut into 8 equal pieces
1 egg, beaten
Vegetable oil
1 small avocado, peeled, and cut into 8
  pieces
Lemon or lime juice
4 cherry tomatoes
¼ pound Monterey Jack cheese, cut
  into 4 equal pieces

Fry bacon until transparent; drain.
Combine flour, salt, and pepper, stirring well. Dip chicken into egg, and dredge in flour mixture. Fry chicken in deep hot oil (375°) until golden brown. Drain on paper towels.

Dip avocado pieces into lemon juice, and set aside.

Alternate chicken, avocado, tomato, bacon, and cheese on skewers. Broil 6 inches from heat, turning several times, until cheese begins to melt. Yield: 2 to 4 servings.

Mrs. Bob Joe,
Austin, Texas.

GUACAMOLE SANDWICHES

3 avocados, peeled and quartered
1 small tomato, peeled and quartered
½ cup cottage cheese
2 tablespoons lemon juice
1½ teaspoons garlic salt
6 (8-inch) flour tortillas
12 ounces Cheddar cheese
1 cup bean sprouts
1 cup alfalfa sprouts
Commercial taco sauce (optional)
Crushed tortilla chips (optional)

Combine first 5 ingredients in container of an electric blender. Blend mixture until smooth, and set aside.

Place tortillas on a lightly greased baking sheet. Cut cheese into twelve 2- x 5-inch slices; place 2 slices on surface of each tortilla. Broil 6 inches from heat just until cheese melts.

Spoon ⅓ cup avocado mixture on each tortilla; top with sprouts. Fold tortillas in half; serve with taco sauce and crushed tortilla chips, if desired. Yield: 6 servings. *Jan K. Sliwa, Temple, Texas.*

MEXICAN CHEESE PIE

6 (6-inch) flour tortillas
1 small onion, sliced and separated into rings
1 large tomato, peeled and chopped
1 (4-ounce) can diced green chiles, drained
1 cup (4 ounces) shredded Cheddar cheese
3 tablespoons all-purpose flour
½ teaspoon baking powder
½ teaspoon salt
½ cup milk
3 eggs, beaten
1 medium avocado, peeled and sliced
Commercial taco sauce

Line bottom and sides of a well-greased 9-inch quiche dish with tortillas. Top with onion, tomato, green chiles, and cheese.

Combine flour, baking powder, salt, milk, and eggs, stirring until smooth. Pour mixture into quiche dish. Bake at 350° for 40 to 45 minutes. Top with avocado. Serve with taco sauce. Yield: 6 servings. *Becky Holzhaus, Castroville, Texas.*

AVOCADO SALAD

½ large head iceberg lettuce, torn
10 cherry tomatoes, halved
1 large avocado, peeled and chopped
3 pitted ripe olives, thinly sliced
⅓ cup commercial Thousand Island dressing
1 teaspoon chili powder

Combine lettuce, tomatoes, avocado, and olives, tossing gently. Stir together Thousand Island dressing and chili powder; serve over salad. Yield: 6 servings. *Mary Thielman, San Marcos, Texas.*

ZIPPY AVOCADO DIP

2 ripe avocados, peeled and coarsely chopped
2 tablespoons picante sauce
2 teaspoons lemon or lime juice
1 teaspoon chopped onion
⅛ teaspoon seasoned salt

Combine all ingredients in container of electric blender. Blend and chill. Serve dip with corn chips. Yield: about 1½ cups.

Note: Avocado seed may be placed in dip to prevent mixture from darkening. *Jean Westmoreland, Manvel, Texas.*

Build A Sandwich For Lunch

These recipes prove that a sandwich lunch can be as satisfying as any meal. For our Chicken-Almond Pocket Sandwiches, rounds of pocket bread are cut in half and stuffed with shredded lettuce, alfalfa sprouts, and a yogurt-flavored chicken filling.

EGGS-TRA SPECIAL SANDWICHES

4 slices bologna, chopped
4 hard-cooked eggs, chopped
1 stalk celery, chopped
¼ cup sweet pickle relish, drained
¼ cup mayonnaise
1 teaspoon instant minced onion
Leaf lettuce
4 onion rolls

Combine first 6 ingredients; stir well. Chill. Arrange lettuce on bottom half of each onion roll; top with filling, and cover with roll top. Yield: 4 servings. *Peggy Fowler Revels, Woodruff, South Carolina.*

BROILED REUBEN SANDWICHES

½ cup mayonnaise
1 tablespoon chili sauce
About 3 tablespoons butter or margarine, softened
12 slices rye bread
6 slices Swiss cheese
2 (4-ounce) packages thinly sliced corned beef
1 (16-ounce) can sauerkraut, well drained

Combine mayonnaise and chili sauce, stirring well.

Spread butter on one side of each slice of bread; spread other side with mayonnaise mixture. Arrange cheese, corned beef, and sauerkraut on mayonnaise side of 6 bread slices. Top with remaining bread, buttered side out.

Place sandwiches on a cookie sheet, and broil each side until browned. Yield: 6 servings. *Mrs. Ron Bain, Nashville, Tennessee.*

TEMPTING TWOSOME

1 (3-ounce) package cream cheese, softened
2 tablespoons sliced green onion
1 tablespoon soy sauce
1 tablespoon dry sherry
About 3 tablespoons butter or margarine, softened
12 slices rye bread
Lettuce leaves
2 (3-ounce) packages thinly sliced roast beef
4 (3-ounce) packages thinly sliced smoked pork

Combine cream cheese, onion, soy sauce, and sherry; mix well.

Spread butter on one side of each slice of bread; spread cream cheese mixture over butter. On 6 bread slices, arrange lettuce, roast beef, and pork evenly over cream cheese mixture. Top with remaining bread. Yield: 6 servings. *Mrs. Parke LaGourgue Cory, Neosho, Missouri.*

CHICKEN-ALMOND POCKET SANDWICHES

3 cups cubed cooked chicken
½ cup plain yogurt
½ cup chopped toasted almonds
1½ tablespoons lemon juice
½ teaspoon salt
¼ teaspoon pepper
⅛ teaspoon dried dillweed
4 (6-inch) pocket bread rounds
2 cups shredded lettuce
1 cup alfalfa sprouts

Combine first 7 ingredients, mixing well; set aside.

Cut bread rounds in half; fill each about half full with lettuce and alfalfa sprouts. Spoon in chicken mixture. Chill at least 1 hour. Yield: 8 sandwiches. *Martha Edington, Oak Ridge, Tennessee.*

Create A Light Crêpe

Everyone knows crêpes are fattening—or are they? The elegant, French-inspired crêpe has that reputation, but it's actually what goes in and on the skinny pancake that sends the calorie count up.

We recommend letting the batter stand 1 hour to allow flour particles to expand and air bubbles to collapse. Batter may be stored in the refrigerator overnight; just stir well, and add 1 or 2 tablespoons milk if necessary to thin batter.

Eliminate excess calories in the crêpes themselves by using skim milk instead of whole. Also, cook the crêpes in a skillet coated with vegetable cooking spray or in a nonstick crêpe pan. Each 10-inch crêpe adds about 69 calories to a main dish, while 6-inch crêpes are about 48 calories each.

PLAIN CREPES

3 eggs
1½ cups skim milk
1⅓ cups all-purpose flour
½ teaspoon salt
2 teaspoons vegetable oil
Vegetable cooking spray

Combine first 5 ingredients in container of an electric blender; process 30 seconds. Scrape down sides of blender container with rubber spatula; process an additional 30 seconds or until smooth. Refrigerate batter 1 hour. (This allows flour particles to swell and soften so crêpes are light in texture.)

Coat the bottom of a 10- or 6-inch crêpe pan or nonstick skillet with cooking spray; place pan over medium heat until just hot, not smoking.

Pour about 3 tablespoons batter into 10-inch pan or 2 tablespoons batter into 6-inch pan. Quickly tilt pan in all directions so batter covers pan in a thin film; cook about 1 minute.

Lift edge of crêpe to test for doneness. Crêpe is ready for flipping when it can be shaken loose from pan. Flip the crêpe, and cook about 30 seconds on the other side. (This side is rarely more than spotty brown, and is the side on which the filling is placed.)

When crêpe is done, place on a towel to cool. Stack between layers of waxed paper to prevent sticking. Repeat until all batter is used, stirring occasionally. Yield: 14 (10-inch) crêpes (about 69 calories per crêpe) or 20 (6-inch) crêpes (about 48 calories per crêpe).

WHOLE WHEAT CREPES

1½ cups whole wheat flour
3 eggs
¾ cup skim milk
¾ cup water
¼ teaspoon salt
1 tablespoon vegetable oil
Vegetable cooking spray

Combine first 6 ingredients in container of an electric blender; process 30 seconds. Scrape down sides of blender container with rubber spatula; process an additional 30 seconds or until smooth. Refrigerate batter 1 hour. (This allows flour particles to swell and soften so crêpes are light in texture.)

Coat the bottom of a 10- or 6-inch crêpe pan or nonstick skillet with cooking spray; place pan over medium heat until just hot, not smoking.

Pour about 3 tablespoons batter into 10-inch pan or 2 tablespoons batter into 6-inch pan. Quickly tilt pan in all directions so batter covers pan in a thin film; cook about 1 minute.

Lift edge of crêpe to test for doneness. Crêpe is ready for flipping when it can be shaken loose from pan. Flip the crêpe, and cook about 30 seconds. (This side is rarely more than spotty brown, and is the side on which the filling is placed.)

When crêpe is done, place on a towel to cool. Stack between layers of waxed paper to prevent sticking. Repeat until all batter is used, stirring occasionally. Yield: 15 (10-inch) crêpes (about 68 calories per crêpe) or 21 (6-inch) crêpes (about 48 calories per crêpe).

BRAN CREPES

3 eggs
1½ cups skim milk
1 cup all-purpose flour
⅓ cup 100% bran cereal
1 tablespoon sugar
¼ teaspoon salt
2 teaspoons vegetable oil
Vegetable cooking spray

Combine first 7 ingredients in container of an electric blender; process 30 seconds. Scrape down sides of blender container with rubber spatula; process

an additional 30 seconds or until smooth. Refrigerate batter 1 hour. (This allows flour particles to swell and soften so crêpes are light in texture.)

Coat the bottom of a 10- or 6-inch crêpe pan or nonstick skillet with cooking spray; place pan over medium heat until just hot, not smoking.

Pour about 3 tablespoons batter into a 10-inch pan or 2 tablespoons batter into a 6-inch pan. Quickly tilt pan in all directions so batter covers the pan in a thin film; cook crêpe about 1 minute.

Lift edge of crêpe to test for doneness. Crêpe is ready for flipping when it can be shaken loose from pan. Flip the crêpe, and cook about 30 seconds. (This side is rarely more than spotty brown, and is the side on which the filling is placed.)

When crêpe is done, place on a towel to cool. Stack between layers of waxed paper to prevent sticking. Repeat until all batter is used, stirring occasionally. Yield: 14 (10-inch) crêpes (about 67 calories per crêpe) or 20 (6-inch) crêpes (about 47 calories per crêpe).

CHICKEN-VEGETABLE CREPES

6 chicken breast halves, skinned and boned
½ teaspoon garlic powder
1 tablespoon soy sauce
1 teaspoon cornstarch
½ teaspoon salt
¼ teaspoon pepper
Vegetable cooking spray
1 tablespoon vegetable oil
1 large green pepper, coarsely chopped
1 cup diagonally sliced celery
4 scallions, sliced
1 (6-ounce) package frozen Chinese pea pods, thawed and drained
1 tablespoon soy sauce
2 tablespoons plus 2 teaspoons cornstarch
¾ cup water
⅛ teaspoon ground ginger
¾ teaspoon chicken-flavored bouillon granules
2 medium tomatoes, peeled and coarsely chopped
12 (10-inch) plain or whole wheat crêpes
Mushroom Sauce

Cut chicken breasts into ¾-inch pieces, and set aside.

Combine garlic powder, 1 tablespoon soy sauce, 1 teaspoon cornstarch, salt, pepper, and chicken; mix well, and let stand 20 minutes at room temperature.

Coat wok with cooking spray; add oil. Allow to heat at medium high (325°) for 2 minutes. Add green pepper, and stir-fry 2 minutes. Add celery, scallions, and pea pods; stir-fry 2 minutes. Remove vegetables from wok, and set aside.

Combine 1 tablespoon soy sauce and 2 tablespoons plus 2 teaspoons cornstarch; stir in water, ginger, and bouillon granules. Set mixture aside.

Add chicken to wok, and stir-fry 3 minutes; add stir-fried vegetables, tomatoes, and bouillon mixture. Stir-fry over low heat (225°) 3 minutes or until thickened and bubbly.

Spoon ½ cup chicken mixture in center of each crêpe; roll up. Spoon Mushroom Sauce evenly over crêpes, and serve immediately. Yield: 6 servings (about 309 calories per serving).

Mushroom Sauce:

1 cup sliced fresh mushrooms
Vegetable cooking spray
1 tablespoon cornstarch
1 teaspoon chicken-flavored bouillon
    granules
1 cup water

Sauté mushrooms until tender in a small skillet coated with cooking spray; remove mushrooms from skillet, and set aside. Combine cornstarch, bouillon granules, and water in a small saucepan. Bring to a boil, and cook 1 minute, stirring constantly. Stir in sautéed mushrooms. Yield: 1⅓ cups.

Note: Filled crêpes may be heated if necessary. Place in a shallow baking dish; cover with foil, and bake at 375° for 10 to 12 minutes or until thoroughly heated.

CHEESE BLINTZES

2 (12-ounce) cartons dry curd cottage
    cheese
1 egg, beaten
3 tablespoons sugar
1½ teaspoons grated lemon rind
¼ teaspoon vanilla extract
16 (6-inch) plain or bran crêpes
Vegetable cooking spray
½ cup reduced-calorie strawberry
    preserves
Mock Sour Cream (optional)

Combine first 5 ingredients; stir well. Spoon about 3 tablespoons cheese filling in center of each crêpe. Fold right and left sides over filling; then fold bottom and top over filling, forming a square.

Coat a baking sheet with cooking spray. Place blintzes, seam side down, on baking sheet; bake at 350° for 12 minutes or until thoroughly heated. Top each blintz with ½ tablespoon preserves. Serve with Mock Sour Cream, if desired. Yield: 8 servings (about 208 calories per serving plus 3 calories per teaspoon Mock Sour Cream).

Mock Sour Cream:

½ cup low-fat cottage cheese
1 tablespoon skim milk
1½ teaspoons lemon juice

Combine all ingredients in the container of an electric blender; process on medium-high speed until smooth and creamy. Cover and chill thoroughly. Yield: about ½ cup.

LIGHT CREPES SUZETTES

2 cups unsweetened orange juice
2 tablespoons cornstarch
1 tablespoon grated orange rind
2 medium oranges, peeled and sectioned
16 (6-inch) plain crêpes
¼ cup Grand Marnier or other
    orange-flavored liqueur

Combine orange juice, cornstarch, and orange rind in a large skillet or chafing dish; cook over medium heat until mixture comes to a boil, stirring constantly. Boil 1 minute. Stir in orange sections, and cool slightly.

Dip both sides of crêpe in orange sauce; fold in half, then in quarters. Repeat procedure with the remaining crêpes.

Arrange crêpes in remaining sauce; place over low heat until thoroughly heated. Heat liqueur in a saucepan over medium heat. (Do not boil.) Ignite and pour over crêpes. After flames die down, serve immediately. Yield: 8 servings (about 146 calories per serving).

Crêpes For An Easy Brunch

Brunch can be easy with a make-ahead entrée like Cheesy Sausage Crêpes. Fill a batch of crêpes with cooked sausage, cheese, and mushrooms; refrigerate it overnight, or freeze for later use.

CHEESY SAUSAGE CREPES

1 pound bulk pork sausage
¼ cup chopped onion
½ cup (2 ounces) shredded sharp Cheddar
    cheese
1 (3-ounce) package cream cheese,
    softened
¼ teaspoon ground thyme
1 (4½-ounce) jar sliced mushrooms,
    drained
¼ teaspoon garlic salt
Crêpes (recipe follows)
½ cup commercial sour cream
¼ cup butter or margarine, softened

Cook sausage and onion in a heavy skillet until sausage is brown, stirring to crumble; drain well. Stir in next 5 ingredients.

Fill each crêpe with about 2 tablespoons sausage mixture. Roll up, and place seam side down in two greased 12- x 8- x 2-inch baking dishes. Cover and bake at 350° for 25 minutes. Combine sour cream and butter, mixing well; spoon over crêpes. Bake, uncovered, 5 minutes. Yield: 8 servings.

Crêpes:

3 eggs
1 cup all-purpose flour
1 cup milk
1 tablespoon vegetable oil
Additional vegetable oil

Combine first 4 ingredients in container of electric blender; process 1 minute. Scrape down sides of blender container with rubber spatula; process an additional 15 seconds. Refrigerate 1 hour. (This allows flour particles to swell and soften so crêpes are light in texture.)

Brush the bottom of a 6-inch crêpe pan with oil; place pan over medium heat until oil is just hot, not smoking.

Pour 2 tablespoons batter into pan; quickly tilt pan in all directions so batter covers the pan in a thin film. Cook about 1 minute.

Lift edge of crêpe to test for doneness. Crêpe is ready for flipping when it can be shaken loose from pan. Flip crêpe, and cook about 30 seconds on the other side. (This side is rarely more than spotty brown.) Place on a towel to cool. Stack crêpes between layers of waxed paper to prevent sticking. Yield: 16 crêpes.

Note: Cheesy Sausage Crêpes may be frozen; thaw, and bake as directed.
                    Mrs. Leslie Villeneuve,
                    Neptune Beach, Florida.

Tip: Rub hands with parsley to remove any odor.

There's Rum In The Beans

Mrs. Roger Williams of Arden, North Carolina, discovered a way to turn ordinary dried navy beans into a spirited main dish—by adding rum.

RUM-LACED BEAN BAKE

1 pound dried navy beans
2 whole cloves
1 small onion
½ pound lean salt pork
1 small bay leaf
1½ teaspoons salt
2 medium onions, chopped
½ pound smoked ham, chopped
2 small cloves garlic, minced
1 tablespoon dry mustard
¼ cup light rum

Sort and wash beans; place in a large Dutch oven. Cover with water 2 inches above beans; let soak overnight. Drain.

Insert cloves in small onion. Add onion, salt pork, bay leaf, and salt to beans. Cover beans with water 3 inches above beans; bring to a boil. Cover, reduce heat, and simmer 1 hour or until beans are tender. Drain, reserving liquid. Add enough water to bean liquid to make 2¼ cups; set aside. Discard cloves, onion, and bay leaf. Remove salt pork; dice and set aside.

Layer half of beans in a 2½-quart casserole. Combine salt pork with chopped onion, ham, and garlic; spoon over beans. Top with remaining beans.

Combine reserved bean liquid and dry mustard, stirring well; pour over beans. Bake at 350° for 1 hour. Pour rum over top, and bake an additional 45 minutes. Yield: 10 to 12 servings.

Mrs. Rodger Williams,
Arden, North Carolina.

Baked Crabmeat At Its Best

William Phillips of Guntersville, Alabama, shares this outstanding recipe for Crabmeat Imperial.

The fresh crabmeat is enhanced by sautéed green pepper, celery, and pimiento and is lightly seasoned to complement the fresh ocean taste.

CRABMEAT IMPERIAL

¼ cup chopped green pepper
¼ cup chopped celery
1 (2-ounce) jar chopped pimiento, drained
2 tablespoons butter or margarine
1 teaspoon Old Bay seasoning
1 teaspoon butter-flavored salt
2 teaspoons chopped fresh parsley
½ teaspoon prepared mustard
Dash of hot sauce
Dash of red pepper
1 egg, beaten
3 tablespoons mayonnaise
1 pound fresh crabmeat, drained and flaked
Mayonnaise
Pimiento strips (optional)
Sliced pimiento-stuffed olives (optional)

Sauté green pepper, celery, and chopped pimiento in butter until pepper and celery are tender. Stir in next 6 ingredients.

Combine egg and 3 tablespoons mayonnaise; stir in vegetable mixture. Gently stir in crabmeat. Spoon into four 6-ounce individual baking shells or dishes. Bake at 375° for 15 minutes. Broil 5 inches from heat for 3 minutes. Top each with a dollop of mayonnaise, and garnish with 2 pimiento strips and 1 olive slice, if desired. Yield: 4 servings.

William Phillips,
Guntersville, Alabama.

Pipe Cakes To Canapés From A Decorating Bag

If you call a bakery when you need a decorated cake, learn the art of decorating yourself. Once you learn to use a decorating bag, you can also pipe filling into eggs and canapés, or turn mashed potatoes into an elegant side dish.

Working With Icing

There are two basic types of icing: Buttercream Icing and Royal Icing. Most cakes are decorated with Buttercream, which stays soft and moist. Royal Icing dries hard and is used to decorate cookies or make decorations last indefinitely.

The key to decorating is to have icing of ideal consistency. It must be firm enough to hold swirls and designs, yet pliable enough to mold. If the icing seems too thin, stir in extra powdered sugar; add a little water if it's too thick. Color icing with paste food coloring.

Decorating Equipment

You'll need decorating bags, metal tips, and plastic couplers to change tips without refilling bags. To make elaborate shaped flowers, you'll also need a metal flower nail.

To assemble the decorating bag, drop coupler into bag and push as far down into bag as possible. Insert metal tip over tip of coupler, and screw coupler ring over metal tip. Spoon icing into decorating bag, filling it about half full; fold corners of bag over, and crease until all air is pressed out. To change tips, simply unscrew the coupler ring and replace tip.

Metal decorating tips can be categorized into five basic groups that determine the type of decorations they will produce. The size and the shape of the opening on a decorating tip determines which group it belongs to. The basic tips available are represented in our step-by-step photographs.

Decorating Techniques

Skillful use of a decorating bag requires practice. Before actually decorating, mix up a batch of icing to practice the designs, and pipe onto a cookie sheet.

The amount of pressure will determine the size and uniformity. Some decorations require even pressure, others a varying application of pressure. If icing ripples, you are squeezing too hard. If icing breaks, you are moving too quickly or the icing is too thick.

There are six decorating techniques requiring different pressure and tip positions. Follow these basic instructions:

Dots, stars, and drop flowers: Hold the bag at a 90-degree angle with tip almost touching the surface. Steadily squeeze out icing. Lift the bag slightly as the icing builds up in desired design; keep the tip buried in the icing, then stop the pressure, and pull tip away.

Straight lines: To pipe a straight line, touch the decorating tip to the cake at a 45-degree angle, letting a small amount of icing flow. Continue squeezing bag, and draw tip across cake about ½ inch from surface. Touch cake with tip, and release pressure to end line.

Leaves: Hold bag at a 45-degree angle to cake. Squeeze bag to build up a base, then pull bag away as you relax pressure; stop squeezing, and lift tip.

Borders: For most borders, hold bag at a 45-degree angle. Touch tip to cake, and squeeze out icing as you pull tip in desired border design.

Duplicate the techniques in the following step-by-step photographs, and decorate this beautiful cake.

Step 1—To make a decorating bag, roll an obtuse triangle made from parchment paper so two ends meet at the center point of triangle; staple or tape in place.

Step 4—Pipe simpler, smaller flowers directly from a fluted drop flower tip.

Writing: Use small round tip, holding it at 45-degree angle to cake; move tip with motion of arm, not wrist, to form desired letters. The tip should lightly touch the cake as you write.

Shaped flowers: Those more intricate than drop flowers are generally shaped on a flower nail then transferred.

ROYAL ICING

3 large egg whites
½ teaspoon cream of tartar
1 (16-ounce) package powdered sugar, sifted

Combine egg whites (at room temperature) and cream of tartar. Beat at medium speed of electric mixer until frothy. Gradually add powdered sugar, mixing well. Beat for 5 to 7 minutes. Yield: about 2 cups.

Note: Icing dries very quickly; keep covered at all times with plastic wrap.

BUTTERCREAM ICING

2 cups shortening
1 teaspoon salt
2 teaspoons almond or vanilla extract
1 cup water
3 (16-ounce) packages powdered sugar, sifted

Combine shortening, salt, and extract; beat at medium speed of electric mixer until blended. Alternately add water and powdered sugar, beating constantly at low speed, until blended. Beat 8 minutes at medium speed.

Icing may be stored at room temperature for several days or in refrigerator for 2 weeks. Yield: about 7 cups.

Step 2—Pipe borders using fluted star tip, moving bag to make zigzag or desired design; this tip also produces stars, shells, and drop flowers.

Step 5—Squeeze leaves among flowers using a special forked leaf tip; same tip makes decorative borders.

Step 3—Make roses on a flower nail using rose tip: Pipe a mound of icing, then petals. Move up and down turning counterclockwise.

Step 6—Use a plain round tip for writing, as well as making lines, stems, dots, and latticework.

Fold Wontons With Imagination

Have some fun folding wontons. With just a little imagination, you can create triangles, envelopes, and spirals, in addition to a traditional Chinese shape.

If you want a traditional Chinese shape, follow the directions with our Spinach Wontons. You can also fold triangles or envelopes such as those that hold our cheese and sausage fillings. The Sugar Flip fold is used for frying crisp shells that have no filling.

Here are some simple rules to follow:

—Always keep wonton skins covered with a towel or wrapped in plastic before and after folding. Their thinness makes them dry out quickly, and when dry, they crack and crumble.

—For wontons that have a filling, always finely chop the filling ingredients so wontons can be folded easily and sealed tightly. It is important to seal them well so oil doesn't seep inside.

—To seal wontons, dampen the edges with water, and press firmly together. Dampen with a pastry brush, your finger, or the top of a chopstick.

—You don't need a special pan to fry wontons; a regular or electric skillet will work fine. A wok is best, however, because much less oil is required to fill its rounded bottom.

—Peanut oil is best for frying wontons because it can be heated to high temperatures without smoking. Vegetable oil will do, however.

—Use a thermometer to make sure you have an accurate frying temperature (375°). If the oil is too cool, the wontons will be greasy; if too hot, the oil will smoke and burn.

—Drain wontons on paper towels.

SAUSAGE ROLLS WITH SWEET-AND-SOUR SAUCE

¼ pound hot bulk pork sausage
1 (2-ounce) can mushroom stems and
    pieces, drained and finely chopped
1 small clove garlic, minced
2 dozen frozen wonton skins, thawed
Peanut or vegetable oil
Commercial sweet-and-sour sauce

Combine sausage, mushrooms, and garlic in a skillet; cook until sausage is browned, stirring to crumble. Drain off pan drippings.

Mound 2 teaspoons sausage mixture in center of each wonton. Fold top corner of wonton over filling. Fold left and right corners over filling. Lightly brush exposed corner of wonton with water. Tightly roll the filled end of wonton toward the exposed corner, and gently press to seal.

Heat 1½ inches of oil to 375° in wok or large skillet. Place several rolls at a time in hot oil, and fry 30 seconds on each side or until golden brown; drain on paper towels. Repeat with remaining rolls. Serve with sweet-and-sour sauce. Yield: about 2 dozen.

CHEESE WONTONS WITH HOT SAUCE

¾ cup (3 ounces) shredded Cheddar
    cheese
2 tablespoons drained, chopped green
    chiles
2 dozen frozen wonton skins, thawed
Peanut or vegetable oil
Hot sauce (recipe follows)

Mound 1½ teaspoons cheese and ¼ teaspoon green chiles in center of each wonton skin; brush edges of wonton lightly with water. Fold in half diagonally, and press edges together to seal.

Heat 1½ inches oil to 375° in wok or large skillet. Place 6 wontons in hot oil, and fry 30 seconds on each side or until golden brown; drain on paper towels. Repeat with remaining wontons. Serve with hot sauce. Yield: 2 dozen.

Hot Sauce:

⅓ cup chopped onion
1 small clove garlic, minced
1 tablespoon vegetable oil
½ cup chopped tomato, drained
1 tablespoon chopped canned jalapeño
    pepper
¼ teaspoon dried whole oregano
¼ teaspoon ground cumin
¼ teaspoon salt
1 (8-ounce) can tomato sauce
1½ tablespoons vinegar

Sauté onion and garlic in hot oil until tender. Add remaining ingredients, and cook until thoroughly heated. Yield: 1⅓ cups.

SPINACH WONTONS

1 (10-ounce) package frozen chopped
    spinach
2 tablespoons butter or margarine
2 tablespoons finely chopped onion
¼ cup (1 ounce) shredded Cheddar
    cheese
2 tablespoons grated Parmesan cheese
¼ cup commercial sour cream
⅛ teaspoon salt
⅛ teaspoon ground nutmeg
2½ dozen frozen wonton skins,
    thawed
Peanut or vegetable oil

Cook spinach according to package directions, omitting salt; drain well, and press dry.

Melt butter in a medium skillet; add onion, and sauté until tender. Remove from heat; stir in next 5 ingredients.

Place 1 teaspoon of spinach mixture in center of each wonton. Tuck top corner over and under the filling, rolling until tight. Lightly brush left and right corners of wonton with water. Holding center back of the wonton with your middle finger, fold left and right corners back, around your finger. Overlap left and right corners and seal, letting the remaining corner flap loosely.

Heat 1½ inches oil to 375° in wok or large skillet. Place several wontons at a time in hot oil, and fry 30 seconds on each side or until golden brown; drain on paper towels. Repeat with remaining wontons. Yield: 2½ dozen.

SUGAR FLIPS

1 cup sugar
1 teaspoon ground cinnamon
¼ teaspoon ground nutmeg
2 dozen frozen wonton skins,
    thawed
Peanut or vegetable oil

Combine first 3 ingredients in a large plastic bag, mixing well; set aside.

Cut each wonton skin into 3 lengthwise strips; lay strips on cutting board. Cut a slit down center of each strip using a sharp knife, cutting to within ½ inch of ends. Invert one end of strip through center slit. Gently straighten the strip, rolling twist to center of strip. Repeat with remaining strips.

Heat 1 inch oil to 375° in wok or large skillet. Fry strips, a few at a time, in hot oil for a few seconds or until crisp and golden brown, turning once. Drain. While warm, place a few at a time in sugar mixture in bag; shake gently to coat. Store in airtight container. Yield: 6 dozen.

Shape Sausage Rolls like an envelope. Fold the top corner over filling, fold side corners over filling, then roll toward the tip, jellyroll fashion.

For unfilled Sugar Flips, cut a wonton wrapper into 3 strips; slit strip down the center, and invert one end of strip through slit.

Cheese Wontons are simple to shape; just add filling, moisten edges of wrapper, and fold into a triangle.

For a more traditional Chinese fold, try Spinach Wontons. Tuck the top corner over the filling, and overlap right and left corners behind it. The remaining corner flaps loosely.

Casseroles For Busy Days

When you come home after a busy day at work, you may not have time or energy left to prepare supper. That's when you'll appreciate these convenient main-dish casseroles.

BEEF-AND-BISCUIT CASSEROLE

1¼ pounds ground beef
½ cup chopped onion
1 (8-ounce) can tomato sauce
¼ cup diced green chiles
2 teaspoons chili powder
1 egg
½ cup commercial sour cream
1½ cups (6 ounces) shredded Cheddar cheese, divided
1 (10-ounce) can refrigerated buttermilk flaky biscuits

Combine beef and onion in a large skillet; cook until meat is browned, stirring to crumble meat. Drain off pan drippings. Stir in tomato sauce, chiles, and chili powder. Cook over low heat, uncovered, 10 minutes, stirring occasionally; remove from heat. Beat egg in a small bowl; stir in sour cream and ½ cup cheese. Add to meat mixture, and mix well; set aside.

Separate each biscuit into two halves, making 20 biscuit rounds. Press 10 rounds into an ungreased 9-inch square baking dish. Spread meat mixture over biscuit layer. Arrange remaining biscuit rounds over meat mixture; sprinkle with remaining 1 cup cheese. Bake, uncovered, at 375° for 25 to 30 minutes or until biscuits are golden. Yield: 4 to 6 servings.

Sue James,
Nucla, Colorado.

SAUSAGE-RICE CASSEROLE

2 pounds bulk pork sausage
1 medium onion, chopped
1 medium-size green pepper, chopped
1 cup chopped celery
1 cup uncooked regular rice
½ cup slivered almonds, toasted
2 (0.375-ounce) envelopes instant chicken noodle soup mix
1 (8-ounce) can water chestnuts, drained and chopped
2½ cups water

Cook sausage in a large skillet until browned, stirring to crumble; drain off pan drippings, and remove from heat. Stir in next 7 ingredients, mixing well. Place mixture in a lightly greased 13- x 9- x 2-inch baking dish; pour water over top. Cover and bake at 350° for 1 hour and 15 minutes. Yield: 8 servings.

Darlene Codding,
Bartlesville, Oklahoma.

TANGY TUNA-BROCCOLI CASSEROLE

1 (10-ounce) package frozen broccoli spears
2 tablespoons butter or margarine
1 cup sliced fresh mushrooms
¼ cup chopped green onion
¼ teaspoon dried whole dillweed
3 tablespoons lemon juice
1 (10¾-ounce) can cream of celery soup, undiluted
1 (7-ounce) can tuna, drained and flaked
2 tablespoons diced pimiento
3 tablespoons dry white wine
3 tablespoons grated Romano cheese

Cook broccoli according to package directions; drain. Arrange in a lightly greased 10- x 6- x 2-inch baking dish, and set aside.

Melt butter in a large skillet. Add mushrooms, onions, and dillweed; sauté until tender. Stir in next 5 ingredients, and cook until heated. Spoon mixture over broccoli, and sprinkle with cheese. Place under broiler for 4 to 5 minutes or until bubbly. Yield: 4 servings.

Regyna Carbone Day,
Westminster, Colorado.

CHICKEN-ASPARAGUS CASSEROLE

1 (10-ounce) package frozen asparagus
    spears
½ cup all-purpose flour
⅛ teaspoon salt
⅛ teaspoon pepper
⅛ teaspoon paprika
6 chicken breast halves, skinned and
    boned
¼ cup butter or margarine
1 (10¾-ounce) can cream of mushroom
    soup, undiluted
1 cup whipping cream
¼ cup diced pimiento
¼ teaspoon salt
⅛ teaspoon hot sauce
¼ cup grated Parmesan cheese

Cook asparagus according to package directions; drain. Arrange in a greased 12- x 8- x 2-inch baking dish; set aside.

Combine next 4 ingredients; mix well. Dredge chicken in flour mixture. Melt butter in a large skillet; add chicken, and cook until golden brown on both sides. Drain on paper towels, and arrange on top of asparagus.

Combine soup, whipping cream, pimiento, ¼ teaspoon salt, and hot sauce; stir until blended. Spoon over chicken; sprinkle with cheese. Bake, uncovered, at 400° for 15 to 20 minutes or until bubbly. Yield: 6 servings.
Mrs. James R. Jehle,
Robins Air Force Base, Georgia.

Flavor Stacks Up In Layered Desserts

With just a single bite of Frozen Chocolate Dessert, you'll enjoy vanilla ice cream, chocolate-marshmallow sauce, coconut, and pecans. It's perfect for unexpected guests because it's made ahead and waiting.

FROZEN CHOCOLATE DESSERT

1 (13-ounce) can evaporated milk
1 (10½-ounce) package miniature
    marshmallows
1 (6-ounce) package semisweet chocolate
    morsels
½ cup butter or margarine
1 (3½-ounce) can flaked coconut
2 cups graham cracker crumbs
½ gallon vanilla ice cream
1 cup chopped pecans or walnuts

Combine first 3 ingredients in top of double boiler; bring water to a boil. Reduce heat to low; cook until chocolate and marshmallows are melted. Remove from heat, and set aside to cool.

Combine butter and coconut in a small saucepan over medium heat. Cook, stirring often, until the coconut is lightly browned. Remove from heat, and stir in graham cracker crumbs. Press three-fourths of crumb mixture into a 13- x 9- x 2-inch baking pan.

Cut ice cream crosswise into ½-inch-thick slices. Arrange half of slices over graham cracker crust. Pour half of chocolate mixture over ice cream; then repeat the layers.

Combine remaining crumb mixture and pecans; sprinkle over top of dessert. Cover and freeze until firm.

Let stand at room temperature 5 minutes before serving. Yield: 15 servings.
Pearle E. Evans,
North Myrtle Beach, South Carolina.

SPEEDY PARFAITS

1 (4⅛-ounce) package milk chocolate
    instant pudding mix
1½ cups milk
½ cup commercial sour cream
2 tablespoons powdered sugar
2 tablespoons crème de cacao
1 cup finely crushed chocolate sandwich
    cookies (about 12)
¼ cup chopped pecans

Combine pudding mix and milk; beat for 2 minutes at medium speed of electric mixer.

Gently stir the sour cream, sugar, and liqueur into pudding.

Combine cookie crumbs and pecans. Spoon alternate layers of pudding mixture and cookie crumb mixture into 6 parfait glasses. Yield: six 5-ounce parfaits.
Marietta Marx,
Louisville, Kentucky.

BUTTERSCOTCH FANTASTIC

½ cup butter or margarine, melted
1½ cups all-purpose flour
½ cup chopped pecans or walnuts
1 (8-ounce) package cream cheese,
    softened
1 cup sifted powdered sugar
1 (8-ounce) container frozen whipped
    topping, thawed and divided
2 (3¾-ounce) packages butterscotch instant
    pudding mix
3 cups milk

Combine first 3 ingredients, mixing well. Press flour mixture into a 13- x 9- x 2-inch baking pan. Bake at 350° for 20 minutes; let cool completely.

Combine cream cheese and sugar, beating until fluffy; fold in 2 cups whipped topping. Spread over crust.

Combine pudding mix and milk; beat 2 minutes at medium speed of electric mixer. Spread over cream cheese layer. Spread remaining whipped topping over pudding layer. Chill thoroughly. Yield: 15 servings.
Margaret Myers,
Amherst, Virginia.

Another Way To Stuff A Potato

Ever tried stuffing your potatoes with garden-fresh vegetables? Cynthia Kannenberg, of Milwaukee, Wisconsin, did just that, and came up with Garden Potato Cups. Featuring cabbage, carrots, onion, and green pepper, the stuffed potatoes are not only economical, but nutritious as well.

GARDEN POTATO CUPS

4 medium baking potatoes
Vegetable oil
1 small onion, chopped
¼ cup butter or margarine
2 cups shredded cabbage
1 cup grated carrots
½ cup water
⅓ cup chopped green pepper
½ teaspoon salt
⅛ teaspoon white pepper
Carrot curls (optional)

Wash potatoes, and rub with oil. Bake at 400° for 1 hour.

Sauté onion in butter in a large skillet until tender. Add cabbage, carrots, and water; cover and simmer 10 minutes. Stir in green pepper; cook, uncovered, an additional 5 minutes or until liquid is absorbed.

Cut potatoes in half lengthwise; carefully scoop out pulp, leaving a ¼-inch shell. Mash pulp.

Combine cabbage mixture and mashed potato pulp, mixing well. Stir in salt and pepper. Stuff shells with potato mixture. Bake at 400° for 15 minutes. Garnish with carrot curls, if desired. Yield: 8 servings. *Cynthia Kannenberg,*
Milwaukee, Wisconsin.

April

Talk about good—the highlight of our April testing was tasting recipes shared by some of the finest Louisiana Cajun chefs. In addition, these chefs offered secrets and tips for authentic Cajun cooking, such as how to make a *good* roux. Our task was to scale down the restaurant-size proportions to serving sizes you can duplicate in your kitchen, and we loved every minute of it.

In this chapter we'll also take you to Richmond, Virginia, where the azaleas are the center of an annual party. Amidst the pink and white blossoms, our host and hostess bring on musicians and an impressive menu including Hot Sherried Mushroom Tarts, Caviar Crown, Steak Tartare, and a luscious Double Chocolate Sauce for dipping fruits.

When the parties are over, get back to watching calories with recipes from our "Cooking Light" feature. Here we'll explain the techniques of trimming calories with simple cooking methods such as poaching, sautéing, and grilling.

Azaleas Bring On A Richmond Party

Colorful azaleas decorate the garden, and tables are filled with an assortment of delicious food. What's the occasion? Jan and J. Robert Carlton's annual azalea party in Richmond, Virginia.

As guests arrive, Jan serves Hot Sherried Mushroom Tarts on the sunporch; J. Robert stays busy helping guests to refreshing drinks. A wall of pink and white azaleas borders a cozy courtyard next to the Carlton home. What better setting for a table filled with such delicacies as Caviar Crown, Brandied Meatballs, Salmon Mousse, fresh vegetables with Tarragon Dip, and J. Robert's Steak Tartare.

Another table on the back lawn includes a tempting selection of desserts: Elegant Sour Cream Pound Cake, Chocolate Tea Brownies, and Lemon Tarts. There's also assorted fresh fruit, including slices of ripe banana rolled in toasted coconut. Jan says her guests really enjoy dipping their favorite fruit into the luscious Double Chocolate Sauce she includes on the tray of fruit.

Hot Sherried Mushroom Tarts
Caviar Crown
Steak Tartare
Fresh Vegetables With Tarragon Dip
Brandied Meatballs
Old-Fashioned Chicken Salad
Salmon Mousse
Elegant Sour Cream Pound Cake
Lemon Tarts
Fresh Fruit With
Double Chocolate Sauce
Chocolate Tea Brownies

HOT SHERRIED MUSHROOM TARTS

1 pound fresh mushrooms, chopped
½ cup butter or margarine
¼ cup plus 2 tablespoons all-purpose flour
1½ cups half-and-half
2 tablespoons dry sherry
1 tablespoon plus 1 teaspoon diced chives
2 teaspoons lemon juice
1 teaspoon Worcestershire sauce
¾ teaspoon salt
2 to 3 drops hot sauce
2½ dozen 2-inch tart shells, partially baked
Fresh artichoke (optional)

Sauté mushrooms in butter in a heavy skillet until tender. Remove mushrooms, reserving drippings.

Add flour to reserved drippings, stirring until smooth. Cook for 1 minute, stirring constantly. Gradually add half-and-half; cook over medium heat, stirring constantly, until thickened. Add mushrooms and next 6 ingredients, stirring well.

Spoon 2 tablespoons mushroom filling into each tart shell. Place tarts on an ungreased baking sheet; bake at 350° for 15 minutes or until lightly browned. Garnish with fresh artichoke, if desired. Yield: about 2½ dozen.

CAVIAR CROWN

3 (8-ounce) packages cream cheese, softened
3 tablespoons lemon juice
3 tablespoons finely chopped green onion
1½ teaspoons Worcestershire sauce
¼ to ½ teaspoon garlic juice
4 to 6 drops hot sauce
1 (4-ounce) jar red caviar
1 (2-ounce) jar black caviar
Lemon wedges (optional)
Fresh parsley sprigs (optional)

Combine first 6 ingredients; beat on medium speed of electric mixer until smooth and fluffy. Place on serving plate, and shape into a 10-inch circle. Spoon red caviar into center of cream cheese; spread caviar into an 8-inch circle. Spread a 1-inch ring of black caviar around red caviar circle, leaving a 1-inch border of cream cheese mixture. Garnish with lemon wedges and parsley sprigs, if desired. Serve with party bread or melba toast. Yield: 3½ cups.

STEAK TARTARE

2 pounds boneless sirloin steak
½ onion, grated
8 anchovy fillets, finely chopped
1 clove garlic, crushed
2 egg yolks, slightly beaten
1½ tablespoons lemon juice
1 tablespoon capers
1 teaspoon salt
2 teaspoons Worcestershire sauce
¼ teaspoon dry mustard
Dash of hot sauce
Lettuce leaves
Capers (optional)
Chopped fresh parsley (optional)
Anchovy fillets (optional)

Have butcher grind sirloin 3 times. Combine sirloin and next 10 ingredients; mix well. Shape meat mixture into a loaf; cover and chill 2 hours.

Place meat mixture on a lettuce-lined platter; top with capers, parsley, and anchovies, if desired. Serve with party rye bread or crackers. Yield: 4½ cups.

TARRAGON DIP

1½ cups commercial sour cream
1 (3-ounce) package cream cheese, softened
½ cup mayonnaise
1 teaspoon lemon juice
½ teaspoon dried whole tarragon
½ teaspoon Worcestershire sauce
⅛ teaspoon garlic juice
5 to 6 drops hot sauce

Combine all ingredients, mixing well. Cover and chill overnight. Serve with assorted fresh vegetables. Yield: 2 cups.

BRANDIED MEATBALLS

2 pounds ground beef
¾ cup milk
½ cup soft breadcrumbs
1 tablespoon Worcestershire sauce
1 teaspoon salt
½ teaspoon garlic powder
¼ teaspoon ground nutmeg
¼ teaspoon ground ginger
⅛ teaspoon pepper
2 drops hot sauce
2 tablespoons vegetable oil
1 (18-ounce) jar peach preserves
¼ cup firmly packed brown sugar
½ cup brandy
½ cup peach-flavored brandy
¼ teaspoon ground nutmeg
1 tablespoon cornstarch
1 tablespoon cold water

Combine first 10 ingredients, mixing well; shape into 1-inch meatballs. Cook meatballs in hot oil in a large skillet over medium heat 10 to 15 minutes or until browned. Drain meatballs on paper towels; pour off pan drippings.

Combine next 5 ingredients in skillet, mixing well; simmer 10 minutes. Add meatballs; cover and simmer 1 hour, stirring occasionally. Combine cornstarch and water, mixing well; stir into sauce. Cook over medium heat, stirring constantly, until thickened and bubbly. Serve in a chafing dish. Yield: 6 dozen.

Tip: To easily remove waxed paper or aluminum foil from frozen food, place package in 300° oven for 5 minutes.

OLD-FASHIONED CHICKEN SALAD

4 cups chopped cooked chicken
2 hard-cooked eggs, chopped
1 cup chopped celery
¼ cup chopped onion
¾ teaspoon salt
½ teaspoon celery salt
⅛ to ¼ teaspoon white pepper
Dash of red pepper
2 tablespoons lemon juice
½ to ¾ cup mayonnaise
Paprika
Fresh parsley sprigs
Cherry tomatoes

Combine first 9 ingredients; toss gently. Fold in mayonnaise; cover and chill 2 hours.

Spoon into a serving dish; sprinkle with paprika. Garnish with parsley and tomatoes. Yield: 16 appetizer servings.

SALMON MOUSSE

1 (15½-ounce) can red salmon
2 envelopes unflavored gelatin
¼ cup cold water
¼ cup boiling water
1 small onion, minced
1 cup mayonnaise
¼ cup lemon juice
1 tablespoon dried whole dillweed
2 teaspoons paprika
1½ cups whipping cream
½ cup commercial sour cream
½ teaspoon Worcestershire sauce
Pimiento-stuffed olives (optional)
Cucumber slices (optional)
Pimiento slice (optional)
Watercress (optional)
Lemon wedges (optional)

Drain salmon, and flake with a fork.
Soften gelatin in cold water; add boiling water, stirring until gelatin is dissolved. Place half of gelatin mixture, half of salmon, and half each of next 6 ingredients in container of electric blender; process until smooth. Pour mixture into a lightly oiled 5½-cup fish mold. Repeat blending procedure; add to mold. Chill.

Combine sour cream and Worcestershire sauce in a small bowl, mixing well. Chill 5 hours.

Unmold mousse on a chilled serving plate; frost with sour cream mixture. Decorate fish with pimiento-stuffed olive slices for eyes, cucumber slices for gills and tail, and a pimiento slice for mouth, if desired. Garnish tray with watercress and lemon wedges, if desired. Serve immediately with crackers. Yield: 5½ cups.

ELEGANT SOUR CREAM POUND CAKE

½ cup butter, softened
½ cup shortening
3 cups sugar
6 eggs, separated
3 cups sifted cake flour
¼ teaspoon baking powder
¼ teaspoon baking soda
¼ teaspoon salt
1 (8-ounce) carton commercial sour cream

Cream butter and shortening; gradually add sugar, beating well. Add egg yolks, one at a time, beating well after each addition.

Combine flour, baking powder, soda, and salt; add to creamed mixture alternately with sour cream, beginning and ending with flour mixture. Beat egg whites (at room temperature) until stiff; gently fold into batter.

Pour batter into a greased and floured 10-inch tube pan. Bake at 325° for 1½ hours or until a wooden pick inserted in center comes out clean. Cool 10 minutes; remove from pan, and cool completely. Yield: one 10-inch cake.

LEMON TARTS

½ cup butter or margarine, softened
2 cups sugar
6 eggs
¼ cup all-purpose flour
¾ cup sugar
⅔ cup lemon juice
1 tablespoon grated lemon rind
Ground nutmeg
3 dozen 2-inch commercial tart shells, partially baked

Cream butter; gradually add 2 cups sugar, beating well. Add eggs, one at a time, beating well after each addition.

Combine flour and ¾ cup sugar; add to creamed mixture alternately with lemon juice, beginning and ending with flour mixture. Stir in rind.

Lightly sprinkle nutmeg into each tart shell. Spoon 2 tablespoons lemon filling into each tart shell. Place tarts on an ungreased baking sheet, and bake at 350° for 15 to 20 minutes or until lightly browned. Yield: 3 dozen.

DOUBLE CHOCOLATE SAUCE

1 (6-ounce) package semisweet chocolate morsels
2 (1-ounce) squares unsweetened chocolate, quartered
1 cup sifted powdered sugar
⅔ cup half-and-half
½ cup light corn syrup
2 tablespoons butter
½ teaspoon salt
1 tablespoon vanilla extract
Assorted fresh fruit

Place chocolate in container of an electric blender. Combine next 5 ingredients in a medium saucepan; cook over medium heat until bubbly. Pour sugar mixture over chocolate; add vanilla. Process mixture 1 minute or until smooth. Serve warm with fresh fruit. Yield: 2 cups.

CHOCOLATE TEA BROWNIES

5 (1-ounce) squares unsweetened chocolate
⅔ cup butter or margarine
5 eggs
2½ cups sugar
2 teaspoons vanilla extract
½ teaspoon salt
1¼ cups all-purpose flour
1½ cups chopped pecans
Chocolate frosting (recipe follows)
Pecan halves

Combine chocolate and butter in a medium saucepan over low heat. Cook until chocolate and butter melt.

Combine next 4 ingredients; beat on medium speed of electric mixer until well blended. Stir in flour, chopped pecans, and chocolate mixture.

Pour batter into a lightly greased 15- x 10- x 1-inch jellyroll pan. Bake at 350° for 25 minutes or until a wooden pick inserted in center comes out clean. Spread with chocolate frosting while brownies are still warm. Cut into squares; top each square with a pecan half. Yield: about 3½ dozen.

Chocolate Frosting:

¼ cup plus 2 tablespoons butter or margarine
1½ (1-ounce) squares unsweetened chocolate, melted
3 tablespoons half-and-half
3 cups sifted powdered sugar
2 tablespoons kirsch

Combine first 3 ingredients in a medium saucepan; cook until butter and chocolate melt. Remove from heat, and stir in sugar and kirsch; beat until smooth. Yield: enough frosting for 3½ dozen brownies.

Spring Arrives With Colorful Salads

Few foods do more to tempt the appetite than a salad. In these recipes, our readers have combined fruit, vegetables, meats, eggs, cheese, and grain products into some refreshing salad creations.

Salad experts agree on two basic principles for great salads. The first is to purchase only the prettiest and freshest produce. Heads of lettuce should be crisp and firm, but give slightly when squeezed. Fruit should always be free of blemishes. Skip over any that are wilted, wrinkled, or dirty.

Secondly, keep your carefully selected ingredients at their freshest by storing them correctly. For maximum crispness, wash greens as soon as you get home by rinsing under cold, running water. Then drain and pat with paper towels or shake until almost dry in a salad spinner or basket; a little moisture will keep them crisp. Place clean greens in a plastic bag or covered bowl, and refrigerate.

Most other vegetables and fruits should also be kept in the refrigerator, and washed just before using. However, potatoes, dry onions, and tomatoes are exceptions. They retain more flavor and a better texture if they are stored at room temperature or in a cool, dry place. When tomatoes have fully ripened, store in the refrigerator.

CHICKEN SALAD MOLD

2 envelopes unflavored gelatin
1 cup cold water
1 (10¾-ounce) can cream of chicken soup, undiluted
1 cup diced celery
1 (7-ounce) jar diced pimiento, drained
1 (6¾-ounce) can boned chicken, drained and flaked
½ cup sweet pickle relish
½ cup chopped pecans
1 (3-ounce) package cream cheese, softened
1 tablespoon finely chopped onion
½ teaspoon sugar
2 tablespoons mayonnaise
Celery leaves (optional)
Pimiento slices (optional)

Combine gelatin and cold water; let stand 2 minutes.

Place soup in a large saucepan over medium heat; cook until thoroughly heated. Add gelatin mixture; cook, stirring often, until gelatin is dissolved.

Combine next 9 ingredients, mixing well; stir into soup mixture. Pour into a lightly oiled 8-cup mold, and chill until firm. Unmold on serving platter, and garnish with celery leaves and pimiento, if desired. Yield: 6 to 8 servings.
Frances Bowles,
Mableton, Georgia.

CHICKEN STACK-UP SALAD

2 cups diced cooked chicken
¼ teaspoon salt
¼ teaspoon paprika
⅛ teaspoon lemon-pepper seasoning
4 cups shredded lettuce
1 cup chopped celery
1 (10-ounce) package frozen English peas, thawed
1½ cups (6 ounces) shredded Cheddar cheese
1 cup cooked elbow macaroni
1 cup mayonnaise
1 (8-ounce) carton commercial sour cream

Combine first 4 ingredients, tossing gently. Layer lettuce, chicken mixture, celery, peas, cheese, and macaroni in a 4-quart bowl. Combine mayonnaise and sour cream, mixing well; spread evenly over top, sealing to edge of bowl. Cover tightly, and chill 24 hours. Yield: 8 servings.
Mrs. Ellis W. Golson,
Evergreen, Alabama.

PINEAPPLE-NUT CHICKEN SALAD

1½ cups chopped cooked chicken
½ cup chopped celery
2 hard-cooked eggs, chopped
¼ cup chopped almonds, toasted
¼ to ⅓ cup mayonnaise
½ teaspoon salt
⅛ teaspoon pepper
1½ teaspoons lemon juice
1 (15½-ounce) can sliced pineapple, drained
Lettuce leaves
¼ cup crumbled cooked bacon

Combine first 8 ingredients; toss gently. Arrange 6 pineapple slices on lettuce leaves (reserve remaining pineapple for use in other recipes). Spoon chicken salad over pineapple slices, and sprinkle with bacon. Yield: 6 servings.
Darlene George,
Bon Aqua, Tennessee.

GREEN BEAN-POTATO SALAD

1 dozen small new potatoes, unpeeled
1 pound fresh green beans
1 small red onion, sliced and separated into rings
1 medium-size green pepper, sliced into rings
½ cup sliced celery
¼ cup olive oil
¼ cup chopped fresh parsley
3 tablespoons vinegar
½ teaspoon salt
¼ teaspoon pepper
⅛ teaspoon dried whole oregano
Curly endive leaves (optional)

Cook potatoes in boiling water 20 minutes or until tender; drain and cool. Slice potatoes thinly; set aside.

Remove strings from beans; cut beans into 1½-inch pieces. Wash thoroughly. Cover and cook in boiling water 10 to 15 minutes or until beans are crisp-tender; drain and cool.

Combine potatoes, green beans, onion, green pepper, and celery in a mixing bowl. Combine next 6 ingredients in a jar. Cover tightly, and shake vigorously. Pour over vegetables, and toss gently. Chill salad thoroughly. Serve over endive, if desired. Yield: 6 to 8 servings. *Mrs. Jonnie Carroll,*
Duck Hill, Mississippi.

OVERNIGHT FIESTA SALAD

1 (15½-ounce) can kidney beans, drained
1 medium onion, chopped
2 medium tomatoes, unpeeled and coarsely chopped
½ cup chopped celery
½ cup chopped green pepper
½ cup commercial French salad dressing
1 small head iceberg lettuce, torn into bite-size pieces
1 cup (4 ounces) shredded Cheddar cheese
3 hard-cooked eggs, chopped
1 cup crushed corn chips

Layer first 9 ingredients in order listed in a large salad bowl. Cover tightly; refrigerate several hours or overnight. Top with corn chips; toss gently before serving. Yield: 6 to 8 servings. *Mrs. George Lance,*
Madison, Tennessee.

Tip: For perfect hard-cooked eggs, place eggs in a saucepan and cover with water; bring to a boil, lower heat to simmer, and cook 14 minutes. Pour off hot water and add cold water; shells will come off easily.

CUCUMBER-BEAN SALAD

1 (10-ounce) package frozen English peas
1 (10-ounce) package frozen baby lima
   beans
2 (3-ounce) packages cream cheese,
   softened and cubed
1 medium cucumber, chopped
1 small onion, chopped
¼ cup mayonnaise or salad dressing

Cook frozen vegetables according to package directions; drain and let cool to room temperature. Combine vegetables and remaining ingredients; stir gently until blended. Chill. Yield: 8 servings.

Joyce Eastham,
Proctorville, Ohio.

CUCUMBER SALAD MOLD

1 (3-ounce) package lime-flavored gelatin
1 cup boiling water
1 cup diced, peeled cucumber, drained
¼ cup cold water
1 tablespoon vinegar
½ teaspoon grated onion
1 (3-ounce) package cream cheese,
   softened
1 cup diced celery
¼ cup diced green pepper
Lettuce leaves

Dissolve gelatin in boiling water; stir in next 4 ingredients. Pour half of cucumber mixture into a lightly oiled 4-cup mold; chill until set.

Combine cream cheese and remaining cucumber mixture, stirring well; stir in celery and green pepper. Pour over cucumber layer in mold; chill until firm. Unmold salad on lettuce leaves. Yield: 6 to 8 servings.   *Mrs. H. A. Wagner,*
Hendersonville, North Carolina.

NEXT-DAY VEGETABLE SALAD

½ medium head cauliflower
½ large bunch broccoli
1 medium head iceberg lettuce, torn into
   bite-size pieces
1 pound bacon, cooked and crumbled
1 medium-size red onion, sliced and
   separated into rings
¼ cup grated Parmesan cheese
2 cups mayonnaise
1 tablespoon sugar
Dash of white pepper
Shredded lettuce (optional)
Chopped green onion (optional)

Wash cauliflower, and cut flowerets into bite-size pieces. Trim off large leaves of broccoli, and remove tough ends of lower stalks. Wash broccoli thoroughly, and cut flowerets into bite-size pieces (reserve stems for use in other recipes).

Layer lettuce, cauliflower, broccoli, bacon, onion, and cheese in a 4-quart bowl. Combine mayonnaise, sugar, and pepper; mix well. Spread evenly over top, sealing to edge of bowl. Cover tightly; chill 24 hours. Garnish with shredded lettuce and chopped onion, if desired. Yield: 8 to 10 servings.

Sally Pedigo,
Dallas, Texas.

CRISP SPINACH SALAD WITH CREAMY DRESSING

1 pound fresh spinach, torn into bite-size
   pieces
½ cup sliced celery
½ cup chopped green onion
3 hard-cooked eggs, sliced
2 to 3 slices bacon, cooked and crumbled
1 cup (4 ounces) shredded Cheddar cheese
Creamy Dressing

Combine first 6 ingredients in a large bowl; toss well. Serve with Creamy Dressing. Yield: 6 servings.

Creamy Dressing:

1 cup mayonnaise
2 teaspoons prepared horseradish
1½ teaspoons cider vinegar
½ teaspoon hot sauce
Paprika (optional)

Combine first 4 ingredients; stir well. Sprinkle with paprika, if desired. Yield: 1 cup.   *Diana McConnell,*
Arlington, Texas.

FRUIT CUPS WITH PINEAPPLE CREAM DRESSING

1 (15½-ounce) can pineapple chunks in
   heavy syrup, undrained
1 (11-ounce) can mandarin oranges,
   drained
2 medium bananas, sliced
1 large red apple, unpeeled and chopped
1 pound seedless green grapes, halved
Pineapple Cream Dressing

Drain pineapple, reserving 1 tablespoon syrup for dressing recipe; set aside. Combine pineapple chunks and next 4 ingredients; toss. Spoon into individual serving dishes; top with Pineapple Cream Dressing. Yield: 8 servings.

Pineapple Cream Dressing:

1¼ cups marshmallow creme
3 tablespoons mayonnaise
1 tablespoon pineapple syrup
¼ teaspoon vanilla extract

Combine all ingredients, stirring well. Spoon over fruit. Yield: 1½ cups.

Marie Bilbo,
Meadville, Mississippi.

DELUXE WALDORF SALAD

2 large tart red apples, unpeeled
   and diced
1 large green apple, unpeeled and diced
½ teaspoon ascorbic-citric powder
½ pound seedless green grapes, halved
½ cup coarsely chopped pecans
½ cup finely diced celery
⅓ cup raisins
2 tablespoons maraschino cherries, sliced
¼ cup plus 2 tablespoons mayonnaise
Lettuce leaves

Sprinkle diced apple with ascorbic-citric powder. Add next 6 ingredients; mix well. Spoon into a lettuce-lined bowl. Yield: 6 to 8 servings.

Betty Howlett,
Homewood, Alabama.

Quench Your Thirst With Sangría

Harold Tate of Birmingham traveled a long way to get his recipe for Spanish Sangría. During a visit to Spain, he watched carefully as a Spanish waiter prepared the drink at a restaurant. Harold says he experimented at home until he duplicated the fruity, smooth taste of the drink.

SPANISH SANGRIA

1 (25.4-ounce) bottle Burgundy or other
   dry red wine
¼ cup brandy
2 tablespoons Cointreau or other
   orange-flavored liqueur
3 cups red Hawaiian punch
3 oranges, thinly sliced
2 lemons, thinly sliced
2 bananas, sliced

Combine first 4 ingredients in a 3-quart pitcher; mix well. Add fruit, stirring gently. Cover; refrigerate at least 4 hours before serving. Serve over ice. Yield: 3 quarts.   *Harold Tate,*
Birmingham, Alabama.

Citrus Flavors This Stir-Fry

The delicate sweetness of orange juice and the zesty flavor of grated orange rind make this chicken stir-fry unique. Combine bite-size pieces of chicken, cashews, sliced carrots, and celery in an orange-flavored sauce for a great wok recipe.

STIR-FRY CHICKEN A L'ORANGE

4 chicken breast halves, skinned and boned
1 tablespoon grated orange rind
¾ cup orange juice
1 tablespoon cornstarch
3 tablespoons soy sauce
⅓ cup corn syrup
¼ teaspoon ground ginger
2 tablespoons peanut or vegetable oil
2 large carrots, scraped and diagonally sliced
2 stalks celery, diagonally sliced
1 tablespoon peanut or vegetable oil
½ cup cashews
Hot cooked rice

Cut chicken breasts into 1-inch pieces; set aside. Combine next 6 ingredients; stir well.

Pour 2 tablespoons oil around top of preheated wok, coating sides; allow to heat at medium high (325°) 2 minutes. Add carrots and celery, and stir-fry 3 minutes. Remove vegetables from wok, and set aside.

Pour 1 tablespoon oil around top of wok, coating sides; allow to heat at medium high 2 minutes. Add chicken, and stir-fry 3 minutes. Add orange juice mixture, vegetables, and cashews; stir constantly until thickened. Serve over hot cooked rice. Yield: 4 servings.
Janice Elder,
Spartanburg, South Carolina.

Accent With Green Onions

Did you know that scallions are the same as green onions? The only difference is that green onions are more mature and have a tiny bulb at their base. In spite of this, both scallions and green onions can add zesty flavor and bright color to your menu.

ZESTY STIR-FRIED CHICKEN

4 chicken breast halves, skinned and boned
¼ cup sherry
2 to 3 tablespoons soy sauce
½ teaspoon sugar
Dash of ground ginger
Dash of garlic powder
Dash of dry mustard
3 tablespoons peanut or vegetable oil
½ pound fresh mushrooms, sliced
1 (6-ounce) package frozen Chinese pea pods, thawed and drained
5 scallions or green onions, diagonally cut into ½-inch pieces
1 cup chicken broth
1 tablespoon cornstarch
Hot cooked rice

Cut chicken breasts into 2-inch strips, and set aside. Combine next 6 ingredients, stirring well; add chicken. Cover and refrigerate 1 hour. Drain chicken, reserving marinade.

Pour oil around top of preheated wok, coating sides; allow to heat at medium high (325°) for 2 minutes. Add chicken, and stir-fry 2 to 3 minutes. Remove chicken from wok, and set aside. Add mushrooms, pea pods, and scallions; stir-fry 2 minutes.

Combine chicken broth, reserved marinade, and cornstarch, stirring well; pour over vegetables. Cook, stirring constantly, until slightly thickened. Return chicken to wok; stir well. Serve over rice. Yield: 4 to 6 servings.
Paula Patterson,
Houston, Texas.

CHEESY SCALLOPED POTATOES

2 pounds potatoes
12 slices bacon, cooked and crumbled
¼ cup sliced green onion
3 tablespoons butter or margarine
3 tablespoons all-purpose flour
1½ cups milk
¼ teaspoon salt
¼ teaspoon pepper
¼ teaspoon celery seeds
1 cup (4 ounces) shredded sharp Cheddar cheese

Peel potatoes, and cut into ¼-inch slices; cook in boiling water 5 minutes. Drain well. Place potatoes in a lightly greased 10- x 6- x 2-inch baking dish; sprinkle with bacon and onion.

Melt butter in a heavy saucepan over low heat; add flour, stirring until smooth. Cook 1 minute, stirring constantly. Gradually add milk; cook over medium heat, stirring constantly, until thickened and bubbly. Stir in salt, pepper, and celery seeds. Remove from heat; add cheese, stirring until cheese melts. Pour sauce over potatoes; cover and bake at 350° for 30 minutes. Yield: 6 to 8 servings.
John L. Wood,
Memphis, Tennessee.

RICE-AND-SHRIMP SALAD

1½ cups uncooked regular rice
3 (4½-ounce) cans shrimp, drained and rinsed
1 cup frozen English peas, thawed
½ cup minced fresh parsley
½ cup chopped green onion or scallions with tops
½ cup sliced ripe olives
¼ cup chopped green pepper
⅓ cup vinegar
¼ cup vegetable oil
½ teaspoon salt
¼ teaspoon dried whole tarragon
¼ teaspoon pepper

Cook rice according to package directions, omitting butter. While hot, combine with remaining ingredients; toss gently. Cover and chill at least 2 hours. Yield: 8 servings.
Mina De Kraker,
Holland, Michigan.

CREAMED GREEN ONION SOUP

1½ cups sliced green onion
¼ cup butter or margarine
2 tablespoons all-purpose flour
1 quart milk
½ teaspoon salt
3 egg yolks

Sauté onion in butter in a heavy saucepan over low heat until tender. Stir in flour; cook 1 minute, stirring constantly. Gradually add milk; cook over medium heat until slightly thickened. Stir in salt.

Beat egg yolks until thick and lemon colored. Gradually stir about 2 tablespoons hot mixture into yolks; stir yolks into remaining hot mixture. Yield: 4½ cups.
Lois Rodriquez,
Henryetta, Oklahoma.

Easter Bread

According to legend, breads similar to this rich, sweet loaf were baked for Greek Easter celebrations. Since it's similar to a coffee cake, you can enjoy Trinity Feast Bread for breakfast or brunch. Just slice and serve the bread with butter.

TRINITY FEAST BREAD

2 packages dry yeast
5 to 6 cups all-purpose flour, divided
¾ cup sugar
¼ teaspoon salt
¾ cup half-and-half
¼ cup water
½ cup butter or margarine
4 eggs, beaten
1 tablespoon grated lemon rind
2 teaspoons vanilla extract
1 egg white
1 tablespoon water
Powdered sugar glaze (recipe follows)
Decorator candies

Combine yeast, 1½ cups flour, sugar, and salt in a large bowl; stir well.

Combine half-and-half, ¼ cup water, and butter in a small saucepan; place over low heat until very warm (120° to 130°). Gradually add cream mixture to flour mixture, stirring well; beat at medium speed of electric mixer 2 minutes. Add eggs, lemon rind, and vanilla; beat well. Gradually add 1 cup flour; beat at high speed 2 additional minutes. Stir in enough remaining flour (2½ to 3½ cups) to make a soft dough.

Turn dough out onto a lightly floured surface, and knead 8 to 10 minutes or until smooth and elastic. Place dough in a well-greased bowl, turning to grease top. Cover and let rise in a warm place (85°), free from drafts, 1 hour or until doubled in bulk.

Punch dough down; turn out on a lightly floured surface. Divide dough in half; shape each portion into a ball. Divide 1 ball of dough into 3 equal portions, and shape each into a smooth round ball; place in a 3-leaf clover design on a greased baking sheet. Repeat procedure with remaining dough. Cover and let rise in a warm place (85°), free from drafts, 1 hour or until doubled in bulk.

Combine egg white and 1 tablespoon water, mixing well; gently brush over each loaf. Bake at 350° for 20 minutes. Cover loaves loosely with aluminum foil; continue to bake at 350° for 20 minutes or until loaves sound hollow when tapped. Cool loaves on wire racks. Drizzle with powdered sugar glaze. Sprinkle with decorator candies. Yield: 2 loaves.

Powdered Sugar Glaze:

1 cup sifted powdered sugar
½ teaspoon vanilla extract
1½ tablespoons milk

Combine all ingredients, mixing well. Yield: about ½ cup.

Eggs For Easter And More

The sale of eggs skyrocket just before Easter as families across the South prepare for the traditional egg hunt. Here are tips for cooking eggs followed by recipes to help you use them.

Never boil an egg—high temperatures toughen them and cause an ugly (but harmless) green ring to form around the yolks. Follow this simple hard-cook method instead.

Place the eggs in a saucepan with enough water to come at least 1 inch above the eggs. Cover and bring rapidly to a boil; remove from heat immediately. Let the eggs stand in hot water 15 to 17 minutes for large eggs, adjusting the time by 3 minutes for each size larger or smaller. Then quickly cool the eggs under cold running water.

Refrigerate hard-cooked eggs as soon as decorating is completed and again immediately after the hunt; use them within a week.

TUNA-STUFFED EGGS

6 hard-cooked eggs
3 to 4 tablespoons mayonnaise
1 (3¼-ounce) can tuna, drained and flaked
1 teaspoon sweet pickle relish
1 teaspoon prepared mustard
½ teaspoon grated onion
⅛ teaspoon salt
Dash of pepper

Slice eggs in half lengthwise, and carefully remove yolks. Mash yolks, and stir in mayonnaise. Add remaining ingredients; stir well. Stuff egg whites with yolk mixture. Yield: 6 servings.
Ruby Bonelli,
Pearland, Texas.

CREAMED EGGS IN TOAST CUPS

4 hard-cooked eggs
2 tablespoons butter or margarine
2 tablespoons all-purpose flour
1 cup milk
½ teaspoon salt
⅛ teaspoon pepper
4 slices bread
3 tablespoons butter or margarine, melted

Slice one egg in half; remove yolk. Press yolk through a sieve; set aside for garnish. Coarsely chop egg white and remaining eggs. Set aside.

Melt 2 tablespoons butter in a heavy saucepan over low heat; add flour, stirring until smooth. Cook 1 minute, stirring constantly. Gradually add milk; cook over medium heat, stirring constantly, until thickened and bubbly. Stir in salt, pepper, and chopped egg.

Trim crust from bread. Brush both sides of each slice with melted butter. Press each slice into a 6-ounce custard cup. Bake at 400° for 8 to 10 minutes or until lightly toasted. Remove toast from custard cups, and place on serving plates. Spoon egg mixture into toast cups; garnish each with the sieved yolk. Yield: 4 servings. *Helen McCauley,*
Fort Myers, Florida.

BRUNCHEON EGGS

18 hard-cooked eggs, coarsely chopped
1 (10¾-ounce) can cream of mushroom soup, undiluted
1 (3-ounce) can sliced mushrooms, drained
1 (2-ounce) jar diced pimiento, drained
1 (8-ounce) can sliced water chestnuts, drained
1 cup (4 ounces) shredded sharp Cheddar cheese
⅔ cup milk
¼ cup dry sherry
1 tablespoon Worcestershire sauce
¼ teaspoon salt
¼ teaspoon pepper
Dash of hot sauce
1½ cups herb seasoned stuffing mix
¼ cup chopped almonds, toasted

Combine first 12 ingredients; mix well. Spoon mixture into a lightly greased 13- x 9- x 2-inch baking dish. Sprinkle stuffing mix and almonds over egg mixture. Bake at 325° for 20 to 25 minutes or until bubbly. Yield: 8 servings. *Mrs. Rex Clements, Jr.,*
Birmingham, Alabama.

SAUCY EGGS

6 hard-cooked eggs
8 slices bacon
½ pound fresh mushrooms, sliced
1 (10¾-ounce) can cream of mushroom
   soup, undiluted
½ cup mayonnaise
½ cup milk
1 (2-ounce) jar diced pimiento, drained
1 tablespoon chopped chives
Paprika (optional)
Chopped fresh parsley (optional)
1 (3-ounce) can chow mein noodles

Slice eggs in half lengthwise; place in a lightly greased 8-inch baking dish.

Cook bacon in a large skillet until crisp; remove bacon, reserving 2 tablespoons drippings in skillet. Crumble bacon, and set aside. Sauté mushrooms in drippings until tender; drain well, and spoon over eggs.

Combine soup, mayonnaise, milk, pimiento, and chives; mix well, and spoon over mushrooms. Sprinkle with reserved bacon. Bake at 350° for 20 minutes. Sprinkle with paprika and parsley, if desired. Serve over chow mein noodles. Yield: about 6 servings. *Jean Sparnon, Lutz, Florida.*

BROCCOLI AND CREAMED EGGS

6 hard-cooked eggs
2 (10-ounce) packages frozen broccoli
   spears
2 tablespoons lemon juice
¼ cup butter or margarine
¼ cup all-purpose flour
2 cups milk
½ teaspoon Worcestershire sauce
½ teaspoon salt
½ teaspoon dry mustard
⅛ teaspoon pepper

Slice 2 eggs in half; remove yolks. Press yolks through a sieve; set aside for garnish. Slice egg whites and remaining eggs into quarters; set aside.

Cook broccoli according to package directions, omitting salt; drain well. Arrange in a serving dish, and drizzle lemon juice over top.

Melt butter in a heavy saucepan over low heat; add flour, stirring until smooth. Cook 1 minute, stirring constantly. Gradually add milk; cook over medium heat, stirring constantly, until thickened and bubbly. Stir in Worcestershire, salt, mustard, and pepper. Add egg quarters; mix well. Pour sauce over broccoli, and garnish with sieved egg yolks. Yield: 6 to 8 servings.
*Mrs. J. M. Hamilton,
Fort Mill, South Carolina.*

Sweet Treats From Dried Fruit

Some of the best fruit flavors are preserved in dried fruit like apples, peaches, and apricots. It usually helps to "plump" or rehydrate dried fruit so it will be tender and more chewable. Soaking it in boiling water is the best way to soften the fruit. When a recipe calls for chopped dried fruit, like our recipe for Delicious Fried Pies, chop the fruit before plumping. You can coat your knife or kitchen shears with vegetable oil or run them under hot water occasionally to prevent stickiness.

APRICOT KOLACHES

1 cup butter or margarine, softened
2 (3-ounce) packages cream cheese,
   softened
2 tablespoons sugar
2 cups all-purpose flour
Apricot filling (recipe follows)
Powdered sugar (optional)

Cream butter and cream cheese; add sugar, beating well. Add flour, and mix well. Shape dough into a ball; cover and chill 1 hour.

Work with half of dough at a time. Turn dough out onto a well-floured working surface. Roll dough out to ⅛-inch thickness; cut into 2-inch squares. Spoon about ½ teaspoon apricot filling in center of each square. Bring corners of square to center, pinching edges to seal. Place cookies on ungreased cookie sheets. Bake at 400° for 15 minutes. Cool on wire racks. Sprinkle with powdered sugar, if desired. Yield: about 7 dozen.

Apricot Filling:

¾ cup dried apricots
1½ cups water
¾ cup sugar

Combine apricots and water in a heavy saucepan; cook, covered, over medium heat about 10 minutes or until apricots are soft. Cook, uncovered, 5 minutes or until most of water has been absorbed. Remove from heat. Mash apricots, and stir in sugar. Yield: 1 cup.
*Dora S. Hancock,
Malakoff, Texas.*

DELICIOUS FRIED PIES

1 cup chopped dried peaches
1 cup chopped dried apples
¾ cup sugar
Dash of salt
¼ teaspoon ground nutmeg
1 tablespoon butter or margarine
Pastry (recipe follows)
Vegetable oil

Combine peaches, apples, and water to cover in a medium saucepan. Cook over medium heat 10 to 15 minutes or until tender. Stir in next 4 ingredients.

Divide pastry evenly into 7 balls; roll each ball to ¼-inch thickness on waxed paper. Cut into 6-inch circles.

Place about 2 tablespoons fruit mixture on half of each pastry circle. To seal pies, dip fingers in water, and moisten edges of circles; fold in half, making sure edges are even. Using a fork dipped in flour, press pastry edges firmly together.

Heat ½ inch of oil to 375° in a large skillet. Cook pies until golden brown on both sides, turning only once. Drain well on paper towels. Yield: 7 pies.

Pastry:

2 cups all-purpose flour
1 teaspoon salt
1½ teaspoons baking powder
⅓ cup shortening
About ½ cup milk

Combine flour, salt, and baking powder; cut in shortening until mixture resembles coarse meal. Sprinkle milk over flour mixture; stir lightly until mixture forms a ball. Yield: pastry for seven 6-inch pies.
*Mrs. Ottis Watson,
Fayetteville, Arkansas.*

He Favors Hot, Spicy Dishes

After gaining fame among his friends for his Fried Onion Rings, Augusta, Georgia, attorney Trey Obenshain decided to take his cooking interest more seriously. Classes in gourmet, French, Italian, and Oriental cooking led him to his favorite—Szechwan-style Chinese.

For Szechwan Chicken, Trey combines hot peppers, onion, garlic, and Szechwan chili sauce to add a fiery flavor to a mixture of chicken, water chestnuts, and green peppers.

Following Trey's specialties you'll find recipes from other Southern men who love to cook.

MEXICAN RICE

1 cup chopped onion
¼ cup butter or margarine
4 cups cooked regular rice
1 (16-ounce) carton commercial sour cream
1 (8-ounce) carton cream-style cottage cheese
1 bay leaf, crumbled
½ teaspoon salt
¼ teaspoon pepper
3 (4-ounce) cans chopped green chiles, drained
2 cups (8 ounces) shredded sharp Cheddar cheese

Sauté onion in butter in a large saucepan until tender. Remove from heat; stir in rice, sour cream, cottage cheese, bay leaf, salt, and pepper.

Spoon half the rice mixture into a lightly greased 2-quart casserole. Top with half the chiles and cheese. Repeat layers, except for cheese.

Bake at 375°, uncovered, 20 minutes. Sprinkle with remaining cheese; bake an additional 5 minutes. Yield: 8 to 10 servings.

SZECHWAN CHICKEN

¼ cup soy sauce
1 tablespoon cornstarch
10 chicken thighs, skinned, boned, and diced
¼ cup vegetable oil
1 medium-size green pepper, coarsely chopped
1 medium onion, coarsely chopped
1 (8-ounce) can sliced water chestnuts, drained
2 hot peppers, seeded and chopped
2 cloves garlic, minced
1 teaspoon chopped fresh gingerroot
2 tablespoons soy sauce
2 tablespoons cornstarch
1 tablespoon sugar
1 teaspoon dried crushed red pepper
¼ cup plus 1 tablespoon water
1 tablespoon vinegar
1 tablespoon Chablis or other dry white wine
2 teaspoons Szechwan chili sauce
Hot cooked rice

Combine ¼ cup soy sauce and 1 tablespoon cornstarch in a large bowl; stir in chicken, and let stand 30 minutes.

Pour oil around top of preheated wok, coating sides. Allow to heat at medium high (325°) 2 minutes. Add undrained chicken, and stir-fry about 2 to 3 minutes until chicken is lightly browned. Remove chicken; reserving pan drippings in wok. Set chicken aside.

Add next 6 ingredients; stir-fry 2 minutes. Combine next 8 ingredients, mixing well; add to vegetable mixture in wok. Add chicken; cook, stirring constantly, until thickened. Serve over rice. Yield: 6 to 8 servings.

FRIED ONION RINGS

2 large Spanish onions
3 cups all-purpose flour
1½ teaspoons baking powder
2 teaspoons salt
¼ teaspoon pepper
3 eggs
1 cup milk
Vegetable oil

Peel onions; cut into ¼-inch slices, and separate into rings.

Combine next 4 ingredients; stir well. Combine eggs and milk in a separate bowl; beat well. Dip onion rings into flour mixture, then into egg mixture, and back into flour mixture. Fry onion rings in deep hot oil (375°) until golden brown. Drain on paper towels. Yield: 6 to 8 servings.

OPEN-FACE PIZZA SANDWICHES

2 cups biscuit mix
½ cup cold water
1 pound ground beef
¼ cup chopped onion
2 tablespoons chopped green pepper
2 (6-ounce) cans tomato paste
½ cup grated Parmesan cheese
1 teaspoon dried whole oregano
½ teaspoon salt
⅛ teaspoon pepper
2 to 3 tomatoes, thinly sliced
4 (8- x 4-inch) slices mozzarella cheese

Combine biscuit mix and water; stir until a soft dough is formed. Divide dough in half. Using floured hands, pat each half into a 16- x 4-inch rectangle on a greased baking sheet. Bake at 450° for 10 to 15 minutes or until lightly browned.

Combine next 3 ingredients in a heavy skillet; cook until beef is browned and vegetables are tender, stirring to crumble meat. Drain well. Add next 5 ingredients, and stir well.

Spoon beef mixture evenly over each pizza crust, leaving a ¼-inch border around edges. Bake pizza at 350° for 10 minutes. Arrange tomato slices over pizza; top with cheese slices. Bake 5 minutes until cheese melts. Yield: 6 servings.
O. W. Dollison,
Albany, Georgia.

COMPANY BEEF STEW

1 cup Burgundy or other dry red wine
1 clove garlic, minced
1 bay leaf
2 whole cloves
1 teaspoon salt
½ teaspoon freshly ground pepper
¼ teaspoon dried whole thyme
2 pounds lean beef for stewing, cut into 1-inch cubes
¼ cup olive oil
2 (10½-ounce) cans beef broth, undiluted
12 small boiling onions
12 fresh mushroom caps
3 carrots, cut into 2-inch slices
1 (10-ounce) package frozen green beans

Combine first 7 ingredients; mix well. Pour over beef in a shallow baking dish; cover and refrigerate overnight.

Drain meat, reserving marinade. Discard bay leaf and cloves. Heat oil in a Dutch oven over medium heat; brown beef in oil. Add broth and reserved marinade; bring to a boil. Cover, reduce heat, and simmer 1½ hours. Add onions, mushrooms, and carrots; cover and cook 30 minutes. Stir in beans; cover and cook 15 minutes. Yield: 6 servings.
Andrew Heatwole,
Virginia Beach, Virginia.

SWEET POTATO POUND CAKE

½ cup shortening
½ cup butter or margarine, softened
2 cups sugar
6 eggs
3 cups all-purpose flour
½ teaspoon salt
¼ teaspoon baking soda
1 teaspoon baking powder
1 cup buttermilk
1 cup cooked pureed sweet potatoes
½ teaspoon almond extract
¼ teaspoon coconut extract
¼ cup slivered almonds, toasted and finely chopped
¼ cup flaked coconut

Cream shortening and butter; add sugar, beating well. Add eggs, one at a time, beating after each addition. Combine next 4 ingredients, stirring well; add to creamed mixture alternately with buttermilk, beginning and ending with flour mixture. Stir in sweet potatoes and flavorings.

Grease and flour a 10-inch Bundt pan; sprinkle almonds and coconut over bottom. Pour batter into pan; bake at 350° for 1 hour and 15 minutes. Cool 10 minutes; remove from pan. Yield: one 10-inch cake.
Brent Elswick,
Betsy Layne, Kentucky.

CAULIFLOWER QUICHE

1 unbaked 9-inch pastry shell
1½ cups cooked regular rice
2 cups cauliflower flowerets, coarsely
   chopped
1 cup milk
2 eggs, beaten
1 cup (4 ounces) shredded sharp Cheddar
   cheese
1 tablespoon fine, dry breadcrumbs
½ teaspoon salt
⅛ teaspoon white pepper
Pinch of ground nutmeg

Line a 9-inch quiche dish with pastry; trim excess pastry around edge. Prick bottom and sides of pastry with fork. Bake at 400° for 3 minutes; remove from oven, and gently prick with a fork. Bake 5 minutes. Let cool on rack.

Gently press rice on bottom and sides of pastry shell.

Steam cauliflower 10 minutes or until crisp-tender. Spoon into pastry.

Combine remaining ingredients; pour over cauliflower. Bake at 375° for 30 to 35 minutes. Yield: one 9-inch quiche.

Tony Jones,
Atlanta, Georgia.

Fresh Vegetables With Ease

When it comes to preparing fresh vegetables, the simplest way is often the best. Simplicity is the key to Almond Asparagus, Sautéed Zucchini, and these other vegetable ideas. Not only do you taste more fresh flavor, but the reduced cooking time preserves the color and nutrients.

You'll minimize loss of thiamine, vitamin C, and other important nutrients if you steam vegetables or cook them in only a small amount of boiling water. Either way, add vegetables to the pan after the water is boiling, and quickly return the water to a boil. Cover the saucepan, and cook until just tender.

ALMOND ASPARAGUS

1 pound fresh asparagus spears
2 tablespoons butter or margarine
1 tablespoon lemon juice
½ cup slivered almonds, toasted
⅛ teaspoon salt
Dash of pepper

Snap off tough ends of asparagus, and remove scales from stalks with a knife or vegetable peeler.

Melt butter in a large skillet; add asparagus, and sauté 3 to 4 minutes. Cover skillet; simmer 2 minutes or until asparagus is crisp-tender. Add remaining ingredients; toss gently. Yield: 4 servings. *Georgia F. Chapman,*
Bedford, Virginia.

SAUCY CABBAGE WEDGES

1 medium head cabbage
⅓ cup mayonnaise
¼ cup milk
1 tablespoon plus 1 teaspoon vinegar
1 teaspoon sugar
½ teaspoon prepared mustard

Cut cabbage into 8 wedges, removing core. Cover and cook in a small amount of boiling water 8 to 10 minutes or until crisp-tender. Drain well; arrange wedges on a serving platter.

Combine mayonnaise and milk in a small saucepan, stirring until smooth; stir in vinegar, sugar, and mustard. Cook over low heat, stirring constantly, until thoroughly heated. Spoon over cabbage wedges. Yield: 8 servings.

Marion Gilmore,
Lake Placid, Florida.

CARROTS IN BRANDY SAUCE

3 cups sliced carrots
2 tablespoons butter or margarine
2 tablespoons all-purpose flour
1 cup chicken broth
2 tablespoons brandy
¼ cup diced green pepper
1 teaspoon diced onion
½ teaspoon chopped fresh parsley

Cook carrots, covered, in a small amount of boiling salted water for 18 to 20 minutes or until tender; drain.

Melt butter in a heavy saucepan over low heat; add flour, stirring until smooth. Cook 1 minute, stirring constantly. Gradually add broth; cook over medium heat, stirring constantly, until thickened and bubbly. Stir in brandy. Gently stir in carrots and remaining ingredients; cook until thoroughly heated. Yield: 4 to 6 servings.

Mrs. Rodger Giles,
Augusta, Georgia.

CREOLE EGGPLANT

1 small onion, chopped
1 small green pepper, chopped
1 (8-ounce) can tomato sauce
1 clove garlic, minced
½ teaspoon salt
¼ teaspoon dried whole oregano
¼ teaspoon pepper
¼ teaspoon hot sauce
1 small eggplant, peeled and coarsely
   chopped

Combine first 8 ingredients in a heavy skillet; cover and cook over low heat 10 minutes. Stir in eggplant; cover and cook an additional 20 minutes, stirring occasionally. Yield: 4 servings.

Patrick I. Greer,
Meridian, Mississippi.

SAUTEED ZUCCHINI

1 small onion, chopped
2 tablespoons vegetable oil
1 cup sliced fresh mushrooms
1 pound zucchini, sliced
1 teaspoon salt
¼ teaspoon pepper
½ teaspoon dried whole thyme
¼ cup grated Parmesan cheese

Sauté onion in hot oil until tender. Add next 5 ingredients; cook over low heat, stirring often, 5 to 7 minutes or until zucchini is crisp-tender. Sprinkle with cheese, and serve immediately. Yield: 4 servings. *Judy Hamby,*
Montgomery, Alabama.

MICROWAVE COOKERY

Speed Up Dinner With Microwave Casseroles

Casseroles are perfect for quick, one-dish meals, and with a microwave, they can be even more convenient.

For a casserole that starts with raw vegetables, cook the vegetables in a small amount of water until done, then stir them into the remaining casserole ingredients. This method promotes even cooking because you can stir the vegetables as they cook.

Following are some additional pointers for cooking casseroles in your microwave oven.

—You can convert almost any favorite recipe to microwave cooking. The best way to adapt a recipe is to compare its ingredients, cooking times, and temperature setting with a microwave recipe that is similar.

—Less evaporation takes place when microwaving than when cooking conventionally, so reduce the amount of liquid when converting a recipe for the microwave oven. Seasonings may also need to be reduced since there is less liquid to dilute them.

—When preparing casseroles, cut ingredients into a similar size and shape to promote even cooking. Also, rotate the dish periodically during cooking to ensure even doneness.

—Microwave any casserole that contains cheese or sour cream at less than full power. MEDIUM HIGH (70% power) is usually low enough to cook without overcooking or curdling. If a casserole calls for cheese sprinkled over the top, add it during the last few minutes of cooking.

—Casseroles do not brown or develop a crisp topping in the microwave oven. A sprinkling of cracker crumbs over a casserole will simulate a crisp, browned crust, if desired.

—Many casseroles continue to cook after the microwave cycle is complete, so let them stand as the recipe directs before checking for doneness. If they are still not done after standing, microwave again briefly.

MEXI CASSEROLE

1 pound ground beef
¾ cup chopped onion
½ cup chopped celery
1 teaspoon seasoned salt
½ teaspoon pepper
1½ teaspoons chili powder
1 (12-ounce) can whole kernel corn, drained
1 (15½-ounce) can red kidney beans, drained
½ cup sliced ripe olives
1 (8-ounce) can tomato sauce
½ cup (2 ounces) shredded Cheddar cheese
½ cup coarsely crushed corn chips

Combine ground beef, onion, and celery in a 2½-quart casserole. Cover with heavy-duty plastic wrap, and microwave at HIGH for 5 to 7 minutes or until meat is done; stir twice. Drain.

Stir in next 7 ingredients; microwave at HIGH for 4 to 5 minutes, giving dish a half turn after 3 minutes. Sprinkle with cheese, then corn chips. Microwave at MEDIUM HIGH (70% power) for 1 minute or until cheese melts. Yield: 6 servings.

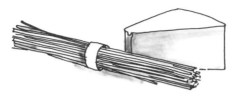

CHEESY CHICKEN TETRAZZINI

6 cups water
½ teaspoon salt
1 tablespoon olive oil
1 (7-ounce) package spaghetti
4 chicken breast halves, skinned and boned
1 cup water
¼ teaspoon salt
⅛ teaspoon pepper
¼ cup butter or margarine
1 medium-size green pepper, chopped
2½ tablespoons all-purpose flour
1 cup milk
1 (10¾-ounce) can cream of mushroom soup, undiluted
1 (2-ounce) jar diced pimiento
⅛ teaspoon garlic powder
¼ cup dry white wine
1 (4-ounce) can sliced mushrooms, drained
½ cup grated Parmesan cheese
3 cups (12 ounces) shredded process American cheese, divided
½ cup sliced almonds

Combine first 3 ingredients in a 12- x 8- x 2-inch baking dish. Cover with heavy-duty plastic wrap, and microwave at HIGH for 10 minutes. Add spaghetti; cover with heavy-duty plastic wrap, and microwave at HIGH for 6 minutes, stirring after 4 minutes. Let stand 3 minutes; drain well, and set aside.

Cut chicken into ¼-inch cubes. Combine chicken, 1 cup water, ¼ teaspoon salt, and pepper in a 1½-quart casserole. Cover with heavy-duty plastic wrap; microwave at MEDIUM HIGH (70% power) for 6 to 9 minutes or until done. Drain chicken.

Combine butter and green pepper in a 2-quart dish. Cover with heavy-duty plastic wrap, and microwave at HIGH for 4 minutes or until crisp-tender. Add flour, and stir well. Stir in next 7 ingredients and 2 cups shredded cheese. Cover with heavy-duty plastic wrap, and microwave at MEDIUM HIGH for 6 to 8 minutes or until thoroughly heated, stirring twice.

Spread half of spaghetti in a greased 12- x 8- x 2-inch baking dish; spread half of chicken mixture evenly over spaghetti. Repeat layers once using remaining spaghetti and chicken mixture. Sprinkle remaining cheese over casserole; top with almonds. Cover with heavy-duty plastic wrap, and microwave at MEDIUM HIGH for 5 minutes or until heated, giving dish a half turn after 3 minutes. Yield: 8 to 10 servings.

HAM-AND-POTATO CASSEROLE

2 cups cubed potatoes
1 cup sliced carrots
1 cup chopped celery
½ cup water
2 cups cubed cooked ham
2 tablespoons chopped green pepper
2 tablespoons chopped onion
3 tablespoons butter or margarine
¼ cup butter or margarine
3 tablespoons all-purpose flour
1½ cups milk
½ cup (2 ounces) shredded Cheddar cheese
½ teaspoon salt
⅛ teaspoon pepper
4 round buttery crackers, crushed

Combine potatoes, carrots, celery, and water in a 1½-quart glass bowl. Cover with heavy-duty plastic wrap; microwave at HIGH for 7 to 8 minutes or until crisp-tender, stirring once. Drain and set aside.

Combine ham, green pepper, onion, and 3 tablespoons butter in a 1-quart glass bowl. Microwave at HIGH for 3 to 4 minutes or until green pepper is tender, stirring once. Combine potato mixture and ham mixture in a deep, greased 2-quart casserole; stir well.

Place ¼ cup butter in a 4-cup glass measure. Microwave at HIGH for 55 seconds or until melted. Add flour; stir until smooth. Gradually add milk, stirring well. Microwave at HIGH for 3 to 5 minutes or until thickened and bubbly, stirring at 1-minute intervals. Add cheese, salt, and pepper; stir until cheese melts. Pour cheese sauce over ham mixture; sprinkle with cracker crumbs. Microwave at MEDIUM HIGH (70% power) for 8 to 9 minutes, turning once. Yield: 4 to 6 servings.

Tip: Reheat single servings in a microwave or toaster oven; these use less energy than a standard range.

Talk About Good!

Come to New Orleans. Direct your cabbie to 416 Chartres Street and prepare to stand in line. K-Paul's Louisiana Kitchen is open for dinner.

While you stand outside studying the handwritten menu, you'll make friends with the truly hungry. At each opening, the door exhales a tangible temptation. By the time you're welcomed in, you are willing to submit.

At the back, wearing denim overalls and a "Totally Hot" button, Chef Paul Prudhomme guards his kitchen door. At one elbow is a diet pop—Paul's one concession to his "joy proportions"—and at the other, a tongue-tickling lemon. He intercepts a plate of Blackened Redfish, places a sliver in his mouth. The look that crosses his face is pure. "Taste," he says.

You taste. Smoky, tangy, tender as air—every fish ever caught should aspire to this condition.

Chef Paul smiles. His eyes take on some devilment. "Now. Taste again."

This time the smoke is subtler, and a faint sweetness has crept in. "It's different now," you might say.

"Of course it is." He sends the waiter for another plate. "That's the thing of Cajun food. Every bite tastes different, start to finish. Exciting. You wind up somewhere else from where you started. We got some stuffed soft-shell crawfish comin' in a minute. Talk about good . . . ."

Cajun Louisiana is the southern third of the state, 22 parishes (or 23, or 21, depending upon who tells you). The land is so flat that seawater sometimes travels 100 miles up the bayous. Roughly half is the familiar marsh, draped in moss and legend, and the other half is ripe wide farmland. From swamps and fields came the Cajun's ingredients: seafood and game in terrific abundance, sugar cane, rice, chickens and ducks, the inglorious crawfish, two vegetable crops every year—plus enough good spices to set it all afire.

These things, combined a million ways by people who knew how, created Cajun cooking. African, French, Spanish influences abound. Some dishes went to New Orleans, got dressed up, and evolved into Creole cuisine—which, Louisianians will tell you, is the same as Cajun, only different.

Yet Cajuns hold on to their style of cooking, and so to the taste of the old days, the bayous, before oil fields and bridges. Crowds of many thousands come to two dozen Louisiana festivals devoted to one food or the other, or to

Cajuns in general. K-Paul's is just one of the restaurants drawing two-hour lines. A trademarked flavor called Tabasco leaves Avery Island in tiny bottles with red caps, bound for tables everywhere. Cajun is alive, well, and hot.

"First You Make a Roux"

Miss Tootie Guirard is on the phone from Catahoula. "Well, honey," she says, "a good cook can cook anything you got. What you got?"

The word crawfish is mentioned.

"An étouffée, mm-*hmmm!*" The taste of it is audible on the line. A date is set, which Miss Tootie repeats three times. "Honey, I tell you," she says, "the charm of livin' over here is you don't know what day it is and you don't care."

"Over here" is just this side of the Atchafalaya levee, by the vast cypress swamp that bisects Cajun country. Under live oaks, in a rambling house with a tree growing through its porch roof, Miss Tootie and her clan gather for dinner.

"First you make a roux," Miss Tootie begins, as every Cajun must. The all-vital roux is a simple blend of flour and fat, cooked and stirred for an hour to a deep bubbling brown (or copper—again, depending). A good roux is the starting place for gumbos and gravies and countless *sauces piquantes.*

"Lock the front door," she says, "and take the receiver off the telephone hook if you plan to make a roux. You can't leave it, else it burns. If it burns, throw it out and start over." She stirs and stirs, adding pinches and dashes, searching in vain for a measuring cup. "I had one once," she says.

Dessert that evening is fresh blackberry pie with cream from a friend's cow, the music of crickets through the screen, and a story from Miss Tootie. When the Acadians were driven from Nova Scotia in the 1700's, it seems, the lobster was left to make the trip by land. The longer the lobster walked, the smaller he got. By the time he reached the bayou, he was shrunk down to crawfish size.

That Famous Red-Hot Smell

Until he died last summer, Walter Doré ran the general store on Avery Island with his wife Eula, who lives there still. The Dorés came there in 1952; managing the store was a nice step up from farming. Walter's enthusiasm for life was general. His love of hot food was specific.

For a family dinner in early spring, Walter concocted a *sauce piquante* with crabs and shrimp for 15. On the stove at the rear of his store, he began with a roux. "If a child come along and interrupt you while you makin' a roux," he said, "you got to whip him twice. Once for whatever he did, and once cause he made you burn the roux."

When the mixture was nutty brown, Walter added tomatoes so the sauce bubbled up crimson. He turned down the flame. "Now let it cook oh, say, one hour to two days. It'll make your tongue go crazy."

In their house a hundred yards away, Eula made her mother's best dessert. "We'd go to church first, come home, have the big Sunday dinner, then Mama would always make the *tarte à la bouilli,*" she remembered. "They made us children little bitty ones. Or pies, fruit pies, fresh peaches, fresh berries, when it was season. You could make pear pies like you do apple, with braided tops for company. A baked chicken or fried, or pork roast or beef—always two meats. And then this custard pie."

After the sweet-crusted *tarte* had cooled, Eula tried to explain the secret: "The dough—it needs the touch of a hand, you know? And good feelings, in the kitchen."

At dinner, Walter revealed that he learned how to cook about the time he learned to eat (provoking laughter all around). All tongues, it may be noted, went crazy.

Chef Paul Comes Home

The 13th child of a sharecropping family from Opelousas, Paul Prudhomme learned to cook at his mother's side and rose to celebrity at his own stove. Top chef for years at New Orleans' Commander's Palace, he struck out on his own with K-Paul's, determined to sell good Cajun food, inventively prepared.

On a little farm near Cankton, Paul's brother Elden lives with wife Odelia.

In pens near his house, Elden raises all the ducks, chickens, geese, and rabbits that are served in K-Paul's Louisiana Kitchen. He offers a huge fresh egg to Paul as evidence of his chickens' health.

"That's a serious egg, *mon frère*," says Paul.

Odelia says, "We got some duck egg too, Paul, how many you want?"

"Four dozen, how about."

"Nearly strawberry time, too," Elden puts in.

"I got a lady in Ponchatoula, her strawberries, they're red all the way to the heart," says Paul. "Put some cream on 'em, that's all you got to do."

"Mm-*hmmmm*," Odelia says. "It all depends how you hungry or not." And later, she tries (like Eula) to reach the truth of the matter. "If you interesting in cooking," she says, "and you like to do it, you learn something from everybody. But if somebody's not, why, you can't eat they cooking, cause it taste not a thing in this world. Can't get a taste from it no way.

"That ain't the way we eat, over here," she says. "We got to have a *taste*. That's what we like."

As Chef Paul Prudhomme likes to say, every taste in a Cajun meal is a brand-new experience. We've gathered some of the best recipes we could find in Louisiana, from Paul's traditional Red Beans and Rice and Seafood Gumbo to Miss Tootie Guirard's Crawfish Étouffée.

■ At K-Paul's Louisiana Kitchen, the menu changes every day, depending on what's fresh and what Chef Paul feels like serving. His Seafood Gumbo and Sautéed Seafood Platter present fish and shellfish in different fashions; Red Beans and Rice is the essence of tradition. Roast Duck With Sweet Potato-Eggplant Gravy may be the best duck you have ever prepared. And the Sweet Potato-Pecan Pie, topped with Chantilly Cream, is a specialty of Paul's sister, Enola.

RED BEANS AND RICE

1 pound dried red kidney beans
4 quarts water
¾ cup chopped onion
¾ cup chopped celery
¾ cup chopped green pepper
2 teaspoons minced garlic
½ cup butter or margarine
2 bay leaves
2 teaspoons salt
2 teaspoons Hungarian paprika
1 teaspoon dried whole thyme
½ teaspoon ground red pepper
½ teaspoon dried whole oregano
1 pound andouille sausage or smoked
   Polish sausage, cut into 1-inch pieces
½ cup finely chopped fresh parsley
Oven Rice

Sort and wash beans; place in a 6-quart Dutch oven. Cover with water 2 inches above beans; let soak overnight. Drain beans. Add 4 quarts water; bring to a boil. Reduce heat to medium; cook, uncovered, 1½ hours, stirring beans occasionally.

Sauté onion, celery, green pepper, and garlic in butter in a large skillet until tender. Stir sautéed vegetables and next 6 ingredients into beans; cook, uncovered, 1 hour, stirring occasionally and adding water if necessary.

Bake sausage at 350° for 20 minutes; drain well. Stir sausage into bean mixture. Cook, uncovered, 30 minutes, stirring occasionally. Remove bay leaves. Stir in chopped parsley. Serve over Oven Rice. Yield: 6 servings.

Oven Rice:

1½ cups uncooked regular rice
2½ cups chicken broth
1½ tablespoons finely chopped celery
1½ tablespoons finely chopped onion
1½ tablespoons finely chopped green
   pepper
1½ tablespoons butter or margarine
½ teaspoon salt
⅛ teaspoon garlic powder
Dash of ground red pepper
Pinch of white pepper

Combine all ingredients in a 2-quart baking dish, stirring well. Cover and bake at 350° for 1 hour or until all liquid is absorbed. Yield: 6 servings.

SAUTEED SEAFOOD PLATTER

18 medium shrimp with heads
3½ cups water
½ cup Worcestershire sauce
½ teaspoon minced garlic
½ teaspoon salt
1 tablespoon all-purpose flour
1½ cups unsalted butter, softened
¾ teaspoon salt
¼ teaspoon ground red pepper
⅛ teaspoon white pepper
⅛ teaspoon garlic powder
⅛ teaspoon onion powder
⅛ teaspoon Hungarian paprika
⅛ teaspoon dried whole thyme
⅛ teaspoon dried whole oregano
⅛ teaspoon black pepper
1 cup all-purpose flour
1 egg, beaten
1 cup milk
6 (4-ounce) fish fillets
Vegetable oil
3 tablespoons butter, divided
3 tablespoons chopped green onion,
   divided
1½ dozen fresh oysters, shucked
¼ pound fresh lump crabmeat

Remove shrimp heads and shells, reserving both. Devein shrimp, and set aside in refrigerator.

Combine 3½ cups water, shrimp heads, and shells in a 2-quart saucepan; bring to a boil. Reduce heat and simmer, uncovered, 30 minutes, adding additional water as necessary to maintain 3 cups liquid in pan. Strain the shrimp stock through layers of cheesecloth; discard all solids. Let stock cool. (Stock may be prepared early in the day and refrigerated until needed.)

Place 1 cup shrimp stock in a small saucepan, and bring to a boil; add Worcestershire sauce, ½ teaspoon minced garlic, and ½ teaspoon salt.

Combine 1 tablespoon flour and 1 tablespoon cooled shrimp stock, stirring until smooth; stir into stock mixture. Cook over medium heat until mixture thickens enough to coat a metal spoon.

Add butter, 3 to 4 tablespoons at a time, and stir with a wire whisk until butter melts and mixture is smooth. Simmer over low heat, uncovered, 1½ minutes, stirring occasionally. Cover and remove from heat; set aside.

Combine next 9 ingredients in a small bowl, stirring well. Combine 1 cup flour and ½ teaspoon seasoning mixture in a shallow bowl; set aside.

Combine egg, milk, and ⅛ teaspoon seasoning mixture in a shallow bowl; mix well.

Sprinkle fish fillets with seasoning mixture. Dredge in seasoned flour, and dip in egg mixture; dredge fillets in flour again.

Heat ½ inch oil in a large skillet to 350°; add fillets, and fry 4 to 5 minutes or until golden brown, turning once. Drain on paper towels. Place in a 250° oven to keep warm.

Sprinkle shrimp with seasoning mixture. Melt 1 tablespoon butter in a small skillet. Add 1 tablespoon green onion, 1 tablespoon shrimp stock, ⅛ teaspoon seasoning mixture, and shrimp; sauté 3 to 4 minutes or just until shrimp are pink. Remove from pan, and place in oven with fillets to keep warm.

Repeat seasoning and sautéing procedure with oysters (sauté 2 to 3 minutes) and crabmeat (sauté 1 to 2 minutes), using 1 tablespoon butter, 1 tablespoon green onion, 1 tablespoon shrimp stock, and ⅛ teaspoon seasoning mixture for each. (Reserve any remaining stock for another use.)

To serve, spoon about ⅓ cup sauce on each plate. Place a fish fillet on top of sauce; arrange 3 oysters and 3 shrimp on the side. Sprinkle fillets with crabmeat. Yield: 6 servings.

SEAFOOD GUMBO

1 pound fresh jumbo shrimp with heads
Carcasses or heads of 2 (3- to 5-pound) fish
1 medium onion, quartered
1 stalk celery, quartered
1 medium tomato, peeled and quartered
2 quarts water
3 tablespoons gumbo filé
1 teaspoon salt
½ teaspoon white pepper
½ teaspoon black pepper
1½ teaspoons ground red pepper
1½ teaspoons Hungarian paprika
1 teaspoon minced garlic
½ teaspoon dried whole thyme
½ teaspoon dried whole oregano
1 bay leaf, crushed
¾ cup butter or margarine
2 cups coarsely chopped onion
2 cups coarsely chopped celery
2 cups coarsely chopped green pepper
1 tablespoon hot sauce
1 (15-ounce) can tomato sauce with tomato bits
1 dozen fresh oysters, shucked
1½ cups flaked crabmeat
Hot cooked rice

Remove shrimp heads and shells, reserving both. Devein shrimp, and set aside in refrigerator. Combine shrimp heads and shells, fish carcasses, and next 4 ingredients in a 6-quart Dutch oven; bring to a boil. Reduce heat and simmer, uncovered, 6 to 8 hours. (Add water as necessary to maintain 2 quarts.) Strain stock through cheesecloth, discarding solids; set stock aside.

Combine next 10 ingredients; set aside.

Melt butter in a 4-quart Dutch oven over medium heat; stir in next 4 ingredients and seasoning mixture. Increase heat to high; cook 6 minutes, stirring constantly. Add tomato sauce; cook over medium heat 5 minutes, stirring constantly and scraping bottom. Stir in seafood stock; bring to a boil. Reduce heat and simmer, uncovered, 45 minutes to an hour, stirring occasionally. Stir in shrimp, oysters, and crabmeat; cover and turn off heat. Let stand 6 to 10 minutes or until edges of oysters curl and shrimp are pink. Serve over rice. Yield: about 2 quarts.

Tip: For ingredients listed in recipes: If the direction comes before the ingredient—for example, sifted flour—first sift the flour, then measure. If the direction comes after the ingredient—for example, pecans, chopped—first measure pecans, then chop.

ROAST DUCK WITH SWEET POTATO-EGGPLANT GRAVY

3 (4- to 5-pound) dressed ducklings
2 tablespoons salt
1 tablespoon garlic powder
1 tablespoon black pepper
1½ teaspoons white pepper
1½ teaspoons ground cumin
1½ teaspoons Hungarian paprika
1½ teaspoons onion powder
1 teaspoon ground red pepper
6 quarts cold water
2 onions, quartered
3 cups coarsely chopped onion, divided
3 cups uncooked regular rice
½ cup finely chopped green onion tops
2 cups diced peeled eggplant
4 cups diced sweet potatoes, divided
1¾ teaspoons salt
½ teaspoon ground red pepper
½ teaspoon black pepper
¼ teaspoon white pepper
¼ teaspoon garlic powder
⅛ teaspoon ground cumin
¾ cup sugar, divided
2 tablespoons Grand Marnier or other orange-flavored liqueur
1 teaspoon cornstarch
2 tablespoons cold water

Remove giblets and neck from ducklings; reserve for other uses. Prick fatty areas of duckling (not breast) with a fork at intervals. Combine next 8 ingredients; rub over surface and in cavity of each duckling. Fold neck skin under and place ducklings, breast side up, on a rack in large roasting pans. Bake, uncovered, at 325° for 2 hours and 45 minutes or until drumsticks and thighs move easily. Remove from oven; let cool to touch.

Remove ducklings from roasting pans, reserving ½ cup plus 2 tablespoons pan drippings. Split each duckling in half lengthwise. Carefully remove all bones, except the large bone in wing, keeping each half of duck intact and skin in place; set bones aside. Place ducklings on a platter, and keep warm. Reserve meat scraps remaining after boning ducklings.

Combine bones, 6 quarts water, and 2 onions in an 8-quart Dutch oven; bring to a boil. Continue to boil, uncovered, 1 hour or until stock is reduced to 1 gallon. Strain stock through layers of cheesecloth. Discard the bones and onion; set aside stock.

Heat ¼ cup reserved pan drippings in roasting pan used for ducklings (place pan over 2 heating elements, if necessary). Add 1 cup chopped onion; cook over medium heat, stirring occasionally, 15 to 20 minutes, or until onion is golden brown. Stir in rice; cook over medium heat 10 minutes, stirring constantly. Stir in 5 cups stock and reserved meat scraps. Cover and bake at 350° for 30 to 35 minutes or until all liquid is absorbed. Stir in green onion. Set rice aside, and keep warm.

Heat remaining ¼ cup plus 2 tablespoons pan drippings in a heavy 2-quart saucepan; add remaining 2 cups onion. Cook over medium heat, stirring occasionally, 15 to 20 minutes, or until onion is golden brown. Add eggplant and 2 cups sweet potatoes; cook over medium heat 10 to 15 minutes, stirring constantly, until potatoes are tender. Stir in next 6 ingredients and 2 quarts stock; reduce heat and simmer, uncovered, 20 minutes, stirring occasionally.

Cook ½ cup sugar in a small skillet over low heat, stirring constantly, about 8 to 10 minutes or until sugar dissolves and forms a smooth, caramel-colored liquid. Carefully stir caramelized sugar into potato mixture. (The mixture will foam.) Stir in remaining potatoes, remaining sugar, and Grand Marnier. Bring to a boil; reduce heat and simmer, uncovered, 10 minutes. Combine cornstarch and 2 tablespoons water, mixing until smooth; stir into potato mixture. Cook over medium-high heat, stirring constantly, until thickened.

Serve ducklings with rice and sweet potato-eggplant gravy. Yield: 6 servings.

SWEET POTATO-PECAN PIE

1 cup cooked, mashed sweet potato
1 tablespoon butter, softened
¼ cup firmly packed light brown sugar
1 tablespoon vanilla extract
¼ teaspoon ground cinnamon
⅛ teaspoon ground nutmeg
⅛ teaspoon ground allspice
¼ teaspoon salt
½ beaten egg
2 tablespoons sugar
1 tablespoon whipping cream
Pastry (recipe follows)
½ cup chopped pecans
¾ cup sugar
2 eggs
¾ cup dark corn syrup
1½ tablespoons butter, melted
Pinch of salt
Pinch of ground cinnamon
2 teaspoons vanilla extract
Chantilly Cream

Combine first 11 ingredients; beat at medium speed of an electric mixer until smooth. Spread on bottom of pastry shell; sprinkle with pecans.

Combine next 7 ingredients, beating well. Pour over pecans. Bake at 300° for 1½ hours. Cool. Top each slice with a dollop of Chantilly Cream. Yield: one 9-inch pie.

Pastry:

3 tablespoons butter, softened
2 tablespoons sugar
½ beaten egg
2 tablespoons milk
1 cup all-purpose flour

Cream butter and sugar, beating until light and fluffy. Add egg and milk; beat about 2 minutes. Add flour, stirring just until ingredients are moistened. Refrigerate dough at least 1 hour.

Roll dough out to a 14-inch circle on lightly floured waxed paper. Invert pastry and waxed paper onto a deep-dish 9-inch pieplate. Carefully remove waxed paper, and press pastry into pieplate. (Dough will be soft and fragile.) Yield: one 9-inch pastry shell.

Chantilly Cream:

¾ cup whipping cream
1 tablespoon plus 2 teaspoons sugar
1 teaspoon Grand Marnier or other orange-flavored liqueur
1 teaspoon Cognac

Combine whipping cream and sugar; beat at medium speed of electric mixer until foamy. Increase speed to high, and beat until soft peaks form. Add Grand Marnier and Cognac; beat just until blended. Yield: 1½ cups.

■ Chez Marcelle, a restaurant in Broussard, has become very popular with its *nouvelle* Cajun cooking—a lighter approach to old favorites. Crème d'Ange, a caramelized dessert that once was Marcelle's reward for a good report card, seems too delicious for such a simple recipe. Chef Joe Gonsoulin's Stuffed Soft-Shell Crabs are always a hit—when they're in season.

CREME D'ANGE

1 (14-ounce) can sweetened condensed milk
Whipped cream
Chopped pecans

Pour sweetened condensed milk into an 8-inch glass pieplate. Cover with foil.

Pour about ¼ inch hot water into a larger shallow pan. Place covered pieplate in pan. Bake at 425° for 1 hour and 20 minutes or until milk is thick and caramel colored (add hot water to pan as needed). Chill at least 2 hours. Garnish each serving with a dollop of whipped cream; sprinkle with chopped pecans. Yield: 5 servings.

STUFFED SOFT-SHELL CRABS

1 pound fresh lump crabmeat
½ cup dry white wine
1 bunch green onion with tops, finely chopped
1 clove garlic, minced
1 pound medium shrimp, peeled, deveined, and ground
3 cups stale bread cubes
½ pound fresh mushrooms, sliced
3 egg yolks, beaten
½ teaspoon salt
⅛ teaspoon ground red pepper
12 fresh jumbo soft-shell crabs
Salt and pepper
All-purpose flour
Peanut oil
Fresh parsley sprigs (optional)
Creolaise Sauce

Remove any cartilage or shell from lump crabmeat. Heat wine in a heavy skillet. Add green onion, garlic, shrimp, and crabmeat; cook until vegetables are tender, stirring frequently. Remove from heat. Stir in next 5 ingredients; chill at least 1 hour.

To clean crabs, remove spongy substance (gills) that lies under the tapering points on either side of back shell. Place crabs on back, and remove the small piece at lower part of shell that terminates in a point (the apron). Wash crabs thoroughly; drain well.

Stuff about ½ cup crabmeat-shrimp mixture into cavity of each crab; sprinkle lightly with salt and pepper, and dredge in flour. Fry crabs in deep hot peanut oil (320°) for 1 to 2 minutes. Drain well on paper towels.

Place crabs upside down on a serving platter; garnish with parsley sprigs, if desired. Serve with Creolaise Sauce. Yield: 12 crabs.

Creolaise Sauce:

About 1¼ cups butter
8 egg yolks
1 tablespoon water
Juice of 1 lemon
⅓ cup Creole-style mustard
3 dashes of hot sauce

Melt butter over low heat; let stand until milk solids settle to bottom. Skim off white froth on surface. Pour off clear, yellow liquid, leaving sediment in pan. Set aside 1 cup clarified butter.

Combine yolks and water in top of a double boiler; beat with a whisk until blended. Cook over warm water, stirring constantly, until thick and opaque.

Remove top of double boiler, and set in pan of cold water to stop cooking process. Gradually add clarified butter, stirring constantly. Stir in the lemon juice, mustard, and hot sauce. Yield: about 1½ cups.

■ Crawfish Étouffée, from the kitchen of Miss Tootie Guirard of Catahoula, is a Cajun classic prepared in her own relaxed style. Miss Tootie insists that the crawfish fat is the most essential ingredient in her étouffée—"that's where you get your taste," she says.

CRAWFISH ETOUFFEE

4 pounds crawfish tails with fat
Hot sauce to taste
Ground red pepper to taste
½ cup vegetable oil
½ cup all-purpose flour
4 stalks celery, chopped
4 large onions, chopped
4 large green peppers, chopped
1 bunch green onions with tops, chopped
½ cup water
1 teaspoon salt
½ teaspoon black pepper
¼ to ½ teaspoon ground red pepper
½ cup chopped fresh parsley
Hot cooked rice

Remove package of fat from crawfish tails; set aside. Sprinkle crawfish with hot sauce and red pepper; set aside.

Combine oil and flour in a 4-quart Dutch oven. Cook mixture over medium heat 10 to 15 minutes, stirring constantly, until roux is the color of a copper penny.

Stir in the next 4 ingredients; cook until vegetables are tender, stirring often. Add crawfish tails and ½ cup water; cook over low heat, uncovered, 15 minutes, stirring occasionally. Stir in 2 tablespoons crawfish fat (reserve remaining fat for other uses), salt, and pepper; simmer 5 minutes. Stir in parsley. Serve over rice. Yield: 12 servings.

■ Walter Doré, who ran Avery Island's general store, prepared a Crab and Shrimp Sauce Piquante that "makes your tongue go crazy." He only allowed one crab per person, but the recipe may serve more than 15. His wife Eula's Tarte à la Bouilli was her mother's special dessert—and makes enough custard for the family to get an extra taste.

CRAB AND SHRIMP SAUCE PIQUANTE

15 large live blue crabs
1 cup vegetable oil
¾ cup all-purpose flour
6 medium tomatoes, coarsely chopped
1 teaspoon sugar
3 pounds onion, chopped
2 large green peppers, chopped
3 stalks celery, chopped
4 cloves garlic, minced
3 (12-ounce) cans tomato paste
1 (8-ounce) can tomato sauce
1 (10-ounce) can tomatoes and green chiles, undrained
2 cups water
1 teaspoon hot sauce
½ teaspoon ground red pepper
4 bay leaves
Salt and pepper to taste
5 pounds jumbo shrimp, peeled and deveined
Hot cooked rice

Wash crabs under cold running water, removing all sand. Drop crabs, several at a time, into a large pot of boiling water. Cover and cook 5 to 10 minutes or until shells are bright red. Remove the crabs, and set aside to cool. Repeat with remaining crabs.

Break off crab claws, and crack; set aside. Place each crab on its back; remove and discard the small piece at lower part of shell that terminates to a point (the apron). Remove fat beneath apron and set aside. Holding crab in both hands, insert thumb under shell by the apron hinge; remove and discard top shell. Remove the spongy substance (gills) that lies under the tapering points on either side of crab back. Set crab body aside.

Combine oil and flour in a 20-quart kettle; cook over very low heat about 45 minutes, stirring constantly, until roux is the color of light peanut butter.

Add tomatoes, sugar, onion, green peppers, celery, and garlic to roux, stirring well. Cook over low heat 5 minutes, stirring frequently. Stir in next 4 ingredients; simmer, uncovered, 10 minutes, stirring frequently. Add crab fat,

hot sauce, red pepper, bay leaves, salt, and pepper; cover and simmer 2 to 2½ hours, stirring occasionally.

Add crab claws; cover and simmer 5 minutes. Add crabs; cover and simmer an additional 10 minutes. Stir in shrimp; cover and simmer 30 minutes, stirring mixture occasionally.

Remove from heat; uncover and let stand 10 minutes. Remove bay leaves. Serve over rice. Yield: 15 servings.

TARTE A LA BOUILLI

1 quart milk
2 egg yolks
1 cup sugar
1 (13-ounce) can evaporated milk
1 teaspoon vanilla extract
¾ cup all-purpose flour
¼ cup butter
¼ cup butter, softened
1 cup sugar
2 cups all-purpose flour
1 teaspoon baking powder
¼ cup milk
1 teaspoon vanilla extract
2 tablespoons all-purpose flour

Scald 1 quart milk in a heavy Dutch oven; set aside.

Beat egg yolks until thick and lemon colored at low speed of electric mixer; add 1 cup sugar, and beat well. Add evaporated milk and 1 teaspoon vanilla, mixing well at low speed of electric mixer. Stir in ¾ cup flour.

Gradually stir about one-fourth of hot milk into egg mixture; add to remaining hot milk, stirring constantly. Cook over medium heat about 15 minutes, stirring constantly, until thick and smooth. Gently stir in ¼ cup butter, and remove from heat.

Cream ¼ cup softened butter; gradually add 1 cup sugar, beating well. Add 2 cups flour and baking powder, beating at low speed of electric mixer until mixture resembles coarse meal. Add ¼ cup milk and vanilla, stirring until well blended. (Dough will be crumbly at first but will form a smooth ball with continued mixing.) Turn dough out, and knead 4 or 5 times. Divide in half.

Sprinkle 2 tablespoons flour on waxed paper; press one portion of dough into a 14-inch circle. Carefully transfer pastry (floured side down) to a buttered 9-inch deep-dish pieplate. Fill pastry shell with custard, reserving 1¼ cups custard. Place remaining dough on waxed paper; press into an 11-inch circle. Carefully place pastry over filling. (Do not slit top crust.) Seal and flute

edges. Bake at 350° for 35 minutes or until browned. Cool.

Spoon the reserved custard into individual serving dishes; chill and serve as desired. Yield: one 9-inch pie and 1¼ cups custard.

Appetizers Open The Party

Wanda Wood, of Memphis, spends a lot of time coming up with new recipes. "I love to have parties, so my favorite creations are appetizers," she says. The result is a hot appetizer dip with broccoli, mushrooms, hot sauce, onion, and garlic cheese.

CHEESY BROCCOLI DIP

1 (10-ounce) package frozen chopped broccoli
¼ cup sliced fresh mushrooms
¼ cup chopped celery
¼ cup chopped onion
3 tablespoons butter or margarine
1 (10¾-ounce) can cream of mushroom soup, undiluted
1 (6-ounce) roll process cheese food with garlic, cut into cubes
Dash of hot sauce

Cook broccoli according to package directions; drain well, and set aside.

Sauté mushrooms, celery, and onion in butter in a large skillet until tender. Add broccoli and remaining ingredients; cook over low heat, stirring until cheese melts. Serve warm with corn chips. Yield: about 3 cups. *Wanda Wood, Memphis, Tennessee.*

QUICK PARTY MIX

¼ cup butter or margarine, melted
1 (12-ounce) can mixed nuts
¼ cup grated Parmesan cheese
Dash of ground celery seeds
Dash of garlic powder
¼ teaspoon dried whole oregano
4 cups honey graham cereal

Combine all ingredients in a large mixing bowl; stir well. Place in a 15- x 10- x 1-inch jellyroll pan; bake at 300° for 15 minutes. Cool completely, and store in an airtight container. Yield: 5½ cups. *Ramona Land, Live Oak, Florida.*

ALOHA SPREAD

1 (8-ounce) package cream cheese, softened
1 cup drained, crushed pineapple
1 cup flaked coconut
1½ teaspoons ground ginger
2 teaspoons lemon juice
½ cup chopped pecans

Beat cream cheese until light and fluffy. Add remaining ingredients, mixing well. Chill. Serve with crackers. Yield: 2¼ cups. *Mrs. John W. Betts, Virginia Beach, Virginia.*

DILLED CAULIFLOWER

1 medium head cauliflower
¾ cup Italian reduced-calorie salad dressing
1 tablespoon chopped pimiento
1 tablespoon finely chopped onion
½ teaspoon whole dried dillweed

Wash cauliflower, and break into flowerets. Cook, covered, in a small amount of boiling salted water about 8 to 10 minutes or until crisp-tender; drain. Place in a shallow dish.

Combine remaining ingredients, mixing well. Pour marinade over cauliflower, and toss lightly. Cover and chill at least 4 hours, stirring occasionally. Drain before serving. Yield: 18 appetizer servings. *Mrs. A. J. Amador, Decatur, Alabama.*

MINIATURE BACON-CHEESE QUICHE

1 egg, beaten
½ cup milk
¼ teaspoon salt
Pinch of pepper
½ cup (2 ounces) shredded Cheddar cheese
2 slices bacon, cooked and crumbled
2½ tablespoons minced onion
1 tablespoon minced green pepper
Pastry shells (recipe follows)

Combine first 8 ingredients; stir well, and pour into prepared pastry shells. Bake at 350° for 20 minutes. Yield: 2½ dozen.

Pastry Shells:

1 (3-ounce) package cream cheese, softened
½ cup butter or margarine, softened
1½ cups all-purpose flour

Combine cream cheese and butter, creaming until smooth. Add flour, and mix well.

Shape dough into thirty 1-inch balls. Place dough balls in lightly greased 1¾-inch muffin pans; shape each into a shell. Prick bottom and sides of pastry shell with a fork; bake at 400° for 5 minutes. Let cool on a rack. Yield: 2½ dozen. *Mary Windell, Fort Mill, South Carolina.*

ZESTY ANCHOVY APPETIZERS

2 cups (8 ounces) shredded Swiss cheese
1 (2-ounce) can flat anchovies, drained and minced
1 tablespoon minced fresh parsley
1 tablespoon mayonnaise
1 tablespoon lemon juice
⅛ teaspoon pepper
1 (8-ounce) loaf sliced party rye bread

Combine first 6 ingredients; mix well. Spread 1 scant tablespoon cheese mixture on each slice of bread. Broil 2 minutes; serve hot. Yield: about 3 dozen.
Note: Cheese mixture may be frozen. Chill well; shape into a log about 1½ inches in diameter. Wrap securely, and freeze. To serve, thaw cheese and cut into ¼-inch slices; place on bread, and broil 2 minutes. *Ella C. Stivers, Abilene, Texas.*

CRAB SNACKS

1 (6½-ounce) can crabmeat, drained and flaked
1 (5-ounce) jar sharp process cheese spread
¼ cup butter or margarine, softened
1½ teaspoons mayonnaise
6 English muffins, split
Paprika

Combine first 4 ingredients; mix well. Spread on each muffin half; sprinkle with paprika. Cut each muffin half into quarters. Broil 3 minutes or until lightly browned. Yield: 4 dozen.
Note: Crab Snacks may be frozen. Wrap each muffin half in aluminum foil and freeze. Remove from freezer; thaw. Cut into quarters before broiling. *Margot Foster, Hubbard, Texas.*

Pimientos Pack Color And Flavor

Want to add sparkle to plain vegetables or routine rice? Then spoon on some diced pimiento; the bright-red color will perk up any dish.

SAVORY PILAF

1 cup uncooked regular rice
1 medium onion, chopped
1 medium-size green pepper, chopped
¼ cup plus 2 tablespoons butter or margarine, melted
1 (10¾-ounce) can chicken broth, diluted
1 (4-ounce) can mushroom stems and pieces, undrained
1 (4-ounce) jar diced pimiento, undrained
¼ teaspoon powdered saffron (optional)
2 tablespoons grated Parmesan cheese (optional)

Sauté rice, onion, and green pepper in butter in a 2-quart casserole until rice is golden brown. Remove from heat; stir in next 3 ingredients. Add saffron, if desired. Cover and bake at 350° for 55 minutes or until liquid is absorbed. Sprinkle cheese over top, if desired; bake 5 additional minutes. Yield: 6 servings. *Stanley L. Evans II, Bidwell, Ohio.*

PIMIENTO CHEESE SPREAD

2 cups (8 ounces) shredded Cheddar cheese
1 (4-ounce) jar diced pimiento, undrained
½ teaspoon prepared mustard
2 tablespoons mayonnaise

Combine all ingredients; mix well. Cover and refrigerate. Yield: 1½ cups. *Debra Rich, Vancouver, Washington.*

PIMIENTO TOPPING

2 (4-ounce) jars diced pimiento, undrained
½ cup cracker crumbs
½ cup grated Parmesan cheese
½ cup finely chopped, unsalted peanuts
½ cup finely chopped fresh mushrooms
½ cup butter or margarine, melted

Combine all ingredients, mixing well. Spoon over cooked asparagus, broccoli, or cauliflower. Broil 3 minutes. Yield: 2 cups. *Mrs. T. J. Compton, Lampasas, Texas.*

From Our Kitchen To Yours

Quite often there's a fine line between refrigerated items that are safe to eat and those that need to be thrown out. Our storage chart for the refrigerator will show you how long you can safely keep products such as milk, cottage cheese, mayonnaise, fish, and meats on hand.

See March, page 65, for a chart on safe food storage in the pantry.

REFRIGERATOR

Food Item	Length of Storage
MEATS	
Fresh beef, lamb, pork, and veal	
roasts	3 to 5 days
steaks, chops	3 days
ribs	2 days
stew meat	2 days
ground meat	1 to 2 days
Processed meats (after package is opened)	
hams, whole and half	7 days
bacon	5 to 7 days
frankfurters	4 to 5 days
luncheon meats, sliced	3 days
Fresh fish	1 to 2 days
Poultry	1 to 2 days
DAIRY	
Butter and margarine	1 month
Buttermilk	1 to 2 weeks
Cheese (opened)	
hard cheese: Cheddar, Swiss	3 to 4 weeks
Parmesan, grated	1 year
soft cheese: cream, Neufchâtel	2 weeks
cottage cheese	5 to 7 days or date on package
Eggs	1 month
Half-and-half	7 to 10 days
Milk, whole and skimmed	1 week
Sour cream	3 to 4 weeks
Whipping cream	7 to 10 days
Yogurt	10 days or date on package
CANNED FOODS (Opened)	
Fruit	5 to 7 days
Jams and jellies	6 months
Mayonnaise	1 to 2 months
Meats	1 to 2 days
Pickles	2 to 3 months
Vegetables	2 to 3 days

FRESH FRUIT AND VEGETABLES

Most fresh fruit is best used within 3 to 5 days. Apples maintain freshness about 3 weeks and citrus fruits 10 days to 2 weeks. Try to use fresh vegetables as soon as possible after purchasing or after picking from the garden. Corn in the husk will only hold up 1 day in the refrigerator. Carrots and radishes will last 2 to 3 weeks, but most other vegetables should be eaten within 3 to 7 days. (Can or freeze vegetables the day they are bought or picked.)

Bite Into A Fresh, Hot Doughnut

It's easy to mix up a batch of homemade doughnuts—just try our Pineapple Drop Doughnuts and see. Drop a spoonful of batter into hot oil, and cook until browned; drain and sprinkle with powdered sugar. For our Chocolate Doughnuts, you'll want to make sure you save the holes. Dip the doughnuts and the holes in our cinnamon-flavored sugar glaze and enjoy.

We think you'll love velvety Glazed Doughnuts. The secret to their featherlight texture is bread flour.

GLAZED DOUGHNUTS

1 package dry yeast
2 tablespoons warm water (105° to 115°)
¾ cup warm milk (105° to 115°)
¼ cup sugar
½ teaspoon salt
½ teaspoon ground nutmeg
⅛ teaspoon ground cinnamon
1 egg
3 tablespoons shortening
2½ cups bread flour, divided
Vegetable oil
Glaze (recipe follows)

Dissolve yeast in warm water in a large mixing bowl. Add next 7 ingredients and 1 cup flour; beat at medium speed of an electric mixer about 2 minutes until blended. Stir in remaining flour.

Cover and let rise in a warm place (85°), free from drafts, 1 hour or until doubled in bulk.

Punch dough down; turn out onto a well-floured surface, and knead several times until smooth and elastic. Roll dough out to ½-inch thickness; cut with a 2½-inch doughnut cutter. Place doughnuts on a lightly floured surface. Cover and let rise in a warm place, free from drafts, 30 minutes or until doubled in bulk.

Heat 2 to 3 inches of oil to 375°; drop in 4 or 5 doughnuts at a time. Cook about 1 minute or until golden on one side; turn and cook other side about 1 minute. Drain well. Dip each doughnut in glaze while warm; cool on wire racks. Yield: 1½ dozen.

Glaze:
2 cups sifted powdered sugar
¼ cup milk

Combine ingredients, and stir until smooth. Yield: 1 cup. *Charlie Payne, Birmingham, Alabama.*

CHOCOLATE DOUGHNUTS

2 eggs
1¼ cups sugar
¼ cup vegetable oil
1 teaspoon vanilla extract
4 cups all-purpose flour
⅓ cup cocoa
1 tablespoon plus 1 teaspoon baking
   powder
1 teaspoon ground cinnamon
¾ teaspoon salt
¼ teaspoon baking soda
¾ cup buttermilk
Vegetable oil
Glaze (recipe follows)

Beat eggs with electric mixer at medium speed until frothy. Gradually add sugar, beating until mixture is thick and lemon-colored; stir in ¼ cup vegetable oil and vanilla extract.

Combine next 6 ingredients; add to egg mixture alternately with buttermilk, beginning and ending with flour mixture. Cover dough; chill several hours.

Divide dough in half. Working with one portion at a time, place dough on a lightly floured surface; roll out to ½-inch thickness. Cut dough with a floured 2½-inch doughnut cutter.

Heat 2 to 3 inches of oil to 375°; drop in 4 or 5 doughnuts at a time. Cook about 1 minute or until golden on one side; turn and cook other side about 1 minute. Drain well on paper towels. Dip each doughnut in glaze; cool on waxed paper. Yield: 2 dozen.

Glaze:

4 cups sifted powdered sugar
½ teaspoon ground cinnamon
1 teaspoon vanilla extract
¼ cup plus 2 tablespoons milk

Combine all ingredients, and beat until smooth. Yield: about 2 cups.
Mrs. Roderick W. McGrath,
Orlando, Florida.

PINEAPPLE DROP DOUGHNUTS

3 cups all-purpose flour
¾ cup sugar
2 tablespoons baking powder
¾ teaspoon salt
3 eggs, beaten
1 cup milk
1 (20-ounce) can crushed pineapple,
   drained
Vegetable oil
Powdered sugar

Combine first 4 ingredients, mixing well. Add next 3 ingredients, stirring until smooth.

Heat 3 to 4 inches oil to 375°; carefully drop batter by heaping tablespoonfuls into hot oil, cooking 5 or 6 doughnuts at a time. Cook 1 minute or until golden on one side; turn and cook other side about 1 minute. Drain well on paper towels; sprinkle with powdered sugar. Yield: 3 dozen.
Mrs. Daniel F. Citak,
Titusville, Florida.

Oats—More Than A Cereal

Oats make a nutritious, hot breakfast cereal, but you can do a lot more with oats than just cook them into a cereal. Stir oats into waffle batter with whole wheat flour, honey, and pecans. Or, bake them with whole bran cereal for a high-fiber breakfast or snack muffin. The fiber in oats can make dessert more nutritious as well.

DUTCH OATMEAL CAKE

1½ cups boiling water
1 cup quick-cooking oats, uncooked
½ cup shortening
1 cup firmly packed brown sugar
2 eggs
1½ cups all-purpose flour
1 teaspoon baking soda
1 teaspoon ground cinnamon
½ teaspoon salt
½ cup raisins
¼ cup plus 2 tablespoons butter or
   margarine, melted
½ cup firmly packed brown sugar
½ teaspoon vanilla extract
1 cup flaked coconut
½ cup chopped pecans

Combine boiling water and oats, stirring well; let cool.

Cream shortening; add sugar, and beat well. Add eggs, one at a time, beating well after each addition.

Combine next 4 ingredients; add to creamed mixture, beating well. Stir in oats mixture and raisins.

Pour batter into a greased and floured 13- x 9- x 2-inch baking pan.

Combine remaining ingredients; spoon over batter. Bake at 350° for 40 minutes. Yield: 15 to 18 servings.
Mrs. Clayton Turner,
DeFuniak Springs, Florida.

PEANUTTY OATMEAL COOKIES

1½ cups quick-cooking oats, uncooked
1 cup raisins
¾ cup shelled, raw peanuts
1 cup butter or margarine, softened
2 cups sugar
⅓ cup molasses
3 eggs, beaten
⅔ cup buttermilk
2 teaspoons baking soda
5 cups all-purpose flour
2 teaspoons baking powder
½ teaspoon salt
½ teaspoon ground cinnamon

Combine first 3 ingredients in container of electric blender. Process until mixture is crumbly; set aside.

Cream butter; add sugar and molasses, beating well. Add eggs; mix well.

Combine buttermilk and soda; set aside. Combine dry ingredients; add to creamed mixture alternately with buttermilk mixture, beginning and ending with dry ingredients. Stir in oat mixture. Drop dough by 1½ teaspoonfuls onto greased baking sheets; bake at 375° for 10 to 12 minutes. Yield: about 7 dozen.
Carol Forcum,
Marion, Illinois.

OATMEAL-HONEY MUFFINS

¾ cup whole bran cereal
¾ cup milk
1 egg
¼ cup vegetable oil
¼ cup honey
¼ cup firmly packed brown sugar
1 cup quick-cooking oats, uncooked
⅔ cup all-purpose flour
1 tablespoon baking powder
¼ teaspoon salt

Combine cereal and milk in a medium bowl; let stand 15 minutes. Add next 4 ingredients, stirring well.

Combine remaining ingredients in a large bowl; make a well in center of mixture. Add liquid mixture to dry ingredients; stir just until moistened. Spoon into greased muffin pans, filling two-thirds full. Bake at 400° for 15 minutes. Yield: 1 dozen.
Mrs. John H. Kolek,
Lakeland, Florida.

OAT CRISPIES

1½ cups all-purpose flour
1½ cups regular oats, uncooked
½ cup sugar
¾ teaspoon salt
½ teaspoon baking soda
¾ cup butter or margarine, softened
2 to 4 tablespoons cold water

Combine first 5 ingredients; cut in butter with pastry blender until mixture resembles coarse meal. Sprinkle cold water evenly over surface; stir with a fork until all dry ingredients are moistened. Roll dough to ¼-inch thickness on a lightly floured surface; cut into rounds with a 2-inch cookie cutter. Place cookies on lightly greased cookie sheets; bake at 350° for 15 minutes. Yield: 3½ dozen. *Mrs. Everett Smith, Candler, North Carolina.*

OATMEAL-NUT WAFFLES

1½ cups whole wheat flour
2 teaspoons baking powder
½ teaspoon salt
2 cups milk
2 eggs
¼ cup butter or margarine, melted
2 tablespoons honey
1 cup regular oats, uncooked
1 cup finely chopped pecans

Combine first 3 ingredients in a medium mixing bowl; mix well. Add milk, eggs, butter, and honey; beat at medium speed of an electric mixer until smooth. Stir in oats and pecans.

Bake in a preheated, lightly oiled waffle iron about 5 minutes. Yield: twelve 4-inch waffles. *Julie Converse, Knoxville, Tennessee.*

These Muffins Are Plum Good

Muffins are the easiest bread to make—they require no rising, shaping, or rolling out, and they bake in only a few minutes. But the best thing about muffins is the variety of flavors that you can stir into them.

Unlike most bread batters or dough, the ingredients for muffins should be mixed just until moistened, leaving the batter lumpy. Overmixing will make the muffins tough and heavy with sharp peaks and an irregular texture.

APPLE MUFFINS

1 egg, beaten
¼ cup shortening, melted
½ cup sugar
2½ cups finely chopped peeled and cored apples
2 cups all-purpose flour
1 tablespoon plus 1 teaspoon baking powder
½ teaspoon salt
½ teaspoon ground cinnamon
⅛ teaspoon ground nutmeg
1 cup milk
1 tablespoon sugar
½ teaspoon ground cinnamon

Combine first 3 ingredients, stirring well. Add apples, and mix well.

Combine next 5 ingredients; add to egg mixture alternately with milk, beginning and ending with flour mixture, stirring just until moistened.

Spoon into greased muffin pans, filling two-thirds full. Combine 1 tablespoon sugar and ½ teaspoon cinnamon; sprinkle over muffins. Bake at 375° for 20 to 25 minutes. Yield: 15 muffins.
Donna Friend, Chantilly, Virginia.

ORANGE-PECAN MUFFINS

1 (3-ounce) package cream cheese, softened
3 cups biscuit mix
½ cup sugar
1 egg, beaten
1¼ cups orange juice
½ cup chopped pecans

Beat cream cheese with electric mixer until light and fluffy. Add biscuit mix and sugar; mix well. Add remaining ingredients, stirring just until moistened.

Spoon into greased muffin pans, filling two-thirds full. Bake at 375° for 20 to 25 minutes. Yield: 1½ dozen.
Mrs. David A. Gibson, Martin, Tennessee.

PLUM GOOD MUFFINS

1¾ cups all-purpose flour
2 tablespoons sugar
2½ teaspoons baking powder
¾ teaspoon salt
1 egg, beaten
¾ cup milk
⅓ cup vegetable oil
¼ cup plum jam

Combine first 4 ingredients in a large bowl; make a well in center of mixture.

Combine egg, milk, and oil. Add to dry ingredients; stir just until moistened.

Spoon into greased muffin pans, filling two-thirds full. Spoon 1 teaspoon jam in center of each batter-filled muffin cup. Bake at 400° for 20 minutes or until golden brown. Yield: 1 dozen.
Mrs. W. A. Ellis, Talbott, Tennessee.

MARVELOUS CHEESE MUFFINS

1¾ cups all-purpose flour
1 tablespoon baking powder
½ teaspoon salt
2 tablespoons sugar
¾ cup (3 ounces) grated sharp Cheddar cheese
1 egg
1 cup milk
¼ cup butter or margarine, melted

Combine first 4 ingredients in a large bowl; add cheese, and mix well. Make a well in center of mixture. Combine egg, milk, and butter; add to dry ingredients, stirring just until moistened.

Spoon into greased muffin pans, filling two-thirds full. Bake at 400° for 25 minutes. Yield: 1 dozen.
Janet M. Filer, Arlington, Virginia.

HONEY-WHEAT MUFFINS

2 cups whole wheat flour
2 teaspoons baking powder
1 teaspoon salt
1 egg
¾ cup milk
¼ cup vegetable oil
¼ cup honey

Combine first 3 ingredients in a large bowl; make a well in center of mixture. Combine egg, milk, oil, and honey; add to dry ingredients, stirring just until moistened.

Spoon into greased muffin pans, filling two-thirds full. Bake at 400° for 20 minutes. Yield: 10 muffins.
Vickie Mullins, Norfolk, Virginia.

Right: *Shrimp-Cucumber Aspic and Peaches-and-Cream Salad are pretty enough to serve straight form the mold, with or without a garnish. Chicken Liver Pâté, however, benefits immensely from its garnish of blanched green onion tops, carrot flowers, and parsley sprigs (recipes on page 108).*

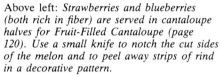

Above: *A bowl of chilled Cantaloupe Soup (page 120) is so delicious you'll forget it's good for you. For this refreshing appetizer, cantaloupe (rich in vitamin A) is whirled in a blender with vitamin C-rich orange juice, a dash of lemon, ginger, and allspice.*

Above left: *Strawberries and blueberries (both rich in fiber) are served in cantaloupe halves for Fruit-Filled Cantaloupe (page 120). Use a small knife to notch the cut sides of the melon and to peel away strips of rind in a decorative pattern.*

Left: *Honeydew-Berry Dessert (page 120) features honeydew, strawberries, and unsweetened orange juice, all rich in vitamin C. Calories scale in at only 140 per serving.*

Above right: *Spoon a flaming mixture of kiwi and unsweetened apple juice over half-cup scoops of ice milk for Kiwi Jubilee (page 120). This elegant dessert provides a good amount of vitamin C (from the kiwi) and totals just 157 calories.*

Right: *Surround low-fat cottage cheese with a colorful combination of fresh fruit. A simple strawberry garnish and a creamy dressing on the side give Main Dish Fruit Salad (page 119) added appeal.*

Start With A Cream Soup

To introduce dinner on a formal note, serve one of these first-course cream soups. Our selection of soups offers a variety of flavors so you're sure to find one to complement any menu. Each is scaled to serve small portions because just a few sips is enough to stimulate the appetite.

CREAM OF CHEESE SOUP

½ cup minced carrots
¾ cup minced celery
2 cups chicken broth
2 tablespoons minced onion
3 tablespoons butter or margarine, melted
¼ cup plus 1½ teaspoons all-purpose flour
2 cups milk
½ pound process American cheese, cut into ½-inch cubes
Chopped fresh parsley (optional)

Combine first 3 ingredients in a small saucepan; simmer 10 minutes or until vegetables are tender.

Sauté onion in butter in a medium saucepan; add flour, stirring well. Cook 1 minute, stirring constantly. Gradually add milk and chicken broth mixture; cook over medium heat, stirring constantly, until thickened and bubbly. Remove from heat; add cheese, and stir until cheese melts. Garnish with parsley, if desired. Serve immediately. Yield: 4 cups. *Frances V. Skuca,*
El Campo, Texas.

CREAM OF ZUCCHINI SOUP

2 to 3 tablespoons finely chopped onion
2 tablespoons butter or margarine, melted
2 cups chicken broth
1 teaspoon curry powder
½ teaspoon salt
¼ teaspoon pepper
2½ pounds zucchini, coarsely chopped
1 (8-ounce) carton commercial sour cream

Sauté onion in butter until tender. Add chicken broth, curry powder, salt, and pepper; bring to a boil. Add zucchini. Cover, reduce heat, and simmer until zucchini is tender. Stir in sour cream. Pour about one-third of mixture into container of electric blender; process until smooth. Pour into a bowl or pitcher; repeat procedure with remaining mixture. Cover and chill. Yield: about 6 cups. *Vern Stevenson,*
Murrells Inlet, South Carolina.

CREAMY BROCCOLI SOUP

3 cups broccoli flowerets
1 medium onion, chopped
1 carrot, shredded
¼ cup butter or margarine, melted
2 cups milk
1 (10¾-ounce) can cream of chicken soup, undiluted
White pepper
Paprika

Sauté broccoli, onion, and carrot in butter in a large saucepan until vegetables are tender. Stir in milk and soup; cook mixture just until thoroughly heated. Sprinkle with pepper and paprika. Yield: about 4 cups.
Alice G. Pahl,
Raleigh, North Carolina.

SUMMER SQUASH SOUP

2 medium onions, chopped
¼ cup plus 2 tablespoons butter or margarine, melted
4 cups diced yellow squash
2 cups chicken broth
½ teaspoon white pepper
1 teaspoon celery salt
½ teaspoon dried whole tarragon
2 cups milk

Sauté onion in butter until tender. Add next 5 ingredients; cook over low heat 10 minutes or until squash is tender. Remove from heat, and stir in the milk.

Place squash mixture in container of electric blender; process until smooth. Serve hot or cold. Yield: 6½ cups.
Cindy Turner Overall,
Baton Rouge, Louisiana.

ELEGANT MUSHROOM SOUP

¾ cup chopped green onion
2 cups chopped fresh mushrooms
¼ cup butter or margarine, melted
2 tablespoons all-purpose flour
2 teaspoons chicken-flavored bouillon granules
2 cups boiling water
1 cup milk

Sauté onion and mushrooms in butter in a Dutch oven until onion is tender. Stir in flour.

Dissolve bouillon granules in boiling water. Gradually add bouillon mixture and milk to mushroom mixture; cook over low heat 10 minutes or just until thoroughly heated. Yield: 4 cups.
Linda Ewing,
Lilburn, Georgia.

What's New With Mayonnaise?

Mayonnaise, that thick mixture of egg yolks and vegetable oil, is used mainly in sandwich spreads or salads. But some creative Southern cooks are also adding mayonnaise to other foods.

CREAMY VEGETABLE DIP

½ small onion, minced
2 tablespoons green pepper, minced
1 teaspoon chopped fresh parsley
1 small carrot, minced
2 tablespoons vinegar
¼ teaspoon salt
½ teaspoon curry powder
1 cup mayonnaise

Combine all ingredients; mix well. Serve with fresh vegetables. Yield: 1¼ cups. *Mrs. Clifford B. Smith, Sr.,*
White Hall, Maryland.

CHOCOLATE MAYONNAISE CAKE

2 cups all-purpose flour
¼ cup plus 1 tablespoon cocoa
1 cup sugar
1 teaspoon baking soda
Pinch of salt
1 cup water
1 cup mayonnaise
1½ teaspoons vanilla extract
Chocolate frosting (recipe follows)

Combine first 5 ingredients; mix well. Add next 3 ingredients; stir until smooth. Pour batter into a greased and floured 9-inch square pan; bake at 350° for 25 to 30 minutes or until cake tests done. Cool. Spread with frosting. Yield: 9 servings.

Chocolate Frosting:

2¾ cups sifted powdered sugar
¼ cup plus 1 tablespoon cocoa
¼ cup butter or margarine, melted
2 egg yolks
2 tablespoons milk
1 teaspoon vanilla extract
⅛ teaspoon salt

Combine all ingredients; beat until smooth. Yield: enough frosting for one 9-inch cake. *Myrna Johns,*
Gastonia, North Carolina.

CHEESE TOAST TREATS

1 egg, beaten
⅓ cup mayonnaise
1 cup (4 ounces) shredded sharp Cheddar
  cheese
½ teaspoon Worcestershire sauce
⅛ teaspoon dry mustard
Dash of red pepper
8 slices white bread
4 slices bacon, cooked and crumbled
  (optional)

Combine first 6 ingredients; mix well.
Trim crust from bread; lightly toast
both sides. Spread cheese mixture on
each slice; cut each slice into 4 squares.
Bake at 350° for 12 minutes. Sprinkle
with bacon, if desired. Yield: 32 appetizer servings.   *Mrs. J. F. McDaniel,*
                         San Antonio, Texas.

EASY PULL-APART BUNS

⅔ cup finely chopped walnuts
⅓ cup sugar
½ teaspoon ground cinnamon
1 (10-ounce) can refrigerated buttermilk
  biscuits
⅓ cup mayonnaise

Lightly grease a muffin pan. Combine
first 3 ingredients; set aside. Cut each
biscuit into quarters; shape quarters into
balls. Coat balls with mayonnaise; roll
in sugar mixture. Place 4 balls in each
muffin cup. Bake at 400° for 15 to 17
minutes or until golden brown. Serve
warm. Yield: 10 buns.
                         Mrs. Charles Lister,
                         Danville, Kentucky.

Great Pies Begin With The Crust

Although the filling of a delicious pie
often gets the most attention, the crust
hardly ever goes unnoticed. Our three
flavorful pie shells are sure to get plenty
of attention on their own; in fact, we
predict that you'll have plenty of re-
quests for a repeat performance.

Two very different alternatives to a
traditional piecrust are rich Chocolate-
Coconut Pie Shell and Crisp Cereal Piecrust. Fill them with ice cream or any
other favorite pie filling. Make-Ahead
Pastry is a tender, flaky crust with the
advantage of keeping well and making
four shells.

MAKE-AHEAD PASTRY

4 cups all-purpose flour
2 teaspoons salt
1 tablespoon sugar
1¾ cups shortening
1 egg, beaten
1 tablespoon vinegar
½ cup cold water

Combine dry ingredients; cut in shortening until mixture resembles coarse
meal. Combine egg, vinegar, and water
in a small bowl; stir into flour mixture.
Divide dough into 4 equal parts, shape
each into a ball, and wrap tightly. Chill.
Roll each portion to ⅛-inch thickness
on a lightly floured surface. Place in a
9-inch pieplate; trim off excess pastry
along edges. Fold edges under and
flute. For a baked shell, prick bottom
and sides with a fork; bake at 450° for
10 to 12 minutes or until golden brown.
It is unnecessary to prick shell if it will
be filled before baking. Yield: four 9-
inch pastry shells.
Note: Dough may be stored up to one
week in refrigerator or stored in freezer
for longer periods.   *Susan Erickson,*
                        Pocahontas, Arkansas.

CRISP CEREAL PIECRUST

2 cups quick-cooking oats, uncooked
¼ teaspoon salt
½ cup sifted powdered sugar
½ teaspoon ground cinnamon
¼ cup plus 2 tablespoons butter or
  margarine, melted
Vegetable cooking spray

Combine first 4 ingredients in a mixing bowl; stir in butter.
Spray a 9-inch pieplate with vegetable
cooking spray; press piecrust mixture on
bottom and sides of pieplate. Bake at
350° for 20 minutes; cool. Yield: one
9-inch piecrust.   *Greta Pinkston,*
                        Harrison, Arkansas.

CHOCOLATE-COCONUT PIE SHELL

2 tablespoons butter or margarine
2 (1-ounce) squares unsweetened chocolate
⅔ cup sifted powdered sugar
2 tablespoons hot water
1½ cups flaked coconut
Vegetable cooking spray

Combine butter and chocolate in top
of double boiler; bring water to a boil.
Reduce heat to low; stir until chocolate
melts. Combine powdered sugar and
hot water; add to chocolate mixture,
stirring well. Stir in coconut.

Spray a 9-inch pieplate with vegetable
cooking spray; firmly press piecrust mixture onto bottom and sides of pieplate.
Cover and chill until firm. Yield: one
9-inch pie shell.
Note: Crust may be filled with softened ice cream and frozen. Before serving, drizzle chocolate syrup over each
slice.   *Lib Cunningham,*
                        Atlanta, Georgia.

COOKING LIGHT

A Guide To Light Cooking

Once you've become familiar with a
few of the techniques used in "Cooking
Light," you'll find it easy to trim away
unwanted calories from your own recipes. Instead of frying vegetables and
meats, get rid of excess fat (and calories) by poaching, sautéing, grilling, and
steaming.

Poaching

You don't have to fry fish to enjoy it.
When frying, fish acts as a sponge,
soaking up the high-calorie shortening
or oil. But when poached in a flavorful
mixture of lemon and wine, fish stays
tender, moist, and low in calories.

Fish is poached by cooking it in a
small amount of simmering liquid, such
as wine or stock. The fish poacher or
skillet is covered so steam won't escape;
the steam keeps the fish moist.

We recommend poaching other foods,
such as eggs and fruit, too. Eggs can be
poached in water, but try poaching eggs
in milk or tomato juice.

Sautéing and Stir-Frying

Sautéing and stir-frying are both light
methods of cooking when the amount of
oil or margarine is kept to a minimum.
By using nonstick cookware or a regular
skillet coated with cooking spray, vegetables and meat can be cooked
quickly—often with no fat added.

We do recommend a small amount of
oil for sautéing some foods such as
green pepper and celery, which dry out
if cooked with cooking spray alone.
Other foods, such as mushrooms,
onion, meat, fish, and poultry, release

some liquid as they cook and can be sautéed using cooking spray or a non-stick skillet without oil.

Slice vegetables thinly for sautéing and stir-frying. Meat, fish, and poultry should be cut into small, even pieces. Shake or stir for uniform browning.

Grilling and Broiling

When grilled over hot coals or broiled on a rack in the oven, meat, fish, and poultry lose extra calories as natural fat drips away. Remove as much fat as possible before cooking by skinning chicken and trimming visible fat from meat. Coat the broiler or grill rack with cooking spray to prevent sticking.

Wine, vinegar, and lemon juice tenderize meat and are good ingredients for low-calorie marinades. Basting frequently keeps food moist during grilling; use a low-calorie marinade that adds moisture, not fat, to the meat.

Steaming

Vegetables are more flavorful and nutritious when placed in a basket above a small amount of boiling water and steamed just until crisp-tender.

You can season vegetables without adding calories by placing herbs or spices in the water. Arrange vegetables in the steaming rack after bringing the water to a boil; cover the pan with its lid. The water should be kept at boiling point during the entire time of cooking.

Many types of steaming baskets and racks are available. Place the basket in a pan with a tight-fitting lid. Since steam can burn, be careful to open the cover slowly and away from you.

POACHED SNAPPER

1 cup Chablis or other dry white wine
½ to 1 cup water
1 lemon, sliced
5 green onions, sliced
5 sprigs fresh parsley
4 whole peppercorns
2 bay leaves
½ teaspoon salt
1½ pounds dressed red snapper
Additional lemon slices

Combine first 8 ingredients in a fish poacher or large skillet; bring to a boil, and add snapper. Cover, reduce heat, and simmer 20 minutes or until snapper flakes easily.

Remove snapper from skillet carefully, and garnish with additional lemon slices. Yield: 3 servings (about 109 calories per serving).

GRILLED SCALLOP KABOBS

1 (15¼-ounce) can unsweetened pineapple chunks, undrained
¼ cup Chablis or other dry white wine
¼ cup soy sauce
2 tablespoons lemon juice
2 tablespoons chopped fresh parsley
½ teaspoon pepper
¼ teaspoon garlic powder
1 pound fresh scallops
18 medium-size fresh mushrooms
2 large green peppers, cut into 1-inch squares
18 cherry tomatoes

Drain pineapple, reserving ¼ cup plus 2 tablespoons juice. Combine pineapple juice and next 6 ingredients in a large shallow baking dish, mixing well. Add pineapple, scallops, and vegetables; toss well to coat, and marinate in the refrigerator 1 to 1½ hours.

Alternate pineapple, scallops, and vegetables on skewers.

Place kabobs 4 to 5 inches from hot coals; grill 10 to 12 minutes, turning kabobs and basting frequently with marinade. Yield: 6 servings (about 149 calories per serving).

STEAMED BROCCOLI WITH TANGY CHIVE SAUCE

1 (1-pound) bunch fresh broccoli
2 tablespoons all-purpose flour
⅛ teaspoon salt
Dash of white pepper
⅔ cup chicken broth
⅓ cup skim milk
2 teaspoons chopped chives
1 teaspoon prepared mustard
1 teaspoon lemon juice

Trim off large leaves of broccoli, and remove tough ends of lower stalks. Wash broccoli thoroughly, and separate into spears. Arrange broccoli on steaming rack with stalks to center of rack. Place over boiling water; cover and steam 10 to 15 minutes or to desired degree of doneness. Arrange broccoli spears in serving dish, and keep warm.

Combine flour, salt, and pepper in a small saucepan; gradually add chicken broth and milk, stirring with a wire whisk until smooth. Place over medium heat and cook, stirring constantly, until mixture thickens. Add remaining ingredients, mixing well. Cook 2 additional minutes, stirring constantly.

Spoon sauce over steamed broccoli to serve. Yield: 4 servings (about 23 calories per serving plus 10 calories per tablespoon sauce).

SAUTEED VEGETABLE MEDLEY

Vegetable cooking spray
1 large clove garlic, minced
1 small onion, sliced and separated into rings
1 small green pepper, chopped
2 medium-size yellow squash, sliced
2 medium zucchini, sliced
2 small tomatoes, peeled and chopped
¼ teaspoon dried whole basil
⅛ teaspoon pepper

Coat a large skillet with cooking spray; place over medium heat until hot. Add garlic and onion; cook until onion is transparent, stirring constantly. Add green pepper; cook 5 minutes, stirring constantly. Add yellow squash and zucchini; cover and cook 5 minutes.

Stir in tomatoes, basil, and pepper; cover and cook about 10 to 15 minutes. Yield: 4 servings (about 55 calories per ¾-cup serving).
Doris S. Shortt,
Leesburg, Florida.

Lamb, Family-Style

Don't wait until your next dinner party to serve our Hearty Lamb Pilaf; it's well-suited for a casual family meal.

HEARTY LAMB PILAF

1 pound ground lamb
2 large onions, chopped
2 cloves garlic, minced
3 (10¾-ounce) cans chicken broth, undiluted
2 (28-ounce) cans whole tomatoes, undrained and quartered
2 cups uncooked brown rice
1 teaspoon dried whole oregano
1 (10-ounce) package frozen English peas
½ cup raisins
1 (4-ounce) jar diced pimiento, undrained
½ teaspoon salt
½ teaspoon pepper

Combine lamb, onion, and garlic in a large Dutch oven; cook until lamb is browned and onion is tender. Stir in chicken broth, tomatoes, rice, and oregano; bring to a boil. Reduce heat and simmer, uncovered, 40 minutes; stir mixture occasionally.

Add remaining ingredients, stirring well. Simmer, uncovered, an additional 40 minutes, stirring occasionally. Yield: 8 servings.

A Smorgasbord Of Pork Chops

Bake, broil, simmer in a skillet, or stuff them with a tasty filling. You can do a lot with pork chops. What's more, they're a good source of protein, iron, and B vitamins.

CHEESY PORK CHOPS

4 (1-inch-thick) pork chops
Salt and pepper
1 large onion, cut into 4 slices
1 tablespoon plus 1 teaspoon mayonnaise
¼ to ½ cup grated Parmesan cheese

Sprinkle pork chops lightly with salt and pepper; place in a lightly greased 12- x 8- x 2-inch baking dish. Top each chop with an onion slice; spread each slice with 1 teaspoon mayonnaise. Sprinkle with Parmesan cheese. Bake, uncovered, at 325° for 1 hour or until chops are tender. Yield: 4 servings.
George Barr,
Birmingham, Alabama.

RICE-STUFFED PORK CHOPS

¼ cup chopped onion
¼ cup chopped celery
¼ teaspoon rubbed sage
¼ teaspoon ground thyme
2 tablespoons butter or margarine
⅔ cup cooked rice
1 (10¾-ounce) can cream of mushroom soup, undiluted and divided
1 tablespoon chopped fresh parsley
4 (1-inch-thick) pork chops
2 tablespoons vegetable oil
1 to 1½ cups water
¼ teaspoon rubbed sage
¼ teaspoon ground thyme
⅛ teaspoon pepper

Sauté onion, celery, sage, and thyme in butter in a small saucepan until vegetables are tender. Stir in rice, 2 tablespoons soup, and parsley; set aside.

Make pockets in pork chops, cutting from rib side just to beginning of fat edge of each chop. Stuff pockets of pork chops with rice mixture.

Heat oil in a large skillet over medium heat. Brown pork chops on both sides; drain off pan drippings. Combine next 4 ingredients and remaining soup; pour over pork chops. Cover, reduce heat, and simmer 50 to 55 minutes or until pork chops are tender. Yield: 4 servings.
Elizabeth Moore,
Huntsville, Alabama.

CREOLE PORK CHOPS

¼ cup all-purpose flour
½ teaspoon salt
¼ teaspoon pepper
¼ teaspoon dried whole rosemary, crushed
6 (½-inch-thick) pork chops
2 tablespoons vegetable oil
1 medium onion, finely chopped
1 medium-size green pepper, finely chopped
2 stalks celery, thinly sliced
2 cloves garlic, minced
¼ cup butter or margarine
2 cups beef broth
½ pound fresh mushrooms, halved
4 medium tomatoes, peeled and quartered
1 (6-ounce) can tomato paste
1 tablespoon chopped fresh parsley
1 bay leaf
Hot cooked rice

Combine first 4 ingredients. Dredge pork chops in flour mixture.

Heat oil in a large skillet over medium heat; brown pork chops on both sides. Drain pork chops, and place in a lightly greased 13- x 9- x 2-inch baking dish; set aside.

Sauté onion, green pepper, celery, and garlic in butter in skillet until tender. Add next 6 ingredients; simmer, uncovered, 20 minutes, stirring occasionally. Remove bay leaf; discard. Pour sauce over pork chops. Cover and bake at 325° for 1 hour or until pork chops are tender. Serve over rice. Yield: 6 servings.
Lynn Aigner,
Woodsboro, Texas.

SAUCY COMPANY PORK CHOPS

½ cup all-purpose flour
½ teaspoon dried whole thyme
½ teaspoon salt
¼ teaspoon pepper
6 (1-inch-thick) pork chops
2 tablespoons butter or margarine
2 tablespoons vegetable oil
1 cup dry vermouth
½ pound fresh mushrooms, sliced
6 (1-ounce) slices Swiss cheese

Combine first 4 ingredients. Dredge pork chops in flour mixture.

Heat butter and oil in an electric skillet over medium heat. Brown pork chops on both sides; drain off pan drippings. Add vermouth; cover, reduce heat, and simmer 25 minutes. Add mushrooms; cover and simmer an additional 20 minutes. Turn off heat; top each pork chop with a slice of cheese. Cover and let stand until cheese melts. Yield: 6 servings.
Meta Davis,
St. Charles, Missouri.

PORK CHOPS WITH SOUR CREAM SAUCE

2 tablespoons vegetable oil
2 (¾-inch-thick) pork chops
1 small onion, thinly sliced
¼ teaspoon caraway seeds
¼ teaspoon paprika
⅛ teaspoon salt
⅛ teaspoon dried whole dillweed
Dash of garlic powder
¾ to 1 cup water
⅓ cup commercial sour cream

Heat oil in a heavy skillet over medium heat. Brown pork chops on both sides; drain off pan drippings. Add next 7 ingredients. Cover, reduce heat, and simmer 1 hour, adding additional water if needed to prevent sticking. Remove pork chops from skillet. Stir sour cream into drippings; serve over pork chops. Yield: 2 servings.
Carol Bowen,
Tifton, Georgia.

POLYNESIAN PORK AND PINEAPPLE

6 (½- to ¾-inch-thick) pork chops
Salt and pepper
2 tablespoons vegetable oil
1 (15¼-ounce) can pineapple chunks, undrained
1 large onion, chopped
¼ cup finely chopped celery leaves
1 clove garlic, minced
12 pitted prunes
2 tablespoons soy sauce
½ teaspoon dried whole marjoram
1 cup diagonally sliced celery
Fluffy Ginger Rice

Sprinkle pork chops with salt and pepper. Heat oil in an electric skillet over medium heat. Brown pork chops on both sides; drain off pan drippings.

Combine next 7 ingredients, mixing well; pour over pork chops. Cover, reduce heat, and simmer 25 minutes. Add celery; cover and simmer an additional 15 minutes. Serve over Fluffy Ginger Rice. Yield: 6 servings.

Fluffy Ginger Rice:

2 cups water
1 teaspoon salt
1 cup uncooked regular rice
1 teaspoon minced crystallized ginger

Bring water and salt to a boil; stir in rice and ginger. Cover, reduce heat, and simmer 20 minutes or until water is absorbed. Yield: 6 servings.

Pat Boschen,
Ashland, Virginia.

PORK CHOPS AND SPANISH RICE

1 (28-ounce) can whole tomatoes
2 tablespoons vegetable oil
5 (½-inch-thick) pork chops
1 teaspoon salt
1 teaspoon chili powder
⅛ teaspoon pepper
¾ cup uncooked regular rice
½ cup chopped onion
¼ cup chopped green pepper
5 green pepper rings
¾ cup (3 ounces) shredded sharp Cheddar
 cheese

Drain tomatoes, reserving the liquid; coarsely chop tomatoes, and set aside. Add enough water to liquid to equal 1¾ cups, and set aside.

Heat oil in an electric skillet over medium heat. Brown pork chops on both sides; drain off pan drippings. Combine next 3 ingredients; sprinkle over chops. Add rice, onion, chopped green pepper, tomatoes, and reserved liquid. Cover, reduce heat, and simmer 30 to 35 minutes or until pork and rice are tender; stir occasionally. Top each pork chop with a green pepper ring; cover and cook an additional 5 minutes. Sprinkle with cheese, and cook just until cheese melts. Yield: 5 servings.
Mrs. C. E. Owens,
Houston, Texas.

Bake A Batch Of Chocolate Snaps

A handful of crisp chocolate cookies with a glass of cold milk makes a great afternoon snack, especially when the cookies are flavored with a surprising dash of mint.

CHOCOLATE MINT SNAPS

4 (1-ounce) squares unsweetened chocolate
1¼ cups shortening
2 cups sugar
2 eggs
⅓ cup corn syrup
2½ tablespoons water
2 teaspoons peppermint extract
1 teaspoon vanilla extract
4 cups all-purpose flour
2 teaspoons baking soda
½ teaspoon salt
¼ cup plus 2 tablespoons sugar

Melt chocolate over hot water in top of double boiler. Remove from heat.

Cream shortening; gradually add 2 cups sugar, beating until light and fluffy. Add melted chocolate, eggs, corn syrup, water, and flavorings; mix well. Combine flour, soda, and salt; add to creamed mixture, beating just until blended.

Shape dough into 1-inch balls, and roll in remaining sugar. Place on ungreased cookie sheets; bake at 350° for 10 minutes. Cool on cookie sheets 5 minutes. Remove to wire racks, and cool completely. Yield: 10½ dozen.
Lawrence L. Clapp,
Cantonment, Florida.

Barbecue Straight From The Oven

Forget the grill and charcoal. With an oven, some good cuts of meat, and these recipes, you can have that tender, juicy, sauce-dripping barbecue you're longing for.

BARBECUED BEEF ROAST

1 (4- to 5-pound) eye-of-round roast
½ teaspoon salt
½ teaspoon pepper
½ teaspoon garlic salt
½ teaspoon meat tenderizer
1 cup water
¾ cup peeled chopped tomato
¼ cup vinegar
¼ cup catsup
2 tablespoons chopped onion
1 clove garlic, minced
2 stalks celery, sliced
1 tablespoon Worcestershire sauce
1 teaspoon lemon juice
¼ cup butter or margarine
1 cup commercial barbecue sauce

Rub roast on all sides with salt, pepper, garlic salt, and meat tenderizer; place roast in a 13- x 9- x 2-inch baking pan, and set aside.

Combine next 9 ingredients in a large saucepan; bring to a boil. Reduce heat and simmer 15 minutes. Stir butter and barbecue sauce into liquid.

Pour half the sauce mixture over roast; bake at 300° for 2½ hours, basting frequently with pan drippings and half of remaining sauce. Thinly slice roast, and serve with remaining sauce. Yield: 16 to 18 servings. *Billie Taylor,*
Afton, Virginia.

OLD SOUTH BARBECUED CHICKEN

1 (2½- to 3-pound) broiler-fryer, cut up
Salt
½ cup all-purpose flour
⅓ cup vegetable oil
1 medium onion, diced
½ cup chopped celery
1 cup catsup
1 cup water
¼ cup lemon juice
3 tablespoons Worcestershire sauce
2 tablespoons brown sugar
2 tablespoons vinegar
1 small hot pepper
Hot cooked rice or noodles

Sprinkle chicken with salt. Dredge chicken in flour, and brown in hot oil in a Dutch oven.

Remove chicken from Dutch oven. Drain off excess oil. Combine remaining ingredients except rice in Dutch oven; add chicken. Cover and bake at 350° for 1 hour. Remove hot pepper; discard. Serve over rice or noodles. Yield: 4 servings.
Mrs. J. O. Branson,
Thomasville, North Carolina.

BARBECUED CHICKEN

1 cup all-purpose flour
2 teaspoons paprika
1 teaspoon salt
¼ teaspoon pepper
1 (2½- to 3-pound) broiler-fryer, cut up
¼ cup butter or margarine, melted
½ cup catsup
¼ cup water
½ medium onion, thinly sliced
1 tablespoon sugar
1 tablespoon vinegar
1 tablespoon Worcestershire sauce
1 teaspoon salt
½ teaspoon chili powder
¼ teaspoon pepper

Combine first 4 ingredients; mix well. Dredge chicken in flour mixture. Pour butter into a 13- x 9- x 2-inch baking pan. Arrange chicken in pan, skin side down. Bake at 350° for 30 minutes.

Combine remaining ingredients in a medium saucepan; mix well. Bring mixture to a boil; reduce heat and simmer 15 minutes.

Remove chicken from oven, and turn; spoon sauce over chicken. Bake an additional 30 minutes. Yield: 4 servings.
Sue-Sue Hartstern,
Louisville, Kentucky.

PORK ROAST BARBECUE

1 (4- to 5-pound) pork loin roast
1½ cups water
1 cup vinegar
½ cup catsup
½ cup Worcestershire sauce
1 medium onion, chopped
3 tablespoons dry mustard
3 tablespoons brown sugar
1½ teaspoons salt
¼ teaspoon crushed red pepper
¼ teaspoon pepper

Place roast, fat side up, in a 13- x 9- x 2-inch baking pan. Insert meat thermometer (not touching bone or fat).

Combine remaining ingredients; mix well, and pour over roast. Bake, uncovered, at 325° for 2½ to 3 hours or until thermometer reaches 170°, basting frequently with pan drippings. Let stand 10 to 15 minutes; serve with any remaining sauce. Yield: 8 to 10 servings.

Kathy Plowman,
Concord, North Carolina.

EASY BARBECUED SPARERIBS

3 pounds spareribs
1 (14-ounce) bottle catsup
1¼ cups water
¼ cup vinegar
3 tablespoons brown sugar
1 tablespoon dry mustard
3 tablespoons Worcestershire sauce
2 teaspoons chili powder
Pinch of ground cloves
Pinch of garlic powder

Cut ribs into serving-size pieces; place in a 13- x 9- x 2-inch baking pan. Bake at 400° for 30 minutes.

Combine remaining ingredients; mix well. Spoon over ribs. Reduce heat to 350°; bake an additional 1½ hours or until tender. Yield: 3 to 4 servings.

Gail Thomas,
White Hall, Maryland.

Cooked Cabbage Specialties

You'll find all these cooked cabbage dishes full of flavor and easy to prepare. Louise Denmon's recipe for Cabbage With Polish Sausage cooks in only 20 minutes, so you can have a one-dish dinner in less than one hour.

CORNED BEEF AND CABBAGE

1 (3-pound) corned beef brisket
1 medium head cabbage, coarsely chopped
8 medium potatoes, peeled and quartered
1 medium onion, sliced

Combine corned beef and water to cover in a large Dutch oven; bring to a boil. Reduce heat, cover, and simmer 2 to 2½ hours or until tender. Add cabbage, potatoes, and onion; cover and simmer an additional 20 to 30 minutes or until vegetables are tender. Yield: about 8 servings.

Ethel Evans,
St. Petersburg, Florida.

CABBAGE ROLLS

6 large cabbage leaves
1½ pounds lean ground beef
2 eggs
1 cup milk
⅓ cup finely chopped onion
2 tablespoons all-purpose flour
2 teaspoons salt
½ teaspoon pepper
½ teaspoon ground allspice
4 beef-flavored bouillon cubes
1 cup boiling water
6 small new potatoes
4 medium carrots, scraped and cut into 2-inch pieces

Cook cabbage leaves in a small amount of salted water for 3 minutes or until limp; set aside.

Combine next 8 ingredients, stirring well. Place equal portions of meat mixture in center of each cabbage leaf; fold ends of cabbage leaves over, and fasten with wooden picks. Place in a large skillet. Dissolve bouillon in 1 cup water; pour over cabbage. Bring to a boil; cover, reduce heat, and simmer 1½ hours.

Peel a thin strip around center of each potato. Add potatoes and carrots to skillet; cover and simmer an additional 30 minutes. Yield: 6 servings.

Mary Bengtson,
Dallas, Texas.

CABBAGE AND TOMATOES

2 tablespoons chopped onion
2 tablespoons bacon drippings
1 medium head cabbage
1¼ cups water
1 teaspoon salt
½ teaspoon sugar
2 tablespoons all-purpose flour
2 cups peeled, chopped tomatoes
2 tablespoons butter or margarine, melted
¼ cup dry breadcrumbs
3 tablespoons grated Parmesan cheese

Sauté onion in bacon drippings in a Dutch oven until tender.

Cut cabbage into 8 wedges, removing core. Add cabbage and next 3 ingredients to onion; boil, uncovered, 8 minutes, turning cabbage once.

Stir flour into tomatoes; stir into cabbage mixture. Cook over medium heat, stirring constantly until thickened. Spoon into serving dish. Combine butter, breadcrumbs, and grated Parmesan cheese; sprinkle over top. Yield: 8 servings.

Sarah Watson,
Knoxville, Tennessee.

CABBAGE WITH POLISH SAUSAGE

1 cup chopped onion
2 tablespoons butter or margarine
2 tablespoons all-purpose flour
1 cup water
¼ cup vinegar
¾ teaspoon salt
½ teaspoon sugar
¼ teaspoon pepper
12 cups coarsely chopped cabbage
1 to 1¼ pounds Polish sausage, cut into 1-inch slices

Sauté onion in butter in a Dutch oven over low heat until tender. Add flour, stirring until smooth. Cook 1 minute, stirring constantly. Gradually add water and vinegar; cook over medium heat, stirring constantly, until mixture thickens. Stir in remaining ingredients. Reduce heat, cover, and simmer for 20 minutes. Yield: 4 to 6 servings.

Louise Denmon,
Silsbee, Texas.

CABBAGE MEDLEY

5 or 6 slices bacon
¾ cup Italian salad dressing
¼ cup water
½ small head cabbage, coarsely chopped
¾ cup thinly sliced mushrooms
½ cup coarsely chopped cauliflower
½ cup coarsely chopped broccoli flowerets
3 green onions with tops, sliced

Cook bacon in a large skillet until crisp; remove bacon, reserving 2 tablespoons drippings in skillet. Crumble bacon, and set aside.

Stir dressing and water into drippings. Add vegetables, stirring to coat well. Simmer, uncovered, 10 minutes. Sprinkle with bacon. Yield: 6 servings.

Janet Queen,
Arlington, Texas.

Do Something Different With Spaghetti

Pepperoni, anchovies, chicken, and English peas are just a few of the ingredients in these spaghetti recipes.

Three-Cheese Spaghetti is a meatless dish made with a cream sauce featuring Gouda, Parmesan, and Swiss cheese, mushrooms, and parsley. The sauce is stirred into the pasta before serving.

Anchovies, bacon, ripe olives, and mushrooms make Joanna Delman's Spaghetti Etcetera something new. But if you prefer tomato sauce with your spaghetti, try Pepperoni Pasta. It's similar to a traditional spaghetti sauce, but with pepperoni slices instead of ground beef.

PEPPERONI PASTA

1 large onion, sliced
2 cloves garlic, minced
2 medium-size green peppers, cut into strips
½ pound pepperoni, thinly sliced
3 tablespoons olive oil
1 (16-ounce) can whole tomatoes, undrained and chopped
1 teaspoon dried whole oregano
½ teaspoon salt
Hot cooked spaghetti
Grated Parmesan cheese

Sauté onion, garlic, green pepper, and pepperoni in oil in a Dutch oven 5 minutes. Add tomatoes, oregano, and salt; cover and cook 5 minutes, stirring occasionally. Uncover and cook 1 minute to thicken. Spoon sauce over spaghetti, and sprinkle with cheese. Yield: 4 servings. *Tammy Smith, Talbott, Tennessee.*

CHICKEN SPAGHETTI

1 (4- to 5-pound) hen
3 large onions, chopped
3 green peppers, chopped
½ cup butter or margarine
1 (17-ounce) can English peas, drained
2 (16-ounce) cans whole tomatoes, undrained and chopped
2 (10¾-ounce) cans tomato soup
3 tablespoons Worcestershire sauce
1 (12-ounce) package thin spaghetti, cooked and drained
½ cup (2 ounces) shredded sharp Cheddar cheese

Place chicken in a Dutch oven, and cover with water. Bring to a boil; cover and reduce heat. Simmer 1 hour or until tender. Remove chicken, and let cool. Reserve broth for other uses. Bone chicken, and chop meat; set aside.

Sauté onion and green pepper in butter in a large Dutch oven until tender. Add next 4 ingredients and chicken to sautéed ingredients; cook over medium heat 15 to 20 minutes, stirring occasionally. Stir in spaghetti, and sprinkle with cheese. Yield: 8 servings.

Nancy Houston, Birmingham, Alabama.

SPAGHETTI ETCETERA

2 onions, thinly sliced
2 cloves garlic, crushed
3 tablespoons olive oil
½ pound fresh mushrooms, sliced
3 slices bacon, chopped
6 ripe olives, sliced
5 anchovy fillets, chopped
⅓ cup chopped fresh parsley
Hot cooked spaghetti
Grated Parmesan cheese

Sauté onion and garlic in oil in a large skillet 3 to 5 minutes. Stir in next 4 ingredients and cook, covered, 15 minutes over low heat. Stir in parsley. Spoon over spaghetti, and sprinkle with cheese. Yield: 2 to 3 servings.

Joanna R. Delman, Greensboro, North Carolina.

THREE-CHEESE SPAGHETTI

1 tablespoon butter or margarine
1 tablespoon all-purpose flour
1 cup milk
½ cup (2 ounces) shredded Swiss cheese
½ cup (2 ounces) shredded Gouda cheese
1 (2½-ounce) jar sliced mushrooms, drained
¼ teaspoon salt
1 (7-ounce) package spaghetti
2 tablespoons butter or margarine, melted
1 tablespoon dried parsley flakes
½ cup grated Parmesan cheese

Melt 1 tablespoon butter in a heavy saucepan over low heat; add flour, stirring until smooth. Cook 1 minute, stirring constantly. Gradually add milk; cook over medium heat, stirring constantly, until thickened and bubbly. Stir in cheese, mushrooms, and salt.

Cook spaghetti according to package directions; drain. Combine spaghetti, 2 tablespoons butter, parsley, and Parmesan cheese; stir well. Pour cheese sauce over spaghetti, stirring until combined. Yield: 6 servings. *Marietta Marx, Louisville, Kentucky.*

Four Ways To Frost A Cake

Good cakes deserve good frostings. The tangy flavor of Cream Cheese Frosting will complement many of your favorite layer cakes. Or, if you prefer chocolate, just spread on our Chocolate Fudge Frosting, which doesn't require cooking. Its irresistible flavor will have everyone licking the bowl.

CHOCOLATE FUDGE FROSTING

¼ cup butter or margarine, softened
⅓ cup light corn syrup
½ teaspoon vanilla extract
¼ teaspoon salt
½ cup cocoa
1 (16-ounce) package powdered sugar, sifted
2 to 3 tablespoons milk

Cream butter; add next 3 ingredients, beating well. Add cocoa, mixing well. Gradually add sugar and milk alternately to reach spreading consistency; beat until smooth. Yield: enough for one 2-layer cake. *Elizabeth Marcantel, DeQuincy, Louisiana.*

CREAM CHEESE FROSTING

1 (8-ounce) package cream cheese, softened
½ cup butter or margarine, softened
1 (16-ounce) package powdered sugar, sifted
2 to 3 teaspoons milk or whipping cream
¼ cup chopped pecans or walnuts

Combine cream cheese and butter; beat until smooth. Gradually add powdered sugar and milk, beating until light and fluffy. Spread immediately on cooled cake; sprinkle pecans on top. Yield: enough for one 2-layer cake.
Margaret M. Worthy, Birmingham, Alabama.

FAVORITE CARAMEL FROSTING

3 cups sugar, divided
¾ cup milk
1 egg, beaten
Pinch of salt
½ cup butter, cut up

Sprinkle ½ cup sugar in a heavy saucepan; place over medium heat. Cook, stirring constantly, until sugar melts and syrup is light golden brown.

Combine remaining 2½ cups sugar and next 3 ingredients, mixing well; stir in butter. Stir butter mixture into hot caramelized sugar. (The mixture will tend to lump, becoming smooth with further cooking.) Cook over medium heat 15 to 20 minutes, stirring frequently, until mixture reaches thread stage (230°). Cool 5 minutes. Beat to almost spreading consistency, and spread immediately on cooled cake. Yield: enough for one 2-layer cake.

DECORATOR FROSTING

8 cups sifted powdered sugar
2 cups shortening
¾ cup milk
2 teaspoons vanilla extract
1 teaspoon almond extract

Combine all ingredients in a mixing bowl; beat at high speed of electric mixer 5 minutes or until light and fluffy. Yield: enough to frost and decorate one 2-layer cake. *Judy Cunningham, Roanoke, Virginia.*

Puddings Perfect For Two

Most pudding recipes and commercial mixes serve four or more, which spells leftovers when you're cooking for two. Our readers have solved the problem with recipes for puddings that make just enough for two people.

LEMON PUDDING CAKE

½ cup sugar
2½ tablespoons all-purpose flour
⅛ teaspoon salt
1 egg, separated
½ cup milk
1½ teaspoons grated lemon rind
1 tablespoon lemon juice
Whipped cream (optional)

Combine first 3 ingredients in a medium bowl; set aside.

Beat egg yolk; add milk, lemon rind, and juice. Add to dry ingredients, and mix well. Beat egg white (at room temperature) until soft peaks form; fold into milk mixture.

Pour into 2 lightly greased 10-ounce custard cups; place in a pan of warm water. Bake at 350° for 30 to 35 minutes or until a knife inserted in center comes out clean. Serve warm; top with whipped cream, if desired. Yield: 2 servings. *Sharon Saullo, Dallas, Texas.*

CREAMY CHOCOLATE PUDDING

⅓ cup sugar
1 tablespoon cornstarch
1 tablespoon cocoa
Dash of salt
1 cup milk
1 egg yolk, slightly beaten
½ teaspoon vanilla extract
Whipped cream (optional)
Chopped pecans (optional)

Combine first 4 ingredients in a medium saucepan; stir in milk and egg yolk. Cook over medium heat, stirring constantly, until mixture comes to a boil; cook 1 additional minute, stirring constantly. Remove from heat, and stir in vanilla.

Pour into 2 individual serving dishes. Serve warm or chilled; top with whipped cream and pecans, if desired. Yield: 2 servings. *Sandra Edmondson, Walnut Ridge, Arkansas.*

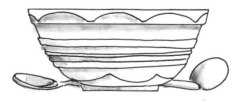

Make The Bread Whole Grain

Help improve your family's nutrition by baking whole grain breads. The flavor of a homemade whole grain loaf or muffin will convert even the staunchest of white-bread fans.

Bread becomes whole grain when white flour is replaced with whole wheat or rye. Or you can stir unprocessed bran or granola into the dough to achieve a full, fiber-rich texture. In addition to dietary fiber, whole grain breads also provide trace vitamins and minerals not present in white bread.

BEST EVER NUT CRUNCH MUFFINS

1½ cups unbleached all-purpose flour
½ cup sugar
¼ cup cornmeal
¼ cup wheat germ
2 tablespoons baking powder
½ teaspoon salt
1½ cups unprocessed bran
½ cup granola
2 cups buttermilk
1½ tablespoons crunchy peanut butter
2½ tablespoons vegetable oil
2 eggs, beaten

Combine the first 6 ingredients in a large mixing bowl; set mixture aside.

Combine bran, granola, and buttermilk, mixing well; soak 5 minutes. Add peanut butter, oil, and eggs; mix well.

Make a well in center of dry ingredients; pour in liquid ingredients. Stir just until moistened.

Fill greased muffin pans two-thirds full. Bake at 400° for 25 minutes. Remove from pans immediately. Yield: about 2 dozen. *Kim Chutter, San Antonio, Texas.*

WHOLE WHEAT HONEY BREAD

2½ cups warm water (105° to 115°)
⅓ cup instant nonfat dry milk powder
⅓ cup shortening
¼ cup honey
2 packages dry yeast
1 tablespoon salt
3½ cups whole wheat flour
About 3½ cups all-purpose flour

Combine first 6 ingredients in a large mixing bowl; let stand 5 minutes. Add whole wheat flour; beat with electric mixer at low speed until blended. Increase speed to medium, and beat 3 minutes. Gradually add remaining flour.

Turn dough out onto a heavily floured surface (dough will be sticky), and knead until smooth and elastic. Cover and let rest in a warm place (85°), free from drafts, for 15 minutes. (Dough will be soft.)

Divide dough in half; place each half in a greased 9- x 5- x 3-inch loafpan. Cover and let rise in a warm place (85°), free from drafts, about 1½ hours or until doubled in bulk. Bake at 375° for 40 minutes or until loaves sound hollow when tapped. Cool on wire racks. Yield: 2 loaves. *Teri Isenhour, Charlotte, North Carolina.*

May

Grills are made ready in May as Southerners get fired up for warm weather cookouts. Use the grill for some of our steak recipes such as Saucy Beef Kabobs and Herb Marinated Tenderloin. Other key recipes call for broiling, stir-frying, or sautéing, so choose your favorite way to prepare it. Take note of the tips we offer as well, and find out how to select the tenderest cut of meat and cook it just right.

Microwaving becomes even more popular as the weather gets warm, and you can whip up one of our elegant microwave desserts without heating up your kitchen. Save time and win compliments with fancy desserts like our Brandy Alexander Soufflé.

You'll also find some unique ideas for shaped salads, appetizers, and desserts that are cool and refreshing. Whether they're congealed in a colorful layered aspic or molded into a creamy pâté, these dishes are worth the additional effort to make a springtime brunch or luncheon something extra special.

Unmold A Showy, Shaped Dish

Delicate, pretty, and so delicious are our elegant, chilled pâté, aspic, and salad dishes shaped in dainty fluted molds or simple loafpans. They take time to make, but may be assembled the day before serving.

Chicken Liver Pâté is an attractive appetizer spread seasoned with onion, brandy, and a dash of nutmeg. To be sure the pâté has smooth sides with no cracks, mold it in a dish with straight sides and few indentations.

Making an aspic requires more care and technique. Defined as a jelly made with meat, fish, or vegetable stock, an aspic is usually served as a salad, side dish, or sometimes as an entrée. Meat or fish and vegetables may be congealed in patterns in the shimmering stock.

To create patterns of food in an aspic, or in any congealed food, prepare the recipe in steps. Pour a thin layer of gelatin mixture into the bottom of the mold, allow to set, then arrange a layer of food in a pattern over the gelatin. Barely cover with gelatin, and chill until set. Speed the process by chilling the mold in the freezer prior to filling with the first gelatin layer.

Another tip: To get prettier slices of congealed mixtures containing large chunks of food, use an electric knife.

See page 124 for the article "From Our Kitchen To Yours" for more tips on preparing molded dishes.

SHRIMP-CUCUMBER ASPIC

6 cups water
2 pounds medium-size fresh shrimp
4¼ cups water
3 chicken-flavored bouillon cubes
½ cup celery leaves
3 envelopes unflavored gelatin
1 cup cold water
1½ tablespoons dry white wine
⅛ teaspoon white pepper
10 cucumber slices
2½ cups chopped cucumber
1 cup chopped celery
1 small onion, chopped
Additional celery leaves (optional)

Bring 6 cups water to a boil; add shrimp and reduce heat. Simmer 3 to 5 minutes. Drain well, and rinse with cold water; chill. Peel and devein shrimp. Measure 2 cups shrimp, and coarsely chop. Set aside remaining shrimp.

Bring 4¼ cups water to a boil in a Dutch oven; add bouillon cubes, stirring until dissolved. Add ½ cup celery leaves, and boil 30 seconds; remove leaves with slotted spoon, and discard. Boil broth about 20 minutes until reduced to 2¼ cups. Add additional water if necessary to measure 2¼ cups liquid.

Sprinkle gelatin over 1 cup cold water, and let stand 5 minutes. Add to broth in saucepan; cook over medium heat until gelatin dissolves, stirring constantly and scraping sides occasionally. Stir in wine and pepper.

Pour ½ cup gelatin mixture into an oiled 9- x 5- x 3-inch loafpan. Chill until set. Arrange about 15 whole shrimp in desired pattern over chilled gelatin layer; spoon enough gelatin over shrimp to cover. Chill until set.

Chill remaining gelatin until the consistency of unbeaten egg white. Dip cucumber slices and 4 whole shrimp into slightly thickened gelatin; arrange around sides of pan. Chill until set. Stir chopped shrimp and vegetables into remaining slightly thickened gelatin; carefully spoon into pan. Chill until firm. Unmold on a serving platter. Garnish with remaining whole shrimp and celery leaves, if desired. Slice with an electric knife. Yield: 10 servings.

CHICKEN LIVER PATE

½ cup butter or margarine
1 pound chicken livers
2 small onions, quartered
½ teaspoon salt
¼ teaspoon pepper
Dash of ground nutmeg
¼ cup brandy
Boston lettuce leaves
Fresh parsley sprigs
Green onion tops, blanched
Carrot flowers, blanched

Melt butter in a large skillet; add chicken livers and cook 8 minutes, stirring often. Cool. Pour livers into container of electric blender. Add next 5 ingredients; process until smooth. Spoon mixture into a lightly oiled 7½- x 3½- x 3-inch loafpan; cover and chill 8 hours or overnight.

Arrange lettuce leaves on serving dish; unmold pâté onto lettuce. Garnish with parsley sprigs, green onion tops, and carrot flowers. Serve with crackers. Yield: about 2 cups. *Julie B. Kennedy, Kingwood, Texas.*

PEACHES-AND-CREAM SALAD

1 (3-ounce) package peach-flavored gelatin
1 cup boiling water
¾ cup cold water
3 cups sliced peaches
1 small banana, sliced
1 envelope unflavored gelatin
3 tablespoons cold water
½ cup half-and-half
1 (8-ounce) package cream cheese, softened
1 cup whipping cream
½ cup plus 2 tablespoons sugar
1 cup pureed peaches

Dissolve peach gelatin in 1 cup boiling water; stir until dissolved. Add cold water and mix well. Chill until the consistency of unbeaten egg white. Stir in sliced peaches and banana. Pour into a lightly oiled 8-cup mold. Chill until set.

Soften unflavored gelatin in 3 tablespoons cold water. Scald half-and-half, and stir into gelatin mixture. Beat cream cheese with electric mixer. Add whipping cream, sugar, and pureed peaches; mix well. Add to gelatin mixture, and stir well. Pour over peach and banana layer; chill at least 8 hours or until firm. Yield: 10 to 12 servings.
*Patricia Flint,
Staunton, Virginia.*

RASPBERRY DREAM

1 envelope unflavored gelatin
¼ cup cold water
1 (8-ounce) package cream cheese, softened
½ cup sugar
½ teaspoon almond extract
Dash of salt
1 cup milk
1 cup whipping cream
Raspberry Sauce

Combine gelatin and water in a small saucepan; cook over low heat, stirring until gelatin dissolves. Set aside.

Combine cream cheese, sugar, almond extract, and salt; beat until smooth and creamy. Gradually add milk and gelatin mixture to creamed mixture, mixing well. Beat whipping cream until soft peaks form (do not overbeat); fold into the gelatin mixture.

Pour into a lightly oiled 4-cup mold; chill until set. Unmold dessert onto serving dish, and serve with Raspberry Sauce. Yield: 8 servings.

Raspberry Sauce:

1 (10-ounce) package frozen raspberries, thawed
1 tablespoon cornstarch
2 tablespoons cream sherry

Drain raspberries, reserving juice. Put raspberries through a food mill; discard seeds. Set berry pulp aside.

Combine juice, cornstarch, and sherry in a small saucepan; mix well. Cook over low heat, stirring constantly, until smooth and slightly thickened. Stir in raspberries. Cool. Yield: about 1 cup.

Give Beef A Turn

What's your favorite way to enjoy steak? Grilled whole and sliced, cut into chunks and threaded on kabob skewers, or cut into thin strips and stir-fried? No matter which method you prefer, one thing is certain. You want the steak to be tender, juicy, and flavorful.

To help ensure perfect results every time, start by paying close attention to which steak you select. Remember that some cuts of steak are naturally more tender than others. The rib-eye, sirloin, and tenderloin are more tender than flank and round steaks. Tender cuts of beef come from the muscles that are used less, while tougher cuts come from the harder working muscles.

The tenderness of a steak is also determined by the amount of marbling or veinlike fat running through the meat.

When preparing lean meat, you must be especially careful to avoid overcooking. The tenderest, juiciest steaks will be those cooked only to rare, medium rare, or medium. If grilling or broiling, place your steak on a preheated broiler or over hot coals. This way the exterior of the steak will brown quickly, holding in the juices. For even more juiciness, baste the steak as it cooks with a flavorful sauce or marinade.

You can create your own basting sauce or marinade from a variety of ingredients. Try combining herbs and spices with oils, wines, vinegars, fruit juices, and soy sauce. An easy and efficient way to marinate steak is in a plastic bag. Place the bag in a shallow dish, add the steak and marinade, then close the bag and refrigerate. Turning the bag will help distribute the marinade.

Allow flank steak to marinate several hours or overnight to make it tender. Cook it briefly—just a few minutes on each side—and cut into thin slices.

Round steak can be sliced into thin strips, marinated, and quickly stir-fried. Tossed with vegetables and served over rice, round steak becomes a flavorful, tender meat course in minutes.

STEAK WITH HAM-AND-MUSHROOM SAUCE

½ cup sliced fresh mushrooms
¼ cup finely diced Prosciutto ham
¼ cup finely chopped onion
1 small clove garlic, minced
1 tablespoon olive oil
¼ teaspoon salt
Dash of dried whole oregano
Dash of coarsely ground black pepper
Dash of red pepper
3 tablespoons brandy
1 pound sirloin strip steak

Sauté mushrooms, ham, onion, and garlic in olive oil until onion is tender; add salt, oregano, and pepper. Stir in brandy, and simmer 1 minute; set aside.

Grill steak over medium coals 20 to 25 minutes or until desired doneness. Pour sauce over steak before serving. Yield: 2 to 3 servings.   *Don Yost,*
Miami, Florida.

STEAK ON A STICK

¼ cup sherry
1 tablespoon soy sauce
1½ teaspoons wine vinegar
1½ teaspoons catsup
1½ teaspoons honey
Dash of garlic powder
1 pound boneless sirloin steak, cut into 1-inch cubes

Combine first 6 ingredients in a large shallow dish. Add steak; cover and marinate at least 2 hours in refrigerator, turning occasionally.

Drain steak, reserving marinade. Thread steak on 7-inch skewers. Grill 5 minutes on each side over medium coals or until desired degree of doneness, basting with marinade. Yield: 4 servings.   *Cynthia Aaron,*
Tallahassee, Florida.

SAUCY BEEF KABOBS

2 cups tomato juice
½ cup butter or margarine
¼ cup finely chopped onion
¼ cup catsup
1 teaspoon dry mustard
¾ teaspoon salt
½ teaspoon paprika
½ teaspoon pepper
1 clove garlic, minced
1 tablespoon Worcestershire sauce
Dash of hot sauce
2 pounds (1½-inch-thick) boneless sirloin steak, cut into 1-inch cubes
¼ pound fresh mushroom caps
½ pint cherry tomatoes
1 large onion, cut into eighths
1 large green pepper, cut into 1-inch pieces

Combine first 11 ingredients in a medium saucepan; simmer, uncovered, for 30 minutes.

Alternately thread steak and vegetables on 6 skewers.

Grill kabobs over medium-hot coals 10 to 15 minutes or until desired degree of doneness, turning kabobs and brushing frequently with sauce. Yield: 6 servings.   *Lucille James,*
New Orleans, Louisiana.

HERB MARINATED TENDERLOIN

1 cup Burgundy or other dry red wine
1 small onion, chopped
1 tablespoon chopped fresh parsley
1 bay leaf
½ teaspoon salt
¼ teaspoon dried whole thyme
½ clove garlic, crushed
2 pounds (1½-inch-thick) tenderloin steak

Combine first 7 ingredients, mixing well; pour into a large shallow dish. Add steak; cover dish and marinate at least 24 hours in the refrigerator, turning steak occasionally.

Remove steak from marinade. Grill 8 to 9 minutes on each side over medium coals or until desired degree of doneness. Yield: 6 servings.
DeLea Lonadier,
Montgomery, Louisiana.

CRACKED PEPPER STEAK

2 (8- to 12-ounce) rib-eye steaks, 1½ inches thick
¼ teaspoon garlic powder
Salt
¼ cup chopped green onion
¼ cup butter or margarine
1 teaspoon cracked black pepper, divided

Sprinkle both sides of the steaks with garlic powder and salt; set aside.

Sauté onion in butter in a large skillet until crisp-tender. Remove onion and set aside.

Sprinkle ½ teaspoon pepper in the skillet; add steaks, and cook over medium heat 5 to 7 minutes. Sprinkle remaining ½ teaspoon pepper over top of steaks; turn and continue cooking 5 to 7 minutes or until desired degree of doneness. Remove steaks to serving platter, and sprinkle with sautéed onion. Yield: 2 servings.

SWEET-AND-SOUR MARINATED STEAKS

4 (8- to 12-ounce) rib-eye steaks, 1 inch
  thick
½ cup soy sauce
¼ cup firmly packed brown sugar
¼ cup pineapple juice
¼ cup vinegar
½ teaspoon garlic salt

Place steaks in a large shallow dish.
Combine remaining ingredients; stir
well and pour over steaks. Cover and
marinate 4 hours in refrigerator, turning
steaks occasionally.

Remove steaks from marinade. Grill
5 inches from hot coals about 5 minutes
on each side. Yield: 4 servings.

Mrs. Michael R. Hill,
Montgomery, Alabama.

BROILED ORIENTAL STEAKS

2 (1-pound) flank steaks
⅓ cup vegetable oil
⅓ cup soy sauce
2 tablespoons instant minced onion
2 tablespoons red wine vinegar
2 tablespoons chutney
⅛ teaspoon onion powder
Dash of garlic salt

Prick both sides of steaks with a fork,
and place in a large shallow dish. Combine remaining ingredients; pour over
steaks. Cover; marinate 4 to 6 hours in
refrigerator, turning occasionally.

Remove steaks from marinade. Broil
4 inches from heat, 3 to 5 minutes on
each side or until desired degree of
doneness. To serve, thinly slice steaks
across grain. Yield: 6 to 8 servings.

Margaret O. Kaminsky,
Manassas, Virginia.

DELICIOUS MARINATED FLANK STEAKS

2 (1- to 1¼-pound) flank steaks
½ cup vegetable oil
¼ cup teriyaki sauce
1 tablespoon minced onion
3 tablespoons honey
½ teaspoon garlic powder
½ teaspoon ground ginger
Green onion fan

Prick both sides of steaks with fork,
and place in a large shallow dish.

Combine remaining ingredients; pour
over steaks. Cover; marinate 24 hours
in refrigerator, turning occasionally.

Remove steaks from marinade. Grill
over hot coals 4 to 5 minutes on each
side or until desired degree of doneness.
To serve, thinly slice steaks across
grain, and garnish with green onion fan.
Yield: 6 to 8 servings.

Mrs. John S. Gregory, Jr.,
Naples, Florida.

STIR-FRY BROCCOLI AND BEEF

1 pound boneless round steak
⅓ cup soy sauce
¼ cup water
2 tablespoons brown sugar
1 clove garlic, crushed
1 teaspoon ground ginger
1 teaspoon cornstarch
3 tablespoons vegetable oil
4 cups fresh broccoli flowerets
1 large onion, cut into 8 wedges
¼ cup water
Hot cooked rice

Partially freeze steak; slice across
grain into 3- x ¼-inch strips, and set
aside. Combine next 6 ingredients, mixing well; add steak. Cover and refrigerate 1 hour.

Drain steak, reserving marinade.
Pour oil around top of preheated wok,
coating sides; allow to heat at medium
high (325°) for 1 minute. Add steak;
stir-fry 2 to 3 minutes or just until
browned. Remove steak, and set aside.

Add broccoli, onion, and ¼ cup
water to wok. Cover and reduce heat to
low (225°); cook 3 to 5 minutes or until
broccoli is crisp-tender. Stir in steak and
marinade; cook 1 minute, stirring constantly, until thickened. Serve over rice.
Yield: 4 to 6 servings. *Cindy Murphy,*
Cleveland, Tennessee.

TERIYAKI STIR-FRY

1½ pounds boneless round steak
¼ cup firmly packed brown sugar
¼ cup water
¼ cup soy sauce
2 tablespoons Worcestershire sauce
½ teaspoon minced garlic
1 tablespoon vegetable oil
1½ cups diagonally sliced carrots
1½ cups diagonally sliced celery
1 cup chopped onion
1 tablespoon vegetable oil
1 tablespoon cornstarch
1 cup uncooked regular rice, cooked

Partially freeze steak; slice across
grain into 3- x ¼-inch strips.

Combine next 5 ingredients, mixing
well; pour into a shallow dish. Add
steak; cover and marinate 4 to 6 hours
in refrigerator, stirring occasionally.

Pour 1 tablespoon oil around top of
preheated wok, coating sides; allow to
heat at medium high (325°) for 2 minutes. Add carrots, celery, and onion;
stir-fry 4 minutes. Remove vegetables
from wok, and set aside.

Add 1 tablespoon oil to wok. Drain
steak, reserving marinade. Add steak to
the wok; stir-fry 2 to 3 minutes or just
until browned.

Combine cornstarch and marinade,
mixing well; stir into steak. Cook, stirring constantly, until thickened.

Combine vegetables and rice, tossing
gently; place on serving dish. Spoon
steak mixture over rice. Yield: 6
servings. *Deanna Bleasdell,*
Weatherford, Texas.

Salads For Any Occasion

Looking for a bright, colorful salad to
serve with dinner? Here are some refreshing new salad ideas.

FROZEN FRUIT SALAD

2 eggs, slightly beaten
2 tablespoons vinegar
¼ cup sugar
2 tablespoons butter or margarine
1 (15¼-ounce) can pineapple chunks,
  undrained
2 medium bananas, sliced
1 (11-ounce) can mandarin oranges,
  drained
1 (16-ounce) can sliced peaches, drained
1 (6-ounce) jar maraschino cherries,
  drained
1 (7-ounce) package miniature
  marshmallows
½ cup whipping cream, whipped

Combine first 4 ingredients in a small
saucepan. Cook over medium heat, stirring constantly, until thickened; set
aside to cool.

Drain pineapple, reserving liquid.
Add bananas to reserved liquid, and
toss gently; drain.

Combine fruit and marshmallows in a
large bowl. Add egg mixture, and stir
gently. Fold in whipped cream. Pour
mixture into a lightly greased 10-inch
tube pan; cover and freeze until firm.
Let salad stand at room temperature 20
minutes before serving. Yield: 12 to 15
servings. *Linda C. Hawkins,*
Cushing, Oklahoma.

COCONUT FRUIT BOWL

1 (1.25-ounce) envelope whipped topping mix
1 (16-ounce) can fruit cocktail, drained
1 (11-ounce) can mandarin oranges, drained
1 (16-ounce) can pear halves, drained and chopped
1 (10-ounce) jar maraschino cherries, drained and chopped
1 (3½-ounce) can flaked coconut

Prepare whipped topping mix according to package directions.

Combine fruit and coconut in a large mixing bowl; toss well. Fold in whipped topping; cover salad and chill. Yield: 8 to 10 servings. *Marie Davis, Morganton, North Carolina.*

RAINBOW VEGETABLE SALAD

1 (10-ounce) package frozen English peas
1 cup shredded cabbage
1 cup grated carrots
1 cup chopped green pepper
1 cup torn lettuce
1 cup chopped tomato
1 cup sliced celery
1 cup (4 ounces) shredded Cheddar cheese
½ cup chopped cucumber
1 small onion, thinly sliced and separated into rings
½ cup white wine vinegar
1 teaspoon sugar
½ teaspoon salt
⅛ teaspoon pepper

Cook peas according to package directions; drain. Combine peas and next 9 ingredients in a large bowl; toss well.

Combine vinegar, sugar, salt, and pepper; pour over vegetables, tossing well. Cover salad and chill. Yield: 8 to 10 servings. *Thelma B. Scott, Meadows of Dan, Virginia.*

TOMATO RELISH SALAD

3 tomatoes, sliced
1 medium cucumber, thinly sliced
1 medium onion, thinly sliced and separated into rings
½ cup sliced carrots
½ cup sliced celery
½ cup tarragon vinegar
½ cup water
¼ cup sugar
1 teaspoon salt
1 teaspoon paprika
Dash of pepper

Combine the first 5 ingredients, and toss gently.

Combine remaining ingredients; mix well, and pour over vegetables. Cover salad, and chill 4 to 6 hours. Yield: 6 to 8 servings. *Barbara Burrows, Livonia, Michigan.*

Pick Vegetable Recipes For Spring

Green beans, zucchini, carrots, English peas, and snow peas—all fresh from your garden. There's no better way to enjoy them than when they are fresh in these simple recipes.

GOLDENROD BEANS

1½ pounds fresh green beans
2½ cups water
½ teaspoon salt
3 hard-cooked eggs
1½ tablespoons butter or margarine
2 tablespoons all-purpose flour
½ cup evaporated milk
½ teaspoon salt
⅛ teaspoon pepper
2 tablespoons mayonnaise

Wash beans; trim ends and remove strings. Cut beans into 1½-inch pieces. Combine beans, water, and ½ teaspoon salt in a heavy saucepan; bring to a boil. Reduce heat, cover, and simmer 30 to 35 minutes or until tender. Drain, reserving ½ cup bean liquid; set beans aside and keep warm.

Slice eggs in half; remove yolks. Press yolks through a sieve, and set aside. Chop egg whites, and set aside.

Melt butter in a heavy saucepan over low heat; add flour, stirring until smooth. Cook 1 minute, stirring constantly. Gradually add milk and reserved bean liquid; cook over medium heat, stirring constantly, until thickened and bubbly. Stir in ½ teaspoon salt, pepper, mayonnaise, and egg whites.

Place beans in a serving dish; pour sauce over top. Sprinkle egg yolks over sauce. Yield: 6 servings. *Kay Stubbs, Mauk, Georgia.*

LEMON CARROTS

8 carrots, scraped and cut into 1-inch diagonal slices
¾ cup water
¼ cup sugar
1½ tablespoons lemon juice
⅛ teaspoon salt
2 tablespoons butter
Fresh parsley sprigs (optional)

Combine first 5 ingredients in a saucepan. Cover and cook over medium heat 15 minutes or until carrots are tender. Add butter; stir until melted. Garnish with parsley, if desired. Yield: 4 servings. Serve immediately. *Betty J. Moore, Belton, Texas.*

SNOW PEAS AND TOMATOES

1 pound fresh snow peas
¼ cup chopped onion
2 tablespoons butter or margarine
½ teaspoon salt
1 tablespoon minced fresh oregano or 1 teaspoon dried whole oregano
1 tablespoon soy sauce
3 medium tomatoes, cut into wedges

Wash pea pods; trim ends and remove tough strings. Set aside.

Sauté onion in butter in a large skillet until tender. Stir in peas, salt, oregano, and soy sauce; cook, stirring constantly, until peas are crisp-tender. Add tomatoes; cover and cook 1 minute. Yield: 4 to 6 servings. *Marian Cox, Deming, New Mexico.*

GLAZED ENGLISH PEAS

2 pounds fresh English peas
¼ cup chopped green onion
2 tablespoons butter or margarine
½ teaspoon all-purpose flour
¼ teaspoon sugar
¼ cup milk
¼ teaspoon salt
⅛ teaspoon pepper

Shell and wash peas; cover with water, and bring to a boil. Reduce heat, cover, and simmer 8 to 10 minutes or until tender; drain well. Set aside.

Sauté onion in butter in a large skillet until tender. Add flour and sugar, stirring until smooth. Cook 1 minute, stirring constantly. Gradually add milk, stirring until smooth; stir in peas. Cook over medium heat, stirring constantly, until thickened and bubbly. Stir in salt and pepper. Yield: about 4 servings. *Daisy Cotton, Edcouch, Texas.*

GARDEN SURPRISE

1 (1-pound) bunch broccoli
1 small head cauliflower, broken into flowerets
1 pound carrots, scraped and cut into ½-inch slices
¼ cup finely chopped onion
¾ cup mayonnaise
3 to 4 tablespoons prepared horseradish
¼ teaspoon salt
¼ teaspoon pepper
⅓ cup cracker crumbs
2 tablespoons butter or margarine, melted
⅛ teaspoon paprika

Trim off large leaves of broccoli, and remove tough ends of lower stalks; slice remaining stalks into 1-inch pieces. Separate tops into flowerets.

Arrange broccoli, cauliflower, and carrots in a steaming rack. Place over boiling water; cover and steam 7 minutes or until tender.

Combine onion, mayonnaise, horseradish, salt, and pepper. Add to vegetables; toss until well coated. Spoon mixture into a lightly greased 2-quart baking dish. Combine cracker crumbs, butter, and paprika, stirring well. Sprinkle over top. Bake at 350° for 5 to 10 minutes or until thoroughly heated. Yield: 8 servings. *Esther Wrobel, Chaseburg, Wisconsin.*

VEGETABLE MEDLEY

2 tablespoons vegetable oil
3 medium zucchini, sliced
2 green peppers, cut into lengthwise strips
1 large onion, sliced and separated into rings
½ pound fresh mushrooms, sliced
1 large clove garlic, minced
1 teaspoon dried whole basil
½ teaspoon salt
½ teaspoon pepper
½ cup Chablis or other dry white wine
1 tablespoon butter or margarine
½ cup grated Parmesan cheese

Heat oil in a large skillet. Add next 8 ingredients; cover and cook 5 minutes. Stir in wine; simmer, uncovered, 10 additional minutes. Add butter, and stir gently until melted. Sprinkle with cheese. Yield: 6 servings.
Doris Fritz Phillips, Springdale, Arkansas.

VEGETABLES WITH SESAME SAUCE

1 cup scraped and sliced carrots
1 cup coarsely chopped zucchini
1 cup cauliflower flowerets
1 cup sliced fresh green beans
1 tablespoon sliced red chile pepper
1 tablespoon butter or margarine
2 tablespoons all-purpose flour
1 cup beef broth
1 teaspoon Dijon mustard
¼ teaspoon salt
2 tablespoons sesame seeds
Grated Parmesan cheese

Arrange vegetables and chile pepper in a steaming rack. Place over boiling water; cover and steam 7 minutes or to desired degree of doneness. Spoon into serving dish; set aside.

Melt butter in a heavy saucepan over low heat; add flour, stirring until smooth. Cook 1 minute, stirring constantly. Gradually add beef broth; cook over medium heat, stirring constantly, until thick and bubbly. Stir in mustard, salt, and sesame seeds; simmer 1 minute, stirring constantly. Pour over vegetables, and sprinkle with cheese. Yield: 4 to 6 servings. *Marie Raney, Dogpatch, Arkansas.*

These Goodies Start With Biscuit Mix

Biscuit mix provides a favorite shortcut for baking. The flour, leavening, salt, and dry milk powder are premixed to save you time.

SAUSAGE-ONION SQUARES

1 pound mild bulk pork sausage
1 large onion, chopped
2 cups biscuit mix
¾ cup milk
2 eggs
2 teaspoons caraway seeds
1½ cups commercial sour cream
¼ teaspoon salt
¼ teaspoon paprika

Cook sausage and onion until sausage is browned and onion is tender; drain.

Combine biscuit mix, milk, and 1 egg; mix well. Spread mixture in a greased 13- x 9- x 2-inch baking dish. Sprinkle with caraway seeds; top with sausage mixture.

Combine sour cream, salt, and 1 egg; blend well. Pour over sausage mixture, and sprinkle with paprika. Bake at 350° for 25 to 30 minutes. Cut into squares. Yield: 12 servings. *Mary Blue, Cape Girardeau, Missouri.*

RASPBERRY COFFEE CAKE

1 (3-ounce) package cream cheese, softened
2 tablespoons butter or margarine, softened
2 cups biscuit mix
⅓ cup milk
½ cup raspberry preserves
Glaze (recipe follows)

Cut cream cheese and butter into biscuit mix with a pastry blender until mixture resembles coarse meal. Add milk, stirring with a fork until dry ingredients are moistened.

Turn dough out onto a well-floured surface and knead 10 times. Roll dough into a 12- x 8-inch rectangle on waxed paper. Spread preserves over rectangle, leaving a ½-inch margin around edges; carefully fold each side to center of dough. Firmly pinch ends to seal. Transfer to a greased baking sheet.

Using kitchen shears, make 1½-inch cuts about 1 inch apart on each side of coffee cake, cutting one-third of the way through dough at each cut. Bake at 400° for 20 to 25 minutes.

Pour glaze over coffee cake while still warm. Yield: 8 servings.

Glaze:

1 cup sifted powdered sugar
2 tablespoons milk
½ teaspoon vanilla extract

Combine all ingredients, mixing well. Yield: ⅓ cup. *Cindi Rawlins, Dunwoody, Georgia.*

ONION-CHEESE SUPPER BREAD

½ cup chopped onion
1 tablespoon vegetable oil
½ cup milk
1 egg, beaten
1½ cups biscuit mix
1 cup (4 ounces) shredded sharp Cheddar cheese, divided
2 tablespoons chopped fresh parsley
2 tablespoons butter, melted

Sauté onion in oil in a small skillet until tender. Set aside.

Combine milk, egg, and biscuit mix in a medium mixing bowl; stir just until moistened. Add onion, ½ cup cheese, and parsley; stir well.

Spread batter in a greased 8-inch round cakepan; drizzle with melted butter. Bake at 400° for 15 minutes. Sprinkle with remaining ½ cup cheese. Bake an additional 5 minutes. Yield: 6 to 8 servings.   *Mrs. Peter Rosato III, Memphis, Tennessee.*

PEACH CRISP

1 (29-ounce) can sliced peaches, drained
1 cup biscuit mix
¾ cup firmly packed brown sugar
½ teaspoon ground cinnamon
¼ cup butter or margarine, softened
Ice cream (optional)

Arrange peach slices in an ungreased 8-inch square pan; set aside.

Combine next 3 ingredients in a large bowl; mix well. Cut butter into mixture with pastry blender until mixture resembles coarse meal. Sprinkle over peaches. Bake, uncovered, at 400° for 18 to 20 minutes or until golden brown. Serve warm with ice cream, if desired. Yield: 6 to 8 servings.   *Carolyn Sutton, Savannah, Georgia.*

Fresh Cookies Draw A Crowd

When the aroma of freshly baked cookies drifts throughout the house, cookie making quickly becomes a family affair. Children will find Frosted Orange Cookies are not only good to eat, but fun to make, too. They'll enjoy dropping the dough on baking sheets and frosting the cookies with an orange-flavored glaze.

SOUTHERN SOUR CREAM COOKIES

⅓ cup shortening
⅔ cup sugar
1 egg
1¾ cups all-purpose flour
1 teaspoon baking powder
¼ teaspoon baking soda
½ teaspoon salt
½ cup commercial sour cream
½ cup chopped walnuts
Sugar
2 tablespoons sugar
½ teaspoon ground cinnamon

Combine shortening and ⅔ cup sugar in a large mixing bowl; beat well. Add egg, and beat well. Combine flour, baking powder, soda, and salt; add to creamed mixture alternately with sour cream, beginning and ending with flour mixture. Stir in walnuts.

Drop dough by heaping teaspoonfuls onto lightly greased cookie sheets. Dip bottom of a glass in water; dip in sugar, and gently press each cookie until 2 inches in diameter. Combine 2 tablespoons sugar and cinnamon; lightly sprinkle over cookies. Bake at 400° for 10 to 12 minutes. Cool on wire racks. Yield: 3½ dozen.   *Lois Gloer, Atlanta, Georgia.*

CRISPY SHORTBREAD COOKIES

½ cup butter or margarine, softened
½ cup shortening
1½ cups sifted powdered sugar
1½ teaspoons vanilla extract
1¼ cups all-purpose flour
1½ cups corn flake cereal
½ cup finely chopped pecans

Cream butter and shortening; gradually add sugar, beating until smooth. Add vanilla and flour, beating well. Stir in cereal.

Shape dough into a long roll, 2 inches in diameter; gently roll in pecans. Wrap in waxed paper, and chill overnight or until firm.

Let roll stand at room temperature about 10 minutes. Cut dough into ¼-inch slices; place 2 inches apart on ungreased cookie sheets. Bake at 350° for 15 minutes or until lightly brown. Cool on wire racks. Yield: 3½ dozen.
   Mrs. E. F. Whitt, Attalla, Alabama.

PEANUT BUTTER-COCONUT COOKIES

½ cup butter or margarine, softened
½ cup chunky peanut butter
1 cup firmly packed brown sugar
1 egg
½ teaspoon vanilla extract
1¼ cups all-purpose flour
¾ teaspoon baking soda
½ teaspoon baking powder
½ teaspoon salt
1 cup flaked coconut

Cream butter and peanut butter. Gradually add sugar, beating well. Beat in egg and vanilla. Combine flour, soda, baking powder, and salt; add to creamed mixture, stirring well. Stir in coconut.

Divide dough in half; shape each half into a roll 1½ inches in diameter. Wrap in waxed paper, and chill 3 to 4 hours or until firm.

Cut dough into ¼-inch slices; place 2 inches apart on lightly greased cookie sheets. Bake at 350° for 8 to 10 minutes or until lightly browned. Cool on wire racks. Yield: 4 dozen.   *Lynette Walther, East Palatka, Florida.*

PECAN-BUTTER COOKIES

1 cup butter or margarine, softened
1 cup sugar
2 egg yolks
¾ teaspoon vanilla extract
¾ teaspoon almond extract
½ teaspoon lemon extract
2 cups all-purpose flour
1 teaspoon baking powder
¼ teaspoon salt
About 1 cup pecan halves

Cream butter; gradually add sugar, beating until light and fluffy. Add egg yolks, one at a time, beating well after each addition. Stir in flavorings. Combine flour, baking powder, and salt. Add to creamed mixture; beat well.

Roll dough into 1-inch balls; place about 2 inches apart on ungreased cookie sheets. Press a pecan half into center of each cookie. Bake at 300° for 20 minutes or until lightly browned. Cool on wire racks. Yield: about 3½ dozen.   *L. W. Goshert, Houston, Texas.*

ORANGE-CHOCOLATE COOKIES

½ cup shortening
1 (3-ounce) package cream cheese, softened
½ cup sugar
1 egg, beaten
1 teaspoon vanilla extract
1 teaspoon grated orange rind
1 cup all-purpose flour
½ teaspoon salt
1 (6-ounce) package semisweet chocolate morsels

Combine first 4 ingredients in a large bowl; beat until smooth and creamy. Add vanilla and orange rind; beat well. Combine flour and salt; add to creamed mixture, beating well. Stir in semisweet chocolate morsels.

Drop dough by heaping teaspoonfuls onto ungreased cookie sheets; bake at 350° for 15 minutes or until edges just begin to brown. Cool on wire racks. Yield: 3 dozen.   *Hazel Slucher, Taylorsville, Kentucky.*

DIFFERENT CHOCOLATE CHIP COOKIES

1 cup butter or margarine, softened
¾ cup firmly packed brown sugar
¾ cup sugar
2 eggs
1 teaspoon vanilla extract
1¼ cups all-purpose flour
1 cup whole wheat flour
½ teaspoon baking powder
1 teaspoon baking soda
¼ teaspoon salt
1 (12-ounce) package semisweet chocolate morsels
½ cup salted sunflower kernels
¼ cup sesame seeds

Cream butter; gradually add sugar, beating until light and fluffy. Add eggs and vanilla, beating well. Combine flour, baking powder, soda, and salt; add to creamed mixture, beating well. Stir in remaining ingredients.

Drop dough by heaping teaspoonfuls onto lightly greased cookie sheets. Bake at 375° for 8 to 10 minutes. Cool slightly on cookie sheets; remove to wire racks. Yield: 5 dozen.   *Betty R. Allen,*
Raleigh, North Carolina.

FROSTED ORANGE COOKIES

1½ cups sugar
1 cup shortening
2 eggs, beaten
1 (8-ounce) carton commercial sour cream
2 tablespoons grated orange rind
3 tablespoons orange juice
4 cups plus 2 tablespoons all-purpose flour
1 tablespoon baking powder
1 teaspoon baking soda
¼ teaspoon salt
Orange glaze (recipe follows)

Combine first 4 ingredients in a large bowl; beat until smooth and creamy. Add orange rind and juice; beat well.

Combine flour, baking powder, soda, and salt; gradually add to creamed mixture, beating well. Drop dough by teaspoonfuls onto greased cookie sheets; bake at 350° for 14 to 16 minutes or until edges just begin to brown. Cool on wire racks. Spread tops of cookies with orange glaze. Yield: 8½ dozen.

Orange Glaze:

1 (16-ounce) package powdered sugar, sifted
2 tablespoons grated orange rind
¼ cup plus 1 tablespoon orange juice
1 teaspoon vanilla extract

Combine all ingredients; beat until smooth. Yield: about 2 cups.
Judy Todd,
Belleville, Michigan.

MICROWAVE COOKERY

Microwave An Elegant Dessert

If there's anything that guarantees the success of a dinner party, it's a fancy dessert. But if your hectic schedule leaves you little time to devote to lavish sweets, then let your microwave oven come to the rescue. Some of these impressive desserts can be prepared and refrigerated well ahead of your party, and the actual microwave time for each one is 15 minutes or less.

BRANDY ALEXANDER SOUFFLE

2 envelopes unflavored gelatin
½ cup cold water
1½ cups hot water
4 eggs, separated
¾ cup sugar
1 (8-ounce) package cream cheese, softened
3 tablespoons crème de cacao
3 tablespoons brandy
¼ cup sugar
1 cup whipping cream, whipped
Chocolate curls (optional)
Chocolate shavings (optional)

Cut a piece of aluminum foil or waxed paper long enough to fit around a 1½-quart soufflé dish, allowing a 1-inch overlap; fold lengthwise into thirds. Lightly oil one side of the foil; wrap around outside of dish, oiled side of foil against dish, allowing it to extend 3 inches above rim to form a collar. Secure the foil with freezer tape.

Combine gelatin and ½ cup cold water; stir well. In a 2½-quart casserole, microwave 1½ cups hot water at HIGH for 5 to 9 minutes until boiling. Add gelatin mixture; stir to dissolve.

Beat egg yolks until thick and lemon colored; gradually add ¾ cup sugar, beating well. Gradually stir in about one-fourth of hot gelatin mixture; then stir into remaining hot mixture. Microwave at HIGH for 3 to 5 minutes or until thickened, stirring at 2-minute intervals. Beat cream cheese until smooth; gradually add yolk mixture, beating well. Stir in crème de cacao and brandy; chill until slightly thickened.

Beat egg whites (at room temperature) until foamy; gradually add ¼ cup sugar, beating until stiff peaks form. Gently fold whipped cream and beaten egg whites into cream cheese mixture.

Spoon mixture into a 1½-quart soufflé dish, and chill until firm. Remove collar from dish. Garnish soufflé with chocolate curls and shavings, if desired. Yield: 8 servings.

BANANAS FOSTER

¼ cup butter or margarine
¼ cup firmly packed brown sugar
½ teaspoon ground cinnamon
4 medium bananas, split and quartered
2 tablespoons banana-flavored liqueur
2 tablespoons light rum
Vanilla ice cream

Place butter in a 2-quart shallow casserole. Microwave at HIGH for 55 seconds or until melted. Stir in sugar and cinnamon. Microwave at HIGH for 30 to 45 seconds or just until hot; stir well. Gently mix in bananas. Microwave at HIGH for 1½ to 2 minutes; stir gently.

Place liqueur and rum in a 1-cup glass measure; microwave at HIGH for 40 to 45 seconds or until hot. Quickly pour over bananas, and ignite with a long match. Serve immediately over vanilla ice cream. Yield: 6 servings.

PEACH MELBA

1 (10-ounce) package frozen raspberries
½ cup red currant jelly
1 tablespoon water
1 tablespoon Cointreau or other orange-flavored liqueur
1 tablespoon cornstarch
6 canned peach halves
Vanilla ice cream

Place raspberries in a 1½-quart glass bowl; microwave at MEDIUM (50% power) for 3 to 4½ minutes or until thawed. Press raspberries through a food mill or sieve; discard seeds. Add jelly to raspberry puree; microwave at MEDIUM for 3 to 5 minutes or until jelly melts. Stir well.

Combine water and Cointreau; stir in cornstarch. Add cornstarch mixture to raspberry mixture, stirring well; microwave at HIGH for 2 to 4 minutes or until mixture thickens. Stir well. Chill.

Place each peach half cut side up in an individual dessert dish; top each peach with a scoop of vanilla ice cream. Pour raspberry sauce over top of ice cream. Yield: 6 servings.

VANILLA CREAM

2 cups milk
¼ cup plus 2 tablespoons sugar, divided
2 egg yolks, beaten
1 tablespoon plus 1 teaspoon cornstarch
½ teaspoon vanilla extract
Fresh strawberries

Combine milk and 3 tablespoons sugar in a 2-quart casserole. Microwave at HIGH for 6½ to 9 minutes or just until mixture reaches boiling point, stirring at 3-minute intervals.

Combine egg yolks and remaining 3 tablespoons sugar in a medium mixing bowl; gradually add cornstarch, stirring well. Gradually stir one-fourth of hot milk mixture into egg mixture; add to remaining hot milk mixture, stirring constantly. Microwave at HIGH for 2 to 2½ minutes or until thickened, stirring at 1-minute intervals. Remove from microwave; stir for 3 minutes. Stir in vanilla. Pour custard into stemmed glasses. Chill until set. Top with fresh strawberries. Yield: 4 servings.

Perk Up The Dish With Parmesan Cheese

Parmesan cheese can turn your favorite food into something special by lending an irresistible flavor to pasta, vegetables, breads, and more.

You'll find Parmesan cheese fresh in rounds or wedges (often with a brown or black coating) or packaged in a convenient grated form. The flavor varies according to the length of time the cheese was aged; the older the cheese, the sharper the flavor.

CRISPY CHICKEN BAKE

½ cup all-purpose flour
⅛ teaspoon pepper
6 chicken breast halves, skinned
1 cup crispy rice cereal, crushed
1 cup grated Parmesan cheese
1 (1⅜-ounce) envelope onion soup mix
2 eggs, beaten
2 tablespoons water
¼ cup plus 2 tablespoons butter or margarine, melted

Combine flour and pepper; dredge chicken in flour; set aside.

Combine next 3 ingredients, and set aside. Combine eggs and water; dip chicken in egg mixture, and coat with cereal mixture.

Place chicken breasts in a 13- x 9- x 2-inch baking dish. Drizzle with melted butter. Bake, uncovered, at 350° for 30 minutes; turn chicken, and bake an additional 30 minutes or until tender. Yield: 6 servings. *Dorothy Campbell, Mayfield Village, Ohio.*

PARMESAN STUFFED MUSHROOMS

20 large fresh mushrooms
1 clove garlic, minced
¼ cup olive oil
½ cup soft breadcrumbs
½ cup grated Parmesan cheese
1 tablespoon dried parsley flakes

Clean mushrooms with damp paper towels. Remove mushroom stems and chop; set caps aside.

Sauté mushroom stems and garlic in oil until tender; remove from heat. Stir in remaining ingredients; spoon into mushroom caps. Place in a shallow baking dish. Bake at 350° for 20 to 25 minutes. Yield: 6 to 8 servings.

Betty Baird, Utica, Kentucky.

FETTUCCINE WITH PARSLEY

1 (8-ounce) package fettuccine
½ cup butter or margarine, melted
¼ cup whipping cream
¼ cup minced fresh parsley
½ teaspoon dried whole basil
Dash of black pepper
1 cup grated Parmesan cheese

Cook fettuccine according to package directions; drain well. Add next 5 ingredients; toss until noodles are well coated. Add Parmesan cheese, and toss gently. Yield: 6 servings. *Patsy Hull, Florence, Alabama.*

SOFT BREADSTICKS

2¾ to 3 cups all-purpose flour
1 package dry yeast
1 tablespoon sugar
1½ teaspoons salt
1¼ cups warm water (105° to 115°)
1 tablespoon vegetable oil
1 cup grated Parmesan cheese
1 clove garlic, minced
Melted butter or margarine
Sesame seeds or additional grated Parmesan cheese

Combine 1½ cups flour, yeast, sugar, and salt in a large bowl. Add water and oil; beat at medium speed of electric mixer 3 to 4 minutes or until smooth. Stir in 1 cup Parmesan cheese, garlic, and enough of remaining flour to make a stiff dough; turn out onto a lightly floured surface, and knead 4 to 5 times or until smooth and elastic.

Divide dough into fourths; shape each fourth into a ball. Cut each ball into 10 pieces. Shape each piece into an 8-inch rope. (Cover remaining dough while working to prevent drying.) Dip rope in butter, and roll in sesame seeds or Parmesan cheese.

Place 2 inches apart on greased baking sheets. Cover and let rise in a warm place (85°), free from drafts, 50 minutes. (Dough will not double in bulk.) Bake at 400° for 12 to 15 minutes or until lightly browned. Yield: 40 breadsticks. *Cecilia Breithaupt, Boerne, Texas.*

Delicious Desserts The Easy Way

Last minute company coming? Or are you just short on time? Try topping canned sliced peaches with a crumbly sugar mixture. Pop it in the oven to bake during dinner, and by dessert time you can serve Easy Peach Crumble. What could be simpler?

QUICK COCONUT PIE

4 eggs
2 cups milk
1½ cups sugar
½ cup all-purpose flour
¼ cup butter or margarine, melted
1 teaspoon vanilla extract
1 (7-ounce) can flaked coconut

Combine first 6 ingredients in the container of an electric blender; blend on low speed 3 minutes. Pour mixture into 2 lightly greased 8-inch pieplates, and let stand 5 minutes. Sprinkle coconut over egg mixture; press coconut into mixture. Bake at 350° for 35 to 40 minutes or until set. Chill before serving. Yield: two 8-inch pies. *Rose Kuehnle, Brenham, Texas.*

CHILLED COCONUT DESSERT

2 envelopes unflavored gelatin
¼ cup cold water
1 cup sugar
1 cup boiling water
1 (15¼-ounce) can crushed pineapple, undrained
2 tablespoons lemon juice
1 (5-ounce) package whipped topping mix
1 (10¾-ounce) loaf angel food cake, cut into ¼-inch pieces
1 (6-ounce) package frozen coconut, thawed

Soften gelatin in cold water. Combine gelatin mixture, sugar, and boiling water; stir until gelatin dissolves. Stir in pineapple and lemon juice; chill until consistency of unbeaten egg white.

Prepare whipped topping according to package directions. Fold pineapple mixture into whipped topping.

Gently fold cake pieces into pineapple mixture, coating all pieces well. Spoon into a lightly greased 13- x 9- x 2-inch dish; sprinkle with coconut. Chill several hours. Yield: 15 servings.
Alma Durden,
Pelham, Georgia.

EASY PEACH CRUMBLE

1 (29-ounce) can sliced peaches, drained
¾ cup firmly packed brown sugar
½ cup all-purpose flour
½ teaspoon ground cinnamon
¼ cup butter or margarine, softened

Place peaches in a lightly greased 9-inch pie plate.

Combine sugar, flour, and cinnamon; cut butter into mixture with a pastry blender until mixture resembles coarse meal. Sprinkle mixture over the peaches. Bake at 375° for 25 minutes. Yield: 4 servings. *Sherry Smith,*
Afton, Tennessee.

PEANUT BUTTER SQUARES

1 cup all-purpose flour
½ cup sugar
½ cup firmly packed brown sugar
½ teaspoon baking soda
¼ teaspoon salt
½ cup butter or margarine, softened
⅓ cup crunchy or smooth peanut butter
1 egg, slightly beaten
1 cup quick-cooking oats, uncooked
1 (12-ounce) package semisweet chocolate morsels
½ cup sifted powdered sugar
¼ cup smooth peanut butter
3 to 5 tablespoons milk

Combine first 9 ingredients in a large mixing bowl; mix well.

Press dough into a lightly greased 13- x 9- x 2-inch pan. Bake at 350° for 20 minutes. Remove from oven, and sprinkle with chocolate morsels. Let stand until chocolate melts; spread evenly.

Combine powdered sugar, ¼ cup peanut butter, and enough milk to make a thin consistency; beat well. Drizzle over cookies. Cut into squares. Yield: 24 squares. *Anne Murphy,*
Abbeville, Alabama.

One Pound Of Meat Serves Six

One pound of meat ordinarily feeds four, but with a little help, it can be stretched to make six servings. The recipes below add pasta, rice, or mashed potatoes to a single pound of meat, turning it into a hearty meal for six.

CHINESE MEATBALLS

1½ cups uncooked regular rice
1 (4-ounce) can mushroom stems and pieces, undrained
1 pound ground beef
½ cup soft breadcrumbs
2 tablespoons soy sauce
2 cloves garlic, minced
1 egg, beaten
2 tablespoons vegetable oil
1 beef-flavored bouillon cube
1 cup hot water
2 large onions, coarsely chopped
1 large green pepper, cut into 1-inch pieces
1 large red pepper, cut into 1-inch pieces
2 stalks celery, diagonally sliced
¼ cup soy sauce
2 teaspoons cornstarch

Cook rice according to package directions; set aside.

Drain mushrooms, reserving liquid; set mushrooms aside. Combine mushroom liquid and next 5 ingredients; shape into ¾-inch meatballs. Brown meatballs in oil over medium heat in a Dutch oven. Remove meatballs and drain on paper towels, reserving 2 tablespoons pan drippings in Dutch oven.

Dissolve bouillon cube in hot water; set aside. Add onion, pepper, and celery to pan drippings; cook over medium heat 5 minutes, stirring constantly, until vegetables are crisp-tender.

Combine soy sauce and cornstarch, mixing well. Add cornstarch mixture, bouillon mixture, mushrooms, and meatballs to vegetables. Cook over medium-high heat, stirring constantly, until thickened. Serve over rice. Yield: about 6 servings. *Mrs. Arthur R. Bartolo,*
Clearwater, Florida.

SHEPHERD PIE

1 pound ground beef
½ cup chopped onion
½ cup chopped celery
1 (10½-ounce) can vegetable soup
½ to 1 teaspoon dried whole thyme
3 cups mashed potatoes
1 cup (4 ounces) shredded Cheddar cheese

Cook ground beef, onion, and celery in a large skillet until meat is browned, stirring to crumble. Drain off pan drippings; stir in soup and thyme. Spoon meat mixture into a lightly greased 2-quart shallow casserole. Spread potatoes evenly over meat mixture.

Bake at 350° for 20 minutes. Remove from oven; sprinkle with cheese. Bake 5 additional minutes or until cheese melts. Yield: 6 servings. *Becky Broersma,*
Chattanooga, Tennessee.

PORK CASSEROLE

1 pound boneless pork, cut into 1-inch pieces
2 tablespoons vegetable oil
½ cup chopped onion
½ cup chopped celery
1 medium-size green pepper, chopped
1 teaspoon salt
⅛ teaspoon pepper
½ teaspoon dried whole basil
1 teaspoon Worcestershire sauce
1 (10¾-ounce) can cream of mushroom soup, undiluted
½ cup milk
1 (4-ounce) can sliced mushrooms, undrained
1 (8-ounce) package thin spaghetti
1 medium tomato, peeled and sliced
1 cup (4 ounces) shredded sharp Cheddar cheese

Brown pork in oil in a large skillet. Add onion, celery, and green pepper; sauté until vegetables are tender. Stir in salt, pepper, basil, and Worcestershire sauce; cover, reduce heat, and simmer 25 minutes. Stir in soup, milk, and sliced mushrooms; cover and simmer 5 minutes.

Cook spaghetti according to package directions; drain. Combine pork mixture and spaghetti; spoon into a shallow 2-quart casserole. Arrange tomato slices over top of casserole; sprinkle with cheese. Bake at 350° for 5 minutes or until cheese melts. Yield: 6 servings.

Kay Castleman Cooper,
Burke, Virginia.

SAUSAGE SKILLET EXPRESS

1 pound smoked sausage, cut into ¼-inch slices
⅔ cup sliced celery
¼ cup chopped green onion
1 (4-ounce) can mushroom stems and pieces, undrained
1½ cups water
¼ teaspoon salt
¼ teaspoon pepper
1½ teaspoons chili powder
2 (.75-ounce) envelopes instant tomato soup mix
1½ cups uncooked instant rice

Combine sausage, celery, and onion in a large skillet; cook over medium heat, stirring often, until vegetables are tender. Drain well. Add the next 6 ingredients; bring to a boil. Stir in rice; remove from heat. Cover and let stand 10 minutes. Yield: 6 servings.

Rosalee DeJarnette,
Owasso, Oklahoma.

CHICKEN LIVERS IN ITALIAN SAUCE

1 pound chicken livers
¼ cup vegetable oil
½ cup minced onion
½ cup minced celery
1 (8-ounce) can tomato sauce
1 (6-ounce) can tomato paste
1 (4-ounce) can sliced mushrooms, undrained
½ cup water
1 tablespoon minced fresh parsley
1 clove garlic, minced
½ teaspoon salt
⅛ teaspoon pepper
¼ teaspoon dried whole marjoram
¼ teaspoon dried whole basil
¼ teaspoon dried rosemary, crushed
Dash of red pepper
1 (8-ounce) package fine egg noodles
½ cup grated Parmesan cheese

Sauté chicken livers in oil in a large skillet 5 to 8 minutes or until livers are browned. Remove livers from skillet; chop and set aside. Add onion and celery to skillet; sauté until tender.

Return livers to skillet, and add next 12 ingredients; cover, reduce heat, and

simmer 25 to 30 minutes. Cook noodles according to package directions; drain. Serve liver mixture over noodles, and sprinkle with cheese. Yield: 6 servings.

Loren Martin,
Knoxville, Tennessee.

What's New With Carrots?

Bite into a crisp, raw carrot and enjoy a low-calorie vegetable that's rich in vitamin A. But if you'd rather have your carrots cooked, try Harvard Carrots in a sweet-and-sour glaze.

CARROT-NUT LOAF

1½ cups all-purpose flour
1 teaspoon baking soda
½ teaspoon salt
1 teaspoon ground cinnamon
¾ cup vegetable oil
2 eggs
1 cup sugar
1 cup grated carrots
1 cup chopped pecans

Combine first 4 ingredients in a small mixing bowl. Set aside.

Combine oil, eggs, and sugar in a large mixing bowl; beat at medium speed of electric mixer for 1 minute. Add dry ingredients; mix at low speed just until blended. Fold in carrots and pecans. (Batter will be stiff.)

Spoon batter into a greased and floured 8½- x 4½- x 3-inch loafpan; bake at 350° for 1 hour and 25 minutes or until a wooden pick inserted in center comes out clean. Cool 10 minutes in pan; remove to wire rack, and cool completely. Yield: 1 loaf.

Deborah Mullinax,
Killeen, Texas.

CARROT-RAISIN SALAD

3 cups shredded carrots
½ cup flaked coconut
½ cup raisins
⅓ cup salad dressing or mayonnaise
¼ cup pineapple juice
⅓ cup salted peanuts (optional)
Lettuce leaves

Combine all ingredients except lettuce; stir well. Cover and chill for 2 to 3 hours. Serve on lettuce leaves. Yield: 6 servings.

Mrs. James S. Stanton,
Richmond, Virginia.

HARVARD CARROTS

2 pounds carrots, scraped
½ cup sugar
1½ tablespoons cornstarch
¼ cup vinegar
¼ cup water
¼ cup butter or margarine

Cut carrots crosswise into ½-inch slices. Cook, covered, in a large saucepan in a small amount of boiling salted water 15 minutes or until tender; drain.

Combine sugar and cornstarch in a small saucepan. Add vinegar and water; cook over medium heat, stirring constantly, until thickened. Add sauce and butter to carrots; cook over low heat until butter melts and carrots are heated. Yield: 6 to 8 servings.

Velva Ross,
Barboursville, West Virginia.

CARROT PIE

2 eggs
½ cup sugar
1 tablespoon cornstarch
1½ cups cooked, mashed carrots (about 1¼ pounds)
1 teaspoon pumpkin pie spice
⅔ cup evaporated milk
1 unbaked 9-inch pastry shell

Combine first 6 ingredients in container of electric blender; process on high speed until smooth. Pour into pastry shell; bake at 375° for 35 to 40 minutes until set. Cool. Yield: one 9-inch pie. *Mrs. Gillis Van Der Kamp, Holland, Michigan.*

GLAZED CARROTS

6 medium carrots, scraped
2 tablespoons sugar
2 tablespoons butter or margarine
¼ teaspoon grated orange rind

Cut carrots in half lengthwise. Cook, covered, in a skillet in a small amount of boiling salted water 8 to 10 minutes until crisp-tender. Drain.

Combine sugar, butter, and rind; cook over medium heat, stirring constantly, until bubbly. Pour butter mixture over carrots; simmer 2 to 3 minutes. Yield: 4 servings. *Dianne Rogers, Falkville, Alabama.*

Entertain Eight Economically

If your checkbook balance takes a nosedive every time you have company for dinner, consider this menu for eight. It will please your guests and keep you within your budget.

Chicken Cacciatore
Parmesan Noodles
Broccoli With Olive-Butter Sauce
Pineapple-Cucumber Congealed Salad
Refrigerator Yeast Rolls
Frozen Lemon Cream
Iced Tea   Coffee

CHICKEN CACCIATORE

½ cup all-purpose flour
½ teaspoon poultry seasoning
½ teaspoon salt
½ teaspoon pepper
2 (2½- to 3-pound) broiler-fryers, cut up
½ cup butter or margarine, divided
1 large onion, chopped
1 large green pepper, chopped
½ pound fresh mushrooms, sliced
½ cup thinly sliced celery
2 cloves garlic, minced
2 (16-ounce) cans whole tomatoes, undrained and coarsely chopped
1 (8-ounce) can tomato sauce
1 teaspoon dried Italian seasoning
1 teaspoon pepper
½ teaspoon dried whole oregano

Combine first 4 ingredients; mix well. Dredge chicken in flour mixture. Melt ¼ cup plus 2 tablespoons butter in a large skillet; add chicken, several pieces at a time, and brown on both sides. Remove chicken from skillet; place in a lightly greased, shallow roasting dish.

Sauté onion, green pepper, mushrooms, celery, and garlic in remaining 2 tablespoons butter in skillet until tender. Stir in remaining ingredients; simmer, uncovered, 5 to 10 minutes, stirring occasionally. Pour mixture over chicken. Cover and bake at 350° for 30 minutes. Remove cover, and bake an additional 15 to 20 minutes or until chicken is tender. Yield: 8 servings.

Maxine Moses,
Birmingham, Alabama.

PARMESAN NOODLES

1 (12-ounce) package medium egg noodles
½ cup butter or margarine, melted
⅛ teaspoon garlic powder
¼ cup chopped fresh parsley
¼ cup grated Parmesan cheese

Cook noodles according to package directions; drain well. Pour butter over noodles; add garlic powder and parsley, tossing gently. Place noodles in a serving dish. Sprinkle with grated cheese. Yield: 8 servings.

BROCCOLI WITH OLIVE-BUTTER SAUCE

2 (1-pound) bunches fresh broccoli
½ cup butter or margarine
½ cup sliced pimiento-stuffed olives
3 tablespoons lemon juice
1 clove garlic, minced

Trim off large leaves of broccoli, and remove tough ends of lower stalks. Wash broccoli thoroughly, and separate into spears. Arrange broccoli in steaming rack with stalks to center of rack. Place over boiling water; cover and steam 10 to 15 minutes or to desired degree of doneness. Arrange broccoli in a serving dish. Melt butter and stir in remaining ingredients. Spoon sauce over broccoli. Yield: 8 servings.

Cindy Turner Overall,
Baton Rouge, Louisiana.

PINEAPPLE-CUCUMBER CONGEALED SALAD

2 envelopes unflavored gelatin
½ cup cold water
½ cup boiling water
½ cup sugar
1⅓ cups canned pineapple juice
½ cup white vinegar
2 tablespoons lemon juice
½ teaspoon salt
1 (20-ounce) can pineapple tidbits, drained
1 cup peeled, diced cucumber
Leaf lettuce (optional)
Cucumber slices (optional)

Soften gelatin in cold water; let stand 5 minutes. Add boiling water; stir until gelatin dissolves. Add sugar, pineapple juice, vinegar, lemon juice, and salt; stir well. Chill until the consistency of unbeaten egg white.

Stir pineapple and diced cucumber into gelatin; pour into a lightly oiled 7-cup mold. Chill until firm. Unmold on lettuce; garnish with cucumber slices, if desired. Yield: 8 servings.

Mary Carden,
Hartford, Kentucky.

REFRIGERATOR YEAST ROLLS

2 packages dry yeast
1 cup warm water (105° to 115°)
1 cup shortening
½ cup sugar
1½ teaspoons salt
1 cup boiling water
2 eggs, beaten
6 to 7 cups all-purpose flour
Melted butter or margarine (optional)

Dissolve yeast in 1 cup warm water; set aside. Combine shortening, sugar, and salt in a large mixing bowl. Add boiling water, stirring until shortening melts. Cool to 105° to 115°. Add yeast mixture and eggs; mix well. Gradually stir in enough flour to make a soft dough.

Turn dough out onto a floured surface, and knead about 3 to 5 minutes. Place dough in a well-greased bowl, turning to grease top. Cover and chill until needed. (Dough may be stored in refrigerator up to 1 week.)

Lightly grease muffin pans. Shape dough into 1-inch balls; place 3 balls in each muffin cup. Cover and let rise in a warm place (85°), free from drafts, 1 hour or until doubled in bulk. Bake at 400° for 12 to 15 minutes or until golden brown. Brush with melted butter, if desired. Yield: about 3 dozen.

Mrs. Paul C. Hollis,
Rolling Fork, Mississippi.

FROZEN LEMON CREAM

1½ cups sugar
1 cup water
Peel of 1 lemon
3 egg whites
2 cups whipping cream
¼ cup lemon juice
8 maraschino cherries (optional)

Combine first 3 ingredients in a heavy saucepan. Cook over medium heat, stirring constantly, until clear. Cook, without stirring, until mixture reaches thread stage (230°). Remove lemon peel and discard.

Beat egg whites (at room temperature) until soft peaks form; continue to beat, slowly adding syrup mixture. Beat until stiff peaks form. Cool completely.

Beat whipping cream until stiff peaks form. Fold whipped cream and lemon juice into egg white mixture. Spoon into a 13- x 9- x 2-inch baking pan; freeze. Stir mixture 3 to 4 times during freezing process. Spoon into individual serving dishes; garnish with maraschino cherries, if desired. Yield: 8 servings.

Jennie Kinnard,
Mabank, Texas.

No Meat In These Entrées

You don't need to be a vegetarian to enjoy these meatless entrées. Made with eggs and cheese instead of meat, they provide plenty of protein in each nutritious bite. A variety of vegetables and seasonings lends extra flavor.

GARDEN LASAGNA

4 medium zucchini, coarsely chopped
1 large onion, chopped
1 medium-size green pepper, chopped
1 medium carrot, scraped and diced
½ cup chopped celery
1 clove garlic, minced
3 tablespoons peanut or vegetable oil
2 (16-ounce) cans stewed tomatoes, undrained
1 (8-ounce) can tomato sauce
1 (6-ounce) can tomato paste
¼ cup dry white wine
2 tablespoons chopped fresh parsley
2 teaspoons dried Italian seasoning
1 teaspoon dried whole basil
½ teaspoon seasoning salt
¼ teaspoon freshly ground pepper
3 quarts water
2 teaspoons salt
9 lasagna noodles
1 (16-ounce) carton ricotta cheese
2 cups (8 ounces) shredded Swiss cheese
1 cup grated Parmesan cheese

Sauté zucchini, onion, green pepper, carrot, celery, and garlic in oil in a Dutch oven over medium heat 15 minutes. Stir in next 9 ingredients; bring to a boil. Cover, reduce heat, and simmer 30 minutes. Uncover and simmer an additional 45 minutes or until sauce is thickened, stirring occasionally.

Combine water and salt in a large Dutch oven; bring to a boil. Gradually add noodles. Boil, uncovered, 12 to 15 minutes or until noodles are just tender; drain well.

Spread one-fourth of sauce in a lightly greased 13- x 9- x 2-inch baking dish. Top with 3 noodles, one-third of ricotta cheese, one-fourth of Swiss cheese, and one-fourth of Parmesan cheese; repeat layers twice. Top with remaining sauce, Swiss, and Parmesan cheese. Bake, uncovered, at 350° for 35 to 40 minutes. Let stand 5 minutes before serving. Yield: 8 servings.
Cynthia Kannenberg,
Brown Deer, Wisconsin.

SPINACH-CHEESE OMELET

1 (10-ounce) package frozen chopped spinach
1 small onion, chopped
1 clove garlic, minced
1 tablespoon vegetable oil
½ teaspoon ground nutmeg
8 eggs
¾ teaspoon salt
½ teaspoon pepper
2 tablespoons vegetable oil, divided
¼ cup grated Parmesan cheese, divided

Cook spinach according to package directions. Drain; place on paper towels, and squeeze until barely moist.

Sauté onion and garlic in 1 tablespoon oil until tender; reduce heat to low. Stir in spinach and nutmeg; keep warm, stirring occasionally.

Combine eggs, salt, and pepper; beat well. Heat 1 tablespoon oil in a 10-inch omelet pan or heavy skillet over medium heat. Pour half the egg mixture into skillet. As the mixture starts to cook, gently lift edges of omelet with a spatula, and tilt pan so the uncooked portion flows underneath.

When egg mixture is set, spoon half of spinach mixture over half of omelet; sprinkle with 2 tablespoons Parmesan cheese. Fold unfilled side over filling, and remove to a serving plate. Repeat procedure with remaining ingredients. Yield: 4 servings. *Lona B. Shealy,*
Leesville, South Carolina.

EGG AND RICE BAKE

1 (10-ounce) package frozen English peas
3 cups cooked regular rice
2 tablespoons diced pimiento
2 tablespoons chopped fresh parsley
1 tablespoon minced onion
⅓ cup butter or margarine, melted
¼ teaspoon salt
½ cup (2 ounces) shredded American cheese, divided
6 eggs

Cook peas according to package directions; drain.

Combine peas, next 6 ingredients, and ¼ cup cheese; toss well. Spoon into a greased 10- x 6- x 2-inch baking dish. Make six 2-inch wells in rice mixture using back of a spoon; break an egg into each well. Sprinkle remaining ¼ cup cheese on top; bake at 350° for 30 minutes or until the eggs are set. Yield: 6 servings. *Alice Citak,*
Titusville, Florida.

Feel Free To Enjoy Fruit

Dieters often get tired of living by a list of foods to avoid. But fruit is one food group that everyone should enjoy more often. The storehouse of vitamins, minerals, and fiber combined in a low-calorie, low-sodium package is what makes fruit so valuable.

Many folks enjoy fruit in its simplest form—alone as an easy snack. We want to show you how to turn nutritious fruit into appetizers, salads, and elegant desserts. The secret to keeping these fruit recipes light lies in limiting the addition of sugar and fat. The natural sweetness of fruit is highlighted instead.

Use ripe, unblemished fruit for your light recipes. The riper fruit usually has sweeter flavor. Notice how spices such as cinnamon, ginger, and allspice enhance the natural taste of fruit when sugar is reduced.

Try our recipes, and then experiment with some of your own. Use fruit often to add color, flavor, and nutrients to your low-calorie diet.

MAIN DISH FRUIT SALAD

½ cup reduced-calorie mayonnaise
1 tablespoon lemon juice
2 teaspoons sugar
2 medium bananas, sliced
1½ cups cantaloupe balls
1 medium peach, peeled and cubed
1 cup cubed fresh pineapple
1 cup seedless green grapes
1 cup fresh strawberries, halved
1½ cups watermelon balls
Lettuce leaves
3 cups low-fat cottage cheese
6 fresh strawberries

Combine mayonnaise, lemon juice, and sugar; stir well and set aside.

Combine next 7 ingredients; toss gently. Spoon into 6 individual lettuce-lined serving dishes, and top each with ½ cup cottage cheese. Slice 6 strawberries lengthwise, keeping stem end intact; place atop each salad. Serve with mayonnaise dressing. Yield: 6 servings (about 178 calories per serving plus 40 calories per tablespoon dressing).

Tip: Store cottage cheese containers upside down after opening—cheese stays fresh longer.

BLUEBERRY-KIRSCH SORBET

2 cups unsweetened apple juice
2 tablespoons sugar
1 quart fresh blueberries
½ cup kirsch
1 tablespoon lemon juice
Lemon rind strips (optional)

Combine apple juice and sugar in a small saucepan; bring to a boil, and boil 1 minute.

Process blueberries in container of an electric blender until smooth. Combine blueberries, apple juice mixture, kirsch, and lemon juice; pour into ice cream freezer, and freeze according to manufacturer's directions. Garnish each serving with lemon rind strips, if desired. Yield: 7½ cups (about 68 calories per ½-cup serving).

CANTALOUPE SOUP

1 large cantaloupe (about 3 pounds)
4½ cups unsweetened orange juice, divided
3 tablespoons lemon juice
¼ teaspoon ground ginger
¼ teaspoon ground allspice
Fresh mint leaves (optional)

Cut cantaloupe in half, and remove seeds. Peel each, and cut fruit into 1-inch cubes. Combine half of cantaloupe and ½ cup orange juice in container of an electric blender; process until mixture is smooth. Repeat processing with remaining cantaloupe cubes and an additional ½ cup orange juice.

Combine cantaloupe mixture, remaining 3½ cups orange juice, and next 3 ingredients, blending well; cover and chill thoroughly. Garnish with mint leaves, if desired. Yield: 6 cups (about 112 calories per 1-cup serving).

FRUIT-FILLED CANTALOUPE

2 medium cantaloupes (about 2¼ pounds each)
1 pint fresh strawberries, halved
1 cup fresh blueberries
¼ cup gin
1½ tablespoons lemon juice
2 teaspoons sugar
Fresh mint leaves (optional)

Cut each cantaloupe in half, and remove seeds; prick cavities with a fork (do not puncture rind). Combine next 5 ingredients, and toss lightly. Spoon fruit mixture into cantaloupe halves. Chill at least 2 hours. Garnish with mint, if desired. Yield: 4 servings (about 172 calories per serving). *Wilmina R. Smith, St. Petersburg, Florida.*

FRESH CHERRY SALAD

2 cups fresh cherries, pitted
2 cups cantaloupe balls
2 nectarines, cut into wedges
Lettuce leaves
Lime Dressing

Combine fruit, and place in a lettuce-lined bowl. Serve with Lime Dressing. Yield: 8 servings (about 63 calories per serving plus 35 calories per tablespoon dressing).

Lime Dressing:

½ cup reduced-calorie mayonnaise
½ teaspoon grated lime rind
2 tablespoons lime juice
1 tablespoon honey

Combine all ingredients, mixing well. Chill. Yield: ½ cup plus 3 tablespoons.

GRAPE SALAD MOLD

1 envelope unflavored gelatin
2 cups unsweetened white grape juice, divided
1½ cups green grapes, halved
Vegetable cooking spray
Lettuce leaves

Soften gelatin in 1 cup grape juice; let stand 10 minutes. Bring remaining grape juice to a boil; add gelatin mixture, stirring until dissolved. Chill until consistency of unbeaten egg white. Stir in the grapes. Coat five ½-cup molds with cooking spray; pour gelatin mixture into molds. Chill until firm. Unmold on lettuce leaves. Yield: 5 servings (about 105 calories per serving).
Mrs. Blair Cunnyngham, Cleveland, Tennessee.

HONEYDEW-BERRY DESSERT

½ cup reduced-calorie strawberry jam
¼ teaspoon grated orange rind
½ cup unsweetened orange juice
Dash of ground cinnamon
1 tablespoon cornstarch
2 tablespoons water
1 cup sliced fresh strawberries
¼ teaspoon almond extract
4 cups honeydew balls
Grated orange rind

Combine first 4 ingredients in a small saucepan. Combine cornstarch and water, mixing well; add to strawberry jam mixture. Bring to a boil over medium heat, stirring frequently; reduce heat and simmer until the strawberry jam melts and mixture is thickened. Remove sauce from heat; stir in the sliced strawberries and almond extract. Cool sauce to room temperature.

Spoon 1 cup honeydew balls into each of 4 individual serving dishes; divide sauce evenly over fruit, and sprinkle with grated orange rind. Yield: 4 servings (about 140 calories per serving).

KIWI JUBILEE

½ cup unsweetened apple juice
½ teaspoon grated orange rind
4 kiwis, peeled and sliced
¼ cup rum
3 cups vanilla ice milk

Combine apple juice and orange rind in a small skillet; bring to a boil. Add kiwi; reduce heat and simmer until kiwi is thoroughly heated.

Place rum in a small, long-handled pan; heat just until warm. Ignite with a long match, and pour over kiwi mixture. Serve sauce over ½-cup servings of ice milk. Yield: 6 servings (about 157 calories per serving).

MANGO SAUCE

1 cup cubed mango
2 tablespoons Cointreau or other orange-flavored liqueur
3 tablespoons unsweetened orange juice
2½ cups lemon sherbet

Combine first 3 ingredients in container of an electric blender; process until smooth. Serve over lemon sherbet. Yield: 1¼ cups (about 42 calories per ¼ cup sauce plus 130 calories per ½ cup sherbet).

PEACH SOUP

3½ cups peeled, diced peaches
½ cup Chablis or other dry white wine
1½ cups unsweetened white grape juice
1 cup water
1 (3-inch) stick cinnamon
½ teaspoon ground cardamom
½ teaspoon vanilla extract

Combine first 5 ingredients in a medium saucepan. Bring to a boil; cover, reduce heat, and simmer 30 minutes. Remove from heat, and stir in cardamom and vanilla; discard cinnamon. Pour half the mixture into container of an electric blender; process until smooth. Repeat with remaining mixture. Chill thoroughly. Yield: 6 cups (about 104 calories per 1-cup serving).

Bake These Garden-Fresh Breads

Stir garden flavor into breads with our recipes for quick vegetable muffins, biscuits, and loaves. Our sweet Zucchini Muffins, Spicy Squash Bread, or onion-flavored Hearty Biscuits all use fresh produce.

HEARTY BISCUITS

¼ cup plus 2 tablespoons shortening
2 cups self-rising flour
5 slices bacon, cooked and crumbled
½ cup (2 ounces) shredded Cheddar cheese
¼ cup finely chopped green onion
¾ cup milk

Cut shortening into flour with a pastry blender until mixture resembles coarse meal. Stir in bacon, cheese, and green onion. Add milk, stirring with a fork until dry ingredients are moistened. Turn dough out onto a lightly floured surface, and knead 4 or 5 times.

Roll dough to ½-inch thickness, and cut with a 2½-inch biscuit cutter. Place biscuits on an ungreased baking sheet; bake at 450° for 10 to 12 minutes or until lightly browned. Yield: about 1 dozen. *Mrs. E. R. Hendrix, Augusta, Georgia.*

SPINACH BREAD

2 (10-ounce) packages frozen chopped spinach
½ teaspoon garlic salt
1 loaf frozen bread dough, thawed
1½ cups (6 ounces) shredded mozzarella cheese
1 egg, beaten

Cook spinach according to package directions, omitting salt. Drain well, and press spinach in paper towels until barely moist. Combine spinach and garlic salt, stirring well.

Divide dough in half. Roll each half into a 13- x 6½-inch rectangle. Spread half of spinach evenly over dough, and sprinkle with half of cheese. Roll up jellyroll fashion, starting at long side. Pinch seams and ends together to seal. Place roll, seam side down, on a lightly greased baking sheet.

Repeat procedure with remaining ingredients, and brush loaves with egg. Bake at 400° for 20 minutes. Cut into 1-inch slices and serve warm. Yield: about 2 dozen appetizer servings. *Viola V. Hudson, Hampton, Virginia.*

JALAPENO PEPPER BREAD

1½ cups self-rising cornmeal
1 (8-ounce) carton commercial sour cream
½ cup shortening, melted
3 eggs, beaten
1 (7-ounce) can whole kernel corn, undrained
2 jalapeño peppers, seeded and chopped

Combine all ingredients, mixing well. Pour batter into a well-greased 10½-inch cast-iron skillet. Bake at 425° for 20 minutes or until golden brown. Yield: about 8 servings. *Mrs. Robert A. Bailey, Knoxville, Tennessee.*

SPICY SQUASH BREAD

1¾ cups all-purpose flour
1¼ teaspoons baking powder
½ teaspoon baking soda
½ teaspoon salt
½ teaspoon ground ginger
¾ teaspoon ground cinnamon
¼ teaspoon ground nutmeg
⅛ teaspoon ground cloves
2 eggs
¾ cup sugar
⅓ cup vegetable oil
⅓ cup commercial sour cream
3 tablespoons apricot preserves
1¾ cups unpeeled shredded yellow squash

Combine first 8 ingredients in a mixing bowl; set aside.

Combine eggs, sugar, oil, sour cream, and preserves in a large mixing bowl; stir in shredded squash. Gradually add dry ingredients, stirring well.

Spoon the mixture into a greased and floured 8½- x 4½- x 3-inch loafpan. Bake at 350° for 1 hour and 5 minutes or until a wooden pick inserted in center of bread comes out clean.

Cool 10 minutes in pan; remove to wire rack, and let cool completely. Yield: 1 loaf. *Warren S. Martin, Birmingham, Alabama.*

ZUCCHINI MUFFINS

2 eggs
1 cup sugar
½ cup vegetable oil
1 tablespoon vanilla extract
2 cups unpeeled shredded zucchini
2 cups all-purpose flour
1 teaspoon baking soda
¼ teaspoon baking powder
½ teaspoon salt
1½ teaspoons ground cinnamon
1 cup raisins
½ cup chopped pecans

Combine first 4 ingredients, mixing well. Stir in shredded zucchini; set mixture aside.

Combine next 5 ingredients in a mixing bowl. Reserve ¼ cup flour mixture, and toss with raisins and pecans.

Make a well in center of flour mixture. Add zucchini mixture to dry ingredients, stirring just until moistened. Stir in dredged raisins and pecans.

Spoon mixture into greased muffin pans, filling two-thirds full. Bake at 350° for 20 minutes. Yield: about 2 dozen. *Mrs. O. V. Elkins, Chattanooga, Tennessee.*

Quiche, Rich And Cheesy

A luscious quiche begins with eggs, cheese, and milk. Stir in some bacon, sausage, or vegetables, and you have a delicious main dish to serve any time.

ONION QUICHE

Pastry for 9-inch pie
6 slices bacon
2½ cups chopped onion
1 clove garlic, minced
1 cup (4 ounces) shredded sharp Cheddar cheese
4 eggs
1 (13-ounce) can evaporated milk
1 teaspoon dry mustard
1 teaspoon soy sauce
½ teaspoon salt
½ teaspoon paprika
Dash of hot sauce

Line a 9-inch quiche dish with pastry; trim excess pastry around edges. Prick bottom and sides of pastry with a fork. Bake at 400° for 3 minutes; remove from oven, and gently prick with a fork. Bake 5 minutes longer. Cool.

Cook bacon in a large skillet until crisp; remove bacon, reserving 2 tablespoons drippings in skillet. Crumble bacon, and set aside.

Sauté onion and garlic in drippings until tender; drain and spoon into pastry shell. Sprinkle with bacon and cheese.

Beat eggs; add remaining ingredients, beating well. Pour into pastry shell. Bake at 325° for 1 hour or until set. Let stand 10 minutes before serving. Yield: one 9-inch quiche. *Pat Weaver, Leicester, North Carolina.*

SPRINGTIME QUICHE

Pastry for 11-inch pie
1½ pounds fresh asparagus
8 slices bacon, cooked and crumbled
2 cups (8 ounces) shredded Swiss cheese
4 eggs
1½ cups half-and-half
⅛ teaspoon salt
⅛ teaspoon ground nutmeg
Dash of pepper
6 cherry tomatoes, halved

Line an 11-inch pieplate with pastry; trim excess pastry around edges; fold edges under and flute. Prick bottom and sides of pastry with a fork. Bake at 400° for 3 minutes; remove from oven, and gently prick with a fork. Bake an additional 5 minutes. Cool on rack.

Snap off tough ends of asparagus. Remove the scales with a knife or vegetable peeler.

Cook asparagus, covered, in a small amount of boiling salted water 6 to 8 minutes or until crisp-tender; drain. Set aside 16 asparagus spears; chop remaining spears into ½-inch pieces.

Sprinkle bacon, cheese, and chopped asparagus in pastry shell. Beat eggs. Add half-and-half, salt, nutmeg, and pepper; beat well. Pour into pastry shell. Bake at 350° for 35 minutes. Remove from oven and arrange remaining asparagus spears, spoke fashion, on quiche. Arrange tomato halves between asparagus spears and in center of quiche. Return to oven, and continue to bake 20 minutes or until set. Let stand 10 minutes before serving. Yield: one 11-inch quiche. *Mary Mae Herring, Wichita, Kansas.*

ZUCCHINI-SAUSAGE QUICHE

Pastry for 9-inch deep-dish pie
½ pound Italian link sausage, thinly sliced
½ pound fresh mushrooms, sliced
1 tablespoon butter or margarine
1 medium zucchini, thinly sliced
1 cup (4 ounces) shredded mozzarella cheese
3 eggs
¾ cup milk
½ teaspoon dried whole basil
½ teaspoon dried whole oregano

Line a 9-inch deep-dish pieplate with pastry; trim excess pastry around edges; fold edges under and flute. Prick bottom and sides of pastry with a fork. Bake at 400° for 3 minutes; remove from oven, and gently prick with a fork. Bake 5 minutes longer. Cool.

Cook the sausage in a skillet until browned; remove sausage, reserving 1 tablespoon drippings in skillet. Drain

sausage, and set aside. Sauté mushrooms in pan drippings 5 minutes or until tender; drain and set aside.

Melt butter in skillet, add zucchini, and sauté until tender; drain.

Place sausage in pastry shell; sprinkle with half of cheese. Spoon mushrooms on top of cheese; sprinkle with remaining cheese. Top with zucchini.

Beat eggs; add remaining ingredients, beating well. Pour into pastry shell. Bake at 350° for 55 minutes or until set. Let stand 10 minutes before serving. Yield: one 9-inch quiche.

*Cheryll Tuthill,
Virginia Beach, Virginia.*

It's Strawberry Time

What could be better than the sweet goodness of fresh strawberries? With just a little sugar and cream, they're hard to beat. But we think they taste even better in one of these tempting strawberry desserts.

Strawberries are a delicate fruit and deserve special care. Always select fully ripened, bright red berries—strawberries won't ripen after they're picked. To store, spread berries in a single layer on a shallow pan or tray and refrigerate. Never wash the fruit or remove caps until just before using. The caps protect and preserve flavor and texture.

STRAWBERRY SHORTCAKE

4 cups sliced strawberries
4 to 6 tablespoons sugar
2 cups biscuit mix
2 tablespoons sugar
⅔ cup half-and-half
¼ cup butter or margarine, melted
1 egg, beaten
Sweetened whipped cream or frozen whipped topping, thawed

Combine strawberries and 4 to 6 tablespoons sugar; chill. Combine next 5 ingredients, and beat at high speed of electric mixer 30 seconds. Spoon batter into a greased 8-inch cakepan. Bake at 425° for 15 to 20 minutes or until golden brown. Turn out onto wire rack to cool.

Slice shortcake crosswise into 2 equal parts. Place bottom half of shortcake, cut side up, on a serving plate; spoon

half of strawberries onto bottom layer. Top with second layer of shortcake, cut side down; spoon on remaining strawberries. Top with whipped cream. Yield: 6 to 8 servings.

Note: 4 cups sliced, fresh peaches may be substituted for strawberries.

*Debra Lancaster,
Hawkinsville, Georgia.*

STRAWBERRY DESSERT CREPES

2 cups sliced strawberries
½ cup firmly packed light brown sugar
Crêpes (recipe follows)
2 to 2½ cups commercial sour cream or whipped cream
Powdered sugar
Whole strawberries

Combine sliced strawberries and brown sugar; toss lightly until sugar dissolves. Spoon about ¼ cup strawberry mixture into center of each crêpe; do not spread. Spoon about 3 tablespoons of sour cream or whipped cream over strawberries.

Roll up crêpes, leaving ends open. Place crêpes, seam side down, in a serving dish. Sprinkle powdered sugar over crêpes; garnish with remaining sour cream or whipped cream and whole strawberries. Yield: 8 to 10 servings.

Crêpes:

1 cup all-purpose flour
⅛ teaspoon salt
1 cup milk
3 eggs
2 tablespoons butter or margarine, melted
Vegetable oil

Combine first 3 ingredients, beating until smooth. Add eggs and beat well. Stir in butter. Refrigerate 1 hour. (This allows flour particles to swell and soften so the crêpes will be light in texture.)

Brush the bottom of a 10-inch crêpe pan with oil. Place over medium heat until just hot, not smoking.

Pour ¼ cup batter into pan; quickly tilt pan in all directions so batter covers pan in a thin film. Cook about 1 minute. Lift edge of crêpe to test for doneness. Crêpe is ready for flipping when it can be shaken loose from pan. Flip the crêpe, and cook about 30 seconds on other side. (This side is rarely more than spotty brown, and is the side on which filling is placed.) Remove crêpe from pan, and repeat procedure until all batter is used.

Place crêpes on a towel to cool. Stack between layers of waxed paper. Yield: 8 to 10. *Scarlet Keck, Williamson, West Virginia.*

STRAWBERRY-CREAM CHEESE DESSERT

1½ cups graham cracker crumbs
½ cup butter or margarine, melted
3 tablespoons sugar
½ cup chopped pecans
½ cup chopped almonds
1 (3-ounce) package strawberry-flavored gelatin
2 cups strawberries, sliced
1 (8-ounce) package cream cheese, softened
3 tablespoons powdered sugar
1 (1.25-ounce) envelope whipped topping mix
9 whole strawberries (optional)

Combine graham cracker crumbs, butter, sugar, and nuts; stir well. Press mixture into an 8-inch square pan. Bake at 350° for 8 to 10 minutes or until light brown. Cool completely on wire rack.

Prepare gelatin according to package directions; chill until consistency of unbeaten egg white. Stir sliced strawberries into gelatin. Spoon gelatin mixture over crust; chill until firm.

Combine cream cheese and powdered sugar; beat until light and fluffy.

Prepare whipped topping mix according to package directions. Add cream cheese mixture, and beat until fluffy. Spread topping mixture over strawberry filling, and chill several hours. Cut into squares. Top each with a whole strawberry, if desired. Yield: 9 servings.

Mrs. Artie B. Lowe,
Milledgeville, Georgia.

CHILLED FRUIT COMPOTE

1 (20-ounce) can pineapple chunks, undrained
2 cups strawberries, sliced
2 medium apples, chopped
1 cup fresh cherries, halved and pitted
2 medium bananas, sliced
3 cups sliced fresh peaches
1 tablespoon plus 1 teaspoon ascorbic-citric powder
¼ cup plus 2 tablespoons water
1 teaspoon coconut extract
1 teaspoon almond extract

Combine first 6 ingredients in a large mixing bowl; toss gently.

Combine remaining ingredients, mixing well. Pour over fruit. Chill until ready to serve. Yield: 8 to 10 servings.

Mrs. C. F. Colbert III,
Pittsburgh, Pennsylvania.

STRAWBERRY DESSERT

¼ cup firmly packed brown sugar
½ cup butter or margarine, softened
1 cup all-purpose flour
¾ cup chopped pecans
⅔ cup milk
30 large marshmallows
1 (1.25-ounce) envelope whipped topping mix
1 (3-ounce) package strawberry-flavored gelatin
1 cup boiling water
¾ cup cold water
2 cups sliced strawberries

Cream brown sugar and butter until smooth. Add flour and stir until mixture resembles coarse crumbs. Add pecans. Press into a 13- x 9- x 2-inch pan. Bake at 350° for 15 minutes; cool.

Combine milk and marshmallows in a medium saucepan; stir over low heat until marshmallows melt. Prepare whipped topping mix according to package directions. Fold into marshmallow mixture. Pour over crust; chill.

Dissolve gelatin in boiling water; stir in cold water. Chill until consistency of unbeaten egg white. Fold in strawberries; pour over marshmallow layer. Chill until firm. Yield: 12 to 15 servings.

Mrs. Galen Johnson,
Transylvania, Louisiana.

Highlight The Meal With A Congealed Salad

Pack vitamins and minerals into congealed salads by filling them with eggs, fruit, or vegetables. To serve one of these salads, invert mold on serving dish, then wrap the mold with a hot towel. The salad will slip out easily.

APRICOT SALAD

1 (6-ounce) package apricot-flavored gelatin
⅔ cup boiling water
1 (8-ounce) package cream cheese, softened
1 (15¼-ounce) can crushed pineapple, undrained
2 (7¾-ounce) jars apricot baby food
1 (8-ounce) carton frozen whipped topping, thawed
Lettuce leaves

Dissolve gelatin in boiling water; cool slightly. Beat cream cheese until smooth. Gradually add gelatin; beat well. Stir in pineapple and apricot baby food; fold in whipped topping. Pour mixture into a 12- x 8- x 2-inch dish; cover and chill. Cut into squares and place on lettuce. Yield: 12 servings.

Mrs. Billy Scheffer,
Brenham, Texas.

APPLE CIDER SALAD

4 cups apple cider, divided
1 (6-ounce) package orange-flavored gelatin
1 cup raisins
1 cup coarsely chopped apple
1 cup chopped celery
Grated rind and juice of 1 lemon
Lettuce leaves

Bring 2 cups apple cider to a boil; remove from heat. Add gelatin and stir until dissolved. Stir in raisins. Let cool.

Add remaining 2 cups cider; chill until consistency of unbeaten egg white. Stir in apple, celery, lemon rind, and juice. Pour into a lightly oiled 6-cup mold. Chill until set. Unmold onto lettuce leaves. Yield: 8 to 10 servings.

Mrs. Charles Judy,
Daleville, Virginia.

FROSTED ORANGE SALAD

1 (6-ounce) package orange-flavored gelatin
1 envelope unflavored gelatin
1 cup boiling water
1 pint orange sherbet, softened
1 (20-ounce) can crushed pineapple, undrained
1 (11-ounce) can mandarin oranges, drained
½ cup orange juice
1 egg, beaten
½ cup sugar
1 tablespoon all-purpose flour
1 (1.25-ounce) envelope whipped topping mix

Dissolve gelatin in water in a large bowl. Gently stir in sherbet, pineapple, and oranges. Pour into a 12- x 8- x 2-inch dish; set aside.

Combine orange juice, egg, sugar, and flour in a small saucepan; cook over medium heat, stirring constantly, until thickened. Allow to cool.

Prepare topping mix according to package directions. Fold into cooked orange mixture; spread evenly over salad. Cover and chill overnight. Yield: 12 servings.

Barbara D. Walker,
Rocky Mount, North Carolina.

GRAPEFRUIT SALAD

2 pink grapefruit
1 (15¼-ounce) can crushed pineapple,
    undrained
2 (3-ounce) packages lemon-flavored
    gelatin
¾ cup boiling water
1 tablespoon all-purpose flour
3 tablespoons sugar
1 egg yolk, beaten
2 tablespoons lemon juice
6 large marshmallows, quartered
½ cup whipping cream
⅓ cup chopped pecans
8 maraschino cherries

Cut grapefruit in half lengthwise; scoop out pulp, removing membranes and seeds. Reserve shells, pulp, and juice. Drain pineapple, reserving ⅓ cup juice. Set aside.

Dissolve gelatin in boiling water; cool 15 minutes. Stir in grapefruit pulp, juice, and pineapple; pour into grapefruit shell halves. Chill until firm.

Combine flour, sugar, egg yolk, lemon juice, and reserved pineapple juice in top of double boiler; place over boiling water and cook, stirring constantly, until thickened. Remove from heat; add marshmallows, and stir until melted. Cool completely. Beat whipping cream until stiff peaks form. Fold whipped cream and pecans into sauce.

To serve, cut each shell in half; top each serving with a dollop of sauce and a maraschino cherry. Yield: 8 servings.
*Mrs. Bob Nester,
Charleston, West Virginia.*

DEVILED EGG SALAD

1 envelope unflavored gelatin
¼ cup cold water
¼ cup catsup
2 tablespoons cider vinegar
1 (3-ounce) package cream cheese,
    softened
½ cup mayonnaise
1 teaspoon grated onion
3 drops hot sauce
6 hard-cooked eggs, finely chopped
¼ cup finely chopped green pepper
¼ cup finely chopped celery
2 tablespoons finely chopped pimiento
1 tablespoon finely chopped fresh parsley
Leaf lettuce

Soften gelatin in water in a saucepan; let stand 1 minute. Place over medium heat; stir until dissolved. Remove from heat; stir in catsup and vinegar.

Combine cream cheese and mayonnaise; beat until smooth. Add gelatin mixture, onion, and hot sauce; stir well,

and chill until consistency of unbeaten egg white. Fold in next 5 ingredients; spoon into lightly oiled ½-cup molds. Cover and chill until firm. Unmold on a lettuce-lined plate. Yield: 5 servings.
*Rita Bufkin,
Mansfield, Louisiana.*

GREEN SPRING SALAD

1 (3-ounce) package lime-flavored gelatin
1⅓ cups boiling water
½ cup mayonnaise
1½ cups chopped cabbage
¼ cup chopped celery
2 tablespoons diced pimiento
1 tablespoon chopped green pepper
¼ teaspoon salt
¼ teaspoon paprika
Leaf lettuce

Dissolve gelatin in boiling water; chill until consistency of unbeaten egg white.

Combine next 7 ingredients; add to gelatin, stirring well. Pour into a lightly oiled 1-quart mold; cover and chill until firm. Unmold on a lettuce-lined plate. Yield: 6 servings.   *Mrs. R. L. Lyerly,
Mocksville, North Carolina.*

TANGY TOMATO ASPIC

4 cups tomato juice
1 (6-ounce) package lemon-flavored gelatin
2 tablespoons lemon juice
2 tablespoons prepared horseradish
Leaf lettuce
Cottage cheese

Bring tomato juice to a boil; remove from heat. Add gelatin and stir until dissolved. Stir in lemon juice and horseradish. Pour into an oiled 4½-cup ring mold; chill until firm. Unmold on a lettuce-lined serving plate; fill center with cottage cheese. Yield: 8 to 10 servings.
*Mrs. W. J. Scherffius,
Mountain Home, Arkansas.*

From Our Kitchen To Yours

Our test kitchen home economists discovered that it's just plain fun preparing dishes as pretty and tasty as shaped or molded aspics, pâtés, and salads. While working on these recipes, we came across a lot of information on preparation that helped make our testing both successful and fun. We thought

you'd find this information useful too. Try our recipes, but also try creating your own shaped treasures.

Using gelatin—As we tested and evaluated, we were very concerned that each recipe contain enough gelatin to unmold easily and hold its shape. A general guideline we follow is that 1 envelope of unflavored gelatin will support 2 cups of liquid. If you're adding solids, chopped fruit, vegetables, or meat, then reduce the amount of liquid by ¼ cup. If you're using flavored gelatin, just follow the instructions on the package for adding solids. Also, lemon juice, vinegar, wine, and other acids will make the mold softer and more fragile. One to two tablespoons of an acid per cup of liquid is probably the most you'll want to add.

When you're working with gelatin, always make sure all the gelatin granules have dissolved before proceeding to the next step of the recipe. If you don't let the entire dissolving process take place, the gelatin will not congeal enough to support the other ingredients and the mold will not hold its shape.

Selecting and preparing a mold—Always use the size mold called for in the recipe. If your mold is too small, then you'll end up with extra gelatin mixture. If it's too large, then the ingredients won't fill up the container and you'll lose the effect of the shape.

To prepare a mold before adding the ingredients, do what the recipe tells you. Our recipes usually say to lightly oil the mold. We use vegetable oil when preparing the container.

Chill to the consistency of unbeaten egg white—Don't let this description confuse you. When a recipe says to chill the gelatin mixture to the consistency of unbeaten egg white, put your mixture in the refrigerator and let it chill until it's only slightly thick. Just imagine what an egg white looks like after you break an egg. The chilling will take anywhere from 20 to 40 minutes, depending on the temperature of your refrigerator. Do be careful; don't let the mixture congeal too much because then the solids are difficult to add. If the gelatin does get too firm, set the container of gelatin in a bowl of warm water, and stir until the mixture softens enough to add the solids.

Unmolding—After your shaped dish has completely chilled and congealed, carefully unmold. To help break the suction, run a knife around the edge of the mold. If the mold has very curved, fluted sides, then press the edge of the congealed mixture lightly with your finger and gently pull away from the sides of the mold. There are several ways to proceed, but our favorite method in the test kitchen is the hot towel method. Wet a dish towel with hot water, and wring it out. Wrap the towel around the bottom and sides of the container, and let it stand for a few seconds. Place a serving platter on top of the mold and invert. If it doesn't unmold, repeat the process until the mold releases.

Uncork The Flavor Of Wine

See how our readers have used wine, then experiment with your own recipes. If you're a beginner in wine cookery, start with a small amount, and add more to taste. Remember that too little is better than too much—you can always stir in more. Add wine in the beginning if you want it to blend with the flavors of other ingredients. Wait until near the end of preparation if you want more wine flavor.

BURGUNDY STEW WITH DROP DUMPLINGS

¼ cup all-purpose flour
1½ teaspoons salt
¼ teaspoon pepper
1 pound round steak, cut into 1-inch squares
¼ cup vegetable oil
2½ cups water
1¼ cups Burgundy
2 tablespoons minced fresh parsley
Pinch of dried whole thyme
3 medium carrots, scraped and chopped
3 medium onions, chopped
2 medium potatoes, peeled and chopped
¼ cup finely chopped celery
1½ cups all-purpose flour
2¼ teaspoons baking powder
½ teaspoon salt
¾ cup milk
1 (10-ounce) package frozen English peas

Combine ¼ cup flour, 1½ teaspoons salt, and pepper; dredge meat in flour mixture. Heat oil in a Dutch oven; add meat, and brown well. Add next 4 ingredients; cover and bring to a boil. Reduce heat and simmer 1 hour, stirring often.

Add carrot, onion, potatoes, and celery; simmer 30 minutes.

Combine next 3 ingredients in a small bowl; make a well in center of mixture. Add milk, stirring just until moistened.

Add frozen peas to stew; return to a boil. Drop dumpling mixture by tablespoonfuls onto stew; cover, reduce heat, and cook 15 minutes without removing cover. Yield: 8 cups. *Greydon Baker, Venice, Florida.*

BEEF BURGUNDY

1 tablespoon vegetable oil
2 pounds round steak, cut into bite-size pieces
2 medium onions, sliced and separated into rings
½ pound fresh mushrooms, sliced
1½ tablespoons all-purpose flour
1 teaspoon salt
¼ teaspoon pepper
1 cup Burgundy
½ cup beef broth
Hot cooked rice

Heat oil in a heavy Dutch oven; add beef. Cook, stirring constantly, until browned; remove beef, and set aside. Add onion and mushrooms to drippings; sauté until tender. Remove and set aside.

Return beef to skillet; sprinkle with flour, salt, and pepper. Stir in wine and broth; bring to a boil. Cover, reduce heat, and simmer 1 hour and 15 minutes or until tender. Add onion and mushrooms; cook until thoroughly heated. Serve over rice. Yield: 6 to 8 servings. *Patsy Wear, Fort Payne, Alabama.*

VEAL SCALLOPINI

1 pound veal cutlets
3 tablespoons all-purpose flour
½ teaspoon salt
⅛ teaspoon pepper
¼ cup butter or margarine
¼ pound fresh mushrooms, coarsely chopped
¼ cup chopped onion
⅓ cup chicken broth
¼ cup dry white wine
½ teaspoon dried whole marjoram
½ cup commercial sour cream
Chopped fresh parsley (optional)
Hot cooked rice

Flatten cutlets to ¼-inch thickness, using a meat mallet or rolling pin. Cut into serving-size pieces.

Combine flour, salt, and pepper; dredge cutlets in flour mixture, coating well. Sauté cutlets in butter in a large skillet about 3 minutes on each side or

until browned. Remove cutlets from skillet; place in a 1-quart casserole, reserving pan drippings.

Sauté mushrooms and onion in pan drippings; remove from heat. Add broth, wine, and marjoram; pour over cutlets. Cover and bake at 325° for 25 to 30 minutes or until veal is tender. Remove veal to a serving dish.

Combine mushroom mixture and sour cream; heat thoroughly. Pour over veal, and sprinkle with parsley, if desired. Serve over rice. Yield: 4 servings.
Mrs. Lloyd E. Reynolds, York, Pennsylvania.

COMPANY CHICKEN

¼ cup all-purpose flour
½ teaspoon salt
⅛ teaspoon pepper
8 chicken breasts halves, skinned and boned
¼ cup butter or margarine
1 cup dry white wine
8 (1-ounce) slices cooked ham
¼ cup chopped onion
1 tablespoon dried parsley flakes
¼ cup butter or margarine
¼ cup all-purpose flour
1 cup milk
1 cup half-and-half
1 avocado, peeled and sliced

Combine ¼ cup flour, salt, and pepper; dredge chicken in flour mixture. Melt ¼ cup butter in a large skillet; add chicken, and cook over medium heat until golden brown on each side. Add wine; cover, reduce heat, and simmer 20 minutes. Remove the chicken, reserving pan drippings.

Place ham in a lightly greased 13- x 9- x 2-inch baking dish. Arrange chicken over ham. Cover and bake at 325° for about 45 minutes.

Sauté onion and parsley flakes in ¼ cup butter and pan drippings in skillet until tender. Add ¼ cup flour, stirring until smooth. Cook 1 minute, stirring constantly. Gradually add milk and half-and-half; cook over medium heat, stirring constantly, until thickened and bubbly. Pour sauce over chicken. Garnish with sliced avocado. Yield: 8 servings.
Patsy M. Smith, Lampasas, Texas.

STUFFED MUSHROOMS

12 large fresh mushrooms
Melted butter or margarine
½ cup finely chopped celery
½ cup finely chopped green onion, with tops
¼ cup finely chopped green pepper
2 tablespoons butter or margarine
¼ cup dry white wine
½ teaspoon Worcestershire sauce
¼ cup Italian-style breadcrumbs
1½ teaspoons grated Parmesan cheese

Clean mushrooms with damp paper towels. Remove stems and chop; set aside. Brush caps with butter.

Sauté mushroom stems, celery, onion, and green pepper in 2 tablespoons butter in a large skillet until tender. Add wine and Worcestershire sauce; simmer 5 minutes. Stir in breadcrumbs.

Spoon vegetable mixture into mushroom caps; sprinkle with cheese, and place in a shallow baking pan. Bake at 350° for 18 to 20 minutes. Yield: 1 dozen.   *Mrs. J. K. Garrett, Jr.,*
Jonesboro, Georgia.

FRENCH ONION SOUP

¾ cup butter or margarine
4 medium onions (about 3 pounds), thinly sliced
1 tablespoon all-purpose flour
5 (10½-ounce) cans beef broth, undiluted
⅓ cup Burgundy or other dry red wine
½ teaspoon white pepper
½ teaspoon dried whole thyme
8 slices French bread, toasted
¾ cup (3 ounces) shredded Muenster cheese
¾ cup (3 ounces) shredded Swiss cheese
½ cup grated Parmesan cheese

Melt butter in a large Dutch oven over medium heat; add onion, and cook 40 to 45 minutes, stirring frequently. Sprinkle flour over onion; cook 2 minutes, stirring constantly. Add broth, wine, pepper, and thyme; bring to a boil. Cover, reduce heat, and simmer 30 minutes.

Ladle soup into 8 individual baking dishes; top each with a toasted bread slice. Sprinkle each with 1½ tablespoons Muenster cheese, 1½ tablespoons Swiss cheese, and 1 tablespoon Parmesan cheese. Place under broiler 2 to 3 minutes until cheese melts. Yield: 8 cups.   *Lynne DeWitt,*
Roanoke, Virginia.

He Cooks With A French Flair

New Orleans Attorney Ron Naquin has come a long way since his bachelor days when he didn't know how to cook. "I learned to cook when I found myself craving my mother's good Creole cooking," he says. And since Creole is an offspring of French cuisine, he buried himself in French cookbooks and started experimenting.

Now, Ron is well known among friends as a creative cook. He especially enjoys developing his own recipes.

One of his favorite creations is Dilled Crawfish Salad. "I developed it for my daughter's christening party," he says. "It's my own adaptation of a French recipe, which is basically crawfish tails in a vinaigrette dressing. I added the mayonnaise and the dill."

Desserts, especially crêpes, also are one of his favorites. "Crêpes are basic," says Ron, "but you can change them so much. I use different liqueurs in desserts for a special flavor, such as in the Crêpes Gelée Amandine." For this recipe, Ron particularly likes red currant jelly filling but suggests that cherry, grape, or raspberry jelly would be just as tasty.

Like Ron, many men across the South enjoy cooking. You'll also find some of their best recipes listed.

DILLED CRAWFISH SALAD

¼ cup finely chopped carrot
¼ cup finely chopped onion
¼ cup finely chopped celery
¼ cup plus 1 tablespoon butter or margarine, melted
1 pound peeled crawfish tails
2 tablespoons dry white wine or vermouth
1 tablespoon brandy or Cognac
1 bay leaf
½ teaspoon salt
¼ teaspoon white pepper
¼ teaspoon dried whole thyme
3 dashes of hot sauce
½ cup mayonnaise
1 tablespoon lemon juice
2 teaspoons dried whole dillweed
Lettuce leaves
Whole cooked crawfish (optional)
Lemon twists (optional)

Sauté carrot, onion, and celery in butter in a large skillet until tender. Add next 7 ingredients; simmer 4 minutes. Stir in hot sauce. Remove mixture from skillet, and drain well. Chill 20 minutes.

Combine crawfish mixture, mayonnaise, lemon juice, and dillweed; chill mixture thoroughly. Remove bay leaf. Serve on lettuce leaves. Garnish salad with whole crawfish and lemon twists, if desired. Yield: 4 servings.

CREAM OF CAULIFLOWER AND WATERCRESS SOUP

1 medium head cauliflower, broken into flowerets
2 cups sliced onion
¼ cup plus 1 tablespoon butter or margarine
¼ cup all-purpose flour
4 cups milk
4 cups chicken broth
1 teaspoon salt
½ teaspoon white pepper
½ pound watercress, washed and stems removed
¾ cup whipping cream

Cook cauliflower, covered, in a small amount of boiling water for 2 minutes; drain well. Set aside.

Sauté onion in butter in a large Dutch oven until tender. Add flour, stirring until smooth. Cook 1 minute, stirring constantly. Gradually stir in milk and chicken broth; cook over medium heat, stirring constantly, until thickened. Stir in salt and pepper.

Add cauliflower to the sauce and simmer 15 minutes, stirring occasionally.

Add watercress to soup mixture, and simmer an additional 10 minutes.

Pour soup into container of electric blender, and process until smooth. Add whipping cream; blend well. Serve hot or cold. Yield: about 11 cups.

CREPES GELEE AMANDINE

½ cup red currant jelly
12 crêpes (recipe follows)
½ cup sliced almonds
2 tablespoons sifted powdered sugar
Zest of 1 orange
4 to 6 tablespoons Curaçao
4 to 6 tablespoons amaretto

Spoon 2 teaspoons jelly onto center of each crêpe. Roll up crêpes, and place seam side down in a 13- x 9- x 2-inch baking dish. Top with almonds; sprinkle with powdered sugar and orange zest. Place dish under broiler 1 to 2 minutes or until almonds are toasted and sugar is partially dissolved. Pour Curaçao and amaretto over crêpes. Serve immediately. Yield: 6 servings.

Crêpes:

2 eggs
2 egg yolks
½ cup milk
½ cup water
3 tablespoons vegetable oil
¼ cup sugar
1 tablespoon Grand Marnier or other
   orange-flavored liqueur
½ teaspoon almond extract
1 cup instant-blending flour
Vegetable oil

Combine all ingredients in container of electric blender; process 1 to 1½ minutes. Scrape down sides of blender container with a rubber spatula; process an additional 15 seconds. Refrigerate batter 1 hour. (This allows the flour particles to swell and soften so the crêpes are light in texture.)

Brush the bottom of a 6-inch crêpe pan with oil; place the pan over medium heat until just hot, not smoking. Pour 3 tablespoons batter into pan; quickly tilt pan in all directions so batter covers the pan in a thin film. Cook about 1 minute.

Lift edge of crêpe to test for doneness. The crêpe is ready for flipping when it can be shaken loose from pan. Flip crêpe, and cook about 30 seconds on other side. (This side is rarely more than spotty brown and is the side on which filling is placed.)

Remove crêpe from pan, and repeat procedure until all batter is used. Place crêpes on a towel to cool. Stack between layers of waxed paper to prevent sticking. Yield: 12 crêpes.

NUTTY FRUIT BAKE

1 (8-ounce) can pineapple chunks,
   undrained
5 cooking apples, peeled, cored, and sliced
½ cup chopped walnuts
½ cup raisins
2 tablespoons butter or margarine
⅓ cup sugar
2 tablespoons all-purpose flour
1 teaspoon ground cinnamon
1 teaspoon vanilla extract

Drain pineapple chunks, reserving ⅓ cup juice.

Layer fruit, walnuts, and raisins in a 12- x 8- x 2-inch baking dish. Melt butter in a small saucepan; add reserved pineapple juice and remaining ingredients, mixing well. Pour over fruit mixture. Cover and bake at 350° for 30 minutes. Remove cover and bake an additional 15 minutes. Yield: 6 servings.

Jim Boatman,
Memphis, Tennessee.

ITALIAN SAUSAGE-STUFFED MUSHROOMS

About 20 large fresh mushrooms
½ pound hot bulk Italian sausage
1 clove garlic, pressed
¼ teaspoon pepper
Grated Parmesan cheese
2 teaspoons chopped fresh parsley

Clean mushrooms with damp paper towels. Remove mushroom stems and set aside. Place caps in a lightly greased 13- x 9- x 2-inch baking dish.

Combine sausage and garlic in a medium skillet. Brown sausage, stirring to crumble; drain well.

Position knife blade in processor bowl; add the mushroom stems, sausage, and pepper, and top with cover. Process 30 seconds.

Spoon sausage mixture into mushroom caps, and sprinkle with Parmesan cheese. Bake at 375° for 15 minutes. Garnish mushrooms with parsley. Yield: about 20 appetizer servings.

Joseph E. Bland,
Louisville, Kentucky.

Put A Chill On Appetizers

If you're planning a party, count on serving a variety of cold appetizers. These appealing snacks are easy to prepare ahead, and will wait in the refrigerator until your guests arrive.

SALMON PARTY ROLL

1 (15½-ounce) can red salmon
1 (8-ounce) package cream cheese,
   softened
1 tablespoon lemon juice
2 teaspoons grated onion
1 teaspoon prepared horseradish
¼ teaspoon liquid smoke
½ cup chopped pecans
3 tablespoons minced fresh parsley

Drain salmon; flake with a fork. Add cream cheese, lemon juice, onion, horseradish, and liquid smoke; stir well. Chill several hours or overnight.

Shape salmon mixture into a log. Combine pecans and parsley; stir well. Roll log in pecan mixture, and chill several hours. Yield: one 10-inch log.

Mrs. Fred C. Powers,
Newport, Arkansas.

LAYERED CRABMEAT SPREAD

4 (3-ounce) packages cream cheese,
   softened
1 small onion, grated
2 tablespoons Worcestershire sauce
2 tablespoons mayonnaise
1 tablespoon lemon juice
Dash of garlic salt
½ cup chili sauce
1 (6½-ounce) can crabmeat, drained and
   flaked
Chopped fresh parsley

Combine first 6 ingredients; beat until smooth, using an electric mixer or food processor. Spread mixture evenly onto a 12-inch pizza plate. Spread chili sauce evenly over cream cheese mixture, leaving a ¾-inch margin. Sprinkle with crabmeat. Garnish with parsley. Yield: 3½ cups.

Lilyan Oulehla,
New Port Richey, Florida.

PARTY BEAU MONDE DIP IN RYE BREAD

1 large round loaf Jewish or onion rye
   bread
1 (16-ounce) carton commercial sour
   cream
1 (48-ounce) jar mayonnaise
¼ cup dried parsley flakes
¼ cup Beau Monde seasoning
¼ cup dried whole dillweed
¼ cup instant minced onion
Fresh parsley sprigs

Scoop out center portion of bread, leaving crust intact. Tear removed portion into bite-size pieces; set aside.

Combine next 6 ingredients, mixing well. Pour dip into cavity of bread. Garnish with parsley sprigs, and serve with reserved pieces of rye bread. Yield: 2 quarts dip.

Sara Abraham,
Vicksburg, Mississippi.

PECAN CHEESE BALL

1 (8-ounce) package cream cheese,
   softened
1 cup (4 ounces) shredded Cheddar cheese
2 teaspoons chopped pimiento
2 teaspoons chopped green pepper
2 teaspoons minced onion
1 teaspoon Worcestershire sauce
½ teaspoon lemon juice
Dash of red pepper
Dash of salt
½ cup finely chopped pecans

Combine all ingredients except pecans; mix well. Shape into a ball, and roll in chopped pecans. Yield: one 4-inch cheese ball.

Jolene Christian,
Harrison, Tennessee.

CUCUMBER-CHEESE VEGETABLE DIP

1 (8-ounce) package cream cheese, softened
2 tablespoons whipping cream
⅓ cup minced cucumber
1 teaspoon grated onion
½ teaspoon salt
¼ teaspoon ground cumin

Combine cream cheese and whipping cream; beat on medium speed of electric mixer 2 minutes until smooth. Stir in remaining ingredients; chill. Serve with vegetables. Yield: 1⅓ cups dip.

Mrs. John R. Allen,
Dallas, Texas.

MARINATED MUSHROOM CAPS

⅓ cup white wine vinegar
⅓ cup corn oil
2 green onions, chopped
2 tablespoons chopped fresh parsley
½ teaspoon salt
½ teaspoon dry mustard
½ teaspoon dried whole basil
Dash of pepper
1 pound large fresh mushrooms

Combine first 8 ingredients in a medium bowl; stir well. Rinse mushrooms, and pat dry. Carefully remove caps; reserve stems for other uses. Add caps to vinegar mixture, tossing gently to coat. Chill mushrooms 4 to 6 hours. Yield: about 1 dozen appetizer servings.

Nora Henshaw,
Castle, Oklahoma.

Which Grill Is Best For You?

Grills on today's market range from lightweight foldup braziers to permanently installed gas grills. They can vary greatly in price as well. If you're planning to purchase a new grill, you'll save money if you keep in mind that the most expensive model isn't necessarily best suited for your needs.

When buying a grill, you should consider these four points: where you grill, how often you grill, what kind of food you cook, and the number of people you usually serve. Here are some specifics on the different type grills to help you select the right one for you.

Braziers—The most popular and least expensive grill is the lightweight brazier. It is basically a shallow bowl set on three or four legs and is available in foldup models or with such options as draft controls, wheels, and a cover or windshield.

This type of grill is perfect for cooking serving-size food items (such as hamburgers, hotdogs, steaks, and fish) and is convenient for grilling in small areas. If you only grill occasionally, one of the least expensive braziers should work well.

If you opt for an inexpensive model without draft controls, a 1-inch layer of gravel in the bottom of the grill will help air circulate more freely and allow for more even heating. A foil lining also makes cleanup easy and can be used 10 to 12 times before discarding. When you change the foil, wash the gravel and allow it to dry before replacing.

Hibachis—Made of heavy cast iron, hibachis come with air dampers for controlled heat, adjustable grates, and coal racks for ashes to sift to the bottom. The grate size can range from 4 to 20 inches across, so these grills are best used for small cooking tasks such as appetizers or grilling for two or three people.

Most hibachis have short legs for tabletop grilling and are ideal for apartment dwellers. Their small size and heavy weight make them space saving and safe from accidental tipovers.

Kettle grills—These are the most versatile and most expensive charcoal grills you'll find. They're constructed of heavy cast metal and are spherical in shape, with the lid comprising the top half of the sphere. They're designed to work like a Dutch oven and are suitable for roasting large cuts of meat in addition to grilling.

The deep grill base makes smoking by indirect heat a possible option. Most models are equipped with draft controls on the lid and the base, which allows cooking with minimum watching. Kettle grills may come with a coal rack in the bottom or an ash catcher fastened outside and underneath the grill. The cover adds weather protection.

Gas grills—The main advantage of a gas grill is the number of convenience options it provides. It's quick starting, allows accurate heat control and even cooking, and is easy to clean.

Gas grills use ceramic or volcanic pumice briquets instead of charcoal, eliminating ash cleanup. The briquets are placed on a rack between the heat source and the grate; heat radiated from the hot briquets cooks the food.

Models available include permanently installed grills attached to a natural gas line and portable grills of any size fueled by LP (liquefied petroleum) gas. If you're selecting a stationary grill, be sure that it will rotate so you can adjust the position according to the wind.

Gas grill bodies are generally made of heavy, cast aluminum with rust and oxidation resistance, which permits outdoor storage. Covered grills allow year-round barbecuing and can be used for smoking meats as well as grilling.

Electric grills—Like gas grills, electric grills are hot and ready to use in minutes, offer temperature selections, better heat control, and easy cleanup. Some models come with ceramic or rock briquets.

Countertop electric grills, designed for use indoors, produce no smoke. The drippings run from the grill into a shielded tray. These models are excellent for broiling steaks, hamburgers, or hot dogs on a rainy day.

Of course, grilling is limited to locations with available electrical outlets. But, it is an ideal appliance for grilling indoors or on an apartment balcony.

Season With Aromatic Chervil

Lacy green chervil looks so much like parsley, it may be hard to tell the difference. But just one sniff reveals an herb that is much more aromatic than parsley. The aromas of both tarragon and anise come to mind.

Herb growers will want to include chervil in their garden; it follows a growing pattern similar to parsley.

CHERVIL SAUCE

2 tablespoons butter or margarine
2 tablespoons all-purpose flour
3 tablespoons minced fresh chervil
   or 1 tablespoon dried whole chervil
1 green onion, chopped
½ teaspoon grated lemon rind
1¼ cups half-and-half
1 teaspoon lemon juice
½ teaspoon salt
Dash of pepper

Melt butter in a heavy saucepan over low heat; add flour, stirring until smooth. Cook 1 minute, stirring constantly. Stir in chervil, onion, and lemon rind. Gradually add half-and-half; cook over medium heat, stirring constantly, until thickened. Stir in lemon juice, salt, and pepper. Serve over fish or vegetables. Yield: 1½ cups.

CHERVIL BUTTER

1 cup butter or margarine,
  softened
4 to 6 tablespoons minced fresh
  chervil or 1 to 2 tablespoons dried
  whole chervil

Cream butter until light and fluffy; blend in chervil. Refrigerate several hours or overnight. Serve over baked potatoes. Yield: 1 cup.

The Ice Cream's In The Cake

You'll find our Strawberry Cake Roll surprisingly easy to make—just soften vanilla ice cream, and stir in whipped topping and fresh strawberries for the filling. Then freeze the mixture, spread on the cake, roll it up, and freeze the cake until firm.

Our home economists found a secret to spreading the ice cream filling on the cake: be sure that the frozen mixture is spreadable but still frozen hard enough to hold its shape. If ice cream oozes from the ends as you're rolling the cake, it should still be firm enough to stuff back between the cake layers with a spatula.

STRAWBERRY CAKE ROLL

1½ pints vanilla ice cream, softened
1 cup frozen whipped topping, softened
1 cup chopped fresh strawberries
4 eggs, separated
¼ cup sugar
½ teaspoon vanilla extract
½ cup sugar
¾ cup all-purpose flour
1 teaspoon baking powder
¼ teaspoon salt
2 to 3 tablespoons powdered sugar
Whipped cream
Strawberry slices

Combine first 3 ingredients. Freeze about 3½ hours until firm.

Grease a 15- x 10- x 1-inch jellyroll pan with vegetable oil, and line with waxed paper. Grease waxed paper lightly with vegetable oil, and set aside.

Beat egg yolks until light and lemon colored; gradually add ¼ cup sugar and vanilla, stirring well. Set aside.

Beat egg whites (at room temperature) until foamy in a large mixing bowl; gradually add ½ cup sugar, 1 tablespoon at a time, beating until stiff but not dry. Fold in egg yolk mixture. Combine flour, baking powder, and salt; mix well, and fold into egg mixture. Spread batter evenly in prepared pan. Bake at 350° about 12 minutes.

Sift powdered sugar in a 15- x 10-inch rectangle on a linen towel. When cake is done, immediately loosen from sides of pan, and turn out onto sugar. Peel off waxed paper. Starting at narrow end, roll up cake and towel together; cool on a wire rack, seam side down.

Unroll cake, and remove the towel. Quickly spread cake with ice cream mixture, leaving a 1-inch margin around edges. Immediately reroll cake, and wrap in aluminum foil. Freeze.

Place cake on a serving plate, with seam side down. Garnish with whipped cream and strawberry slices. Slice cake with an electric knife. Yield: 8 to 10 servings. *Gayle Wallace, Memphis, Tennessee.*

Stir Variety Into Rice

Our readers have discovered some tasty ways to turn plain rice into something special.

Be sure to use long grain regular rice for these recipes; it cooks up into fluffy, separate grains. Medium and short grain varieties are moister and tend to cling together when cooked. Use these varieties for molded dishes, such as rice rings or desserts.

RICE AU GRATIN

3 cups cooked regular rice
1 small onion, chopped
1 small green pepper, chopped
1 (4-ounce) jar diced pimiento,
  drained
1 (10¾-ounce) can cream of mushroom
  soup, undiluted
¼ cup milk
½ cup (2 ounces) shredded Cheddar
  cheese

Combine first 6 ingredients; spoon into a 10- x 6- x 2-inch baking dish. Bake at 350° for 40 minutes; top with cheese, and bake 5 minutes. Yield: 6 servings. *Sue McLean, Brownwood, Texas.*

FRIED RICE

1 tablespoon vegetable oil
2 eggs, beaten
6 slices bacon
6 green onions, chopped
1 (8-ounce) can sliced water chestnuts,
  drained
½ cup frozen green peas, cooked
Dash of garlic powder
3 cups cooked regular rice
1 to 2 tablespoons soy sauce

Heat oil in a small skillet; add eggs and cook, stirring constantly, until firm but still moist. Set aside.

Cook bacon in a large skillet until crisp; remove bacon, reserving 2 tablespoons drippings in skillet. Crumble bacon, and set aside. Add next 4 ingredients to drippings; cook until onions are tender. Stir in rice, soy sauce, eggs, and bacon. Cook until thoroughly heated. Yield: 6 servings.
Ann Elsie Schmetzer, Madisonville, Kentucky.

BACON-CHIVE RICE

3 slices bacon, diced
3 cups cooked regular rice
¼ cup chopped chives
1 tablespoon Worcestershire sauce
¼ teaspoon pepper

Cook bacon in a large skillet until crisp; pour off pan drippings, reserving 1½ tablespoons drippings in skillet. Add remaining ingredients; stir well, and cook until thoroughly heated. Yield: 6 servings. *Cindy Freeman, Hereford, Texas.*

GLORIFIED RICE

1 tablespoon butter or margarine
½ cup slivered almonds
2 cups cooked regular rice
½ cup raisins
1 teaspoon sugar

Melt butter in a large skillet. Add almonds; cook over medium heat, stirring frequently, until golden brown. Stir in rice, raisins, and sugar; cook until thoroughly heated. Yield: 4 servings.
Mrs. Jack Besst, St. Petersburg, Florida.

Sandwiches Can Be Special

Sandwiches make the perfect lunch or supper during the warmer months when meals are more relaxed. You'll find the convenience of deviled ham and corned beef especially appealing on busy days.

BARBECUED CORNED BEEF SANDWICHES

½ cup catsup
½ cup water
1 tablespoon cider vinegar
1 tablespoon Worcestershire sauce
1 teaspoon chili powder
⅛ teaspoon pepper
1 (12-ounce) can corned beef, coarsely chopped
4 hamburger buns, split and toasted

Combine first 6 ingredients in a skillet. Bring mixture just to boiling point. Add corned beef; reduce heat to low. Simmer 15 to 20 minutes, stirring frequently, until most of liquid is absorbed. Spoon corned beef mixture on bottom half of buns; cover with bun tops. Yield: 4 servings. *Beth Dillard, Cantonment, Florida.*

OVEN BURGERS

1 cup catsup
½ cup water
¼ cup plus 2 tablespoons chopped onion
2 tablespoons sugar
3 tablespoons vinegar
2 tablespoons Worcestershire sauce
1½ pounds ground beef
¾ cup regular oats, uncooked
1 cup evaporated milk
3 tablespoons chopped onion
1½ teaspoons salt
¼ teaspoon pepper
10 hamburger buns

Combine first 6 ingredients in a medium saucepan; simmer 15 minutes.

Combine next 6 ingredients; mix well. Shape into 10 patties about ¾ inch thick. Cook patties over medium heat in a large skillet until browned, turning only once.

Arrange patties in a 13- x 9- x 2-inch baking dish. Pour catsup mixture over patties. Bake at 350° about 40 minutes. Serve on buns. Yield: 10 servings.
Mrs. Al Van Loo, Norborne, Missouri.

SUPER SLOPPY JOES

1 pound ground beef
2 teaspoons instant minced onion
1 (5¾-ounce) can mushroom steak sauce
1 (4-ounce) can tomato sauce
1 (2½-ounce) jar sliced mushrooms, drained
3 tablespoons chili sauce
1½ teaspoons chili powder
½ teaspoon salt
Dash of pepper
6 hamburger buns, buttered and toasted

Cook ground beef and onion until meat is browned, stirring to crumble; drain well. Stir in the next 7 ingredients; simmer 10 minutes, stirring occasionally. Spoon ground beef mixture onto buns. Yield: 6 servings.
Ella Rae Poehls, Houston, Texas.

DEVILED DELIGHT

1 (4-ounce) can deviled ham
2 hard-cooked eggs, finely chopped
3 tablespoons finely chopped dill pickle
1 teaspoon minced onion
1 teaspoon prepared mustard

Combine all ingredients, stirring well. Chill. Spread on your favorite bread. Yield: about 1 cup. *Janice Finn, Greensburg, Kentucky.*

Try A Boysenberry Dessert

If you haven't tried boysenberries, look for some this summer. They're great in our Berry Crisp or Peachy Berry Cream Mold.

The season for boysenberries is short, so enjoy them while you can. They're a delicious flavor blend of blackberries and raspberries and taste good plain or in a variety of desserts.

PEACHY BERRY CREAM MOLD

1 envelope unflavored gelatin
½ cup milk
2 (3-ounce) packages cream cheese, softened
3 tablespoons powdered sugar
1 cup milk
½ teaspoon vanilla extract
Pinch of salt
½ cup whipping cream, whipped
Sweetened sliced fresh peaches
Sweetened fresh boysenberries

Combine gelatin and ½ cup milk in top of double boiler; let stand 1 minute. Bring water to a boil; reduce heat to low, and cook until gelatin dissolves.

Beat cream cheese at medium speed of electric mixer until fluffy; add sugar, mixing well. Add gelatin mixture, 1 cup milk, vanilla, and salt; beat until smooth. Fold in whipped cream; pour into an oiled 3-cup mold. Chill; unmold and serve with peaches and boysenberries. Yield: 6 servings. *Mrs. Ron Bain, Nashville, Tennessee.*

BERRY CRISP

1½ cups fresh boysenberries
2 tablespoons sugar
2 tablespoons butter or margarine
1 cup sugar
1 cup all-purpose flour
1 teaspoon baking powder
1 egg, beaten
Whipped cream

Combine boysenberries and 2 tablespoons sugar; stir. Place in a greased 8-inch square pan; dot with butter.

Combine 1 cup sugar, flour, baking powder, and egg; stir until mixture resembles coarse crumbs. Sprinkle over berries. Bake at 350° for 30 minutes. Serve with whipped cream. Yield: 6 servings. *Mrs. Jack W. Slade, Helen, Georgia.*

Right: Three of the best ways we know to enjoy steak to the fullest are Delicious Marinated Flank Steak (page 110), Stir-Fry Broccoli and Beef (page 110), and Saucy Beef Kabobs (page 109).

Page 132: Perk up summer meals by offering sandwiches with a variety of breads and fillings. The Garden features spinach and three types of cheese on pumpernickel bread. Pita bread neatly holds the vegetable filling within Pita Salad Sandwich. Tuna Club Sandwich sports two different fillings between three thin slices of whole wheat bread (recipes on page 134).

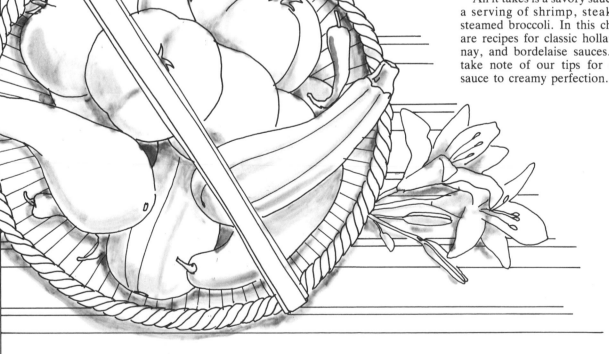

June

Prime time for vegetables is June, and we know just the way to show off prize produce—use the shells of your prettiest squash, tomatoes, and green peppers to stuff with savory fillings. Try some of our recipes for salads, side dishes, and entrées all served in edible vegetable containers.

Vegetables make very tasty sandwiches as well. See for yourself in our recipes for spectacular summer sandwiches such as Pita Salad Sandwiches in which marinated vegetables are stuffed in a pita bread pocket. A sandwich called The Garden attracted our tastebuds with toasted pumpernickel bread hosting a filling of three types of cheese, spinach, mushrooms, alfalfa sprouts, and sunflower kernels. You'll never settle for a plain sandwich again.

All it takes is a savory sauce to dress up a serving of shrimp, steak, or tender steamed broccoli. In this chapter, there are recipes for classic hollandaise, mornay, and bordelaise sauces. Be sure to take note of our tips for cooking any sauce to creamy perfection.

A Spread Of Summer Sandwiches

Piled high with meat and vegetables, grilled with cheese, or battered and fried until golden brown, these sandwiches are perfect for a warm summer day. They're great for a casual outdoor luncheon or a light family supper.

You don't have to dine at a restaurant to enjoy a Monte Cristo Sandwich. Our version of this unique fried sandwich is just as delicious, and you can make it at home. To guarantee success, our staff suggests skewering the sandwiches to hold them together as they're battered and fried. Use a frying basket or slotted metal spoon or spatula to lower each sandwich into the oil.

PITA SALAD SANDWICHES

2 small avocados, peeled, seeded, and sliced
1 large cucumber, unpeeled and thinly sliced
1 medium-size green pepper, chopped
2 medium tomatoes, unpeeled and coarsely chopped
2 stalks celery, thinly sliced
3 green onions with tops, thinly sliced
Dash of pepper
Dash of garlic powder
1 (8-ounce) bottle Italian dressing
4 (6-inch) pocket bread rounds
Commercial sour cream (optional)

Combine first 8 ingredients in a large bowl. Add dressing and toss gently.

Cut each bread round in half. Using a slotted spoon, fill pockets with vegetable mixture. Serve immediately with sour cream, if desired. Yield: 4 servings.
Maria Lilly,
Charleston, West Virginia.

TUNA CLUB SANDWICHES

1 small cucumber, peeled and thinly sliced
1 tablespoon vinegar
1 tablespoon vegetable oil
Dash of pepper
Dash of dried whole dillweed
1 (7-ounce) can tuna, drained and flaked
½ cup chopped celery
¼ cup chopped fresh parsley
¼ cup mayonnaise
12 thin slices whole wheat bread
About 3 tablespoons butter or margarine, softened
2 hard-cooked eggs, sliced

Combine first 5 ingredients, tossing well. Cover and chill 30 minutes.

Combine tuna, celery, parsley, and mayonnaise; mix well, and set aside.

Toast bread on both sides. Spread butter on one side of 8 toast slices. Spread tuna mixture on buttered side of 4 toast slices; top each with an unbuttered toast slice. Layer one-fourth of egg slices and one-fourth of cucumber slices on top of each unbuttered toast slice. Top with remaining toast slices, buttered side down. Cut each sandwich in half diagonally; secure with wooden picks. Serve immediately. Yield: 4 servings.
Agnes Kolk,
Arlington, Texas.

THE GARDEN

2 (10-ounce) packages frozen chopped spinach, thawed
½ cup minced green onion
¼ cup plus 2 tablespoons mayonnaise
1 tablespoon minced green pepper
1 tablespoon lemon juice
¼ teaspoon salt
½ pound fresh mushrooms, sliced
1 tablespoon butter or margarine
¼ cup butter or margarine, softened
12 slices pumpernickel bread
¾ cup fresh alfalfa sprouts, washed and drained
2 tablespoons salted sunflower kernels
6 (1-ounce) slices Provolone cheese
6 (1-ounce) slices Cheddar cheese
6 (1-ounce) slices Swiss cheese

Squeeze spinach to remove excess liquid. Combine spinach and next 5 ingredients in a bowl; stir well, and set aside.

Sauté mushrooms in 1 tablespoon butter in a skillet until tender; set aside.

Spread 1 teaspoon softened butter on one side of each bread slice. Lightly brown 6 bread slices, buttered side down, on a hot griddle; remove from heat. Spread spinach mixture evenly on unbuttered sides of toasted bread; sprinkle with alfalfa sprouts, mushrooms, and sunflower kernels. Set aside.

Place 1 slice each of Provolone, Cheddar, and Swiss cheese on unbuttered side of remaining 6 bread slices. Place bread, buttered side down, on hot griddle; cook over medium heat, just until cheese softens and bread lightly browns. To serve, put cheese-topped bread slices and spinach-topped bread slices together. Yield: 6 sandwiches.
Note: Sandwiches may be served open-face.
James O. Weisman,
Little Rock, Arkansas.

MONTE CRISTO SANDWICHES

¼ cup mayonnaise
2 teaspoons prepared mustard
8 slices white bread
4 (1-ounce) slices cooked turkey
4 (1-ounce) slices fully cooked ham
4 (1-ounce) slices Swiss cheese
2 egg whites
3 eggs
½ cup commercial sour cream
2 tablespoons milk
About 1 cup fine, dry breadcrumbs
Vegetable oil

Combine mayonnaise and mustard, mixing well; spread on one side of each bread slice. Place one slice each of turkey, ham, and cheese on top of 4 bread slices. Top with remaining bread. Cut each sandwich in half diagonally; secure with wooden picks.

Beat egg whites (at room temperature) until stiff; set aside. Beat eggs; add sour cream and milk, mixing well. Fold in egg whites. Dip sandwich halves in batter; coat with breadcrumbs. Carefully lower sandwich halves, one at a time, into deep hot oil (375°); fry until golden brown, turning once. Drain; remove wooden picks. Serve sandwiches immediately. Yield: 4 servings.

Summer Vegetables Invite A Filling

Ruby red tomatoes, yellow squash, and shiny purple eggplant look pretty whole, but they offer more flavor possibilities when blended with other foods. So slice an opening into the vegetable, scoop out pulp, and spoon in a filling.

Any vegetable that is firm and plump works well for stuffing—from a large eggplant right down to a tiny cherry tomato. Either slice the vegetable in half or cut a small hole in the top; remove the pulp, leaving a shell thick enough to support the stuffed vegetable.

BEEF-STUFFED SQUASH

5 large yellow squash
½ pound ground beef
1 medium onion, chopped
1 medium-size green pepper, chopped
1 (16-ounce) can whole tomatoes, drained and chopped
½ cup (2 ounces) shredded Cheddar cheese

Wash squash thoroughly; cook in boiling salted water to cover 8 minutes or until tender but still firm. Drain and cool slightly. Trim off stems. Cut squash in half lengthwise; remove pulp, leaving a firm shell. Coarsely chop the pulp, and set aside.

Cook ground beef, onion, and green pepper in a skillet until beef is browned, stirring to crumble. Drain. Stir in squash pulp and tomatoes.

Place squash shells in a 13- x 9- x 2-inch baking dish. Spoon ground beef mixture into shells; bake at 350° for 25 minutes. Sprinkle with cheese, and bake 5 minutes. Yield: 10 servings.

Alice G. Pahl,
Raleigh, North Carolina.

GARDEN-STUFFED LETTUCE

1 large head iceberg lettuce
1 large carrot, scraped
4 radishes
4 green onions
1 tomato, cut into wedges
1 small cucumber, sliced
4 ounces cooked ham, sliced into strips
4 ounces Cheddar cheese, sliced into strips
Ripe olives
Thousand Island Dressing

Carefully remove outer green leaves of lettuce, and set aside. Cut a 1- to 2-inch slice from stem end of lettuce; hollow out 1 to 2 inches from center of lettuce, leaving a 1-inch margin at edges. Stack reserved outer leaves to form a bowl, and place lettuce shell in bowl of leaves. Reserve remaining lettuce for other uses.

Slice carrot into 8 thin lengthwise strips using a vegetable peeler. Roll strips jellyroll fashion, and secure with wooden picks. Place in bowl of ice water to curl the strips. Remove wooden picks.

Trim stem ends from radishes. Cut radishes into roses using a radish rose cutter or slice petals into radishes using a sharp paring knife. Place in bowl of ice water to open petals.

Trim both ends of green onions, leaving about 3 inches of green tops. Place green onions on a cutting board. Using a sharp knife, cut several slits into both ends of green onions, cutting almost to the center. Place in bowl of ice water to curl ends.

Arrange tomato wedges, cucumber slices, ham, cheese, carrots, radishes, green onions, and olives in lettuce shell and around base of lettuce. To serve, slice lettuce into wedges. Pour Thousand Island Dressing over each serving. Yield: 2 to 4 servings.

Thousand Island Dressing:

½ cup mayonnaise
¼ cup chili sauce
1½ tablespoons coarsely chopped pimiento-stuffed olives
⅛ teaspoon onion powder
1½ teaspoons chopped fresh parsley
1½ teaspoons chopped pimiento
¼ teaspoon lemon juice
6 capers

Combine all ingredients, stirring well. Chill before serving. Store in refrigerator. Yield: about 1 cup.

PIZZA PEPPERS

6 large green peppers
⅓ pound bulk Italian sausage
1 (16-ounce) can whole tomatoes, undrained and chopped
1⅓ cups water
⅔ cup uncooked regular rice
1 teaspoon dried whole oregano
½ teaspoon dried Italian seasoning
¾ cup (3 ounces) shredded mozzarella cheese

Cut off tops of green peppers; remove seeds. Cook peppers 5 minutes in boiling salted water to cover; drain peppers and set aside.

Cook sausage until browned, stirring to crumble; drain. Combine sausage and next 5 ingredients; cover and cook over medium heat 20 minutes or until rice is done. Fill green peppers with meat mixture; place in a shallow baking dish. Bake at 350° for 15 minutes. Sprinkle with cheese, and bake 5 minutes. Yield: 6 servings.

K. E. Kelleher,
Wilmington, Delaware.

BAKED STUFFED ONIONS

6 large Spanish onions
½ pound hot bulk pork sausage
¼ cup chopped green pepper
1 egg, beaten
1 cup cooked rice
½ cup soft breadcrumbs
½ teaspoon dried whole oregano
2 tablespoons chopped fresh parsley
2 tablespoons butter or margarine, melted
½ teaspoon paprika

Peel onions and cut a slice from top. Cook onions in boiling salted water 12 minutes or until tender but not mushy. Cool. Remove center of onions, leaving shells intact; chop onion centers, and reserve ½ cup.

Cook sausage until browned, stirring to crumble; drain, reserving pan drippings. Sauté green pepper and reserved

½ cup onion in drippings until tender. Combine sausage, sautéed vegetables, egg, rice, breadcrumbs, oregano, and parsley. Fill onion shells with sausage mixture; place in a greased shallow pan.

Combine butter and paprika; brush on onions. Cover and bake at 400° for 15 minutes. Uncover and bake an additional 5 minutes. Yield: 6 servings.

Jean Pashby,
Memphis, Tennessee.

POTATO SALAD 'N' PEPPERS

6 medium-size green peppers
5 to 6 medium-size new potatoes
½ cup finely chopped celery
⅓ cup finely chopped onion
2 hard-cooked eggs, chopped
½ cup mayonnaise
¼ cup butter or margarine, melted
1 tablespoon vinegar
1 teaspoon sugar
¾ teaspoon salt
Pepper to taste
3 slices bacon, cooked and crumbled

Cut off tops of green peppers; discard seeds. Set aside.

Cook potatoes in boiling water about 30 minutes or until tender. Drain and cool. Peel potatoes, and cut into ½-inch cubes. Combine potatoes and next 3 ingredients; toss lightly.

Combine next 6 ingredients; mix thoroughly. Add to potato mixture; stir to coat vegetables.

Fill green peppers with potato mixture, and top with bacon. Yield: 6 servings.

Ann Elsie Schmetzer,
Madisonville, Kentucky.

CHEESY CHERRY TOMATOES

1 pint (about 20) cherry tomatoes
1 (8-ounce) package cream cheese, softened
¼ teaspoon celery salt
Dash of onion powder
4 slices bacon, cooked and crumbled
Fresh parsley sprigs

Wash tomatoes thoroughly. Cut a thin slice from top of each tomato; carefully scoop out pulp, leaving the shells intact. Reserve pulp for other uses. Invert shells to drain 30 minutes.

Combine next 4 ingredients in a mixing bowl; beat at low speed of an electric mixer until smooth. Spoon cream cheese mixture into tomato shells, and garnish each with parsley. Yield: about 20 appetizer servings.

Gay Evaldi,
East Windsor, New Jersey.

CUCUMBER TUNA BOATS

3 medium cucumbers
Salt
1 (7-ounce) can tuna, drained and flaked
¾ cup (3 ounces) shredded process
    American cheese
½ cup finely chopped celery
2 hard-cooked eggs, chopped
⅓ cup mayonnaise or salad dressing
2 tablespoons sweet pickle relish
1 tablespoon minced onion
1 teaspoon lemon juice
Paprika

Wash cucumbers thoroughly. Cut cucumbers in half lengthwise, and scrape out seeds. Cut a thin slice from bottom of each half so cucumbers lie flat; lightly salt cavities. Set aside.

Combine next 8 ingredients; mix well. Fill cucumber shells with tuna mixture, and sprinkle with paprika. Chill until ready to serve. Yield: 6 servings.

Margaret L. Hunter,
Princeton, Kentucky.

MUSHROOM-STUFFED EGGPLANT

1 medium eggplant
½ cup chopped onion
¼ cup butter or margarine
1 (4-ounce) can sliced mushrooms, drained
¾ cup soft breadcrumbs
¼ teaspoon pepper
1 cup (4 ounces) shredded Cheddar cheese

Cut eggplant in half lengthwise. Remove pulp, leaving a ¼-inch shell; set shells aside. Dice pulp.

Sauté diced eggplant and onion in butter in a large skillet until tender. Add mushrooms and sauté 5 minutes. Stir in breadcrumbs and pepper. Stuff eggplant shells with mushroom mixture, and place shells in a 9-inch square baking pan.

Bake at 350° for 15 minutes. Remove from oven; sprinkle cheese on eggplant halves, and bake an additional 5 minutes. Yield: 2 servings. *Nancy Moore,*
Memphis, Tennessee.

STUFFED MUSHROOMS

1¼ pounds large fresh mushrooms
¼ cup butter or margarine
4 green onions, finely chopped
⅓ cup finely chopped green pepper
3 tablespoons finely chopped celery
1 clove garlic, minced
1 (12-ounce) package frozen spinach
    soufflé, thawed

Clean mushrooms with damp paper towels; remove the stems and reserve for other uses.

Melt butter in a skillet. Roll mushroom caps in butter; place in a shallow baking dish, cap side down. Sauté green onion, green pepper, celery, and garlic in butter remaining in skillet; stir in soufflé, and cook until thoroughly heated.

Spoon spinach mixture into mushroom caps; cover and bake at 350° for 15 minutes. Yield: about 2 dozen.

Patsy Layer,
Galveston, Texas.

STUFFED ZUCCHINI SUPREME

4 medium zucchini
¼ cup chopped onion
1 tablespoon butter or margarine
1 (8¾-ounce) can whole kernel corn,
    drained
1½ cups (6 ounces) shredded Monterey
    Jack cheese, divided
2 tablespoons chopped pimiento
½ teaspoon salt
Dash of pepper

Wash zucchini thoroughly; cook in boiling water to cover 10 minutes or until tender but still firm. Drain and cool slightly. Trim off stems. Cut squash in half lengthwise; remove pulp, leaving a firm shell. Coarsely chop the pulp, and set aside.

Sauté onion and chopped zucchini in butter in a large skillet until tender. Stir in corn, 1 cup cheese, pimiento, salt, and pepper.

Stuff zucchini shells with cheese mixture, and place in a 12- x 8- x 2-inch baking dish.

Bake at 350° for 35 to 40 minutes. Sprinkle with remaining cheese, and return to oven until cheese melts. Yield: 8 servings.

Edith Askins,
Greenville, Texas.

BROCCOLI-STUFFED TOMATOES

6 medium tomatoes
Salt and pepper
1 (10-ounce) package frozen chopped
    broccoli
1 cup (4 ounces) shredded Swiss cheese
1 cup soft breadcrumbs
½ cup mayonnaise
2 tablespoons chopped onion
2 tablespoons grated Parmesan cheese
Green onion fans (optional)

Wash tomatoes thoroughly. Cut tops from tomatoes; scoop out pulp, leaving

shells intact. Reserve pulp for other uses. Sprinkle cavities of tomatoes with salt and pepper, and invert on wire rack to drain 30 minutes.

Cook broccoli according to package directions, omitting salt; drain well.

Combine broccoli and next 4 ingredients; mix well. Stuff tomato shells with broccoli mixture; sprinkle with Parmesan cheese. Bake at 350° for 30 minutes. Arrange tomatoes on serving platter, and garnish with green onion fans, if desired. Yield: 6 servings.

Betty Hornsley,
Columbia, South Carolina.

Chicken's Cooking For Two

Chicken is an ideal choice when you're cooking for two. It's inexpensive, nutritious, and offers lots of versatility.

Although chicken is usually packaged to serve four or more, you can ask the butcher to custom-wrap a smaller amount. If you buy enough chicken for several meals, divide it into servings for two and tightly wrap it for freezing, using heavy-duty aluminum foil, freezer paper, or plastic freezer bags. When stored at 0°F or below, chicken will keep from 4 to 6 months.

GOLDEN BARBECUED CHICKEN

1 tablespoon butter or margarine, melted
1 tablespoon sugar
1 tablespoon lemon juice
1 tablespoon prepared mustard
1 tablespoon Worcestershire sauce
¼ teaspoon garlic salt
⅛ teaspoon pepper
3 drops of hot sauce
2 chicken quarters

Combine first 8 ingredients in a small bowl; mix well. Place chicken in a lightly greased 8-inch square baking dish; pour sauce over chicken. Bake, uncovered, at 350° for 45 minutes. Increase temperature to 400°; bake an additional 10 minutes. Yield: 2 servings.

Violet Moore,
Montezuma, Georgia.

BAKED CHICKEN PARMESAN

1 egg
¼ cup commercial sour cream
¼ cup Italian-style breadcrumbs
2 tablespoons grated Parmesan cheese
2 chicken breast halves, skinned

Beat egg in a shallow bowl; stir in sour cream, and set aside.

Combine breadcrumbs and cheese in a shallow bowl. Dip each chicken breast in egg mixture, and coat with breadcrumb mixture; place in a greased 10- x 6- x 2-inch baking dish. Bake, uncovered, at 350° for 45 minutes or until tender. Yield: 2 servings.

Mrs. John R. Styles,
Titusville, Florida.

CHICKEN MARSALA

2 chicken breast halves, skinned and boned
2 tablespoons butter or margarine
6 mushrooms, sliced
½ cup Marsala wine
⅛ teaspoon salt
Dash of pepper
1 teaspoon lemon juice
2 teaspoons chopped fresh parsley

Place each piece of chicken between 2 sheets of waxed paper, and flatten to ¼-inch thickness using a meat mallet or rolling pin.

Melt butter in a medium skillet; add chicken and cook over low heat 3 to 4 minutes on each side or until golden brown. Remove chicken breasts to serving platter. Add next 5 ingredients to skillet; cook until mushrooms are tender. Pour wine mixture over chicken; sprinkle with parsley. Yield: 2 servings.

Note: Instead of Marsala wine, ½ cup white wine plus 2 teaspoons brandy may be used. *Cyn Hickey,*
Dallas, Texas.

CHICKEN WITH SNOW PEAS

2 chicken breast halves, skinned and boned
Salt and pepper
1 tablespoon vegetable oil
1 cup diagonally sliced celery
1 small onion, sliced and separated into rings
1 (6-ounce) package frozen pea pods, thawed
½ cup chicken broth, divided
1 tablespoon soy sauce
1 teaspoon cornstarch
¼ teaspoon sugar
Hot cooked rice

Cut chicken into thin strips; sprinkle with salt and pepper. Sauté chicken in hot oil in a large skillet until lightly browned. Add celery, onion, pea pods, and 2 tablespoons broth; cover skillet and cook 1½ minutes.

Combine soy sauce, cornstarch, and sugar, stirring well; stir into chicken mixture. Gradually add remaining ¼ cup plus 2 tablespoons broth; cook, stirring constantly, until thickened. Serve over rice. Yield: 2 servings.

Margaret Oldfield,
Fort Myers, Florida.

CHICKEN A LA KING

1 tablespoon butter or margarine
1 tablespoon all-purpose flour
1 cup milk
¼ cup half-and-half
1 cup chopped cooked chicken
1 tablespoon chopped pimiento
1 teaspoon chopped pimiento-stuffed olives
½ teaspoon paprika
¼ teaspoon salt
⅛ teaspoon white pepper
2 slices toast

Melt butter in a heavy saucepan over low heat; add flour, stirring until smooth. Cook 1 minute, stirring constantly. Gradually add milk and half-and-half; cook over medium heat, stirring constantly, until thickened and bubbly. Stir next 6 ingredients into the sauce. Cook until thoroughly heated. Serve over toast. Yield: 2 servings.

Thelma Graybeal,
Cushing, Oklahoma.

Stir Up A Classic Sauce

Start with something simple, like steamed broccoli—smother it in hollandaise sauce, and suddenly it's fancy fare. Grilled steak is always good, but covered with Bordelaise sauce, it becomes a masterpiece.

The names of these classic sauces bring visions of complicated gourmet meals to mind. But the sauces themselves are simple to prepare. They turn out perfectly every time if you carefully follow the instructions.

The basis of several of our sauces is a butter and flour mixture called a roux. The 1 minute of cooking and stirring specified for the roux is essential, as this releases the starch from the flour, prevents the sauce from lumping, and eliminates any pasty flavor.

When the recipes say to stir, they mean to stir constantly. Stirring or beating with a wire whisk will help ensure a smooth sauce.

Some recipes call for a heavy saucepan; it will keep your sauces from scorching. A double boiler is sometimes necessary because the sauce may curdle if cooked over direct heat.

A sauce may also curdle or become lumpy if the liquid, butter, or oil is added too quickly.

If you take your time, try your best, and still end up with a problem sauce, there are solutions. Lumps can be removed by pouring the sauce through a fine sieve or by whirling it in the blender. An overly thick sauce can be thinned by gradually adding milk, a tablespoon at a time, as the sauce cooks. If too thin, blend additional flour and butter together and add it to the sauce, cooking and beating until thickened.

To rescue an overheated hollandaise or béarnaise sauce that has curdled, place a teaspoon of lemon juice and a tablespoon of the curdled sauce in a mixing bowl. Beat with a wire whisk until the mixture is thick and creamy. Gradually beat in the remaining sauce, a tablespoon at a time, making sure each addition has thickened before adding the next.

See page 146 for the article "From Our Kitchen To Yours" for more tips on preparing sauces.

HOLLANDAISE SAUCE

3 egg yolks
2 tablespoons lemon juice
½ cup butter or margarine, softened
¼ teaspoon salt

Combine egg yolks and lemon juice in top of a double boiler; beat with a wire whisk until blended. Add one-third of butter. Bring water to a boil (water in bottom of double boiler should not touch top pan). Reduce heat to low; cook, stirring constantly, until butter melts. Add second third of butter; stir constantly until butter begins to melt. Add the remaining butter, stirring constantly until melted. Cook, stirring constantly, 2 to 3 minutes or until smooth and thickened. Remove from heat and stir in salt.

Serve sauce over poached eggs, poultry, seafood, or vegetables. Yield: about ⅔ cup.

CURRY SAUCE

2 tablespoons butter or margarine
3 tablespoons minced onion
1½ teaspoons curry powder
¾ teaspoon sugar
⅛ teaspoon ground ginger
2 tablespoons all-purpose flour
1 cup milk
⅛ teaspoon salt
Dash of white pepper
1 teaspoon lemon juice

Melt butter in a heavy saucepan over low heat; add next 4 ingredients, and sauté until onion is tender. Add flour, stirring until smooth. Cook 1 minute, stirring constantly. Gradually add milk; cook over medium heat, stirring constantly, until thickened and bubbly. Stir in salt, pepper, and lemon juice.

Serve sauce over poached eggs, poultry, or vegetables. Yield: 1¼ cups.

PARSLEY-GARLIC SAUCE

2 egg yolks
1½ tablespoons lemon juice
1 tablespoon minced fresh parsley
2 cloves garlic, crushed
1 tablespoon chopped chives
¼ teaspoon dry mustard
⅛ teaspoon ground red pepper
Dash of salt
½ cup butter or margarine, softened

Combine first 8 ingredients in top of a double boiler. Place over hot water (not boiling). Beat with a wire whisk until smooth. Add butter, 1 tablespoon at a time, beating constantly until melted. Continue beating until thickened.

Serve sauce over seafood, beef, or vegetables. Yield: ¾ cup.

BEARNAISE SAUCE

3 tablespoons tarragon vinegar
1 teaspoon minced green onion
¼ teaspoon coarsely ground black pepper
Dash of dried whole tarragon
Dash of dried whole chervil or parsley flakes
1 tablespoon cold water
4 egg yolks
½ cup butter, softened
1 teaspoon minced fresh parsley
⅛ teaspoon salt

Combine first 5 ingredients in a small saucepan; bring to a boil over medium heat. Reduce heat to low, and simmer until half the liquid evaporates. Pour mixture through a strainer, reserving liquid. Discard herb mixture. Combine vinegar mixture and water.

Beat egg yolks in top of a double boiler with a wire whisk. Gradually add vinegar mixture in a slow, steady stream. Bring water to a boil (water in bottom of double boiler should not touch top pan). Reduce heat to low; add butter, 2 tablespoons at a time, beating constantly, until butter melts. Continue beating until smooth and thickened. Remove from heat. Stir in fresh parsley and salt.

Serve sauce over beef, poultry, or seafood. Yield: about 1 cup.

BORDELAISE SAUCE

2 tablespoons butter or margarine
2 tablespoons all-purpose flour
1 tablespoon minced green onion
1 tablespoon chopped fresh parsley
1 bay leaf
¼ teaspoon dried whole thyme
⅛ teaspoon salt
⅛ teaspoon coarsely ground black pepper
1 (10½-ounce) can beef broth, undiluted
3 tablespoons dry red wine

Melt butter in a heavy saucepan over low heat; add flour, stirring until smooth. Cook 1 minute, stirring constantly. Stir in next 6 ingredients. Gradually add broth and wine; cook over medium-high heat, stirring constantly, until thickened and bubbly. Remove bay leaf.

Serve sauce over beef. Yield: about 1½ cups.

WHITE SAUCE

Thin White Sauce:

1 tablespoon butter or margarine
1 tablespoon all-purpose flour
1 cup milk
¼ teaspoon salt
Dash of white pepper

Medium White Sauce:

2 tablespoons butter or margarine
2 tablespoons all-purpose flour
1 cup milk
¼ teaspoon salt
Dash of white pepper

Thick White Sauce:

3 tablespoons butter or margarine
3 tablespoons all-purpose flour
1 cup milk
¼ teaspoon salt
Dash of white pepper

Melt butter in a heavy saucepan over low heat; add flour, stirring until smooth. Cook 1 minute, stirring constantly. Gradually add milk; cook over medium heat, stirring constantly, until thickened and bubbly. Stir in salt and pepper.

Serve sauce over poached eggs, poultry, seafood, or vegetables. Yield: about 1 cup.

MORNAY SAUCE

1 egg yolk
2 tablespoons whipping cream
1 cup thin white sauce
1 tablespoon minced onion
2 tablespoons shredded Swiss cheese
¼ teaspoon salt
Dash of white pepper

Beat egg yolk and whipping cream with a wire whisk; set aside.

Combine warm white sauce and onion in a heavy saucepan. Cook over low heat, stirring constantly, 3 or 4 minutes until onion is tender. Gradually stir about one-fourth of hot mixture into the yolk mixture; add to remaining hot mixture, stirring constantly. Add cheese to sauce; cook, stirring constantly, until cheese melts. Stir in salt and pepper.

Serve sauce over poached eggs, seafood, or vegetables. Yield: 1 cup.

CHEESE SAUCE

1 cup (4 ounces) shredded sharp American cheese
1 cup medium white sauce

Add cheese to warm white sauce; cook over low heat, stirring constantly, until cheese melts.

Serve sauce over poached eggs, poultry, or vegetables. Yield: 1⅓ cups.

It's Cherry-Picking Time

Summer months bring plump, fresh cherries to produce stands, tempting passersby with thoughts of fresh fruit salads, savory sauces, or flaming cherries jubilee.

You may find both sweet and tart cherries at the market, but the sweet ones are most plentiful since commercially grown tart cherries are generally used for processing. If you have your own tree and an abundance of sour cherries, you'll find the bright red fruit excellent for pies, tarts, sauces, and canning. Sour cherries also freeze well and retain their flavor better than frozen sweet cherries.

The best known sweet cherries are the Bing and Lambert selections. Bings are dark red, large, round, and plump. Lamberts differ only in shape—the fruit is heart shaped. Generally, the darker the cherries, the sweeter the flavor. So, try to select sweet cherries with a reddish-brown color. The Royal Ann selection offers golden-colored sweet cherries, but these are usually reserved for commercial use and rarely found.

Both sour and sweet cherries are most abundant in June and July. They're best used just after purchasing or picking but can be stored in the refrigerator for a few days. Place them unwashed in plastic bags, and wash just before serving.

CHERRY SALAD WITH HONEY-LIME DRESSING

2 cups pitted fresh sweet cherries
½ honeydew melon, cut into wedges
2 medium peaches, peeled and sliced
1 banana, cut into ½-inch slices
Lettuce leaves
Honey-Lime Dressing

Arrange fruit on 6 lettuce-lined plates; serve with Honey-Lime Dressing. Yield: 6 servings.

Honey-Lime Dressing:
¼ to ½ teaspoon grated lime rind
2 tablespoons lime juice
2 tablespoons honey
¼ teaspoon salt
½ cup mayonnaise

Combine all ingredients; mix well. Yield: about ¾ cup.

CHERRIES JUBILEE

1 pound fresh sweet cherries, frozen
3 tablespoons sugar
1 tablespoon cornstarch
½ teaspoon grated orange rind
½ cup orange juice
½ cup water
¼ cup brandy
Vanilla ice cream

Partially thaw cherries; stem and pit. Set aside.

Combine sugar, cornstarch, and orange rind in a saucepan. Stir in orange juice and water; bring to a boil, stirring constantly. Add cherries and simmer 10

minutes, stirring gently. Transfer cherry sauce to a chafing dish or flambé pan, and keep warm.

Rapidly heat brandy in a small saucepan to produce fumes (do not boil). Pour over cherries and ignite; stir until flames die down. Serve immediately over ice cream. Yield: 4 to 6 servings.

CHERRY COMPOTE

2 cups pitted fresh sweet cherries
1 large orange, peeled and sectioned
½ cup seedless green grapes
1 cup pineapple chunks
⅓ cup orange juice
1 tablespoon lime juice
Pineapple sherbet
Stemmed cherries (optional)

Combine fruit. Combine juice; pour over fruit. Chill 1 hour. Spoon into compotes or stemmed glasses. Top with sherbet. Garnish with stemmed cherries, if desired. Yield: 6 to 8 servings.

CHERRY SLUMP

1 quart pitted fresh sweet cherries
¾ cup sugar
2½ tablespoons all-purpose flour
1 cup all-purpose flour
½ teaspoon baking powder
¼ teaspoon salt
⅓ cup shortening
½ cup milk
Vanilla ice cream

Combine first 3 ingredients; stir well. Spoon into an 8-inch square baking dish.

Combine 1 cup flour, baking powder, and salt; cut in shortening with pastry blender until mixture resembles coarse meal. Sprinkle milk evenly over flour mixture; stir with a fork until all ingredients are moistened. Drop by rounded teaspoonfuls over cherries. Bake at 350° for 45 minutes or until crust is browned. Serve with ice cream. Yield: 6 to 8 servings.   *Mary M. Hoppe,*
Kitty Hawk, North Carolina.

Sweet Bread Loaves In A Jiffy

You can offer one of these quick loaves as a sweet breakfast bread or even as a dessert.

BLUEBERRY-OATMEAL BREAD

2 cups all-purpose flour
1 cup quick-cooking oats, uncooked
½ cup sugar
1 tablespoon baking powder
½ teaspoon baking soda
½ teaspoon salt
½ teaspoon ground cinnamon
¼ cup plus 2 tablespoons butter or
  margarine, softened
2 eggs, slightly beaten
1 cup milk
¼ cup light corn syrup
1 cup fresh blueberries

Combine first 7 ingredients in a large mixing bowl. Cut in butter with a pastry blender until mixture resembles coarse meal. Combine eggs, milk, and corn syrup; mix well. Add to the dry ingredients, stirring just until moistened. Fold in blueberries.

Pour batter into a greased and floured 9- x 5- x 3-inch loafpan; bake at 350° for 1 hour and 10 minutes or until a wooden pick inserted in center comes out clean. Cool loaf in pan 10 minutes; remove from pan, and cool completely on a wire rack. Yield: 1 loaf.
Mrs. Roland Guest, Jr.,
Tupelo, Mississippi.

PINEAPPLE BREAD

½ cup butter or margarine, softened
½ cup sugar
2 eggs
2 cups all-purpose flour
2 teaspoons baking powder
½ teaspoon salt
1 (8-ounce) can crushed pineapple,
  undrained
1 teaspoon vanilla extract

Cream butter; gradually add sugar, beating well. Add eggs, one at a time, beating well after each addition.

Combine flour, baking powder, and salt; add to creamed mixture alternately with pineapple, mixing well. Stir in vanilla extract.

Spoon batter into a greased and floured 9- x 5- x 3-inch loafpan. Bake at 350° for 55 minutes to 1 hour or until a wooden pick inserted in center comes out clean. Cool loaf in pan 10 minutes; remove from pan, and cool completely on a wire rack. Yield: 1 loaf.
Dorothy Davenport,
North Wilkesboro, North Carolina.

STRAWBERRY BREAD

3 cups all-purpose flour
2 cups sugar
1 teaspoon baking soda
1 teaspoon salt
1 teaspoon ground cinnamon
4 eggs, beaten
1¼ cups vegetable oil
2 (10-ounce) packages frozen strawberries,
    thawed and chopped

Combine first 5 ingredients in a large mixing bowl; make a well in center of mixture. Combine remaining ingredients; add to the dry ingredients, stirring until well combined.

Spoon mixture into 2 greased and floured 9- x 5- x 3-inch loafpans. Bake at 350° for 1 hour. Cool loaves in pans about 10 minutes; remove from pans, and let cool completely on wire racks. Yield: 2 loaves. *Linda Cardwell, Grand Prairie, Texas.*

COCONUT BREAD

2¾ cups all-purpose flour
1¼ cups flaked coconut, toasted
1 cup sugar
1 tablespoon plus 1 teaspoon baking
    powder
1 teaspoon salt
1½ cups milk
2 tablespoons vegetable oil
1 egg
1 teaspoon coconut extract

Combine first 5 ingredients in a large bowl; make a well in center of mixture. Combine remaining ingredients; add to dry ingredients, stirring until moistened.

Spoon into a greased and floured 9- x 5- x 3-inch loafpan. Bake at 350° for 1 hour or until wooden pick inserted in center comes out clean. Cool in pan about 10 minutes. Remove from pan, and cool completely on a wire rack. Yield: 1 loaf. *Lynette L. Walther, East Palatka, Florida.*

POPPY SEED BREAD

3 cups all-purpose flour
2 cups sugar
3 eggs
1½ teaspoons baking powder
1½ teaspoons salt
1½ tablespoons poppy seeds
1½ cups milk
¾ cup vegetable oil
1½ teaspoons vanilla extract
1½ teaspoons almond extract
1½ teaspoons butter flavoring
Orange Glaze

Combine first 11 ingredients in a large bowl; beat 2 minutes at medium speed of electric mixer. Spoon batter into 2 greased and floured 8- x 4- x 3-inch loafpans; bake at 350° for 1 hour or until a wooden pick inserted in center comes out clean. Cool loaves in pans 10 minutes; remove from pans, and cool completely on wire racks. Drizzle bread with Orange Glaze. Yield: 2 loaves.

Orange Glaze:

1 cup sifted powdered sugar
2 tablespoons orange juice
¼ teaspoon vanilla extract
¼ teaspoon almond extract
¼ teaspoon butter flavoring

Combine all ingredients, mixing well. Yield: about ½ cup. *Carol Craighead, Newport News, Virginia.*

Taste Summer In A Garden Soup

When fresh vegetables fill gardens and produce bins, it's time to think of soups. Hot or cold, homemade vegetable soups make enticing summer appetizers or combine perfectly with sandwiches or salads for a light meal.

FRESH TOMATO SOUP

½ cup chopped onion
¼ cup butter or margarine
¼ cup all-purpose flour
1 cup water
6 medium tomatoes, peeled and coarsely
    chopped
1 tablespoon minced fresh parsley
1 tablespoon sugar
1 teaspoon salt
½ teaspoon dried whole thyme
¼ teaspoon pepper
1 bay leaf
Lemon slices (optional)
Additional bay leaves (optional)

Sauté onion in butter in a large Dutch oven 3 minutes or until tender. Reduce heat to low; add flour, stirring until smooth. Cook 1 minute, stirring constantly. Gradually add water; cook over medium heat, stirring constantly, until thickened and bubbly.

Add next 7 ingredients; bring to a boil. Cover, reduce heat, and simmer 30 minutes; remove and discard bay leaf.

Spoon one-third of tomato mixture into container of electric blender, and process until smooth. Repeat procedure with remaining mixture. Garnish with lemon and additional bay leaves, if desired. Yield: 6 cups. *Gwen Louer, Roswell, Georgia.*

COOL GAZPACHO

4 cups tomato juice
½ cup finely chopped unpeeled cucumber
½ cup chopped unpeeled tomato
¼ cup finely chopped green pepper
¼ cup finely chopped onion
¼ cup finely chopped celery
¼ cup diced pimiento
2 tablespoons olive oil
2 tablespoons wine vinegar
½ teaspoon salt
¼ teaspoon pepper

Combine all ingredients, stirring well; cover and chill at least 3 hours. Stir before serving. Yield: 5½ cups.
James E. Boggess, North Miami, Florida.

GARDEN VEGETABLE SOUP

2 (16-ounce) cans whole tomatoes,
    undrained and chopped
1 quart water
½ pound okra, sliced
½ pound green beans, cut into 1-inch
    pieces
1 large onion, chopped
2 stalks celery, chopped
2 carrots, thinly sliced
1½ cups coarsely chopped cabbage
1¼ teaspoons salt
½ teaspoon dried parsley flakes
Dash of pepper
Dash of onion powder
Dash of garlic powder

Combine all ingredients in a large Dutch oven; cover and simmer 1 hour and 20 minutes, stirring occasionally. Yield: 11 cups. *Mrs. E. L. Earnhardt, Rose Hill, North Carolina.*

CREAMY ZUCCHINI SOUP

2 pounds zucchini, cut into ½-inch pieces
1 medium onion, sliced
2 (10¾-ounce) cans chicken broth,
    undiluted
1 (8-ounce) carton commercial sour cream
⅛ teaspoon salt
⅛ teaspoon pepper
⅛ teaspoon garlic powder

Combine zucchini, onion, and chicken broth in a large Dutch oven; bring to a boil. Cover, reduce heat, and simmer 10 minutes or until zucchini is tender.

Spoon half of squash mixture into container of electric blender; process until smooth. Repeat procedure with remaining squash mixture.

Return pureed squash mixture to Dutch oven; stir in remaining ingredients. Cook over low heat, stirring constantly, until heated (do not boil). Yield: 6½ cups.   *Lynn Lockwood, Glencoe, Missouri.*

A Harvest Of Fresh English Peas

Shelling fresh English peas is a routine part of spring for many Southerners, especially those with gardens. So is savoring the delicate sweetness of the peas when they are simmered and topped with melted butter.

When selecting English peas, choose large, bright green pods that are plump and snap easily. Use the peas as soon as possible. If storage is necessary, place the unshelled peas in the refrigerator.

SPRING PEA MEDLEY

3 pounds fresh English peas
1 cup sliced green onion with tops
12 tiny new potatoes
2 tablespoons butter or margarine
3 tablespoons all-purpose flour
1 cup milk
½ teaspoon salt
⅛ teaspoon pepper
1 tablespoon chopped pimiento

Shell and wash peas; cover peas and onion with water, and bring to a boil. Cover, reduce heat, and simmer 8 to 12 minutes or until peas are tender. Drain.

Cook potatoes, covered, in boiling water 15 minutes or until tender; drain and gently toss with peas and onion.

Melt butter in a heavy saucepan over low heat; add flour, stirring until smooth. Cook 1 minute, stirring constantly. Gradually add milk; cook over medium heat, stirring constantly, until thickened and bubbly. Stir in salt and pepper. Spoon sauce over vegetable mixture, stirring until coated. Sprinkle with pimiento. Yield: 6 servings.

Note: 3 cups frozen peas may be substituted for fresh peas. *Mary D. Duffy, Roanoke, Virginia.*

PEAS-AND-ASPARAGUS SALAD

3 pounds fresh English peas
2 pounds fresh asparagus spears
1 cup sliced pimiento-stuffed olives
3 egg yolks
2 tablespoons lemon juice
2 tablespoons chopped fresh mint or 2 teaspoons dried mint flakes
⅔ cup butter or margarine, melted
⅓ cup whipping cream, whipped
Shredded lettuce
2 hard-cooked eggs, sliced
Additional pimiento-stuffed olives
Fresh parsley sprigs

Shell and wash peas; cover with water, and bring to a boil. Cover, reduce heat, and simmer 8 to 12 minutes or until peas are tender. Drain.

Snap off tough ends of asparagus. Remove scales from stalks with a knife or vegetable peeler, if desired. Cook asparagus, covered, in boiling water 6 to 8 minutes or until crisp-tender; drain. Cut asparagus into 1½-inch pieces.

Combine peas, asparagus, and 1 cup sliced olives in a large bowl; chill.

Combine next 3 ingredients in container of electric blender; process until smooth. Slowly add melted butter in a steady stream, processing well. Fold in whipped cream. Pour over chilled vegetables; toss gently. Cover and chill 4 hours. Serve over shredded lettuce. Top with egg slices, additional olives, and parsley. Yield: 6 to 8 servings.

Note: 3 cups frozen peas and 2 (10-ounce) packages frozen asparagus may be substituted for fresh. *Mary Hensley, Jonesboro, Tennessee.*

MINTED PEAS

2½ pounds fresh English peas
½ cup mayonnaise
¼ cup commercial sour cream
¼ cup minced onion
¼ cup chopped fresh mint or 1 tablespoon plus 1 teaspoon dried mint flakes
¼ teaspoon prepared mustard
¼ teaspoon salt
⅛ teaspoon pepper
6 to 8 strips pimiento (optional)

Shell and wash peas; cover with water, and bring to a boil. Cover, reduce heat, and simmer 6 to 8 minutes or until peas are crisp-tender; drain. Rinse with cold water, and drain again.

Combine next 7 ingredients in a mixing bowl; mix well. Add peas; stir

gently. Spoon into a serving dish; garnish with pimiento, if desired. Yield: 4 servings.

Note: 2½ cups frozen peas may be substituted for fresh peas.

Bettie Glidden, Lake Montezuma, Arizona.

PEAS AND MUSHROOMS

2 pounds fresh English peas
1 cup pearl onions
½ pound fresh mushrooms, sliced
2 tablespoons olive oil
¼ teaspoon salt
⅛ teaspoon pepper

Shell and wash peas; cover peas and onions with water, and bring to a boil. Cover, reduce heat, and simmer 8 to 12 minutes or until peas are tender. Drain.

Sauté mushrooms in oil in a large skillet until tender. Stir in peas and onions, salt, and pepper; cook, stirring constantly, until thoroughly heated. Yield: 4 servings.

Note: 2 cups frozen peas may be substituted for fresh peas.   *Gay Evaldi, East Windsor, New Jersey.*

Summertime Coolers Served Icy Cold

On hot summer days, nothing is more welcome than a tall, frosty glass of a refreshing fruit drink. Here is an assortment of new ideas for ice cold drinks filled with fresh fruits and juices, sherbet, and ginger ale.

CITRUS PARTY PUNCH

1½ cups crushed pineapple
2 cups orange juice
1½ cups ginger ale
2 tablespoons lemon juice
2 teaspoons cherry juice
8 maraschino cherries, halved

Spoon equal amounts of pineapple into 3 custard cups; freeze.

Combine remaining ingredients in a punch bowl; chill. Run a knife around inside edge of cups containing frozen pineapple; turn into punch. Yield: about 1 quart.   *Carolyn Beyer, Fredericksburg, Texas.*

BANANA CRUSH

3 bananas
1 (6-ounce) can frozen lemonade
   concentrate, thawed and undiluted
3 quarts lemon-lime carbonated beverage
1 (12-ounce) can frozen orange juice
   concentrate, thawed and undiluted
3 cups pineapple juice
3 cups water
2 cups sugar

Combine bananas and lemonade concentrate in container of electric blender; process until smooth.

Combine banana mixture and remaining ingredients; mix well. Pour into freezer containers; freeze until slushy. Yield: 5 quarts. *Pauline Lester, Saluda, South Carolina.*

CRANAPPLE PUNCH

1 quart cranberry-apple juice
2 cups water
1 (6-ounce) can frozen lemonade
   concentrate, thawed and undiluted
3 tablespoons orange-flavored instant
   breakfast drink
3 cups ginger ale, chilled

Combine first 4 ingredients; chill. Add ginger ale just before serving. Yield: about 2½ quarts.

Mrs. James Cook, Columbia, Louisiana.

LIME-PINEAPPLE PUNCH

1 cup sugar
2 cups water, divided
2 teaspoons grated lime rind
½ cup lime juice
1 pint pineapple sherbet
1 pint lime sherbet
3½ cups lemon-lime carbonated beverage,
   chilled

Combine sugar and 1 cup water in a saucepan; cook, stirring constantly, until sugar dissolves. Add remaining water, lime rind, and juice; chill. Spoon sherbet into punch; add lemon-lime beverage. Yield: about 2½ quarts.

Mickie Morrow, Bernice, Louisiana.

ORANGE BLOSSOM PUNCH

1½ quarts orange juice
1 cup lemon juice
⅓ cup maraschino cherry juice
½ cup sugar
1 (33.8-ounce) bottle ginger ale, chilled

Combine fruit juice and sugar, mixing well. Add ginger ale just before serving; serve over ice. Yield: about 3 quarts.
Mabel B. Couch, Chelsea, Oklahoma.

ORANGE SHERBET PARTY PUNCH

2 (3-ounce) packages strawberry-flavored
   gelatin
1½ cups sugar
2 cups boiling water
2 cups cold water
1 (46-ounce) can pineapple juice
1 (46-ounce) can orange juice
1 cup lemon juice
½ gallon orange sherbet, softened
1 (33.8-ounce) bottle ginger ale, chilled

Combine gelatin and sugar; add boiling water, and stir until dissolved. Stir in cold water and fruit juice; chill. Spoon sherbet into punch; add ginger ale. Yield: about 6½ quarts.

Barbara Anz, Clifton, Texas.

TANGY PUNCH

2½ cups orange-flavored instant breakfast
   drink
3 quarts water
2 (46-ounce) cans pineapple juice, chilled
1 (6-ounce) can frozen lemonade
   concentrate, thawed and undiluted
4 (33.8-ounce) bottles ginger ale, chilled

Dissolve breakfast drink in water; add pineapple juice and lemonade concentrate. Chill well. Pour mixture over ice in a punch bowl; add ginger ale. Yield: about 2½ gallons. *Mrs. Nelson Jones, Richlands, North Carolina.*

His Cooking Is Spiced With Imagination

In Charlotte, North Carolina, friends of Dr. Loy Witherspoon eagerly await invitations to his frequent dinner parties. Loy is one bachelor cook who has fun with food and loves sharing his creations with friends.

He's been cooking since an early age. Loy grew up in an orphanage where all the children shared cooking duties. By the time he was in high school, Loy was helping to plan daily menus for 80 people.

One of the culinary highlights of Loy's dinner parties is a slice of his creamy Glazed Cheesecake served with a selection of liqueur-flavored fruit glazes. Loy whips up cherry, pineapple, blueberry, and strawberry toppings and lets guests choose a favorite. If he has glaze left over, he saves it to spoon into tart shells for another dessert.

You'll enjoy Loy's cheesecake and Cornish Hens With Tarragon. The recipes are given here, along with recipes from other men who love to cook.

GLAZED CHEESECAKE

2 tablespoons graham cracker crumbs
1 (16-ounce) carton cream-style cottage
   cheese
2 (8-ounce) packages cream cheese,
   softened
1½ cups sugar
4 eggs, slightly beaten
1 (16-ounce) carton commercial sour
   cream
½ cup butter or margarine, melted
⅓ cup cornstarch
2 tablespoons lemon juice
1 teaspoon vanilla extract
About 2 cups whole strawberries, washed
   and hulled
Strawberry Glaze

Grease a 9-inch springform pan; dust generously with graham cracker crumbs. Combine cheese; beat on high speed of electric mixer until smooth. Gradually add sugar, beating after each addition. Add eggs; beat well. Add next 5 ingredients; beat on low speed until mixture is smooth.

Pour batter into pan; bake at 325° for 1 hour and 10 minutes. Turn oven off; let cheesecake stand in oven 2 hours. Cool completely; cover and chill at least 4 hours. Arrange whole strawberries on top of cheesecake; drizzle with Strawberry Glaze. Chill thoroughly. Yield: 10 to 12 servings.

Strawberry Glaze:

1 cup strawberries, washed and hulled
½ cup sugar
1½ tablespoons cornstarch
2 tablespoons Grand Marnier

Mash strawberries. Combine strawberries, sugar, and cornstarch in a heavy saucepan; stir well. Cook over medium heat until thick, stirring constantly. Stir in Grand Marnier; cover and chill. Yield: ¾ cup.

Note: If desired, one of the following glazes may be substituted for the whole strawberries and Strawberry Glaze.

Blueberry Glaze:
½ cup fresh blueberries, washed and drained
¼ cup water
¼ cup sugar
¼ cup kirsch
1½ tablespoons cornstarch
3 tablespoons water

Combine blueberries and ¼ cup water in a heavy saucepan; cook over medium heat, stirring constantly, for 15 minutes or until berries are very soft. Press through a sieve, and return to saucepan. Stir in sugar and kirsch; cook over medium heat 10 minutes, stirring often, or until slightly thickened. Dissolve cornstarch in 3 tablespoons water; add to blueberry mixture. Cook, stirring constantly, until thickened. Cover and chill. Yield: 1 cup.

Pineapple Glaze:
1 (21-ounce) can pineapple pie filling
¼ cup Triple Sec or other orange-flavored liqueur

Heat pie filling in a saucepan, stirring constantly; stir in Triple Sec. Cover and chill. Yield: 2¼ cups.

Cherry Glaze:
1 (21-ounce) can cherry pie filling
2 to 4 tablespoons kirsch

Heat pie filling in a saucepan, stirring constantly; stir in kirsch. Cover and chill. Yield: 2 cups.

CORNISH HENS WITH TARRAGON

4 (1- to 1¼-pound) Cornish hens
Salt and pepper
1 teaspoon dried whole tarragon
2 tablespoons butter or margarine, melted
3 tablespoons finely chopped shallots
⅓ cup dry white wine
½ cup whipping cream
¼ teaspoon dried whole tarragon
Chopped fresh parsley

Remove giblets from hens, and reserve for another use. Rinse hens with cold water, and pat dry; sprinkle each cavity with salt, pepper, and ¼ teaspoon tarragon. Close cavities, and secure with wooden picks; truss. Place hens, breast side up, in a 13- x 9- x 2-inch baking pan.

Pour melted butter over hens. Bake at 450° for 15 minutes. Cover hens with aluminum foil; reduce heat to 350° and bake an additional 45 minutes, basting every 15 minutes.

Place hens on a serving platter; keep warm. Transfer pan drippings to a skillet; stir in shallots, and cook until tender. Add wine; cook over medium heat until mixture is reduced by half. Stir in whipping cream and ¼ teaspoon tarragon. Cook until thoroughly heated. Spoon sauce over hens just before serving. Sprinkle hens with parsley. Yield: 4 servings.

ZUCCHINI CHEF'S SALAD

4 cups diced zucchini
1 cup chopped red onion
1 cup peeled, diced cucumber
1 tablespoon lemon juice
1 teaspoon salt
¼ teaspoon white pepper
1 teaspoon sugar
1½ to 2 pounds fish fillets
1 quart water
1 teaspoon salt
2 hard-cooked eggs, finely chopped
½ cup cubed Cheddar cheese
¾ cup mayonnaise
Lettuce leaves
Chopped fresh parsley

Combine first 7 ingredients; stir gently. Chill thoroughly.

Wrap each fish fillet in cheesecloth; secure ends with string. Combine water and salt in a large skillet; bring to a boil. Add fish fillets; simmer 10 minutes or until fish flakes easily. Drain fillets, and unwrap; flake with a fork.

Add flaked fish, eggs, cheese, and mayonnaise to chilled vegetable mixture; toss gently. Chill 1 hour; serve on lettuce. Sprinkle with parsley. Yield: 6 servings.   *Milton, E. Bass,*
Salter Path, North Carolina.

PEANUTTY CLUSTERS

2 cups sugar
1 cup evaporated milk
¼ cup butter or margarine
18 large marshmallows
½ cup milk chocolate morsels
½ cup semisweet chocolate morsels
1 (8-ounce) jar dry-roasted peanuts

Combine first 4 ingredients in a heavy 3-quart saucepan; cook over medium heat, stirring constantly, until mixture reaches soft ball stage (234°).

Remove from heat; add chocolate, and beat on medium speed of electric mixer until chocolate melts. Stir in peanuts. Drop by rounded teaspoonfuls onto lightly greased waxed paper; cool thoroughly, and store at room temperature. Yield: 3½ dozen.   *Bill Hodges,*
Guntersville, Alabama.

Fancy Ways With Frankfurters

Did you ever think of adding frankfurters to spaghetti or serving them as a party appetizer? In the recipes below, we offer some different ways to use ever-popular frankfurters. You'll find recipes for all-time favorites as well— enjoy our versions of old-fashioned corn dogs and baked beans.

PICNIC BAKED BEANS

1 (16-ounce) can pork and beans
1 (15½-ounce) can kidney beans, drained
1 (17-ounce) can lima beans, drained
½ pound frankfurters, cut diagonally into 1½-inch pieces
½ cup firmly packed brown sugar
¼ cup catsup
2 tablespoons chopped onion
½ teaspoon salt
⅛ teaspoon garlic salt

Combine all ingredients; spoon into a lightly greased 2-quart casserole. Cover and bake at 375° for 35 minutes. Yield: 6 servings.   *Marie Davis,*
Morganton, North Carolina.

CHAFING DISH FRANKS

1½ cups catsup
½ cup firmly packed brown sugar
½ cup water
¼ cup bourbon
2 tablespoons minced onion
2 pounds frankfurters, cut into ½-inch slices

Combine first 5 ingredients in a large skillet; mix well. Add frankfurters; bring to a boil. Cover, reduce heat, and simmer 30 minutes, stirring occasionally. Transfer to a chafing dish; use wooden picks to serve. Yield: about 16 appetizer servings.   *DeLois Gates,*
Blue Springs, Mississippi.

FAVORITE CORN DOGS

¾ cup self-rising flour
¼ cup self-rising cornmeal
2 tablespoons minced onion
1 tablespoon sugar
1 teaspoon dry mustard
½ cup milk
1 egg, beaten
1 pound frankfurters

Combine flour, cornmeal, onion, sugar, and mustard; stir well. Combine milk and egg; add to dry ingredients, stirring well. Set aside.

Wipe each frankfurter dry, and insert a wooden stick into one end. Dip frankfurters in batter; fry in deep hot oil (375° to 400°) for 2 to 3 minutes or until browned, turning once. Drain well on paper towels. Repeat with the remaining frankfurters. Serve with mustard and catsup. Yield: 8 to 10 servings.
Mrs. Carl Ziglar,
Madison, North Carolina.

BARBECUED FRANKFURTERS

12 frankfurters, scored diagonally
1 small onion, sliced
1 tablespoon butter or margarine
½ cup catsup
½ cup water
1 tablespoon plus 1 teaspoon sugar
¼ cup vinegar
1 tablespoon plus 1 teaspoon
    Worcestershire sauce
1 teaspoon celery salt
1 teaspoon dry mustard
½ teaspoon paprika
½ teaspoon hot sauce

Place frankfurters in a 12- x 8- x 2-inch baking dish; set aside.

Sauté onion in butter in a medium saucepan until tender. Remove from heat; stir in remaining ingredients. Pour over frankfurters. Bake, uncovered, at 325° for 25 minutes. Yield: 6 servings.
Mrs. Robert Bryce,
Fairport, New York.

HOT DOG AND SPAGHETTI SKILLET

½ (8-ounce) package spaghetti
8 frankfurters, cut into thirds
⅓ cup chopped green pepper
2 tablespoons butter or margarine
1 (10¾-ounce) can cream of chicken soup,
    undiluted
1 small tomato, chopped
¼ cup water
Dash of ground thyme
¼ cup grated Parmesan cheese

Cook spaghetti according to package directions, omitting salt. Drain.

Sauté frankfurters and green pepper in butter in a large skillet 5 minutes or until green pepper is tender. Stir in next 4 ingredients. Cook over medium heat 3 to 5 minutes. Add spaghetti; heat. Sprinkle with cheese. Yield: 4 to 6 servings.
Mrs. Robert I. Ballard,
Houston, Texas.

Scallops Fresh From The Sea

Simmered to perfection, these fresh scallop dishes are all excellent choices for a special dinner. Your guests will savor every sweet, delicate bite.

You can find fresh scallops in most seafood markets. They vary in color from creamy white to pale pink and have a mild, sweet odor. Store them in the coldest part of the refrigerator, and use within two days after purchase. Wash the scallops thoroughly in cold water before using.

CREAMY SCALLOPS AND MUSHROOMS

½ pound fresh mushrooms, sliced
1 medium onion, sliced
1 tablespoon butter or margarine
1 pound fresh scallops
¼ cup dry sherry
3 tablespoons butter or margarine
¼ cup all-purpose flour
1 cup half-and-half
½ teaspoon salt
⅛ teaspoon white pepper
4 frozen patty shells, baked

Sauté mushrooms and onion in 1 tablespoon butter until tender. Add scallops and sherry; bring to a boil. Reduce heat and simmer, uncovered, 8 minutes, stirring occasionally.

Melt 3 tablespoons butter in a medium saucepan over low heat; add flour, stirring until smooth. Cook 1 minute, stirring constantly. Gradually add half-and-half; cook over medium heat, stirring constantly, until mixture is thickened and bubbly. Stir in salt and pepper. Add sauce to scallops, stirring gently; cook, uncovered, just until heated. Spoon filling into patty shells. Yield: 4 servings. *Sherry Phillips,*
Knoxville, Tennessee.

SCALLOPS VERONIQUE

¼ cup chopped green onion
3 tablespoons butter or margarine
1 pound fresh scallops
1 teaspoon cornstarch
2 tablespoons dry sherry
⅓ cup mayonnaise
1 (2½-ounce) jar sliced mushrooms,
    drained
½ cup halved seedless green grapes
½ teaspoon salt
Dash of pepper
2 tablespoons fine, dry breadcrumbs

Sauté green onion in butter in a large skillet over medium heat until tender. Add scallops; cover and cook 5 minutes. Combine cornstarch and sherry, stirring until smooth; add to scallops. Cook, stirring constantly, until slightly thickened. Stir in mayonnaise, mushrooms, grapes, salt, and pepper.

Spoon scallop mixture into four individual baking shells or four 10-ounce custard cups. Sprinkle with breadcrumbs. Broil 5 inches from heat 2 minutes or until lightly browned. Yield: 4 servings. *Mrs. C. D. Chamberlin,*
Charlotte, North Carolina.

SAUTEED SCALLOPS WITH CRANBERRY RELISH

¼ cup butter or margarine
3 tablespoons lemon juice
½ teaspoon celery salt
½ teaspoon paprika
Dash of white pepper
2 pounds fresh scallops
1 tablespoon chopped fresh parsley
Cranberry Relish

Melt butter in a large skillet over medium heat. Add next 5 ingredients, and sauté 6 to 7 minutes. Place scallops on a serving platter; sprinkle with parsley. Serve with Cranberry Relish. Yield: 4 to 6 servings.

Cranberry Relish:

1 (16-ounce) can whole berry cranberry
    sauce
½ cup finely chopped celery
1 tablespoon lemon juice

Combine all ingredients, mixing well. Chill. Yield: 2 cups. *Joyce Maurer,*
Christmas, Florida.

Here's A Meal You Don't Cook

Some summer days are just too hot to spend in the kitchen. So, we've devised a cool refreshing menu that will keep you away from the range or oven.

Cheesy Onion Dip   Crackers
Summer Chicken Salad
Oregano Tomatoes
Marinated Green Beans
Commercial Hard Rolls
Grasshopper Pie
Iced Tea

CHEESY ONION DIP

1 (8-ounce) package cream cheese, softened
1 cup (4 ounces) shredded sharp Cheddar cheese
1 (1⅜-ounce) envelope onion soup mix
¾ cup half-and-half

Combine first 3 ingredients; beat at medium speed of an electric mixer until smooth. Gradually add half-and-half, beating well. Chill. Serve with crackers. Yield: 2½ cups. *Carol S. Noble, Burgaw, North Carolina.*

SUMMER CHICKEN SALAD

¾ cup mayonnaise
¾ cup frozen whipped topping, thawed
3 (5-ounce) cans chunk chicken, drained
1½ cups sliced celery
¾ cup seedless grapes, halved
¾ cup slivered almonds, toasted
⅓ cup sliced pimiento-stuffed olives
Lettuce leaves

Combine mayonnaise and whipped topping. Add chicken, celery, grapes, almonds, and olives; toss mixture well. Serve salad on lettuce leaves. Yield: 6 servings. *Frances Bowles, Mableton, Georgia.*

OREGANO TOMATOES

4 medium tomatoes, sliced
¼ cup vegetable oil
1½ tablespoons lemon juice
1 small clove garlic, minced
½ teaspoon salt
½ teaspoon dried whole oregano
⅛ teaspoon pepper

Place tomatoes in a shallow dish. Combine remaining ingredients; stir well, and pour over tomatoes. Cover and refrigerate several hours, stirring twice. Yield: 6 servings. *Carole May, Shawmut, Alabama.*

MARINATED GREEN BEANS

2 (16-ounce) cans whole green beans, drained
1 small onion, sliced and separated into rings
3 tablespoons sugar
½ cup white wine vinegar
3 tablespoons chopped fresh parsley
½ cup vegetable oil
1 teaspoon salt
½ teaspoon dry mustard
½ teaspoon dried whole basil
½ teaspoon dried whole tarragon

Combine green beans and sliced onion; set aside.

Combine sugar and vinegar; stir until sugar dissolves. Add remaining ingredients; stir well. Pour over green beans. Cover and chill 8 hours. Yield: about 6 servings. *Bobby McVey, Hutchinson, Kansas.*

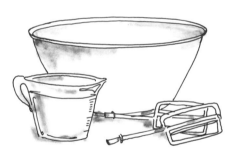

GRASSHOPPER PIE

2 cups cold milk
2 tablespoons green crème de menthe
2 tablespoons white crème de cacao
1 (5⅜-ounce) package vanilla instant pudding mix
1 (1.25-ounce) envelope whipped topping mix
1 (9-inch) prepared chocolate crumb crust
Additional whipped topping (optional)
Chocolate curls (optional)

Combine first 5 ingredients, and beat at low speed of an electric mixer until blended. Gradually increase beating speed to high, and beat 3 to 6 minutes or until soft peaks form.

Spoon mixture into prepared crumb crust; freeze until firm. Remove pie from freezer; let stand 5 to 10 minutes before serving. Garnish with whipped topping and chocolate curls, if desired. Yield: 6 to 8 servings. *Shirley Hodge, Delray Beach, Florida.*

Salads Suited For Summer Meals

Prepare Individual Shrimp Salads for lunch or a light supper, and you'll only need a bread and beverage to round out the menu. Try Wild Rice-Chicken Salad or Chef's Garden Salad when you have leftover chicken in the refrigerator. Our main-dish salad recipes are refreshing, satisfying, and easy to prepare.

TACO SALAD

1 pound ground beef
2 large onions, chopped
2 green onions, chopped
5 cloves garlic, pressed
1 cup thinly sliced celery
2 tablespoons picante sauce
1 teaspoon chili powder
1 medium head lettuce
2 cups (8 ounces) shredded Cheddar cheese
1 cup quartered cherry tomatoes
½ cup chopped salad olives
1 cup crushed tortilla chips

Cook ground beef in a large skillet until browned, stirring to crumble; add next 4 ingredients, and cook until vegetables are tender. Drain well. Stir in picante sauce and chili powder.

Combine next 4 ingredients in a large bowl, tossing well. Add meat mixture and tortilla chips, tossing well. Yield: 8 servings. *Mrs. A. W. Gathright, Baton Rouge, Louisiana.*

TUNA-MACARONI SALAD

1 (8-ounce) package small seashell macaroni
1 (8½-ounce) can small English peas
1 (6½-ounce) can tuna, drained and flaked
1 cup diced Cheddar cheese
1 (2-ounce) jar diced pimiento, drained
1 small green pepper, finely chopped
2 stalks celery, thinly sliced
½ cup chopped sweet pickle
½ cup mayonnaise
¼ teaspoon pepper

Cook macaroni according to package directions, omitting the salt; drain. Rinse with cold water, and drain.

Combine macaroni and remaining ingredients in a large salad bowl; toss gently. Cover salad, and chill. Yield: 6 to 8 servings. *Joan B. Piercy, Memphis, Tennessee.*

INDIVIDUAL SHRIMP SALADS

4½ cups water
1½ pounds unpeeled medium shrimp
2 tablespoons butter or margarine, melted
1 cup coarsely chopped pecans
Salt
1 small head Bibb lettuce
6 slices tomato
1 (15¼-ounce) can sliced pineapple, drained
2 small ripe avocados, peeled and chopped
Pear Dressing
½ to ¾ cup plain croutons

Bring water to a boil; add shrimp, and return to a boil. Reduce heat, and simmer 3 to 5 minutes. Drain well; rinse with cold water. Peel and devein shrimp; chill.

Place butter in an 8-inch square baking pan; add pecans, stirring well. Bake at 350° for 15 to 20 minutes, stirring occasionally. Drain on paper towels; sprinkle lightly with salt. Cool.

Arrange lettuce leaves on 6 individual salad plates. Layer 1 slice tomato, 1 slice pineapple, equal amounts of shrimp, and chopped avocado on lettuce. Spoon Pear Dressing over each. Sprinkle with croutons and pecans. Yield: 6 servings.

Pear Dressing:

1 (16-ounce) can pear halves, undrained
1 cup mayonnaise or salad dressing
½ cup peeled and finely chopped cucumber
½ cup minced onion

Drain pears, reserving 2 tablespoons juice; finely chop pears. Add 2 tablespoons pear juice and remaining ingredients to pears; mix well. Chill 1 hour. Yield: about 3½ cups.   *Beth Martin, Charleston, South Carolina.*

WILD RICE-CHICKEN SALAD

1 (6-ounce) package long-grain and wild rice mix
2 cups diced cooked chicken
¼ cup chopped green pepper
2 tablespoons chopped pimiento
½ cup mayonnaise
2 tablespoons commercial Russian dressing
1 tablespoon lemon juice
2 large ripe avocados
2 tablespoons lemon juice

Cook rice according to package directions; let cool.

Add chicken, green pepper, and pimiento to rice; toss gently. Combine mayonnaise, Russian dressing, and 1 tablespoon lemon juice; stir into rice mixture. Chill.

Cut avocados in half lengthwise; remove seed, and peel. Cut into ½-inch slices. Gently rub slices with 2 tablespoons lemon juice. Arrange avocado slices on serving plate; spoon chicken mixture over avocado. Yield: 6 servings.   *Cindy Murphy, Cleveland, Tennessee.*

CHEF'S GARDEN SALAD

1 large head lettuce, torn into bite-size pieces
1 tomato, cut into wedges
1 small cucumber, sliced
½ cup sliced celery
½ cup chopped green pepper
½ cup commercial French dressing
½ pound thinly sliced cooked ham or chicken, cut into strips
¼ pound Cheddar cheese, cut into thin strips
2 hard-cooked eggs, sliced
Additional commercial French dressing (optional)

Combine vegetables in a large bowl. Add ½ cup French dressing, tossing well. Place ham, cheese, and eggs on salad. Serve with additional French dressing, if desired. Yield: 4 to 6 servings.   *Mrs. Robert L. Humphrey, Palestine, Texas.*

SALMAGUNDI SALAD

1 head endive, torn
1 head Boston lettuce, torn
1 head romaine lettuce, torn
1 pound thinly sliced cooked ham, cut into 2-inch strips
1 pound thinly sliced cooked chicken or turkey, cut into 2-inch strips
24 pitted ripe olives
16 sweet whole gherkin pickles
4 hard-cooked eggs, sliced
4 celery hearts, quartered
3 (4⅜-ounce) cans sardines, drained
2 (2-ounce) cans anchovy fillets, drained
½ pound fresh mushrooms, sliced
Honey dressing (recipe follows)

Arrange salad greens on individual salad plates or a large platter. Roll up ham and chicken strips, jellyroll fashion; place ham, chicken, and remaining ingredients except honey dressing on salad greens. Serve with honey dressing. Yield: 8 to 10 servings.

Honey Dressing:

1 cup vegetable oil
⅓ cup tarragon vinegar
¼ cup honey
1 tablespoon lemon juice
1 tablespoon sugar
½ teaspoon dry mustard
½ teaspoon paprika
¼ teaspoon salt
¼ teaspoon celery seeds
¼ teaspoon grated onion

Combine all ingredients in a jar. Cover tightly, and shake vigorously. Chill several hours. Yield: 1¾ cups.   *Helen L. Berman, Dover, Delaware.*

From Our Kitchen To Yours

Thin sauces, curdled custards, lumpy gravies, and runny pie fillings are disasters we've all experienced. We put our heads together and collected some tips that might prevent the lumps and curdles from appearing in your kitchen.

Thickening with cornstarch. We're using cornstarch more and more in our test kitchens. This thickener works especially well in pie fillings, gravies, cake fillings, sauces, and Chinese stir-fry dishes. It's easy to use, but there are some specific rules to follow when working with cornstarch.

We never add cornstarch directly to a hot mixture because it will lump. Before adding it to a hot mixture, combine the cornstarch with about twice as much cold liquid and stir until smooth. Then gently stir the cornstarch mixture into the hot mixture. (Overstirring can cause the mixture to thin.) Usually, you'll cook over medium-low to medium heat. Cook, stirring gently, until the mixture comes to a full boil. (This is when bubbles rise rapidly to the surface and break.) Boil for at least 1 minute. It only takes a short time for the starch granules to swell, absorb some of the liquid, and thicken the mixture.

Don't think the longer you cook the cornstarch mixture the thicker it will get. Overcooking can cause the mixture to become thin and runny. Carefully watch the clock when cooking with cornstarch. We usually set a timer to let us know when the cooking time is over. The mixture may look too thin while cooking but thickens as it cools.

If you're making a fruit or lemon pie filling or anything with an acid ingredient, cook the cornstarch mixture until thickened. Then remove from heat, and gently stir in the acid, such as lemon juice or fruit. Acid tends to reduce the thickening ability of cornstarch.

When substituting cornstarch for flour, remember that one tablespoon cornstarch has the same thickening power as two tablespoons flour. If you're making a soup, sauce, or gravy, use half as much cornstarch as flour. Blend the cornstarch with a cold liquid, and add at the end of the cooking time instead of the beginning.

Arrowroot and tapioca thicken, too. We don't use arrowroot very often in the test kitchens, but when we have, we've been especially pleased with the results. Thickening with this delicate starch produces an extremely clear sauce. It has a little more than twice the thickening power of flour. Arrowroot is usually preferred over flour for thickening fruit sauces or soups because acids do not diminish its thickening strength. Serve an arrowroot-thickened dish as soon as possible after preparation; it will not hold well at room temperature and will not reheat.

Tapioca is a thickener especially suited for sauces that are to be frozen. They reheat well without watering out and breaking down like some frozen flour-based sauces. For freezing, use 1 to 2½ tablespoons tapioca to 1 cup liquid. Be careful not to overcook tapioca because it becomes stringy.

Don't let the eggs curdle. Eggs are also thickening agents. Custards and sauces such as hollandaise and béarnaise get their luscious consistency from eggs. Eggs must be handled carefully to prevent curdling.

Custards and sauces will be smooth if care is taken not to overcook the egg or use heat that's too high. This can easily happen when making a hollandaise. Try using a thermometer and cooking the hollandaise to 140°; that's usually a safe temperature to obtain the right consistency. When thickening with eggs, heat slowly and stir constantly.

When adding eggs to a hot mixture, there's a special technique called tempering that usually prevents instant cooking. First, beat the eggs slightly; warm them by gradually stirring in about one-fourth of the hot mixture. Then stir the tempered egg mixture into the remaining hot mixture. Cook, stirring constantly, until the mixture thickens. By taking the time to follow this method, you'll be ensuring yourself of a creamy, smooth mixture.

MICROWAVE COOKERY

Team Vegetables And Herbs For The Microwave

Fresh vegetables are at their best when seasoned just right with herbs then cooked in a microwave oven. Along with speeding preparation, the microwave oven retains more of the vegetable's crisp texture and color and keeps herb flavor at a peak.

You'll find that vegetables need only a small amount of water to microwave. The oven uses the natural moisture of the vegetable to provide most of the cooking liquid. Only a few tablespoons up to about ½ cup additional liquid is needed. Cover the vegetables with heavy-duty plastic wrap before microwaving to hold in steam and heat.

Be sure to pierce vegetables, such as new potatoes, that are microwaved whole in their skins. This allows steam to escape; otherwise, they may burst.

A sprinkling of fresh or dried herbs will highlight the natural flavor of garden produce. One word of caution—use a light hand in adding herbs to microwaved recipes. Because the herbs are not diluted with the additional liquid, they tend to taste more potent.

Keep in mind that dried herbs are three or four times stronger than fresh herbs. Use about one-third of the dried leaves to replace the fresh. For example, one teaspoon of dried basil leaves can replace one tablespoon of minced fresh basil.

HERBED GREEN BEANS

½ pound fresh green beans
½ cup water
⅓ cup chopped green pepper
¼ cup sliced green onion
1 tablespoon vegetable oil
1 medium tomato, peeled and diced
¼ to ½ teaspoon salt
¼ teaspoon sugar
¾ teaspoon minced fresh basil or ¼ teaspoon dried whole basil
¼ teaspoon minced fresh rosemary or ⅛ teaspoon dried whole rosemary

Wash beans; trim ends, and remove strings. Cut beans into 1½-inch lengths. Place beans in a 1½-quart casserole; add water. Cover with heavy-duty plastic wrap and microwave at HIGH for 9

to 10 minutes, stirring after 3 minutes. Let stand, covered, for 3 to 4 minutes.

Place green pepper, onion, and oil in a 1-quart casserole. Cover and microwave at HIGH for 3 minutes or until tender. Drain beans. Add green pepper mixture and remaining ingredients; stir well. Cover and microwave at HIGH for 2 to 3 minutes or until hot. Yield: 4 servings.

SEASONED FRESH CORN

2 tablespoons butter or margarine
2 cups fresh corn cut from cob
¼ cup water
1½ teaspoons chopped chives
¾ teaspoon minced fresh basil or ¼ teaspoon dried whole basil
¼ teaspoon sugar
¼ teaspoon salt
⅛ teaspoon white pepper

Place butter in a 1-quart casserole, and microwave at HIGH for 40 seconds or until melted; stir in corn and water. Cover with heavy-duty plastic wrap. Microwave at HIGH for 2 minutes; stir well, and give dish a half-turn. Cover and microwave at HIGH for 5 to 7 minutes or until corn is tender. Drain well.

Stir in remaining ingredients. Cover and microwave at HIGH for 1 to 2 minutes or until hot. Yield: 4 servings.

ITALIAN ZUCCHINI

2 cups thinly sliced zucchini
1 medium onion, thinly sliced and separated into rings
1 clove garlic, minced
1 medium-size green pepper, cut into 1-inch pieces
1 tablespoon vegetable oil
1½ teaspoons minced fresh basil or ½ teaspoon dried whole basil
1 teaspoon minced fresh parsley
¼ teaspoon salt
Dash of pepper
1 medium tomato, unpeeled and coarsely chopped
1 tablespoon grated Parmesan cheese

Combine first 9 ingredients in a 2-quart casserole. Cover with heavy-duty plastic wrap and microwave at HIGH for 4 to 5 minutes or until zucchini is crisp-tender, stirring after 2 minutes.

Stir in tomato. Cover and microwave at HIGH for 1 to 2 minutes or until tomato is tender. Sprinkle with cheese. Yield: 4 to 6 servings.

SAUTEED ONIONS AND PEPPERS

1 small green pepper, cut into
  2- x ¼-inch strips
1 small red pepper, cut into 2- x ¼-inch
  strips
1 cup sliced fresh mushrooms
6 green onions, cut into 1-inch pieces
2 tablespoons vegetable oil
1 clove garlic, minced
¼ teaspoon salt
Dash of white pepper

Combine all ingredients in a 2-quart casserole. Cover with heavy-duty plastic wrap and microwave at HIGH for 4 to 5 minutes or until peppers are crisp-tender, stirring mixture at 2-minute intervals. Yield: 4 servings.

HERBED NEW POTATOES

12 medium new potatoes
2 tablespoons water
3 tablespoons butter or margarine
2 tablespoons minced fresh parsley
1 tablespoon lemon juice
1½ teaspoons minced fresh dillweed or ½
  teaspoon dried whole dillweed
1 teaspoon chopped chives

Wash potatoes. Prick each potato twice with a fork. Place potatoes in a 2-quart casserole; add water. Cover with heavy-duty plastic wrap and microwave at HIGH for 8 to 10 minutes, stirring after 4 minutes. Let stand 3 to 4 minutes.

Place butter in a 1-cup glass measure. Microwave at HIGH for 50 seconds or until melted. Stir in parsley, lemon juice, dillweed, and chives. Drain potatoes. Pour butter mixture over potatoes. Yield: 4 to 6 servings.

Chiles Put The Heat On

A sprinkling of chopped chile peppers can give a flavor boost to almost any type of recipe. Mexicans are skillful in their use of this versatile seasoning, and you can be, too.

Because varieties and availability of chiles vary so greatly, it's important to become acquainted with the different types of this popular seasoning. Chiles range from red to green, small to large, and hot to mild or even sweet. In general, the smallest ones are the strongest.

Fresh or canned chiles—Chiles are available fresh, canned, or dried. California, serrano, and jalapeño chiles are the most common types found fresh or canned. *California chiles,* often called green chiles, are long and green and are the mildest of the three. The *jalapeño* is a small green pepper that ranges in flavor from hot to very hot. The *serrano* is the hottest of all; it's picked green, but it ripens to a bright red.

Dried chiles—In the dried form you'll most frequently find mulato, ancho, or pasilla chiles. *Mulato* is blackish-brown in color and tastes almost sweet. The brownish-red *ancho* is mildly hot in flavor, while the red *pasilla* is the fieriest of the dried chiles.

Working With Chiles

For many recipes, and whenever the outer skin on fresh chiles is tough, you'll want to peel them before using. To peel, place chiles on a baking sheet and broil 3 to 4 inches from heat, turning often with tongs, until blistered on all sides. Immediately place chiles in a plastic bag; fasten securely, and let steam 10 to 15 minutes. Tear the peel from each chile.

To remove seeds from chiles, cut a small slit in the side of each, and rinse under cold running water while removing seeds. Wear rubber gloves when rinsing or cutting chiles if you have sensitive skin; they're as fiery to the touch as they are to the taste.

Summer's Brimming With Yellow Squash

Yellow squash brightens summer dining with color, nutrition, and variety.

The stem can indicate the quality of squash. If it's hard, dry, shriveled, or darkened, the squash is no longer fresh. Also, look for squash that's well developed, with a glossy, blemish-free skin.

SQUASH CROQUETTES

3 pounds yellow squash, sliced
3 eggs, beaten
2 cups cornbread crumbs
2 tablespoons finely chopped onion
3 tablespoons butter or margarine, melted
1 cup cracker crumbs
Vegetable oil

Cook squash, covered, in a small amount of boiling salted water 10 to 15 minutes or until tender. Drain well and mash. Combine squash and next 4 ingredients; mix well.

Shape mixture into 12 croquettes; roll in cracker crumbs. Fry in deep hot oil (375°) for 3 to 5 minutes or until golden brown. Drain on paper towels. Yield: 12 servings. *Mrs. Gene O. Cross, Montgomery, Alabama.*

SQUASH, BEANS, AND TOMATOES

1 pound fresh green beans
1 large onion, sliced
1 clove garlic, minced
¼ cup chopped fresh parsley
1 teaspoon salt
¼ teaspoon pepper
¼ teaspoon dried whole thyme
¼ teaspoon rubbed sage
2 tablespoons vegetable oil
⅓ cup water
1 pound yellow squash, sliced
3 large tomatoes, peeled and coarsely
  chopped

Wash beans thoroughly. Remove the strings, and cut beans into 1½-inch pieces; set aside.

Sauté onion, garlic, parsley, and seasonings in oil in a large skillet over medium heat until onion is tender. Add beans and water; cover and simmer 10 to 15 minutes. Add squash and tomatoes; cover and simmer 10 minutes. Yield: 8 to 10 servings. *Ruby Bonelli, Bastrop, Texas.*

STUFFED SQUASH WITH GREEN CHILES

6 medium-size yellow squash
2 tablespoons butter or margarine
2 tablespoons all-purpose flour
½ cup milk
1 teaspoon salt
⅛ teaspoon pepper
1 (4-ounce) can chopped green chiles,
  drained
2 tablespoons minced onion
1 cup (4 ounces) shredded Cheddar
  cheese, divided
6 slices bacon, cooked
⅓ cup buttered breadcrumbs
Paprika

Cook squash, covered, in boiling salted water 8 to 10 minutes or until crisp-tender. Drain and cool slightly. Remove and discard stems. Cut each squash in half lengthwise; remove and reserve pulp, leaving a ¼-inch shell.

Mash pulp, and drain well; set pulp and shells aside.

Melt 2 tablespoons butter in a heavy saucepan over low heat; add flour, stirring until smooth. Cook 1 minute, stirring constantly. Gradually stir in milk; cook over medium heat, stirring constantly, until thickened and bubbly. Stir in salt and pepper.

Combine squash pulp, white sauce, green chiles, onion, and ½ cup cheese. Crumble 4 slices bacon, and stir into squash mixture.

Place squash shells in a lightly greased 13- x 9- x 2-inch baking dish. Spoon squash pulp mixture into shells, and top with buttered breadcrumbs. Bake, uncovered, at 375° for 20 minutes. Crumble remaining bacon; sprinkle over squash. Top with remaining cheese. Bake 5 additional minutes. Sprinkle with paprika. Yield: 6 servings.
Louise Turpin,
Birmingham, Alabama.

BAKED SQUASH CASSEROLE

8 medium-size yellow squash, sliced
1 medium onion, chopped
4 slices bacon, cooked and crumbled
¼ cup butter or margarine, melted
2 eggs, beaten
1 cup milk
1 tablespoon sugar
1 cup cracker crumbs or 1 cup fine, dry breadcrumbs
1 cup (4 ounces) shredded Cheddar cheese
½ teaspoon salt
¼ teaspoon pepper
Dash of hot sauce
1 teaspoon Worcestershire sauce

Cook squash and onion in a small amount of boiling water 5 to 7 minutes or until squash is tender; drain well. Place vegetables in container of electric blender, and process until smooth.

Combine squash mixture and remaining ingredients; mix well and spoon into a lightly greased 2-quart shallow casserole. Bake, uncovered, at 350° for 35 minutes. Yield: 8 servings.
Mrs. Cody Coggins,
Brundidge, Alabama.

Cookies Made For Snacking

When children come in tired and hungry from playing, perk them up with a homemade cookie snack.

CARROT-ORANGE COOKIES

¾ cup shortening
¾ cup sugar
1 cup mashed, cooked carrots
1 egg
1 teaspoon vanilla extract
¾ teaspoon orange extract
2 cups all-purpose flour
2 teaspoons baking powder
½ teaspoon salt
½ cup raisins
¼ cup chopped pecans

Cream shortening and sugar until light and fluffy. Add mashed carrots, egg, and flavorings; beat well.

Combine flour, baking powder, and salt; gradually add to creamed mixture. Stir in raisins and pecans.

Drop by rounded teaspoonfuls onto greased cookie sheets. Bake at 350° for 12 to 15 minutes. Yield: about 5½ dozen.
Gail Marshall,
Camden, Tennessee.

MIRACLE COOKIES

1 cup peanut butter
1 cup sugar
1 egg, beaten
1 teaspoon vanilla extract

Combine peanut butter and sugar; mix well. Stir in egg and vanilla. Roll dough into ¾-inch balls. Place balls on ungreased cookie sheets. Flatten with a floured fork.

Bake cookies at 350° for 10 minutes. Allow to cool before removing from cookie sheets. Yield: about 4 dozen.
Carolyn Stewart,
Collinsville, Oklahoma.

GINGER CRINKLES

⅔ cup vegetable oil
1 cup sugar
1 egg
¼ cup molasses
2 cups all-purpose flour
½ teaspoon salt
2 teaspoons baking soda
1 teaspoon ground cinnamon
1 teaspoon ground ginger
¼ cup sugar

Combine oil and 1 cup sugar in a large mixing bowl; add egg, and beat well. Stir in molasses. Combine flour, salt, soda, cinnamon, and ginger; add to molasses mixture, stirring well.

Roll dough into 1-inch balls; roll each ball in remaining ¼ cup sugar. Place balls 2 inches apart on greased cookie sheets. Bake at 350° for 10 to 12 minutes or until lightly browned. Remove to wire rack to cool. Yield: about 4 dozen.
Sue Ellen Buchanan,
Jackson, Alabama.

CRINKLE SUNFLOWER COOKIES

¾ cup shortening
1 cup sugar
1 cup firmly packed light brown sugar
2 eggs, slightly beaten
1 teaspoon vanilla extract
2 cups all-purpose flour
½ teaspoon baking powder
1 teaspoon baking soda
¼ teaspoon salt
2 cups regular oats, uncooked
1 cup flaked coconut
1 (4-ounce) package salted sunflower kernels

Combine shortening and sugar, creaming well; beat in eggs and vanilla. Add flour, baking powder, soda, and salt; mix well. Add remaining ingredients, stirring until blended. Drop by rounded teaspoonfuls onto greased cookie sheets; bake at 350° for 13 to 15 minutes or until edges brown. Yield: about 9½ dozen.
Mrs. John Evanson,
Judsonia, Arkansas.

DUTCH SOUR CREAM COOKIES

½ cup butter or margarine, softened
1 cup sugar
1 egg
½ teaspoon orange or lemon extract
½ teaspoon vanilla extract
3 cups all-purpose flour
¼ teaspoon baking soda
¼ cup commercial sour cream

Cream butter; gradually add sugar, beating until light and fluffy. Add egg and flavorings; beat well.

Combine flour and soda; add to creamed mixture alternately with sour cream, beating just until blended.

Shape dough into a long roll, 2 inches in diameter; wrap in waxed paper, and chill 2 to 3 hours or until firm. Unwrap roll, and cut into ¼-inch slices; place on ungreased cookie sheets. Bake at 375° for 8 to 10 minutes. Yield: 4 dozen.
Melissa Walker,
Maryville, Tennessee.

Bite Into A Juicy Mango

When tasting a mango you're in for a refreshing surprise. It tastes like a cross between a pineapple and apricot with a hint of peaches and bananas.

Mangoes vary in color—green, yellow, and red—so the only test of ripeness is to squeeze the fruit. It should give slightly. Ripe mangoes will keep in the refrigerator for several days, but firm mangoes should be stored at room temperature until they ripen. To prepare, score the skin into four quarters and peel as you would a banana. Then slice the fruit from the large seed.

MANGO PAN DOWDY

¼ cup butter or margarine, softened
8 slices bread, crust removed
6 cups peeled and sliced ripe mango
2 tablespoons brown sugar
1 teaspoon ground cinnamon
½ teaspoon salt
½ teaspoon ground nutmeg
½ teaspoon ground cloves
½ cup water
2 tablespoons molasses
½ teaspoon ground cinnamon
2 tablespoons sugar

Spread butter over one side of each slice of bread; place 4 slices of bread, buttered side up, in a 2-quart baking dish. Arrange mango over bread.

Combine next 7 ingredients, mixing well; pour over mango. Cover with remaining bread slices, buttered side up. Cover and bake at 350° for 30 minutes.

Combine remaining ingredients, stirring well; sprinkle over bread. Bake 20 minutes. Yield: 6 to 8 servings.

Jo Johnson,
Bokeelia, Florida.

MANGO CAKE

2½ cups peeled and mashed ripe mango
2 cups sugar
2 eggs
2 cups all-purpose flour
2 teaspoons baking soda
1 cup chopped pecans or walnuts
1 teaspoon vanilla extract
½ (8-ounce) package cream cheese, softened
¼ cup butter or margarine, softened
2¼ cups sifted powdered sugar
1 teaspoon vanilla extract

Combine first 3 ingredients in a medium mixing bowl; mix well. Stir in flour, soda, pecans, and 1 teaspoon vanilla. Pour into a greased and floured 13- x 9- x 2-inch baking pan; bake at 350° for 35 to 40 minutes or until a wooden pick inserted in center comes out clean. Cool.

Combine remaining ingredients, mixing well. Spread over top of cake. Yield: 15 to 18 servings.

Janet B. Grochouski,
Bokeelia, Florida.

Fry Cheesy Chiles Rellenos

If you like Tex-Mex food, then Chiles Rellenos is sure to be a favorite. The mild green chile can be stuffed with a variety of fillings, but this recipe is one of the most popular versions.

CHILES RELLENOS

6 canned whole mild green chiles
6 (3- x ½- x ½-inch) strips Monterey Jack, Longhorn, or mild Cheddar cheese
3 eggs, separated
3 tablespoons all-purpose flour
1 tablespoon water
¼ teaspoon salt
All-purpose flour
Vegetable oil
Seasoned Tomato Sauce

Rinse chiles and remove seeds; pat dry. Place strips of cheese inside chiles. (If chiles tear, overlap torn sides; batter will hold them together.)

Beat egg yolks 3 to 5 minutes with an electric mixer until fluffy and pale yellow. Add 3 tablespoons flour, water, and salt; mix well. Beat egg whites (at room temperature) until stiff; fold into yolk mixture. Dredge stuffed chiles in flour, coating well. Dip chiles into egg mixture.

Fry chiles on both sides in ½ inch hot oil (370°) about 3 to 5 minutes until browned. Drain. Serve warm with Seasoned Tomato Sauce. Yield: 6 servings.

Seasoned Tomato Sauce:

¼ cup finely chopped green onion
1 clove garlic, minced
1 tablespoon vegetable oil
1 (15-ounce) can tomato sauce
½ teaspoon salt
½ teaspoon dried whole oregano

Sauté onion and garlic in hot oil. Stir in tomato sauce, salt, and oregano. Heat thoroughly. Serve warm over chiles. Yield: 1⅔ cups. *Olivia Taylor, Port Arthur, Texas.*

COOKING LIGHT

A Light Menu With Oriental Flair

Get out the chopsticks, and heat up your wok. Here's a lesson in "Cooking Light"—Oriental style. Since many Oriental ingredients and techniques are well suited to low-calorie cooking, dieters can enjoy this food often. To get you started, we've planned a menu that totals about 500 calories.

Both of our entrée choices are cooked by stir-frying, the most popular of all Oriental cooking procedures. Stir-frying involves constant lifting and turning of small pieces of food in a wok over high heat. While a wok is the traditional utensil, you may use a deep, heavy skillet with high sides instead. We recommend a nonstick surface so that very little, if any, oil is necessary during cooking. But if your wok or skillet isn't the nonstick kind, just coat the bottom and sides well with vegetable cooking spray before heating; then use as little oil as possible for stir-frying.

Oriental cooks know the importance of slicing vegetables and meat into small pieces to ensure quick, even cooking. It's easier to slice meat for stir-fries by partially freezing it first (45 to 60 minutes for a 1-inch-thick steak); slice meat across the grain into thin strips.

Most Oriental entrées call for a variety of nutritious, low-calorie vegetables. Bamboo shoots, Chinese cabbage, snow peas, water chestnuts, celery, onion, mushrooms, and carrots are all excellent choices for adding color and texture. Since the meat and vegetables are combined in one dish, you'll only need rice to complete the main course. (Cook the rice the low-calorie way—and in Oriental fashion—without butter.)

Oriental Spinach Soup goes well with either of our entrées; the flavorful combination of low-fat chicken broth and spinach checks in at only 55 calories per serving.

The calorie-conscious dieter is rarely tempted by sweet desserts when eating a typical Oriental meal. However, fresh fruit is often served as a ending to a hot menu. We've included a simple dessert of Gingered Fruit, as well as a recipe for Light Almond Cookies.

Oriental Spinach Soup
Chinese Beef Stir-Fry
or
Chicken-Vegetable Stir-Fry
Rice
Gingered Fruit
Light Almond Cookies

ORIENTAL SPINACH SOUP

1 (10-ounce) package frozen chopped spinach
1 tablespoon cornstarch
1½ cups water, divided
2 (10½-ounce) cans chicken broth, undiluted
½ cup diagonally sliced celery
2 tablespoons sliced green onion
2 teaspoons soy sauce

Cook spinach according to package directions, omitting salt; drain well.

Dissolve cornstarch in ¼ cup water; add to remaining 1¼ cups water. Combine cornstarch mixture and chicken broth in a saucepan. Add spinach and remaining ingredients; bring to a boil. Reduce heat and simmer 5 minutes. Yield: 8 cups (about 55 calories per 1⅓-cup serving).   *Thelma Olson, Lexington, Oklahoma.*

CHINESE BEEF STIR-FRY

1 pound boneless flank steak
½ cup water
1 tablespoon cornstarch
1½ teaspoons sugar
¼ cup soy sauce
2 tablespoons oyster-flavored sauce
1 medium onion
Vegetable cooking spray
3 stalks celery, diagonally sliced
½ pound fresh mushrooms, sliced
½ cup sliced water chestnuts
½ pound fresh snow peas
3 cups hot cooked rice

Trim excess fat from steak. Partially freeze steak; slice across grain into 2- x ¼-inch strips. Set aside.

Combine water, cornstarch, sugar, soy sauce, and oyster sauce; set aside.

Peel onion, and cut into ¼-inch slices; quarter each slice. Set aside.

Coat wok or skillet well with cooking spray; allow to heat at medium high

(325°) for 2 minutes. Add steak, and stir-fry about 3 minutes. Remove meat from wok, reserving pan drippings.

Place onion, celery, mushrooms, and water chestnuts in wok; stir-fry 2 to 3 minutes. Add meat and snow peas; cover and reduce heat to medium (275°). Simmer 2 to 3 minutes.

Stir in soy sauce mixture. Cook on medium high (325°), stirring constantly, until thickened and bubbly. Serve over rice. Yield: 6 servings (about 176 calories per serving plus 80 calories per ½ cup of rice).

Note: One 6-ounce package frozen Chinese pea pods, thawed and drained, may be substituted for fresh snow peas.

CHICKEN-VEGETABLE STIR-FRY

6 chicken breast halves, skinned and boned
Vegetable cooking spray
¼ cup plus 1 tablespoon soy sauce
1 (4-ounce) can sliced mushrooms, undrained
1 large onion, coarsely chopped
2 small green peppers, cut into 1-inch strips
1 (8-ounce) can sliced water chestnuts, drained
1 teaspoon cornstarch
½ teaspoon sugar
⅛ teaspoon red pepper
3 cups hot cooked rice

Cut chicken breasts into 1½-inch cubes; set aside.

Coat wok or skillet well with cooking spray; allow to heat at medium high (325°) for 1 to 2 minutes. Add chicken and soy sauce; stir-fry 3 to 4 minutes or until lightly browned. Remove chicken from wok, reserving the pan drippings.

Drain mushrooms, reserving the liquid; set aside.

Add onion and green pepper to wok; stir-fry 4 minutes or until vegetables are crisp-tender. Return chicken to wok. Stir in mushrooms and water chestnuts.

Combine reserved mushroom liquid, cornstarch, sugar, and red pepper; mix well. Pour over chicken and vegetables, stirring well. Reduce heat to low (225°); simmer 2 to 3 minutes or until slightly thickened. Serve over rice. Yield: 6 servings (about 175 calories per serving plus 80 calories per ½ cup rice).
Mrs. J. Edward Ebel, Louisville, Kentucky.

GINGERED FRUIT

2 medium apples, cored and sliced
2 medium oranges, peeled and sectioned
2 medium bananas, sliced
½ cup unsweetened orange juice
1 tablespoon grated fresh ginger

Combine all ingredients; cover and chill 2 hours. Yield: 6 servings (about 85 calories per serving).

LIGHT ALMOND COOKIES

¼ cup plus 2 tablespoons margarine, softened
¼ cup sugar
1 egg yolk
½ teaspoon almond extract
¼ teaspoon vanilla extract
¼ teaspoon lemon extract
1 cup all-purpose flour
½ teaspoon baking powder
Dash of salt
1 tablespoon (about 2 dozen) almond slices

Cream margarine; gradually add sugar, and beat until light and fluffy. Add egg yolk, and beat well. Stir in flavorings.

Combine dry ingredients; add to creamed mixture, beating until thoroughly combined. Shape dough into 1-inch balls. Place about 2 inches apart on ungreased cookie sheets. Press an almond slice in center of each cookie.

Bake at 300° for 20 minutes or until edges begin to brown. Remove cookies to wire racks, and cool completely. Yield: 2 dozen (about 54 calories each).

Three Ideas For Rice

Although rice is one of the more common staples, its versatility is very often overlooked. Here we share some exciting ways to discover its flavor in delicious side dishes.

RICE LYONNAISE

¾ cup chopped onion
2 tablespoons butter or margarine
3 cups cooked regular rice
¼ cup chopped pimiento

Sauté onion in butter in a heavy skillet until tender. Stir in rice and pimiento; cook, stirring constantly, until heated. Yield: 4 to 6 servings.
Mrs. Edward R. Haug, Sulphur, Louisiana.

SPANISH-STYLE RICE

2 (8-ounce) cans tomato sauce
½ cup water
⅓ cup chopped onion
⅓ cup chopped green pepper
¼ cup butter or margarine
1 teaspoon sugar
½ teaspoon prepared mustard
¼ teaspoon salt
Dash of pepper
6 cups cooked regular rice

Combine first 9 ingredients in a 2½-quart saucepan, stirring well. Bring to a boil; cover and boil 15 minutes. Stir in cooked rice. Remove from heat; cover and let stand 5 minutes. Stir well before serving. Yield: 8 servings. *Elaine Bay, Point, Texas.*

RICE AND GREEN CHILES

4 cups cooked regular rice
1 (16-ounce) carton commercial sour
    cream
1 teaspoon salt
¾ cup (3 ounces) shredded Monterey Jack
    cheese
¾ cup (3 ounces) shredded sharp Cheddar
    cheese
1 (4-ounce) can whole green chiles, seeded
    and cut into strips

Combine rice, sour cream, and salt; stir well. Spoon half into a buttered 10- x 6- x 2-inch baking dish. Layer half the cheese and half the green chiles on top; repeat layers with remaining ingredients. Bake at 350° for 20 minutes or until thoroughly heated and cheese is melted. Yield: 6 to 8 servings.

Kathryn Watkins, Justin, Texas.

Sparkling Ice Cools And Refreshes

Ice is very much a part of summer entertaining, and imaginative use of ice makes party food more appealing. Here are some suggestions.

Ice bowl: For serving cold foods, nothing is quite as spectacular as an ice bowl. Use it to hold ice cream or sherbet balls, cold soup, or a festive salad.

You can make an ice bowl any size you need. It's a good idea to make it well in advance of the party to be sure of getting the effect you want.

Fill a large container, such as a plastic pan, about three-fourths full of water. Place a small, clear-glass bowl in the center of the water-filled container, and add some water to the glass bowl to weight it. Use masking tape to hold the glass bowl in position. Freeze.

Check the ice bowl as it freezes, since you may need to adjust the position of the small bowl in the center.

When it's time to use the ice bowl, let it stand at room temperature for a few minutes; then remove both the outside container and the piece of ice that has formed inside the small bowl. Smooth any uneven edges of the ice bowl by applying warm water with a sponge. Leave the glass bowl in place to hold the food being served.

Place the ice bowl on a tray that has a raised edge. The edge of the tray will hold water as the ice melts. Arrange ivy leaves, other greenery, or some flowers around the base of the ice. Place the tray on a thick mat or trivet to protect the table surface from the condensate. Use a bulb baster (plastic tube used to baste meat) if you need to remove water from the tray during the party.

Ice cubes: Add an unexpected dash of flavor and color to fruit punches and other summer drinks with colorful bits of fruit frozen in ice. Use strawberries, cherries, lemon or lime slices, grapes, mint leaves, or pineapple wedges.

Place a mint leaf or a piece of fruit in each section of an ice cube tray or muffin tin. Add water until each section is nearly full; then freeze.

Frozen punch ring: Make a frozen ring to keep the punch cool at a tea or party. Fill a metal ring mold with

For fruit-filled ice, place fruit in each section of a muffin tin or ice cube tray (left); *add water and freeze. These cubes add color and flavor to beverages* (right).

For a frozen ring, fill a metal ring mold with punch (left); *freeze. This frozen ring* (right) *won't dilute the punch as it melts, since it's made with punch instead of water.*

punch, add sliced fruit or mint leaves to the mold if you wish, and freeze.

When you're ready to use the frozen ring, let it stand at room temperature for a few minutes. Fill the punch bowl with chilled punch, invert the mold to remove the ring, and place ice ring in the punch.

Some tips: Ice will be clearer if you boil the water and let it cool before freezing. Since water expands as it freezes, never fill a container full. Use only metal, plastic, or freezer-proof glass containers in the freezer.

Fruit In A Pineapple

Frances Bowles of Mableton, Georgia, likes to serve Fresh Pineapple Boats whenever her daughter brings college friends home for a visit. "It's cool, refreshing, and a little bit fancy," she says. Each boat is heaped with fresh fruit and coconut and served with Frances' special Poppy Seed Dressing.

FRESH PINEAPPLE BOATS

1 fresh pineapple
1 medium-size red apple, unpeeled
2 medium oranges, peeled and sectioned
1 to 1½ cups strawberries, halved
½ cup flaked coconut, divided
Poppy Seed Dressing

Cut the pineapple in half lengthwise. Scoop out pulp, leaving shells ¼ to ½ inch thick; set aside.

Cut pineapple pulp and apple into bite-size pieces, discarding cores. Combine fruit and ¼ cup plus 2 tablespoons coconut; toss gently.

Spoon mixture into pineapple shells, and sprinkle with remaining coconut. Pour Poppy Seed Dressing over fruit. Yield: 4 to 6 servings.

Poppy Seed Dressing:
⅓ cup vegetable oil
¼ cup plus 1 tablespoon sugar
2 tablespoons vinegar
1½ teaspoons poppy seeds
½ teaspoon salt
½ teaspoon prepared mustard

Combine all ingredients in container of electric blender. Process on high speed 30 seconds. Yield: about ½ cup.
Frances Bowles,
Mableton, Georgia.

Citrus Puts Sparkle In These Favorites

The fresh flavor of citrus fruit and juice adds a special touch to meals. Remember to select firm, well-rounded fruit that is heavy for its size. And, if possible, store citrus in the refrigerator. This prolongs storage.

GRAPEFRUIT ASPIC

1 (3-ounce) package lemon- or lime-flavored gelatin
1 tablespoon sugar
¾ cup boiling water
1 cup unsweetened grapefruit juice
2 medium grapefruit, peeled, seeded, and sectioned
¾ cup sliced almonds
Lettuce leaves

Dissolve gelatin and sugar in boiling water; stir in grapefruit juice. Chill until the consistency of unbeaten egg white.

Chop grapefruit sections; drain. Stir grapefruit and almonds into thickened gelatin. Pour mixture into lightly oiled ⅓-cup molds. Chill until firm. Serve on lettuce leaves. Yield: 8 servings.
Mrs. E. C. Holloway,
Murfreesboro, Tennessee.

ORANGE PUDDING

2 eggs, separated
¼ cup sugar
¼ teaspoon salt
2 tablespoons all-purpose flour
2 tablespoons butter or margarine, softened
1 tablespoon orange rind
¼ cup orange juice
1 tablespoon lemon juice
¼ cup sugar
1 cup milk

Beat egg whites (at room temperature) until frothy. Add ¼ cup sugar and salt; continue beating until soft peaks form. Set aside.

Beat egg yolks until thick and lemon colored; add flour, butter, orange rind, juice, and ¼ cup sugar. Gradually beat in milk. Fold egg white mixture into pudding. Spoon into six 6-ounce buttered custard cups. Place in a pan of hot water; bake at 350° for 35 to 40 minutes or until a knife inserted in center comes out clean. Chill. Yield: 6 servings.
Varniece Warren,
Hermitage, Arkansas.

LEMON MOIST CUPCAKES

¾ cup butter or margarine, softened
1 cup sugar
2 eggs
2 cups self-rising flour
½ cup milk
1 teaspoon vanilla extract
1 cup sugar
Grated rind of 1 lemon
Grated rind of 1 orange
Juice of 2 lemons
Juice of 2 oranges

Combine butter and 1 cup sugar in a large mixing bowl, creaming until light and fluffy. Add eggs, beating well. Stir in flour. Add milk and vanilla, mixing just until blended.

Spoon batter into paper-lined muffin pans, filling each cup half full. Bake at 350° for 20 to 25 minutes.

Combine remaining ingredients, stirring until blended. Spoon glaze over warm cupcakes. Yield: about 2 dozen.
Mrs. Lyman Clayborn,
Kinston, North Carolina.

Freezing Ahead Is Easy—And Smart

Wouldn't it be nice to be able to go to the freezer and take out a whole meal that's already prepared and waiting? These recipes let you do just that.

SLOPPY JOES

3 pounds ground beef
1 medium onion, finely chopped
1 cup finely chopped celery
1 (10¾-ounce) can tomato soup, undiluted
1 cup catsup
1 teaspoon salt
⅛ teaspoon pepper
8 hamburger buns, halved
Shredded Cheddar cheese

Brown meat in a large skillet, stirring to crumble. Add onion and celery; cook until tender. Drain. Stir in tomato soup, catsup, salt, and pepper; simmer 30 minutes.

Freeze in a plastic freezer container. To serve, thaw in refrigerator, and heat in a saucepan. Spoon over warm bun halves, and sprinkle with cheese. Yield: 16 servings.
Nell Little,
Jonesboro, Tennessee.

INDIVIDUAL MEAT LOAVES

2 pounds ground beef
1 cup round buttery cracker crumbs
1 egg, beaten
½ cup finely chopped green pepper
½ cup finely chopped onion
½ cup evaporated milk
1 teaspoon salt
¼ teaspoon pepper
1 teaspoon seasoned meat tenderizer
1¼ cups catsup, divided
3 tablespoons dark corn syrup

Combine first 9 ingredients and ¼ cup catsup; mix well. Shape mixture into 6 loaves, and wrap individually in freezer paper or aluminum foil. Freeze. To serve, thaw in refrigerator; bake at 350° for 35 minutes. Combine corn syrup and remaining 1 cup catsup; brush on tops of meat loaves. Bake 10 additional minutes. Yield: 6 servings.

Mary H. Gillian,
Cartersville, Virginia.

FREEZER SLAW

1 large cabbage
½ green pepper
6 large carrots
1 teaspoon salt
2 cups sugar
1 teaspoon dry mustard
½ cup water
1 cup vinegar
1 teaspoon celery seeds

Shred cabbage, green pepper, and carrots. Sprinkle with salt; let stand 1 hour. Drain if water accumulates.

Combine remaining ingredients in a saucepan. Bring to a boil; boil 3 minutes. Cool. Pour over cabbage mixture, and let stand 3 minutes. Stir well. Freeze in plastic freezer bags or containers. To serve, thaw in refrigerator. Yield: about 10 servings.

Mrs. Ken Keller,
Alcoa, Tennessee.

STRAWBERRY FROST

½ cup butter
1 cup all-purpose flour
¼ cup firmly packed brown sugar
½ cup finely chopped pecans
1 (10-ounce) package frozen sliced
    strawberries, slightly thawed
2 egg whites
⅔ cup sugar
2 tablespoons lemon juice
1 cup whipping cream
Whole fresh strawberries
    (optional)

Melt butter in a 13- x 9- x 2-inch baking pan. Add flour, brown sugar, and pecans; mix well. Pat out evenly in pan. Bake at 350° for 10 minutes. Stir and bake 10 additional minutes. Cool; remove one-third of crumbs for topping. Pat remaining crumbs smoothly in pan.

Combine sliced strawberries, egg whites (at room temperature), sugar, and lemon juice. Beat on high speed of electric mixer for 15 minutes.

Beat whipping cream until light and fluffy; fold into strawberry mixture. Spread mixture over crust in pan, and sprinkle with remaining crumbs.

Cover tightly with aluminum foil, and freeze. Cut into squares, and garnish with whole strawberries, if desired. Yield: 12 to 16 servings.

Mrs. W. G. Greenlee,
Inverness, Florida.

Select A Yeast Bread For Dinner

Light and airy yeast breads, fresh from the oven and smothered with butter, are an ideal addition to meals. The delectable aroma of these dinner breads is reason enough for serving them!

HONEY OATMEAL BUNS

¼ cup sugar
2 packages dry yeast
2 teaspoons salt
1 cup regular oats, uncooked
4½ to 5 cups all-purpose flour,
    divided
½ cup water
1 cup milk
¼ cup butter or margarine
2 eggs
Honey Topping
⅔ cup chopped pecans or walnuts
¼ cup butter or margarine, melted
½ cup firmly packed brown sugar
2 teaspoons ground cinnamon

Combine ¼ cup sugar, yeast, salt, oats, and 1½ cups flour in a large bowl.

Heat water, milk, and ¼ cup butter in a small saucepan to 120° to 130°. Add to dry ingredients; beat 2 minutes at medium speed of electric mixer, scraping bowl occasionally. Add 1 cup flour and eggs; beat 2 minutes at high speed. Stir in enough remaining flour to make a soft dough.

Turn dough out onto a lightly floured surface and knead about 8 to 10 minutes until smooth and elastic. Place in a greased bowl, turning to grease top. Cover and let rise in a warm place (85°), free from drafts, 1 hour or until doubled in bulk. Punch dough down. Let rest 10 minutes.

Prepare Honey Topping; pour into 2 lightly greased 9-inch square nonstick pans. Tilt pans to cover evenly. Sprinkle half of pecans in each pan. Set aside.

Divide dough in half. Roll each half into a 12- x 9-inch rectangle on a lightly floured board. Brush each rectangle with half of melted butter. Combine brown sugar and cinnamon. Sprinkle half of cinnamon mixture over each rectangle, leaving a ½-inch margin on all sides. Roll up each rectangle, starting at long end, jellyroll fashion. Pinch edge and ends to seal. Cut each roll into twelve 1-inch slices. Arrange slices cut side down in prepared pans. Cover and let rise 45 minutes until doubled in bulk.

Bake at 375° for 25 minutes. Cool 5 minutes on a rack; invert onto plate. Yield: 2 dozen.

Honey Topping:

½ cup honey
½ cup firmly packed brown sugar
¼ cup butter or margarine
¼ teaspoon salt

Combine all ingredients in a small saucepan; bring to a boil, stirring constantly. Simmer for 1½ to 2 minutes. Yield: 1 cup. *Dorothy L. Anderson,*
Manor, Texas.

COTTAGE CHEESE-DILL BREAD

2 packages dry yeast
½ cup warm water (105° to 115°)
2 teaspoons sugar
2 cups cream-style cottage cheese
2 tablespoons finely chopped onion
2 tablespoons dried whole dillweed
1 teaspoon baking powder
1 teaspoon salt
2 tablespoons sugar
2 eggs, beaten
4½ cups all-purpose flour
Melted butter

Dissolve yeast in warm water in a large bowl; stir in 2 teaspoons sugar.

Combine next 7 ingredients in a small bowl; add to yeast mixture, mixing well. Gradually add flour; stir well.

Turn dough out onto a floured surface, and knead 8 to 10 minutes until smooth and elastic (dough will be sticky). Place in a well-greased bowl, turning to grease top. Cover and let rise in a warm place (85°), free from drafts, 1 hour or until doubled in bulk.

Punch dough down, and divide in half. Shape each half into a loaf. Place in 2 well-greased 8½- x 4½- x 3-inch loafpans. Cover and let rise 45 minutes or until doubled in bulk. Bake at 350° for 30 to 35 minutes or until loaves sound hollow when tapped. Remove from pans, and brush with melted butter. Yield: 2 loaves. *Rachel V. Youree, Murfreesboro, Tennessee.*

NO-KNEAD REFRIGERATOR BREAD

1 package dry yeast
1½ cups warm water (105° to 115°)
⅔ cup sugar
⅔ cup shortening
2 eggs
1 cup warm mashed potatoes
1½ teaspoons salt
About 7½ cups all-purpose flour

Dissolve yeast in warm water in a large mixing bowl. Add sugar, shortening, eggs, potatoes, salt, and 4 cups flour. Beat 30 seconds at low speed of electric mixer; beat 2 minutes at medium speed, scraping bowl occasionally. Stir in remaining flour, mixing well. Place dough in a well-greased bowl, turning to grease top. Cover tightly, and refrigerate 8 hours or up to 3 days before shaping.

Divide dough in half; shape each half into a loaf. Place in 2 greased 9- x 5- x 3-inch loafpans. Cover and let rise in a warm place (85°), free from drafts, 3 hours or until doubled in bulk. Bake at 400° for 15 to 20 minutes or until loaves sound hollow when tapped. Yield: 2 loaves.

Note: To make rolls, shape as desired. Place in greased pans. Cover and let rise in a warm place, free from drafts, until doubled in bulk. Bake at 400° for 10 to 15 minutes. Yield: 2 dozen. *Mrs. Max E. Ayer, Elizabethton, Tennessee.*

YEAST BREAD SQUARES

1 package dry yeast
1¼ cups warm water (105° to 115°)
¼ cup shortening
2 tablespoons sugar
1 teaspoon salt
2⅔ cups all-purpose flour
1 tablespoon poppy seeds
Melted butter

Combine yeast and warm water in a large bowl. Add shortening, sugar, salt,

and 2 cups flour. Beat 3 minutes at low speed of electric mixer. Stir in the remaining flour.

Cover and let rise in a warm place (85°), free from drafts, 30 minutes or until doubled in bulk.

Stir dough and spread evenly in a well-greased 13- x 9- x 2-inch baking pan. Sprinkle poppy seeds over top; cover and let rise 40 minutes or until doubled in bulk.

Bake at 375° for 25 to 30 minutes or until golden brown. Brush with melted butter, and cut into squares. Yield: 2 dozen. *Mrs. Ray Harp, Shawnee, Oklahoma.*

QUICK BUTTERMILK ROLLS

4 to 4½ cups all-purpose flour, divided
2 packages dry yeast
3 tablespoons sugar
1 teaspoon salt
½ teaspoon baking soda
1¼ cups buttermilk
½ cup water
½ cup shortening

Combine 1½ cups flour, yeast, sugar, salt, and soda in a large mixing bowl. Combine buttermilk, water, and shortening in a small saucepan; place over low heat until very warm (120° to 130°). Gradually add milk mixture to dry ingredients, mixing at low speed of electric mixer; beat 3 minutes on medium speed. Stir in remaining flour.

Turn dough out onto a lightly floured surface, and knead about 5 minutes until smooth and elastic.

Place dough in a greased bowl, turning to grease top. Cover and let rise in a warm place (85°), free from drafts, for 45 minutes or until doubled in bulk.

Punch dough down, and shape into 1½-inch balls; place balls on a greased 15- x 10- x 1-inch jellyroll pan. Let rise 35 minutes or until doubled in bulk. Bake at 400° for 18 to 20 minutes. Yield: 2 dozen.

Mrs. Robert D. Burgess, Fort Smith, Arkansas.

More Than A Casserole—It's A Pie

Easy Chicken Pot Pie is a casserole you must try. It's a basic recipe with an easy-to-make crust. Country Pie has an unusual crust made with ground beef.

COUNTRY PIE

1 pound lean ground beef
½ cup fine, dry breadcrumbs
¼ cup finely chopped onion
¼ cup finely chopped green pepper
1½ teaspoons salt
¼ teaspoon pepper
2 (8-ounce) cans tomato sauce, divided
3 cups cooked regular rice
½ cup (2 ounces) shredded process American cheese
2 (1-ounce) slices process American cheese, cut diagonally
Fresh parsley sprigs (optional)
Tomato wedges (optional)

Combine first 6 ingredients and one can of tomato sauce, mixing well. Spread mixture into a 10-inch pieplate; mold to sides of pan to form a shell.

Combine rice, shredded cheese, and remaining tomato sauce, stirring well; spoon rice mixture into meat shell. Arrange cheese slices over top of rice mixture. Bake at 350° for 30 to 40 minutes. Garnish with parsley and tomato wedges, if desired. Yield: 6 servings.

Florence L. Costello, Chattanooga, Tennessee.

ENCHILADA PIE

2 pounds ground beef
1 medium onion, finely chopped
½ teaspoon garlic powder
1 (8-ounce) can tomato sauce
2 cups canned whole tomatoes, chopped
1 (4-ounce) can chopped green chiles
1 (1½-ounce) package taco seasoning mix
½ teaspoon salt
¼ teaspoon pepper
1 tablespoon chili powder
1 (14-ounce) package corn tortillas
1 (10¾-ounce) can cream of chicken soup, undiluted
¾ cup milk
2 cups (8 ounces) shredded Cheddar cheese

Combine ground beef, onion, and garlic powder in a large skillet; cook over medium heat until meat is browned, stirring to crumble. Drain well. Add next 7 ingredients; cook mixture 5 minutes, stirring occasionally.

Tear each tortilla into 8 pieces. Place half of tortilla pieces in a 13- x 9- x 2-inch baking pan; top with meat mixture. Arrange remaining tortilla pieces evenly over meat mixture. Combine soup and milk in a small bowl, mixing well; pour over tortillas. Sprinkle cheese evenly over top. Bake at 350° for 45 minutes. Yield: 8 to 10 servings.

Nina Bebout, Purcell, Oklahoma.

CORN BURGER PIE

1 pound ground chuck
1 medium onion, chopped
1 (1½-ounce) package spaghetti sauce mix
1 (16-ounce) can green beans, drained
1 (6½-ounce) package cornbread mix

Combine ground chuck and onion in a large skillet; cook over medium heat, stirring occasionally, until meat is browned and onion is tender. Drain.

Prepare spaghetti sauce mix according to package directions; add spaghetti sauce and green beans to meat mixture. Bring to a boil, stirring well; remove from heat, and pour into a 12- x 8- x 2-inch baking dish.

Prepare cornbread mix according to package directions; pour over meat mixture. Bake at 425° for 25 minutes. Yield: 6 servings. *Ellen Darrow, Choctaw, Oklahoma.*

EASY CHICKEN POT PIE

3 tablespoons butter or margarine
¼ cup all-purpose flour
1¼ cups chicken broth
1 cup milk
2 cups cubed, cooked chicken
1 (16-ounce) can peas and carrots, drained
1 hard-cooked egg, thinly sliced
½ teaspoon salt
¼ teaspoon poultry seasoning
⅛ teaspoon pepper
Flaky Pastry

Melt butter in a heavy Dutch oven; add flour, stirring until smooth. Cook 1 minute, stirring constantly. Gradually add broth and milk; cook over medium heat, stirring constantly, until thickened and bubbly. Stir in next 6 ingredients.

Pour chicken mixture into a deep 1½-quart casserole. Top with Flaky Pastry; cut slits in pastry to allow steam to escape. Bake at 400° for 25 to 30 minutes or until the crust is golden brown. Yield: 6 servings.

Flaky Pastry:

1 cup all-purpose flour
¾ teaspoon baking powder
½ teaspoon salt
⅓ cup shortening
3 tablespoons ice water

Combine flour, baking powder, and salt in a mixing bowl; cut in shortening with a pastry blender until mixture resembles coarse meal. Sprinkle ice water evenly over surface; stir with a fork until all dry ingredients are moistened. Roll dough out onto a lightly floured surface to fit casserole dish. Yield: enough pastry for a 1½-quart casserole. *Mrs. Galen Jones, Ackerman, Mississippi.*

Start Dinner With Escargots

Snails, commonly referred to by their French name, escargots, are considered a delicacy of the first order. Baked in their own shells along with a highly seasoned combination of butter, garlic, and parsley, snails are usually served as a savory light appetizer.

The final cooking may be done in a special snail pan (available in most gourmet shops) designed to keep the shells from moving. Or, simply fill a baking pan with rock salt and nestle the shells in the salt to keep them still.

ESCARGOTS PROVENCAL

1 (7½-ounce) can snails, drained and rinsed
½ cup Chablis or other dry white wine
½ cup beef broth
⅛ teaspoon salt
⅛ teaspoon pepper
Dash of ground nutmeg
18 snail shells, rinsed and drained
½ cup butter or margarine, softened
1 cup coarsely chopped fresh parsley
4 cloves garlic, minced
Rock salt (optional)
Fresh parsley sprigs (optional)

Combine first 6 ingredients; stir well. Cover and chill at least 3 hours. Drain; insert each marinated snail into a shell.

Combine butter, parsley, and garlic in container of electric blender; blend well. Pack about 2 teaspoons of butter mixture into each shell.

Place filled shells in snail pan, or pour enough rock salt into an 8-inch square baking dish to cover bottom (salt helps shells sit upright); arrange filled shells, open end up, on salt. Bake at 400° for 15 minutes. Garnish with parsley sprigs, if desired; serve immediately. Yield: 6 appetizer servings. *Maryse H. Rose, Mary Esther, Florida.*

Simmer These Okra Favorites

As the fresh crops of okra make their way into the market, Southerners everywhere are enjoying the tender green pods in a variety of dishes.

When shopping, select bright, green okra less than 4½ inches in length. You can easily test for tenderness by gently pressing on the tips of the pods. Tender pods bend easily; tough pods are stiff and resist bending.

MEATBALL-OKRA CREOLE

1 pound ground beef
¾ cup soft breadcrumbs
1 egg, beaten
½ teaspoon salt
¼ teaspoon pepper
2 tablespoons vegetable oil
1 pound okra, cut into ½-inch slices
1 small onion, chopped
¼ cup chopped green pepper
¼ cup chopped celery
1 clove garlic, minced
1 (16-ounce) can whole tomatoes, undrained and coarsely chopped
1½ cups water
½ teaspoon red pepper
Hot cooked rice

Combine first 5 ingredients; mix well. Shape into 1-inch balls.

Heat oil in a Dutch oven; add meatballs, and brown on all sides. Drain, reserving 3 tablespoons drippings in pan. Add okra, onion, green pepper, celery, and garlic; sauté 5 minutes. Stir in meatballs, tomatoes, water, and red pepper. Bring mixture to a boil; cover, reduce heat, and simmer for 20 minutes. Serve over hot cooked rice. Yield: 6 servings. *Carol Barclay, Portland, Texas.*

EASY CHICKEN GUMBO

¼ cup butter or margarine
1 tablespoon bacon drippings
2 cups sliced okra
1 small onion, chopped
¼ cup chopped green pepper
5 cups chicken broth
2 cups peeled, chopped tomato
1 bay leaf
¼ teaspoon salt
⅛ teaspoon pepper
½ cup uncooked regular rice
1 cup diced, cooked chicken
1 tablespoon chopped fresh parsley

Melt butter and bacon drippings in a Dutch oven. Add okra, onion, and green pepper; sauté until onion is tender. Stir in broth, tomato, bay leaf, salt, and pepper. Bring to a boil; stir in rice. Cover, reduce heat, and simmer 20 minutes. Stir in chicken and parsley; cook just until thoroughly heated. Remove bay leaf. Yield: about 7 cups.

Karen Cregor,
Bidwell, Ohio.

OKRA-CORN CREOLE

3 tablespoons bacon drippings
¼ cup chopped onion
1 small green pepper, chopped
1¼ cups sliced fresh okra
¾ cup chopped tomato
1 cup fresh corn cut from cob
¼ teaspoon salt
⅛ teaspoon pepper

Heat bacon drippings in a large skillet over medium heat. Add onion and green pepper; sauté until tender, stirring frequently. Add the remaining ingredients; cover, reduce heat, and simmer 10 to 15 minutes. Yield: 4 servings.

Kay Stubbs,
Mauk, Georgia.

OKRA-TOMATO COMBO

6 slices bacon
1 large onion, chopped
1 cup chopped celery
2½ cups sliced okra
1 (16-ounce) can tomatoes, undrained and chopped
¾ cup water
1 teaspoon salt
¼ teaspoon pepper
½ teaspoon chili powder

Cook bacon in a large skillet until crisp; remove bacon, reserving ¼ cup drippings in skillet. Crumble bacon, and set aside. Sauté onion and celery in drippings until tender. Add bacon and remaining ingredients; bring to a boil. Cover, reduce heat, and simmer 20 minutes, stirring occasionally. Yield: about 8 servings.

Audrey Donahew,
Garland, Texas.

Tip: When you are out of canned tomatoes for a recipe—do not panic! Try substituting 1 (6-ounce) can tomato paste plus 1 cup water. The substitution will make very little difference in most recipes.

OKRA PUFFS

½ cup plain cornmeal
½ cup evaporated milk
1 egg, beaten
1 large onion, finely chopped
¼ teaspoon dried whole marjoram
¼ teaspoon dried whole thyme
¼ to ½ teaspoon salt
¼ teaspoon pepper
2 cups thinly sliced okra
Hot vegetable oil

Combine first 8 ingredients, mixing well. Stir in okra. Drop mixture by tablespoonfuls into ¼ inch hot oil (350°); cook until golden brown, turning once. Yield: 2 dozen.

Mrs. Bruce Fowler,
Woodruff, South Carolina.

Take A Fresh Look At Chicken Salad

For an interesting and refreshing main dish salad, toss together tender bits of chicken with a variety of fruit, vegetables, and nuts.

FRUITY CHICKEN SALAD

1 (15¼-ounce) can pineapple tidbits, undrained
4 cups chopped, cooked chicken
1 (11-ounce) can mandarin oranges, drained
1 (8-ounce) can sliced water chestnuts, drained
1 (2½-ounce) package sliced almonds, toasted
1 cup chopped celery
1 cup seedless green grapes, cut in half
1½ cups mayonnaise
1 tablespoon soy sauce
1 teaspoon curry powder
1 (3-ounce) can chow mein noodles
Lettuce leaves (optional)

Drain pineapple, reserving 2 tablespoons juice. (Reserve remaining juice for use in other recipes.)
Combine pineapple tidbits and next 6 ingredients; mix well.
Combine 2 tablespoons pineapple juice, mayonnaise, soy sauce, and curry powder; stir well, and add to chicken mixture. Chill. Stir in noodles just before serving. Serve on lettuce leaves, if desired. Yield: 8 servings.

Mrs. Ronald D. Smith,
Houston, Texas.

CHICKEN-AND-SPINACH TOSSED SALAD

½ pound fresh spinach, torn into bite-size pieces
2 cups chopped, cooked chicken
2 cups fresh broccoli flowerets
1 (8-ounce) can sliced water chestnuts, drained
4 slices bacon, cooked and crumbled
Dressing (recipe follows)
¼ cup grated Parmesan cheese
½ cup chow mein noodles

Combine spinach and next 4 ingredients in a large bowl; toss with dressing until coated. Sprinkle with cheese and noodles. Yield: 4 to 6 servings.

Dressing:

3 tablespoons soy sauce
3 tablespoons wine vinegar
3 tablespoons vegetable oil
1 teaspoon minced onion
1 teaspoon sugar
⅛ teaspoon pepper

Combine all ingredients in a jar. Cover tightly, and shake vigorously. Yield: ½ cup.

Mrs. James Tuthill,
Virginia Beach, Virginia.

NUTTY CHICKEN-RICE SALAD

2 cups chopped, cooked chicken
1½ cups cooked regular rice, cooled
1 cup diced celery
1 (8-ounce) can crushed pineapple, drained
¾ cup chopped pecans
¼ cup chopped green pepper
¼ cup finely chopped onion
½ cup mayonnaise or salad dressing
2 tablespoons vegetable oil
1 tablespoon red wine vinegar
1 teaspoon salt
½ to ¾ teaspoon curry powder
2 teaspoons lemon juice
Lettuce leaves (optional)
Tomato wedges (optional)

Combine first 7 ingredients in a large bowl; mix well. Combine next 6 ingredients, stirring well; add to chicken mixture, and toss gently. Chill.
Serve on lettuce leaves with tomato wedges, if desired. Yield: 4 to 6 servings.

Lillian M. Clendenin,
Charleston, West Virginia.

Whip The Meringue Problem

Tired of a weeping meringue? Mrs. Roy E. Gunnells of Dearing, Georgia, sent us her recipe for a cooked meringue that doesn't shrink or collect water droplets, even after refrigeration. And the chocolate filling that goes with it nets a high rating from us, too.

CHOCOLATE MERINGUE PIE

1¼ cups sugar
½ cup cocoa
⅓ cup cornstarch
¼ teaspoon salt
3 cups milk
3 egg yolks
3 tablespoons margarine
1½ teaspoons vanilla extract
1 baked 9-inch pastry shell
Easy Cooked Meringue

Combine sugar, cocoa, cornstarch, and salt in a heavy saucepan. Mix well to remove lumps. Gradually add milk, stirring until blended. Cook over medium heat, stirring constantly, until mixture thickens and comes to a boil; boil 1 minute, stirring constantly. Remove mixture from heat.

Beat egg yolks until thick and lemon colored. Gradually stir about one-fourth of hot mixture into yolks; add to remaining hot mixture, stirring constantly. Cook over medium heat 2 minutes, stirring constantly. Remove from heat; stir in margarine and vanilla. Immediately pour into pastry shell. Spread meringue over filling, sealing to edge of pastry. Bake at 425° for 5 to 7 minutes or until meringue is lightly browned. Cool before serving. Yield: one 9-inch pie.

Easy Cooked Meringue:

½ cup water
¼ cup plus 2 tablespoons sugar
1 tablespoon cornstarch
3 egg whites
Dash of salt

Combine water, sugar, and cornstarch in a small saucepan, stirring well; cook over medium heat, stirring constantly, until transparent and thickened. Combine egg whites (at room temperature) and salt; beat until foamy. Continue beating while gradually pouring cooked mixture into egg whites. Beat 3 minutes or until stiff, but not dry. Do not overbeat. Yield: enough for one 9-inch pie.
Mrs. Roy E. Gunnells,
Dearing, Georgia.

Southern Pies Make Special Desserts

Pie ranks high on the list of the South's favorite desserts. Everyone has a favorite pie, whether it be chocolate topped with a fluffy meringue, devilishly rich pecan, or an old-fashioned buttermilk pie. Try the recipes we offer here. We think they'll soon be favorites at your house, too.

BUTTERSCOTCH MERINGUE PIE

1 cup firmly packed brown sugar
1 tablespoon plus 1 teaspoon sugar
¼ cup all-purpose flour
⅛ teaspoon salt
1½ cups milk
¼ cup butter or margarine
2 eggs, separated
1 teaspoon vanilla extract
1 baked 8-inch pastry shell
¼ cup sugar

Combine first 4 ingredients in top of a double boiler; add milk and butter, stirring well. Cook over boiling water, stirring constantly, 30 minutes until thickened.

Beat egg yolks until thick and lemon colored. Gradually stir about one-fourth of hot mixture into yolks; add to remaining hot mixture. Cover; cook 15 minutes over boiling water, stirring frequently. Remove from water; stir in vanilla. Cool; pour into pastry shell.

Beat egg whites (at room temperature) until foamy. Gradually add ¼ cup sugar; continue beating until stiff peaks form. Spread meringue over pie; bake at 425° for 6 to 8 minutes or until lightly browned. Cool. Refrigerate until chilled. Yield: one 8-inch pie.
Mrs. Willis J. Dewar,
Selma, North Carolina.

EASY CHOCOLATE PIE

1 cup sugar
3 tablespoons cornstarch
Dash of salt
2 cups milk
3 eggs, separated
1 (1-ounce) square unsweetened chocolate
1 tablespoon butter or margarine
1 teaspoon vanilla extract
1 baked 9-inch pastry shell
½ teaspoon cream of tartar
¼ cup plus 2 tablespoons sugar

Combine 1 cup sugar, cornstarch, and salt in a heavy saucepan; mix well.

Combine milk and egg yolks; beat with a wire whisk 1 to 2 minutes or until frothy. Gradually stir into sugar mixture, mixing well. Cook over medium heat, stirring constantly, until thickened and bubbly. Remove from heat; add chocolate, butter, and vanilla, stirring until chocolate and butter melt. Spoon into pastry shell; set aside.

Beat egg whites (at room temperature) until frothy; add cream of tartar, beating slightly. Gradually add remaining sugar, 1 tablespoon at a time, beating until stiff peaks form. Spread meringue over filling, sealing to edge of pastry. Bake at 350° for 10 to 12 minutes or until golden brown. Yield: one 9-inch pie.
Bonita Loewe,
Carmine, Texas.

BUTTERMILK PIE

1⅓ cups sugar
3 tablespoons all-purpose flour
2 eggs, beaten
½ cup butter or margarine, melted
1 cup buttermilk
2 teaspoons vanilla extract
1 teaspoon lemon extract
1 unbaked 9-inch pastry shell

Combine sugar and flour, mixing well; add eggs, butter, and buttermilk, beating well. Stir in flavorings. Pour into pastry shell. Bake at 400° for 10 minutes. Reduce heat, and bake at 325° for 30 to 35 minutes. Yield: one 9-inch pie.
Varniece Warren,
Hermitage, Arkansas.

HEAVENLY PIE

4 eggs, separated
¼ teaspoon cream of tartar
1½ cups sugar, divided
1 tablespoon grated lemon rind
3 tablespoons lemon juice
⅛ teaspoon salt
1 cup whipping cream, whipped
Additional whipped cream

Beat egg whites (at room temperature) until frothy; add cream of tartar, beating slightly. Gradually add 1 cup sugar, beating well after each addition; continue beating mixture until stiff and glossy. Do not underbeat.

Spoon meringue into a well-greased 9-inch pieplate. Use a spoon to shape meringue into a pie shell, swirling sides high. Bake at 275° for 50 minutes. Cool.

Beat egg yolks until thick and lemon colored. Gradually add remaining ½ cup sugar, lemon rind, lemon juice, and salt. Cook in top of a double boiler, stirring constantly, until smooth and thickened. Cool mixture.

Fold 1 cup whipped cream into lemon mixture; spoon into meringue shell, and spread evenly. Cover and refrigerate at least 12 hours. Top with additional whipped cream. Yield: one 9-inch pie.
Mrs. Warren D. Davis,
Yulee, Florida.

TEXAS PECAN PIE

⅓ cup butter or margarine, melted
1 cup sugar
1 cup light corn syrup
½ teaspoon salt
2 teaspoons vanilla extract
4 eggs
1 cup coarsely chopped pecans
1 unbaked 9-inch pastry shell

Combine butter, sugar, corn syrup, salt, and vanilla in a medium mixing bowl; beat well. Add eggs, and beat well. Stir in pecans. Pour into pastry shell. Bake at 375° for 45 to 50 minutes. Yield: one 9-inch pie. *Flora Bowie,*
Splendora, Texas.

Churn Your Own Pralines And Cream

When you try Susan Temple's Pralines and Cream Ice Cream, you'll find it hard to believe it didn't come from the ice cream parlor. Toasted pecans are lightly coated with caramelized sugar to give it flavor and crunch.

PRALINES AND CREAM ICE CREAM

2 to 2½ cups chopped pecans
2 tablespoons butter or margarine
6 eggs
1 (14-ounce) can sweetened condensed milk
1 (13-ounce) can evaporated milk
1 tablespoon vanilla extract
1 pint whipping cream
2 cups sugar, divided
1 cup evaporated milk
2 cups milk

Sauté chopped pecans in butter, stirring constantly, about 5 minutes or until toasted. Set aside to cool.

Beat eggs in a large bowl at medium speed of electric mixer until frothy. Add next 4 ingredients; mix well.

Combine 1 cup sugar and 1 cup evaporated milk in a saucepan. Cook over low heat, stirring constantly, until the mixture begins to bubble; remove pan from heat.

Place remaining 1 cup sugar in a small saucepan; cook over medium heat, stirring constantly, until sugar dissolves and forms a smooth liquid. Stir in pecans. (Mixture may form lumps.)

Stir pecan mixture into sugar and milk mixture; break apart pecan lumps. Stir into egg mixture.

Pour into freezer can of a 1-gallon hand-turned or electric freezer. Add enough milk to fill can three-fourths full. Freeze according to manufacturer's instructions using one part rock salt to six parts ice. Let ice cream ripen at least 1 hour. Yield: about 1 gallon.
Susan Temple,
Longview, Texas.

A New Peach Ice Cream

After a year of experimenting, Jenny Heinzmann of Lothian, Maryland, perfected this unusual recipe for scrumptious Peach Ice Cream.

PEACH ICE CREAM

1¼ cups sugar
1½ tablespoons all-purpose flour
1½ tablespoons cornstarch
¼ teaspoon salt
3 eggs, beaten
2 cups milk
2 cups sliced fresh peaches
⅓ cup sugar
1 (3-ounce) package peach-flavored gelatin
¾ cup boiling water
3 pints frozen non-dairy coffee creamer, thawed
¼ cup sugar
½ cup commercial sour cream

Combine first 5 ingredients in a large saucepan, mixing well. Stir in milk. Cook over medium heat, stirring constantly, until smooth and thickened. Remove from heat; chill 2 to 3 hours.

Place peaches in a saucepan; cook over medium heat until bubbly, stirring constantly. Stir in ⅓ cup sugar. Place in container of electric blender; blend until smooth. Set aside.

Dissolve gelatin in boiling water, and let cool.

Combine coffee creamer and ¼ cup sugar in a large bowl; stir well. Gradually stir in egg mixture. Add pureed peaches, gelatin mixture, and sour cream; beat with a wire whisk until smooth. Pour into freezer can of a 1-gallon freezer. Freeze according to manufacturer's instructions. Let ripen 2 hours before serving. Yield: about 1 gallon.
Jenny Heinzmann,
Lothian, Maryland.

Bake Bread In Rounds

You can serve these Individual Bread Rounds in a variety of ways. Try cutting pockets into them and stuffing with a tasty filling. Or split the rounds lengthwise and use as sandwich buns. For dinner, cut each round into four wedges and serve hot with butter.

INDIVIDUAL BREAD ROUNDS

2 cups warm water (105° to 115°), divided
2 teaspoons sugar
1 package dry yeast
About 6½ cups all-purpose flour, divided
1½ teaspoons salt
3 tablespoons vegetable oil

Combine ¼ cup warm water, sugar, and yeast; stir until yeast dissolves.

Combine 4½ cups flour and salt; add oil, yeast mixture, and remaining 1¾ cups water, stirring until smooth. Add enough of remaining flour to form a moderately stiff dough, stirring well.

Turn dough out onto a lightly floured surface, and knead 8 to 10 minutes until smooth and elastic. Place in a greased bowl, turning to grease top. Cover and let rise in a warm place (85°), free from drafts, 1 hour or until doubled in bulk.

Divide dough into 12 equal portions; shape each portion into a smooth ball. Pat each ball into a 5-inch circle. Place circles on lightly greased baking sheets.

Let rise, uncovered, in a warm place, free from drafts, 1 hour or until doubled in bulk. Bake at 500° for 4 to 6 minutes or until lightly browned. Yield: 1 dozen.
Debra Rich,
Vancouver, Washington.

Make Pork The Main Attraction

Whether you're planning simple family meals or cooking for company, pork provides a multitude of ways to brighten everyday menus.

PORK CHALUPAS

1 (1-pound) package dried pinto beans
1 (3-pound) pork loin roast
1 (4-ounce) can green chiles, undrained
2 tablespoons cumin seeds
1 tablespoon salt
2 cloves garlic, chopped
1 teaspoon dried whole oregano
Corn chips
Shredded Cheddar cheese
Shredded lettuce
Chopped onion
Diced tomato
1 (7½-ounce) jar jalapeño relish

Sort beans, and wash thoroughly. Combine beans, roast, chiles, cumin seeds, salt, garlic, and oregano in a large Dutch oven. Add enough water to cover. Cover and simmer 6 hours, stirring occasionally, and adding water as needed.

Remove roast from Dutch oven; cut meat from bone, and break meat apart. Return meat to Dutch oven. Cook, uncovered, 1 to 1½ hours or until mixture is thick.

To serve, place corn chips on individual serving plates. Top each with meat mixture, cheese, lettuce, onion, and tomato. Serve with jalapeño relish. Yield: 8 to 10 servings. *Mrs. Gary Denson, Lineville, Alabama.*

SWEET-AND-SOUR PORK CHOPS

4 lean pork chops
Salt
All-purpose flour
2 tablespoons vegetable oil
1 (13¼-ounce) can pineapple chunks, drained
1 small green pepper, cut into rings
1 cup chicken broth
1 cup sugar
1 cup vinegar
⅓ cup catsup
2 tablespoons cornstarch
¼ cup water
Hot cooked rice

Sprinkle chops with salt; dredge in flour. Brown chops in hot oil on both sides. Place chops in a shallow 10-inch square casserole; top with pineapple and green pepper rings.

Combine next 4 ingredients in a small saucepan; bring to a boil. Reduce heat to medium. Combine cornstarch and water; stir well. Add cornstarch mixture to chicken broth mixture; stir constantly until thickened and bubbly. Pour chicken broth mixture over chops. Cover and bake at 325° for 1 hour or until done. Serve over rice. Yield: 4 servings. *Zelda Dawson, Altus, Arkansas.*

SAUSAGE SPAGHETTI

1 pound bulk pork sausage
1 cup chopped onion
½ cup chopped green pepper
½ teaspoon salt
½ to 1 teaspoon pepper
¼ teaspoon garlic powder
⅛ teaspoon chili powder
⅛ teaspoon ground thyme
1½ cups tomato juice
1 cup tomato sauce
1 teaspoon Worcestershire sauce
2 teaspoons vinegar
Dash of red pepper
1 (8-ounce) package spaghetti
½ cup grated Parmesan cheese

Crumble sausage in a Dutch oven; cook over medium heat until browned, stirring frequently. Add next 7 ingredients; cook 5 minutes, stirring frequently. Drain off pan drippings. Stir in the next 5 ingredients; cover and simmer 10 minutes.

Cook spaghetti according to package directions; drain. Add spaghetti to meat sauce, mixing well. Remove to platter, and sprinkle with Parmesan cheese. Yield: 6 to 8 servings. *Bonnie S. Baumgardner, Sylva, North Carolina.*

TANGY BARBECUED RIBS

¼ cup chopped onion
2 tablespoons vegetable oil
1 cup chili sauce
½ cup tomato juice
¼ cup lemon juice
¼ cup firmly packed brown sugar
2 tablespoons Worcestershire sauce
6 drops of hot sauce
3 pounds country-style pork ribs or backbones
Salt and pepper

Sauté onion in oil in a small saucepan until tender. Add next 6 ingredients; simmer 20 minutes.

Cut ribs into serving-size pieces; season with salt and pepper.

Place ribs on grill, 5 inches from heat, over slow coals. Grill 45 minutes to 1 hour or until desired degree of doneness, turning frequently. Brush ribs with sauce during last 20 minutes of cooking.

Place ribs on platter; spoon remaining sauce over ribs. Yield: 4 servings. *Mrs. S. R. Griffith, Memphis, Tennessee.*

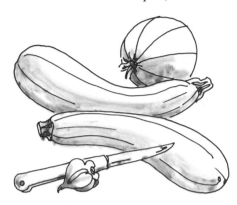

A New Way With Zucchini

Other parts of the country are not so lucky, but in the South you'll find fresh zucchini in the marketplace year-round. This has led many Southern cooks to develop new recipes for this versatile vegetable.

ZUCCHINI SPAGHETTI

1 pound ground beef
1 small onion, chopped
½ cup chopped green pepper
1 clove garlic, minced
2 cups chopped zucchini
1 (15-ounce) can tomato sauce
½ cup water
1 tablespoon minced fresh oregano or
    1 teaspoon dried whole oregano
½ teaspoon dried Italian seasoning
Salt and pepper to taste
Hot cooked spaghetti
Grated Parmesan cheese (optional)

Cook ground beef, onion, green pepper, and garlic in a large skillet until meat is browned. Add zucchini and cook, stirring constantly, 2 minutes; drain well. Add next 4 ingredients; stir in salt and pepper to taste. Reduce heat and simmer, stirring often, 5 to 10 minutes or until desired thickness.

Serve sauce over spaghetti, and sprinkle with cheese, if desired. Yield: 4 servings. *Kay Crocker, Spearman, Texas.*

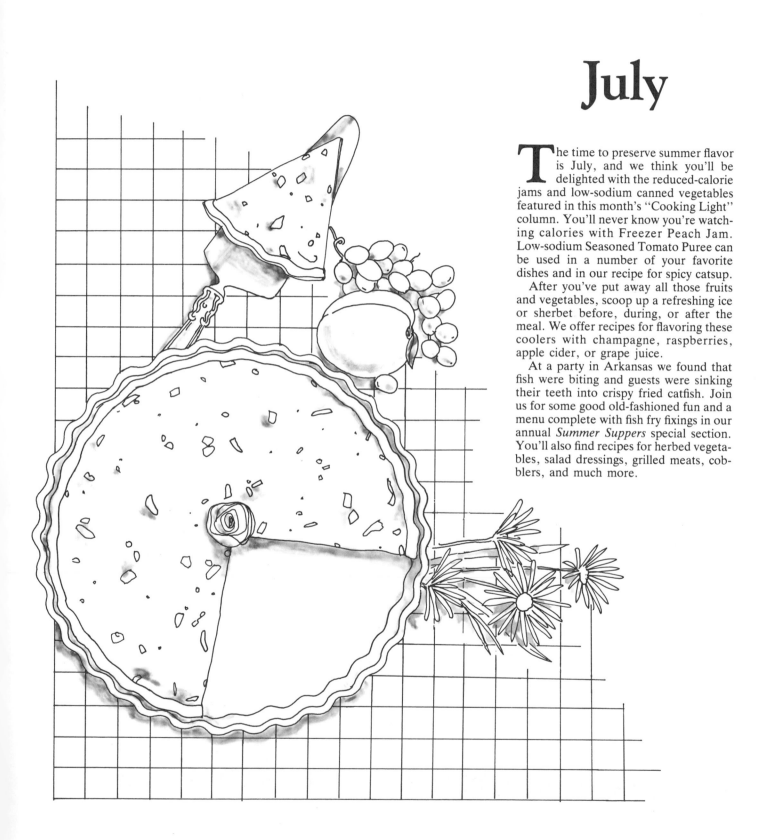

July

The time to preserve summer flavor is July, and we think you'll be delighted with the reduced-calorie jams and low-sodium canned vegetables featured in this month's "Cooking Light" column. You'll never know you're watching calories with Freezer Peach Jam. Low-sodium Seasoned Tomato Puree can be used in a number of your favorite dishes and in our recipe for spicy catsup.

After you've put away all those fruits and vegetables, scoop up a refreshing ice or sherbet before, during, or after the meal. We offer recipes for flavoring these coolers with champagne, raspberries, apple cider, or grape juice.

At a party in Arkansas we found that fish were biting and guests were sinking their teeth into crispy fried catfish. Join us for some good old-fashioned fun and a menu complete with fish fry fixings in our annual *Summer Suppers* special section. You'll also find recipes for herbed vegetables, salad dressings, grilled meats, cobblers, and much more.

Appetizing Ices And Sherbets

Summer is the right time to spoon into an ice or sherbet. These cold, tangy treats are a delicious way to cool off or to end a fine meal. But culinary experts will tell you they aren't just for dessert. When served as an appetizer or midway through dinner, a refreshing ice or sherbet cleanses the palate so the food that follows will taste its best.

Ices are tart, containing fruit juice, water, and sugar. Some have egg whites, which lend a fluffy texture.

Sherbets (or sorbets, as they're called in France) are also tart, yet unlike ices, they may contain milk or egg yolk. Sherbets are sweeter than ice cream, yet not as rich.

Although most of our sherbets and ices are frozen in the freezer, Raspberry Sherbet is churned in the ice cream freezer. To guarantee a firm consistency, use 3 parts ice to 1 part rock salt and let the sherbet ripen 1½ to 2 hours after churning. The mixture may appear to curdle when adding milk, but don't worry—the frozen sherbet will be smooth, creamy, and delicious.

AVOCADO SHERBET

2 ripe avocados, peeled, seeded, and
  coarsely chopped
2 to 3 tablespoons lemon juice
½ cup sugar
1½ cups orange juice
¼ cup water
1 teaspoon unflavored gelatin
1½ tablespoons cold water
2 egg whites
2 tablespoons sugar

Place avocado in container of electric blender and process until smooth. Combine 1 cup avocado puree and lemon juice; mix well and set mixture aside. Reserve remaining avocado puree for another use.

Combine ½ cup sugar, orange juice, and ¼ cup water in a medium saucepan; place over medium heat, and bring to a boil. Reduce heat and simmer, uncovered, 5 minutes, stirring occasionally. Remove from heat.

Soften gelatin in 1½ tablespoons cold water; add to orange juice mixture, stirring until gelatin dissolves. Let cool. Stir in avocado mixture; pour into container of electric blender, and process until smooth. Pour mixture into freezer trays; freeze until almost firm.

Beat egg whites (at room temperature) until foamy. Gradually add 2 tablespoons sugar, beating until stiff peaks form.

Spoon avocado mixture into a medium mixing bowl; beat with an electric mixer until smooth. Fold in beaten egg whites. Spoon into freezer trays; freeze until firm, stirring several times during freezing process. Yield: 1 quart.

Loy Witherspoon,
Charlotte, North Carolina.

BANANA-ORANGE SHERBET

1 egg, separated
½ cup sugar
½ cup orange juice
3 tablespoons lemon juice
1 medium banana, mashed
1 cup water

Combine egg yolk and sugar; beat well at medium speed of electric mixer. Add fruit juice, banana, and water, mixing well. Beat egg white (at room temperature) until stiff peaks form; stir into fruit mixture.

Pour mixture into a freezer tray; freeze until firm, stirring several times during freezing process. Yield: about 3 cups. *Mrs. Walter R. Robertson,*
Virgilina, Virginia.

STRAWBERRY-CHAMPAGNE SORBET

1 (10-ounce) package frozen strawberries,
  thawed
1 cup whipping cream
½ cup sugar
1½ cups champagne
2 egg whites
¼ teaspoon cream of tartar
¼ cup sugar

Mash strawberries; set aside.

Combine whipping cream and ½ cup sugar in a medium saucepan; cook over low heat, stirring constantly, until sugar dissolves. Stir in strawberries and champagne. Place mixture in a 13- x 9- x 2-inch pan; freeze until almost firm.

Beat egg whites (at room temperature) and cream of tartar until foamy.

Gradually add ¼ cup sugar, 1 tablespoon at a time, beating until stiff peaks form; fold into frozen mixture. Freeze. Yield: 1 quart. *Lenore Picard,*
Birmingham, Alabama.

RASPBERRY SHERBET

2 (10-ounce) packages frozen raspberries,
  thawed
1 (3-ounce) package raspberry-flavored
  gelatin
¼ cup sugar
2 cups boiling water
3 cups milk

Press raspberries through a sieve or food mill; set raspberry puree aside, and discard seeds.

Dissolve gelatin and sugar in boiling water. Add raspberries and milk, stirring well. (Mixture will appear curdled.)

Pour mixture into freezer can of a 1-gallon hand-turned or electric freezer. Freeze according to the manufacturer's instructions. Let ripen 1½ to 2 hours before serving. Yield: about 7 cups.

GRAPE ICE

3½ cups water
¾ cup sugar
1 tablespoon lemon juice
1 (12-ounce) can frozen grape juice
  concentrate, undiluted

Combine water and sugar in a large saucepan; cook over medium heat, stirring constantly, until sugar dissolves. Add remaining ingredients, stirring until grape juice melts.

Pour mixture into freezer trays. Freeze until firm; stir several times during freezing process. Yield: 5½ cups.

CIDER ICE

2 cups apple cider
½ cup sugar
½ cup orange juice
¼ cup lemon juice

Combine cider and sugar in a saucepan; bring to a boil. Reduce heat and simmer 5 minutes; cool. Stir in fruit juice. Pour mixture into a freezer tray, and freeze until firm.

Spoon frozen mixture into a mixing bowl; beat with an electric mixer until fluffy. Return to freezer tray; freeze until firm. Yield: about 3 cups.

Margaret L. Hunter,
Princeton, Kentucky.

WINE ICE

1 cup water
1 cup sugar
2 teaspoons grated lemon rind
½ cup lemon juice
1 (25-ounce) bottle rosé

Combine water and sugar in a small saucepan; bring to a boil, stirring constantly. Reduce heat and simmer 5 minutes, stirring occasionally; cool.

Combine sugar syrup and remaining ingredients; pour into freezer trays. Freeze until almost firm. Spoon mixture into a bowl, and beat with an electric mixer until slushy. Return to freezer trays; freeze until firm. Yield: 4½ cups.

Gail Thompson,
Brundidge, Alabama.

Summer Calls For Chilled Pasta

The days are gone when spaghetti was served only under a thick blanket of sauce. Our readers are quickly discovering how delightful chilled pasta can be for light summer meals. Combined with such Southern staples as seafood and garden-fresh vegetables, chilled pastas make delightful main dishes, side dishes, and even appetizers if you reduce the serving size.

It's fun to experiment with different pastas since commercial pasta makers have stretched the famous dough into hundreds of shapes and sizes. You're probably already familiar with egg noodles and elbow macaroni, but how about acini di pepe and margheritina?

Our recipes call for an assortment of pastas, though the types are generally interchangeable in these and other recipes. When substituting one type of pasta for another, it's a good idea to choose a size similar to the original.

For whatever type of pasta you choose, the cooking time will vary with the size and thickness of the pasta. Check package directions for specifics. Just be careful not to overcook it; pasta is done when it is tender but still firm to the bite.

Pasta that is to be served hot is generally not rinsed after cooking, but cold pasta has the tendency to stick together if not rinsed. Our test kitchen home economists have had good luck rinsing the pasta with cold water before proceeding with each recipe.

PASTA-AND-SHRIMP SALAD

3 cups water
1 pound unpeeled fresh shrimp
⅓ (16-ounce) package margheritina
½ cup diced celery
½ cup sliced ripe olives
½ cup sliced fresh mushrooms
½ cup sliced water chestnuts
¾ cup mayonnaise or salad dressing
2 tablespoons sugar (optional)
1 tablespoon vinegar
½ teaspoon salt
⅛ teaspoon pepper

Bring water to a boil; add shrimp, and return to a boil. Reduce heat and simmer 3 to 5 minutes. Drain well; rinse with cold water. Chill. Peel and devein shrimp.

Cook margheritina according to package directions; drain. Rinse with cold water; drain.

Combine shrimp, pasta, and next 4 ingredients. Combine mayonnaise, sugar, if desired, vinegar, salt, and pepper; pour over pasta mixture, and toss until coated. Cover salad and chill. Yield: 4 to 6 servings. *Betty J. Moore, Belton, Texas.*

PASTA WITH VEGETABLE SAUCE

3 cloves garlic, minced
⅓ cup pine nuts or sliced almonds
3 tablespoons olive oil
1½ cups sliced broccoli flowerets
1½ cups fresh or frozen snow peas
1 cup sliced zucchini
1 cup frozen English peas
10 large mushrooms, sliced
6 fresh or frozen asparagus spears, cut into 1-inch pieces
¼ cup chopped fresh parsley
2 teaspoons dried whole basil
½ teaspoon salt
¼ teaspoon pepper
12 cherry tomatoes, halved
1 (12-ounce) package spaghetti
⅓ cup butter or margarine
1 cup whipping cream
½ cup grated Parmesan cheese

Sauté garlic and pine nuts in oil in a large Dutch oven, stirring frequently, 2 to 3 minutes or until pine nuts are lightly browned. Add next 10 ingredients; cook, stirring occasionally, 5 minutes or until vegetables are crisp-tender. Stir in tomatoes. Chill vegetable mixture at least 1 hour.

Cook spaghetti according to package directions; drain. Rinse with cold water, and drain.

Melt butter over low heat in a large saucepan; stir in whipping cream and cheese. Cook, stirring constantly, until cheese melts. Add spaghetti; toss gently. Cover and chill spaghetti mixture at least 1 hour. To serve, spoon vegetable mixture over spaghetti. Yield: 6 servings.

Note: Pasta With Vegetable Sauce may be served hot.

Mrs. Walter Sebaste,
Charlotte, North Carolina.

ACINI DI PEPE SALAD

½ (14.5-ounce) package acini di pepe macaroni
1 egg yolk, beaten
½ cup sugar
1 tablespoon all-purpose flour
¾ cup plus 2 tablespoons pineapple juice
1 (8-ounce) carton frozen whipped topping, thawed
2 cups miniature marshmallows
1 (8-ounce) can crushed pineapple, drained
1 (8-ounce) can pineapple tidbits, drained
2 (11-ounce) cans mandarin oranges, drained

Cook macaroni according to package directions; drain. Rinse with cold water; drain. Place macaroni in a large bowl.

Combine next 4 ingredients in a medium saucepan; cook over medium heat, stirring constantly, until thickened. Cool. Pour sauce over macaroni. Stir in remaining ingredients, and chill thoroughly. Yield: 10 to 12 servings.

Barbara B. Seidel,
Ocean Springs, Mississippi.

CORKSCREW MACARONI TOSS

1 cup uncooked corkscrew macaroni
2 small carrots, cut into 2-inch julienne strips
2 green onions, chopped
1 (2-ounce) jar diced pimiento, drained
¾ cup sliced celery
¼ cup frozen English peas, thawed
2 tablespoons chopped fresh parsley
10 cherry tomatoes, halved
¼ cup commercial Italian salad dressing
2 tablespoons mayonnaise
⅛ teaspoon pepper
Lettuce leaves

Cook macaroni according to package directions, omitting salt; drain. Rinse with cold water; drain.

Combine pasta and remaining ingredients except lettuce, tossing well; chill at least 1 hour. Spoon into a lettuce-lined bowl. Yield: 4 servings.

FRESH SCALLOPS AND PASTA

1 large purple onion, thinly sliced
1 medium-size green pepper, cut into
    1-inch strips
1 medium-size red pepper, cut into
    1-inch strips
½ cup sliced carrots
1 pound fresh scallops
¾ cup olive oil
⅔ cup vinegar
½ cup lemon juice
½ teaspoon dry mustard
¼ teaspoon salt
⅛ teaspoon freshly ground pepper
Pinch of red pepper
1 clove garlic, crushed
1 cup Chablis or other dry white
    wine
1 cup water
¼ cup chopped purple onion
1 tablespoon chopped fresh parsley
2 bay leaves
2 cups uncooked spinach egg noodles
2 cups uncooked egg noodles

Cut onion slices in half. Arrange onion, green and red pepper, and carrots in a steamer rack. Place rack over boiling water; cover and steam 4 to 6 minutes or until vegetables are crisp-tender. Place the vegetables and scallops in a shallow container.

Combine next 8 ingredients; stir well. Pour over scallop mixture. Cover and marinate 12 hours or overnight in refrigerator, turning scallops occasionally.

Remove scallops from marinade with a slotted spoon. Combine Chablis, water, chopped onion, parsley, and bay leaves in a medium saucepan; bring to a boil and add scallops. Cover, reduce heat, and simmer 3 to 5 minutes. Drain scallop mixture; discard bay leaves.

Cook egg noodles according to package directions; drain. Rinse with cold water; drain.

Drain vegetables from marinade. Combine vegetables, scallop mixture, and noodles; toss gently. Cover and chill thoroughly. Yield: 4 servings.

VERMICELLI WITH TOMATO SAUCE

3 tablespoons olive oil
½ cup chopped onion
3 cups peeled, chopped tomatoes
1 teaspoon paprika
½ teaspoon salt
½ teaspoon dried whole basil
½ teaspoon dried whole oregano
¼ teaspoon sugar
¼ teaspoon pepper
½ (8-ounce) package vermicelli

Heat oil in a large skillet; add onion, and sauté until tender. Add next 7 ingredients; cover and simmer 5 minutes, stirring occasionally.

Cook vermicelli according to package directions; drain. Rinse with cold water, and drain.

Arrange vermicelli on serving platter, and top with tomato sauce. Cover and chill. Yield: 4 servings. *Betty Holtum, Charlotte, North Carolina.*

SNAPPY PASTA

1 cup uncooked pasta dumplings
1 (6-ounce) package frozen Chinese
    pea pods, thawed and drained
3 tablespoons minced green pepper
3 tablespoons commercial sour cream
2 tablespoons cider vinegar
1 tablespoon minced onion
1 tablespoon diced pimiento
1 tablespoon vegetable oil
¾ teaspoon salt
¼ teaspoon dried whole basil
¼ teaspoon pepper
6 large tomatoes, chilled

Cook dumplings according to package directions; drain. Rinse with cold water, and drain.

Combine dumplings and next 10 ingredients. Cover and marinate for several hours in the refrigerator.

With stem ends up, cut each tomato into 6 wedges, cutting to, but not through, base of tomato. Spread wedges slightly apart; spoon pasta mixture into tomatoes. Yield: 6 servings.

Back To Basics With Ground Beef

Meatballs and hamburgers are two of the oldest uses for ground beef. The following recipes offer some tasty variations on these favorite standbys.

Beef Balls Heidelberg adds an international flavor—meatballs seasoned with caraway seeds are simmered with sauerkraut and potatoes. For a hamburger version we're sure you'll enjoy,

try broiling or grilling some juicy Party Burgers. The ground beef mixture is seasoned with Burgundy and spices, and it's full of mushrooms.

PARTY BURGERS

2 pounds ground beef
1 cup soft breadcrumbs
¾ cup Burgundy
1 (4-ounce) can mushroom stems and
    pieces, drained
2 teaspoons onion salt
1 teaspoon dry mustard
1 teaspoon Worcestershire sauce
¼ teaspoon garlic powder
¼ teaspoon pepper
8 hamburger buns (optional)

Combine first 9 ingredients, mixing well. Shape into 8 patties. Broil or grill 4 to 5 inches from heat 5 minutes on each side, or until desired degree of doneness. Serve in hamburger buns, if desired. Yield: 8 servings.

*Mrs. R. P. Vinroot,
Matthews, North Carolina.*

BEEF BALLS HEIDELBERG

1½ pounds ground beef
1½ teaspoons caraway seeds
1 tablespoon vinegar
1½ cups soft rye breadcrumbs
¼ cup chopped onion
⅓ cup milk
1 egg, beaten
1 teaspoon salt
1 tablespoon vegetable oil
1 (16-ounce) can whole potatoes, drained
    and cut into ¼-inch slices
1 (16-ounce) can sauerkraut, undrained

Combine first 8 ingredients, mixing well. Shape mixture into 1½-inch balls; brown in hot oil over medium heat in a large skillet.

Add potatoes and sauerkraut; cover, reduce heat, and simmer 10 minutes. Yield: about 6 servings.

*Norma Cowden,
Shawnee, Oklahoma.*

Right: Chilled pasta and vegetables are combined in refreshing summer side dishes: Pasta With Vegetable Sauce (page 163), Snappy Pasta (page 164), and Corkscrew Macaroni Toss (page 163).

Page 168: You'll enjoy the cool refreshment of these fruity ices and sherbets anytime. Raspberry Sherbet and Grape Ice may be served before, during, or after dinner (recipes on page 162).

Far left: *While planning your menus for summertime entertaining, plan on a colorful fruit and vegetable centerpiece. Place a bouquet of radishes and green onions in a carved melon vase; fresh chives provide graceful leaves (instructions on page 171).*

Far left inset: *A tray of vegetables and dip can be an eye-catching centerpiece when there's a plan to the arrangement (instructions on page 171).*

Left: *Serve spicy, chilled Shrimp Remoulade (page 173) at your warm-weather parties for a refreshing appetizer or side dish.*

Below left: *Parsley, chives, and thyme highlight the flavor of marinated tomato wedges in Herbed Tomatoes (page 173).*

Below: *Each bite of Peach Cobbler (page 175) promises a taste of spicy peaches and crisp pastry.*

summer Suppers.

Bring The Party Outside

It's time to sit under a shade tree sipping a cool, icy beverage or to ramble through the berry patch searching for the juiciest berries. Or maybe you'd rather sear a tender steak over a fire or find a new recipe for vegetables and herbs at the peak of flavor.

Whatever your preference, this year's "Summer Suppers" special section offers a range of recipes and features to suit you. You'll find some edible centerpieces for fancy party decor, along with recipes for fruit cobblers, grilled meat, and beverage coolers.

Then come along with us to Arkansas for some real old-fashioned summer fun. There's a fish fry in El Dorado you won't want to miss.

It's a Fish Fry— Arkansas Style

No party typifies summer fun like a fish fry. At least that's what Bob and Betty Linda Nolan and their friends in El Dorado think. When the Nolans are ready to entertain, Bob grabs a fishing pole and a friend, and reels in enough fish to feed a crowd.

Bob and a friend spend that afternoon at the pond catching and cleaning catfish, bass, and bream. "I love to fish," says Bob, "and have it down to a pretty good art now. We always catch our fish, and the kids like to help, too."

Bob is known among his guests for his potatoes, as well. He uses a device that cuts the potatoes into long, thin spirals. Then he coats the curls in cornmeal and fries them to a crispy golden brown.

While Bob specializes in the fish and potato frying, Betty Linda adds her personal touch to recipes like Creamy Coleslaw, Marinated Salad, tangy Lemon Ice Cream, and an El Dorado favorite, Squash Puppies.

According to Bob and Betty Linda, it takes more than a platter of crispy fried catfish, crunchy coleslaw, or a churn of homemade ice cream for a successful fish fry. A healthy helping of fun, friends, and family is a must to create the perfect party—Arkansas style.

Fresh Vegetables With Blue Cheese Dip
Tomato-Orange Juice Cocktail
Fried Catfish   Special Potatoes
Squash Puppies
Cheesy Hominy Casserole
Marinated Salad   Creamy Coleslaw
Tea Cookies
Chocolate Chip Squares
Lemon Ice Cream
Iced Mint Tea

BLUE CHEESE DIP

⅔ cup cottage cheese
½ cup plain yogurt
1 (4-ounce) package blue cheese, crumbled
⅛ teaspoon seasoning salt
Dash of red pepper
Paprika

Combine first 5 ingredients in container of electric blender; process until smooth. Sprinkle with paprika. Serve with fresh vegetables. Yield: 1½ cups.

TOMATO-ORANGE JUICE COCKTAIL

1 (46-ounce) can tomato juice
1 (6-ounce) can frozen orange juice concentrate, thawed and undiluted
¾ cup vodka
Orange slice halves

Combine first 2 ingredients; stir well. Chill. Add vodka; serve over ice. Garnish with orange slices. Yield: 7½ cups.

FRIED CATFISH

12 catfish fillets, halved
1 cup prepared mustard, divided
1¼ cups white cornmeal
½ teaspoon salt
1 to 1½ teaspoons ground red pepper
½ teaspoon pepper
Vegetable oil
Fresh parsley sprigs
Lemon wedges
Purple onion rings

Brush fillets lightly with half the mustard. Place cornmeal, salt, and pepper in a plastic bag; drop in catfish one at a time, and shake until completely coated. Brush fillets lightly with remaining mustard; return them to bag and shake again.

Fry fillets in deep hot oil (330°) until they float to the top and are golden brown; drain well. Transfer to serving platter; garnish with parsley, lemon wedges, and onion rings. Serve hot. Yield: 12 servings.

SPECIAL POTATOES

10 to 12 medium-size red potatoes, peeled
½ cup white cornmeal
Vegetable oil
Salt

Cut potatoes into curlicued ringlets using special potato-cutting machine, or cut potatoes into French fries ⅜ inch thick. Cover potatoes with cold water.

Drain potatoes well in a large colander just before frying. Sprinkle with cornmeal, tossing to coat well.

Fry potatoes in deep hot oil (330°), a small amount at a time, 2 minutes or until golden. (Stir well while frying to prevent potatoes from becoming soggy.) Drain well on paper towels. Sprinkle with salt. Yield: 12 servings.

SQUASH PUPPIES

5 medium-size yellow squash
1 egg, beaten
½ cup buttermilk
1 medium onion, chopped
¾ cup self-rising cornmeal
¼ cup all-purpose flour
Vegetable oil

Trim ends off squash; slice and place in a Dutch oven. Cover squash with water; cook over medium heat 20 minutes or until tender. Drain squash well; mash and drain again.

Combine squash and next 5 ingredients. Drop mixture by scant tablespoonfuls into hot oil (350°); fry 5 minutes. Yield: about 2½ dozen.

CHEESY HOMINY CASSEROLE

4 (15½-ounce) cans hominy, drained
2 (3-ounce) cans chopped green chiles, drained
3 (8-ounce) cartons commercial sour cream
2 cups (8 ounces) shredded Monterey Jack cheese
¼ cup plus 2 tablespoons minced onion
1 to 2 jalapeño peppers, seeded and finely chopped
¼ cup fine, dry breadcrumbs
¼ cup butter or margarine
Whole green chiles, sliced crosswise
Pimiento strips

Combine first 6 ingredients in a large mixing bowl; spoon into a lightly greased 13- x 9- x 2-inch baking dish. Sprinkle with breadcrumbs; dot with butter. Bake, uncovered, at 350° for 30 minutes. Garnish with green chiles and pimiento strips. Yield: 12 servings.

MARINATED SALAD

6 to 8 medium tomatoes, sliced
3 medium cucumbers, sliced
2 medium onions, sliced
¼ cup prepared mustard
¼ cup cider vinegar
½ cup vegetable oil
2 teaspoons salt
2 teaspoons sugar
½ teaspoon pepper
1 clove garlic, crushed
Fresh parsley sprigs

Layer about one-fourth of each vegetable in a large deep refrigerator container. Combine mustard, vinegar, oil, salt, sugar, pepper, and garlic; stir well. Pour about one-fourth of marinade over vegetables; repeat layers 3 times with remaining vegetables and marinade.

Cover salad, and chill 3 to 4 hours; transfer to a large serving bowl. Garnish with parsley sprigs. Serve with slotted spoon. Yield: 12 servings.

CREAMY COLESLAW

1 (8-ounce) carton commercial sour cream
¼ cup mayonnaise
2 teaspoons celery seeds
2 teaspoons lemon juice
2 teaspoons sugar
½ to 1 teaspoon salt
½ teaspoon white pepper
8 cups shredded cabbage
Cabbage leaves
Red and green pepper rings

Combine first 7 ingredients; mix well. Just before serving, spoon mixture over cabbage; toss lightly. Serve in a bowl lined with cabbage leaves; garnish with red and green pepper rings. Yield: 12 servings.

TEA COOKIES

½ cup butter or margarine, softened
¼ cup vegetable oil
1½ cups powdered sugar
1 egg
2 cups all-purpose flour
1 teaspoon baking soda
1 teaspoon cream of tartar
1 teaspoon vanilla extract
Green sugar sprinkles

Combine first 4 ingredients, mixing well. Set aside.

Combine flour, soda, and cream of tartar; add to butter mixture, stirring until well blended. Stir in vanilla. Chill dough at least 1 hour.

Shape dough into 1-inch balls; place about 2 inches apart on ungreased cookie sheets. Bake at 350° for 10 to 12 minutes. Sprinkle cookies with sugar sprinkles immediately after baking. Yield: about 2½ dozen.

CHOCOLATE CHIP SQUARES

¾ cup butter or margarine, softened
1 cup firmly packed brown sugar
2 cups all-purpose flour
1 teaspoon vanilla extract
1 (6-ounce) package chocolate morsels
¾ cup chopped pecans

Cream butter; gradually add sugar, beating well. Stir in flour and vanilla.

Press mixture evenly into an ungreased 13- x 9- x 2-inch baking pan. Sprinkle with chocolate morsels and pecans. Bake at 350° for 15 to 20 minutes. Cool; cut into squares. Yield: about 4 dozen.

LEMON ICE CREAM

1½ cups lemon juice
4 cups sugar
1 tablespoon grated lemon rind
1 cup whipping cream
6 cups milk
Lemon twists

Combine lemon juice and sugar; stir well. Let stand 30 minutes.

Add lemon rind, whipping cream, and milk; mix well. Pour mixture into freezer can of a 1-gallon hand-turned or electric freezer. Freeze according to manufacturer's instructions. Let ripen 1½ to 2 hours; spoon into serving dishes. Garnish with lemon twists. Yield: about 1 gallon.

ICED MINT TEA

2 quart-size tea bags
1 cup fresh mint leaves
Juice of 2 lemons
1 cup sugar
1 quart boiling water
1 quart water
Lemon slices
Fresh mint sprigs

Combine first 4 ingredients. Pour boiling water over tea mixture; cover and let stand 5 minutes.

Remove tea bags and mint leaves; discard. Transfer tea to a 2-quart pitcher, and add 1 quart water and lemon slices. Serve over ice. Garnish with mint sprigs. Yield: 2 quarts.

Summer Blooms With Fruit And Vegetable Centerpieces

While planning your menus for summertime entertaining, give some thought to table arrangements, too. You'll want attractive centerpieces that are as bright and colorful as the season.

Fruit and Cheese Tray

Summer is noted for its gorgeous fresh fruit; combine your favorites with cheeses for a buffet centerpiece that guests can nibble on.

It's easier to assemble an attractive arrangement when you have a variety of colors, shapes, and sizes to work with. Place larger foods toward the back (or center) and smaller items toward the front. Fill in empty spaces with crackers and small fruit such as strawberries or sliced kiwi, and tuck in an exotic flower, if you like. Be sure to include a knife so your guests can serve themselves from the centerpiece.

Grapes Light Up the Party

For an especially dramatic arrangement, try a cluster of grapes and candles. Lay a rectangle of plastic foam or florist foam on a serving tray or cutting board, and arrange grapes in clusters to cover the foam; secure grapes with florist picks, if necessary. Then insert tall, slim candles into the foam.

Remember that the narrower the candle, the shorter the burning time. The ⅛-inch-wide candles will burn for about 30 minutes. Choose those ¼ inch wide or larger for longer burning times.

Dip and Dippers in a Basket

Vegetables and dip can be attractive enough for a centerpiece if you take a few extra minutes in their preparation and assembly. See page 166 for our colorful arrangement.

Scallop the edges of a green pepper with a sharp knife, and fill with dip. Place in the center of the arrangement.

Carefully cut and arrange groups of vegetables to radiate from the green pepper. Try using a fluted knife when slicing vegetables.

For a final touch, surround the green pepper with vegetable daisies. To make the daisies, slice a turnip ⅛ inch thick and cut into flower shapes using a canapé cutter. Cut an equal number of ⅛-inch slices from thin carrots. Assemble carrot circles on turnip flowers, and insert wooden picks up through the flowers and just into the circles.

A Blooming Melon

You'll get lots of compliments on a charming bouquet of radish and green onion flowers. See page 166 for our Blooming Melon. First cut an assortment of radish flowers as follows:

Make accordian-type flowers by cutting radishes into narrow crosswise slices, not quite cutting through bottom.

Shape radish mums by cutting narrow intersecting slices.

To make tulips, cut a small circle into the stem end of a radish; then scrape the pulp from the circle about ½ inch deep. Zigzag the standing rim of the radish into petals using a sharp knife. Slice a small red circle from another radish, and attach it in the center of the tulip using a wooden pick.

Make flat radish flowers by first cutting several strips down the length of a radish using a citrus zester, then slicing the radish into rounds. Attach a small radish square in the center of each sliced flower using a wooden pick.

To make green onion flowers, trim both ends of green onions, leaving just about 1 inch of the green stems and 2 inches of the white tops. Place the green onions on a cutting board, and carefully slice through the white part of each onion in several places.

Place green onion and radish flowers in ice water to "bloom." (Petals will open and curl.)

To make a melon vase, slice the top from a small watermelon or cantaloupe. Cut a small slice from the bottom to make vase sit level, if necessary. Using a sharp knife or a V-shaped cutter, wedge the top of the melon.

Make stems for your flowers by inserting narrow wooden skewers up through the stems of green onions, and secure flowers on the top of each stem.

Insert flowers into vase. Also insert a few sprays of fresh chives into vase, if desired, using florist picks.

Garden Salad Centerpiece

An arrangement of greens and vegetables can double as a centerpiece and garden salad. The salad is composed of a backdrop of leafy greens, with vegetables carefully arranged in the foreground. Special attention is given to the size, shape, and color of each.

To make the garden salad centerpiece, choose several types of leafy greens; cut off the core end of the heads and stand leaves upright in the back half of a bowl. Arrange attractively cut vegetables in front of the greens, and toss a few bright red radishes throughout the arrangement.

Stack plates on the side with dressing and croutons; then let guests build their own salads.

Blend A Frosty Beverage

When it's time to cool off, get out your blender and whirl up one of these refreshing beverages.

Since they contain ice or ice cream, these beverages are best if prepared just before serving. However, if you have any left over, place the blender container in the freezer for up to 45 minutes and whirl the mixture just before serving it again.

CRANBERRY SHAKE

2 cups cranberry juice cocktail, chilled
½ cup orange juice, chilled
1 pint vanilla ice cream

Combine all ingredients in container of electric blender; process until smooth. Serve immediately. Yield: 4½ cups.
Barbara C. Witt,
San Antonio, Texas.

AMARETTO BREEZE

1 quart vanilla ice cream
¼ cup brandy
¼ cup amaretto

Combine all ingredients in container of electric blender; process until smooth. Serve immediately. Yield: 4½ cups.
Mary Pappas,
Richmond, Virginia.

COCONUT-PINEAPPLE DRINK

2 bananas, peeled and quartered
1½ cups milk
1½ cups pineapple juice, chilled
1 (8.5-ounce) can cream of coconut, chilled
¼ cup banana liqueur
¼ cup light rum
Crushed ice

Combine first 6 ingredients in container of electric blender; process until smooth. Pour over crushed ice, and serve immediately. Yield: 6 cups.
Mrs. Harlan J. Stone,
Ocala, Florida.

FROSTY MARGARITAS

¼ cup plus 2 tablespoons tequila
3 tablespoons Triple Sec or other orange-flavored liqueur
2 tablespoons sweet-and-sour beverage mix
1 (6-ounce) can frozen limeade concentrate, thawed and undiluted
About 4 cups ice cubes

Combine first 4 ingredients in container of electric blender; process until smooth. Gradually add ice, processing until mixture reaches desired consistency. Serve immediately. Yield: 1 quart.
Bonnie Haley,
Palestine, Texas.

STRAWBERRY-ORANGE SLUSH

½ cup milk
1 tablespoon sugar
1 (10-ounce) package frozen strawberries, thawed
2 cups orange juice
About 2 cups ice cubes
Fresh strawberries (optional)
Orange wedges (optional)

Combine first 4 ingredients in container of an electric blender; process until smooth. Gradually add ice; process until mixture reaches desired consistency. Garnish each serving with a strawberry and orange wedge, if desired. Serve immediately. Yield: 5½ cups.
Jan Johnson,
Louisville, Kentucky.

ICY RUM COFFEE CREAM

⅓ cup water
¼ cup firmly packed brown sugar
2 tablespoons instant coffee granules
1½ cups vanilla ice cream
1 cup milk
½ cup dark rum
2 tablespoons Cointreau or other orange-flavored liqueur
4 ice cubes
Whipped cream (optional)
Chocolate curls (optional)

Combine water, sugar, and coffee in a small saucepan; cook over low heat, stirring constantly, until sugar dissolves. Cool completely.
Combine coffee mixture and next 5 ingredients in container of an electric blender; process 30 seconds or until smooth. Garnish with whipped cream and chocolate curls, if desired. Serve immediately. Yield: 3 cups.

Dress Up Vegetables With Herbs

Each summer more Southerners are discovering that vegetables and herbs are natural partners. Many gardeners are growing herbs alongside vegetables, then combining them in dishes that enhance the flavors of both. If you're not lucky enough to have your own garden, then turn to your spice rack and market produce bins.

Keep in mind that dried herbs always taste stronger than fresh. This means you should use about one-third of the dried leaves to replace the fresh. Be sure to add herbs with a light hand; you can always add more later.

BASIL BEANS AND TOMATOES

1 pound fresh green beans
2 tablespoons vegetable oil
⅓ cup sliced green onion
1 clove garlic, crushed
1½ tablespoons minced fresh basil or 1½ teaspoons dried whole basil
½ teaspoon salt
¼ teaspoon pepper
2 medium tomatoes, peeled and chopped

Wash beans; trim ends and remove strings. Cut beans into 1-inch pieces.
Heat oil in a medium skillet; add beans and remaining ingredients except tomatoes, stirring well. Cover and cook over medium heat 20 minutes, stirring occasionally. Stir in tomatoes; cover and cook 5 minutes. Serve immediately. Yield: 6 servings.
Ann Dunstan,
Elizabeth City, North Carolina.

VEGETABLE-HERB TRIO

½ pound fresh green beans, cut into 1½-inch pieces
½ cup chopped onion
2 tablespoons chopped fresh parsley
1 teaspoon salt
¾ teaspoon minced fresh thyme or ¼ teaspoon dried whole thyme
¾ teaspoon minced fresh sage or ¼ teaspoon rubbed sage
⅛ teaspoon pepper
½ cup water
2 cups sliced yellow squash
¼ cup water
3 large tomatoes, unpeeled and cut into wedges
2 tablespoons butter or margarine, softened

Combine first 7 ingredients and ½ cup water in a large skillet; bring to a boil. Cover, reduce heat, and simmer 10 minutes. Add squash and ¼ cup water; bring to a boil. Cover, reduce heat, and

simmer 10 minutes. Drain well. Add tomatoes and butter; cook, stirring often, until butter melts. Yield: 6 servings.
Sarah Bergey,
Quakertown, Pennsylvania.

TARRAGON CARROTS

¼ cup plus 2 tablespoons butter or
　margarine
6 large carrots, scraped and shredded
1½ teaspoons minced fresh tarragon or ½
　teaspoon dried whole tarragon
¼ teaspoon salt
Dash of coarsely ground black pepper

Melt butter in a large skillet; add carrots and cook, stirring constantly, 3 to 5 minutes or until thoroughly heated. Sprinkle with tarragon, salt, and pepper. Yield: 4 to 6 servings.
Sallie Chasteen,
Atlanta, Georgia.

STEAMED AND MINTED
GARDEN TOSS

8 new potatoes, scraped
8 baby carrots, scraped
1 (1-pound) bunch broccoli
4 small onions, peeled and quartered
4 small apples, peeled, cored, and
　quartered
¼ cup butter or margarine, melted
2 tablespoons chopped fresh mint
2 tablespoons lemon juice
1 tablespoon honey

Arrange potatoes and carrots in steaming rack. Place over boiling water; cover and steam the vegetables for 8 to 10 minutes.

Trim off large leaves of broccoli. Remove tough ends of lower stalks, and wash broccoli thoroughly. Make lengthwise slits in thick stalks. Arrange broccoli and onion in steaming rack over potatoes and carrots; cover and steam 10 minutes.

Arrange apples over broccoli in rack; cover and steam 5 minutes. Place vegetables in serving dish. Combine remaining ingredients, mixing well. Pour sauce over vegetables. Yield: 4 to 6 servings.
Jane C. Perkins,
DeQueen, Arkansas.

LEMON-HERB
STUFFED POTATOES

6 large baking potatoes
Vegetable oil
⅓ cup chopped onion
1 clove garlic, minced
1 tablespoon butter or margarine
½ cup milk
1 tablespoon minced fresh dillweed or 1
　teaspoon dried whole dillweed
1 teaspoon chopped fresh parsley
1 teaspoon grated lemon rind
⅛ teaspoon pepper
Paprika

Wash potatoes, and rub with oil. Bake at 400° for 1 hour or until done.

Sauté onion and garlic in a small skillet until onion is tender. Set aside.

Split tops of potatoes lengthwise; scoop out pulp, leaving skins intact. Mash pulp. Add sautéed onion mixture, milk, dillweed, parsley, lemon rind, and pepper; mix well. Spoon pulp mixture into potato skins. Sprinkle with paprika. Bake at 400° for 30 minutes. Yield: 6 servings.
Saralyn Bone Lundy,
Tallahassee, Florida.

DILLED ZUCCHINI AND CORN

¼ cup butter or margarine
4 cups sliced zucchini
1½ cups fresh corn cut from cob
½ cup chopped onion
⅓ cup chopped green pepper
½ teaspoon salt
1 tablespoon minced fresh dillweed or 1
　teaspoon dried whole dillweed

Melt butter in a large skillet; add vegetables and salt. Cover and cook over medium heat 10 to 12 minutes, stirring occasionally. Sprinkle with dillweed. Yield: 4 to 6 servings. *Pat Sanders,*
Austin, Texas.

HERBED TOMATOES

½ cup chopped fresh parsley
½ cup chopped fresh chives
⅔ cup vegetable oil
¼ cup vinegar
¼ teaspoon pepper
Pinch of dried whole thyme
6 tomatoes, unpeeled and quartered
Lettuce leaves

Combine first 6 ingredients; mix well. Place tomatoes in a shallow container; pour dressing over tomatoes. Cover and refrigerate overnight. Drain tomatoes, reserving dressing. Arrange tomatoes on lettuce-lined serving plates; spoon dressing over tomatoes. Yield: 12 servings.
Noel Todd McLaughlin,
Chapel Hill, North Carolina.

Serve A Cool,
Refreshing Snack

Summer parties call for cool snacks and appetizers—something you can make a day ahead and serve chilled.

SHRIMP REMOULADE

9 cups water
1 small onion
1 stalk celery
1 bay leaf
3 whole peppercorns
3 pounds unpeeled fresh shrimp
¾ cup vegetable oil
½ cup prepared mustard
⅓ cup vinegar
1 cup chopped celery
¼ cup chopped fresh parsley
1 hard-cooked egg, chopped
1 tablespoon chopped green pepper
2 teaspoons finely chopped onion
1 teaspoon salt
2 teaspoons paprika
¾ teaspoon hot sauce
Lettuce leaves
Lemon wedges

Combine first 5 ingredients in a large Dutch oven. Bring to a boil; add shrimp, and return to a boil. Reduce heat, and simmer 3 to 5 minutes. Drain well; cool completely. Peel and devein shrimp. Combine remaining ingredients; stir well. Add shrimp; cover and chill 8 hours. Remove bay leaf; serve in lettuce-lined bowls and garnish with lemon. Yield: 12 appetizer servings.
Mrs. W. D. Schmitt,
Montrose, Alabama.

TUNA SPREAD

1 (6½-ounce) can tuna, drained and flaked
1 (8-ounce) package cream cheese, softened
2 tablespoons mayonnaise
2 tablespoons chili sauce
4 green onions with tops, chopped
⅛ teaspoon white pepper

Combine all ingredients in container of electric blender; blend until smooth. Spoon into serving dish, and refrigerate at least 2 hours before serving. Serve with crackers. Yield: 2 cups.
Nancy Everett,
Cleveland, Tennessee.

PICKLED PARTY FRANKS

2 cups water
3 (5½-ounce) packages cocktail frankfurters
½ medium onion, thinly sliced
1 teaspoon salt
½ teaspoon peppercorns
10 whole cloves
1 cup vinegar
3 tablespoons sugar
4 small cloves garlic

Bring water to a boil; add next 5 ingredients. Cover, reduce heat, and simmer 10 minutes. Drain; place frankfurters in a 1-quart container.
Combine remaining ingredients; mix well, and pour over frankfurters. Cover and refrigerate several hours or overnight. Yield: 4 dozen appetizers.
Ann Elsie Schmetzer,
Madisonville, Kentucky.

DRUNK MUSHROOMS

2 medium onions, thinly sliced
¾ cup water
½ cup vinegar
¼ cup Burgundy or other dry red wine
1 teaspoon salt
½ teaspoon butter or margarine
½ teaspoon celery seeds
½ teaspoon mustard seeds
¼ teaspoon whole cloves
½ pound fresh mushrooms
¼ cup vegetable oil

Combine first 9 ingredients in a medium saucepan; bring to a boil, and

cook 5 minutes. Add mushrooms; reduce heat, and simmer 5 minutes.
Remove mushrooms with a slotted spoon, and place in a medium bowl. Strain liquid, discarding onions. Add oil to the reserved liquid; pour over mushrooms, tossing gently to coat. Cover and chill about 6 hours before serving. Yield: 4 appetizer servings.
Annie F. Stark,
La Marque, Texas.

COCKTAIL CHEESE BALL

2 (3-ounce) packages cream cheese, softened
1 (6-ounce) roll smoke-flavored process cheese food
1½ ounces blue cheese, crumbled
1 teaspoon Worcestershire sauce
1 tablespoon finely chopped onion
1 tablespoon chopped olives
2 tablespoons chopped fresh parsley
½ cup finely chopped walnuts

Combine first 2 ingredients; beat at medium speed of an electric mixer until smooth. Add blue cheese, and beat well. Stir in Worcestershire sauce, onion, and olives; mix well. Chill mixture at least 1 hour.
Combine parsley and walnuts; set aside. Shape chilled mixture into a ball, and roll in parsley mixture. Refrigerate several hours or overnight. Serve with crackers. Yield: 1 cheese ball.
Millie Ebel,
Louisville, Kentucky.

VEGETABLE SANDWICH SPREAD

¼ cup finely chopped celery
1 small onion, finely chopped
¾ cup grated carrot
¼ cup finely chopped green pepper
¼ cup grated unpeeled cucumber
1 (8-ounce) package cream cheese, softened
1 tablespoon lemon juice
¼ teaspoon white pepper

Drain vegetables well. Beat cream cheese and lemon juice until smooth; stir in vegetables and pepper. Spread on rye or pumpernickel bread. Yield: about 2½ cups. *Mrs. Joe DeJournette,*
Thurmond, North Carolina.

CREAMY GUACAMOLE

2 medium-size ripe avocados
2 tablespoons lemon juice
2 teaspoons finely chopped onion
1 teaspoon olive oil
½ teaspoon salt
3 drops of hot sauce
Grated Cheddar cheese
Chopped green onion
Chopped tomatoes

Peel and slice avocados. Combine avocados with next 5 ingredients in the container of electric blender; process mixture until almost smooth.
Place in serving dish; sprinkle with cheese, onion, and tomatoes. Serve with taco chips. Yield: about 2⅔ cups.
Karyl Curlee,
Charlotte, North Carolina.

Fancy A Fruit Cobbler

One of the best ways to capture the flavor of summer is in a freshly baked cobbler. With each bite comes a taste of golden pastry and sweet, syrupy fruit.

EASY APPLE COBBLER

5 cups peeled, sliced apples
¾ cup sugar
2 tablespoons all-purpose flour
½ teaspoon ground cinnamon
¼ teaspoon salt
¼ cup water
1 teaspoon vanilla extract
1 tablespoon butter or margarine, softened
½ cup all-purpose flour
½ cup sugar
½ teaspoon baking powder
¼ teaspoon salt
2 tablespoons butter or margarine, softened
1 egg, slightly beaten

Combine the first 7 ingredients; mix gently. Spoon into a lightly greased 9-inch square baking pan; dot with 1 tablespoon butter. Set aside.

Combine remaining ingredients; mix well. Spoon over apple mixture in 9 equal portions (batter will spread during baking). Bake at 375° for 35 to 40 minutes. Yield: 6 servings. *Nell S. Harper, Russellville, Kentucky.*

PEACH COBBLER

About 8 cups sliced fresh peaches
⅓ cup all-purpose flour
2 cups sugar
1 teaspoon ground cinnamon
1 cup water
½ cup butter or margarine, melted
1 teaspoon almond extract
Pastry (recipe follows)

Dredge peaches in flour; add next 5 ingredients, and mix well. Set aside.

Roll three-fourths of pastry to ⅛-inch thickness on a lightly floured surface; fit into a 13- x 9- x 2-inch baking dish. Spoon in peach mixture.

Roll remaining pastry out to ¼-inch thickness on a lightly floured surface; cut into ½-inch strips. Arrange in lattice fashion over peaches. Bake at 350° for 1 hour. Yield: 8 to 10 servings.

Pastry:

3 cups all-purpose flour
1½ teaspoons salt
¾ teaspoon baking powder
¾ cup shortening
6 to 8 tablespoons ice water

Combine dry ingredients; cut in shortening with pastry blender until mixture resembles coarse meal. Sprinkle ice water evenly over surface; stir with a fork until all dry ingredients are moistened. Shape dough into a ball. Yield: pastry for 1 cobbler. *Thelma Robinson, Birmingham, Alabama.*

BLUEBERRY COBBLER

½ cup sugar
¼ cup all-purpose flour
¼ teaspoon ground cinnamon
¼ teaspoon ground nutmeg
4½ cups fresh blueberries
1 tablespoon lemon juice
3 tablespoons butter or margarine
Pastry for 9-inch pie

Combine sugar, flour, cinnamon, and nutmeg; add blueberries, stirring until coated. Spoon mixture into an 8-inch square baking dish. Sprinkle with lemon juice, and dot with butter.

Roll pastry out on a lightly floured surface into an 8-inch square; place over blueberries, sealing edges to sides of dish. Cut slits in crust. Bake at 400° for 30 minutes or until golden brown. Yield: 6 servings. *Margaret Ryalls, Troy, Virginia.*

BLACKBERRY COBBLER

4 cups fresh blackberries or 2 (16-ounce) packages frozen blackberries, thawed
¾ cup sugar
¼ cup all-purpose flour
2 tablespoons butter or margarine
1 cup all-purpose flour
½ teaspoon salt
⅓ cup shortening
2 tablespoons ice water

Combine blackberries, sugar, and ¼ cup flour; stir well. Spoon into an 8-inch square baking dish; dot with butter.

Combine 1 cup flour and salt; cut in shortening with a pastry blender until mixture resembles coarse meal. Sprinkle ice water evenly over surface, stirring with a fork until all dry ingredients are moistened. Shape dough into a ball. Roll pastry out on a lightly floured surface into an 8-inch square; place over blackberries, sealing edges to sides of dish. Cut slits in crust. Bake at 375° for 45 minutes or until golden brown. Serve warm. Yield: 6 servings.

Mrs. Harlan J. Stone, Ocala, Florida.

Sipping, Mexican Style

Some of the most delightful ways to quench a thirst come from Mexico. Salt-rimmed glasses of margaritas, frothy mugs of rich hot chocolate, and eye-opening Tequila Sunrises are just a few of the delicious offerings.

MEXICAN COFFEE

24 cups hot coffee
1 (16-ounce) can chocolate syrup
1 cup Kahlúa or other coffee-flavored liqueur
½ teaspoon ground cinnamon
Whipped cream

Combine coffee, chocolate syrup, Kahlúa, and cinnamon in a large container; stir well. Top servings with a dollop of whipped cream. Serve immediately. Yield: 25 to 30 servings.

Note: Mexican Coffee may also be served cold with a scoop of ice cream.

Carol Barclay, Portland, Texas.

TEQUILA SUNRISE

3 tablespoons tequila
½ cup orange juice
2 teaspoons lime juice
1½ tablespoons grenadine
Orange slice
Maraschino cherry

Fill a tall thin glass with ice. Add tequila, orange juice, and lime juice; mix well. Slowly pour grenadine down inside of glass (do not stir before serving). Garnish with orange slice and maraschino cherry. Yield: 1 serving.

Retta Miller, Stillwater, Oklahoma.

PITCHER MARGARITAS

Lime juice
Salt
4 cups crushed ice
1½ cups tequila
⅔ cup lime juice
2 tablespoons Triple Sec
½ cup powdered sugar
1 egg white
Lime slices

Dip rims of cocktail glasses in lime juice, then in a shallow dish of salt; shake to remove excess salt.

Combine remaining ingredients except lime slices in container of an electric blender; process until very frothy. Transfer to a pitcher; garnish with lime slices. Yield: about 6 servings.

Dottie Placke, Katy, Texas.

TEQUILA SLUSH

4½ cups water
2 (6-ounce) cans frozen limeade
    concentrate, thawed and undiluted
1 (6-ounce) can frozen orange juice
    concentrate, thawed and undiluted
¾ cup lime juice
1 (28-ounce) bottle grapefruit soda
1 cup tequila

Combine first 4 ingredients, mixing well. Stir in soda and tequila. Pour mixture into a freezer container; freeze overnight or until firm. Remove from freezer 30 minutes before serving; stir until slushy. Yield: 3 quarts.

Rita W. Cook,
Corpus Christi, Texas.

MEXICAN SLUSH

7 cups water
2 cups light rum
1 (12-ounce) can frozen lemonade
    concentrate, thawed and undiluted
1 (12-ounce) can frozen orange juice
    concentrate, thawed and undiluted
2 tablespoons plus 1 teaspoon
    lemon-flavored instant tea powder
3 (33.8-ounce) bottles ginger ale
Maraschino cherries

Combine first 5 ingredients in a large bowl; stir well. Cover and freeze overnight or until frozen.

Let stand at room temperature 15 minutes. Fill half of each serving glass with slush mixture; fill with ginger ale. Garnish with cherries. Serve immediately. Yield: about 24 servings.

Carolyn Morris,
Baton Rouge, Louisiana.

TROPICAL FRUIT PUNCH

Juice of 5 oranges
Juice of 3 lemons
2 large bananas, sliced
½ cup rum
½ cup honey
¼ cup crushed pineapple, drained
¼ cup banana-flavored liqueur
2 tablespoons grenadine syrup

Combine all ingredients in a large bowl, stirring well. Pour half of punch

mixture into container of electric blender; process until smooth. Repeat process with remaining punch mixture. Serve over ice. Yield: 5½ cups.

FROSTY PINA COLADAS

1 (8½-ounce) can cream of coconut
1 (8-ounce) can crushed pineapple,
    undrained
½ cup flaked coconut
¼ cup light rum
¼ cup milk
1 tablespoon powdered sugar
15 to 20 ice cubes

Combine first 6 ingredients in container of electric blender; process until smooth. Gradually add ice, processing until mixture is smooth and thickened. Yield: about 4 cups.

COOKING LIGHT

Welcome Guests With A Light Menu

Many a dieter claims great success in keeping calories low on a routine day. The problem often comes when it's time to entertain. Lest our "Cooking Light" readers feel discouraged, we've put together a 575-calorie menu that's perfect for a warm-weather party.

Ruby Red Borscht
Cucumber-Stuffed Red Snapper Rolls
or
Wine-Baked Chicken Breasts
Herbed Green Beans
Fresh Fruit With
Yogurt-Honey Poppy Seed Dressing
Chilled Chocolate Dessert
or
Orange Alaska

RUBY RED BORSCHT

5 large beets (about 1¾ pounds), peeled
    and grated
2 medium onions, finely chopped
6 cups chicken broth
1 tablespoon lemon juice
¼ teaspoon sugar
¼ teaspoon pepper
2 eggs, slightly beaten
Fresh dillweed (optional)

Combine first 3 ingredients in a Dutch oven. Cover and bring to a boil; reduce heat, and simmer 45 minutes. Add lemon juice, sugar, and pepper; simmer 15 additional minutes.

Remove Dutch oven from heat. Gradually stir about one-fourth of hot mixture into beaten eggs; add to the remaining hot mixture, stirring constantly. Chill thoroughly. Garnish with dillweed, if desired. Yield: 8 cups (about 75 calories per 1-cup serving).

Note: Soup may also be served hot.

Gwen Louer,
Roswell, Georgia.

CUCUMBER-STUFFED RED SNAPPER ROLLS

¼ cup sliced green onion
2 tablespoons reduced-calorie margarine
1½ cups French bread cubes (½-inch
    cubes), toasted
2 cups peeled, seeded, and chopped
    cucumber
2 tablespoons plain low-fat yogurt
1 tablespoon minced fresh parsley
2 teaspoons lemon juice
½ teaspoon dried whole dillweed
¼ teaspoon salt
8 (⅓-pound) red snapper fillets with skin

Sauté onion in margarine until tender. Combine onion and next 7 ingredients; set aside.

Cut each snapper fillet in half lengthwise. Spread ¼ cup stuffing over each piece of fish, leaving a ½-inch margin. Starting at narrow end, roll up fish fillets, jellyroll fashion, and secure them with wooden picks.

Stand fish rolls vertically in a large glass baking dish; cover and bake at 350° for 30 to 35 minutes or until fish flakes easily with a fork. Yield: 8 servings (about 183 calories per serving).

WINE-BAKED CHICKEN BREASTS

8 chicken breast halves, skinned
1 pound fresh mushrooms, halved
1 cup Chablis or other dry white wine
⅓ cup chopped fresh parsley
1 teaspoon dried whole tarragon
½ teaspoon salt
½ teaspoon freshly ground pepper

Arrange chicken breasts, bone side down, in a 13- x 9- x 2-inch baking dish. Arrange mushrooms around chicken. Pour wine over chicken; sprinkle with parsley, tarragon, salt, and pepper. Cover and bake at 350° for 50 to 60 minutes or until done. Yield: 8 servings (about 154 calories per serving).
Paula Beckham,
Surfside Beach, South Carolina.

HERBED GREEN BEANS

1½ pounds fresh green beans
¼ cup reduced-calorie margarine
½ cup sliced green onion
1 (4½-ounce) jar sliced mushrooms, drained
1 (4-ounce) jar diced pimiento, drained
½ teaspoon dried whole basil
½ teaspoon dried whole marjoram
¼ teaspoon pepper
Lemon wedges (optional)
Strips of lemon rind (optional)

Wash beans; trim ends and remove strings, if necessary. Cook in a small amount of boiling water 10 to 15 minutes or just until tender; drain.

Melt margarine in a medium saucepan; add onion, and cook just until tender. Add green beans and next 5 ingredients; cook over medium heat until thoroughly heated, stirring constantly. Garnish with lemon wedges and strips of lemon rind, if desired. Yield: 8 servings (about 51 calories per serving). *Mrs. Rudolph F. Watts,*
Glasgow, Kentucky.

Tip: Cooking vegetables with the least amount of water possible will preserve vitamins and maintain flavor.

YOGURT-HONEY POPPY SEED DRESSING

1 (8-ounce) carton plain low-fat yogurt
¼ cup honey
1 tablespoon plus 1 teaspoon lemon juice
1 teaspoon poppy seeds

Combine all ingredients, mixing well. Chill. Serve dressing over fresh fruit. Yield: 1⅓ cups (about 18 calories per tablespoon).
Eileen Wehling,
Austin, Texas.

CHILLED CHOCOLATE DESSERT

1 envelope unflavored gelatin
⅔ cup skim milk
¼ cup sugar
3 tablespoons cocoa
¼ cup skim milk
1 (12-ounce) carton low-fat cottage cheese
2 eggs, separated
1½ teaspoons vanilla extract
2 tablespoons sugar
⅓ cup graham cracker crumbs
¼ teaspoon ground cinnamon
1 tablespoon reduced-calorie margarine
1 cup frozen whipped topping, thawed
1 cup fresh strawberries

Combine gelatin and ⅔ cup milk in a small saucepan; let stand 1 minute. Cook over medium heat, stirring constantly, about 1 minute or until gelatin is dissolved; set aside to cool.

Combine ¼ cup sugar and cocoa in a small bowl; gradually add ¼ cup milk, stirring until smooth. Combine cocoa mixture, cottage cheese, egg yolks, and vanilla in container of an electric blender; process until smooth. Add gelatin mixture, blending well. Set aside.

Beat egg whites (at room temperature) until foamy. Gradually add 2 tablespoons sugar, 1 tablespoon at a time, beating until stiff peaks form. Fold one-fourth of the chocolate mixture into egg whites; fold in the remaining chocolate mixture.

Combine graham cracker crumbs and cinnamon; cut in margarine with a pastry blender or fork. Firmly press mixture evenly into bottom of an 8- or 9-inch springform pan. Pour chocolate mixture over crust; cover and chill 4 hours or until firm. Spread whipped topping over top of cheesecake, and garnish with strawberries. Yield: 8 servings (about 157 calories per serving).
Linda Morgan,
Roanoke, Virginia.

ORANGE ALASKA

8 large oranges
1 pint orange sherbet, softened
2 (8-ounce) cartons peach low-fat yogurt
⅓ cup Cointreau or other orange-flavored liqueur
2 teaspoons grated orange rind
3 egg whites
½ teaspoon vanilla extract
¼ teaspoon cream of tartar
¼ cup sugar

Cut a small slice from the top of each orange. Clip membranes, and carefully remove pulp (do not puncture bottom). Strain pulp, reserving ½ cup juice.

Combine ½ cup orange juice, sherbet, yogurt, Cointreau, and orange rind in a large bowl; pour into orange shells. Place shells on a baking sheet; freeze about 4 hours or until mixture is firm.

Beat the egg whites (at room temperature), vanilla, and cream of tartar until foamy. Gradually add sugar, 1 tablespoon at a time, beating until stiff peaks form.

Spread meringue over top opening of each orange shell, making sure edges are sealed. Freeze until ready to serve.

When ready to serve, broil orange shells 6 inches from heat for 1 or 2 minutes or until tops are golden. Yield: 8 servings (approximately 188 calories per serving). *Maryanne Southard,*
Delmar, Maryland.

summer Suppers

Flavorful Meats Hot Off The Grill

Many meats taste better when cooked outdoors over glowing coals. Grilled beef, pork, and chicken take on an irresistible smoky flavor and fill the air with a tantalizing aroma.

BARBECUED BEEF SHORT RIBS

1 tablespoon butter or margarine
⅓ cup chopped onion
1 tablespoon plus 1 teaspoon all-purpose flour
1 cup apple cider or apple juice
3 tablespoons sweet pickle relish
1 tablespoon catsup
¼ teaspoon salt
¼ teaspoon dried whole basil
⅛ teaspoon ground allspice
Dash of ground cloves
4 pounds beef short ribs

Melt butter in a heavy saucepan; add onion, and sauté until tender. Add flour, stirring well. Gradually add cider; cook over medium heat, stirring constantly, until thickened. Stir in next 6 ingredients.

Cut ribs into serving-size pieces; grill over slow coals 1 hour and 10 minutes.

Brush ribs with sauce, and cook 20 additional minutes, basting and turning frequently. Serve with remaining sauce. Yield: 4 servings. *Sophie Baugher, Shrewsbury, Pennsylvania.*

ORIENTAL FLANK STEAK

1 (1½-pound) flank steak
5 green onions, chopped
¾ cup vegetable oil
½ cup soy sauce
1½ teaspoons ground ginger
1½ teaspoons garlic powder
3 tablespoons honey
2 tablespoons vinegar

Place steak in a large shallow dish. Combine remaining ingredients, mixing well. Pour over steak; cover and marinate in refrigerator 8 hours, turning steak occasionally.

Drain steak, reserving marinade. Grill over hot coals 5 to 10 minutes on each side or until desired degree of doneness, basting with marinade.

To serve, slice steak across grain into thin slices. Yield: about 6 servings. *Jeanne H. Minetree, Dinwiddie, Virginia.*

STEAK CONTINENTAL

1 clove garlic, minced
2 teaspoons salt
2 to 3 tablespoons soy sauce
1 tablespoon catsup
1 tablespoon vegetable oil
½ teaspoon pepper
½ teaspoon dried whole oregano
3 pounds sirloin steak

Mash garlic and salt together; add next 5 ingredients, mixing well.

Score steak ¼ inch deep on both sides; rub in garlic mixture. Place steak in a large shallow dish; cover and refrigerate 8 hours.

Grill over medium coals 15 minutes on each side or until desired degree of doneness. Yield: 4 to 6 servings. *Shirley B. Kennedy, Lynchburg, Virginia.*

BARBECUED CRANBERRY CHICKEN

2 (3- to 3½-pound) broiler-fryers, quartered
Salt and pepper
1 chicken-flavored bouillon cube
½ cup boiling water
1 (16-ounce) can whole berry cranberry sauce
1 cup chili sauce
Juice of 1 small lemon
1 tablespoon Worcestershire sauce
1 tablespoon instant minced onion
1 teaspoon dry mustard

Sprinkle chicken on all sides with salt and pepper.

Dissolve bouillon cube in water; combine with next 6 ingredients in container of electric blender, and process until mixture is smooth.

Grill chicken over hot coals 30 minutes, turning every 10 minutes. Brush chicken with sauce; grill 30 additional minutes, brushing with sauce every 10 minutes. Serve with remaining sauce. Yield: 8 servings. *Mrs. O. V. Elkins, Chattanooga, Tennessee.*

GLAZED PORK STEAKS

1 (29-ounce) can sliced peaches, undrained
1 tablespoon cornstarch
1 teaspoon salt
½ cup catsup
¼ cup sweet pickle relish
2 tablespoons vinegar
1 tablespoon prepared mustard
6 (½- to ¾-inch-thick) pork steaks

Drain peaches, reserving syrup; set peaches aside. Combine cornstarch and salt in a heavy saucepan; gradually stir in reserved syrup. Add next 4 ingredients to syrup mixture. Cook sauce over medium heat, stirring constantly, until thickened and bubbly.

Grill pork steaks over medium coals 30 to 40 minutes, turning occasionally. Brush steaks with sauce, and cook 10 additional minutes, basting and turning frequently. Place steaks on serving platter. Garnish with reserved peach slices, and serve with remaining sauce. Yield: 6 servings. *Cindy Murphy, Cleveland, Tennessee.*

Don't Forget The Fruit

No matter what the menu, most agree that fruit is basic to a Mexican-style meal. So if you're planning a party with a south-of-the-border accent, you'll want to include the fruit in one of these varied and colorful preparations.

AVOCADO ICE

1 cup pineapple juice
¾ cup water
1 cup sugar, divided
¼ cup plus 1 tablespoon lemon juice
¼ teaspoon salt
1 cup pureed avocado
2 egg whites

Combine pineapple juice, water, ¾ cup sugar, lemon juice, and salt in a heavy saucepan; bring to a boil, and cook 5 minutes. Cool; stir in avocado with a wire whisk. Pour avocado mixture into an 11- x 7- x 2-inch pan; freeze 1 hour or until firm.

Beat egg whites (at room temperature) until foamy. Gradually add remaining sugar, 1 tablespoon at a time, beating until stiff peaks form.

Spoon avocado mixture into a medium mixing bowl; beat with an electric mixer until smooth. Fold in meringue. Freeze until firm. Yield: 8 to 10 servings.
Kathleen Stone,
Houston, Texas.

GUACAMOLE

2 large ripe avocados, peeled and mashed
¼ cup mayonnaise
⅓ cup minced onion
2 to 3 tablespoons lemon juice
1 teaspoon dried cilantro leaves or 1 to 2 tablespoons chopped fresh coriander
2 to 4 canned jalapeño peppers, seeded, rinsed, and minced
⅛ teaspoon salt
1 clove garlic, crushed
1 large tomato, chopped

Combine all ingredients; mix well. Cover and chill thoroughly. Serve with tortilla chips. Yield: about 3 cups.
Jana Dominguez, Jr.,
Navasota, Texas.

CANDIED BANANAS

2 tablespoons butter or margarine
¼ cup firmly packed brown sugar
1 teaspoon grated lemon rind
1 tablespoon lemon juice
Dash of ground cinnamon
Dash of ground nutmeg
3 medium-size firm bananas

Melt butter in a heavy skillet. Add next 5 ingredients; cook over low heat, stirring constantly, until bubbly.

Peel bananas, and slice in half lengthwise. Place bananas in skillet; cook over low heat 2 to 3 minutes, turning once. Serve warm. Yield: 6 servings.
Mrs. E. T. Williams,
Baton Rouge, Louisiana.

BAKED PINEAPPLE WITH NATILLAS SAUCE

1 large fresh pineapple
¼ cup sugar
1 teaspoon rum flavoring
2 tablespoons butter or margarine
Natillas Sauce

Cut a lengthwise slice from pineapple, removing about one-third of pineapple (stem should remain intact). Scoop pulp from slice; discard rind. Scoop the pulp from remaining portion of pineapple, leaving shell ½ inch thick; set pineapple shell aside.

Cut pineapple pulp into bite-size pieces, discarding core. Combine pulp, sugar, and flavoring; toss gently.

Spoon pulp mixture into pineapple shell; dot with butter. Cover entire pineapple, including stem, with heavy-duty aluminum foil. Place on a cookie sheet. Bake pineapple at 350° for 30 minutes. Serve warm with Natillas Sauce. Yield: about 6 servings.

Natillas Sauce:

2 cups half-and-half
2 egg yolks
1 egg
¼ cup sugar
1 teaspoon cornstarch
1 teaspoon vanilla extract
¼ teaspoon salt

Scald half-and-half; set aside.

Beat egg yolks and egg with electric mixer at medium speed until frothy. Gradually add sugar, beating until mixture thickens. Add cornstarch, vanilla, and salt; mix well.

Gradually stir about one-fourth of the half-and-half into egg yolk mixture; add to the remaining half-and-half, stirring constantly.

Pour custard into top of a double boiler; bring water to a boil. Reduce heat to low; cook, stirring constantly, until custard is smooth and thickened. Chill 1 hour. Yield: about 2 cups.
Lee Ruth Krieg,
Lubbock, Texas.

PINEAPPLE SOPAIPILLAS

2 cups all-purpose flour
1 tablespoon baking powder
½ teaspoon salt
¾ cup water
1 tablespoon vegetable oil
Vegetable oil
Pineapple filling (recipe follows)
Powdered sugar

Combine flour, baking powder, and salt; stir well. Make a well in center of mixture. Add water and 1 tablespoon oil, mixing well.

Turn dough out on a floured surface; divide dough into 4 portions. Lightly knead one portion four or five times; roll into an 8- x 4-inch rectangle. Cut into 4- x 2-inch rectangles. Repeat procedure with remaining dough.

Place dough rectangles, a few at a time, in deep hot oil (385°); fry until puffed and golden, turning once. Drain on paper towels.

Split each sopaipilla by gently cutting down one long side and one short side. Spoon pineapple filling into each sopaipilla. Sprinkle with powdered sugar, and serve warm. Yield: 16 sopaipillas.

Pineapple Filling:

2½ tablespoons sugar
2 tablespoons cornstarch
1 (20-ounce) can crushed pineapple, undrained

Combine sugar and cornstarch in a heavy saucepan, stirring well. Add undrained pineapple, stirring well. Cook over medium heat, stirring constantly, until sugar dissolves and mixture is thickened and bubbly. Yield: about 2 cups.
Mary Lou McCray,
Jonesboro, Arkansas.

Relax And Enjoy This Menu For Eight

When was the last time you had guests over for a casual dinner outdoors? Our menu for eight is just right for a warm, summer evening. And since most of the dishes may be prepared in advance, you can entertain even if you have a busy schedule.

**White Sangría
Fresh Vegetables With
Creamy Vegetable Dip
Peach Soup
Sherried Crab Quiche
Green Bean Bundles
Buttery Crescent Rolls
Almond Cookies**

WHITE SANGRIA

2 oranges, sliced and seeded
1 lemon, sliced and seeded
1 lime, sliced and seeded
⅔ cup brandy
½ cup sugar
2 (3-inch) sticks cinnamon
2 (25.4-ounce) bottles Chablis, chilled
1 quart club soda, chilled

Combine first 6 ingredients in a large pitcher. Cover and chill at least 4 hours, stirring occasionally. Remove and discard cinnamon sticks. Add wine, stirring well; cover and chill at least 2 hours. Stir in club soda, and serve over ice. Yield: 2½ quarts.   *Rita W. Cook, Corpus Christi, Texas.*

CREAMY VEGETABLE DIP

1 (8-ounce) package cream cheese, softened
1 cup mayonnaise
1 (8-ounce) carton commercial sour cream
1 tablespoon instant minced onion
1 tablespoon chopped fresh parsley
1½ tablespoons minced fresh dillweed or 1½ teaspoons dried whole dillweed
1 teaspoon Beau Monde seasoning
½ teaspoon curry powder
Fresh dillweed (optional)

Beat cream cheese with an electric mixer until smooth. Add next 7 ingredients, and beat well; cover and refrigerate at least 8 hours. Place mixture in a serving bowl; garnish with dillweed, if desired. Serve with fresh vegetables. Yield: 3 cups.   *Lou Kanatzar, Wilmette, Illinois.*

PEACH SOUP

4 cups peeled, diced peaches
2 cups Sauterne
2 cups water
⅓ cup sugar
1 (3-inch) stick cinnamon
1½ tablespoons lemon juice
⅛ teaspoon almond extract
Lemon slices (optional)
Mint sprigs (optional)

Combine first 5 ingredients in a 3-quart saucepan; bring to a boil. Cover and reduce heat; simmer 30 minutes, stirring occasionally. Remove and discard cinnamon stick; stir in lemon juice and flavoring. Pour half of mixture into container of electric blender; process until smooth. Pour into a bowl or pitcher. Repeat with remaining mixture. Cover and chill. Garnish with lemon slices and mint sprigs, if desired. Yield: about 5½ cups.   *Joy Callaway, Decatur, Georgia.*

SHERRIED CRAB QUICHE

Pastry for 9-inch pie
2 tablespoons minced green onion
1 tablespoon butter or margarine
4 eggs
2 cups whipping cream
¾ teaspoon salt
2 (6-ounce) packages frozen crabmeat, thawed and drained
1 cup (4 ounces) shredded Swiss cheese
2 tablespoons sherry
⅛ teaspoon red pepper
Tomato rose (optional)

Line a 9-inch quiche dish with pastry; trim excess pastry around edges. Set dish aside.

Sauté onion in butter in a small skillet until tender. Set aside.

Beat eggs in a large bowl. Add whipping cream and salt, mixing well. Stir in sautéed onion, crabmeat, cheese, sherry, and pepper. Pour into pastry shell. Bake at 425° for 15 minutes. Reduce heat to 325°, and bake an additional 35 to 40 minutes. Garnish with tomato rose, if desired. Yield: one 9-inch quiche.   *Lynne Teal Weeks, Columbus, Georgia.*

GREEN BEAN BUNDLES

2 pounds green beans
¼ cup plus 2 tablespoons olive oil
2 tablespoons lemon juice
½ teaspoon salt
⅛ teaspoon pepper
2 to 3 small red sweet peppers, cut into 8 rings

Wash beans thoroughly; remove strings, and cut beans into 3-inch pieces. Cut each piece in half lengthwise.

Cook beans, covered, in a small amount of boiling water 10 minutes or until crisp-tender. Drain beans; cool.

Combine oil, lemon juice, salt, and pepper. Pour mixture over beans; toss gently. Cover beans, and refrigerate at least 2 hours.

Divide beans into 8 bundles. Carefully place each bundle through a red pepper ring; arrange on a serving platter. Yield: 8 servings.   *Carrie Bartlett, Gallatin, Tennessee.*

BUTTERY CRESCENT ROLLS

1 cup milk
¼ cup butter or margarine
3 tablespoons sugar
1 teaspoon salt
1 package dry yeast
½ cup warm water (105° to 115°)
2 eggs, beaten
4 to 5 cups bread flour
Butter or margarine, melted

Scald milk; add butter, sugar, and salt, stirring until butter melts. Let mixture cool to lukewarm.

Dissolve yeast in water in a large bowl. Add milk mixture, eggs, and 2 cups flour; beat at low speed of an electric mixer until smooth. Stir in enough remaining flour to make a soft dough.

Turn dough out onto a floured surface, and knead about 8 to 10 minutes until smooth and elastic. Place in a well-greased bowl, turning to grease top. Cover and let rise in a warm place (85°), free from drafts, 1 hour or until doubled in bulk.

Divide dough in half. Roll half of dough into a 12-inch circle on a lightly floured surface; cut into 12 wedges. Roll up each wedge tightly, beginning at wide end. Seal points, and place rolls, point side down, on lightly greased baking sheets; curve into crescent shapes. Repeat with remaining dough.

Cover and let rise in a warm place (85°), 30 minutes or until doubled in bulk. Bake at 400° for 8 to 10 minutes or until browned. Brush with butter. Yield: 2 dozen. *Dee Buchfink,*
Oologah, Oklahoma.

ALMOND COOKIES

⅔ cup shortening
1⅔ cups sugar
2 eggs
1 teaspoon almond extract
2½ cups all-purpose flour
2 teaspoons baking powder
½ teaspoon baking soda
¼ teaspoon salt
1 egg white, slightly beaten
About ¼ cup sliced almonds

Cream shortening; gradually add sugar, beating well. Add eggs and flavoring, beating well. Combine flour, baking powder, soda, and salt; stir into creamed mixture.

Shape dough into 1½-inch balls, and place 2 inches apart on greased cookie sheets; flatten slightly. Brush with egg white. Place 3 sliced almonds in center of each cookie. Bake at 375° for 15 minutes or until lightly browned. Cool. Yield: 3 dozen. *Beckie Webster,*
Roanoke, Virginia.

Dressings Suited For Summer Salads

A homemade dressing is all it takes to turn a bowl of mixed fruit or vegetables into a special summer salad. Toss a medley of melon, peaches, and strawberries with Ralph Monin's Delightful Salad Dressing. Ralph suggests using his dressing rather than commercial mayonnaise on Waldorf salads. We found it delicious with vegetable salads, too.

APPLE DRESSING

½ cup applesauce
½ cup commercial sour cream
½ cup mayonnaise
2 tablespoons lemon juice
1 teaspoon celery seeds

Combine all ingredients, mixing well. Chill thoroughly. Serve over fresh fruit. Yield: 1⅔ cups. *Mrs. Doug Hail,*
Moody, Texas.

RUSSIAN-STYLE DRESSING

1 (10¾-ounce) can tomato soup, undiluted
½ cup sugar
½ cup vegetable oil
½ cup vinegar
1 small onion, finely chopped
1 tablespoon Worcestershire sauce
1 teaspoon dry mustard
1 teaspoon paprika
½ teaspoon salt

Combine all ingredients, mixing well. Cover and chill. Serve over salad greens. Yield: 2¾ cups.
Mrs. Robert Collins,
Fairfax, Missouri.

SPINACH SALAD DRESSING

¾ cup chili sauce
¾ cup red wine vinegar
½ cup vegetable oil
½ cup sugar
1 tablespoon soy sauce

Combine all ingredients, mixing well. Chill thoroughly. Serve over spinach or other salad greens. Yield: 2 cups.
Ellen Hanna,
England, Arkansas.

CREAMY SALAD DRESSING

1 cup mayonnaise
½ cup whipping cream
3 tablespoons chopped green onion
2 tablespoons chopped fresh parsley
3 tablespoons anchovy paste
3 tablespoons tarragon vinegar
1 tablespoon lemon juice
1 clove garlic, minced

Combine all ingredients, mixing well. Chill thoroughly. Serve over spinach or other salad greens. Yield: 2 cups.
Anne Frezell,
Bel Air, Maryland.

DELIGHTFUL SALAD DRESSING

6 egg yolks
2 tablespoons sugar
½ cup buttermilk
1½ teaspoons butter, melted
½ cup vinegar
½ teaspoon dry mustard
¼ teaspoon red pepper
Dash of salt

Beat egg yolks at medium speed of electric mixer until thick and lemon colored. Add sugar, beating mixture well. Stir in buttermilk and melted butter. While beating at medium speed of electric mixer, slowly add vinegar to egg yolk mixture. Stir in the mustard, pepper, and salt.

Pour mixture into top of a double boiler. Bring water to a boil (water in bottom of double boiler should not touch top pan). Reduce heat to low; cook, stirring constantly, 8 to 10 minutes or until smooth and thickened. Immediately remove from heat. Chill thoroughly. Serve over fruit or salad greens. Yield: about 1½ cups.
Ralph B. Monin,
Elizabethtown, Kentucky.

COOKING LIGHT

A Lesson In Canning

Start preparing for your wintertime low-calorie and low-sodium menus now. It's easy once you've learned a few lessons about food preservation "Cooking Light" style.

Instead of depending on commercially canned fruit this winter, put up a batch of Nectarines in Apple Juice or Unsweetened Mixed Fruit. No sugar is added to the liquid—we used unsweetened fruit juice instead of syrup to keep calories low and flavor high.

You can cut calories even more by pouring plain boiling water over the fruit instead of juice or syrup, but we felt the addition of unsweetened juice produced a better flavor.

In regular canning, sugar in the syrup helps prevent darkening. Since our recipes are prepared without sugar, we suggest tossing the nectarines in an ascorbic acid mixture before packing. This will prevent browning.

Even if you're a dedicated dieter, you probably like an occasional dollop of jam or preserves with toast for breakfast. We've included a reduced-calorie peach jam just for you.

In regular jam and jelly recipes, sugar is essential. It works with natural fruit pectin for proper gel formation; when sugar is reduced, the result is closer to syrup than jam. However, we've come up with a refrigerator jam recipe that uses very little sugar. Since you don't process this jam in a boiling-water bath, you must store it in the refrigerator.

Since salt is added only for flavor, it may be left out of canned vegetable recipes. (This rule does not apply to pickle recipes, however, where certain amounts of salt and vinegar are necessary to prevent spoilage.)

SEASONED TOMATO PUREE

4 quarts peeled, chopped tomatoes
3 cups chopped onion
2 cups sliced carrots
2 cups chopped celery
1½ cups chopped green pepper
1 teaspoon white pepper

Combine all ingredients in a large Dutch oven; cook until vegetables are tender, stirring mixture frequently.

Pour one-fourth of tomato mixture into container of an electric blender; process until smooth. Repeat with remaining tomato mixture. Pour the processed mixture through a fine sieve, discarding pulp.

Return tomato juice to Dutch oven. Bring to a boil; reduce heat and simmer, uncovered, 1 to 1½ hours or until puree is reduced to about 2 quarts.

Pour the hot tomato puree into hot sterilized jars, leaving ½-inch headspace. Cover jars at once with metal lids, and screw bands tight. Process in boiling-water bath 45 minutes. Yield: 8 half pints (about 85 calories and 40 milligrams sodium per ½ cup).

SPICY TOMATO CATSUP

1 quart Seasoned Tomato Puree
⅔ cup vinegar
¼ cup sugar
¾ teaspoon paprika
½ teaspoon dry mustard
⅛ teaspoon red pepper
1 (3-inch) stick cinnamon
1 teaspoon whole allspice
½ teaspoon whole cloves

Combine first 6 ingredients in a small Dutch oven. Tie cinnamon, allspice, and cloves in a cheesecloth bag; add to tomato mixture. Bring to a boil; reduce heat and simmer, uncovered, 45 to 60 minutes or until desired consistency, stirring frequently. Remove spice bag.

Pour hot mixture into hot sterilized jars, leaving ½-inch headspace. Cover at once with metal lids, and screw bands tight. Process in boiling-water bath 15 minutes. Yield: 1 to 1½ pints (about 25 calories and 9 milligrams sodium per tablespoon).

STEWED TOMATOES

4 quarts peeled, chopped tomatoes
1½ cups chopped celery
1 cup chopped onion
¾ cup chopped green pepper
1 tablespoon sugar (optional)
1 tablespoon dried whole basil
1 tablespoon dried whole oregano
2 bay leaves

Combine all ingredients in a large Dutch oven. Bring to a boil. Reduce heat and simmer, uncovered, 1 hour, stirring occasionally. Remove bay leaves.

Spoon hot mixture into hot sterilized jars, leaving ½-inch headspace. Cover at once with metal lids, and screw bands tight. Process in pressure canner at 10 pounds pressure (240°) for 15 minutes. Yield: 7 pints (about 41 calories and 14 milligrams sodium per ½ cup).

UNSWEETENED MIXED FRUIT

1 pound fresh peaches
1 small fresh pineapple (about 2 pounds)
1 pound fresh seedless white grapes
1 pound fresh sweet cherries, pitted
2½ cups unsweetened apple juice

Peel and slice peaches. Remove leaf and stem ends from pineapple. Peel and core pineapple; cut into 1-inch pieces. Combine fruit and apple juice in a saucepan; bring to a boil. Reduce heat and simmer until thoroughly heated.

Pack hot fruit loosely in hot sterilized jars, leaving ½-inch headspace. Cover with boiling juice, leaving ½-inch headspace. Cover at once with metal lids, and screw bands tight. Process pints in boiling-water bath for 20 minutes and quarts for 25 minutes. Yield: 2 quarts (about 69 calories and 2 milligrams sodium per ½ cup).

FREEZER PEACH JAM

4 cups peeled, coarsely chopped peaches
1 (1¾-ounce) package powdered fruit pectin
1 tablespoon sugar
1 tablespoon lemon juice
½ teaspoon ascorbic acid

Crush peaches in a medium saucepan; stir in remaining ingredients. Bring to a boil; cook 1 minute, stirring constantly. Remove from heat and stir 3 minutes.

Spoon jam into freezer containers, leaving ½-inch headspace. Cover at once with lids. Let stand at room temperature 24 hours; freeze. To serve, thaw jam at room temperature. Yield: 2½ half pints (about 11 calories and 7 milligrams sodium per tablespoon).

Note: Jam may be stored in the refrigerator up to 1 month.

Tip: When squeezing fresh lemons or oranges for juice, first grate the rind by rubbing the washed fruit against surface of grater, taking care to remove only the outer colored portion of the rind. Wrap in plastic in teaspoon portions and freeze for future use.

NECTARINES IN APPLE JUICE

Ascorbic-citric powder
2 pounds nectarines, peeled
1½ cups unsweetened apple juice

Prepare ascorbic-citric solution according to the manufacturer's directions; set aside.

Cut nectarines in half, and discard pits; toss in ascorbic-citric solution. Rinse and drain nectarines. Cook nectarines in boiling water to cover until thoroughly heated. Drain.

Pack hot nectarines loosely in hot sterilized jars, leaving ½-inch headspace. Bring apple juice to a boil; pour over nectarines, leaving ½-inch headspace. Cover at once with metal lids, and screw bands tight. Process in boiling-water bath 20 minutes. Yield: 2 pints (about 92 calories and 7 milligrams sodium per ½ cup).

Here's A Pretty Pepper Relish

Preserving summer bounty in home-canned relishes is tradition. This recipe for Pepper Relish is an excellent way to use red and green peppers.

As with all home canning, be sure to follow safety precautions and recipe directions. Be certain to process half-pint jars of Pepper Relish in a boiling-water bath the full 5 minutes. If you prefer to use pint jars, increase the processing time 10 to 15 minutes.

PEPPER RELISH

6 green peppers, minced
6 sweet red peppers, minced
6 medium onions, minced
2 cups vinegar (5% acidity)
1½ cups sugar
2 tablespoons plus 1 teaspoon mustard
    seeds
1 fresh hot pepper

Combine all ingredients in a large Dutch oven, and bring to a boil. Reduce heat to medium; cook, uncovered, 30 minutes, stirring occasionally. Discard hot pepper.

Pack into hot sterilized jars, leaving ¼-inch headspace. Cover at once with metal lids, and screw bands tight. Process in boiling-water bath 5 minutes. Yield: 11 half pints. *Kathleen Branson, Thomasville, North Carolina.*

Blueberries Sweeten Dessert

Blueberry cobblers, pies, and cakes are favorites when the berries are juicy, ripe, and just ready for picking. You'll find some tasty variations of these summer standbys in the recipes here.

When you select blueberries at the market, look for ones that are plump, firm, clean, and deep blue in color. A reddish tinge indicates immature fruit. If you like to pick your own, be sure to collect only ripe berries since they won't ripen afterward.

Store unwashed berries in the refrigerator. Wash quickly in cold water just before using. Blueberries will keep at room temperature about 2 to 3 days or in the refrigerator about a week.

EASY BLUEBERRY COBBLER

3 cups fresh blueberries
1 tablespoon lemon juice
1 cup all-purpose flour
1 cup sugar
1 egg, beaten
¼ cup plus 2 tablespoons butter or
    margarine, melted

Place blueberries in a 10- x 6- x 2-inch baking dish, and sprinkle with lemon juice.

Combine flour, sugar, and egg; stir until mixture resembles coarse meal. Spread over blueberries. Drizzle melted butter over topping. Bake at 375° for 30 minutes. Serve warm. Yield: about 6 servings.

Note: Any fruit may be substituted for blueberries. *Dottie Dear, Bronson, Florida.*

BLUEBERRY BRUNCH CAKE

1 cup all-purpose flour
⅓ cup sugar
2 teaspoons baking powder
½ teaspoon salt
1 egg
½ cup milk
⅓ cup vegetable oil
1 tablespoon lemon juice
1 cup fresh blueberries
⅓ cup sugar
¼ cup all-purpose flour
¼ teaspoon ground cinnamon
½ cup chopped pecans
2 tablespoons butter or margarine,
    softened

Combine first 4 ingredients in a medium bowl, and set aside. Combine egg, milk, oil, and lemon juice; add to dry ingredients, mixing well. Pour batter into a greased 8-inch square baking pan; sprinkle with blueberries.

Combine remaining ingredients; sprinkle over blueberries. Bake at 350° for 40 minutes. Yield: 9 servings.
Cathy Mumford, Greenville, North Carolina.

FRESH BLUEBERRY PIE

½ cup sugar
⅓ cup all-purpose flour
½ teaspoon ground cinnamon
4½ cups fresh blueberries
1 unbaked 9-inch pastry shell
1 tablespoon lemon juice
Crumb Topping

Combine first 4 ingredients, mixing well. Place blueberry mixture in pastry shell; sprinkle with lemon juice. Spread Crumb Topping over fruit mixture. Bake at 425° for 30 minutes. Cover with aluminum foil and bake an additional 20 minutes. Yield: one 9-inch pie.

Crumb Topping:

1 cup all-purpose flour
½ cup firmly packed brown sugar
½ cup butter or margarine

Combine flour and sugar, mixing well. Cut in butter with a pastry blender until mixture resembles coarse meal. Yield: about 1½ cups. *Diane Lang, Joppa, Maryland.*

BLUEBERRY-SOUR CREAM PIE

1 (16-ounce) carton commercial sour
    cream
3 tablespoons all-purpose flour
3 tablespoons light brown sugar
1 egg, beaten
1 unbaked 9-inch graham cracker crust
2 cups fresh blueberries
½ cup firmly packed light brown sugar

Combine first 3 ingredients in a mixing bowl; add egg, and beat well. Spoon half of mixture into graham cracker crust. Combine blueberries and ½ cup brown sugar in a small mixing bowl; spread evenly over sour cream mixture. Top with remaining sour cream mixture.

Bake at 400° for 25 minutes. Chill several hours before serving. Yield: one 9-inch pie. *Mrs. Roger Williams, Arden, North Carolina.*

Feature Chicken Breast Entrées

Thick and meaty chicken breasts offer a lot of value for the money. Whole, boneless, or chopped into bite-size pieces, they combine with an endless list of ingredients. In fact, you could serve chicken breasts several times a week for a month and never repeat a recipe.

Swiss cheese and ham are natural partners for chicken breasts. Try rolling all three into bundles and cooking in a creamy gravy for Chicken Rollups in Gravy. Enjoy this hearty entrée served over a bed of hot cooked rice.

SWEET-AND-SOUR CHICKEN

3 tablespoons soy sauce
1 tablespoon sherry
1 egg
¼ teaspoon pepper
¼ teaspoon garlic powder
¼ cup cornstarch
1 pound boneless chicken breasts, cut into 1-inch pieces
2 cups vegetable oil
1 (15¼-ounce) can pineapple chunks, undrained
2 tablespoons cornstarch
½ cup sugar
¼ cup catsup
¼ cup vinegar
1 tablespoon soy sauce
1 medium-size green pepper, cut into 1-inch pieces
Hot cooked rice

Combine first 6 ingredients, mixing well; add chicken, stirring to coat. Heat oil in electric skillet to 375°; fry chicken until lightly browned. Drain.

Drain pineapple, reserving liquid. Add enough water to juice to make 1 cup. Add 2 tablespoons cornstarch, stirring well. Combine pineapple, juice mixture, and next 4 ingredients in a medium saucepan; bring mixture to a boil. Stir green pepper and chicken into sauce, cook until thoroughly heated. Serve over rice. Yield: 4 servings.

Mrs. R. P. Vinroot,
Matthews, North Carolina.

CHICKEN ROLLUPS IN GRAVY

6 chicken breast halves, skinned and boned
1 teaspoon garlic powder
½ teaspoon salt
½ teaspoon pepper
6 (1-ounce) slices cooked ham
6 (1-ounce) slices Swiss cheese
All-purpose flour
2 tablespoons vegetable oil
1½ cups chicken broth
1 (10¾-ounce) can cream of chicken soup, undiluted
1 (3-ounce) can sliced mushrooms, undrained
Hot cooked rice

Place each piece of chicken on waxed paper; flatten to ¼-inch thickness using a meat mallet or rolling pin. Sprinkle both sides of chicken with garlic powder, salt, and pepper.

Place a slice of ham and cheese in center of each piece of chicken. Roll up lengthwise, and secure with a wooden pick. Dredge in flour.

Brown chicken in hot oil. Combine chicken broth, soup, and mushrooms. Pour broth mixture over chicken; bring to a boil. Cover, reduce heat, and simmer 30 minutes. Serve over rice. Yield: 6 servings.

Kathy Rich,
Liberty, Texas.

SAUCY CHICKEN BREASTS

3 tablespoons butter or margarine, melted
2 tablespoons olive oil
8 chicken breast halves, skinned and boned
1 medium onion, finely chopped
¼ cup all-purpose flour
1½ cups chicken broth
¾ cup tomato juice
¼ cup dry sherry
2 tablespoons chopped fresh parsley
¼ teaspoon salt
¼ teaspoon pepper
Hot cooked rice

Heat butter and oil in a large skillet. Add chicken, and brown on both sides; remove from skillet.

Add onion to pan drippings; sauté until tender. Add flour; cook 1 minute, stirring constantly. Gradually add the chicken broth and tomato juice; cook over medium heat, stirring constantly, until thickened and bubbly. Stir in sherry, parsley, salt, and pepper.

Add chicken to broth mixture; cover, reduce heat, and simmer 30 minutes until chicken is done. Serve over rice. Yield: 8 servings.

Jan Thompson,
Highland, Maryland.

BAKED ITALIAN CHICKEN

½ cup all-purpose flour
⅛ teaspoon salt
Dash of pepper
4 chicken breast halves, skinned and boned
2 eggs, beaten
2 tablespoons vegetable oil
1 (15½-ounce) jar commercial thick and zesty spaghetti sauce
2 (1-ounce) slices mozzarella cheese
Hot cooked spaghetti (optional)

Combine flour, salt, and pepper. Dip chicken in egg, and dredge in flour mixture. Brown chicken on all sides in hot oil. Remove chicken to an 8-inch square baking dish. Pour spaghetti sauce over chicken. Bake, uncovered, at 350° for 40 minutes. Top with cheese, and bake 5 additional minutes. Serve over spaghetti, if desired. Yield: 4 servings.

Janet B. Farley,
Orange Park, Florida.

CHICKEN PARMESAN

½ cup fine, dry breadcrumbs
¼ cup grated Parmesan cheese
4 chicken breast halves, skinned and boned
1 egg, beaten
3 tablespoons butter or margarine
1 green pepper, thinly sliced
1 (8-ounce) can tomato sauce
½ cup water
¼ teaspoon dried whole oregano
1 cup (4 ounces) shredded mozzarella cheese

Combine breadcrumbs and Parmesan cheese. Dip chicken in egg, and coat with breadcrumb mixture.

Preheat electric skillet to 350°. Add butter, and cook chicken about 3 minutes on each side or until golden brown. Arrange green pepper over chicken.

Combine next 3 ingredients; pour over chicken. Reduce heat to 220°; cover and cook 25 to 30 minutes or until chicken is tender. Sprinkle with mozzarella cheese; cover and cook just until cheese melts. Yield: 4 servings.

Mrs. Gerald A. Speight, Jr.,
Raleigh, North Carolina.

Tip: Make certain your refrigerator or freezer is cold enough. Refrigerator temperature should be maintained at 34°F to 40°F, and freezer temperature at 0°F or lower. To allow the cold air to circulate freely, foods should not be overcrowded.

August

Plump, purple eggplant fill gardens in August, and our recipes show a variety of ways to bring it to the table. Slice and fry it, stuff the shells with a tomato-flavored ratatouille, or slip tasty fried slices between meat and cheese layers for our Eggplant Parmesan.

Omelets seem to conjure thoughts of morning meals, but you're missing something if you've never whipped up one for a midnight snack. The recipes in "Whip Up An Omelet" explain the secret of mixing up a plain or puffy omelet and provide you with some savory filling suggestions. Try stuffing the tender egg layers with a vegetable combination.

When it's time to make a tasty contribution to the spread at a family reunion or church homecoming, take a look at our covered-dish supper casseroles for some economical entrées. Prepare Hot Chicken Salad, Broccoli-Beef Pie, or Sausage and Wild Rice Casserole; then take note of our suggestions for transporting the food and keeping it hot.

Bring On The Eggplant

Richly colored purple eggplant is the vegetable that ripens when other summer produce runs out. Eggplant offers such versatility you can choose to serve it as an appetizer, entrée, or side dish.

Eggplant size makes a difference in the recipe yield, so we've specified small, medium, or large eggplant in the recipes to follow. You can judge the approximate size by just looking, but here's a guide for a more accurate estimate: small—about 1 to 1¼ pounds, medium—about 1½ pounds, and large—about 2 pounds.

Look for a uniform dark-purple to purple-black skin when selecting eggplant. It also should be glossy and free of dark-brown spots.

If eggplant is stored at room temperature, it will keep about 1 week. Eggplant may be stored in the refrigerator if room temperature is unusually warm, but use within 1 or 2 days as temperatures below 45° damage the vegetable.

Step 1—Cut a medium eggplant into ¼-inch slices; sprinkle with 1 teaspoon salt, and let stand 1 hour. Prepare sauce.

Step 2—Dip each of the eggplant slices in the beaten egg; then dredge the eggplant in soft breadcrumbs.

Step 3—Sauté eggplant slices in butter, browning on both sides.

Step 4—Layer one-third of sauce, and top with half of eggplant. Sprinkle with cheese, and repeat layers. Spread remaining sauce on top; sprinkle with Parmesan.

EGGPLANT PARMESAN

1 medium eggplant
1 teaspoon salt
1 tablespoon butter or margarine
1 medium onion, chopped
⅓ cup chopped green pepper
1 pound ground beef
1 (28-ounce) can tomatoes, undrained and coarsely chopped
1 (6-ounce) can tomato paste
½ teaspoon dried whole oregano
½ teaspoon dried whole basil
½ teaspoon dried whole marjoram
1 teaspoon salt
½ teaspoon pepper
2 eggs, beaten
¾ cup dry breadcrumbs
½ cup butter or margarine, divided
2 cups (8 ounces) shredded mozzarella cheese
¾ cup grated Parmesan cheese
Green pepper rings
Fresh parsley sprigs

Peel eggplant, if desired. Cut eggplant into ¼-inch slices. Sprinkle with 1 teaspoon salt; let stand 1 hour.

Melt 1 tablespoon butter in a saucepan; add onion, green pepper, and ground beef. Cook over medium heat, stirring to crumble, until beef is browned. Drain. Add next 7 ingredients. Bring to a boil, reduce heat, and simmer, uncovered, 30 minutes.

Dip eggplant slices in egg; coat with breadcrumbs. Melt ¼ cup butter in a heavy skillet. Arrange a single layer of eggplant slices in skillet and brown on both sides. Drain on paper towels; set aside. Repeat with remaining eggplant slices, adding more butter as needed.

Layer one-third of meat sauce, half of the eggplant, 1 cup mozzarella cheese, and ¼ cup Parmesan cheese in a lightly greased 13- x 9- x 2-inch baking dish. Repeat layers. Add remaining meat sauce, and top with remaining Parmesan cheese. Bake at 350° for 30 to 35 minutes. Garnish with green pepper rings and parsley. Yield: 6 servings.

Chana Johnson,
Oklahoma City, Oklahoma.

EGGPLANT PATTIES

1 medium eggplant, peeled and chopped
1 medium onion, finely chopped
1½ cups coarse cracker crumbs
2 eggs, beaten
½ teaspoon dried whole basil
½ cup butter or margarine

Cook eggplant in boiling, salted water 10 to 15 minutes or until tender. Drain and cool. Mash eggplant. Add chopped onion, cracker crumbs, eggs, and basil; mix well.

Melt butter in a heavy skillet over medium heat; drop in mixture by heaping tablespoonfuls. Cook until golden, turning once. Drain on paper towels; serve immediately. Yield: 16 patties.

Mrs. W. A. Thornburg,
Long Beach, Mississippi.

EGGPLANT APPETIZER

2 cups peeled, chopped eggplant (about 1 medium eggplant)
1 cup (4 ounces) shredded Cheddar cheese
1 cup cracker crumbs
3 tablespoons minced onion
2 tablespoons minced fresh parsley
1 egg, beaten
2 teaspoons Worcestershire sauce
¼ teaspoon dry mustard
¼ teaspoon curry powder
¼ teaspoon salt
¼ teaspoon pepper
⅛ teaspoon hot pepper sauce
½ cup all-purpose flour
¼ cup butter or margarine

Cook eggplant in boiling water 10 to 15 minutes or until tender; drain and mash. Add remaining ingredients except flour and butter; mix well. Cover and chill 1 hour. Shape mixture into 1-inch balls; coat with flour.

Melt butter in a heavy skillet; sauté balls of eggplant mixture, browning on all sides. Drain on paper towels; serve immediately. Yield: about 1½ dozen.

Karen Bozeman,
Longview, Texas.

FRIED EGGPLANT

1 medium eggplant
½ cup dry breadcrumbs
½ cup grated Parmesan cheese
½ teaspoon dried parsley flakes
¼ teaspoon dried whole basil
⅛ teaspoon garlic salt
1 egg
2 teaspoons milk
Vegetable oil

Peel eggplant, if desired. Cut eggplant into ½-inch slices, and set aside.

Combine next 5 ingredients; set aside. Combine egg and milk. Dip eggplant slices in egg mixture; then dredge in breadcrumb mixture. Sauté in hot oil (375°) until golden brown, turning once. Drain on paper towels. Yield: 4 to 6 servings.

Peggy Sisson,
Wimberley, Texas.

EGGPLANT AND SQUASH

1 small onion, chopped
3 tablespoons vegetable oil
1 medium zucchini, cut into ¼-inch slices
1 medium eggplant, peeled and cut into 1-inch cubes
4 tomatoes, peeled and coarsely chopped
1 clove garlic, minced
1 bay leaf
1 tablespoon chopped fresh parsley
½ teaspoon salt
¼ teaspoon pepper
¼ cup grated Parmesan cheese

Sauté onion in oil in a Dutch oven until tender. Add next 8 ingredients; cover and simmer 10 minutes or until vegetables are crisp-tender. Remove bay leaf. Transfer vegetable mixture to a 12- x 8- x 2-inch baking dish; sprinkle with cheese. Place under broiler 1 to 2 minutes or until cheese melts. Yield: 6 to 8 servings.

Pat Sanders,
Austin, Texas.

RATATOUILLE-STUFFED EGGPLANT

2 small eggplant
1 large onion, chopped
2 cloves garlic, crushed
3 tablespoons olive oil
3 medium tomatoes, peeled and cubed
2 small zucchini, cut into ½-inch cubes
1 large green pepper, chopped
½ cup chopped fresh parsley
½ teaspoon dried whole basil
½ teaspoon dried whole oregano
½ teaspoon dried whole thyme
½ teaspoon salt
¼ teaspoon freshly ground pepper
⅔ cup seasoned dry breadcrumbs, divided
½ cup grated Parmesan cheese
1 tablespoon olive oil

Wash eggplant and cut in half lengthwise. Remove pulp, leaving a ¼-inch shell. Chop pulp, and set aside.

Sauté onion and garlic in 3 tablespoons oil in a large skillet 4 minutes or until tender. Stir in eggplant pulp and next 9 ingredients; cook, uncovered, over medium heat 20 minutes or until zucchini is crisp-tender, stirring occasionally. Remove from heat, and stir in ⅓ cup breadcrumbs and cheese.

Place eggplant shells on a baking sheet; mound mixture into shells. Combine remaining ⅓ cup breadcrumbs and 1 tablespoon oil; mix well and sprinkle evenly over eggplant mixture. Bake at 350° for 15 minutes. Yield: 8 servings.

MEXICAN EGGPLANT

1 medium eggplant
Vegetable oil
1 (4-ounce) can chopped green chiles, undrained
1 (4-ounce) can sliced ripe olives, drained
1 (15-ounce) can tomato sauce
½ teaspoon ground cumin
¼ teaspoon garlic powder
1½ cups (6 ounces) shredded Cheddar cheese

Peel eggplant and cut into ½-inch slices. Brush each side of slices with oil; place on a baking sheet, and bake at 450° for 20 minutes. Set aside.

Combine next 5 ingredients in a medium saucepan over medium heat. Bring to a boil, reduce heat, and simmer 10 minutes.

Place half of eggplant slices in a lightly greased 1½-quart casserole; top with half each of tomato mixture and cheese. Repeat layers with remaining ingredients. Bake at 375° for 10 minutes. Yield: 4 to 6 servings.

Charlene Acker,
Bella Vista, Arkansas.

EGGPLANT-AND-TOMATO CASSEROLE

6 slices bacon
1 green pepper, chopped
1 medium onion, chopped
1 large eggplant, peeled and chopped
4 medium tomatoes, peeled and chopped
½ teaspoon salt
¼ teaspoon pepper
½ cup (2 ounces) shredded Cheddar cheese
½ cup soft breadcrumbs

Cook bacon in a large skillet until crisp; remove bacon, reserving 2 tablespoons drippings in skillet. Crumble bacon and set aside. Sauté green pepper and onion in drippings until tender.

Add eggplant and tomatoes; cover and cook 5 minutes, stirring occasionally. Stir in salt and pepper. Spoon eggplant mixture into a lightly greased 2-quart casserole, and top with bacon. Sprinkle cheese over casserole; top with breadcrumbs. Bake casserole, uncovered, at 350° for 25 minutes. Yield: 6 to 8 servings.

Susie M. E. Dent,
Saltillo, Mississippi.

Whip Up An Omelet

Some people serve omelets only for breakfast, but the Southerners who sent us these recipes had a different idea in mind. They fill their omelets with sauces and fillings for delightful brunch, lunch, or dinner offerings.

When making an omelet, take your choice of a plain or a puffy, soufflé-like version. The difference between the two is in the method of mixing and cooking.

Plain omelets are cooked entirely on the range top. Briskly mix the eggs, seasonings, and liquid ingredients together just until blended; then pour the entire mixture into the pan. As soon as the egg mixture begins to set on the bottom, gently lift the edges all around the omelet to allow uncooked portions to run underneath. Cook until the underside is lightly browned and top is set, but still moist.

In contrast, for puffy omelets the eggs are separated, and the omelet is partially baked in the oven. Beat the egg whites (always at room temperature) until stiff peaks form, and beat the egg yolks separately until thick and lemon colored. Stir the seasonings and liquid ingredients into the yolks, fold the egg whites into the yolk mixture, and pour into the pan. Cook on the range top just until the eggs begin to set and are lightly browned on bottom. Then bake in the oven the length of time specified by the individual recipe. (Be sure the skillet handle is ovenproof; if not, cover completely with aluminum foil.)

You don't need a special pan for making omelets, but it is important that the pan you use be well seasoned or of the nonstick type. It's helpful if the pan has sloping sides. Fill the omelet, and gently slide it from the pan as soon as cooking is done. Serve on warm plates to keep from cooling too quickly.

PUFFY VEGETABLE OMELET

5 eggs, separated
2 tablespoons water
¼ teaspoon salt
Dash of white pepper
2 tablespoons butter or margarine
1 small avocado
Lemon juice
⅓ cup chopped tomato
⅓ cup alfalfa sprouts
Cheese sauce (recipe follows)

Beat egg whites (at room temperature) until stiff but not dry; set aside. Beat egg yolks in a medium bowl until thick and lemon colored. Stir water, salt, and pepper into yolks; fold whites into yolks.

Heat an ovenproof 10-inch omelet pan or heavy skillet over medium heat until hot enough to sizzle a drop of water. Add butter; rotate pan to coat bottom. Pour in egg mixture all at once, and gently smooth surface. Reduce heat and cook omelet about 5 minutes or until puffy and lightly browned on bottom, gently lifting omelet at edge to judge color. Bake at 325° for 12 to 15 minutes or until a knife inserted in center comes out clean.

Peel avocado; remove seed. Slice avocado into wedges; then chop enough wedges to equal ⅓ cup. Toss wedges and chopped avocado separately in small amount of lemon juice. Spread chopped avocado, tomato, and alfalfa sprouts over half of omelet. Pour cheese sauce over vegetables. Loosen omelet with spatula, and fold in half. Gently slide omelet onto a warm serving plate. Garnish with avocado wedges, if desired. Yield: 3 to 4 servings.

Cheese Sauce:

1 tablespoon butter or margarine
1 tablespoon all-purpose flour
½ cup milk
¼ cup (1 ounce) shredded sharp Cheddar cheese
⅛ teaspoon salt
Dash of white pepper

Melt butter in a heavy saucepan over low heat, and stir in flour. Cook 1 minute, stirring constantly. Gradually add milk; cook over medium heat, stirring constantly, until thickened and bubbly. Add cheese, salt, and pepper; stir until cheese melts. Yield: ½ cup.

SPANISH-STYLE OMELETS

¼ cup chopped mushrooms
2 tablespoons chopped onion
2 tablespoons chopped celery
2 tablespoons chopped green pepper
¼ cup vegetable oil, divided
1 (8-ounce) can tomato sauce
Salt
Dash of hot sauce
6 eggs
6 tablespoons water

Sauté vegetables in 1 tablespoon hot oil until tender. Add tomato sauce, ¼ teaspoon salt, and hot sauce; bring to a boil. Set aside.

Combine 2 eggs, 2 tablespoons water, and a pinch of salt; mix just until blended.

Heat a 10-inch omelet pan or heavy skillet over medium heat until hot enough to sizzle a drop of water. Add 1 tablespoon oil; rotate pan to coat bottom. Pour egg mixture into skillet. As mixture starts to cook, gently lift edges of omelet with a spatula, and tilt pan so uncooked portion flows underneath.

When egg mixture is set, spoon 3 tablespoons sauce over half of omelet. Loosen omelet with spatula, and fold in half. Slide omelet onto a warm serving plate. Make 2 additional omelets with remaining ingredients. Spoon remaining sauce over omelets. Yield: 3 servings.

Gloria Pedersen,
Brandon, Mississippi.

BEEFY VEGETABLE OMELET

¼ pound ground beef
1 small onion, sliced
½ cup broccoli flowerets (optional)
¼ cup chopped green pepper
¼ cup sliced fresh mushrooms
¼ cup chopped tomatoes
3 slices bacon, cooked and crumbled
¼ teaspoon crushed red pepper
⅛ teaspoon salt
⅛ teaspoon garlic powder
⅛ teaspoon pepper
4 eggs
1 tablespoon milk
¼ teaspoon salt
Dash of pepper
1 tablespoon butter or margarine
½ cup (2 ounces) shredded Swiss cheese

Cook ground beef, onion, broccoli, and green pepper in a medium skillet over medium heat until beef is browned, stirring to crumble meat. Add next 7 ingredients; cook an additional 5 minutes, stirring mixture frequently.

Combine eggs, milk, ¼ teaspoon salt, and pepper; mix just until blended.

Heat a 10-inch omelet pan or heavy skillet over medium heat until hot enough to sizzle a drop of water. Add butter; rotate pan to coat bottom. Pour egg mixture into skillet. As mixture starts to cook, gently lift edges of omelet with a spatula, and tilt pan so uncooked portion flows underneath.

When egg mixture is set, spoon meat mixture over half of omelet. Loosen omelet with a spatula, and fold in half. Top with cheese; cover until cheese is melted. Slide omelet onto a warm serving plate. Yield: 2 servings.

Debbie Brown,
Austin, Texas.

Layer These Desserts With Ice Cream

If ice cream is your weakness, you'll want to try one of these desserts. Richly layered with sauces or nuts, they're excellent choices for occasions that demand something special.

LAYERED ICE CREAM DESSERT

¾ cup chocolate wafer crumbs, divided
1 cup butter or margarine
2 (1-ounce) squares unsweetened chocolate
2 cups sifted powdered sugar
3 eggs, separated
1 cup coarsely chopped pecans
1 quart vanilla ice cream, softened

Sprinkle ½ cup chocolate crumbs evenly in an ungreased 13- x 9- x 2-inch pan. Set aside.

Combine butter and chocolate in a heavy saucepan; cook over low heat until melted. Remove from heat. Add powdered sugar, and beat 2 minutes at medium speed of electric mixer. Add egg yolks, beating until smooth.

Beat egg whites (at room temperature) until stiff peaks form; fold into chocolate mixture. Carefully spoon mixture over crumbs, and sprinkle with pecans. Cover and freeze until firm.

Spread ice cream evenly over pecan layer; sprinkle with remaining ¼ cup crumbs. Cover and freeze until ice cream is firm. Yield: 15 servings.
Mrs. William Poole, Jr.
Jarrettsville, Maryland.

KONA ICE CREAM PIE

2 tablespoons instant coffee granules
1½ cups whipping cream, divided
1 quart vanilla ice cream, softened
1 baked 9-inch pastry shell
2 tablespoons Kahlúa or other coffee-flavored liqueur
1 pint vanilla ice cream, softened
½ cup chopped cashews or macadamia nuts
4 egg whites
¼ teaspoon cream of tartar
½ cup sugar

Dissolve coffee granules in 1 cup whipping cream; beat until soft peaks form. Fold into 1 quart vanilla ice cream. Spread about two-thirds of coffee mixture in pastry shell; make a well in center. Place pie and remaining coffee mixture in the freezer.

Beat remaining ½ cup whipping cream until foamy; add Kahlúa, beating until soft peaks form. Fold into 1 pint vanilla ice cream; add cashews and stir mixture gently. Spoon mixture into well of frozen pie; freeze until firm. Mound remaining coffee mixture over pie. Freeze until firm.

Beat egg whites (at room temperature) and cream of tartar until foamy. Gradually add sugar, 1 tablespoon at a time, beating until stiff peaks form. Remove pie from freezer; quickly spread meringue over the filling, sealing to edge of pastry.

Bake at 450° for 4 to 5 minutes or until peaks are browned. Serve immediately. Yield: one 9-inch pie.

Note: Meringue may be piped onto pie, if desired. From center, pipe meringue in a straight line to edge of pie, increasing pressure. Repeat procedure, forming a cone design and covering the entire surface of the pie.
Debbie Brown,
Austin, Texas.

LAYERED BANANA SPLIT PIE

1 pint vanilla ice cream, softened
1 (9-inch) graham cracker crust
Chocolate sauce (recipe follows)
1 cup chopped pecans, divided
½ pint chocolate ice cream, softened
1 (8-ounce) can crushed pineapple, drained
2 bananas, sliced
1 cup whipping cream
¼ cup sifted powdered sugar
1 tablespoon grated unsweetened chocolate (optional)

Spread half of vanilla ice cream evenly over graham cracker crust; cover and freeze until firm. Spread one-third of chocolate sauce over ice cream layer; sprinkle with ½ cup pecans. Cover and freeze until set.

Spread chocolate ice cream evenly over pie; cover and freeze until firm.

Spoon half of remaining chocolate sauce over chocolate ice cream; top with pineapple. Cover and freeze.

Spread remaining vanilla ice cream evenly over pie; cover and freeze until firm. Spread remaining chocolate sauce over ice cream; top with remaining ½ cup pecans and banana slices.

Beat whipping cream until foamy; gradually add powdered sugar, beating until soft peaks form. Spread whipped cream over pie; sprinkle with grated chocolate, if desired. Freeze. Let stand at room temperature 5 minutes before serving. Yield: one 9-inch pie.

Chocolate Sauce:

½ cup semisweet chocolate morsels
1 (5.33-ounce) can evaporated milk
1 cup sifted powdered sugar
¼ cup butter or margarine

Combine all ingredients in top of a double boiler; bring water to a boil. Reduce heat to low; cook 15 to 20 minutes or until slightly thickened, stirring occasionally. Cool completely. Yield: about 1¼ cups.
Debra Pennell,
Lenoir, North Carolina.

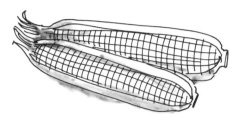

Savor Fresh Corn Flavor

Fresh corn is one of the sweetest joys of summer. When buying fresh corn, remember that 2 medium-size ears of corn equal about 1 cup of kernels. Store the corn unhusked in the refrigerator until ready to use. Use corn as soon after harvesting as possible; the sugar in the kernels turns to starch very soon after corn is picked.

CORN RELISH

4 cups fresh corn, cut from cob
3 medium-size green peppers, chopped
1 cup chopped onion
1 cup chopped cucumber
¼ cup chopped celery
1 (28-ounce) can whole tomatoes, undrained and chopped
1 cup sugar
1 tablespoon salt
1 teaspoon whole mustard seeds
¾ teaspoon ground turmeric
¼ teaspoon dry mustard
1½ cups vinegar (5% acidity)

Combine all ingredients in a large Dutch oven; simmer over low heat 20 minutes. Bring mixture to a boil.

Pack into hot sterilized jars, leaving ¼-inch headspace. Cover at once with metal lids, and screw bands tight. Process in boiling-water bath 15 minutes. Yield: 4 pints.
Mrs. James Pollard,
Brundidge, Alabama.

CORN AND ZUCCHINI

⅓ cup sliced green onion
¼ cup plus 2 tablespoons butter or margarine
4 cups fresh corn, cut from cob
1 large zucchini, cut into ¼-inch slices
1 medium tomato, peeled and chopped
1 tablespoon chopped fresh parsley
½ teaspoon salt
⅛ teaspoon pepper

Sauté onion in butter in a large skillet until tender. Stir in corn and zucchini; cook 10 minutes or until the vegetables are tender.

Add tomato, parsley, salt, and pepper; cook until thoroughly heated. Yield: about 6 servings.
Mrs. Charles R. Field,
Bryson City, North Carolina.

CORN-AND-HAM SKILLET DINNER

½ cup chopped onion
3 tablespoons butter or margarine
½ pound okra, cut into 1-inch pieces
2 cups fresh corn, cut from cob
2 cups chopped cooked ham
2 cups chopped tomatoes
1 teaspoon salt
½ teaspoon dried whole oregano
⅛ teaspoon pepper

Sauté onion in butter in a large skillet 2 minutes. Add okra, and cook, uncovered, 5 to 8 minutes. Stir in the remaining ingredients. Cook, uncovered, over medium heat 8 to 10 minutes, stirring frequently. Yield: 4 to 6 servings.
Geneva P. Tobias,
Albemarle, North Carolina.

SKILLET FRIED CORN

4 slices bacon
1 small green pepper, chopped
¼ cup finely chopped onion
3 cups fresh corn, cut from cob
¼ teaspoon salt

Fry bacon in a large skillet until crisp; remove bacon, reserving the drippings. Crumble bacon, and set aside.

Add green pepper and onion to drippings in skillet; sauté over medium heat, stirring constantly, until vegetables are crisp-tender. Stir in corn, and cook over medium heat 8 to 10 minutes, stirring frequently. Stir in salt. Top with bacon. Yield: 4 servings.
Thelma Peedin,
Newport News, Virginia.

Host A Summer Luncheon

Here's a menu designed especially for a casual summer luncheon. It serves eight generously and includes several dishes that are prepared in advance.

Rice-Stuffed Ham Rolls
Peas Pignoli
Grapefruit Congealed Salad
Zucchini-Carrot Bread
Strawberries With French Cream
Iced Tea   Coffee

RICE-STUFFED HAM ROLLS

1 cup cooked wild rice
1 cup finely chopped cooked chicken
8 (6½- x 4½-inch) cooked ham slices
Mushroom-Cheese Sauce

Combine rice and chicken. Place ¼ cup rice mixture in center of each ham slice. Roll up and place seam side down in a lightly greased 13- x 9- x 2-inch baking dish. Spoon Mushroom-Cheese Sauce over ham rolls. Bake at 350° for 15 minutes or until the sauce is bubbly. Yield: 8 servings.

Mushroom-Cheese Sauce:

¼ cup butter or margarine
1 cup sliced fresh mushrooms
¼ cup all-purpose flour
1 cup chicken broth
1 cup half-and-half
1 cup (4 ounces) shredded sharp Cheddar cheese
Dash of salt

Melt butter in a heavy saucepan over low heat. Add mushrooms, and sauté until tender. Add flour, stirring until mushrooms are coated. Cook 1 minute, stirring constantly. Gradually add broth and half-and-half; cook over medium heat, stirring constantly, until thickened and bubbly. Add cheese and salt; stir until cheese is melted. Yield: about 2¼ cups.
Susan Leftwich,
DeSoto, Texas.

PEAS PIGNOLI

4 pounds fresh English peas
3 tablespoons butter or margarine
¾ cup water
1 teaspoon dried whole basil
½ teaspoon salt
⅓ cup pine nuts or slivered almonds, toasted

Shell and wash peas; drain.

Combine peas, butter, water, basil, and salt in a medium saucepan; bring to a boil. Cover, reduce heat, and simmer 8 to 12 minutes or until peas are tender; drain. Stir in pine nuts just before serving. Yield: 8 servings.

Note: 4 cups frozen English peas may be substituted for fresh peas.
Ruth Moffitt,
Smyrna, Delaware.

GRAPEFRUIT CONGEALED SALAD

2 envelopes unflavored gelatin
1 cup cold water
1 cup boiling water
1 cup sugar
3 large grapefruit, peeled, seeded, and sectioned
1 (8-ounce) can pineapple tidbits, drained
½ cup chopped celery
½ cup chopped pecans
Lettuce leaves

Soften gelatin in cold water. Add boiling water and sugar; stir until gelatin dissolves. Chill until consistency of unbeaten egg white.

Coarsely chop the grapefruit sections; drain well. Stir grapefruit, pineapple, celery, and pecans into the thickened gelatin. Pour mixture into a lightly oiled 5-cup mold, and chill until firm. Unmold salad on lettuce leaves. Yield: 8 to 10 servings.   *Jane Emory Moore,*
Philadelphia, Pennsylvania.

ZUCCHINI-CARROT BREAD

2½ cups all-purpose flour
1 teaspoon baking powder
1 teaspoon baking soda
1 teaspoon salt
1 tablespoon ground cinnamon
¾ cup vegetable oil
3 eggs
1½ cups firmly packed brown sugar
2 teaspoons vanilla extract
1 cup unpeeled shredded zucchini
1 cup shredded carrots
1 cup chopped pecans or walnuts
½ cup crushed bran flakes cereal

Combine first 5 ingredients in a mixing bowl, and set aside.

Combine oil, eggs, sugar, and vanilla in a large bowl; beat well. Stir in zucchini and carrots. Add flour mixture, stirring just until moistened. Stir in the pecans and cereal.

Pour batter into 2 greased and floured 8½- x 4½- x 3-inch loafpans.

Bake at 350° for 1 hour or until a wooden pick inserted in center comes out clean. Cool loaves 10 minutes in pans; remove to wire racks and cool completely. Yield: 2 loaves.

Judy Cunningham,
Roanoke, Virginia.

STRAWBERRIES WITH FRENCH CREAM

1 quart whole strawberries
1 cup whipping cream
⅓ cup sifted powdered sugar
½ cup commercial sour cream
½ teaspoon grated orange rind
Grated chocolate (optional)

Wash and hull strawberries; set aside.

Beat whipping cream until foamy; gradually add powdered sugar, beating until soft peaks form. Fold in sour cream and orange rind.

Spoon strawberries into individual serving dishes. Top each serving with a dollop of whipped cream mixture; sprinkle with grated chocolate, if desired. Yield: about 8 servings.

Joyce M. Maurer,
Christmas, Florida.

From Our Kitchen To Yours

Keep your cool in the kitchen during the summer by following some of these ideas from our test kitchens.

Start with a cool one—Get in the habit of treating yourself to a cool drink before dinner. Serve a tall glass of lemonade with a twist of lemon or fresh mint. Freshly squeezed lemonade is terrific, but use a commercial product if you're short of time. Ginger ale or club soda served over cracked ice with a slice of lime makes a great refresher. And the all-time Southern favorite, iced tea, is perfect to serve before as well as with the meal. If you want something a bit stronger, keep it light with a wine spritzer or frozen daiquiris. Keep your appetizers cold, too. Serve raw vegetables such as carrots, broccoli, zucchini, or cauliflower with a chilled dip. Make it a dieter's appetizer by watching the calories in the dip.

Make the main dish cold—Try salads as the main course for your evening meals. The endless combinations that are possible with salads can make this meal exciting. Serve marinated salads; these can be put together the night before and will often hold up three to four days. Cold meat salads like tuna, ham, chicken, and salmon provide the protein needed in your diet. And don't forget the chef's salad. This is a good way to use up your leftovers.

Remember to include hearty sandwiches in your summer menus. Sliced cold cuts and cheese topped with juicy ripe tomato slices, crisp lettuce, and onion create a meal the family will love. Why not open up a sandwich bar in your kitchen? Offer a variety of sliced meats, cheeses, toppings, and breads and let each person build his own.

Take the cooking outdoors—Fire up that grill or smoker instead of your kitchen. Sure the grill will be hot, but at least your house won't be. Be creative with your outdoor cooking—try cooking the entire meal outside. Corn on the cob is a breeze to grill; just butter the corn, sprinkle with seasonings, wrap in aluminum foil, and place on the grill. Corn usually takes longer to cook than a steak, so begin it first. Slice potatoes or a medley of vegetables, such as yellow squash, green peppers, and onions, and place them on a piece of heavy-duty aluminum foil. Butter and season to your liking. Then wrap up the vegetable packages and put them on the grill. Cook, turning the packages occasionally, until the vegetables are tender.

Try chilled desserts—Instead of making pies or cakes for dessert, which of course involves heating the oven, serve a chilled dessert. Don't forget to churn some ice cream, too. If you're short of time, just serve a bowl of commercial ice cream topped with fudge, butterscotch, or fruit sauce.

Some other cool kitchen tips—When you must stay in your kitchen, remember to use your microwave oven. Rapid cooking is the microwave's main feature, but in the summer its heat-free cooking is just as desirable. The microwave is ideal for cooking fresh vegetables straight from your garden. You'll have delicious vegetables without extra heat. Also, use your wok. By using this small appliance and the quick stir-frying method, you can have a main dish ready for your dinner table in minutes.

When you must turn on your oven, use its heat wisely. Cook several dishes at once, making sure they all bake at the same temperature. Try cooking in the morning, too, while it's still cool. If you use your oven early in the day, then you won't have to fight both its heat and the heat of the late afternoon or evening. Try cooking a chicken, ham, or roast in the morning; then chill it. Slice the cold meat for dinners, or use it to make salads or sandwiches.

Make A Pie For Dessert

Chilled cream pie or hot fruit pie capped with vanilla ice cream are two great ways to end a meal. Here's an assortment of both kinds of pie that you'll be proud to serve.

KAHLUA PIE

1 envelope unflavored gelatin
¼ cup water
2 (1-ounce) squares semisweet chocolate
½ cup sugar
¼ cup water
4 egg yolks
¼ cup Kahlúa or other coffee-flavored liqueur
2 egg whites
1¼ cups whipping cream
2 tablespoons powdered sugar
1 baked 9-inch pastry shell
Chopped toasted almonds

Sprinkle gelatin in ¼ cup water, and set aside.

Combine chocolate, ½ cup sugar, and ¼ cup water in top of a double boiler. Cook over boiling water, stirring constantly, until chocolate melts.

Beat egg yolks until thick and lemon colored. Gradually stir about one-fourth of hot mixture into yolks; add to remaining hot mixture, stirring constantly. Cook, stirring constantly, until mixture thickens. Remove from heat, and gently stir in gelatin and Kahlúa. (Mixture will be thin.) Chill until slightly thickened.

Beat egg whites (at room temperature) until soft peaks form; fold into chocolate mixture. Beat whipping cream until foamy; gradually add powdered sugar, beating until soft peaks form. Fold half the whipped cream into chocolate mixture. Spoon mixture into pastry shell; chill until firm. Top with remaining whipped cream and toasted almonds. Yield: one 9-inch pie.

Sandi Russo,
Springfield, Missouri.

CHOCOLATE CREAM PIE

1 cup sugar
⅓ cup cocoa
⅓ cup all-purpose flour
Pinch of salt
2 eggs, separated
2 cups milk
¼ cup butter or margarine
¼ teaspoon vanilla extract
1 baked 9-inch pastry shell
¼ teaspoon vanilla extract
¼ cup sugar

Combine 1 cup sugar, cocoa, flour, and salt in a heavy saucepan; stir mixture to remove lumps.

Combine egg yolks and milk in a mixing bowl; mix well.

Gradually add milk mixture to cocoa mixture, stirring until well blended. Cook over medium heat, stirring constantly, until mixture thickens and comes to a boil. Cook 1 minute, stirring constantly. Remove from heat; add butter and ¼ teaspoon vanilla, stirring until butter melts. Pour into pastry shell.

Combine egg whites (at room temperature) and ¼ teaspoon vanilla; beat until foamy. Gradually add ¼ cup sugar, 1 tablespoon at a time, beating until stiff peaks form. Spread meringue over filling, sealing to edge of pastry. Bake at 400° for 10 minutes or until golden brown. Cool. Yield: one 9-inch pie. *Susie Timmons, Winston-Salem, North Carolina.*

BRANDY RAISIN-APPLE PIE

¼ cup raisins
¼ cup brandy
Pastry for double-crust 9-inch pie
5 to 7 Granny Smith or other variety green apples
½ cup sugar
¼ cup firmly packed brown sugar
2 tablespoons all-purpose flour
1¼ teaspoons ground cinnamon
Dash of salt
1 tablespoon butter or margarine
1 tablespoon sugar

Combine raisins and brandy in a jar; cover and refrigerate overnight. Drain and set aside.

Line a 9-inch pieplate with half of pastry; set aside. Peel and core apples; thinly slice. Combine ½ cup sugar, brown sugar, flour, cinnamon, and salt; stir mixture to remove lumps. Stir in raisins and apples; spoon into pastry-lined pieplate. Dot with butter.

Cover with top crust. Trim edges of pastry; seal and crimp edges. Cut slits in top of crust for steam to escape. Sprinkle with 1 tablespoon sugar. Bake at 400° for 50 minutes or until brown. Yield: one 9-inch pie. *Marie G. Long, Dayton, Tennessee.*

RED CHERRY PIE

2 (16-ounce) cans pitted tart cherries, undrained
¾ cup sugar
¼ cup plus 1 tablespoon cornstarch
¼ teaspoon ground cinnamon
½ cup sugar
1 tablespoon butter or margarine
½ teaspoon almond extract
5 drops red food coloring (optional)
Pastry for double-crust 9-inch pie

Drain cherries, reserving 1 cup juice; set cherries aside.

Combine ¾ cup sugar, cornstarch, and cinnamon in a medium saucepan; stir mixture to remove lumps. Stir cherry juice into sugar mixture. Cook over medium heat, stirring constantly, until smooth and thickened. Remove from heat; stir in cherries, ½ cup sugar, butter, and almond extract. Stir in food coloring, if desired.

Line a 9-inch pieplate with half of pastry. Pour cherry mixture into the pastry shell. Cover with top crust. Trim edges of pastry; seal and crimp edges. Cut slits in top of crust for steam to escape. Bake at 425° for 45 to 55 minutes or until golden brown. Yield: one 9-inch pie. *Pat Boschen, Ashland, Virginia.*

LEMON SPONGE PIE

3 tablespoons butter or margarine, softened
1¼ cups sugar
4 eggs, separated
3 tablespoons all-purpose flour
1¼ cups milk
2 tablespoons grated lemon rind
⅓ cup lemon juice
Dash of salt
1 unbaked 10-inch pastry shell

Cream butter; gradually add sugar, beating well. Add egg yolks, flour, milk, lemon rind, juice, and salt; beat until smooth.

Beat egg whites (at room temperature) until stiff peaks form; fold into lemon mixture. Pour into pastry shell. Bake at 375° for 15 minutes; reduce heat to 300° and bake 45 to 50 minutes. Cool. Yield: one 10-inch pie.
Janet M. Filer, Arlington, Virginia.

It's Prime Tomato Time

Juicy tomatoes—the big beauties that are such an important part of Southern gardens—are at their peak in midsummer. Enjoy them with a sprinkling of salt, sliced for sandwiches, wedged for salads, or in one of our special recipes.

Remember to select tomatoes carefully. Ripe tomatoes should be completely red or reddish orange, have a sweet, subtle aroma, and give slightly when gently squeezed. Keep unripened tomatoes at room temperature. Once tomatoes are fully ripe, they can be placed in the refrigerator.

TOMATO-ENGLISH PEA BROIL

1 (8½-ounce) can English peas, drained
1 tablespoon butter or margarine, melted
¼ teaspoon pepper
3 medium tomatoes
3 tablespoons grated Parmesan cheese, divided
3 fresh mushrooms, sliced

Combine peas, butter, and pepper; mix well. Cut tomatoes in half. Spoon about 1 tablespoon pea mixture on cut side of each tomato half; sprinkle with 1½ teaspoons cheese. Top each half with a mushroom slice.

Broil 5 inches from heat for 2 to 3 minutes or until cheese is browned. Yield: 6 servings. *Millie Fetzer, Jacksonville, Florida.*

CHERRY TOMATOES WITH RUM

1 pint cherry tomatoes
3 tablespoons butter or margarine, melted
3 tablespoons chopped fresh parsley
1 teaspoon sugar
½ teaspoon salt
¼ teaspoon pepper
2 tablespoons rum

Wash tomatoes; drain on paper towels. Combine butter and tomatoes in a 10- x 6- x 2-inch baking dish; stir gently. Combine remaining ingredients, stirring well. Spoon rum mixture over tomatoes; bake at 300° for 15 to 20 minutes. Yield: 4 to 6 servings.

Pat Boschen,
Ashland, Virginia.

MARINATED TOMATO SLICES

½ cup vegetable oil
¼ cup cider vinegar
1 teaspoon salt
½ teaspoon dried whole oregano
½ teaspoon dried whole thyme
¼ teaspoon pepper
6 large tomatoes, sliced

Combine first 6 ingredients in a jar; cover tightly and shake vigorously. Pour over tomato slices. Cover and marinate in refrigerator for several hours. Yield: 10 to 12 servings.

Marian Cox,
Deming, New Mexico.

FRESH TOMATO
SALAD DRESSING

2 (3-ounce) packages cream cheese, softened
1 large tomato, peeled and quartered
1 small onion, quartered
1 large stalk celery, coarsely chopped
2 cloves garlic
¼ cup mayonnaise
2 tablespoons lemon juice
¼ teaspoon salt
5 to 6 drops of hot sauce

Combine all ingredients in container of electric blender. Process on high speed until smooth; cover and chill 1 to 2 hours. Serve over salad greens. Yield: 2 cups. *Wanda Bishop,*
Little Rock, Arkansas.

Enjoy The Great
Taste Of Garlic

Every cook knows the glory of garlic, and most agree that there's no substitute for fresh. When buying fresh garlic, be sure to choose bulbs with firm cloves and an unbroken skin. If stored in a cool, dry, well-ventilated place, garlic

will keep up to four months without loss of flavor.

Some of our recipes call for chopped or minced garlic—it adds a mild, nut-like flavor in this form. Strong garlic flavor is released by crushing the cloves. If you don't have a garlic press, you can crush cloves between pieces of plastic wrap using a wooden spoon or a wooden utensil handle.

ITALIAN MEAT SAUCE

¼ pound Italian link sausage (2 to 3 links)
1 pound ground beef, crumbled
1 medium onion, chopped
4 cloves garlic, minced
2 (16-ounce) cans whole tomatoes, undrained
2 (6-ounce) cans tomato paste
1 teaspoon dried whole oregano
½ teaspoon dried whole basil
½ teaspoon salt
Hot cooked spaghetti
Parmesan cheese

Cut sausage links into ¼-inch slices; place in a Dutch oven. Add next 3 ingredients. Cook over medium heat until sausage and beef are browned. Drain well. Add tomatoes, tomato paste, and seasonings. Cover, reduce heat, and simmer 45 minutes, stirring occasionally. Serve over spaghetti, and sprinkle with Parmesan cheese. Yield: 6 servings. *Johnabeth Frost,*
Vinita, Oklahoma.

GARLIC-BROILED SHRIMP

2 pounds unpeeled large shrimp
½ cup butter or margarine, melted
½ cup olive oil
¼ cup minced fresh parsley
1 tablespoon minced green onion
3 cloves garlic, minced
1½ tablespoons lemon juice
Coarsely ground black pepper

Peel shrimp, leaving tails on; devein and butterfly. Set shrimp aside.
Combine next 6 ingredients in a large shallow dish. Add shrimp, tossing well to coat. Cover and marinate at least 30 minutes, stirring occasionally.
Broil shrimp 4 inches from heat for 3 to 4 minutes; turn and broil an additional 3 to 4 minutes or until done. Sprinkle with pepper; serve with pan drippings. Yield: 4 to 6 servings.

Lilly B. Smith,
Richmond, Virginia.

GRUYERE POTATOES

3 medium-size baking potatoes, unpeeled and thinly sliced
1½ cups milk
2 tablespoons butter, melted
1 teaspoon salt
¼ teaspoon pepper
1 tablespoon minced garlic
½ cup (2 ounces) shredded Gruyère cheese

Place potatoes in a greased 10- x 6- x 2-inch baking dish. Combine next 5 ingredients, and pour over potatoes. Bake, uncovered, at 400° for 40 minutes. Sprinkle with cheese; bake an additional 5 minutes. Yield: 4 to 6 servings. *Susan Leftwich,*
DeSoto, Texas.

STIR-FRIED VEGETABLES

2 cups fresh snow peas
2 tablespoons vegetable oil
1 cup diagonally sliced carrots
1 cup quartered mushrooms
½ cup sliced water chestnuts
2 large cloves garlic, minced
1 large cucumber, halved, seeded, and cut into julienne strips
½ cup chicken broth
2 teaspoons cornstarch
2 tablespoons dry sherry
1 tablespoon soy sauce

Wash snow peas; trim ends and remove strings. Set aside.
Place oil in a preheated wok, coating sides; heat at medium high (325°) 2 minutes. Add carrots, mushrooms, water chestnuts, and garlic; stir-fry 3 minutes. Add snow peas and cucumber; stir-fry 3 minutes.
Combine remaining ingredients; pour over vegetables, stirring until thickened. Yield: 6 servings. *Daisy Cotton,*
Edcouch, Texas.

GARLIC BUTTER

1 (8-ounce) container whipped butter or margarine
2 to 3 cloves garlic, crushed
1 tablespoon dried parsley flakes

Combine all ingredients; store, covered, in the refrigerator. Serve with crackers, bread, or use on vegetables. Yield: 1 cup. *Pat Belcher,*
Woodstock, Georgia.

Two kinds of cheese, green onions, eggs, and sour cream are baked into the filling of Cheesy Green Onion Quiche.

Green Onions Fill This Quiche

For a simple hot luncheon or supper dish, serve Cheesy Green Onion Quiche. The filling of cheese, bacon, eggs, and sour cream is similar to that of a traditional Quiche Lorraine. But the addition of mild-flavored green onions and two types of cheese—Swiss and Cheddar—makes it different.

CHEESY GREEN ONION QUICHE

Pastry for 9-inch quiche dish or pieplate
8 slices bacon, cooked and crumbled
¾ cup (3 ounces) shredded Cheddar
    cheese
¾ cup (3 ounces) shredded Swiss cheese
4 eggs, beaten
1 (8-ounce) carton commercial sour cream
½ cup half-and-half
¼ cup sliced green onion
1 tablespoon all-purpose flour
¾ teaspoon salt
⅛ teaspoon pepper
Dash of red pepper

Line a 9-inch quiche dish or pieplate with pastry; trim excess pastry around edges. Prick bottom and sides of pastry with a fork. Bake at 400° for 3 minutes; remove from oven, and gently prick with a fork. Bake 5 minutes longer.

Sprinkle bacon and cheese into pastry shell. Combine remaining ingredients, and mix well. Pour into pastry shell. Bake at 375° for 40 to 45 minutes or until set. Yield: one 9-inch quiche.

Grace Bravos,
Timonium, Maryland.

COOKING LIGHT

Microwaving The Light Way

The microwave oven can be a real friend if you're dieting. Since it speeds cooking time, you'll be less tempted to snack before your meal is ready. Also, less water is needed, so fewer vitamins and minerals are lost.

The natural tenderness of chicken and fish makes them both excellent choices for the microwave. They remain moist and tender during cooking, even when no fat is added. You can cook fish in the microwave in only a few minutes. Be careful not to overcook it though, or it will be tough and dry.

When preparing Pineapple Chicken, arrange the meatier pieces of chicken around the outside of the dish since microwave energy enters around the sides of the dish first. As with many of our recipes, we recommend rotating the dish halfway through the microwaving to promote even cooking. You may want to rearrange the chicken pieces in the dish at this time, too.

The secret to microwaving meat loaf for a diet is to cook it on a bacon or meat rack so excess fat drips away. By starting with lean beef, you can keep calories even lower.

ORIENTAL MEAT LOAF

1 pound lean ground beef
1 egg, beaten
¾ cup soft whole wheat breadcrumbs
¼ cup finely chopped onion
¼ cup finely chopped green pepper
¼ cup finely chopped water chestnuts
¼ cup reduced-calorie catsup
1½ tablespoons soy sauce
¼ teaspoon pepper
Vegetable cooking spray

Combine first 9 ingredients; shape into a 5-inch round loaf. Place on a bacon or meat rack coated with vegetable cooking spray. Cover with heavy-duty plastic wrap. Microwave at HIGH for 10 to 14 minutes or until firm, giving dish a half-turn after 5 minutes. Drain off drippings. Let stand 5 minutes. Yield: 4 servings (about 287 calories per serving).

PINEAPPLE CHICKEN

1 (3-pound) broiler-fryer, cut up and
    skinned
¼ teaspoon red pepper
1 (20-ounce) can unsweetened pineapple
    chunks, drained
2 tablespoons raisins
1 cup unsweetened orange juice
⅛ teaspoon ground cinnamon
⅛ teaspoon ground cloves
1 tablespoon cornstarch
¼ cup water

Place chicken in a 3-quart baking dish; sprinkle with red pepper. Combine next 5 ingredients, and pour around chicken. Cover with heavy-duty plastic wrap; microwave at HIGH for 17 to 20 minutes or until done, rotating dish after half the time. Remove chicken to serving platter, and keep warm.

Combine cornstarch and water, stirring until smooth; stir into pan drippings. Cover and microwave at HIGH for 1½ minutes or until the sauce boils and thickens. Spoon sauce over chicken to serve. Yield: 6 servings (about 202 calories per serving).

HALIBUT WITH SWISS SAUCE

3 tablespoons water
3 tablespoons dry white wine
1 medium carrot, scraped and cut into ½-inch pieces
1 stalk celery, cut into 1-inch pieces
5 green onions, cut into 1-inch pieces
½ lemon, sliced
4 peppercorns
1 bay leaf
2 tablespoons chopped fresh parsley
1 pound halibut steaks
Swiss Sauce
Paprika

Combine first 9 ingredients in a 12- x 8- x 2-inch baking dish; stir well, being sure vegetables are evenly distributed in dish. Cover with heavy-duty plastic wrap; microwave at HIGH for 4 to 7 minutes or until the vegetables are crisp-tender.

Arrange fish steaks over vegetables. Cover and microwave at HIGH for 4 to 5 minutes or until fish flakes easily when tested with a fork, rotating dish after half the time. Remove fish steaks, and keep warm. Strain and reserve ¼ cup fish stock; use to prepare Swiss Sauce. Discard vegetables and remaining stock.

Return fish steaks to baking dish; spoon Swiss Sauce over steaks. Sprinkle with paprika. Cover and microwave at MEDIUM (50% power) for 2 to 3 minutes or until bubbly. Yield: 3 servings (about 151 calories per serving plus 24 calories per tablespoon sauce).

Swiss Sauce:
1½ tablespoons reduced-calorie margarine
1½ tablespoons all-purpose flour
⅛ teaspoon salt
⅛ teaspoon white pepper
½ cup skim milk
¼ cup reserved fish stock
¼ cup (1 ounce) shredded Swiss cheese

Place margarine in a 1-quart glass measure. Microwave at HIGH for 15 seconds or until margarine melts; blend in flour, salt, and pepper. Gradually add milk and fish stock, stirring well.

Microwave at HIGH for 2 minutes or until thickened and bubbly, stirring at 1-minute intervals. Add cheese, stirring until melted. Yield: ¾ cup.

HARVARD BEETS

4 medium beets, peeled and cut into ¼-inch slices
½ cup water
2 teaspoons cornstarch
½ cup unsweetened grape juice
¼ cup vinegar
1 teaspoon grated orange rind

Combine beets and water in a 2-quart casserole. Cover with heavy-duty plastic wrap; microwave at HIGH for 11 to 13 minutes or until tender, stirring after half the time; drain.

Combine remaining ingredients in a 2-cup glass measure. Cover and microwave at HIGH for 2 minutes or until mixture boils and thickens.

Pour grape juice mixture over the beets, and microwave at HIGH for 1 minute or until beets are thoroughly heated. Yield: 4 servings (about 44 calories per serving).

ONION-POTATO BAKE

2 medium potatoes (about 1¼ pounds)
Vegetable cooking spray
¼ cup Italian reduced-calorie salad dressing
2 medium onions, thinly sliced and separated into rings
¼ pound fresh mushrooms
1 tablespoon grated Parmesan cheese
¼ teaspoon paprika
¼ teaspoon pepper

Scrub potatoes, and slice ⅛ inch thick. Coat a shallow 2-quart casserole with cooking spray. Combine potatoes and salad dressing in casserole; toss gently. Cover and microwave at HIGH for 10 to 12 minutes, stirring at 4-minute intervals.

Stir in remaining ingredients. Cover and microwave at HIGH for 10 to 12 minutes, stirring at 4-minute intervals. Yield: 6 servings (about 88 calories per serving).

MARINATED VEGETABLE KABOBS

1 medium-size yellow squash
1 small zucchini
8 cherry tomatoes
8 medium-size fresh mushrooms
¾ cup Italian reduced-calorie salad dressing
¼ cup dry white wine

Combine vegetables in a large shallow container. Combine salad dressing and wine; pour over vegetables, and marinate at least 4 hours.

Thread vegetables onto four 8-inch bamboo skewers, reserving marinade. Place in a 12- x 8- x 2-inch baking dish. Drizzle with half of reserved marinade. Cover with heavy-duty plastic wrap. Microwave at HIGH for 5 minutes or until squash is crisp-tender. Let stand, covered, 2 minutes. Yield: 4 servings (about 48 calories per serving).

MIXED VEGETABLES

2 carrots, scraped and diagonally sliced ¼ inch thick
2 stalks celery, diagonally sliced ¼ inch thick
1 clove garlic, minced
¼ cup water
4 green onions, cut into 1-inch pieces
2 medium-size yellow squash, diagonally sliced ¼ inch thick
1 green pepper, cut into ½-inch strips
1 tablespoon soy sauce
¼ teaspoon pepper

Combine first 4 ingredients in a 1¾-quart casserole. Cover with heavy-duty plastic wrap, and microwave at HIGH for 4 minutes; stir well. Add green onions, squash, and green pepper; cover and microwave at HIGH for 3 to 4 minutes or until crisp-tender. Add soy sauce and pepper to the vegetables; toss lightly. Yield: 6 servings (about 30 calories per serving).

Tip: Never microwave an egg in its shell. Steam can build up and the egg will burst.

Take A Covered Main Dish

The next time you go to a covered-dish supper, take along one of these entrées. You'll find they're tasty, economical, and easy to transport.

Your dish will be warmest if you plan for it to come out of the oven just before you're ready to leave, and cover it immediately with a lid or aluminum foil. To help hold in the heat, you can wrap the dish in about eight thicknesses of newspaper. Or for several dishes, try stacking them in a large ice chest.

Casserole dishes that fit into baskets are perfect for covered-dish suppers. With or without handles, a basket makes it easy to carry a hot dish and also acts as a trivet, so you can set the dish directly on the table.

BROCCOLI-BEEF PIE

2 cups chopped fresh broccoli
1 pound ground beef
1 (4-ounce) can mushroom stems and
    pieces, drained
2 cups (8 ounces) shredded Cheddar
    cheese, divided
⅓ cup chopped onion
2 cups biscuit mix
½ cup water
4 eggs
½ cup milk
¼ cup grated Parmesan cheese
½ teaspoon salt
Dash of pepper

Cook broccoli in small amount of boiling water 5 minutes or until tender; drain and set aside.

Brown ground beef in a large skillet, stirring to crumble; drain off pan drippings. Stir in mushrooms, 1½ cups Cheddar cheese, and onion. Remove from heat, and set aside.

Combine biscuit mix and water; stir to form a soft dough. Add remaining ½ cup Cheddar cheese; stir just until blended. With well-floured hands, pat dough into a greased 13- x 9- x 2-inch baking dish, spreading dough halfway up sides of dish. Spoon meat mixture over dough, and top with the chopped broccoli.

Combine remaining ingredients, beating well; pour over broccoli. Bake, uncovered, at 350° for 35 minutes or until a knife inserted in center comes out clean. Yield: about 8 servings.

Kathy Greever,
Mountain City, Tennessee.

BEEF SUPREME

1½ pounds ground beef
1 (14½-ounce) can whole tomatoes,
    undrained
1 (10½-ounce) can pizza sauce with cheese
2 cloves garlic, pressed
1 (8-ounce) package medium egg noodles
1 (8-ounce) carton commercial sour cream
2 (3-ounce) packages cream cheese, cut
    into small chunks
6 green onions with tops, chopped

Brown ground beef in a large skillet, stirring to crumble; drain off pan drippings. Add tomatoes, pizza sauce, and garlic; simmer, uncovered, 10 minutes.

Prepare noodles according to package directions; drain. Combine noodles, sour cream, cream cheese, and green onions, stirring well.

Spoon half of noodle mixture into a greased 12- x 8- x 2-inch baking dish; top with half of meat mixture. Repeat the layers. Cover and bake at 350° for 35 minutes. Yield: 6 to 8 servings.

Mrs. C. W. Kennard,
Anderson, Texas.

SAUSAGE AND WILD RICE CASSEROLE

1 pound bulk pork sausage
½ cup chopped celery
1 tablespoon dried green pepper flakes
1 (10¾-ounce) can cream of mushroom
    soup, undiluted
1½ cups water
1 cup wild rice, uncooked
1 (4-ounce) jar diced pimiento, drained
1 (2½-ounce) jar sliced mushrooms,
    drained
1 cup (4 ounces) shredded Cheddar cheese
1 tablespoon instant minced onion
2 teaspoons chicken-flavored bouillon
    granules
½ teaspoon dried whole marjoram
½ teaspoon dried whole thyme

Brown sausage in a Dutch oven, stirring to crumble. Add celery and green pepper flakes; sauté until celery is tender. Drain off pan drippings.

Stir in remaining ingredients. Pour mixture into a lightly greased 13- x 9- x 2-inch baking dish. Cover and bake at 325° for 1½ hours or until rice is tender. Yield: 8 servings.

Mrs. William F. Collins,
Blacksburg, Virginia.

HOT CHICKEN SALAD

2 cups diced cooked chicken
1½ cups diced celery
½ cup slivered almonds, toasted
2 hard-cooked eggs, chopped
1 tablespoon chopped onion
1 cup mayonnaise
1½ teaspoons grated lemon rind
2 teaspoons lemon juice
½ teaspoon pepper
1½ cups (6 ounces) shredded Cheddar
    cheese
1½ cups crushed potato chips

Combine first 9 ingredients in a large bowl; mix well. Spoon chicken mixture into a lightly greased shallow 2-quart casserole; sprinkle with cheese, and top with potato chips. Bake at 375° for 25 minutes. Yield: 6 servings.

Mildred Sherrer,
Bay City, Texas.

BAKED TUNA AND PEAS IN WINE SAUCE

3 tablespoons butter or margarine
3 tablespoons all-purpose flour
1 cup milk
½ cup dry white wine
¼ teaspoon salt
¼ teaspoon pepper
¼ teaspoon dried whole basil
2 (10-ounce) cans tuna, drained and
    flaked
1 (10-ounce) package frozen English peas,
    thawed
2 hard-cooked eggs, chopped

Melt butter in a heavy saucepan over low heat; add flour, stirring until smooth. Cook 1 minute, stirring constantly. Gradually stir in milk; cook over medium heat, stirring constantly, until mixture is thickened and bubbly. Stir in wine, salt, pepper, and basil.

Place tuna in a greased 2-quart casserole; top with peas and egg. Spoon sauce evenly over casserole. Bake, uncovered, at 350° for 30 minutes. Yield: 8 servings. *Susan Panettiere,*
Little Rock, Arkansas.

Tip: "Light meat" tuna is less expensive than "white meat" tuna. Prices also descend according to the pack—from fancy or solid, to chunks, to flaked or grated. When you intend to use tuna for salads, sandwich fillings, creamed dishes, or even casserole dishes, you can save money by buying the less expensive packs.

September

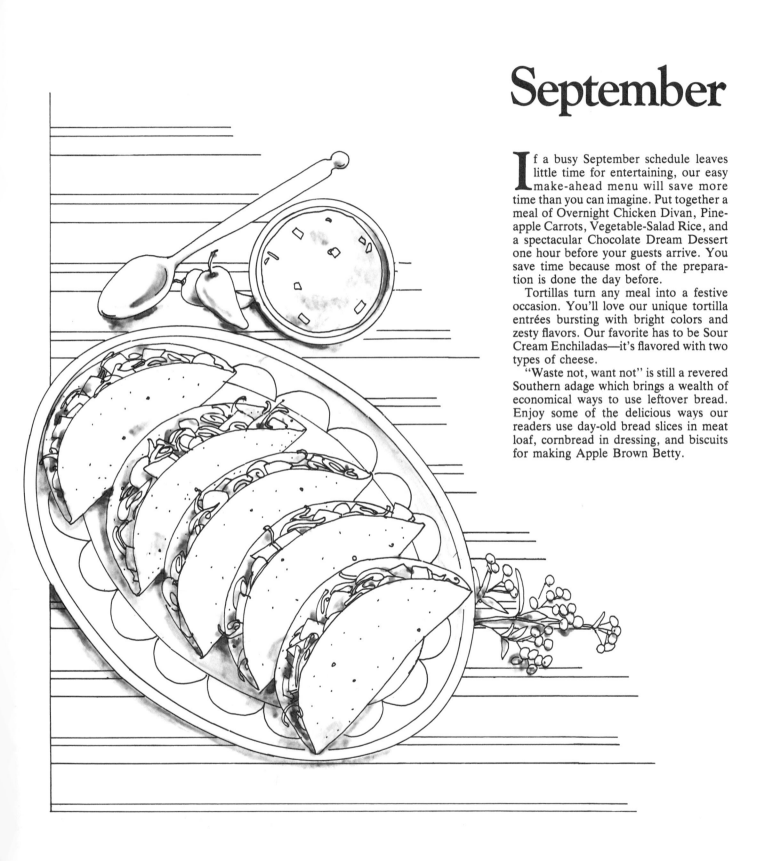

I f a busy September schedule leaves little time for entertaining, our easy make-ahead menu will save more time than you can imagine. Put together a meal of Overnight Chicken Divan, Pineapple Carrots, Vegetable-Salad Rice, and a spectacular Chocolate Dream Dessert one hour before your guests arrive. You save time because most of the preparation is done the day before.

Tortillas turn any meal into a festive occasion. You'll love our unique tortilla entrées bursting with bright colors and zesty flavors. Our favorite has to be Sour Cream Enchiladas—it's flavored with two types of cheese.

"Waste not, want not" is still a revered Southern adage which brings a wealth of economical ways to use leftover bread. Enjoy some of the delicious ways our readers use day-old bread slices in meat loaf, cornbread in dressing, and biscuits for making Apple Brown Betty.

Here's A Menu To Make Ahead

When you're entertaining on a tight schedule, preparation time is as important as the menu. We've designed a meal for eight that can be ready in an hour. Most of the recipes are assembled in advance, but planning of last-minute tasks can save you more time.

Start by mixing up sherry-flavored Overnight Chicken Divan, Vegetable-Rice Salad, and Chocolate Dream Dessert the day before; then refrigerate overnight. The next day, set out the entrée and the butter for bread an hour before dinner, and let them come to room temperature.

During the 10 minutes it takes to cook the carrots, slice the French bread, assemble seasonings to mix with the softened butter, and preheat the oven to 350°. When you put the entrée in the oven, spread bread slices with seasoned butter, wrap in foil, and set aside.

In the remaining time, you can finish preparing the Pineapple Carrots, garnish the dessert, and turn out chilled Vegetable-Rice Salad on a lettuce-lined platter. Don't forget to put the bread in the oven 15 minutes before the entrée is finished baking; both bake at the same temperature.

Overnight Chicken Divan
Pineapple Carrots
Vegetable-Rice Salad
Herb-Seasoned French Bread
Chocolate Dream Dessert
Iced Tea   Coffee

OVERNIGHT CHICKEN DIVAN

8 chicken breast halves
1 teaspoon salt
2 (10-ounce) packages frozen broccoli spears
1 (10½-ounce) can cream of chicken soup, undiluted
½ cup commercial sour cream
½ cup mayonnaise
2 tablespoons dry sherry
1 teaspoon paprika
1 teaspoon prepared mustard
¼ teaspoon curry powder
⅓ cup grated Parmesan cheese
Paprika

Combine chicken and salt in a Dutch oven; cover with water. Bring to a boil; cover, reduce heat, and simmer 1 hour or until tender. Remove chicken, and

let cool. (Reserve broth for other uses.) Remove skin; bone chicken, and coarsely chop meat. Set aside.

Cook broccoli according to package directions; drain well. Arrange in a lightly greased 13- x 9- x 2-inch baking dish. Combine next 7 ingredients; spoon half of sauce over broccoli. Arrange chicken over sauce; top with remaining sauce. Cover; refrigerate overnight.

Let stand at room temperature 30 minutes before baking. Bake at 350° for 25 minutes. Remove from oven; sprinkle with cheese and paprika. Bake an additional 5 minutes. Yield: 8 servings.
*Mrs. Frank J. Yount,
Baldwin, Maryland.*

PINEAPPLE CARROTS

10 medium carrots, diagonally sliced
1 (15¼-ounce) can pineapple tidbits, undrained
1 cup orange juice
1 tablespoon cornstarch
1 teaspoon salt
½ teaspoon ground cinnamon

Cook carrots in boiling water to cover 10 minutes or until tender; drain.

Drain liquid from pineapple; set pineapple aside. Combine pineapple juice, orange juice, cornstarch, salt, and cinnamon in a medium saucepan; mix well. Cook over medium heat, stirring constantly, until smooth and thickened.

Add carrots and pineapple; cook, stirring constantly, until thoroughly heated. Yield: 8 servings. *Jeanne H. Minetree,
Dinwiddie, Virginia.*

VEGETABLE-RICE SALAD

1½ cups uncooked regular rice
1½ cups diced celery
¾ cup diced green pepper
1¾ cups diced tomatoes
⅓ cup chopped onion
¾ cup mayonnaise
1 tablespoon plus 1½ teaspoons Dijon mustard
2 tablespoons creamy garlic dressing
Lettuce leaves
Tomato roses

Cook rice according to package directions. Cool. Combine rice and vegetables; toss lightly. Combine mayonnaise, mustard, and dressing. Pour over rice mixture; toss lightly. Pack into a lightly oiled 6-cup mold. Chill overnight.

Unmold on a lettuce-lined platter; garnish with tomato roses. Yield: 8 servings.
*Darleene J. Lathan,
Sumter, South Carolina.*

HERB-SEASONED FRENCH BREAD

1 loaf unsliced French bread
⅓ cup butter or margarine, softened
1 teaspoon Worcestershire sauce
2 teaspoons dried parsley flakes
½ teaspoon dried whole basil
¼ teaspoon garlic powder

Slice French bread into 1-inch slices. Combine remaining ingredients, mixing well; spread butter mixture between bread slices. Wrap loaf in aluminum foil; bake at 350° for 15 minutes or until thoroughly heated. Yield: 1 loaf.
*L. W. Goshert,
Houston, Texas.*

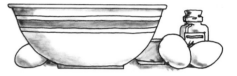

CHOCOLATE DREAM DESSERT

2 dozen ladyfingers, split
¼ cup Kahlúa or other coffee-flavored liqueur
12 (1-ounce) squares semisweet chocolate
2 (8-ounce) packages cream cheese, softened
½ cup sugar
3 eggs, separated
2 teaspoons vanilla extract
2 cups whipping cream, whipped
Sweetened whipped cream
Chocolate curls
Maraschino cherries

Line the bottom and sides of a 9-inch springform pan with ladyfingers, placing the rounded sides of ladyfingers toward pan. Brush cut side of ladyfingers with Kahlúa. Set aside.

Place chocolate in top of double boiler; bring water to a boil. Reduce heat to low; cook until chocolate melts. Let cool.

Beat cream cheese and sugar until light and fluffy. Add egg yolks, one at a time, beating well after each addition. Stir in melted chocolate and vanilla; mix until smooth.

Beat egg whites (at room temperature) until stiff peaks form. Fold egg whites and whipped cream into chocolate mixture; pour into prepared pan. Cover and chill overnight.

Place dessert on a serving platter, and remove rim from springform pan. Garnish with sweetened whipped cream, chocolate curls, and cherries. Yield: 14 to 16 servings. *Cynthia Kannenberg,
Brown Deer, Wisconsin.*

Make A Main Dish From Tortillas

Spicy meats, cheese, chiles, and vegetables are heaped onto tortillas or rolled up inside them for the tasty entrées you'll find here. Our readers have created their own variations of burritos, tacos, enchiladas, tostadas, and more to help you spread a colorful table with south-of-the-border flavor.

If you're confused about the differences in tortilla specialties, remember that the name of the dish indicates the type of tortilla to use and the method of preparation. For example, enchiladas are corn tortillas wrapped around a meat or vegetable filling and basted in a sauce while baking. The sauce helps soften the corn tortillas, which would otherwise be tough and dry after baking. Fillings are the same for burritos, but tender flour tortillas are substituted for corn tortillas. Since baking doesn't toughen flour tortillas, sauce can be served to the side.

BASIC TACOS

1 pound ground beef
1 medium onion, chopped
Commercial taco sauce
2 teaspoons Worcestershire sauce
1½ teaspoons chili powder
1 teaspoon garlic salt
½ teaspoon dried whole oregano
½ teaspoon paprika
¼ teaspoon dried whole rosemary, crushed
¼ teaspoon ground cumin
¼ teaspoon pepper
12 corn tortillas
Vegetable oil
2 to 3 cups shredded lettuce
2 large tomatoes, chopped
1 cup (4 ounces) shredded Cheddar cheese

Combine beef and onion in a skillet; cook over medium heat until beef is browned, stirring to crumble. Drain. Stir in 3 tablespoons taco sauce, Worcestershire sauce, and seasonings; simmer 5 minutes or until heated.

Fry tortillas in ⅛ inch hot oil (375°) until slightly crisp; quickly fold in half, leaving about 1½ inches between edges. Drain.

Place 2 to 3 tablespoons meat in each tortilla; top meat with lettuce, tomatoes, cheese, and 1 to 2 tablespoons taco sauce. Repeat procedure with remaining ingredients. Yield: 6 servings.
Mrs. Johnnie Dominguez, Jr.,
Navasota, Texas.

SUPER TOSTADAS

1 pound ground beef
1 medium onion, chopped
1 (15-ounce) can refried beans
2 medium avocados
1 tablespoon lemon juice
10 corn or flour tortillas
Vegetable oil
2 cups (8 ounces) shredded Cheddar cheese
2 cups shredded lettuce
2 large tomatoes, chopped
Commercial taco sauce

Combine ground beef and onion in a skillet; cook over medium heat until beef is browned, stirring to crumble. Drain. Stir in beans. Set aside.

Peel avocados, and remove seeds. Mash avocados. Stir in lemon juice to prevent browning. Set aside.

Fry tortillas, one at a time, in ¼ inch hot oil (375°) 20 to 30 seconds on each side until crisp and golden brown. Drain on paper towels.

Spoon beef mixture onto tortillas; sprinkle with cheese. Bake at 400° for 2 to 3 minutes or until cheese melts. Top with lettuce, tomato, and avocado. Serve with taco sauce. Yield: 10 servings.
Mrs. Bobbye Bishop,
Alice, Texas.

FLAUTAS

1 (2½- to 3-pound) broiler-fryer, cut up and skinned
2 quarts water
1 medium onion, chopped
2 tablespoons butter or margarine
1 (10-ounce) can tomatoes and green chiles, undrained
1 teaspoon garlic powder
½ teaspoon ground cumin
½ teaspoon salt
⅛ teaspoon pepper
18 corn tortillas
Vegetable oil
Commercial sour cream
Commercial taco sauce

Combine chicken and water in a Dutch oven. Bring to a boil; cover and simmer 1½ hours or until chicken is tender. Remove chicken from broth, reserving broth for use in other recipes. Shred chicken with a fork. Set aside.

Sauté onion in butter in a large skillet until tender. Add chicken, tomatoes and green chiles, garlic powder, cumin, salt, and pepper; cook over medium heat, stirring occasionally, 5 to 8 minutes or until liquid evaporates.

Fry tortillas, one at a time, in ¼ inch hot oil (375°) about 5 seconds on each side or just until softened. Drain thoroughly on paper towels.

Place about 2 tablespoons chicken mixture across center of a tortilla in a narrow strip. Roll up tortilla tightly, and secure with a wooden pick. Repeat with remaining ingredients.

Fry flautas in deep hot oil (375°) 2 to 3 minutes or until golden brown, turning once. Drain well on paper towels. Serve with sour cream and taco sauce. Yield: 9 servings.
Cindie King,
Beaumont, Texas.

MONTEZUMA TORTILLA PIE

2 cups peeled chopped tomatoes
2 small cloves garlic
¼ teaspoon sugar
½ teaspoon salt
½ cup water
3 tablespoons peanut or safflower oil
⅓ cup chopped onion
2 (4-ounce) cans chopped green chiles, drained
24 corn tortillas
Vegetable oil
2 cups chopped cooked chicken
1½ cups commercial sour cream
1¾ cups (7 ounces) shredded Cheddar cheese

Combine first 5 ingredients in container of electric blender. Blend on high speed 1 minute or until smooth. Pour into a skillet; cook 8 minutes over medium heat, stirring often. Set aside.

Heat peanut oil in a skillet; sauté onion until tender. Add chiles; reduce heat and simmer, covered, 4 minutes. Set aside.

Fry tortillas, one at a time, in 2 tablespoons hot oil (375°) about 5 seconds on each side or just until tortillas are softened. Add additional oil, if necessary. Drain on paper towels.

Place 8 tortillas in a lightly greased 13- x 9- x 2-inch baking dish. Layer half the chicken, half the chile mixture, one-third the sauce, one-third the sour cream, and one-third the cheese. Repeat all layers; top with remaining tortillas and remaining sauce, sour cream, and cheese. Bake at 350° for 25 minutes; serve immediately. Yield: 6 to 8 servings.
Tina Alvarez,
Willow Park, Texas.

BROCCOLI BURRITOS

10 flour tortillas
2 (1-pound) bunches fresh broccoli,
    coarsely chopped
1½ cups (6 ounces) shredded Monterey
    Jack cheese
1 large tomato, finely chopped
¾ cup chopped onion
1 (8-ounce) can tomato sauce
1 (8-ounce) carton commercial sour cream
Fresh parsley sprigs (optional)

Wrap tortillas tightly in aluminum foil; bake at 350° for 15 minutes.

Combine broccoli, cheese, tomato, and onion; spoon mixture evenly in center of each tortilla. Roll up each tortilla; place seam side down in a lightly greased 12- x 8- x 2-inch baking dish. Top with tomato sauce. Cover dish, and bake at 350° for 45 minutes. Spread sour cream over top; garnish with parsley, if desired. Yield: 10 servings.

Mary M. Brown,
Richardson, Texas.

VEGETABLE BURRITOS WITH AVOCADO SAUCE

1 clove garlic, crushed
1 medium onion, chopped
2 tablespoons vegetable oil
1 (8-ounce) can water chestnuts, drained
    and cut into julienne strips
1 large zucchini, coarsely shredded
1 cup fresh mushrooms, sliced
1 teaspoon celery salt
1 tomato, chopped
Salt and pepper to taste
10 (6-inch) flour tortillas
2 cups (8 ounces) shredded Cheddar
    cheese
Avocado Sauce

Sauté garlic and onion in hot oil in a large skillet until onion is limp. Reduce heat; stir in water chestnuts, zucchini, and mushrooms. Cook 3 to 4 minutes. Add celery salt and tomato; cook until thoroughly heated. Remove from heat; season with salt and pepper.

Wrap tortillas tightly in aluminum foil; bake at 350° for 15 minutes.

Spoon 2 heaping tablespoons of vegetable mixture on center of each tortilla. Sprinkle with 2 tablespoons of cheese. Fold edge nearest filling up and over filling just until mixture is covered. Fold in sides of tortilla to center; roll up. Repeat with remaining ingredients.

Place burritos in a 13- x 9- x 2-inch baking dish. Bake at 350° for 15 minutes. Top with Avocado Sauce to serve. Yield: 5 servings.

Avocado Sauce:

1 (8-ounce) carton commercial sour cream
1 tablespoon lemon juice
1 medium avocado, chopped

Combine all ingredients in a small bowl, mixing well. Yield: 1 cup.

Marilyn Salinas,
Fort Worth, Texas.

SOUR CREAM ENCHILADAS

1 (1.5-ounce) package enchilada sauce mix
1 (8-ounce) can tomato sauce
1½ cups water
3½ cups (14 ounces) shredded Longhorn
    cheese, divided
1 cup (4 ounces) shredded Monterey Jack
    cheese with jalapeño peppers, divided
1 (16-ounce) carton commercial sour
    cream
1 cup chopped green onion
½ teaspoon ground cumin
12 corn tortillas
Vegetable oil
Additional chopped green onion

Combine enchilada mix, tomato sauce, and water in a small saucepan. Bring to a boil, reduce heat, and simmer 10 minutes. Set aside.

Combine ½ cup of each cheese in a medium mixing bowl. Add sour cream, 1 cup green onion, and cumin; mix well. Set aside.

Fry tortillas, one at a time, in 2 tablespoons hot oil (375°) about 5 seconds on each side or just until tortillas are softened. Add additional oil, if necessary. Drain on paper towels; then dip each tortilla in enchilada sauce.

Place about 1½ tablespoons of sour cream mixture on each tortilla; roll up tightly, and place seam side down in a lightly greased 12- x 8- x 2-inch baking

dish. Pour remaining enchilada sauce over top.

Bake at 375° for 20 minutes. Sprinkle remaining cheese over top, and return to oven 5 minutes. Garnish with chopped onion. Yield: 6 servings.

Cecilia Breithaupt,
Boerne, Texas.

Easy Veal In A Skillet

No matter how it's prepared, veal is always a special treat. But this recipe is especially nice because it's pretty and easy to fix.

SKILLET VEAL

1 (6-ounce) can sliced mushrooms,
    undrained
1½ pounds (¼-inch-thick) boneless veal
    cutlets
½ teaspoon salt
2 tablespoons vegetable oil
1 (16-ounce) can whole tomatoes,
    undrained and chopped
1 (1½-ounce) envelope spaghetti sauce mix
    with mushrooms
⅓ cup sherry
1 (16-ounce) jar pearl onions, drained
1 (16-ounce) can peas and carrots,
    drained

Drain mushrooms, reserving ¼ cup liquid; set aside.

Sprinkle veal with salt. Heat oil in a large skillet; add veal, and brown on both sides. Stir in tomatoes, spaghetti sauce mix, and sherry; bring to a boil. Cover, reduce heat, and simmer 10 minutes, stirring occasionally.

Add onions, peas and carrots, mushrooms, and reserved mushroom liquid; cover and simmer 10 additional minutes. Yield: 6 servings.

Carolyn Brantley,
Greenville, Mississippi.

Right: *Puffy Vegetable Omelet (page 188), filled with vegetables and cheese sauce, is one of the biggest, prettiest omelets ever. It's large enough to serve four people.*

Page 202: *Our Tex-Mex style Basic Tacos (page 199) are stuffed with spicy beef, lettuce, tomato, and cheese.*

Microwave Menu In Time For Breakfast

If breakfast is a busy time for your family, then turn to this microwave menu for help. In about 30 minutes you can put together a complete and nutritious meal to serve 4 to 6 people.

The key to making this meal quick and fuss-free lies in the order the dishes are assembled and microwaved. Begin by combining the ingredients for the coffee cake and then the Tomato Cocktail. After microwaving the cocktail, finish the coffee cake and allow it to stand. In the meantime, microwave the pears and then the grits. Microwave the eggs last so they will be hot and fluffy.

To make this breakfast even more convenient, leave off the coffee cake and prepare the Tomato Cocktail and Marmalade Pears the night before. In the time it takes to microwave the eggs and grits—about 15 minutes—everything will be ready.

**Tomato Cocktail
Creamy Onion Scrambled Eggs
Marmalade Breakfast Pears
Quick Cheese Grits
Cinnamon Coffee Cake**

TOMATO COCKTAIL

2 (12-ounce) cans cocktail vegetable juice
1 (14½-ounce) can beef broth, undiluted
1 tablespoon lemon juice
1 teaspoon Worcestershire sauce
⅛ teaspoon hot sauce
4 thin lemon slices (optional)

Combine first 5 ingredients in a deep 3-quart casserole. Cover and microwave at HIGH for 8 to 11 minutes or until boiling; stir well. Cover and chill. Stir before serving. Garnish with lemon slices, if desired. Yield: 4¾ cups.
Note: Tomato Cocktail may be refrigerated overnight, if desired.

Tip: For a quick juice, place frozen concentrate in a glass or plastic pitcher in the microwave oven. Microwave at HIGH for 30 to 50 seconds or until soft. Add water and stir.

CREAMY ONION SCRAMBLED EGGS

6 eggs
½ cup milk
1 (3-ounce) package cream cheese, cubed
¼ teaspoon salt
⅛ teaspoon pepper
3 tablespoons butter or margarine
⅓ cup chopped green onion with tops

Combine first 5 ingredients in container of electric blender; cover and process at medium speed 7 to 10 seconds until frothy.

Place butter in a 1½-quart casserole. Microwave at HIGH for 50 to 55 seconds or until melted. Add egg mixture; sprinkle with onion, and stir well. Microwave at HIGH for 1 to 2 minutes. Break up set portions of egg with a fork, and push toward center of dish. Microwave at HIGH for 2 to 3 minutes or until eggs are almost set, stirring gently at 1-minute intervals (eggs will be soft and moist). Stir gently again; cover and let stand 1 to 2 minutes. Yield: 4 to 6 servings.

MARMALADE BREAKFAST PEARS

⅓ cup orange marmalade
¼ cup orange juice
2 (16-ounce) cans pear halves, drained
½ cup commercial sour cream
2 teaspoons grated orange rind
½ teaspoon ground cinnamon

Combine marmalade and orange juice in an 8- or 9-inch square baking dish. Arrange pears, cut side down, in dish. Cover and microwave at HIGH for 4 to 5 minutes or until pears are hot. Let stand 2 minutes, basting occasionally with juice mixture.

Spoon pears into individual serving bowls with juice mixture. Combine sour cream, orange rind, and cinnamon, stirring well. Serve over pears. Yield: 4 to 6 servings.
Note: Cooked pear mixture may be refrigerated overnight and served cold.

QUICK CHEESE GRITS

2⅔ cups hot water
⅔ cup quick-cooking grits
¾ teaspoon salt
1 tablespoon butter or margarine
1 cup (4 ounces) shredded Cheddar cheese

Combine water, grits, and salt in a 2-quart casserole. Microwave at HIGH

for 9 to 10 minutes, stirring after 5 minutes. Add butter and cheese, mixing well. Microwave at HIGH for 1 minute or until butter and cheese melt; stir well. Yield: 4 to 6 servings.

CINNAMON COFFEE CAKE

2 tablespoons warm water (105° to 115°)
1 teaspoon sugar
1 package dry yeast
¼ cup shortening
½ cup sugar
1 egg
¼ cup warm milk (105° to 115°)
1¼ cups all-purpose flour
1 teaspoon baking powder
¼ teaspoon salt
Topping (recipe follows)

Combine water, 1 teaspoon sugar, and yeast; let mixture stand 5 minutes.

Cream shortening; gradually add ½ cup sugar, beating until blended. Add egg, beating well.

Combine milk and yeast mixture. Combine flour, baking powder, and salt; add to creamed mixture alternately with milk mixture, beginning and ending with flour mixture. Spoon batter into a greased 9-inch pieplate; sprinkle with topping.

Place pieplate in microwave oven on an inverted custard cup or saucer. Microwave at MEDIUM (50% power) for 7 to 10 minutes or until surface springs back when lightly touched with finger, giving dish a quarter turn at 2-minute intervals. Place dish on a sheet of aluminum foil; let stand 15 minutes. Serve warm. Yield: one 9-inch coffee cake.

Topping:

1½ tablespoons butter or margarine
¼ cup firmly packed brown sugar
1½ tablespoons all-purpose flour
½ teaspoon ground cinnamon
¼ teaspoon ground nutmeg
¼ cup chopped pecans

Place butter in a small glass bowl. Microwave at HIGH for 10 seconds or until softened. Combine brown sugar, flour, cinnamon, and nutmeg; cut in butter with pastry blender until mixture resembles coarse meal. Stir in pecans. Yield: about ½ cup.

Light Ways With Milk, Cheese, And Eggs

Milk, cheese, and eggs are common ingredients in most kitchens. The good news for dieters is that today's market offers a variety of choices that make "Cooking Light" with these products a lot easier. The smart cook will learn to interpret food labels and choose the products best suited for a specific recipe and calorie plan.

Some studies have suggested that high amounts of cholesterol in the blood increase the risk of heart disease. So nutritionists recommend that people who have high blood cholesterol levels should avoid excess cholesterol.

Blood cholesterol levels also seem to be affected by the type of fat eaten. Saturated fats (largely found in animal products, such as meat and whole milk) tend to increase blood cholesterol. Poly-unsaturated fats (found in large proportions in vegetable products, such as corn and soybean oil) tend to decrease blood cholesterol.

Whole milk, most natural cheese, and egg yolks all contain quite a bit of saturated fat and cholesterol. By choosing skim milk instead of whole, you can avoid the saturated fat and cholesterol in milk—and, you'll save about 80 calories per cup. If you choose skim or low-fat milk fortified with vitamins A and D, you'll get all the nutrients present in whole milk, except fat and calories.

Almost all buttermilk is made from skim milk and contains about the same number of calories. Whole buttermilk is available in some areas but, like whole milk, should be avoided.

While whole milk contains some unnecessary fat and calories, whipping cream and half-and-half contain even more. One cup of whipping cream totals 830 calories—that's not counting the calories from sugar added when it's whipped and sweetened!

Keep a box of instant nonfat dry milk powder on hand for cooking or to reconstitute and drink as a beverage. Reconstituted nonfat dry milk is equal to skim milk in calories and other nutrients. Evaporated skim milk is another low-fat milk product to keep on hand.

Yogurt has been increasingly popular among dieters over the past few years, but it isn't always low in calories.

Dieters should be wary of whole milk yogurt and yogurt filled with fruit preserves. The added fruit and sugar can push calories per 8-ounce container up to 280—that's compared to only 140 per 8 ounces of the plain low-fat kind.

Cottage cheese, like yogurt, is another frequent choice of dieters. Look for a label that says "low-fat" (1% fat) to save up to 80 calories per cup. And while ricotta is similar in texture and taste to cottage cheese, it contains about 30 calories more per ounce.

Unlike low-fat cottage cheese, most natural cheeses are made from whole milk and are high in fat. By choosing strong-flavored cheeses, such as extra-sharp Cheddar, you can cut back on the amount you use and still get plenty of cheese flavor. Some cheeses, such as mozzarella, may be made from partially skim milk and are a little lower in calories than most natural cheese.

You'll find several kinds of diet cheese on the market today with labels claiming low-fat, low-calorie, low-cholesterol, and/or low-sodium. (Most natural and processed cheeses are high in sodium.) Read the labels to see what suits you best. Remember that if the label states "low-sodium," the cheese is not necessarily low in calories.

While high on the list of top-quality protein, eggs (specifically the yolks) contain large amounts of cholesterol. Egg whites contain almost no cholesterol, and low-cholesterol egg substitutes are available.

We show you how to keep calories as low as possible in each of our recipes using milk, cheese, and eggs.

CHEESY SPINACH LASAGNA

1 pound lean ground chuck
1 medium onion, chopped
1 green pepper, chopped
2 cloves garlic, minced
1 (16-ounce) can tomato puree
1 teaspoon dried whole oregano, crushed
1 teaspoon dried whole basil, crushed
½ teaspoon salt
⅛ teaspoon pepper
2 (10-ounce) packages frozen chopped spinach, thawed
1½ cups low-fat cottage cheese
1 egg, beaten
3 tablespoons grated Parmesan cheese
⅛ teaspoon ground nutmeg
Dash of hot sauce
6 lasagna noodles
Vegetable cooking spray
½ cup (2 ounces) shredded mozzarella cheese

Combine ground chuck, onion, green pepper, and garlic in a large skillet; cook over medium heat until meat is browned and onion is tender. Drain mixture in a colander, and pat dry with a paper towel; wipe pan drippings from skillet with a paper towel.

Return meat mixture to skillet, and add tomato puree, oregano, basil, salt, and pepper; simmer 5 minutes, stirring often. Set aside.

Place spinach on a paper towel, and squeeze until barely moist. Combine spinach, cottage cheese, egg, Parmesan cheese, nutmeg, and hot sauce.

Cook lasagna according to package directions, omitting the salt. Drain.

Coat a 12- x 8- x 2-inch baking pan with cooking spray. Spoon half of spinach mixture into pan; top with half of noodles. Spread half of meat mixture over noodles, and repeat layering. Cover and bake at 350° for 35 to 40 minutes. Sprinkle with mozzarella, and bake 5 minutes. Yield: 8 servings (about 271 calories per serving).

Note: Lasagna may be prepared in two 8-inch square baking pans. Spoon one-fourth mixture into each pan; cut noodles in half, and place 3 noodle halves over spinach in each pan. Spread one-fourth meat mixture over noodles in each pan; repeat layering. Cover and bake at 350° for 25 minutes. Sprinkle each pan with ¼ cup mozzarella cheese, and bake 5 additional minutes.

Lasagna freezes well. To serve, thaw in refrigerator, and bake as directed.

Patricia Hamby Andrews,
Knoxville, Tennessee.

HAM-AND-EGG CREPES

Vegetable cooking spray
½ cup diced cooked lean ham
4 eggs
¼ cup skim milk
¼ teaspoon pepper
6 crêpes (recipe follows)
Mushroom Sauce

Coat a large nonstick skillet with cooking spray; place over medium-high heat until hot. Add ham, and sauté 3 to 4 minutes or until lightly browned.

Combine eggs, milk, and pepper; beat well. Add egg mixture to ham; cook over low heat, stirring occasionally, until eggs are firm but still moist.

Spoon one-sixth of egg mixture in center of each crêpe; roll up. Spoon Mushroom Sauce evenly over crêpes, and serve immediately. Yield: 3 servings (about 258 calories per serving plus 15 calories per tablespoon sauce).

Crêpes:

2 eggs
1 cup skim milk
¾ cup plus 2 tablespoons all-purpose flour
⅛ to ¼ teaspoon salt
1½ teaspoons vegetable oil
Vegetable cooking spray

Combine first 5 ingredients in container of an electric blender; process 30 seconds. Scrape down sides of blender container with rubber spatula; process an additional 30 seconds or until smooth. Refrigerate batter 1 hour. (This allows flour particles to swell and soften so crepes are light in texture.)

Coat the bottom of a 6-inch crêpe pan or nonstick skillet with cooking spray; place pan over medium heat until just hot, not smoking.

Pour about 2 tablespoons batter into pan. Quickly tilt pan in all directions so batter covers the pan in a thin film; cook crêpe about 1 minute.

Lift edge of crêpe to test for doneness. Crêpe is ready for flipping when it can be shaken loose from pan. Flip the crêpe, and cook about 30 seconds on the other side. (This side is rarely more than spotty brown and is the side on which the filling is placed.)

When crêpe is done, place on a towel to cool. Stack the crêpes between layers of waxed paper to prevent sticking. Repeat until all batter is used, stirring occasionally. Freeze unused crêpes for another use, if desired. Yield: 13 (6-inch) crêpes.

Mushroom Sauce:

2 tablespoons reduced-calorie margarine
¼ pound fresh mushrooms, sliced
2 tablespoons minced onion
1 tablespoon all-purpose flour
¾ cup skim milk
2 tablespoons chopped fresh parsley
1 teaspoon prepared mustard
¼ teaspoon salt
⅛ teaspoon pepper
⅛ teaspoon ground nutmeg

Melt margarine in a heavy medium saucepan; add mushrooms and onion, and sauté 3 to 5 minutes or until onion is tender. Add flour, stirring until vegetables are coated. Cook 1 minute, stirring constantly. Gradually add milk; cook over medium heat, stirring constantly, until thickened and bubbly. Stir in remaining ingredients; cook, stirring constantly, until sauce is thoroughly heated. Yield: 1 cup.

Note: Filled crêpes may be heated if desired. Place seam side down in a shallow baking dish; spoon Mushroom Sauce over crêpes. Cover and bake at 350° for 15 minutes or until heated.

CHEDDAR-VEGETABLE OMELET

Vegetable cooking spray
1 small green pepper, chopped
½ cup sliced fresh mushrooms
1 small tomato, peeled and diced
4 eggs
¼ cup skim milk
2 tablespoons picante sauce
½ teaspoon salt
Dash of pepper
¼ cup (1 ounce) extra-sharp Cheddar cheese

Coat a small skillet with cooking spray; place over medium heat until hot. Add green pepper and mushrooms; sauté until tender. Stir in tomato; cook just until thoroughly heated. Set aside.

Combine next 5 ingredients; beat well. Coat a 10-inch nonstick skillet with cooking spray; place over medium heat until hot enough to sizzle a drop of water. Pour in egg mixture. As mixture starts to cook, gently lift edges of the omelet, and tilt pan to allow any uncooked portion to flow underneath.

Spoon mushroom mixture over half of omelet when eggs are set and top is still moist and creamy; sprinkle with cheese. Fold unfilled side of omelet over filling; place on a warm platter, and serve immediately. Yield: 2 servings (about 257 calories per serving).

MOCK SOUR CREAM

2 cups low-fat cottage cheese
¼ cup plain low-fat yogurt
1 egg
1 tablespoon lemon juice
1 tablespoon water
½ teaspoon dry mustard
¼ teaspoon white pepper
⅛ teaspoon hot sauce

Combine all ingredients in container of electric blender; process until mixture is smooth. Chill. Serve as a topping for baked potatoes or as a base for dips and spreads. Yield: 2 cups (about 14 calories per tablespoon).

CUCUMBER-YOGURT SOUP

2 medium cucumbers, peeled, seeded, and sliced
1 cup water
½ cup chopped onion
½ teaspoon salt
Dash of pepper
2 cups chicken broth, divided
¼ cup all-purpose flour
2 whole cloves
¾ cup plain low-fat yogurt
2 teaspoons dried whole dillweed

Combine first 5 ingredients in a saucepan; bring to a boil over medium heat. Reduce heat to low, cover, and simmer until cucumbers are tender. Spoon mixture into the container of an electric blender; process until mixture is smooth. Set aside.

Gradually add ½ cup chicken broth to flour in a saucepan; cook over low heat 1 minute, stirring constantly. Gradually add remaining 1½ cups broth and cucumber puree. Add cloves; simmer 5 minutes, stirring constantly. Chill well.

Remove cloves. Stir in yogurt and dillweed. Yield: 4 cups (about 89 calories per 1-cup serving).

Martha T. Leoni,
New Bern, North Carolina.

EGGNOG PIE

1 cup graham cracker crumbs
¼ cup reduced-calorie margarine, melted
⅓ cup sugar
⅓ cup instant nonfat dry milk powder
1 envelope unflavored gelatin
2 eggs, separated
1 cup cold water
1 teaspoon vanilla extract
¼ teaspoon rum extract
½ cup ice water
⅔ cup instant nonfat dry milk powder
Ground nutmeg (optional)

Combine graham cracker crumbs and margarine, stirring until well blended. Press mixture into bottom and sides of a 9-inch pieplate. Bake at 375° for 8 minutes; cool.

Combine sugar, ⅓ cup milk powder, and gelatin in a medium-size heavy saucepan; set aside. Beat egg yolks into 1 cup cold water. Stir egg mixture into gelatin mixture, blending well. Let stand 1 minute. Cook over medium heat, stirring constantly, until mixture comes to a full boil; remove from heat. Stir in flavorings. Chill until the consistency of unbeaten egg white.

Combine ½ cup ice water, egg whites, and ⅔ cup milk powder in a cold 1½-quart bowl. Beat with electric mixer at high speed until stiff peaks form. Gradually beat in custard using electric mixer at lowest speed. Pour into crumb crust. Sprinkle with nutmeg, if desired. Chill at least 2 hours or until firm. Yield: 8 servings (about 156 calories per serving). *Doris M. Horst,*
Hagerstown, Maryland.

ORANGE DESSERT SOUFFLE

3 tablespoons margarine
3 tablespoons all-purpose flour
¾ cup skim milk
¼ cup sugar
Dash of salt
1 tablespoon grated orange rind
¼ cup fresh orange juice
4 eggs, separated
½ teaspoon sugar

Melt margarine in a heavy saucepan over low heat; add flour, stirring until smooth. Cook 1 minute, stirring constantly. Gradually add milk; cook over medium heat, stirring constantly, until thickened and bubbly. Stir in ¼ cup sugar, salt, orange rind, and orange juice. Continue to cook over medium heat, stirring constantly, for 3 to 4 minutes. Remove from heat, and cool slightly.

Beat egg yolks until thick and lemon colored. Gradually stir about one-fourth of the hot mixture into egg yolks; add to remaining hot mixture, stirring constantly. Beat egg whites (at room temperature) until stiff peaks form. Gently fold into cooked mixture. Spoon mixture into a 1½-quart soufflé dish; sprinkle with ½ teaspoon sugar. Place dish in larger pan containing about 1 inch hot water; bake at 350° for 45 minutes. Serve immediately. Yield: 6 servings (about 162 calories per serving).

Bunny Campbell,
Gainesville, Florida.

Side Dishes That Rate Attention

Take the routine out of everyday meals by serving one of these exciting side dishes. The recipes aren't elaborate, but their flavors, textures, and colors perk up an ordinary meat loaf or baked chicken, turning it into a glamorous meal.

BROCCOLI WITH HORSERADISH SAUCE

½ cup mayonnaise
2 tablespoons butter or margarine, melted
1 tablespoon prepared horseradish
1 tablespoon grated onion
¼ teaspoon salt
¼ teaspoon dry mustard
Pinch of red pepper
1 (1-pound) bunch broccoli

Combine first 7 ingredients in a bowl; stir well. Chill 3 to 4 hours.

Trim off large leaves of broccoli, and remove tough ends of stalks. Wash broccoli thoroughly, and separate into spears. Cook broccoli, covered, in a small amount of boiling water 8 to 10 minutes or until crisp-tender. Arrange in a dish. Top with horseradish sauce. Yield: 4 servings. *Mrs. Joseph Laux,*
Toney, Alabama.

SAUCY GREEN BEANS

1 pound fresh green beans
1 large onion, thinly sliced
1 medium-size green pepper, chopped
¼ cup butter or margarine
2 large tomatoes, peeled and chopped
1 teaspoon dried whole basil
½ cup commercial sour cream
⅛ teaspoon salt
⅛ teaspoon pepper

Wash beans; trim ends and remove strings. Cut into 1-inch pieces. Cook beans, covered, in a small amount of boiling water 15 to 20 minutes or until tender; drain and set aside.

Sauté onion and green pepper in butter in a skillet until tender. Stir in beans and tomatoes. Combine remaining 4 ingredients; add to bean mixture, stirring gently. Cook until heated. Yield: 4 servings. *Sherri D. Medley,*
Greensboro, North Carolina.

CABBAGE SUPREME

¼ cup water
1 beef-flavored bouillon cube
5 cups shredded cabbage
1 cup thinly sliced carrot
½ cup chopped onion
½ teaspoon salt
½ teaspoon pepper
¼ cup butter or margarine
⅓ cup chopped pecans
1 teaspoon prepared mustard
¼ teaspoon paprika

Bring water to a boil in a large saucepan; add bouillon cube, and stir until dissolved. Add cabbage, carrot, onion, salt, and pepper; stir well. Cover, reduce heat, and simmer about 5 minutes, stirring occasionally.

Melt butter in a small saucepan; stir in pecans and mustard. Cook over medium heat 2 minutes, stirring constantly. Pour over cabbage mixture; stir well. Spoon into serving dish; sprinkle with paprika. Yield: 6 to 8 servings.

Jane Hancock,
Madison, Alabama.

CELERY ORIENTAL

2 cups diagonally sliced celery
1 (10¾-ounce) can cream of chicken soup, undiluted
1 (8-ounce) can sliced water chestnuts, drained
1 (2-ounce) jar diced pimiento, undrained
½ cup herb-seasoned stuffing mix
½ cup slivered almonds
2 tablespoons butter or margarine, melted

Combine first 4 ingredients, mixing well; spoon into a lightly greased 10- x 6- x 2-inch baking dish.

Combine remaining ingredients, and sprinkle over celery mixture. Bake, uncovered, at 350° for 45 minutes. Yield: 6 servings. *Mrs. Donald D. Sisson,*
Wimberley, Texas.

SAUTEED MUSHROOM SPECTACULAR

3 green onions with tops, chopped
¼ cup butter or margarine, melted
1 pound fresh mushrooms, sliced
¼ cup dry white wine
¼ teaspoon salt
¼ teaspoon pepper
⅛ teaspoon garlic powder
2 teaspoons Worcestershire sauce

Sauté green onion in butter until tender. Stir in remaining ingredients; cook, uncovered, over low heat 30 minutes or until mushrooms are tender. Yield: 4 servings.

Mrs. J. K. Garrett, Jr.,
Jonesboro, Georgia.

EASY CHINESE PEAS

1 (8-ounce) can sliced water chestnuts, drained
1 (4-ounce) jar whole mushrooms, drained
2 tablespoons vegetable oil
1 cup chicken broth
1 teaspoon cornstarch
1 teaspoon soy sauce
3 (6-ounce) packages frozen Chinese pea pods, thawed and drained
1 cup coarsely chopped green onion with tops

Sauté water chestnuts and mushrooms in oil in a Dutch oven 1 minute. Add chicken broth. Bring broth to a boil. Reduce heat and simmer, uncovered, for 10 minutes.

Combine cornstarch and soy sauce, stirring well; add to broth mixture. Cook, stirring constantly, until thickened. Add pea pods and onion; cook, stirring constantly, 5 minutes. Yield: 8 servings. *Patty Merritt,*
Jacksonville, North Carolina.

ENGLISH PEA-PIMIENTO CASSEROLE

2 (10-ounce) packages frozen English peas, thawed and drained
1 (10¾-ounce) can cream of mushroom soup, undiluted
1 cup chopped celery
1 (8-ounce) can water chestnuts, drained and chopped
¾ cup chopped onion
1 (2-ounce) jar diced pimiento, undrained
2 tablespoons butter or margarine, melted
½ cup fine, dry breadcrumbs

Combine first 6 ingredients; spoon mixture into a lightly greased 12- x 8- x 2-inch baking dish.

Combine butter and breadcrumbs; sprinkle over casserole. Bake at 350° for 25 to 30 minutes. Yield: 8 servings.

Mrs. Lawrence Clark,
Central City, Nebraska.

Pears For Dessert

Ripe juicy pears are naturally sweet and offer a variety of dessert ideas. You can highlight their flavor by stuffing them with nuts, baking them in a pie, or bathing them in a spicy sauce.

Store fresh pears in the refrigerator, and take them out to ripen about two to three days before needed. You can test for ripeness by applying gentle thumb pressure to the neck of each pear. When ripe, the pear will yield easily.

PEAR CRUMBLE PIE

1 unbaked 9-inch pastry shell
2 (16-ounce) cans sliced pears, undrained
2 tablespoons sugar
1½ tablespoons cornstarch
Dash of ground nutmeg
1 tablespoon butter
½ teaspoon grated lemon rind
2 teaspoons lemon juice
½ cup firmly packed brown sugar
½ cup chopped walnuts
¼ teaspoon ground cinnamon

Prick bottom and sides of pastry shell with a fork. Bake shell at 400° for 3 to 5 minutes.

Drain pears, reserving 1 cup liquid. Arrange pears in pastry shell. Combine 2 tablespoons sugar, cornstarch, and nutmeg in a saucepan; add reserved pear liquid, and stir well. Cook over medium heat, stirring constantly, until thickened. Add butter, lemon rind, and lemon juice, stirring until butter melts. Pour syrup over pears.

Combine remaining ingredients; sprinkle over pie. Bake at 425° for 20 minutes. Yield: one 9-inch pie.

Lucille Hall,
Bakersfield, Missouri.

CRANBERRY-PEAR CRISP

2 cups fresh cranberries
3 medium pears, peeled, cored, and coarsely chopped
1 cup sugar
¼ cup orange juice
2 tablespoons all-purpose flour
½ teaspoon ground cinnamon
¼ teaspoon ground mace
¼ cup firmly packed brown sugar
3 tablespoons all-purpose flour
1 teaspoon grated orange rind
¼ cup butter or margarine
¾ cup regular oats, uncooked
¾ cup chopped walnuts
Whipped cream or ice cream

Combine first 7 ingredients; spoon into a greased 1½-quart casserole.

Combine brown sugar, 3 tablespoons flour, and orange rind; cut in butter with a pastry blender until mixture resembles coarse meal. Stir in oats and walnuts; sprinkle over fruit. Bake at 350° for 50 minutes or until golden brown. Serve warm with whipped cream or ice cream. Yield: 8 servings.

Sandra Russell,
Gainesville, Florida.

ALMOND-STUFFED PEARS

6 medium pears, peeled, halved, and cored
⅓ cup dry sherry
1½ cups water
1 (2¼-ounce) package slivered almonds, toasted and finely chopped
1 tablespoon light brown sugar
⅛ teaspoon almond extract

Place pear halves, cut side down, in a 12- x 8- x 2-inch baking dish. Combine sherry and water; pour over pears. Cover and bake at 350° for 15 minutes.

Turn pear halves over. Combine almonds, sugar, and almond extract; stir well, and spoon equal amounts into cavity of each pear. Bake, uncovered, 5 additional minutes; serve warm. Yield: 6 servings.

Phyllis Fernandez,
St. Petersburg, Florida.

SPICY COCONUT PEARS

1 (29-ounce) can pear halves, undrained
2 tablespoons cornstarch
¼ teaspoon ground cinnamon
¼ teaspoon ground nutmeg
⅛ teaspoon ground cloves
½ cup sugar
¼ cup lemon juice
2 tablespoons butter or margarine
½ cup coconut, toasted

Drain pears, reserving 1 cup liquid. Combine ¼ cup reserved liquid, cornstarch, cinnamon, nutmeg, and cloves; stir until smooth. Set aside.

Combine remaining ¾ cup pear liquid, sugar, lemon juice, and butter in a small saucepan; bring to a boil. Gradually stir in cornstarch mixture; cook over low heat, stirring constantly, until thickened.

Arrange pears in an 8-inch square baking dish. Pour sauce over pears; sprinkle with coconut. Bake at 350° for 15 minutes. Yield: 4 servings.

Mrs. George P. Robinson,
Winston-Salem, North Carolina.

Catch The Aroma Of Homemade Bread

You don't have to be a professional baker to make wonderful homemade bread. These recipes are basic and simple; in no time at all you'll be savoring their enticing aroma and waiting to remove them from the oven.

SAGE-CORN MUFFINS

2 cups yellow cornmeal
1 cup self-rising flour
1 tablespoon baking powder
½ teaspoon baking soda
½ teaspoon salt
1½ teaspoons rubbed sage
3 eggs, slightly beaten
1¾ cups buttermilk
¼ cup plus 2 tablespoons bacon drippings

Combine first 6 ingredients in a large bowl; make a well in center of mixture.

Combine eggs, buttermilk, and bacon drippings; mix well. Add to dry ingredients, stirring just until moistened. Spoon into greased muffin pans, filling two-thirds full. Bake at 400° for 18 to 20 minutes. Yield: about 2 dozen.

Carrie B. Bartlett,
Gallatin, Tennessee.

CHEESE BREAD

2 packages dry yeast
¼ cup warm water (105° to 115°)
1 cup milk, scalded
½ cup butter or margarine
½ cup sugar
¾ teaspoon salt
3 eggs, beaten
5½ to 6 cups all-purpose flour
2 cups (8 ounces) shredded Cheddar
  cheese

Dissolve yeast in warm water in a small bowl. Combine milk, butter, sugar, and salt in a large bowl; stir until butter melts. Cool to lukewarm (105° to 115°). Stir in eggs and yeast mixture.

Gradually add 2 cups flour, beating at medium speed of electric mixer until smooth. Stir in cheese and enough remaining flour to form a stiff dough.

Turn dough out onto a lightly floured surface, and knead 5 to 10 minutes until smooth and elastic. Place dough in a greased bowl, turning to grease top. Cover and let rise in a warm place (85°), free from drafts, 1 hour or until doubled in bulk. Punch dough down.

Divide dough in half, and shape each half into a loaf. Place each loaf in a greased 9- x 5- x 3-inch loafpan. Cover and let rise in a warm place, free from drafts, 1 hour or until doubled in bulk. Bake at 350° for 45 minutes or until loaves sound hollow when tapped. Remove loaves from pans, and cool on wire racks. Yield: 2 loaves.
Evelyn L. Griswold,
Spring City, Tennessee.

BUTTERMILK BISCUITS

1 cup all-purpose flour
1 teaspoon baking powder
½ teaspoon baking soda
1 teaspoon sugar
½ teaspoon salt
¼ cup butter or margarine
⅓ cup buttermilk

Combine first 5 ingredients, mixing well; cut in butter with a pastry blender until mixture resembles coarse meal.

Add buttermilk, stirring until dry ingredients are moistened. Turn dough out onto a lightly floured surface; knead lightly 8 to 10 times.

Roll dough to ¼-inch thickness; cut with a 2-inch biscuit cutter. Place biscuits on an ungreased baking sheet. Bake at 425° for 10 minutes or until golden brown. Yield: 1 dozen.
Betty R. Butts,
Kensington, Maryland.

GIANT PECAN POPOVERS

2 eggs
1 cup all-purpose flour
1 cup milk
¼ teaspoon salt
⅓ cup chopped pecans

Combine first 4 ingredients in container of electric blender; process 10 seconds or until smooth. Stir in pecans.

Pour batter into 6 well-greased 4-ounce custard cups, filling half full. Bake at 475° for 15 minutes; reduce heat to 350°, and bake an additional 25 minutes. Serve immediately. Yield: 6 popovers.
Jean Morgan,
Greenwich, Connecticut.

Try A Vegetable Combo

Turn plain vegetables into fancy side dishes with our recipes for vegetable medleys. You'll add a spark of color, texture contrast, and a delicious blend of flavors to any menu.

STEAMED VEGETABLES WITH MUSTARD SAUCE

1 cup scraped and sliced carrots
1 cup coarsely chopped yellow squash
1 cup cauliflower flowerets
1 cup sliced fresh green beans
1 tablespoon sliced red chile pepper
1 tablespoon butter or margarine
2 tablespoons all-purpose flour
1 cup beef broth
1 teaspoon Dijon mustard
¼ teaspoon salt
2 tablespoons sesame seeds
Grated Parmesan cheese

Arrange first 5 ingredients in steaming rack. Place over boiling water; cover and steam 7 minutes or to desired degree of doneness. Spoon vegetables into serving dish.

Melt butter in a heavy saucepan over low heat; add flour, stirring until smooth. Cook 1 minute, stirring constantly. Gradually add beef broth; cook over medium heat, stirring constantly, until thickened. Stir in mustard, salt, and sesame seeds; simmer 1 minute, stirring constantly. Pour over vegetables; sprinkle with cheese. Yield: 4 to 6 servings.

MIXED VEGETABLE CASSEROLE

2 (10-ounce) packages frozen mixed
  vegetables
1 (16-ounce) can cut green beans, drained
1 cup (4 ounces) shredded Cheddar cheese
¾ cup mayonnaise
1 tablespoon chopped onion
½ cup buttery round cracker crumbs
1 tablespoon butter or margarine, melted

Cook mixed vegetables according to package directions; drain. Add next 4 ingredients; mix well. Spoon into a lightly greased 2-quart shallow baking dish. Sprinkle crumbs over top, and drizzle with butter. Bake at 350° for 30 minutes. Yield: 6 servings.
Marlene Rikard,
Birmingham, Alabama.

SUMMER VEGETABLE MEDLEY

2 tablespoons vegetable oil
4 medium yellow squash, sliced
2 medium-size green peppers, cut into
  lengthwise strips
1 large onion, sliced and separated into
  rings
½ pound fresh mushrooms, sliced
1 large clove garlic, minced
1 teaspoon dried whole basil
½ teaspoon salt
½ teaspoon pepper
½ cup Chablis or other dry white wine
1 tablespoon butter or margarine
½ cup grated Parmesan cheese

Heat oil in a large skillet. Add next 8 ingredients; cover and cook 5 minutes. Stir in wine; simmer, uncovered, 10 minutes. Add butter, stirring gently until melted. Sprinkle with cheese. Yield: 6 servings.

CHINESE SPINACH SAUTE

1 pound fresh spinach
¼ cup sesame oil or peanut oil
2 tablespoons soy sauce
1 tablespoon lime juice
Dash of salt
2 small zucchini, diagonally sliced
1 (8-ounce) can sliced water chestnuts,
  drained

Wash spinach thoroughly, and pat dry. Remove stems, and cut into 1-inch pieces. Tear leaves into bite-size pieces.

Heat oil, soy sauce, lime juice, and salt in a large skillet or wok. Add spinach leaves and stems and remaining ingredients; cover and cook over medium heat 1 to 2 minutes or until spinach leaves are wilted. Remove cover and cook 2 minutes or until zucchini is crisp-tender, stirring gently. Yield: 6 servings. *Alice McNamara, Eucha, Oklahoma.*

FRESH VEGETABLE MARINADE

1 small head cauliflower
1 (1-pound) bunch broccoli
½ pound fresh mushrooms, sliced
2 medium-size green peppers, chopped
1 small red onion, thinly sliced and separated into rings
1 cup vegetable oil
½ cup white wine vinegar
½ cup sugar
1 tablespoon dried Italian seasoning
2 teaspoons dry mustard
1 teaspoon salt

Remove outer green leaves of cauliflower, and break into flowerets; wash thoroughly. Set aside.

Trim off large leaves of broccoli. Remove stalks, separate into flowerets, and wash thoroughly. Reserve stalks for use in other recipes.

Combine vegetables in a large mixing bowl. Combine remaining ingredients; mix well and pour over vegetables, tossing gently. Cover and chill at least 3 hours. Yield: 8 to 10 servings.
Lyn Renwick, Charlotte, North Carolina.

Salads And Side Dishes For Two

If you're cooking for two and don't care to have leftovers, our salad and side dish recipes are just for you. They'll help you cook and serve the correct amount.

ASPIC FOR TWO

1 envelope unflavored gelatin
⅓ cup cold water
1 (6-ounce) can vegetable cocktail juice
¼ teaspoon onion salt
¼ teaspoon soy sauce
¼ teaspoon liquid smoke
Dash of red pepper
½ cup chopped Chinese cabbage
2 hard-cooked eggs, sliced
8 pimiento-stuffed olives, sliced
Lettuce leaves (optional)

Combine gelatin and water in a saucepan; stir until gelatin dissolves. Cook over medium heat, stirring constantly, about 1 minute. Add next 5 ingredients, and stir well. Cool.

Layer Chinese cabbage, eggs, and olives in an oiled 3-cup mold. When gelatin mixture is just cooled, carefully spoon over solids. Chill until firm. Unmold on lettuce leaves. Yield: 2 servings. *Mercena B. Edwards, Orlando, Florida.*

FRUITED COLESLAW

1½ cups shredded cabbage
½ cup chopped apple
2 tablespoons raisins
¼ cup plus 2 tablespoons pineapple tidbits, drained
¼ cup mayonnaise or salad dressing
1 tablespoon lemon juice
1½ teaspoons celery seeds
½ teaspoon sugar
½ teaspoon prepared mustard

Combine first 4 ingredients; set aside. Combine remaining ingredients, and mix well. Pour over cabbage mixture; stir gently to coat. Chill 1 to 2 hours. Yield: 2 servings. *Sonia Robinson, Front Royal, Virginia.*

POTATO BAKE

4 slices bacon, diced
2 tablespoons chopped onion
2 medium baking potatoes, cut into ¼-inch slices
¼ teaspoon salt
⅛ teaspoon pepper
½ cup whipping cream
¼ cup chicken broth

Cook bacon and onion in a heavy skillet until bacon is crisp; drain on paper towels. Set aside.

Place potatoes in a lightly greased 1-quart baking dish; sprinkle with salt and pepper. Add whipping cream and broth; top with bacon and onion. Cover and bake at 350° for 45 minutes until tender. Yield: 2 servings. *Lucille Shaw, Kaufman, Texas.*

BAKED ZUCCHINI

1 small zucchini, thinly sliced
4 fresh mushrooms, sliced
2 scallions or green onions, chopped
1 small red sweet pepper, chopped
1 teaspoon butter or margarine
2 tablespoons water
¼ cup grated Parmesan cheese

Combine first 4 ingredients in a 1-quart casserole. Dot with butter, and add water. Sprinkle with cheese. Cover and bake at 350° for 30 minutes or until zucchini is tender. Yield: 2 servings. *Mrs. Robert L. Fetzer, Jacksonville, Florida.*

SPANISH RICE

½ cup chopped onion
1½ tablespoons chopped green pepper
1 tablespoon butter or margarine
1¼ cups canned tomatoes, undrained and chopped
1 whole clove
1 small bay leaf
1 teaspoon sugar
½ teaspoon salt
1 cup cooked rice

Sauté onion and green pepper in butter in a skillet until tender. Stir in next 5 ingredients; simmer 12 to 15 minutes or until most of the liquid is absorbed. Remove clove and bay leaf; stir in rice. Yield: 2 servings. *Mrs. Steven Carrier, Waynesburg, Kentucky.*

Add Grapes To The Salad

Green grapes make a refreshing addition to these salad recipes. Try them in a fresh fruit mixture, an orange congealed salad, or a chicken salad.

FRUIT SALAD

3 egg yolks
1 tablespoon butter, melted
2 tablespoons vinegar
2 tablespoons sugar
2 tablespoons pineapple juice
1 (20-ounce) can pineapple chunks, drained
1 (11-ounce) can mandarin oranges, drained
2 cups seedless green grapes
2 cups miniature marshmallows
1 cup whipping cream, whipped

Beat egg yolks until thickened. Add next 4 ingredients; place in a saucepan, and cook over medium heat until thickened. Cool. Stir in fruit and marshmallows. Fold in whipped cream. Chill 8 hours. Yield: 8 servings. *Patty Merritt, Jacksonville, North Carolina.*

EXOTIC LUNCHEON SALAD

4 cups coarsely chopped cooked chicken
1 (8-ounce) can water chestnuts, drained
   and diced
1 pound seedless green grapes
1 cup sliced celery
1 (15¼-ounce) can pineapple tidbits,
   drained and divided
¾ cup mayonnaise
¾ cup commercial sour cream
1 tablespoon soy sauce
1½ teaspoons curry powder
2 teaspoons lemon juice
Lettuce leaves
⅓ cup slivered almonds, toasted

Combine chicken, water chestnuts, grapes, celery, and half of the pineapple tidbits. Combine next 5 ingredients, stirring well; add to chicken mixture, and toss well. Chill.

Serve salad on lettuce leaves. Top with remaining pineapple tidbits, and sprinkle with almonds. Yield: 8 servings.   *Mrs. Frank Canady,*
Springfield, Missouri.

JEWELED ORANGE SALAD

1 envelope unflavored gelatin
1¼ cups orange juice, divided
¾ cup apricot nectar
1 (11-ounce) can mandarin oranges,
   drained
½ cup halved seedless green grapes
Lettuce leaves (optional)

Dissolve gelatin in ¼ cup orange juice. Combine remaining 1 cup orange juice and apricot nectar in a saucepan; bring to a boil. Remove from heat; add gelatin, and stir until dissolved. Chill until consistency of unbeaten egg white. Stir in oranges and grapes.

Spoon into a lightly oiled 3-cup mold; chill. Serve on lettuce leaves, if desired. Yield: 6 servings.   *Bettye Cortner,*
Cerulean, Kentucky.

Depend On Potatoes

Whether baked, stuffed, fried, or coated in a creamy sauce, potatoes are a favorite way to round out almost any menu. Here we offer some of our readers' suggestions for turning plain, basic potatoes into showy side dishes or hearty main courses.

When buying potatoes, look them over to make sure they have clean, firm, smooth skins. Beware of any

For a hearty side dish, add butter, cheese, milk, and sour cream to the stuffing of Million Dollar Potatoes.

green spots as this usually means the potato has been sunburned and will taste bitter.

Never wash potatoes before they are stored because it will speed decay. If the recipe calls for peeling, place the peeled potatoes in a bowl of cold water to keep them from turning dark.

MILLION DOLLAR POTATOES

6 medium baking potatoes
Vegetable oil
½ cup butter or margarine, softened
2 cups (8 ounces) Cheddar cheese, divided
1 (8-ounce) carton commercial sour cream
¼ cup milk
1 teaspoon chopped fresh parsley
½ teaspoon salt
¼ teaspoon pepper

Wash potatoes, and rub with oil. Bake at 400° for 1 hour or until done.

Cut potatoes in half lengthwise. Carefully scoop out pulp, leaving shells intact. Mash pulp; stir in butter, 1½ cups cheese, sour cream, milk, parsley, salt, and pepper. Stuff shells with potato

mixture, and sprinkle with remaining cheese. Bake potatoes at 350° for 20 minutes. Yield: 6 servings.

Dena A. Horn,
North Palm Beach, Florida.

CREAMED BEEF AND CHICKEN-TOPPED POTATOES

4 large baking potatoes
Vegetable oil
3 tablespoons butter or margarine
¼ cup finely chopped onion
2 tablespoons minced celery
1 (2½-ounce) jar sliced dried beef, finely
   chopped
3½ tablespoons all-purpose flour
2 cups milk
½ cup diced cooked chicken
1 teaspoon lemon juice
1 teaspoon Worcestershire sauce
¼ teaspoon dried whole thyme
⅛ teaspoon pepper

Wash potatoes, and rub with oil. Bake at 400° for 1 hour or until done.

Melt butter in a medium saucepan; add onion, celery, and dried beef; sauté until onion is tender. Stir in flour; cook 1 minute, stirring constantly. Gradually add milk; cook over medium heat, stirring constantly, until sauce is thickened and bubbly. Stir in next 5 ingredients, and cook until mixture is thoroughly heated.

Split tops of potatoes lengthwise, and fluff pulp with a fork. Spoon topping over potatoes. Yield: 4 servings.

BEER-BATTER POTATO WEDGES

4 medium baking potatoes
Vegetable oil
1 cup all-purpose flour
1 egg, beaten
¼ cup milk
1 tablespoon vegetable oil
¾ teaspoon salt
½ cup beer
Additional vegetable oil
Commercial sour cream (optional)

Wash potatoes, and rub with oil. Bake at 400° for 1 hour or until done.

Combine next 5 ingredients, beating well. Stir in beer. Set aside.

Cut potatoes lengthwise into 4 wedges. Dip wedges in batter, and deep fry in hot oil (375°) until golden brown. Drain on paper towels. Serve with sour cream, if desired. Yield: 6 to 8 servings.
Mrs. M. R. Bennett,
Amarillo, Texas.

SCALLOPED POTATOES

5 to 6 large potatoes, peeled and sliced
1½ cups chicken broth
½ teaspoon salt
¼ teaspoon pepper
1 cup (4 ounces) shredded Swiss cheese
3 tablespoons grated Parmesan cheese

Combine first 4 ingredients in a Dutch oven; bring to a boil. Cover, reduce heat, and simmer 5 minutes. Remove potatoes from broth, reserving broth.

Layer half each of potatoes and Swiss cheese in a lightly greased 2-quart casserole; repeat layers. Pour reserved broth over top; sprinkle with Parmesan cheese. Cover and bake at 350° for 55 minutes. Remove cover, and bake an additional 5 minutes or until potatoes are tender and cheese is golden brown. Yield: 8 servings. *Anita McLemore,*
Knoxville, Tennessee.

Tip: Freeze very soft cheese 15 minutes to make shredding easier.

An Oyster In Every Bite

Even those who prefer oysters on the half shell will like the fresh ocean flavor of these dishes. And you can enjoy oysters year-round.

You can usually find fresh shucked oysters in the meat section of your supermarket. The terms Select and Standard refer to the size of the oysters. Selects are medium size, while Standards are small. Fresh oysters are highly perishable, so use them within 1 to 2 days after you purchase them.

CREAMY OYSTERS AND CRABMEAT

½ cup butter or margarine
3 to 4 green onions, chopped
2 cups chopped fresh parsley
½ cup all-purpose flour
2 cups water
1 teaspoon salt
¼ teaspoon pepper
3 dozen fresh Select oysters, undrained (1 to 1½ pounds)
½ pound fresh crabmeat, drained and flaked
¼ cup plus 2 tablespoons soft breadcrumbs

Melt butter in a heavy skillet. Add green onion and parsley; sauté until green onion is tender. Stir in flour; cook over low heat 1 minute, stirring constantly. Gradually add water; cook over medium heat, stirring constantly, until thickened and bubbly. Stir in salt and pepper.

Place oysters in a saucepan; cook over medium heat 8 to 10 minutes or until edges of oysters begin to curl. Drain.

Place 6 oysters and about 2 tablespoons crabmeat into each of 6 lightly greased 10-ounce ramekins or custard cups. Spoon about ¼ cup sauce over crabmeat. Sprinkle each with 1 tablespoon breadcrumbs; bake at 350° for 20 to 25 minutes. Yield: 6 servings.
Mrs. Bernie Benigno,
Gulfport, Mississippi.

OYSTERS IN BACON

8 slices bacon
1 pint fresh Select oysters, drained
Garlic salt
Pepper
About 1 tablespoon prepared mustard

Cut each bacon slice into thirds. Wrap bacon around each oyster, and secure with a wooden pick. Place oysters on broiling pan; sprinkle with garlic salt and pepper. Spread ⅛ teaspoon mustard on each oyster.

Broil oysters about 4 inches from heat 2 to 3 minutes. Turn and broil an additional 2 to 3 minutes or until golden. Yield: about 12 appetizer servings.
Patricia Boschen,
Ashland, Virginia.

OYSTER-CORN CHOWDER

4 new potatoes, peeled and cubed
1 cup water
1 teaspoon salt
3 stalks celery, chopped
1 (10-ounce) package frozen whole kernel corn
1 tablespoon dried onion flakes
2 pints fresh Standard oysters, undrained
2 cups milk
1 tablespoon butter or margarine
½ teaspoon pepper
4 slices bacon, cooked and crumbled
Chopped fresh parsley (optional)

Combine first 3 ingredients in a Dutch oven; cover and cook over medium heat about 8 minutes. Stir in celery, corn, and onion flakes; cover and cook 10 minutes. Stir in oysters, milk, butter, and pepper; cook over low heat until thoroughly heated, stirring occasionally. Sprinkle each serving with bacon. Garnish with parsley, if desired. Yield: about 2 quarts.
Lt. Col. R. G. Sigman,
Fort Walton Beach, Florida.

OYSTER SOUP

½ cup chopped onion
½ cup chopped green pepper
1 tablespoon butter or margarine, melted
2 cups milk
1 (8-ounce) package cream cheese, softened
1 pint fresh Standard oysters, drained
2 cups chicken broth
½ teaspoon salt
¼ teaspoon white pepper
Chopped celery leaves (optional)

Sauté onion and green pepper in butter in a Dutch oven until tender. Add milk and cream cheese; cook over low heat, stirring until smooth. Add next 4 ingredients; simmer 5 to 8 minutes or until edges of oysters curl. Garnish with celery leaves, if desired. Yield: 7 cups.
Paulette E. Paolozzi,
Annapolis, Maryland.

OYSTERS IN PATTY SHELLS

1 pint fresh Standard oysters, undrained
1 medium onion, finely chopped
2 tablespoons butter or margarine
1 tablespoon all-purpose flour
1 (4-ounce) can mushroom stems and
    pieces, drained
2 tablespoons chopped fresh parsley
¼ teaspoon lemon juice
½ teaspoon salt
⅛ teaspoon pepper
Dash of red pepper
6 commercial patty shells, baked

Place oysters in a saucepan; cook over medium heat 8 to 10 minutes or until edges of oysters begin to curl. Drain.

Sauté onion in butter in a large skillet until tender. Add flour, stirring until blended. Stir in next 6 ingredients and oysters. Simmer, uncovered, 15 minutes, stirring frequently.

Spoon oyster mixture into patty shells, and place on a lightly greased baking sheet. Bake at 375° for 5 minutes or until thoroughly heated. Yield: 6 servings.   *Joan Wilkes,*
Jacksonville, Florida.

DELICIOUS FRIED OYSTERS

1¾ cups all-purpose flour
1¾ teaspoons baking powder
1¾ teaspoons salt
1 teaspoon pepper
¾ to 1 cup milk
1 quart fresh Select oysters, drained
Vegetable oil

Combine first 4 ingredients; gradually stir in milk. Add oysters, stirring to coat. Fry oysters in deep hot oil (375°) until golden, turning once. Drain on paper towels; serve immediately. Yield: 8 servings.   *Helen Rainwater,*
Weslaco, Texas.

He'd Rather Entertain Outdoors

Grilling is the specialty of Jack Millikin of Tallulah, Louisiana, and he considers it serious business. "He's a pharmacist, so he measures everything very precisely," laughs wife Dottie. But Dottie doesn't laugh when Jack puts supper on the table.

A lot of Jack's ideas for recipes come from dishes he's sampled at restaurants visited during his travels. His recipe for Pineapple-Beef Kabobs, in fact, he developed after tasting something similar at a hometown restaurant.

You'll also enjoy his special Sausage Burgers, a delicious variation on regular burgers. You can freeze the burgers either before or after grilling them. Jack keeps them on hand all the time.

Following Jack's recipes are recipes from other men who also enjoy grilling out-of-doors.

PINEAPPLE-BEEF KABOBS

2 (20-ounce) cans pineapple chunks,
    undrained
½ cup firmly packed brown sugar
⅔ cup cider vinegar
⅔ cup catsup
¼ cup soy sauce
2 teaspoons ground ginger
1½ teaspoons liquid smoke
3 pounds boneless sirloin tip roast, cut
    into 1½-inch cubes
½ pound fresh mushroom caps
2 small onions, quartered
2 medium-size green peppers, cut into
    1-inch pieces
Seasoned Rice

Drain pineapple, reserving juice. Combine pineapple juice and next 6 ingredients, mixing well; pour into a large shallow dish. Add meat; cover and marinate overnight in refrigerator.

Drain meat, reserving marinade. Pour marinade in a saucepan; bring to a boil. Add mushrooms; reduce heat and simmer, uncovered, 10 minutes. Drain, reserving marinade. Set mushrooms aside.

Alternate meat, pineapple chunks, mushrooms, onion, and green pepper on 8 to 10 skewers. Grill kabobs over medium-hot coals 10 to 15 minutes or until desired degree of doneness, basting kabobs frequently with marinade. Serve with Seasoned Rice. Yield: 8 to 10 servings.

Seasoned Rice:

1½ cups uncooked regular rice
1½ cups water
1 (10½-ounce) can consommé,
    undiluted
2 tablespoons chopped green pepper
2 tablespoons butter or margarine
1 teaspoon Worcestershire sauce
1 teaspoon soy sauce
Dash of onion powder

Combine all ingredients in a large Dutch oven; bring mixture to a boil. Cover, reduce heat, and simmer 20 minutes or until the rice is done. Yield: 8 to 10 servings.

STEAK WITH MUSHROOM SAUCE

2 tablespoons lemon juice
2 tablespoons Worcestershire sauce
2 tablespoons molasses
1 teaspoon seasoned salt or Creole
    seasoning
1 teaspoon seasoned pepper
2 pounds sirloin steak
Mushroom Sauce

Combine first 5 ingredients, stirring well; pour into a large shallow dish. Add steak; cover and refrigerate at least 1 hour, turning once.

Drain steak, reserving marinade. Grill over hot coals 8 to 12 minutes on each side or to desired degree of doneness, basting frequently with marinade. Serve Mushroom Sauce over steak. Yield: 6 servings.

Mushroom Sauce:

¼ cup butter or margarine
1 pound fresh mushrooms, sliced
2 tablespoons Worcestershire sauce
½ teaspoon hot sauce

Melt butter in a large skillet; add remaining ingredients, and cook over low heat 15 minutes or until mushrooms are tender. Yield: about 1½ cups.

SAUSAGE BURGERS

3 eggs, beaten
¼ cup Worcestershire sauce
½ teaspoon onion salt
½ teaspoon seasoned salt
½ teaspoon seasoned pepper
⅛ teaspoon garlic powder
2 teaspoons hot sauce
3 pounds ground chuck
1 pound hot bulk pork sausage

Combine first 7 ingredients in a large bowl, mixing well. Add beef and sausage; mix well. Cover and refrigerate overnight. Shape meat into 16 patties. Place patties on grill 3 to 5 inches from hot coals; cook 4 to 8 minutes on each side or until done. Yield: 16 servings.

Note: Grilled patties may be frozen. Place patties in a single layer on aluminum foil; seal securely and freeze. Thaw at room temperature. Heat patties in aluminum foil at 350° for 30 minutes or until thoroughly heated. Shaped patties may also be frozen uncooked; stack patties between sheets of waxed paper, and seal stacks securely in plastic bags.

ZIPPY BARBECUED CHICKEN

2 cups apple cider vinegar
½ cup commercial barbecue sauce
¼ cup vegetable oil
½ teaspoon salt
1 tablespoon crushed red pepper
½ teaspoon ground red pepper
1½ teaspoons pepper
2 (2½- to 3-pound) broiler-fryers,
    quartered

Combine first 7 ingredients in a medium saucepan; bring to a boil, and cook 2 to 3 minutes, stirring occasionally. Set sauce aside.

Place chicken, skin side up, on grill. Grill over medium coals 15 minutes.

Dip each chicken quarter in barbecue sauce, and return to grill. Grill an additional 40 minutes or until tender, basting with sauce every 10 minutes. Yield: 8 servings.
William Hawley,
Lucama, North Carolina.

GRILLED FLOUNDER FILLETS

6 (¾-inch-thick) flounder fillets
½ cup butter or margarine
¼ cup lemon juice
1 tablespoon Worcestershire sauce
½ teaspoon seasoned salt
½ teaspoon paprika
¼ teaspoon red pepper

Place fillets in a large shallow dish. Combine remaining ingredients in a small saucepan; cook, stirring constantly, until butter melts. Pour marinade over fish. Cover; marinate 1 hour in refrigerator, turning once.

Drain fillets, reserving marinade; place fillets in a fish basket. Grill over hot coals 3 to 5 minutes on each side, basting often with marinade. Fish is done if it flakes easily when tested with a fork. Yield: 6 servings.
Dr. C. G. Harrington, Jr.,
Memphis, Tennessee.

Cook With Leftover Bread

Recipes for cornbread dressing, meat loaf, and bread pudding have become favorite ways to keep from throwing away leftover bread slices, biscuits, and cornbread. We think you'll enjoy the variations offered here.

TASTY MEAT LOAF

2 slices day-old bread, crumbled
1 cup milk
1½ pounds ground beef
¼ cup finely chopped onion
2 eggs, well beaten
1 teaspoon salt
¼ cup brown sugar
1½ teaspoons dry mustard
⅓ cup catsup

Combine crumbled bread and milk in a small bowl; allow to soak 5 minutes.

Combine beef, onion, eggs, salt, and bread mixture; mix well. Shape meat mixture into a loaf; place in a lightly greased 9- x 5- x 3-inch loafpan.

Combine remaining ingredients, and pour over meat loaf. Bake at 350° for 1 hour or until done. Yield: 6 servings.
Mrs. Carl Layton,
Swainsboro, Georgia.

CORNBREAD-AND-SAUSAGE DRESSING

½ pound bulk pork sausage
¼ cup chopped onion
4 cups coarsely crumbled cornbread
1 cup coarsely crumbled day-old bread
2 eggs
2 cups chicken or turkey broth
¼ cup chopped fresh parsley
½ teaspoon poultry seasoning
¼ teaspoon salt

Combine sausage and onion in a skillet; cook until sausage is browned, stirring to crumble meat. Drain off pan drippings, if necessary.

Combine sausage and remaining ingredients. Spoon the mixture into a lightly greased 12- x 8- x 2-inch baking dish. Cover and bake at 350° for 30 minutes. Remove cover and bake an additional 15 minutes. Yield: 6 to 8 servings.
Susan Wilson,
Johnson City, Tennessee.

APPLE BROWN BETTY

¼ cup butter or margarine
3 cups biscuit crumbs
10 medium-size cooking apples, peeled,
    cored, and sliced
1 cup water
1 cup sugar
½ teaspoon ground cinnamon
2 tablespoons butter or margarine
3 tablespoons brown sugar

Melt ¼ cup butter in a large skillet over medium heat. Add biscuit crumbs and continue to cook, stirring constantly, until browned. Set aside.

Place apples in large Dutch oven with water and bring to a boil. Cover, reduce heat, and simmer until apples are tender; drain. Mash apples until pulpy; stir in sugar and cinnamon.

Alternate layers of apple mixture and biscuit crumbs in a 9-inch square baking dish, beginning with apple mixture and ending with crumbs. Dot top with 2 tablespoons butter, and sprinkle with brown sugar. Bake at 350° about 10 minutes or until thoroughly heated. Serve hot. Yield: 8 servings.
Alida Garrison,
Elizabethton, Tennessee.

OLD-FASHIONED BREAD PUDDING

½ cup raisins
½ cup brandy
¼ cup butter or margarine
8 slices day-old bread, lightly toasted
1 cup firmly packed brown sugar
1 teaspoon ground cinnamon
¼ teaspoon ground allspice
3 eggs
¼ teaspoon salt
1 teaspoon vanilla extract
3 cups milk, scalded and cooled

Cover raisins with brandy; set aside.

Spread 1½ teaspoons butter on each bread slice. Cut bread into 1-inch cubes; set aside.

Combine brown sugar, cinnamon, and allspice; reserve 3 tablespoons of this mixture. Toss bread cubes with remaining sugar mixture. Place half of bread cube mixture in a lightly greased 1½-quart casserole. Drain raisins; place half of raisins over bread cube mixture. Repeat layers.

Combine eggs, salt, and vanilla in a medium mixing bowl. Beat at medium speed of electric mixer 1 minute; gradually stir in milk. Pour over mixture in casserole dish; let stand 5 minutes. Sprinkle with reserved sugar mixture. Bake at 325° for 45 to 50 minutes. Serve warm. Yield: 6 to 8 servings.
Mary Helen Hackney,
Charlotte, North Carolina.

Tip: Use a timer when cooking. Set the timer so it will ring at various intervals, and check the progress of the dish. However, try to avoid opening the oven door unless necessary.

From Our Kitchen To Yours

Since we use so many eggs in our test kitchens, we've learned how to get the most out of them. Here are some ideas you may find handy in your kitchen.

Scrambled, fried, and microwaved— Don't over-scramble the eggs. In our eagerness to get scrambled eggs ready for the breakfast table, we often stir them so much, they look like lifeless yellow shreds instead of soft, fluffy curds. The trick is to let the egg mixture cook until it begins to set. Gently scrape the bottom of the skillet with a pancake turner to form soft curds of eggs. Continue cooking and occasionally turning until the egg mixture thickens. Remove the eggs from the pan before they're completely done. The heat in the eggs will complete the cooking.

When frying eggs (cooking them in a small amount of fat), it is generally best to use moderate heat. If the heat is too high, the white becomes tough and rubbery. The same problem occurs when eggs are cooked too slow. Try this procedure: Heat the fat, butter, or bacon drippings over medium high until a drop of water sizzles. Then add the egg(s), and reduce to medium to medium low. For sunny-side up, don't turn the eggs; just spoon a bit of fat over them to add flavor and help the cooking.

Many homes have microwave ovens these days, and of course you can cook eggs in them. A word of caution: Never microwave eggs in their shells because they can explode. If you want to hard- or soft-cook an egg, break the egg in a microwave-safe bowl. Prick the membrane covering the egg yolk three or four times with a wooden pick; then cover the egg with plastic wrap or waxed paper. Cook on medium to medium-low power until desired degree of doneness. Be sure to allow for standing time, too. Occasionally, eggs cooked this way explode, too. In most cases, cooking on lower power levels prevents this. Hard-cooked eggs for tuna or chicken salads, as well as casseroles, are ready in minutes. When scrambling eggs or making omelets, check your manufacturer's guide for best results.

Thick and lemon-colored yolks— Recipes such as those for sponge cakes and soufflés call for egg yolks to be beaten until thick and lemon colored. When they reach this point, the yolks should have increased to their maximum volume. Beat yolks at high speed with an electric mixer about 3 to 5 minutes or until the yolks thicken and are a pale, lemon-yellow color. If egg yolks are not beaten to this stage, there is the possibility that your recipe may fail.

Meringue— Meringue-making has caused many heartaches in Southern kitchens. It's not an old wive's tale that weather affects meringues. When there's high humidity, the sugar in meringue actually absorbs moisture from the air, making the meringue gooey and limp. So make your meringues on sunny, dry days.

Following are some specific tips that should assure you of good results.

—When making a meringue, carefully separate the whites from the yolks. Eggs separate best when cold, so crack the eggs straight out of the refrigerator. Separate the eggs, one at a time, into small bowls before adding them to a large mixing bowl for beating. This prevents any yolk from getting into other whites. The least bit of yolk will prevent the whites from expanding to maximum volume. (Fatty substances such as shortening, butter, or oil inhibit the whites from holding air. Yolks also contain fat.) Make sure that mixing bowls and beaters are completely grease-free for best results.

—Place the egg whites in either a copper, stainless steel, or glass bowl for beating. Plastic or wooden bowls won't do because they tend to absorb fat. Copper bowls have long had the reputation for being the best bowls to use for preparing meringues. The copper reacts with the egg whites, much like cream of tartar, to stabilize the beaten whites and help them maintain their volume. However, stainless steel and glass bowls are much less expensive and produce exceptionally good meringues.

—Egg whites should come to room temperature before beating. Let them sit out 30 minutes, and they'll easily expand when beaten.

—Beat the whites and cream of tartar until foamy. (Cream of tartar is an acid that stabilizes the whites and helps maintain their volume. Most meringue recipes call for the addition of cream of tartar. A guide we follow is ⅛ teaspoon cream of tartar to 1 egg white.) When the whites are foamy, gradually add the sugar, 1 tablespoon at a time, beating until stiff peaks form.

—If you're unsure of how stiff peaks look, try this. When you lift the beaters from the egg white mixture and the tops of the whites stand straight up without tilting over, then you've reached the stiff-peak stage. When adding sugar to a meringue that will be used on a pie, usually 2 tablespoons sugar to 1 egg white is the rule. About 4 tablespoons sugar per white are needed when making meringue shells. Be sure you don't add the sugar all at once. That could prevent the whites from incorporating air and expanding.

To prevent "weeping" (the appearance of a syrupy liquid between the meringue and the filling) spread the meringue over pie while the filling is hot. Even though this procedure decreases the amount of weeping, it doesn't always eliminate it. To prevent the meringue from shrinking away from the crust, be careful to spread it so that it adheres to the pastry around all edges of the pie.

—Baking instructions will vary from one source to another. We've found baking the meringue at 400° for 10 minutes or until golden brown is best.

Add A Pinch Or More Of Spice

A stick of cinnamon, a pinch of nutmeg, a dash of ground cloves. These and several other spices lend warmth and fragrance to dishes that range from carrot cake to spicy chili.

You can help keep spices potent by storing them away from sources of heat, light, and moisture and keeping each container tightly closed. Check your spices once or twice a year for freshness; discard and replace any that have lost their pungent aromas.

HOT SPICED CHILI

2 pounds ground beef
2 medium onions, chopped
2 cloves garlic, minced
1 (6-ounce) can tomato paste
1 quart tomato juice
3 tablespoons chili powder
1 tablespoon dry mustard
1 tablespoon vinegar
1 tablespoon Worcestershire sauce
1½ teaspoons ground cumin
1 teaspoon salt
1 teaspoon pepper
¾ teaspoon ground allspice
½ teaspoon ground cinnamon
5 bay leaves
Dash of hot sauce
Pinch of red pepper

Combine ground beef, onion, and garlic in a large Dutch oven; cook until beef is browned, stirring to crumble meat. Drain off pan drippings. Add remaining ingredients, mixing well. Cook, uncovered, over low heat 1½ hours, stirring occasionally. Remove bay leaves. Yield: about 2½ quarts.

Marian Cox,
Deming, New Mexico.

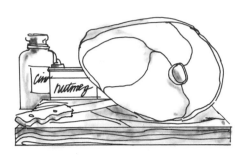

MAPLE-BAKED HAM WITH RAISIN SAUCE

1 (5- to 7-pound) uncooked ham half
14 to 16 whole cloves
1 cup maple-flavored syrup
½ teaspoon ground ginger
¼ teaspoon ground nutmeg
¼ teaspoon ground allspice
Raisin Sauce

Place ham, fat side up, on a cutting board; score fat in a diamond design, and stud with cloves.

Place ham, fat side up, on rack in a shallow roasting pan. Insert meat thermometer, making sure it does not touch fat or bone.

Combine syrup, ginger, nutmeg, and allspice; stir well, and pour over ham. Bake, uncovered, at 325° for 2 to 3 hours until meat thermometer registers 160°, basting ham every 30 minutes. If ham gets too brown, cover lightly with aluminum foil. Serve hot or cold with Raisin Sauce. Yield: 10 to 14 servings.

Raisin Sauce:

1 cup sugar
½ cup water
½ cup raisins
¼ cup red currant jelly
3 tablespoons red wine vinegar
2 tablespoons butter or margarine
1 tablespoon Worcestershire sauce
Pinch of ground mace
Dash of hot sauce
Salt and pepper to taste

Combine sugar and water in a medium saucepan; bring to a boil. Cook 5 minutes, stirring often. Add remaining ingredients; reduce heat and simmer until jelly dissolves, stirring occasionally. Yield: 1½ cups sauce.

Rublelene Singleton,
Scotts Hill, Tennessee.

SPICY RICE

1½ tablespoons vegetable oil
1 small onion, minced
1 (3-inch) stick cinnamon
1 whole clove
1 cardamom seed
1½ cups uncooked regular rice
¼ teaspoon ground turmeric
Pinch of ground ginger
Pinch of ground allspice
3 cups hot water
½ teaspoon salt

Heat oil in a heavy saucepan; add onion, cinnamon, clove, and cardamom seed. Sauté until onion is tender.

Add rice, turmeric, ginger, and allspice; cook over medium heat 10 minutes, stirring frequently. Add water and salt; bring to a boil. Cover, reduce heat, and simmer 20 minutes or until liquid is absorbed. Remove whole spices. Yield: 8 servings.

Mrs. H. J. Grogaard,
Baltimore, Maryland.

EASY CARROT CAKE

2 cups sugar
1 cup vegetable oil
4 eggs
2 (4½-ounce) jars strained baby food carrots
1 teaspoon vanilla extract
2 cups all-purpose flour
½ teaspoon salt
1½ teaspoons baking soda
2 teaspoons ground cinnamon
¼ teaspoon ground nutmeg
¼ teaspoon ground cloves
Cream Cheese Frosting
Pecan halves (optional)

Combine sugar and oil; beat well. Add eggs, carrots, and vanilla; beat mixture until smooth.

Combine next 6 ingredients; add to creamed mixture, beating well. Pour batter into 2 greased and floured 9-inch round cakepans.

Bake at 350° for 30 minutes or until a wooden pick inserted in center comes out clean. Cool in pans 10 minutes; remove layers from pans. Cool on wire racks. Spread Cream Cheese Frosting between layers and on top and sides of cake. Garnish with pecans, if desired. Yield: one 2-layer cake.

Cream Cheese Frosting:

1 (8-ounce) package cream cheese, softened
½ cup butter or margarine, softened
1 tablespoon vanilla extract
4 cups sifted powdered sugar
1¼ cups chopped pecans

Combine cream cheese and butter, beating until light and fluffy. Add vanilla and powdered sugar; beat until smooth. Stir in chopped pecans. Yield: enough for one 2-layer cake.

Robin Roberts,
Decatur, Georgia.

Cheese Makes These Dishes Good

Chances are, your favorite cheese dishes begin with only a few simple ingredients. That's because the goodness of cheese provides all the flavor you need.

When sprinkled on top of a dish, cheese has a tendency to dry out and become tough if it bakes too long. Our home economists recommend sprinkling cheese over the casserole in the last 5 minutes of baking.

CLAM QUICHE

Pastry for 9-inch deep-dish pie
1 (6½-ounce) can minced clams, undrained
1 large onion, chopped
3 tablespoons butter or margarine
½ cup chopped fresh parsley
⅛ teaspoon salt
⅛ teaspoon pepper
1 cup (4 ounces) shredded Swiss cheese
5 eggs
1 cup whipping cream
Paprika

Line a 9-inch quiche dish with pastry; trim excess pastry around edges. Prick bottom and sides of pastry with a fork. Bake at 400° for 3 minutes; remove from oven, and gently prick with a fork. Bake 5 minutes longer. Cool on rack.

Drain clams, reserving liquid; set aside.

Sauté onion in butter in a skillet until tender. Add clams, parsley, salt, and pepper; sauté 30 seconds. Spoon mixture into prepared pastry shell; sprinkle with cheese. Beat eggs; add whipping cream and clam liquid, beating well; pour into pastry shell. Sprinkle with paprika. Bake at 350° for 45 minutes or until set. Let stand 10 minutes before serving. Yield: one 9-inch quiche.

Louise Janin,
New Orleans, Louisiana.

CHEESY MANICOTTI

1 (8-ounce) package manicotti shells
1 (32-ounce) jar extra thick spaghetti
   sauce
2 cups (8 ounces) shredded mozzarella
   cheese, divided
1 (16-ounce) carton ricotta cheese
12 (2-inch) saltine crackers, crushed
2 eggs, beaten
¼ cup chopped chives
½ teaspoon dried whole basil
½ teaspoon dried whole marjoram
¼ teaspoon garlic salt

Cook manicotti shells according to package directions, omitting salt; drain.

Pour half of spaghetti sauce into a lightly greased 13- x 9- x 2-inch baking dish. Combine 1½ cups mozzarella cheese and next 7 ingredients; mix well. Stuff manicotti shells with cheese mixture; arrange in sauce.

Pour remaining spaghetti sauce over manicotti; bake at 350° for 25 minutes. Sprinkle with remaining ½ cup mozzarella; bake an additional 5 minutes. Yield: 7 servings. *Sophie Baugher,*
Shrewsbury, Pennsylvania.

SPINACH-CHEESE CASSEROLE

2 (10-ounce) packages frozen chopped
   spinach
2 cups uncooked medium egg noodles
¼ cup butter or margarine
¼ cup all-purpose flour
2 cups milk
½ teaspoon salt
¼ teaspoon pepper
2 cups (8 ounces) shredded Colby or
   Cheddar cheese
¼ cup grated Parmesan cheese

Cook spinach according to package directions; drain well, and set aside.

Cook noodles according to package directions; drain and set aside.

Melt butter in a heavy saucepan over low heat; add flour, stirring until smooth. Cook 1 minute, stirring constantly. Gradually add milk; cook over medium heat, stirring constantly, until thickened and bubbly. Stir in salt and pepper.

Stir ½ cup white sauce into spinach; spoon spinach mixture into a greased 9-inch square baking dish. Sprinkle with Colby cheese. Combine noodles and ½ cup white sauce; spoon over cheese. Spoon remaining white sauce over noodles; sprinkle with Parmesan cheese. Bake, uncovered, at 350° for 30 minutes or until bubbly. Yield: 6 servings.
Karen L. Foster,
Austin, Texas.

CHEESY ENGLISH PEA CASSEROLE

1 (10-ounce) package frozen English peas
1 (5-ounce) package medium egg noodles
1 (8-ounce) package cream cheese, cubed
   and softened
2 cups (8 ounces) shredded sharp Cheddar
   cheese
1 tablespoon butter or margarine
1 (2½-ounce) jar sliced mushrooms,
   undrained
½ cup chopped onion
½ teaspoon white pepper
5 round buttery crackers, crushed

Cook peas according to package directions; drain and set aside.

Cook noodles according to package directions; drain. Add next 3 ingredients, stirring gently until melted. Stir in peas, mushrooms, onion, and pepper; spoon into a greased 10- x 6- x 2-inch baking dish. Sprinkle cracker crumbs around edge of casserole. Bake at 325° for 20 minutes or until thoroughly heated. Yield: 6 servings.
Susan Settlemyre,
Raleigh, North Carolina.

MUSHROOM-CHEESE CASSEROLE

2 tablespoons butter or margarine,
   softened
5 slices white bread, crust trimmed
2 cups (8 ounces) shredded sharp Cheddar
   cheese
5 eggs, beaten
2 cups milk
1 (4-ounce) can sliced mushrooms, drained
1 teaspoon salt

Spread butter on one side of bread slices. Place bread slices, buttered side down, in a greased 10- x 6- x 2-inch baking dish. Sprinkle cheese over bread. Combine eggs, milk, mushrooms, and salt; pour over bread. Cover and chill overnight. Bake, uncovered, 45 to 50 minutes or until set. Yield: 6 servings. *Mrs. Gene Crow,*
Dallas, Texas.

Plan Ahead With Marinated Salads

If you want a headstart on tomorrow's meal, then make a marinated salad today. Besides offering easy preparation, these salads are full of flavor.

PEPPERONI-AND-BROCCOLI SALAD

1 (0.75-ounce) package Italian salad
   dressing mix
1 (1-pound) bunch broccoli
½ pound fresh mushrooms, sliced
1 cup (4 ounces) diced Swiss cheese
1 (3½-ounce) package sliced pepperoni
1 green pepper, chopped

Prepare dressing mix according to package directions; set aside.

Trim off large leaves of broccoli. Wash broccoli, and break off flowerets; reserve stalks for use in other recipes.

Combine broccoli flowerets and next 4 ingredients in a large bowl. Pour dressing over salad; toss gently. Cover and refrigerate 8 hours or overnight. Yield: 6 to 8 servings.
Cynthia Broderius,
Carrboro, North Carolina.

MARINATED BEET SALAD

2 (16-ounce) cans sliced beets, undrained
½ cup sugar
2¼ teaspoons dry mustard
½ teaspoon salt
¾ cup cider vinegar
1 teaspoon celery seeds
½ cup finely chopped onion

Drain beets, reserving ½ cup juice; set aside. Combine sugar, dry mustard, and salt in a small saucepan; stir well. Add beet juice and vinegar; bring to a boil over medium heat. Remove from heat; stir in celery seeds.

Combine beets and chopped onion. Add the vinegar mixture, tossing gently. Cover and refrigerate salad 8 hours or overnight. Yield: 8 to 10 servings.
Pat Boschen,
Ashland, Virginia.

CRUNCHY VEGETABLE SALAD

1 (28-ounce) can cut green beans, drained
1 (17-ounce) can English peas, drained
1 (2-ounce) jar diced pimiento, drained
4 stalks celery, chopped
1 large green pepper, chopped
1 large cucumber, chopped
1 medium onion, chopped
½ cup sugar
½ cup vinegar
½ cup vegetable oil
¼ cup tarragon vinegar
2 tablespoons water
1 teaspoon salt
Lettuce leaves

Combine first 7 ingredients in a large bowl; set aside.

Combine remaining ingredients, except lettuce, mixing well; pour over vegetables, tossing gently. Cover salad, and refrigerate 8 to 10 hours or overnight. Drain salad, and serve in a lettuce-lined bowl. Yield: 10 to 12 servings.
Mrs. John W. Stevens,
Lexington, Kentucky.

MIXED BEAN SALAD

1 (16-ounce) can garbanzo beans, drained
1 (15½-ounce) can red kidney beans, drained
1 (8-ounce) can wax beans, drained
1 (5.25-ounce) can whole kernel corn, drained
1 (8-ounce) can cut green beans, drained
1 (4-ounce) can whole mushrooms, drained
1 (8½-ounce) can lima beans, drained
1 (8¼-ounce) can sliced carrots, drained
3 small yellow squash, thinly sliced
1 large onion, sliced and separated into rings
1 large green pepper, chopped
¼ teaspoon salt
⅛ teaspoon garlic powder
1 cup vegetable oil
1 cup vinegar
½ cup sugar
1 teaspoon hot sauce
Grated Romano cheese (optional)

Combine first 13 ingredients in a large bowl; toss gently.

Combine oil, vinegar, sugar, and hot sauce in a small saucepan; cook over low heat, stirring occasionally just until sugar dissolves. Pour marinade over vegetables; toss gently. Cover and refrigerate 8 hours or overnight. Sprinkle with cheese before serving, if desired. Yield: 12 to 15 servings. *Lora Blocker,*
Dade City, Florida.

Serve Versatile Ground Beef

There are lots of reasons to serve ground beef. Not only is it a key ingredient in many favorite recipes, but it's nutritious, and, of course, economical.

Ground beef retains its freshness in the refrigerator for only a couple of days. For longer periods, package it in serving-size or meal-size portions, and store it in the freezer. It will keep about three months.

CHEESY BEEF-STUFFED SHELLS

3 quarts water
1½ teaspoons salt
18 jumbo macaroni shells
1 pound ground beef
1 medium onion, chopped
1 clove garlic, minced
2 cups (8 ounces) shredded mozzarella cheese
½ cup Italian-style breadcrumbs
¼ cup chopped fresh parsley
1 egg, slightly beaten
Dash of pepper
1 (15½-ounce) jar meatless spaghetti sauce
¼ cup Burgundy or other dry red wine
½ cup grated Parmesan cheese

Combine water and salt in a Dutch oven; bring to a boil. Add macaroni shells, and cook 15 to 18 minutes or just until tender; drain and set aside.

Cook ground beef, onion, and garlic in a large skillet until beef is browned, stirring to crumble meat; drain off pan drippings. Stir in the next 5 ingredients, and set aside.

Combine spaghetti sauce and Burgundy; spoon one-fourth of sauce into a lightly greased 13- x 9- x 2-inch baking dish. Set aside remaining sauce.

Stuff macaroni shells with beef mixture, and arrange in baking dish. Spoon remaining sauce over shells; sprinkle with Parmesan cheese. Bake, uncovered, at 400° for 20 minutes. Yield: 6 servings.
Marie Greiner,
Baltimore, Maryland.

HOT PITA SANDWICHES

¾ cup chopped onion
1 tablespoon olive oil
1 pound ground beef
3 tablespoons catsup
2½ tablespoons water
½ teaspoon ground allspice
Dash of ground cinnamon
¼ teaspoon salt
Dash of pepper
6 (6-inch) pita bread rounds
1½ cups peeled, chopped tomatoes
5 green onions with tops, chopped
½ cup chopped green pepper
½ cup peeled, chopped cucumber
½ cup feta cheese, crumbled

Sauté ¾ cup onion in hot oil in a large skillet until tender. Add ground beef and cook until browned, stirring to crumble; drain off pan drippings. Stir in next 6 ingredients. Reduce heat and simmer 5 minutes, stirring occasionally.

Place bread rounds on a baking sheet; bake at 250° for 10 minutes or until warm. Cut bread rounds in half; fill

each pocket about half full with meat mixture. Top each with tomatoes, onion, green pepper, cucumber, and cheese. Yield: 6 servings.
Mrs. Bronwen M. Gibson,
Dallas, Texas.

SAUCY COCKTAIL BURGERS

1 pound ground beef
½ cup beer
½ cup catsup
2 tablespoons Worcestershire sauce
½ teaspoon salt
1 teaspoon pepper
20 (2-inch) cocktail buns

Shape ground beef into 20 (2-inch) patties. Place in a single layer in a shallow baking pan. Bake at 475° for 15 minutes or until done; drain well.

Combine next 5 ingredients in a medium saucepan; bring to a boil. Add patties to sauce mixture; reduce heat and simmer, uncovered, 10 minutes. Serve in buns. Yield: 20 appetizer servings.
Norene Brundige,
Amarillo, Texas.

CHEESY BEEF BURGERS

1½ pounds ground beef
½ cup fine, dry breadcrumbs, divided
1 egg, beaten
2 tablespoons commercial barbecue sauce
¾ teaspoon salt
1 cup (4 ounces) shredded sharp Cheddar cheese
¼ cup chopped green pepper
2 tablespoons water

Combine beef, ¼ cup breadcrumbs, egg, barbecue sauce, and salt, mixing well; shape into a 14- x 8-inch rectangle on a sheet of waxed paper. Combine remaining ¼ cup breadcrumbs, cheese, green pepper, and water, mixing well; press gently into meat mixture, leaving a ½-inch margin around edges.

Beginning at short end, roll up meat jellyroll fashion, lifting waxed paper to help in rolling. Press edges and ends together to seal. Cover and chill 1 hour.

Cut roll into 6 slices. Arrange slices on rack of a lightly greased broiler pan. Bake at 350° for 30 minutes or until desired degree of doneness. Yield: 6 servings.
Deann J. Reed,
Staunton, Virginia.

HOT CHILE-BEEF DIP

1 pound ground beef
1 small onion, chopped
1 (8-ounce) can tomato sauce
1 (8-ounce) jar picante sauce
½ cup commercial hot taco sauce
1 tablespoon chili powder
1 (4-ounce) can chopped green chiles,
    drained
¼ teaspoon salt
1 cup (4 ounces) shredded sharp Cheddar
    cheese

Cook ground beef and onion in a large skillet until beef is browned, stirring to crumble meat; drain off pan drippings. Stir in next 6 ingredients. Spoon mixture into a chafing dish; sprinkle with cheese. Serve with tortilla chips. Yield: 4 cups. *Sheree Garvin, Wilkesboro, North Carolina.*

Congeal Flavor In These Salads

Congealed salads are perfect for entertaining on busy workdays. Rely on these make-ahead dishes when expecting company for dinner.

To unmold a congealed salad, first run the tip of a narrow spatula or knife around the inside of the mold. Then, quickly dip the mold up to the rim in a sink of warm water, and invert it onto the serving plate. Or invert the salad onto the plate and warm the mold with a towel soaked in hot water. Shake the mold gently to release the salad.

RANCH TOMATO ASPIC

2 envelopes unflavored gelatin
¼ cup cold water
½ cup water
1 (10¾-ounce) can tomato soup, undiluted
1 (6-ounce) can tomato juice
1 (0.4-ounce) package buttermilk salad
    dressing mix
2 tablespoons lemon juice
½ teaspoon celery seeds
1 cup buttermilk
½ cup mayonnaise
1 cup chopped green pepper
1 cup chopped celery
Lettuce leaves (optional)

Soften gelatin in ¼ cup cold water. Bring ½ cup water to a boil; add gelatin mixture, stirring until dissolved. Add next 5 ingredients; cook over low heat, stirring constantly, until thoroughly heated. Remove from heat, and cool; stir in buttermilk and mayonnaise.

Chill until consistency of unbeaten egg white. Stir in green pepper and celery. Pour mixture into an oiled 6-cup mold; chill until firm. Unmold on lettuce leaves, if desired. Yield: 10 servings. *Nel Beck, Fort Payne, Alabama.*

CHICKEN-PEA SALAD

1 envelope unflavored gelatin
3 tablespoons cold water
1 cup chicken broth
1 tablespoon lemon juice
1 teaspoon onion juice
⅛ teaspoon salt
1 cup finely chopped cooked chicken
¼ cup canned English peas
2 tablespoons finely chopped celery
2 tablespoons diced pimiento

Sprinkle gelatin over cold water; let stand 5 minutes. Bring chicken broth to boil; add to gelatin mixture, and stir until dissolved. Add lemon juice, onion juice, and salt; mix well. Chill until consistency of unbeaten egg white; stir in remaining ingredients. Pour into a lightly oiled 7- x 3½- x 2-inch loafpan; chill until firm. Yield: 4 to 6 servings. *Mrs. Thomas F. Everett, Blackville, South Carolina.*

APRICOT NECTAR SALAD

1 (12-ounce) can apricot nectar
1 (3-ounce) package lemon-flavored gelatin
⅓ cup water
1 tablespoon lemon juice
1 (11-ounce) can mandarin oranges,
    drained
½ cup halved seedless green grapes
¼ cup chopped, unpeeled apple
Apple slices (optional)
Additional mandarin orange sections
    (optional)
Seedless green grapes (optional)

Bring apricot nectar to a boil; add gelatin, stirring until dissolved. Stir in water and lemon juice. Chill until consistency of unbeaten egg white. Stir in next 3 ingredients; pour into an oiled 4-cup mold. Chill until firm. Unmold salad; garnish with apple slices, mandarin orange sections, and grapes, if desired. Yield: 6 to 8 servings. *Maude Crenshaw, Lehigh Acres, Florida.*

PINEAPPLE-ORANGE CONGEALED SALAD

1 (15¼-ounce) can crushed pineapple,
    undrained
1 (6-ounce) package orange-flavored
    gelatin
2 cups buttermilk
1 cup flaked coconut
1 cup chopped pecans
1 (12-ounce) carton frozen whipped
    topping, thawed

Place pineapple in a saucepan; bring to a boil, stirring constantly. Remove from heat. Add gelatin, stirring until dissolved. Stir in buttermilk, coconut, and pecans; cool. Fold in whipped topping; pour into a 13- x 9- x 2-inch dish. Chill until firm. Yield: 15 servings. *Cheryl Landreth, Pleasant Grove, Alabama.*

Let's Have Limas

Lima beans are popular all over the South. Your grandmother probably called them butter beans and seasoned them richly with salt pork or bacon. But there's much more you can do.

Don't shell limas until you're ready to cook them. Refrigerate unshelled limas in a moisture-proof container or plastic bag; they should keep 3 or 4 days.

If you can't find fresh limas, substitute frozen ones for any of these recipes, and cook according to package directions.

LIMA BEAN GARDEN CASSEROLE

2 cups shelled fresh lima beans
1 cup fresh corn cut from cob
2 tablespoons butter or margarine
2 tablespoons all-purpose flour
1 cup milk
1 teaspoon minced fresh dillweed or ¼
    teaspoon dried whole dillweed
½ teaspoon salt
Dash of freshly ground black pepper
1 cup shredded carrots
¼ cup grated Parmesan cheese

Cook lima beans, covered, in boiling salted water 20 minutes or until tender; drain and set aside.

Cook corn, covered, in boiling salted water 10 minutes; drain and set aside.

Melt butter in a heavy saucepan over low heat; add flour, stirring until

smooth. Cook 1 minute, stirring constantly. Gradually add milk; cook over medium heat, stirring constantly, until thickened and bubbly. Stir in dillweed, salt, pepper, and vegetables. Pour into a lightly greased 2-quart casserole; cover and bake at 350° for 25 minutes. Sprinkle with cheese; bake, uncovered, an additional 5 minutes. Yield: 6 servings.
Jan Thompson,
Highland, Maryland.

HOT LIMA AND TOMATO COMBO

2 cups shelled fresh lima beans
2 tablespoons vegetable oil
1½ tablespoons all-purpose flour
1 medium onion, chopped
1 fresh hot pepper, chopped
3 medium tomatoes, peeled and chopped
Dash of pepper

Cook beans in boiling salted water 20 minutes or until tender; drain, reserving liquid. Add enough water to liquid to equal 1 cup. Set beans and liquid aside.

Combine oil and flour in a heavy skillet. Cook over medium heat, stirring constantly, until roux is the color of a copper penny. Add onion and hot pepper; cook, stirring constantly, until tender. Add reserved liquid, tomatoes, and pepper; cook over medium heat, stirring constantly, until slightly thickened. Stir in limas; cook until thoroughly heated. Yield: 4 to 6 servings.
Nell C. Weems,
Pioneer, Louisiana.

SAVORY LIMA BEANS

2 cups shelled fresh lima beans
2 slices bacon
½ cup water
1 tablespoon all-purpose flour
2 tablespoons chopped onion
1 tablespoon brown sugar
¼ teaspoon salt
¼ teaspoon celery salt
¼ teaspoon paprika

Cook lima beans, covered, in boiling salted water 20 minutes or until tender; drain well.

Cook bacon until almost crisp; drain and set aside.

Gradually add water to flour, stirring until smooth. Combine lima beans, flour mixture, onion, and next 4 ingredients, mixing well. Pour into a lightly greased 1-quart baking dish. Place bacon on top. Bake, uncovered, at 375° for 20 minutes. Yield: 4 servings.
Rublelene Singleton,
Scotts Hill, Tennessee.

LIMA BEANS WITH CANADIAN BACON

4 cups shelled fresh lima beans
6 slices Canadian bacon, coarsely chopped
2 tablespoons butter or margarine
2 tablespoons chopped onion
2 tablespoons all-purpose flour
2 teaspoons brown sugar
¼ teaspoon salt
¼ teaspoon ground turmeric
⅛ teaspoon pepper
3 medium tomatoes, peeled and coarsely chopped

Cook lima beans, covered, in boiling salted water 20 minutes or until tender; drain, reserving liquid. Add enough water to reserved liquid to equal 1 cup; set beans and liquid aside.

Fry Canadian bacon in a large skillet about 3 minutes; remove from skillet, and set aside.

Melt butter in skillet; add onion, and sauté until tender. Combine flour, brown sugar, salt, turmeric, and pepper; add to onion, stirring until well blended. Cook 1 minute, stirring constantly. Gradually add reserved liquid; cook over medium heat, stirring constantly, until thickened and bubbly. Stir in beans; cook until thoroughly heated.

Spoon half of bean mixture into a lightly greased 1½-quart casserole. Layer tomatoes and bacon over beans; top with remaining beans. Cover and bake at 350° for 20 minutes. Yield: 6 servings.
Allison Whiteside,
Hinsdale, Illinois.

Tip: Keep butter, margarine, and fat drippings tightly covered in the refrigerator. Vegetable shortening can be kept covered at room temperature. Homemade salad dressing should be kept in the refrigerator; mayonnaise and commercial salad dressings should be refrigerated after opening. Foods mixed with mayonnaise, such as potato salad or egg salad, should be refrigerated and used within a couple of days.

Desserts For A Sweet Victory

When the final points on the scoreboard declare your team the victor, begin the fifth quarter with a celebration. These desserts are fine ways to kick off the party. And, you can make them before the game so they'll be ready to eat when you arrive home.

ECLAIRS WITH PECAN SAUCE

1 cup water
½ cup butter or margarine
1 cup all-purpose flour
4 eggs
1 quart vanilla ice cream
Pecan Sauce

Combine water and butter in a medium saucepan; bring mixture to a boil. Reduce heat to low and add flour, stirring vigorously until the mixture leaves sides of pan and forms a smooth ball. Remove saucepan from heat and allow to cool slightly.

Add eggs, one at a time, beating with a wooden spoon after each addition; beat until batter is smooth.

Drop batter by level one-fourth cupfuls 2 inches apart on ungreased baking sheets, shaping each éclair into a 4½- x 1½-inch rectangle. Bake at 400° for 40 minutes or until golden brown and puffed. Cool away from drafts.

Cut off top of each éclair; pull out and discard soft dough inside. Fill bottom halves with ice cream, and cover with top halves. Freeze.

To serve, drizzle Pecan Sauce over éclairs. Yield: 12 éclairs.

Pecan Sauce:

¼ cup water
3 tablespoons cornstarch
1 cup light corn syrup
¼ cup firmly packed brown sugar
2 tablespoons butter or margarine
1 teaspoon vanilla extract
½ cup chopped pecans

Combine water and cornstarch, stirring until smooth. Combine cornstarch mixture, corn syrup, and brown sugar in a saucepan; cook, stirring constantly, over medium heat until sauce thickens. Add butter, vanilla, and pecans; stir until butter melts. Serve warm or cold. Yield: 1¾ cups.

Note: To form éclairs, batter may also be piped onto ungreased baking sheets.
Mary Ann Turk,
Joplin, Missouri.

BUTTERED RUM POUND CAKE

1 cup butter, softened
2½ cups sugar
6 eggs, separated
3 cups all-purpose flour
¼ teaspoon baking soda
1 (8-ounce) carton commercial sour cream
1 teaspoon vanilla extract
1 teaspoon lemon extract
½ cup sugar
Buttered Rum Glaze

Cream butter; gradually beat in 2½ cups sugar. Add egg yolks, one at a time, beating well after each addition.

Combine flour and baking soda; add to creamed mixture alternately with sour cream, beginning and ending with flour mixture. Stir in flavorings.

Beat egg whites (at room temperature) until foamy; gradually add ½ cup sugar, 1 tablespoon at a time, beating until stiff peaks form. Fold into batter.

Pour batter into a greased and floured 10-inch tube pan. Bake at 325° for 1½ hours or until a wooden pick inserted in center comes out clean. Cool in pan 10 to 15 minutes; remove from pan, and place on a serving plate. While warm, prick cake surface at 1-inch intervals with a wooden pick or meat fork; pour warm Buttered Rum Glaze over cake. Let cake stand several hours or overnight before serving. Yield: one 10-inch pound cake.

Buttered Rum Glaze:

¼ cup plus 2 tablespoons butter
3 tablespoons rum
¾ cup sugar
3 tablespoons water
½ cup chopped walnuts

Combine first 4 ingredients in a small saucepan; bring to a boil. Boil mixture, stirring constantly, 3 minutes. Remove from heat, and stir in walnuts. Yield: enough glaze for one 10-inch cake.
Mary Burk,
Leesburg, Alabama.

RAISIN PIE

Pastry for a double-crust 9-inch pie
1 teaspoon grated lemon rind
⅓ cup lemon juice
2 teaspoons grated orange rind
½ cup orange juice
1 cup firmly packed brown sugar
2 cups raisins
1¼ cups water
¼ cup plus 2 tablespoons all-purpose flour
½ cup water

Line a 9-inch pieplate with half of pastry; set aside.

Combine next 7 ingredients in a heavy saucepan over medium heat; bring to a boil, stirring frequently. Reduce heat to low.

Combine flour and ½ cup water, stirring until smooth. Gradually add to raisin mixture, stirring constantly; simmer 5 minutes or until thickened, stirring frequently. Pour filling into pastry shell. Roll out remaining pastry, and place over filling; seal and flute edges. Cut slits in top of pastry to allow steam to escape. Bake at 400° for 40 minutes. Yield: one 9-inch pie.
Mrs. R. W. Lewis,
Knoxville, Tennessee.

BOSTON CREAM PIE

⅓ cup shortening
⅔ cup sugar
2 eggs
1 cup sifted cake flour
1 teaspoon baking powder
Pinch of salt
½ cup milk
¼ teaspoon butter flavoring
½ teaspoon vanilla extract
Cream filling (recipe follows)
Chocolate glaze (recipe follows)

Cream shortening; gradually add sugar, beating until light and fluffy. Add eggs, one at a time, beating well after each addition.

Combine flour, baking powder, and salt; add to creamed mixture alternately with milk, beginning and ending with flour mixture. Stir in flavorings.

Pour batter into a greased and floured 9-inch round cakepan. Bake at 325° for 25 to 30 minutes or until a wooden pick inserted in center comes out clean. Cool in pan 10 minutes; remove from pan, and cool completely.

Split cake layer in half horizontally to make 2 layers. Spread cream filling between layers; spread chocolate glaze over top. Refrigerate until ready to serve. Yield: about 10 servings.

Cream Filling:

½ cup sugar
¼ cup cornstarch
¼ teaspoon salt
2 cups milk
4 egg yolks, slightly beaten
½ teaspoon vanilla extract

Combine first 3 ingredients in a heavy saucepan. Gradually add milk; stir with a wire whisk until well blended. Cook over medium heat, stirring constantly, until mixture comes to a boil. Boil, stirring constantly, about 1 minute until thickened; remove from heat.

Gradually stir one-fourth of hot mixture into egg yolks; add to remaining hot mixture, stirring constantly. Return to medium heat and bring to a boil, stirring constantly. Boil 1 minute, stirring constantly, until thickened and smooth. Stir in vanilla. Cool. Yield: about 2½ cups.

Chocolate Glaze:

2 tablespoons butter or margarine
1 (1-ounce) square unsweetened chocolate
1 cup sifted powdered sugar
2 tablespoons boiling water

Combine butter and chocolate in top of a double boiler; bring water to a boil. Reduce heat to low; cook until chocolate melts. Cool slightly. Add sugar and water; beat until smooth. Yield: about 1 cup. *Mary Conner,*
Pineview, Georgia.

BLUEBERRY-AMARETTO SQUARES

1¾ cups graham cracker crumbs
½ cup sugar
½ cup butter or margarine, melted
2 eggs
¾ cup sugar
1 (8-ounce) package cream cheese, softened
2½ cups milk
2 (3¾-ounce) packages vanilla instant pudding mix
½ cup amaretto, divided
1¼ cups sugar
¼ cup cornstarch
5 cups frozen blueberries, thawed
1 (8-ounce) carton frozen whipped topping, thawed

Combine first 3 ingredients; press into a greased 13- x 9- x 2-inch baking dish.

Combine eggs, ¾ cup sugar, and cream cheese; beat at medium speed of electric mixer until smooth. Spread mixture over graham cracker crumbs. Bake at 350° for 30 minutes; cool.

Combine milk, pudding mix, and ¼ cup amaretto; beat 2 minutes at low speed of an electric mixer. Spread over cream cheese layer.

Combine 1¼ cups sugar and cornstarch in a large saucepan; gradually add ¼ cup amaretto, stirring until smooth. Stir in blueberries. Cook over medium heat, stirring constantly, until thickened; cool.

Pour blueberry mixture over pudding mixture. Chill thoroughly. To serve, spread whipped topping over blueberries. Yield: 15 to 18 servings.
H. W. Asbell,
Leesburg, Florida.

October

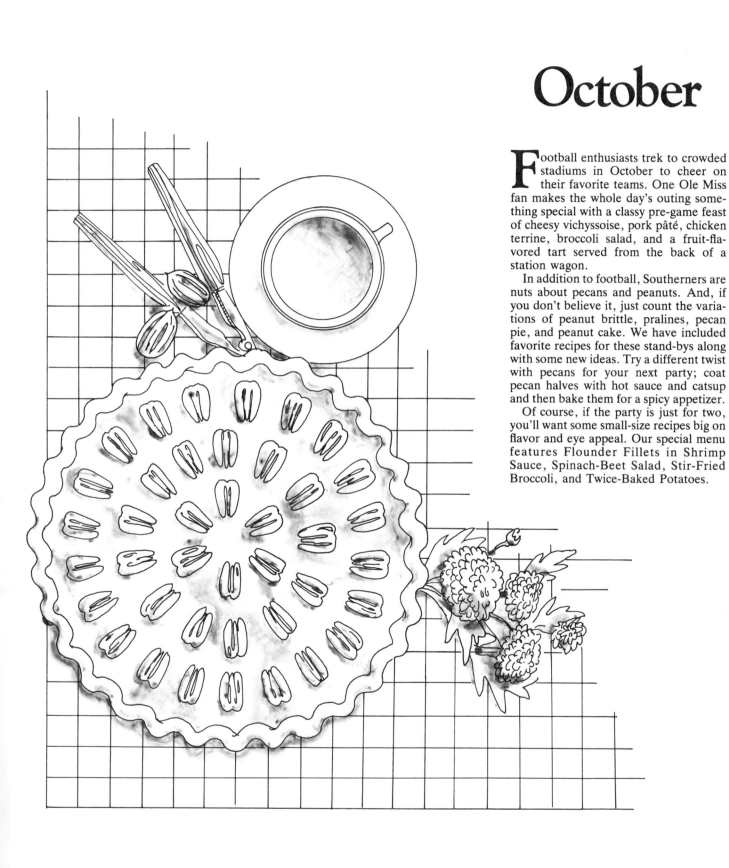

F ootball enthusiasts trek to crowded stadiums in October to cheer on their favorite teams. One Ole Miss fan makes the whole day's outing something special with a classy pre-game feast of cheesy vichyssoise, pork pâté, chicken terrine, broccoli salad, and a fruit-flavored tart served from the back of a station wagon.

In addition to football, Southerners are nuts about pecans and peanuts. And, if you don't believe it, just count the variations of peanut brittle, pralines, pecan pie, and peanut cake. We have included favorite recipes for these stand-bys along with some new ideas. Try a different twist with pecans for your next party; coat pecan halves with hot sauce and catsup and then bake them for a spicy appetizer.

Of course, if the party is just for two, you'll want some small-size recipes big on flavor and eye appeal. Our special menu features Flounder Fillets in Shrimp Sauce, Spinach-Beet Salad, Stir-Fried Broccoli, and Twice-Baked Potatoes.

Capture The Toasty Goodness Of Pecans And Peanuts

When you have a craving for pecans or peanuts, nothing else will do—unless it's a slice of Super Peanutty Layer Cake or a wedge of Orange-Pecan Pie. Following are recipes for these and other delicious treats.

When stocking up on pecans and peanuts, try to find the freshest nuts possible. Nuts in the shell resist aging much longer than those that have been shelled. However, shelling them before storage means that the nuts will take up less space and be much handier to use. Look for nuts that are free of scars, cracks, and holes.

You can purchase peanuts in several different forms. In the shell, they are available raw, roasted, and green. You will probably never purchase green peanuts unless you're planning to boil them. Shelled peanuts come raw, roasted in oil, dry roasted, and chopped. Pecans are available in the shell or in halves, pieces, and chopped.

For cooking purposes, it's helpful to know that 1 pound of unshelled peanuts yields 2 to 2½ cups of shelled nuts. One pound of unshelled pecans produces about 2¼ cups shelled nutmeats.

It's important to store pecans and peanuts properly. Left in the shell, peanuts stay fresh about four months in a dry place, nine months if refrigerated, and two years or longer if frozen. Shelled peanuts keep about six months in the refrigerator and one year when frozen in an airtight container.

Unshelled pecans stay fresh about six months. Shelled pecans are at their best for two months at room temperature, nine months if refrigerated, and two years or longer if frozen.

See page 228 for the article "From Our Kitchen To Yours" for tips on cooking with nuts.

ORANGE-PECAN PIE

3 eggs, beaten
½ cup sugar
1 cup dark corn syrup
1 tablespoon grated orange rind
⅓ cup orange juice
1 tablespoon all-purpose flour
¼ teaspoon salt
1 cup chopped pecans
1 unbaked 9-inch pastry shell
¾ cup pecan halves

Combine first 7 ingredients; beat at medium speed of electric mixer until blended. Stir in chopped pecans. Pour mixture into pastry shell. Arrange pecan halves over top. Bake at 350° for 55 to 60 minutes. Yield: one 9-inch pie.
Ann Elsie Schmetzer,
Madisonville, Kentucky.

MAPLE-PECAN PRALINES

3 cups sugar
1 cup evaporated milk
⅔ cup light corn syrup
2 tablespoons butter or margarine
¼ teaspoon cream of tartar
2 cups pecan pieces
2 teaspoons maple flavoring

Combine first 5 ingredients in a Dutch oven; heat to boiling, stirring constantly. Stir in pecan pieces; cook over medium heat, stirring occasionally, until mixture reaches soft ball stage (236°). Remove from heat; stir in flavoring. Beat with a wooden spoon 5 to 8 minutes or until the mixture is creamy and begins to thicken. Working rapidly, drop by rounded tablespoonfuls onto waxed paper; let cool. Yield: 2 dozen.
Kathleen Pashby,
Memphis, Tennessee.

BARBECUED PECANS

2 tablespoons butter or margarine
¼ cup Worcestershire sauce
1 tablespoon catsup
2 dashes of hot sauce
4 cups pecan halves
Salt to taste

Melt butter in a Dutch oven. Remove from heat; add Worcestershire sauce, catsup, and hot sauce, stirring well. Add pecans, stirring to coat.

Spread pecans evenly in a 15- x 10- x 1-inch jellyroll pan. Bake at 400° for 13 to 15 minutes, stirring every 5 minutes. Place pecans on paper towels; sprinkle lightly with salt and cool completely. Yield: 4 cups. *Mary Rudolph,*
Fort Worth, Texas.

Tip: Shop alone and after you have eaten. Studies show that people tend to buy more when hungry or when accompanied by others.

COUNTRY PECAN MUFFINS

1⅓ cups all-purpose flour
1 cup chopped pecans
½ cup firmly packed brown sugar
2 teaspoons baking powder
Pinch of salt
½ cup milk
¼ cup butter or margarine, melted
2 eggs, beaten
½ teaspoon vanilla extract

Combine first 5 ingredients in a large bowl; make a well in center of mixture. Set aside.

Combine milk, butter, eggs and vanilla; add to dry ingredients, stirring just until moistened.

Spoon the batter into greased and floured muffin pans, filling half full. Bake at 350° for 20 to 25 minutes. Yield: 15 muffins. *Barbara McGlothlin,*
Nashville, Tennessee.

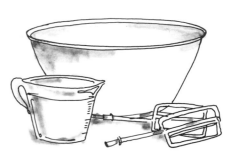

SUPER PEANUTTY LAYER CAKE

¾ cup creamy peanut butter
½ cup shortening
2¼ cups firmly packed brown sugar
3 eggs
3 cups all-purpose flour
1 tablespoon baking powder
½ teaspoon salt
1¼ cups milk
1½ teaspoons vanilla extract
1 cup flaked coconut
1 cup chopped roasted peanuts
Peanut Butter Frosting

Cream peanut butter and shortening; gradually add sugar, beating well. Add eggs, one at a time, beating well after each addition.

Combine flour, baking powder, and salt; add to creamed mixture alternately with milk, beginning and ending with flour mixture. Stir in vanilla.

Pour batter into 3 greased and floured 9-inch round cakepans. Bake at 350° for 18 to 20 minutes or until a wooden pick inserted in center comes out clean. Cool in pans 10 minutes; remove from pans, and cool completely on wire racks.

Brown coconut in a large skillet over low heat, stirring constantly. Remove from heat; stir in peanuts.

Spread Peanut Butter Frosting between layers; sprinkle ½ cup coconut-peanut mixture between each layer. Spread frosting on top and sides of cake. Sprinkle the remaining coconut-peanut mixture on top and sides of cake. Yield: one 3-layer cake.

Peanut Butter Frosting:

½ cup butter or margarine, softened
3 tablespoons creamy peanut butter
2 egg yolks
1 (16-ounce) package powdered sugar, sifted
¼ cup plus 1 tablespoon half-and-half
1 teaspoon vanilla extract

Cream butter and peanut butter; add egg yolks, beating well. Gradually add the sugar alternately with half-and-half, beating well after each addition. Stir in the vanilla. Yield: enough for one 3-layer cake.

Martha Creel,
Dothan, Alabama.

PEANUT BUTTER YUMMIES

2 cups sifted powdered sugar
½ cup creamy peanut butter
1 egg, slightly beaten
1 tablespoon butter or margarine
⅛ teaspoon salt
½ teaspoon vanilla extract
½ cup finely chopped dry roasted peanuts

Combine first 6 ingredients, mixing well. Shape mixture into 1-inch balls; roll each in peanuts. Chill 4 to 5 hours before serving. Store in refrigerator. Yield: about 2½ dozen.

Mrs. William Joseph Hamilton,
Jackson, Tennessee.

CHOCOLATE-PEANUT COOKIES

1 cup butter or margarine, softened
1½ cups sugar
2 eggs
2 teaspoons vanilla extract
2 cups all-purpose flour
⅔ cup cocoa
¾ teaspoon baking soda
½ teaspoon salt
1 cup finely chopped peanuts

Cream butter; gradually add the sugar, beating until light and fluffy. Stir in eggs and vanilla.

Combine flour, cocoa, baking soda, and salt; add to creamed mixture, beating well. Stir in the chopped peanuts.

Drop dough by teaspoonfuls onto ungreased cookie sheets. Bake at 350° for 12 to 14 minutes. Cool cookies on wire racks. Yield: about 5½ dozen.

Rhonda Cox,
Shawnee, Oklahoma.

GOLDEN PEANUT BRITTLE

3 cups shelled raw peanuts
1½ teaspoons baking soda
½ teaspoon salt
2 cups sugar
1 cup light corn syrup
½ cup water
¼ cup butter or margarine

Spread peanuts evenly in a 15- x 10- x 1-inch jellyroll pan; bake at 350° for 15 minutes. Set aside.

Combine soda and salt; set aside. Combine sugar, syrup, and water in a Dutch oven; cook over low heat, stirring occasionally, until mixture reaches soft crack stage (275°). Add peanuts and cook, stirring constantly, until mixture reaches hard crack stage (300°). Remove from heat; stir in butter and soda mixture.

Working rapidly, spread mixture thinly onto 2 buttered 15- x 10- x 1-inch jellyroll pans. Let cool; break into pieces. Yield: about 2½ pounds.

Carolyn Webb,
Jackson, Mississippi.

Pre-Game Picnics Rally Food And Fans

When the University of Mississippi Rebels play football, the real winners are the fans who are invited to Bob and Cissy Coleman's pre-game picnic.

Cissy, as much a food artist as a fabulous cook, invites family and friends to a tailgate spread before each Ole Miss game in Jackson. The result is a spectacular array of food, such as a colorful vegetable-studded terrine and a pâté garnished with tomato wedges and green onion stems in aspic.

Preparation for the picnic begins several days before the game as Cissy plans her menu. She often assigns fellow picnickers a couple of recipes to make, so everyone pitches in on the preparation and transportation of the food. She plans the recipes, however, to minimize

work the day of the game; most can be made a day or two in advance. "The pâté and terrine actually improve in flavor if made several days ahead," confides Cissy.

After the feast any leftovers that remain are carefully packed on ice before everyone leaves for the game.

Velvety Roquefort Vichyssoise
Vegetable-Chicken Terrine
Pork Pâté With Spinach and Cream
Broccoli and Red Pepper Salad
Candied Carrots
Jumbo Popovers
Assorted Commercial Breads
Cherry and Blackberry Tart
Wine

VELVETY ROQUEFORT VICHYSSOISE

2 cups finely chopped onion
¼ cup butter or margarine
4 cups chicken broth
2 cups peeled, diced potatoes
¼ teaspoon salt
Pinch of white pepper
6 ounces Roquefort cheese, divided
½ cup Chablis or other dry white wine
2 cups buttermilk
2 tablespoons minced fresh parsley

Sauté onion in butter in a large Dutch oven until tender and slightly golden. Stir in broth, potatoes, salt, and pepper; bring to a boil. Reduce heat and simmer, uncovered, 15 minutes or until potatoes are tender.

Spoon half of potato mixture into container of an electric blender; process until smooth. Repeat with remaining mixture; return to Dutch oven.

Crumble 4 ounces cheese. Add cheese and wine to potato mixture; cook over low heat, stirring constantly, about 5 minutes or until cheese melts. Let cool; cover and refrigerate about 4 hours until thoroughly chilled. Stir in buttermilk. To serve, pour into soup tureen. Crumble remaining cheese; sprinkle cheese and parsley over soup. Yield: about 8 cups.

Tip: The next time a recipe calls for 1 cup buttermilk, try this handy substitute: Put 1 tablespoon vinegar or lemon juice in a measuring cup, add enough whole milk to make 1 cup, and let stand 5 minutes to thicken slightly.

VEGETABLE-CHICKEN TERRINE

12 fresh whole green beans
1 medium carrot, cut into thin lengthwise strips
½ (10-ounce) package frozen asparagus spears, thawed
1 small zucchini, cut into thin lengthwise strips
¾ pound boneless chicken breast halves, skinned and cut into cubes
2 tablespoons chopped fresh parsley
1 teaspoon salt
½ to 1 teaspoon dried whole tarragon
½ teaspoon ground savory
⅛ teaspoon white pepper
2 cups whipping cream
Fresh Tomato Sauce
Fresh parsley sprigs

Wash beans; trim ends and remove strings. Cook green beans and carrot in boiling water 3 minutes or until tender. Remove vegetables with a slotted spoon, and pat dry. Cook asparagus and zucchini in boiling water 2 minutes or until tender. Remove vegetables with a slotted spoon, and pat dry. Set aside.

Position knife blade in processor bowl; combine chicken and next 5 ingredients in processor bowl, and top with cover. Process 30 to 45 seconds or just until mixture is smooth (do not overprocess). Remove food pusher. Slowly pour whipping cream through food chute with processor running, blending just until mixture is smooth.

Place one-fourth of chicken mixture in a lightly oiled 9- x 5- x 3-inch loaf-pan. Arrange one-third of vegetables over chicken alternating color. Repeat with remaining chicken mixture and vegetables; end with chicken mixture.

Place loafpan in a 13- x 9- x 2-inch baking pan. Pour enough boiling water into larger pan to reach one-third of the way up sides of loafpan. Bake at 325° for 55 to 60 minutes. Let cool. Cover and chill overnight.

Unmold terrine onto serving plate. Pour Fresh Tomato Sauce around base of terrine and in a thin strip across top. Garnish with parsley. Cut into slices to serve. Yield: 8 servings.

Fresh Tomato Sauce:

1½ tablespoons water
1 tablespoon white wine vinegar
1 teaspoon chopped shallots
1 teaspoon tomato paste
¼ teaspoon dried whole tarragon
1 small tomato, peeled, seeded, and diced (about ¼ cup)
¼ cup vegetable oil
½ cup tomato juice
¼ teaspoon salt
⅛ teaspoon pepper

Combine first 5 ingredients in a small saucepan; cook over high heat 2 to 3 minutes or until liquid is reduced to about 1 tablespoon. Cool slightly.

Position knife blade in processor bowl. Combine vinegar mixture and tomato in processor bowl; process until smooth. Add oil; process 20 seconds. Add remaining ingredients; process 20 seconds. Yield: about 1 cup.

PORK PATE WITH SPINACH AND CREAM

2 pounds fresh spinach
¼ pound chicken livers
¼ cup Cognac
⅛ teaspoon freshly ground pepper
1 pound Boston butt, cut into 2-inch pieces
1 (8-ounce) package boiled ham
15 to 17 slices bacon, divided
1 cup whipping cream
4 eggs, beaten
¼ cup plus 1 tablespoon port wine
2 cloves garlic, minced
1 teaspoon salt
1 teaspoon dried whole tarragon
1 teaspoon dried whole thyme
½ teaspoon dried whole marjoram
½ teaspoon dried whole oregano
¼ teaspoon ground savory
¼ teaspoon freshly ground pepper
Pinch of red pepper
Dash of ground nutmeg
¼ pound salt pork, chopped
1 bay leaf
1 cup all-purpose flour
¼ cup plus 2 tablespoons water
Tomato wedges
Green onion stems
Aspic (recipe follows)

Remove stems from spinach. Wash leaves thoroughly in lukewarm water. Cook spinach, covered, in 1 quart boiling salted water 4 to 5 minutes. Drain; place on paper towels, and squeeze until barely moist. Coarsely chop spinach; place in a large bowl.

Combine chicken livers, Cognac, and ⅛ teaspoon pepper; marinate in refrigerator until ready to use.

Position knife blade in food processor bowl; place pork pieces in bowl, and top with cover. Coarsely grind the pork. (A meat grinder may be used instead of processor, if desired.) Add pork to chopped spinach. Coarsely grind ham and 5 slices bacon in processor; add to spinach and pork.

Drain livers, reserving liquid. Add reserved liquid, whipping cream, and next 12 ingredients to the spinach mixture, mixing well.

Line the sides and bottom of a 2-quart round ovenproof mold or soufflé dish with remaining bacon. Spoon one-third of meat mixture into prepared mold. Arrange half of livers and half of salt pork down center of pâté; layer half of remaining meat mixture over salt pork. Arrange remaining livers and salt pork down center of pâté, and top with remaining meat mixture. Tap mold against working surface several times to settle contents. Place bay leaf on top.

Combine flour and water (dough will be sticky); pat dough over pâté, sealing edges carefully. Place mold in a 13- x 9- x 2-inch baking pan; pour hot water into pan to a depth of 1 inch. Bake at 375° for 1½ hours.

Remove mold from water, and peel off flour seal. Set 1½-quart mold or soufflé dish on top of pâté. Place metal weights or dried beans in empty mold to pack pâté as it cools, draining off pan drippings, if necessary.

Refrigerate pâté at least 12 hours. Unmold onto serving dish. Peel away bacon; smooth surface of pâté with the back of a spoon. Arrange tomato wedges and green onion stems as desired on mold; spoon aspic over pâté, and chill until set. Serve with assorted crackers or breads. Yield: 12 servings.

Aspic:

1 envelope unflavored gelatin
¾ cup water
1 teaspoon beef-flavored bouillon granules

Dissolve gelatin in water in a small saucepan. Add bouillon granules to saucepan; bring mixture to a boil, stirring until bouillon granules dissolve. Remove from heat; use when just cooled (before mixture begins to set). Yield: ¾ cup.

BROCCOLI AND RED PEPPER SALAD

4 (1-pound) bunches fresh broccoli
3 sweet red peppers, cut into thin strips
¾ cup olive oil
¼ cup lemon juice
2 teaspoons Dijon mustard
¼ teaspoon salt
⅛ teaspoon pepper

Trim off large leaves of broccoli, and remove tough ends of lower stalks. Wash broccoli thoroughly; cut flowerets into bite-size pieces (reserve the stems for another use). Cook broccoli, covered, in a small amount of boiling salted water 2 to 3 minutes or until slightly tender; drain. Rinse with cold water; drain and set aside.

Combine broccoli and peppers in a large mixing bowl; toss gently. Combine remaining ingredients in a jar; cover tightly and shake vigorously. Pour marinade over vegetables; toss gently. Cover and chill overnight. Drain off marinade before serving. Yield: 8 to 10 servings.

CANDIED CARROTS

About 3 pounds carrots, pared and diagonally sliced
¼ cup plus 2 tablespoons butter or margarine
¾ cup jellied cranberry sauce
¼ cup plus 2 tablespoons firmly packed brown sugar
¾ teaspoon salt

Cook carrots in a small amount of boiling water 8 to 10 minutes or until crisp-tender; drain.

Melt butter in a small saucepan; add remaining ingredients. Cook, stirring constantly, until cranberry sauce melts. Pour cranberry mixture over carrots, stirring well. Yield: 10 servings.

JUMBO POPOVERS

2 cups all-purpose flour
2 cups milk
6 eggs
¼ cup plus 2 tablespoons butter or margarine, melted
1 teaspoon salt

Combine all ingredients; beat at low speed of an electric mixer just until batter is smooth. Fill 12 well-greased 6-ounce custard cups with batter. Bake at 375° for 50 minutes. Quickly cut a small slit in each popover to release steam; bake an additional 5 minutes. Remove popovers from custard cups. Serve warm or cool completely on wire racks. Yield: 1 dozen.

CHERRY AND BLACKBERRY TART

¾ cup unbleached all-purpose flour, chilled
¼ cup unsifted cake flour, chilled
2 tablespoons butter
¼ cup cold water
¼ cup plus 2 tablespoons butter, softened
1 egg yolk
1 teaspoon water
Crème Pâtissière
1 cup maraschino cherries
2 cups fresh or frozen blackberries, thawed and drained
Berry Glaze

Combine flour, and set aside 2 tablespoons. Cut 2 tablespoons butter into larger amount of flour with pastry blender until mixture resembles coarse meal. Sprinkle ¼ cup cold water evenly over surface; stir with a fork until dry ingredients are moistened. Shape into a ball and wrap in waxed paper. Chill for 15 minutes.

Combine ¼ cup plus 2 tablespoons butter and reserved flour; stir with a wooden spoon until smooth. Shape butter mixture into a 4-inch square on waxed paper. Chill 5 minutes.

Roll dough into a 12-inch circle on a lightly floured surface; place chilled butter mixture in center of dough. Fold left side of dough over butter; fold right side of dough over left. Fold upper and lower edges of dough over butter, making a thick square.

Working quickly, place dough, folded side down, on a lightly floured surface; roll dough into a 16- x 8-inch rectangle. Fold rectangle into thirds, beginning with short side. Roll dough into another 16- x 8-inch rectangle; again fold rectangle into thirds. Wrap dough in waxed paper, and chill about 2 hours.

Repeat rolling and folding process 2 additional times. Chill 2 hours.

Roll dough into a 14½- x 7½-inch rectangle. Sprinkle a baking sheet with water and shake off excess water. Place dough on baking sheet.

Working quickly, cut a ¾-inch-wide strip from each long side of pastry. Brush strips with water, and lay them, moist side down, on top of each long side of pastry rectangle, edges flush together. To complete pastry border, repeat procedure on short sides of rectangle, trimming away excess pastry at corners. Prick pastry generously with a fork. Combine egg yolk and 1 teaspoon water; brush border of pastry with egg mixture. Freeze, uncovered, 10 to 15 minutes. Bake at 425° for 15 minutes or until golden brown and puffed. Gently remove pastry from baking sheet with spatulas, and let cool on a wire rack. Transfer to serving platter.

Spread Crème Pâtissière over pastry, and arrange fruit in alternating diagonal rows over filling. Brush fruit with Berry Glaze. Yield: 8 servings.

Crème Pâtissière:

2 egg yolks
2 tablespoons sugar
¼ teaspoon vanilla extract
1½ tablespoons unbleached all-purpose flour
½ cup milk
2 tablespoons butter or margarine, softened

Whisk egg yolks, sugar, and vanilla in a medium saucepan; add flour, and stir until blended. Stir in milk; cook over medium heat, stirring constantly, just until mixture comes to a boil. Reduce heat and simmer 1 minute. Cool to lukewarm; add butter. Stir until butter melts; cover and refrigerate until thoroughly chilled. Yield: ¾ cup.

Berry Glaze:

¼ cup raspberry preserves
¼ cup currant jelly
1 tablespoon water

Put raspberry preserves through a sieve; discard seeds. Combine strained preserves, jelly, and water in a saucepan. Cook over medium heat, stirring constantly, until smooth and thoroughly heated. Use while warm. Yield: ½ cup.

The Sweetest Of All Potatoes

The best thing about sweet potatoes is their flavor. In fact, they are so sweet you may have trouble deciding whether they should be served as a vegetable or as a dessert.

SWEET POTATO MERINGUE PIE

1¼ cups cooked, mashed sweet potatoes
⅔ cup sugar
½ cup evaporated milk
½ cup flaked coconut
¼ cup plus 2 tablespoons butter or margarine, melted
½ teaspoon lemon extract
2 eggs, separated
1 unbaked 9-inch pastry shell
¼ cup sugar
½ teaspoon vanilla extract

Combine first 6 ingredients and egg yolks, mixing well. Spoon mixture into pastry shell. Bake at 350° for 40 to 45 minutes or until knife inserted in center comes out clean.

Beat egg whites (at room temperature) until foamy. Gradually add ¼ cup sugar, 1 tablespoon at a time, and vanilla, beating until stiff peaks form. Spread meringue over filling, sealing to edge of pastry. Bake at 400° for 10 minutes or until meringue is golden brown. Yield: one 9-inch pie.

Mrs. C. T. Eanes,
Hurt, Virginia.

SWEET POTATO-ORANGE BAKE

3 large sweet potatoes
2 medium oranges, peeled and sliced
½ cup firmly packed brown sugar
½ cup water
½ teaspoon salt
¼ cup butter or margarine, melted
¼ cup chopped pecans

Cook sweet potatoes in boiling water 20 to 25 minutes or until tender. Let cool to touch; peel and cut into ½-inch slices. Layer potatoes and oranges in a greased 12- x 8- x 2-inch baking dish.

Combine next 4 ingredients in a small saucepan. Bring to a boil, reduce heat, and simmer 4 to 5 minutes, stirring constantly. Pour glaze over sweet potatoes; sprinkle with chopped pecans. Cover and bake at 350° for 35 minutes. Yield: 6 to 8 servings.   *Mrs. John Rucker,*
Louisville, Kentucky.

FRIED SWEET POTATOES

4 medium-size sweet potatoes
¼ cup Cointreau or other orange-flavored
    liqueur
¼ cup honey
1 teaspoon grated lemon rind
2 cups all-purpose flour
2 cups light beer
Vegetable oil

Cook sweet potatoes in boiling water 5 minutes; let cool to touch. Peel and cut into ¼-inch slices; place in a large shallow dish. Combine Cointreau, honey, and lemon rind, mixing well; pour over potato slices and marinate about 1 hour.

Combine flour and beer, stirring until smooth. Dip sweet potato slices in beer mixture; coat well. Fry in hot oil (390°) until golden; drain on paper towels. Yield: 8 servings.   *Sherri D. Medley,*
Greensboro, North Carolina.

TROPICAL GLAZED SWEET POTATOES

4 large sweet potatoes
1 (8¼-ounce) can crushed pineapple,
    undrained
¾ cup firmly packed brown sugar
1½ tablespoons cornstarch
¼ teaspoon salt
⅛ teaspoon ground cinnamon
2 teaspoons grated orange rind
1 cup canned apricots, undrained and
    pureed
2 tablespoons butter or margarine,
    softened
½ cup chopped pecans

Cook sweet potatoes in boiling water 20 to 25 minutes or until tender. Let cool to touch; peel and cut into ½-inch slices. Arrange slices so edges overlap in a lightly greased 12- x 8- x 2-inch baking dish; set aside.

Drain pineapple, reserving ⅓ cup syrup; set pineapple aside. Combine pineapple syrup, sugar, cornstarch, salt, cinnamon, orange rind, and apricot puree in a heavy saucepan; stir well. Cook over medium heat, stirring constantly, until smooth and thickened. Add butter, pecans, and pineapple, stirring until butter melts; pour over potatoes. Bake at 375° for 20 to 25 minutes. Yield: 8 servings.   *Ann Thomas,*
Huntsville, Alabama.

Two Ways To Create A Pizza

Our readers say you don't have to dine out to enjoy a delicious pizza. And some have given us their own ideas about what makes a pizza good.

SPICY SAUSAGE-PEPPERONI PIZZA

1 (6-ounce) can tomato paste
2 (8-ounce) cans tomato sauce
2 tablespoons vinegar
¼ cup dry red wine
2 cloves garlic, minced
½ teaspoon dried whole oregano
½ teaspoon dried whole thyme
½ teaspoon dried Italian seasoning
Dash of salt
Dash of pepper
Pizza crust (recipe follows)
½ cup grated Parmesan cheese
1 cup (4 ounces) shredded mozzarella
    cheese
1 cup (4 ounces) shredded Monterey Jack
    or provolone cheese
½ pound Italian bulk sausage
½ (3½-ounce) package sliced pepperoni
⅓ cup sliced ripe olives
1 (4-ounce) can sliced mushrooms,
    drained
½ cup chopped onion
½ cup chopped green pepper
1 tablespoon vegetable oil
1 (2-ounce) can anchovy fillets, drained
    (optional)

Combine first 10 ingredients in a small saucepan; bring to a boil. Reduce heat and simmer, uncovered, 20 minutes, stirring occasionally.

Spread sauce evenly over each pizza crust, leaving a ½-inch border around edges. Sprinkle ¼ cup Parmesan cheese over each pizza. Combine mozzarella and Monterey Jack cheese; sprinkle 1 cup cheese mixture over each pizza.

Cook Italian sausage until browned; drain well. Sprinkle sausage over each pizza; top with pepperoni and olives.

Sauté mushrooms, onion, and green pepper in hot oil until tender. Sprinkle evenly over each pizza. Top with anchovies, if desired. Bake at 425° for 20 to 25 minutes. Yield: two 12-inch pizzas.

Pizza Crust:

2 packages dry yeast
1 cup warm water (105° to 115°)
2 tablespoons shortening
1 teaspoon salt
3 to 3½ cups bread flour
1 teaspoon sugar (optional)

Dissolve yeast in warm water in a large bowl; let stand 5 minutes. Stir in shortening, salt, 1 cup flour, and sugar, if desired. Stir in enough remaining flour to make a soft dough.

Turn dough out onto a lightly floured surface, and knead about 8 to 10 minutes until smooth and elastic. Place in a greased bowl, turning to grease top. Cover and let rise in a warm place (85°), free from drafts, 1 hour or until doubled in bulk. Punch dough down, and divide in half. Lightly grease hands, and pat evenly into 2 lightly greased 12-inch pizza pans. Yield: two 12-inch pizza crusts.   *Dee Buchfink,*
Oologah, Oklahoma.

CHEESE-AND-MUSHROOM PIZZA

1 cup chopped onion
2 cloves garlic, minced
2 tablespoons vegetable oil
1 (15-ounce) can tomato sauce
1 to 1½ teaspoons dried whole oregano
1 teaspoon dried whole thyme
½ teaspoon salt
⅛ teaspoon pepper
1 (13¾-ounce) package hot roll mix
1 cup warm water (105° to 115°)
1 (6-ounce) can sliced mushrooms, drained
4 cups (16 ounces) shredded mozzarella
    cheese
¼ cup grated Parmesan cheese

Sauté onion and garlic in oil in a heavy saucepan until tender. Stir in next 5 ingredients. Bring to a boil, reduce heat, and simmer, uncovered, 15 minutes, stirring occasionally. Set aside.

Remove package of yeast from hot roll mix; dissolve in water in a large bowl. Gradually stir in mix. Cover and set aside 10 minutes. Divide dough in half. Lightly grease hands; pat dough evenly into 2 lightly greased 12-inch pizza pans.

Spread sauce evenly over each pizza crust; sprinkle with mushrooms. Bake at 425° for 10 minutes. Sprinkle with cheese; bake an additional 10 minutes. Yield: two 12-inch pizzas. *Marie Davis, Morganton, North Carolina.*

Try This Seafood Menu For Two

This menu for two can make your evening extra-special. It's highlighted by Flounder Fillets in Shrimp Sauce, a delicious dish delicately flavored with wine and tarragon.

Flounder Fillets in Shrimp Sauce
Twice-Baked Potatoes
Stir-Fried Broccoli
Spinach-Beet Salad
Commercial Rolls
Creamy Vanilla Pudding
White Wine   Coffee

FLOUNDER FILLETS IN SHRIMP SAUCE

2 (6-ounce) flounder fillets
1 teaspoon lemon juice
1 tablespoon dry white wine
1½ cups water
½ pound unpeeled small shrimp
2 tablespoons butter or margarine
2 tablespoons all-purpose flour
¾ cup milk
2 tablespoons dry white wine
1½ teaspoons chopped fresh parsley
½ teaspoon salt
¼ teaspoon dried whole tarragon
¼ teaspoon Worcestershire sauce
1 (3-ounce) can sliced mushrooms, drained

Place fillets in a shallow dish. Combine lemon juice and 1 tablespoon wine; pour over fillets. Cover and chill at least 1 hour.

Bring water to a boil; add shrimp, and return to a boil. Reduce heat and simmer, uncovered, 3 to 5 minutes or until shrimp are pink. Drain well and

rinse with cold water. Peel and devein shrimp; set aside.

Melt butter in a heavy saucepan over low heat; add flour, stirring until smooth. Cook 1 minute, stirring constantly. Gradually add milk; cook over medium heat, stirring constantly, until thickened and bubbly. Stir in next 6 ingredients and the shrimp.

Drain fillets; roll up. Place seam side down in a lightly greased baking dish; pour sauce over top. Bake, uncovered, at 375° for 25 minutes or until fish flakes easily, basting occasionally with sauce. Yield: 2 servings.
Elizabeth M. Verbeck, St. Petersburg, Florida.

TWICE-BAKED POTATOES

2 medium baking potatoes
Vegetable oil
½ cup cream-style cottage cheese
2 tablespoons butter or margarine, softened
1 tablespoon mayonnaise
1 tablespoon chopped chives
¼ teaspoon salt
⅛ teaspoon pepper
2 tablespoons shredded Cheddar cheese
Paprika

Scrub potatoes thoroughly, and rub skins with oil; bake at 400° for 1 hour or until done.

Allow potatoes to cool to touch. Cut potatoes in half lengthwise; carefully scoop out pulp, leaving shells intact. Mash pulp.

Combine potato pulp and next 6 ingredients; mix well. Stuff shells with potato mixture; sprinkle with cheese and paprika. Place in a shallow baking dish; bake at 375° for 15 to 20 minutes or until thoroughly heated. Yield: 2 servings. *Mrs. Ben M. Beasley, Orlando, Florida.*

STIR-FRIED BROCCOLI

¼ teaspoon chicken-flavored bouillon granules
¼ cup hot water
1½ teaspoons cornstarch
1 teaspoon sugar
1 tablespoon soy sauce
1 tablespoon dry sherry
2 tablespoons vegetable oil
1 clove garlic, minced
1½ cups coarsely chopped fresh broccoli flowerets

Dissolve bouillon granules in water. Combine cornstarch and sugar; stir into

bouillon mixture. Add soy sauce and sherry. Set aside.

Pour oil around top of preheated wok, coating sides; allow to heat at medium high (325°) for 1 minute. Add garlic; stir-fry 30 seconds. Add broccoli; stir-fry 2 minutes. Pour bouillon mixture over broccoli, stirring well. Cook 1 to 2 minutes or until thickened. Yield: 2 servings.

SPINACH-BEET SALAD

1 (8¼-ounce) can sliced beets, drained
¼ cup commercial Italian dressing
1 stalk celery, chopped
2 green onions, chopped
3 spinach leaves, shredded
Fresh spinach leaves
1 egg yolk, hard-cooked and sieved

Combine beets and dressing; marinate at least 2 hours. Drain. Add next 3 ingredients, and toss gently. Arrange beet mixture on spinach leaves; sprinkle with egg yolk. Yield: 2 servings.
Mercena B. Edwards, Orlando, Florida.

CREAMY VANILLA PUDDING

2 tablespoons sugar
1½ teaspoons cornstarch
Pinch of salt
1 cup milk
1 egg yolk
1½ teaspoons butter or margarine
½ teaspoon vanilla extract

Combine sugar, cornstarch, and salt in a small saucepan; gradually stir in milk. Cook over medium heat, stirring constantly, until mixture comes to a boil. Cook 1 additional minute, stirring constantly. Remove from heat.

Beat egg yolk until thick and lemon colored. Gradually stir about one-fourth of hot mixture into yolk; add to remaining hot mixture, stirring constantly. Bring mixture to a boil over medium heat and cook 1 minute, stirring constantly. Remove from heat; stir in butter and vanilla. Pour mixture into two 6-ounce custard cups. Chill. Yield: 2 servings. *Edna Muddiman, Great Falls, Virginia.*

Spoon Into Chicken And Dumplings

After experimenting with different methods for years, Mrs. Morton Smith finally perfected this recipe for Old-Fashioned Chicken and Dumplings.

Mrs. Smith says buttermilk gives her dumplings a light texture. She recommends kneading them on a well-floured surface; the extra flour in the dumplings will help the broth to thicken correctly.

OLD-FASHIONED CHICKEN AND DUMPLINGS

1 (2½- to 3-pound) broiler-fryer
2 quarts water
2 teaspoons salt
½ teaspoon pepper
2 cups all-purpose flour
½ teaspoon baking soda
½ teaspoon salt
3 tablespoons shortening
¾ cup buttermilk

Place chicken in a Dutch oven; add water and 2 teaspoons salt. Bring to a boil; cover, reduce heat, and simmer 1 hour or until tender. Remove chicken from broth and cool. Bone chicken, and cut meat into bite-size pieces; set aside. Bring broth to a boil; add pepper.

Combine flour, soda, and ½ teaspoon salt; cut in shortening until mixture resembles coarse meal. Add buttermilk, stirring with a fork until dry ingredients are moistened. Turn dough out onto a well-floured surface, and knead lightly 4 or 5 times.

Pat dough to ½-inch thickness. Pinch off dough in 1½-inch pieces, and drop into boiling broth. Reduce heat to medium-low, and cook about 8 to 10 minutes or until desired consistency, stirring occasionally. Stir in chicken. Yield: 4 to 6 servings. *Mrs. Morton Smith, Homewood, Alabama.*

Make Your Own Vanilla Extract

With the following recipes you can mix up your own home brew—of vanilla extract, that is. Just pour vodka or brandy over broken vanilla beans, and let the mixture sit for 6 to 12 weeks. As the flavor is extracted from the beans, the alcohol turns a deep amber color.

The same vanilla beans may be used in several batches of Home-Brewed Vanilla Extract. Just pour more vodka over the beans as the supply of extract gets low. When the vodka will no longer turn dark, then it's time to buy new beans. (Vanilla beans are available on the spice racks at grocery stores.)

HOME-BREWED VANILLA EXTRACT

2 cups vodka
5 vanilla beans, cut into 1-inch pieces

Combine vodka and vanilla beans in a jar with a tight-fitting lid. Cover the jar and let it stand 6 to 8 weeks. (The vodka mixture will turn amber colored after a day or two.)

After half the vanilla extract is used, add more vodka to cover the beans. The flavor in the beans is gone when the vodka no longer turns to a dark color. Yield: 2 cups. *Helen Moore, Matthews, North Carolina.*

HOMEMADE VANILLA EXTRACT

1 cup brandy
2 vanilla beans, cut into 1-inch pieces

Combine brandy and vanilla beans in a jar with a tight-fitting lid. Cover and let stand 3 months, shaking 3 times a week. Yield: 1 cup. *Peggy Grissom, Creedmoor, North Carolina.*

From Our Kitchen To Yours

Welcome autumn into your kitchen with the tantalizing aroma of roasted pecans and peanuts. Cooking with these treats not only makes for delicious eating, but fills your kitchen with warm, harvest-time smells. While testing pecan and peanut recipes we captured the flavor and crunch of these two distinctive Southern nuts in our kitchens. This brought to mind some recent questions readers had asked us about pecans and peanuts. We'll try to answer a few.

How do you boil peanuts?—We did some research and found that you should use peanuts while they're still green, preferably about 2 to 3 weeks before maturity. The peanuts should then be cooked immediately. Wash the peanuts in the shell, and put into a saucepan. Add enough salted water to cover. (For a quart of peanuts, try ¼ cup salt). Cover and bring to a boil. Reduce heat and simmer for 1½ to 2 hours. Add water to keep peanuts covered. Shell a few peanuts at the end of the cooking time and taste. More salt may be needed. Drain the peanuts, shell, and enjoy.

Boiled peanuts in the shell can be frozen in freezer-safe storage bags or containers for up to a year.

What's the best way to roast peanuts and pecans?—The best way we know to roast or parch peanuts in the shell is to spread the nuts in a large, shallow pan, one or two layers deep, and roast at 300° for 45 minutes to an hour. Shell a few after 45 minutes, and test for doneness. The skins should slip off easily, and the nuts should be beige colored.

For shelled peanuts, roast at 300° for 30 to 45 minutes. If you prefer a darker nut, you may want to cook a bit longer. But remember, the nuts continue to darken and crisp after removing from the oven. Salt after roasting, if desired.

Roasted or toasted pecans are an old-time Southern favorite, too. Spread a layer of pecan halves or pieces in a large shallow pan. Pour a bit of melted butter over pecans, and stir well. Bake at 300° for 30 to 45 minutes or until desired degree of doneness, stirring every 15 minutes. Salt to taste.

Why is my peanut brittle not brittle?—The usual cause of this problem is not cooking the candy mixture to the proper temperature. Our test kitchens staff has found that a candy thermometer is essential when making candy, especially with a mixture that has to be cooked to as high a temperature as peanut brittle. A few degrees above or below the designated temperature can make a tremendous difference. If a candy, such as a praline mixture, is cooked to a temperature that's too high, the result may be an extremely hard, rock-like candy. Peanut brittle should be cooked to the hard crack stage (300°). If it's undercooked, the candy will be limp, sticky, and chewy. For successful candymaking, use a thermometer with every batch.

How can I remove the red skins from raw peanuts?—If a recipe calls for skinless or blanched peanuts, but all you have on hand are those with skins, an easy way to remove skins is to spread the shelled peanuts in a shallow pan and bake at 300° for 15 minutes; then, using potholders, carefully shake the pan. As the peanuts bump each other, the loosened skins will rub off. Or after baking, using a cook's mitt, lightly rub the peanuts. This will help remove the skins.

Is it necessary to thaw pecans or peanuts before chopping?—It isn't necessary, but it makes the job easier if the nuts are thawed. To chop the nuts, you can put them in the food processor and chop using the steel blade. However, don't overprocess. Nuts will be ground, not chopped, in mere seconds. Often, we'll use a chef's knife to chop the nuts, especially if using them for a garnish. If you chop the nuts more finely than you'd like, put the nuts in a sieve and gently shake off the ground particles.

Why do we have so many pecans in our freezer?—Visiting tour groups always comment on the amount of pecans we keep. We buy about 100 pounds of shelled pecans every fall and keep them in the freezer until needed for recipe testing during the year.

Coffee Flavors This Cake

When Doris Curls invites friends over to visit, she often serves Coffee Sponge Cake. "It's not too sweet," she says, "and you can serve it year-round." Topped with a luscious Kahlúa and whipped cream frosting, the cake has a delicate coffee flavor.

COFFEE SPONGE CAKE

5 eggs, separated
1 cup sugar
½ teaspoon instant coffee granules
3 tablespoons boiling water
1 teaspoon vanilla extract
1 cup all-purpose flour
1 teaspoon baking powder
Whipped Cream Frosting
About ¼ cup chopped almonds, toasted

Combine egg yolks and sugar in a large bowl; beat at high speed of an electric mixer 3 to 5 minutes or until thick and lemon colored. Combine coffee granules and boiling water, stirring until granules are dissolved. Add coffee and vanilla to egg mixture, beating well.

Combine flour and baking powder; fold into egg mixture.

Beat egg whites (at room temperature) in a large mixing bowl until stiff

peaks form; gently fold into cake batter. Pour batter into an ungreased 10-inch tube pan. Bake at 350° for 30 to 35 minutes or until cake springs back when lightly touched. Remove from oven; invert pan, and cool completely (about 40 minutes) before removing from pan.

Split cake horizontally into 3 layers. Spread Whipped Cream Frosting between layers and on top and sides of cake. Sprinkle with toasted almonds. Chill well before serving. Yield: one 10-inch cake.

Whipped Cream Frosting:

2 tablespoons Kahlúa or other
   coffee-flavored liqueur
1 teaspoon instant coffee granules
1 teaspoon water
2 cups whipping cream
2 tablespoons powdered sugar

Combine Kahlúa, coffee granules, and water, stirring until smooth.

Beat whipping cream until foamy; add sugar and coffee mixture, beating until soft peaks form. Yield: 4 cups.
Doris Curls,
Anniston, Alabama.

Hearty, Satisfying Soups

Nothing is better than a big bowl of hearty soup for warding off chills and satisfying the appetite. Simmered to perfection, these soups fill the house with enticing aromas and, along with bread and salad, make a complete meal.

SPICY SAUSAGE-BEAN SOUP

1 pound bulk pork sausage
2 (16-ounce) cans kidney beans, undrained
1 (28-ounce) can tomatoes, undrained and
   coarsely chopped
1 quart water
1 large onion, chopped
1 bay leaf
1½ teaspoons seasoned salt
½ teaspoon garlic salt
½ teaspoon dried whole thyme
½ teaspoon pepper
1 green pepper, chopped
1 cup peeled, diced potatoes

Brown sausage in a large Dutch oven, stirring to crumble meat. Drain off pan drippings. Stir in next 9 ingredients. Cover and simmer 1 hour, stirring occasionally. Add green pepper and potatoes; cover and simmer 20 minutes. Remove bay leaf before serving. Yield: 11 cups.
Mrs. Frank Patton,
Johnson City, Tennessee.

OYSTER CHOWDER

1 pint oysters, undrained
½ cup chopped onion
½ cup chopped celery
⅓ cup butter or margarine
4 cups milk
1 (8¾-ounce) can whole kernel corn,
   undrained
1 cup peeled, diced, cooked potatoes
½ teaspoon salt
½ teaspoon white pepper
Paprika

Drain oysters, reserving liquid.

Sauté onion and celery in butter in a Dutch oven until tender. Add milk, oyster liquid, corn, potatoes, salt, and pepper. Cook over low heat, stirring constantly, until thoroughly heated (do not boil).

Add oysters; simmer 5 to 8 minutes or until edges of oysters curl. Sprinkle lightly with paprika. Yield: 8 cups.
Ruth E. Hormanski,
Satellite Beach, Florida.

WHITE BEAN SOUP

2 pounds dried Great Northern beans
2½ cups diced cooked ham
2 cups diced celery with leaves
1½ cups sliced carrots
¾ cup chopped green onion with tops
1 pod hot pepper
1 cup peeled, chopped tomatoes
2 teaspoons salt
¾ teaspoon pepper

Sort and wash beans; place in a large Dutch oven. Cover with water 2 inches above beans; let soak overnight. Drain. Add 4 quarts water; bring to a boil. Reduce heat to medium; cook, uncovered, 1½ hours, stirring occasionally.

Add ham, celery, carrots, onion, and hot pepper. Cook, uncovered, 1¼ hours, stirring occasionally.

Add tomatoes, salt, and pepper; cook an additional 15 minutes. Yield: about 5½ quarts.
Rachel Youree,
Murfreesboro, Tennessee.

CREAMY VEGETABLE CHEESE SOUP

1 cup chopped onion
2 tablespoons butter or margarine
2 cups coarsely chopped cabbage
1 (10-ounce) package frozen baby lima beans
1 cup sliced carrots
1 cup peeled, diced potatoes
1 tablespoon chicken-flavored bouillon granules
2 cups water
¼ cup butter or margarine
¼ cup all-purpose flour
3 cups milk
1½ cups (6 ounces) shredded sharp Cheddar cheese
¼ teaspoon paprika
¼ teaspoon pepper

Sauté onion in 2 tablespoons butter; add next 6 ingredients, and bring to a boil. Cover, reduce heat, and simmer 20 minutes or until vegetables are tender. Set aside.

Melt ¼ cup butter in a heavy saucepan over low heat; add flour and cook 1 minute, stirring constantly. Gradually add milk; cook over medium heat, stirring constantly, until thickened and bubbly. Stir in cheese, paprika, and pepper. Stir over low heat until cheese melts. Stir cheese sauce into vegetable mixture. Serve immediately. Yield: about 8 cups. *Helen J. Wright, Leesville, South Carolina.*

When the ball game's over, treat your friends to a delicious supper of Cheese 'n' Beef Ball, Tomato Juice Cocktail, Ambrosia Salad, Muffaletta-Style Po-Boys, and Chocolate Chip Coffee Cake.

Muffalettas Make Supper Easy

Don't let the fun end once the football game is over—invite some friends over for a casual supper of Muffaletta-Style Po-Boys.

Begin by serving Tomato Juice Cocktail and a Cheese 'n' Beef Ball with assorted crackers. Assemble the po-boys, stir bananas into the salad, and your supper is ready. Even dessert, a Chocolate Chip Coffee Cake, can be baked ahead of time.

Tomato Juice Cocktail
Cheese 'n' Beef Ball
Assorted Crackers
Muffaletta-Style Po-Boys
Ambrosia Salad
Chocolate Chip Coffee Cake

TOMATO JUICE COCKTAIL

1 (46-ounce) can tomato juice
2 tablespoons Worcestershire sauce
2 teaspoons chili powder
1 teaspoon dried parsley flakes
½ teaspoon celery seeds
¼ teaspoon garlic salt

Combine all ingredients; cover and chill at least 4 hours. To serve, pour mixture into a Dutch oven, and place over low heat until thoroughly heated. Yield: 1½ quarts. *Rachel Youree, Murfreesboro, Tennessee.*

CHEESE 'N' BEEF BALL

1 (8-ounce) package cream cheese, softened
1 (2½-ounce) package dried beef, finely chopped
¼ cup grated Parmesan cheese
¼ cup chopped pimiento-stuffed olives
2 teaspoons prepared horseradish
¾ cup chopped pecans

Combine all ingredients except pecans. Shape into a ball and coat with pecans. Chill well. Serve with crackers. Yield: 1 cheese ball. *Mrs. Charles DeHaven, Owensboro, Kentucky.*

MUFFALETTA-STYLE PO-BOYS

2 (10-ounce) packages French rolls
¼ cup mayonnaise
1 tablespoon plus 1 teaspoon salad olive juice
4 (1-ounce) slices fully cooked ham
¼ cup plus 2 tablespoons chopped salad olives
4 (1-ounce) slices salami
2 tablespoons chopped ripe olives
8 (1-ounce) slices Mozzarella cheese

Split French rolls; place cut-side up on baking sheet. Combine mayonnaise and olive juice; spread on each roll half. Place one slice ham on bottom half of each roll; top with 1½ tablespoons salad olives. Place one slice salami on top of olives; top with ½ tablespoon ripe olives. Place 2 slices Mozzarella cheese on each remaining roll half.

Set all roll halves under broiler until cheese is melted and bubbly. Place cheese halves on top of meat halves, and slice to serve. Yield: 4 to 8 servings. *Sarah M. Pulling, Pineville, Louisiana.*

AMBROSIA SALAD

1½ cups chopped orange sections
1 cup seedless grapes
1 cup chopped dates
¼ cup lemon juice
4 bananas, sliced
Lettuce leaves
½ cup flaked coconut
Red Fruit Salad Dressing (optional)

Combine first 4 ingredients, tossing lightly; chill. Just before serving, stir in bananas; spoon into a lettuce-lined bowl, and sprinkle with coconut. Serve with Red Fruit Salad Dressing, if desired. Yield: 6 to 8 servings.

Red Fruit Salad Dressing:

½ cup mayonnaise
½ cup jellied cranberry sauce
½ cup whipping cream, whipped

Combine mayonnaise and cranberry sauce; fold in whipped cream. Chill. Yield: about 1¾ cups.
Kay Castleman Cooper, Burke, Virginia.

CHOCOLATE CHIP COFFEE CAKE

1 cup butter or margarine, softened
1 cup sugar
3 eggs
3 cups all-purpose flour
1 tablespoon baking powder
1 teaspoon baking soda
½ teaspoon salt
1 (8-ounce) carton commercial sour cream
1 (12-ounce) package semisweet chocolate morsels
½ cup firmly packed brown sugar
1 teaspoon ground cinnamon

Cream butter; then gradually add the sugar, beating until light and fluffy. Add eggs, one at a time, beating well after each addition.

Combine flour, baking powder, soda, and salt; add to creamed mixture alternately with sour cream, beginning and ending with flour mixture. Spoon half of batter into a greased and floured 13- x 9- x 2-inch baking pan.

Combine chocolate morsels, brown sugar, and cinnamon; sprinkle 1½ cups of chocolate morsel mixture over batter. Top with remaining batter. Sprinkle with the remaining chocolate morsel mixture. Bake at 350° for 35 to 40 minutes. Serve warm or at room temperature. Yield: 15 to 18 servings.
Ann Elsie Schmetzer, Madisonville, Kentucky.

COOKING LIGHT

Try A Meal-In-One, Without Salt

Including one-dish meals in your menus really helps when you are on a tight schedule. But if you're trying to cut back on salt, selecting meal-in-one recipes can be difficult. You need to avoid high-sodium canned and frozen foods and use low-sodium herbs and spices instead of salty seasonings.

Learn to read food labels on canned and frozen vegetables so you'll know if salt has been added. Fresh vegetables are naturally salt free, and plain frozen vegetables are packaged without salt. Fortunately, food companies are expanding their market of low-sodium canned vegetables.

If you're on a low-sodium diet, you should give up regular canned broth and instant bouillon granules and cubes. Low-sodium bouillon granules and cubes are also available. The difference is important—regular bouillon has 50 times as much sodium.

BEEF GOULASH

Vegetable cooking spray
3 cups chopped onion
1½ pounds boneless round steak, trimmed and cut into ½-inch cubes
1 (6-ounce) can low-sodium tomato paste
1 tablespoon paprika
1½ pounds potatoes, peeled and cut into ½-inch cubes
1 quart water
1 tablespoon plus 1 teaspoon low-sodium beef-flavored bouillon granules
2 cloves garlic, minced
1 teaspoon ground marjoram
½ teaspoon caraway seeds
¼ teaspoon pepper

Coat a 4-quart saucepan or Dutch oven with cooking spray; place over medium heat until hot. Add onion; sauté about 10 minutes or until golden brown. Add beef, tomato paste, and paprika; cook 5 minutes, stirring constantly.

Stir in remaining ingredients. Bring to a boil; cover, reduce heat, and simmer for 1½ hours or until thickened, stirring occasionally. Yield: 8 servings (about 88 milligrams sodium per serving).

SPICY BEEF AND RICE

2 pounds lean ground beef
2 medium onions, chopped
1 clove garlic, minced
2 cooking apples, peeled, cored, and chopped
3 small jalapeño peppers, seeded and sliced into thin strips
½ cup raisins
⅛ teaspoon ground cinnamon
⅛ teaspoon ground cloves
⅛ teaspoon pepper
4 cups hot cooked rice (no salt added)

Brown ground beef, onion, and garlic in a Dutch oven. Add next 6 ingredients; cover, reduce heat, and simmer 20 minutes. Serve over hot cooked rice. Yield: 8 servings (about 94 milligrams sodium per serving).

CURRIED RICE AND SHRIMP

6 cups water
2 pounds unpeeled fresh shrimp
1 large onion, minced
2 tablespoons unsalted margarine
1 cup uncooked regular rice
1 teaspoon curry powder
¼ teaspoon freshly ground pepper
2 cups low-sodium chicken broth
2 tomatoes, peeled and chopped
1 cup minced celery

Bring water to a boil; add shrimp, and return to a boil. Reduce heat and simmer 3 to 5 minutes. Drain well. Rinse with cold water. Let cool to touch. Peel and devein shrimp.

Sauté onion in margarine in a Dutch oven until tender. Stir in remaining ingredients except shrimp; bring to a boil. Cover, reduce heat, and simmer 20 minutes. Stir in shrimp; cook 1 minute or until thoroughly heated, stirring occasionally. Yield: 6 servings (about 143 milligrams sodium per serving).
Susan Kamer-Shinaberry, Charleston, West Virginia.

LINGUINE WITH SEAFOOD SAUCE

Vegetable cooking spray
1 teaspoon olive oil
1 medium onion, chopped
1 clove garlic, minced
½ green pepper, chopped
⅓ cup chopped fresh parsley
2 (14½-ounce) cans low-sodium tomatoes, undrained
2 (8-ounce) cans low-sodium tomato sauce
1 teaspoon lemon juice
1 teaspoon dried whole basil
1 teaspoon dried whole oregano
¼ teaspoon garlic powder
¼ teaspoon pepper
1 dozen fresh clams in shells
1 pound unpeeled medium-size fresh shrimp
6 ounces uncooked linguine or spaghetti

Coat a large skillet with cooking spray; add oil and place over medium heat until hot. Add next 4 ingredients, and sauté until tender.

Drain tomatoes, reserving ½ cup liquid; chop tomatoes. Add tomatoes, ½ cup reserved liquid, tomato sauce, lemon juice, and seasonings to sautéed vegetables; simmer, uncovered, about 20 minutes or until thickened.

Scrub clams with a brush under running water; set aside. Peel and devein shrimp; add clams and shrimp to sauce. Cover and simmer about 20 minutes or until clams open.

Cook linguine according to package directions, omitting salt; drain. Place on a warm platter, and top with sauce. Yield: 8 servings (about 169 milligrams sodium per serving).

HEALTHFUL CHICKEN DINNER

2 tablespoons vegetable oil
1 (3-pound) broiler-fryer, cut up and skinned
1½ cups unsweetened apple juice
1 pound sweet potatoes, peeled and cut into 1-inch slices
1 (10-ounce) package frozen whole kernel corn
⅓ cup minced celery leaves
1 bay leaf, crushed
1 green pepper, cut into strips
2 teaspoons cornstarch
2 tablespoons water

Heat oil in a Dutch oven; add chicken, and cook until browned on all sides. Drain on paper towels; then wipe the pan drippings from the Dutch oven with paper towels.

Return chicken to Dutch oven, and add apple juice; cover and cook over medium heat 15 minutes. Add sweet potatoes, corn, celery leaves, and bay leaf; cover and cook an additional 15 minutes. Add green pepper, and cook until peppers are crisp-tender. Using a slotted spoon, remove chicken and vegetables to a warm serving platter.

Combine cornstarch and water, stirring well. Add to remaining liquid in Dutch oven; cook, stirring constantly, until thickened. Pour over chicken. Yield: 6 servings (about 83 milligrams sodium per serving).

Cynthia Kannenberg,
Brown Deer, Wisconsin.

MICROWAVE COOKERY

Layer Cakes From The Microwave

These microwave cake recipes bake into moist and pretty layers in about 8 minutes per layer, and you won't even preheat the oven or heat up the kitchen. For your next layer cake, why not try one of these recipes?

Cakes baked in a microwave oven boast the same tender crumb as those baked in a conventional oven, but there are a few differences in the end product. Cake will not brown in a microwave oven, but our frosting recipes cover the crust and make the cake look like a conventionally baked one. Ingredients in these recipes, such as spices, chocolate, and peanut butter, add color.

Microwave ovens won't accommodate regular metal cakepans, so you'll need to invest in a set made especially for the microwave. Most are made of durable, inexpensive plastic. They have higher sides than regular cakepans, since layers rise slightly higher in a microwave oven than in conventional ones.

The wattage of microwave ovens will vary, so the cooking time will vary also. A time range is given in our recipes to allow for the difference. Cakes bake in such a short period of time that they are easy to overbake. To prevent this, always check for doneness at the lower end of the range.

Cakes continue baking after removal from the microwave oven. So take them from the oven when the cake feels firm and springy but still has a slightly moist area on top. This area will dry and set as the cake cools. Do not overbake the layers, as they will be tough and dry.

Here are some other pointers.

—Grease only the bottom of microwave cakepans; line the bottom with waxed paper, and grease the paper. Don't grease the sides of the pan.

—Cakes tend to rise higher in the microwave oven, so you shouldn't fill the pans more than half full. Cut through the batter in the pan with a knife to remove excess air bubbles.

—Bake microwave cake layers one at a time on an inverted saucer. The saucer allows microwave energy to circulate around the cake, thus baking it more evenly. Rotate the cakepan during baking as the recipe directs.

—Immediately after removing the cakepan from the microwave oven, place it on a sheet of aluminum foil and let stand 10 minutes. Foil will hold heat in as the cake completes cooking. Then remove the layer from the pan, and transfer it to a wire rack to cool.

—Cakes baked in the microwave oven sometimes dry out faster than those baked conventionally. Frost and cover them immediately after cooling.

—The directions and baking times given for these recipes were verified in our test kitchens. When adapting your own recipes for the microwave oven, remember that baking times and other factors vary with each recipe, so you may need to make slight adjustments.

OLD-FASHIONED CARROT CAKE

2 cups all-purpose flour
2 cups sugar
1 teaspoon baking powder
¼ teaspoon baking soda
¼ teaspoon salt
1 teaspoon ground cinnamon
4 eggs
1 cup vegetable oil
2 cups grated carrots
Cream Cheese Frosting

Combine first 6 ingredients; stir gently and set aside. Combine eggs and oil, beating well. Gradually stir dry ingredients into egg mixture, beating just until moistened. Stir in carrots.

Grease bottom (not sides) of two 9-inch microwave-safe cakepans, and line with waxed paper; grease waxed paper. Spoon batter into pans. Cut through batter with a knife to remove the air bubbles.

Place 1 pan in microwave oven on an inverted saucer. Microwave at MEDIUM (50% power) for 5 to 6 minutes, giving pan a half-turn at 2-minute intervals and at end of cooking time. Microwave at HIGH for 2 to 3 minutes or until top is almost dry. Remove from oven and place on a sheet of aluminum foil. Cool in pan 10 minutes; remove from pan, and cool on a wire rack. Repeat with remaining layer.

Spread Cream Cheese Frosting between layers and on top and sides of cake. Yield: one 2-layer cake.

Cream Cheese Frosting:

½ cup butter or margarine
1 (8-ounce) package cream cheese
1 (16-ounce) package powdered sugar, sifted
2 teaspoons vanilla extract
1 cup chopped pecans

Place butter and cream cheese in a 2-quart glass bowl. Microwave at LOW (10% power) for 4 to 5 minutes or until softened. Cream butter and cream cheese until light and fluffy; add sugar and vanilla, mixing well. Stir in pecans. Yield: enough for one 2-layer cake.

GERMAN CHOCOLATE CAKE

1 (4-ounce) package sweet baking chocolate
½ cup water
1 teaspoon vanilla extract
1 cup butter or margarine, softened
2 cups sugar
4 eggs, separated
3 cups sifted cake flour
1 teaspoon baking soda
¼ teaspoon salt
1 cup buttermilk
Coconut-Pecan Frosting

Break chocolate into pieces; combine chocolate and water in a 2-cup glass measure. Microwave at HIGH for 2 to 2½ minutes or until chocolate melts, stirring at 1-minute intervals. Cool; stir in vanilla and set aside.

Cream butter; gradually add sugar, beating until fluffy. Add egg yolks, one at a time, beating well after each. Add chocolate mixture; beat until blended.

Combine flour, soda, and salt; add to creamed mixture alternately with buttermilk, beginning and ending with flour mixture. Beat the egg whites (at room temperature) until stiff peaks form; fold into batter.

Grease bottom (not sides) of three 9-inch microwave-safe cakepans, and line with waxed paper; grease waxed paper. Spoon batter into pans. Cut through batter with a knife to remove air bubbles.

Place 1 pan in microwave oven on an inverted saucer. Microwave at MEDIUM (50% power) for 5 to 6 minutes, giving pan a half-turn at 2-minute intervals and at end of cooking time. Microwave at HIGH for 2 to 3 minutes or until top is almost dry. Remove from oven and place on a sheet of aluminum foil. Cool in pan 10 minutes; remove from pan, and cool on a wire rack. Repeat with remaining layers.

Spread Coconut-Pecan Frosting between layers and on top and sides of cake. Yield: one 3-layer cake.

Coconut-Pecan Frosting:

⅔ cup butter or margarine
1¼ cups evaporated milk
1⅓ cups sugar
4 egg yolks
1½ teaspoons vanilla extract
1⅓ cups flaked coconut
1⅓ cups chopped pecans

Place butter in a 4-cup glass measure. Microwave at HIGH 1 to 1½ minutes or until melted. Add milk, sugar, and egg yolks; beat well. Microwave at MEDIUM (50% power) for 9 to 10 minutes or until slightly thickened, stirring at 2-minute intervals. Add vanilla, coconut, and pecans; mix well. Cool. Stir until frosting is of spreading consistency. Yield: enough for one 3-layer cake.

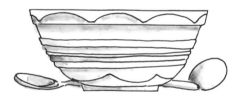

PEANUT BUTTER CAKE

½ cup plus 1 tablespoon butter or margarine, softened
¼ cup plus 2 tablespoons creamy peanut butter
1½ cups firmly packed brown sugar
¾ teaspoon vanilla extract
3 eggs
1½ cups all-purpose flour
2¼ teaspoons baking powder
¼ teaspoon salt
¾ cup milk
Chocolate Frosting
¼ cup chopped peanuts

Cream butter and peanut butter; gradually add sugar, beating until light and fluffy. Stir in vanilla. Add the eggs, one at a time, beating well after each.

Combine flour, baking powder, and salt; add to creamed mixture alternately with milk, beginning and ending with flour mixture.

Grease bottom (not sides) of two 9-inch microwave-safe cakepans, and line with waxed paper; grease waxed paper. Spoon batter into pans. Cut through batter with a knife to remove the air bubbles.

Place 1 pan in microwave oven on an inverted saucer. Microwave at MEDIUM (50% power) for 5 to 6 minutes, giving pan a half-turn at 2-minute intervals and at end of cooking time. Microwave at HIGH for 2 to 3 minutes or until top is almost dry. Remove from oven and place on a sheet of aluminum foil. Cool in pan 10 minutes; remove from pan, and cool on a wire rack. Repeat with remaining layer.

Spread Chocolate Frosting between layers and on top and sides of cake. Sprinkle peanuts over top. Yield: one 2-layer cake.

Chocolate Frosting:

2 (1-ounce) squares unsweetened chocolate
¼ cup butter or margarine
⅓ cup milk
4¾ cups sifted powdered sugar
1 teaspoon vanilla extract

Combine chocolate, butter, and milk in a large microwave-safe mixing bowl; microwave at MEDIUM (50% power) for 3½ minutes or until mixture is softened and blended, stirring after 3 minutes. Stir in remaining ingredients; let stand 10 minutes. Beat with a wooden spoon until spreading consistency. Yield: enough for one 2-layer cake.

Try These Recipes For Fall Fruit

Pears and apples are ripe and juicy in the fall, and ready for enjoying in a fresh fruit salad, dessert, or side dish.

TURKEY FRUIT SALAD

4 cups chopped cooked turkey
1 cup pineapple tidbits, drained
1 cup seedless green grapes, halved
1 cup chopped red apple
1 cup chopped walnuts
1½ cups mayonnaise

Combine all ingredients; mix well. Cover and chill for 2 to 3 hours. Yield: 8 servings. *Mrs. Randall L. Wilson, Louisville, Kentucky.*

SKILLET SPICED APPLES

1 tablespoon vegetable oil
½ teaspoon ground cloves
4 medium cooking apples, peeled, cored, and sliced into wedges
2 tablespoons orange marmalade

Combine vegetable oil and cloves in a medium bowl; add apples, stirring well to coat slices. Fry apples, covered, in a large skillet over medium heat 10 minutes, stirring occasionally. Remove cover; stir in marmalade and continue cooking, uncovered, 3 to 5 minutes. Yield: 4 servings. *Shirley W. Hodge, Delray Beach, Florida.*

HONEY-BAKED APPLES

6 large baking apples
3 tablespoons chopped walnuts
3 tablespoons raisins
1 cup water
⅓ cup honey
1 (3-inch) stick cinnamon
1 tablespoon lemon juice

Core apples; peel top third of each. Place apples in a shallow baking dish. Combine walnuts and raisins; stuff cavities of apples with nut mixture.
Combine water, honey, and cinnamon in a small saucepan; bring to a boil. Reduce heat and simmer 5 minutes. Remove from heat and stir in lemon juice. Remove cinnamon stick; pour liquid over apples. Cover and bake at 350° for 45 to 50 minutes or until apples are tender, basting occasionally. Yield: 6 servings. *Deborah Smith, Salem, Missouri.*

CRUNCHY PEAR SALAD

3 ripe pears, peeled, halved, and cored
2 teaspoons lemon juice
1 (3-ounce) package cream cheese, softened
3 tablespoons milk
¼ teaspoon dried whole tarragon
½ cup sliced celery
½ cup chopped dates
Lettuce leaves
¼ cup chopped walnuts or pecans

Sprinkle pear halves with lemon juice. Combine cream cheese, milk, and tarragon; beat until smooth. Stir in celery and dates. Spoon one-sixth of cheese mixture on each pear half. Arrange the pear halves on a lettuce-lined platter; sprinkle with walnuts. Cover and chill 1 to 2 hours. Yield: 6 servings. *Susan Buckmaster, Charlotte, North Carolina.*

PEAR STREUSEL PIE

½ cup all-purpose flour
¾ cup firmly packed brown sugar
¾ cup flaked coconut
⅓ cup butter, melted
4 large pears, peeled and cubed
1 unbaked 9-inch pastry shell

Combine flour, brown sugar, and coconut; gradually add butter, stirring with a fork. Set aside.
Place 1 cup pears in pastry shell; top with half of coconut mixture. Repeat layers with remaining pears and coconut mixture. Cover pie with aluminum foil, and bake at 450° for 10 minutes. Remove foil; reduce oven to 350°, and bake 30 minutes or until pears are tender. Yield: one 9-inch pie. *Mrs. Clayton J. Turner, De Funiak Springs, Florida.*

Brighten Meals With Beets

Have you ever considered stuffing a beet with potato salad? After cooking the beets whole, peel and prepare them for stuffing by scooping out the centers. Just before serving, fill each beet with potato salad.

PICKLED BEET SALAD

1 (16-ounce) jar whole pickled beets, undrained
1 (3-ounce) package lemon-flavored gelatin
1 cup boiling water
1 teaspoon vinegar
1 cup chopped celery
1 teaspoon prepared horseradish
1½ teaspoons minced onion, divided
3 hard-cooked eggs, sieved
3 tablespoons mayonnaise

Drain beets, reserving ½ cup liquid. Chop beets to measure 1 cup; set aside. Reserve remaining beets for other uses.
Dissolve gelatin in boiling water; stir in reserved beet liquid and vinegar. Chill until consistency of unbeaten egg white. Stir in 1 cup chopped beets, celery, horseradish, and ½ teaspoon onion; pour into a 10- x 6- x 2-inch dish. Chill until firm.
Combine eggs, mayonnaise, and remaining 1 teaspoon onion; spread over salad. Chill. Yield: 8 servings. *Peggy Head, Ennis, Texas.*

STRAWBERRY-GLAZED BEETS

1 tablespoon cornstarch
¼ teaspoon salt
⅛ to ¼ teaspoon pumpkin pie spice
⅓ cup water
2 tablespoons lemon juice
1 (16-ounce) can sliced beets, drained
¼ cup strawberry jam
2 tablespoons butter or margarine

Combine cornstarch, salt, and pumpkin pie spice in a saucepan, stirring well. Gradually stir in water and lemon juice. Cook over medium heat, stirring constantly, until thickened. Stir in beets, jam, and butter; cook until thoroughly heated. Yield: 3 to 4 servings. *Mrs. J. G. Davis, Lilburn, Georgia.*

POTATO-STUFFED BEETS

2 tablespoons vinegar
2 tablespoons mayonnaise
¼ teaspoon salt
⅛ teaspoon pepper
½ cup peeled, diced, cooked potatoes
½ cup chopped celery
1 small green pepper, chopped
1 hard-cooked egg, chopped
6 medium beets
Lettuce leaves

Combine first 4 ingredients in a large bowl; stir in potatoes, celery, green pepper, and egg. Chill.
Leave root and 1 inch of stem on beets; scrub with a brush. Place beets in a large saucepan, and add water to cover; bring to a boil. Cover, reduce heat, and simmer 35 to 40 minutes or until tender; drain and let cool. Trim off beet stems and roots, and rub off skins. Cut a slice from top of each beet. Gently scoop out pulp, leaving ½-inch shells; reserve the pulp for other uses.
Spoon potato mixture into beet shells. Place on lettuce leaves, and serve immediately. Yield: 6 servings. *Dorothy Lewis, Bealeton, Virginia.*

Right: *For simple entertaining try our easy-to-prepare menu of Quick Pizza Casserole (page 266), Sweet-and-Sour Marinated Vegetables (page 266), Toasted Onion-Herb Bread (page 266), and Honey Bee Ambrosia (page 267).*

Page 238: *Slices of fried eggplant are tucked between layers of cheese and a tomato-flavored meat sauce for Eggplant Parmesan (page 186).*

Above: *Nuts add flavor and crunch to Super Peanutty Layer Cake (page 222), Maple-Pecan Pralines (page 222), Orange-Pecan Pie (page 222), and Golden Peanut Brittle (page 223).*

Left: *Simple double-crust pies become fancy with decorative top crusts. Left to right: Peach-Cranberry Pie (page 249), Scrumptious Cherry Pie (page 250), Apple-Pear Pie (page 249), Holiday Mincemeat Pie (page 250), and Dried Fruit Pie (page 249).*

Enjoy The Rich Flavor Of Sour Cream

Our recipes for cheese sauce, chocolate pound cake, pea salad, and lasagna may seem different, but they all rely on sour cream for a rich, creamy taste.

TURKEY LASAGNA

1 (8-ounce) package lasagna
1 (10¾-ounce) can cream of chicken soup, undiluted
1 (10¾-ounce) can cream of mushroom soup, undiluted
1 cup grated Parmesan cheese
1 (8-ounce) carton commercial sour cream
1 cup finely chopped onion
1 cup sliced ripe olives
¼ cup chopped pimiento
½ teaspoon garlic salt
3 cups chopped, cooked turkey
2 cups (8 ounces) shredded Cheddar cheese

Cook lasagna according to package directions; drain.

Combine next 8 ingredients; mix well. Stir in turkey.

Spread about one-fourth of turkey mixture in a lightly greased 13- x 9- x 2-inch baking dish. Layer one-third of lasagna, one-fourth of turkey mixture, and one-third of cheese. Repeat layers twice, beginning with lasagna, and omitting last cheese layer. Cover and bake at 350° for 20 minutes; uncover and sprinkle with remaining cheese. Bake, uncovered, 10 minutes. Yield: 8 servings.   *Nancy Swinney,
Tallahassee, Florida.*

BAKED POTATOES WITH CHEESE SAUCE

4 large baking potatoes
Vegetable oil
1 cup (4 ounces) shredded sharp Cheddar cheese
½ cup commercial sour cream
¼ cup butter or margarine, softened
2 tablespoons chopped green onion

Wash potatoes, and rub with oil. Bake at 400° for 1 hour or until done.

Combine remaining ingredients, and mix well. Split tops of potatoes lengthwise, and fluff pulp with a fork. Spoon one-fourth of cheese mixture over each potato. Serve immediately. Yield: 4 servings.   *Mrs. Harold Wagner,
Hendersonville, North Carolina.*

SPECIAL PEA SALAD

¾ cup commercial sour cream
1 teaspoon seasoned salt
¼ teaspoon garlic powder
¼ teaspoon pepper
2 (10-ounce) packages frozen English peas, thawed
1 tomato, chopped
¼ cup minced green onion
Lettuce leaves
Tomato wedges
5 slices bacon, cooked and crumbled

Combine sour cream, salt, garlic powder, and pepper; stir well. Stir in peas, chopped tomato, and onion. Spoon mixture into a lettuce-lined bowl. Arrange tomato wedges on top, and sprinkle with bacon. Yield: 8 servings.
*Mary Ann Turk,
Joplin, Missouri.*

NACHO DIP

1 (8-ounce) package cream cheese, softened
1 (8-ounce) carton commercial sour cream
1 (10½-ounce) can jalapeño bean dip
1 (1.25-ounce) package chili seasoning mix
5 drops hot sauce
2 teaspoons chopped fresh parsley
¼ cup taco sauce
1¼ cups (5 ounces) shredded Cheddar cheese, divided
1¼ cups (5 ounces) shredded Monterey Jack cheese, divided

Combine cream cheese and sour cream; beat until smooth. Stir in bean dip, chili seasoning mix, hot sauce, parsley, taco sauce, ¾ cup Cheddar cheese, and ¾ cup Monterey Jack cheese. Spoon mixture into a lightly greased 12- x 8- x 2-inch baking dish; top with remaining ½ cup Cheddar cheese and ½ cup Monterey Jack cheese. Bake at 325° for 15 to 20 minutes. Serve hot with tortilla chips. Yield: about 3½ cups.   *Norma Bruce,
Riviera, Arizona.*

PARMESAN TWISTS

¼ cup butter or margarine, softened
1 cup grated Parmesan cheese
½ cup commercial sour cream
1 cup all-purpose flour
½ teaspoon Italian seasoning
1 egg yolk, slightly beaten
1 tablespoon water
Caraway seeds or poppy seeds

Cream butter; gradually add cheese and sour cream, mixing well.

Combine flour and Italian seasoning. Gradually add to creamed mixture, blending until smooth.

Turn dough out onto a lightly floured surface; divide in half. Roll out half of dough to a 12- x 7-inch rectangle, and cut into 6- x ½-inch strips. Twist each strip 2 or 3 times and place on a greased cookie sheet. Repeat procedure with the remaining dough.

Combine egg yolk and water. Brush strips with egg mixture; sprinkle with caraway seeds or poppy seeds. Bake at 350° for 10 to 12 minutes or until light brown. Yield: about 4½ dozen.
*Mrs. Harlan J. Stone,
Ocala, Florida.*

CHOCOLATE-SOUR CREAM POUND CAKE

1½ cups butter, softened
3 cups sugar
5 eggs
3 cups all-purpose flour
½ cup cocoa
1 teaspoon baking soda
¼ teaspoon salt
1 (8-ounce) carton commercial sour cream
1 cup boiling water
2 teaspoons vanilla extract

Cream butter; gradually add sugar, beating well. Add eggs, one at a time, beating well after each addition.

Combine flour, cocoa, soda, and salt; add to creamed mixture alternately with sour cream, beginning and ending with flour mixture. Mix well after each addition. Add boiling water, and mix well. Stir in vanilla.

Pour batter into a greased and floured 10-inch tube pan. Bake at 325° for 1 hour and 20 minutes or until cake tests done. Cool cake in pan 10 to 15 minutes; remove from pan, and cool completely. Yield: one 10-inch cake.
*Mrs. James R. Lineberger,
Gastonia, North Carolina.*

Toss Fall Vegetables In A Salad

These crisp, colorful salads feature cauliflower, broccoli, spinach, onion, and more. Our recipes offer a selection of tasty salads to prepare in advance and some that can be put together at the last minute.

MARINATED BROCCOLI SALAD

2 (1-pound) bunches fresh broccoli
⅓ cup olive oil
¼ cup tarragon vinegar
⅓ cup chopped fresh parsley
1 clove garlic, crushed
1 tablespoon dry mustard
1 teaspoon salt
¼ teaspoon pepper
2 hard-cooked eggs, sliced
10 cherry tomatoes, halved

Trim off large leaves of broccoli. Remove tough ends of lower stalks and wash broccoli thoroughly; cut flowerets and stems into bite-size pieces. Place in a shallow serving dish.

Combine olive oil, vinegar, parsley, garlic, mustard, salt, and pepper in a jar. Cover tightly and shake vigorously. Pour dressing over broccoli, tossing gently. Cover and chill at least 2 hours. Top salad with egg slices and cherry tomatoes before serving. Yield: 8 to 10 servings.
Mrs. B. J. Davis,
Lilburn, Georgia.

LAYERED CAULIFLOWER SALAD

1 medium head cauliflower
1 medium head iceberg lettuce, torn into bite-size pieces
1 large purple onion, chopped
½ pound bacon, cooked and crumbled
1 cup mayonnaise
3 tablespoons sugar
⅓ cup grated Parmesan cheese
Chopped lettuce
Chopped purple onion

Wash cauliflower; cut flowerets into bite-size pieces. Layer lettuce, onion, cauliflower, and bacon in a 3-quart bowl. Combine mayonnaise and sugar; mix well. Spread evenly over top, sealing to edge of bowl. Sprinkle with cheese. Top with chopped lettuce and onion. Cover salad tightly, and refrigerate 24 hours. Toss gently before serving. Yield: 8 to 10 servings.
Betty Atwell,
Vine Grove, Kentucky.

CAULIFLOWER-BRUSSELS SPROUTS SALAD

1 small cauliflower, broken into flowerets
½ pound fresh brussels sprouts
3 tablespoons vegetable oil
2 tablespoons commercial sour cream
1 tablespoon vinegar
¼ teaspoon salt
Freshly ground pepper to taste
Pinch of sugar

Cook cauliflower, covered, in a small amount of boiling salted water 4 minutes. Drain and rinse with cold water. Drain well and set aside.

Remove any discolored leaves from brussels sprouts. Cut off stem ends; wash sprouts thoroughly. Cook, covered, in a small amount of boiling salted water 5 to 8 minutes. Drain and rinse with cold water. Drain well.

Combine remaining ingredients in a jar. Cover and shake vigorously. Combine vegetables and dressing; toss gently. Cover and refrigerate several hours. Yield: 6 to 8 servings.
Jean Pashby,
Memphis, Tennessee.

MEXICAN-STYLE SALAD

1 large head iceberg lettuce, torn and chilled
1 small onion, chopped and chilled
2 small tomatoes, coarsely chopped and chilled
1 (15-ounce) can Ranch-style beans, drained and chilled
2½ cups (10 ounces) shredded Cheddar cheese
1½ cups commercial Catalina salad dressing, chilled
1 (16-ounce) bag corn chips, crushed

Combine all ingredients in a large salad bowl; toss gently. Serve immediately. Yield: 8 to 10 servings.
Mrs. Bronwen M. Gibson,
Dallas, Texas.

CARROT-AND-ZUCCHINI SALAD

4 large carrots, scraped and diagonally sliced
2 cups boiling water
4 medium zucchini, unpeeled and diagonally sliced
1 cup vegetable oil
⅓ cup white wine vinegar
½ teaspoon freshly ground pepper
½ teaspoon dried whole tarragon
½ teaspoon dried whole basil
½ teaspoon dried whole oregano
Leaf lettuce

Cook carrots for 4 minutes in water; add zucchini, and cook 2 to 3 minutes or until crisp-tender. Drain well; place vegetables in a shallow dish.

Combine remaining ingredients, except lettuce, mixing well; pour over hot vegetables, tossing lightly. Cover; chill several hours or overnight. Drain vegetables, and serve in a lettuce-lined bowl. Yield: 8 servings.
W. H. Pinkston,
Knoxville, Tennessee.

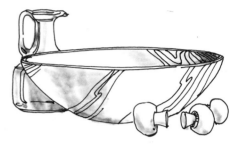

FRESH SPINACH SALAD

6 fresh mushrooms, sliced
1 teaspoon butter or margarine, melted
1 pound fresh spinach, torn into bite-size pieces
½ cup sliced green onion
¼ cup vegetable oil
2 tablespoons white wine vinegar
1 tablespoon lemon juice
½ teaspoon sugar (optional)
½ teaspoon salt
Dash of pepper
1 hard-cooked egg, chopped
2 slices bacon, cooked and crumbled

Sauté mushrooms in butter; set aside. Combine spinach and onion in a large bowl; toss well. Combine next 6 ingredients; mix well. Add dressing and mushrooms to spinach mixture; toss gently. Sprinkle with egg and bacon. Yield: 6 servings.
Jane Hancock,
Madison, Alabama.

Be Creative With These Cupcakes

If your children are eager to help out in the kitchen, get them involved in decorating our Easy Yellow Cupcakes. Let them choose between Creamy Orange Frosting and Chocolate-Almond Frosting. Or double the cupcake recipe and frost with both flavors. With only a small assortment of candies, they can decorate the cupcakes with balloons, faces, or our birthday design.

Be sure to frost the cupcakes just before decorating. If frosted too early, the frosting may harden and keep the candy from adhering properly.

EASY YELLOW CUPCAKES

⅓ cup butter or margarine, softened
3 tablespoons shortening
1 cup sugar
2 eggs
1¾ cups all-purpose flour
1 teaspoon baking soda
½ teaspoon salt
1 cup buttermilk
1 teaspoon vanilla extract
Creamy Orange Frosting or
    Chocolate-Almond Frosting
Assorted candies

Cream butter and shortening; gradually add sugar, beating until light and fluffy. Add eggs, one at a time, beating well after each addition. Combine flour, soda, and salt; add to creamed mixture alternately with buttermilk, beginning and ending with flour mixture. Mix well after each addition. Stir in vanilla.

Spoon batter into paper-lined muffin pans, filling two-thirds full. Bake at 350° for 20 to 25 minutes. Frost with Creamy Orange Frosting or Chocolate-Almond Frosting. Decorate cupcakes with candies. Yield: 1½ dozen.

Creamy Orange Frosting:

2 tablespoons butter or margarine,
    softened
1 (3-ounce) package cream cheese,
    softened
¼ teaspoon vanilla extract
½ teaspoon grated orange rind
1 teaspoon orange juice
1¾ cups sifted powdered sugar

Beat butter and cream cheese; add extract, orange rind, and orange juice. Add sugar; beat until light and fluffy. Yield: about 1 cup.

Chocolate-Almond Frosting:

½ cup semisweet chocolate morsels
¼ cup milk
¼ cup plus 2 tablespoons butter
¼ to ½ teaspoon almond extract
1¼ cups sifted powdered sugar

Combine chocolate morsels, milk, and butter in a saucepan; cook over medium heat, stirring until chocolate melts. Remove from heat; add extract and powdered sugar, mixing well.

Set saucepan in ice; beat until frosting holds its shape and loses its gloss. Add milk if needed to give frosting spreading consistency. Yield: 1 cup.

To make faces, begin with thin black licorice for hair. Use red cinnamon candy for eyes, candy corn for the nose, and red licorice for the mouth.

Children can flatten small, soft gumdrops with a rolling pin and make balloons. Strings are thin licorice.

Instead of a birthday cake, let children make their own birthday cupcakes. All it takes are birthday candles, candy corn, and candies with holes.

Add Bacon For Flavor

Judging from the hundreds of recipes that we receive each month, bacon isn't served just for breakfast. Our readers enjoy sprinkling it over salads, serving it in sandwiches, and jazzing up other foods with its distinctive flavor.

When your recipe calls for bacon, cook it until crisp, and drain it well on paper towels. This way, the calorie count is limited to about 50 per slice.

MARINATED ARTICHOKE SALAD

2 (6-ounce) jars marinated artichoke
    hearts, undrained
¼ pound fresh mushrooms, sliced
4 green onions, chopped
1 small zucchini, thinly sliced
2 tablespoons chopped green pepper
⅛ teaspoon dried whole basil
⅛ teaspoon lemon-pepper seasoning
Lettuce leaves (optional)
1 hard-cooked egg, sliced
4 slices bacon, cooked and crumbled

Drain artichoke hearts, reserving 3 tablespoons liquid. Combine artichoke hearts, reserved liquid, and next 6 ingredients in a shallow container. Cover and refrigerate several hours or overnight. Spoon salad into a lettuce-lined bowl, if desired; garnish with egg slices and bacon. Yield: 6 servings.

Kathy Howe,
Irving, Texas.

BACON-CHEESE SPREAD

2 (8-ounce) packages cream cheese,
    softened
10 slices bacon, cooked and crumbled
⅔ cup finely chopped onion
1 medium-size green pepper, finely
    chopped
1 (3-ounce) can chopped green chiles,
    drained
½ cup mayonnaise
1 tablespoon lemon juice
¼ teaspoon garlic salt
¼ teaspoon seasoned salt

Line a 4-cup bowl with plastic wrap. Beat cream cheese; stir in remaining ingredients, mixing well. Press the mixture firmly into bowl; cover and chill 6 to 8 hours or overnight. Invert onto a serving plate; remove plastic wrap. Serve with assorted crackers. Yield: about 4 cups.

Mrs. Jim Mack,
Midland, Texas.

GRILLED BACON-CHEESE SANDWICHES

½ cup (2 ounces) shredded Swiss cheese
2 tablespoons butter or margarine, softened
⅓ cup sliced fresh mushrooms
1 teaspoon butter or margarine
8 slices day-old sandwich bread
8 slices bacon, cooked and crumbled
4 eggs, beaten
½ cup milk
¼ cup butter or margarine, divided

Combine cheese and 2 tablespoons butter; mix well, and set aside. Sauté mushrooms in 1 teaspoon butter; drain.

Spread cheese mixture evenly on one side of 4 bread slices, leaving a ½-inch margin around edge of bread; sprinkle with mushrooms and bacon. Top with remaining bread; press bread gently to make sandwiches hold together.

Combine eggs and milk; dip sandwiches into egg mixture. Melt 2 tablespoons butter in a large skillet. Add 2 sandwiches, and cook over medium to medium-high heat for 1 to 2 minutes or until golden brown. Turn sandwiches, and continue cooking until golden brown. Drain on paper towels. Repeat with remaining 2 tablespoons butter and sandwiches. Serve immediately. Yield: 4 servings.

Note: Sandwiches may be cooked in a skillet coated with vegetable cooking spray instead of butter, if desired.

Dee Thompson,
Whippany, New Jersey.

PARTY CHICKEN LIVERS

2 dozen chicken livers (about ½ pound)
2 tablespoons butter
½ teaspoon seasoned salt
½ teaspoon seasoned pepper
½ pound bacon
1 (8-ounce) can whole water chestnuts, drained
Hot sauce (optional)

Cut chicken livers in half; sauté in butter until lightly browned. Drain well, and sprinkle with seasoned salt and pepper. Cut bacon slices in half; cook until limp. Wrap a bacon slice around a water chestnut and a piece of chicken liver; secure with a wooden pick. Repeat procedure with remaining chicken livers, water chestnuts, and bacon. Place on an ungreased baking sheet, and bake at 450° for 10 to 12 minutes or until bacon is crisp. Serve with hot sauce, if desired. Yield: 4 dozen.

T. O. Davis,
Waynesboro, Mississippi.

Cake For A Pumpkin Eater

Plan to use all of your jack-o'-lantern this year because you can bake it into some sweet treats. Orange-Pumpkin Cake Squares made from fresh pumpkin, are great as an after-school snack or served as a dessert.

ORANGE-PUMPKIN CAKE SQUARES

½ cup shortening
1½ cups sugar
1 cup cooked, mashed pumpkin
2 eggs, beaten
⅓ cup frozen orange juice concentrate, thawed and undiluted
1⅔ cups all-purpose flour
1 teaspoon baking powder
½ teaspoon baking soda
¾ teaspoon salt
½ teaspoon ground allspice
½ teaspoon ground cloves
½ teaspoon ground cinnamon
½ teaspoon ground nutmeg
Whipped cream (optional)
Walnut halves (optional)

Cream shortening; gradually add sugar, beating well. Add pumpkin, eggs, and orange juice concentrate; mix well. Combine remaining ingredients, mixing well; stir into pumpkin mixture. Pour into a greased and floured 13- x 9- x 2-inch baking pan.

Bake at 350° for 30 to 35 minutes or until a wooden pick inserted in center comes out clean. Cut into squares to serve. Top each square with a dollop of whipped cream and a walnut half, if desired. Yield: 12 to 15 servings.

Virginia Mathews,
Jacksonville, Florida.

It's Time For Turnips And Rutabagas

Fall brings a harvest of turnips and rutabagas bursting with distinctive flavors that Southerners love. You'll find recipes here for both vegetables.

For the best flavor, choose small to medium-size turnips. When purchasing rutabagas or turnips, look for smooth, round vegetables firm to the touch. You may find a thin layer of paraffin on rutabagas used to prevent loss of moisture; it's easily removed by peeling.

TURNIPS AND ONIONS

6 medium turnips, peeled and sliced
2 cups sliced onion
1 chicken-flavored bouillon cube
½ cup boiling water
2 tablespoons butter or margarine, melted
¼ teaspoon salt
¼ teaspoon pepper
1 teaspoon freeze-dried chives

Place turnips and onion in a 2-quart casserole. Dissolve bouillon cube in water; stir in remaining ingredients. Pour over vegetables. Cover and bake at 350° for 1½ hours, stirring occasionally. Yield: 6 servings.

Mrs. Russell T. Shay,
Murrells Inlet, South Carolina.

BOILED TURNIPS

6 medium turnips, peeled and cubed
2 tablespoons butter or margarine
½ teaspoon salt
⅛ teaspoon pepper

Place turnips in a large saucepan; cover with water and bring to a boil. Reduce heat, cover, and simmer 15 to 20 minutes or until tender. Drain. Stir in remaining ingredients. Yield: 4 servings.

Lora Williams,
Macon, Georgia.

TURNIP CASSEROLE

5 small turnips, peeled and sliced
2 tablespoons butter or margarine
1½ cups milk
1 cup soft breadcrumbs
½ cup (2 ounces) shredded Cheddar cheese
¼ teaspoon salt
⅛ teaspoon pepper
½ cup soft breadcrumbs
1 tablespoon butter or margarine, melted

Place turnips in a large saucepan; cover with water and bring to a boil. Reduce heat, cover, and simmer 15 minutes or until turnips are tender. Drain well and set aside.

Melt 2 tablespoons butter in a medium saucepan; stir in milk. Add 1 cup breadcrumbs, cheese, salt, and pepper; cook over low heat, stirring until thickened. Stir in turnips. Spoon mixture into a lightly greased 1½-quart casserole. Combine ½ cup breadcrumbs and 1 tablespoon melted butter; sprinkle over casserole. Bake, uncovered, at 375° for 20 minutes. Yield: 6 to 8 servings.
Hattie Jane Norvell,
Danville, Kentucky.

SIMPLE RUTABAGA

1 medium rutabaga
2 cups water
2 tablespoons sugar
1 teaspoon salt
2 tablespoons butter or margarine
⅛ teaspoon pepper

Peel rutabaga; cut lengthwise into ½-inch-thick slices.

Place next 4 ingredients in a large saucepan; bring to a boil. Add rutabaga; return to a boil. Reduce heat, cover, and simmer 40 minutes or until tender. Stir in pepper. Yield: 4 to 6 servings.
Esther Nethercutt,
Sherwood, Arkansas.

RUTABAGA WITH BACON

1 medium rutabaga, peeled and cubed
1 teaspoon sugar
3 slices bacon

Combine rutabaga and sugar in a medium saucepan; cover with water and bring to a boil. Cook 15 minutes or until rutabaga is tender. Drain well.

Cook bacon until crisp; reserve drippings. Pour drippings over rutabaga, stirring well. Crumble bacon; sprinkle over top. Yield: 4 to 6 servings.
Mrs. Paul M. Connolly,
Deltona, Florida.

Tip: Wash most vegetables; trim any wilted parts or excess leaves before storing in crisper compartment of refrigerator. Keep potatoes and onions in a cool, dark place with plenty of air circulation to prevent sprouting.

Sunday Night Favorites

When you've cooked a large meal for Sunday lunch, it's hard to get excited about cooking supper. So give yourself a break and put together one of these simple main dishes. They'll turn Sunday supper into a relaxing occasion you'll look forward to.

CORNBREAD SKILLET CASSEROLE

2 eggs, slightly beaten
1 cup yellow cornmeal
2 teaspoons baking soda
1 teaspoon salt
1 (17-ounce) can cream-style corn
1 cup milk
¼ cup vegetable oil
1 pound ground beef
2 cups (8 ounces) shredded Cheddar cheese
1 large onion, chopped
2 to 4 jalapeño peppers, finely chopped

Combine first 7 ingredients in a bowl, and set aside. Cook ground beef until browned; drain well and set aside.

Pour half of cornmeal mixture into a greased 10½-inch cast-iron skillet. Sprinkle evenly with beef; top with cheese, onion, and peppers. Pour remaining batter over top. Bake at 350° for 45 to 50 minutes. Let stand 5 minutes before serving. Yield: 6 to 8 servings.
Stephen H. Badgett,
Memphis, Tennessee.

SAUSAGE STRATA

6 slices white bread, crust removed
1 pound bulk pork sausage
1 teaspoon prepared mustard
¾ cup (3 ounces) shredded Swiss cheese
3 eggs, slightly beaten
1¼ cups milk
⅔ cup half-and-half
¼ teaspoon salt
Dash of pepper
1 teaspoon Worcestershire sauce

Line a buttered 13- x 9- x 2-inch baking dish with bread.

Crumble sausage in a medium skillet; cook over medium heat until browned, stirring occasionally. Drain well. Add mustard, stirring well. Spread sausage over bread; sprinkle with cheese.

Combine remaining ingredients; beat well and pour over sausage and cheese.

Bake at 350° for 25 minutes or until set. Cut into squares, and serve immediately. Yield: 6 to 8 servings.
Joy M. Hall,
Lucedale, Mississippi.

SPANISH OMELET

8 eggs
½ cup water
¼ teaspoon salt
1 (4-ounce) can chopped green chiles, drained
¼ cup finely chopped onion
¼ cup butter or margarine, divided
1 cup (4 ounces) shredded Monterey Jack or Cheddar cheese
1 (8-ounce) jar taco or picante sauce

Combine eggs, water, and salt; beat well. Stir in chiles and onion.

For each omelet, melt 1 tablespoon butter in an 8-inch omelet pan or heavy skillet until hot enough to sizzle a drop of water; pour in one-fourth of egg mixture. As mixture begins to cook, lift edges of omelet and tilt pan to allow uncooked portion to flow underneath.

When egg mixture is set and no longer flows freely, sprinkle ¼ cup cheese over half of omelet. Fold omelet in half, and place on a warm platter. Repeat procedure with remaining ingredients. Serve with taco sauce. Yield: 4 servings.
Mrs. Gary Ferguson,
Corsicana, Texas.

BUTTERMILK PANCAKES

1 cup all-purpose flour
1 teaspoon baking soda
1 tablespoon sugar
½ teaspoon salt
1 egg
1 cup plus 2 tablespoons buttermilk
1 tablespoon vegetable oil

Combine first 4 ingredients. Combine egg, buttermilk, and oil; slowly stir into dry ingredients.

For each pancake, pour about ¼ cup batter onto a hot, lightly greased griddle. Turn pancakes when tops are covered with bubbles and edges are browned. Serve with syrup. Yield: eight 4-inch pancakes.
Mrs. Theron L. Trimble,
Pensacola, Florida.

Put Pepperoni In The Rolls

Fill squares of yeast dough with ground pepperoni, green chiles, and mozzarella cheese for our Ground-Pepperoni Rolls. It made quite a hit in our test kitchens.

GROUND-PEPPERONI ROLLS

1 package dry yeast
¼ cup warm water (105° to 115°)
1 cup milk
¼ cup sugar
¾ teaspoon salt
2 tablespoons shortening
1 egg, beaten
3 to 3½ cups all-purpose flour, divided
1 (5-ounce) package pepperoni
1 cup (4 ounces) shredded mozzarella cheese
2 (3-ounce) cans chopped green chiles, drained

Dissolve yeast in warm water; let stand 5 minutes. Combine milk, sugar, salt, and shortening in a small saucepan; cook over medium heat, stirring constantly, until shortening melts. Cool to 105° to 115°. Stir yeast into milk mixture. Add egg and 1½ cups flour; beat on medium speed of electric mixer until smooth. Stir in enough of the remaining flour to make a soft dough.

Turn dough out onto a floured surface, and knead 3 or 4 times. Place in a well-greased bowl, turning to grease top. Cover dough and let rise in a warm place, free from drafts, 1 hour or until doubled in bulk.

Punch dough down. Place on floured surface, and roll out to an 18- x 9-inch rectangle; cut into 18 (3-inch) squares.

Grind pepperoni. Place about 1 tablespoon pepperoni, 1 tablespoon cheese, and 1 tablespoon peppers on each square. Roll up dough, pressing edges to seal; place seam side down in a greased 13- x 9- x 2-inch baking dish. Cover and let rise in a warm place, free from drafts, 45 minutes or until doubled in bulk. Bake at 350° for 15 to 20 minutes or until golden brown. Yield: 1½ dozen.
Betty Leggett,
Fairmont, West Virginia.

Tip: Use an extra set of dry measuring cups as scoops in canisters of flour, sugar, and grains to save time and extra dishwashing.

Cinnamon Adds Some Warmth

If the warm fragrance and flavor of cinnamon is a favorite of yours, you'll love these recipes.

CINNAMON STICKY BUNS

¾ cup butter or margarine, melted
¾ cup firmly packed brown sugar
½ cup light corn syrup
2 tablespoons ground cinnamon
1 package dry yeast
¼ cup warm water (105° to 115°)
¾ cup buttermilk, scalded
¼ cup plus 1 tablespoon butter or margarine
2 tablespoons sugar
¼ teaspoon salt
¼ teaspoon baking soda
1 egg
3 to 3½ cups all-purpose flour

Combine first 4 ingredients; mix well. Spread 1 cup mixture evenly in a 13- x 9- x 2-inch baking pan. Set prepared pan and remaining cinnamon mixture aside.

Dissolve yeast in warm water; set aside. Combine next 5 ingredients in a mixing bowl; stir until butter melts. Cool to 105° to 115°. Add yeast mixture and egg; stir in 1½ cups flour. Beat on medium speed of electric mixer 2½ minutes. Stir in enough remaining flour to make a soft dough.

Turn dough out onto a lightly floured surface; roll into a 16- x 8-inch rectangle. Spread remaining cinnamon mixture over rectangle. Roll up jellyroll fashion, beginning with long side.

Cut roll into ¾-inch slices, and place slices, cut side down, in prepared baking pan. Cover and let rise in a warm place (85°), free from drafts, about 45 minutes or until doubled in bulk. Bake at 375° for 20 to 25 minutes. Invert pan on serving plate; serve warm. Yield: about 16 rolls.
Carole McAllister,
Bixby, Oklahoma.

HOT SPICED TEA

4 (3-inch) sticks cinnamon, halved
1 teaspoon whole cloves
½ teaspoon whole allspice
1 quart hot tea
½ cup sugar
3 cups orange juice
3 cups unsweetened pineapple juice
Orange slice quarters (optional)

Combine first 3 ingredients in a tea ball or cheesecloth bag; set aside.

Combine hot tea and sugar in a large Dutch oven; stir in juice. Add spice mixture, and bring to a boil. Cover, reduce heat, and simmer 30 minutes. Garnish each serving with fresh orange, if desired. Serve hot. Yield: about 10 cups.
Joyce Dean Garrison,
Charlotte, North Carolina.

SPICY CHERRY SAUCE

1 cup sugar
2 tablespoons cornstarch
Dash of salt
1 cup orange juice
1 tablespoon lemon juice
1 (16-ounce) can pitted cherries, undrained
1 (3-inch) stick cinnamon
½ teaspoon whole cloves
4 drops red food coloring

Combine sugar, cornstarch, and salt in a medium saucepan. Add remaining ingredients; stir well. Cook over medium heat, stirring constantly, until thickened and bubbly. Reduce heat and simmer 2 minutes. Remove spices before serving. Serve over ham slices. Yield: 3 cups.
Lily Jo Drake,
Satellite Beach, Florida.

Bake Brownies Plain Or Fancy

A moist, chocolaty brownie is hard to refuse, especially when it's embellished with a special frosting or filling. Here, we feature some fancy brownies, in addition to our Easy Brownies, which are quick and simple to prepare.

CREME DE MENTHE BROWNIES

½ cup butter or margarine, softened
1 cup sugar
4 eggs
1 cup all-purpose flour
½ teaspoon salt
1 (16-ounce) can chocolate syrup
1 teaspoon vanilla extract
¼ cup butter or margarine, softened
2 cups sifted powdered sugar
2 tablespoons crème de menthe
¼ cup butter or margarine
1 (6-ounce) package semisweet chocolate morsels

Cream ½ cup butter; gradually add 1 cup sugar, beating until light and fluffy. Add eggs, one at a time, beating well after each addition.

Combine flour and salt; add to the creamed mixture alternately with chocolate syrup, beginning and ending with flour mixture. Stir in vanilla.

Pour batter into a greased and floured 13- x 9- x 2-inch baking pan. Bake at 350° for 25 to 28 minutes. Cool completely. (Brownies will shrink from sides of pan while cooling.)

Cream ¼ cup butter; gradually add 2 cups powdered sugar and crème de menthe, mixing well. Spread evenly over brownies; chill about 1 hour.

Combine chocolate morsels and remaining ¼ cup butter in top of double boiler; bring water to a boil. Reduce heat to low; cook until chocolate melts. Spread over brownies; chill for at least 1 hour. Cut into squares. Yield: 3½ dozen.
Susan Gann,
Smyrna, Georgia.

EASY BROWNIES

1 cup all-purpose flour
1 cup sugar
3 tablespoons cocoa
½ cup butter or margarine, melted
2 eggs, beaten
1 teaspoon vanilla extract
½ cup chopped pecans

Combine first 3 ingredients in a bowl. Add butter, eggs, and vanilla; stir well. Stir in pecans.

Pour batter into a greased 8-inch square baking pan. Bake at 350° for 20 minutes. Cool and cut into squares. Yield: 1½ dozen.

HEAVENLY HASH BROWNIES

2 (1-ounce) squares unsweetened chocolate
½ cup butter or margarine
2 eggs
1 cup sugar
½ cup all-purpose flour
Chocolate-Marshmallow Frosting

Combine chocolate and butter in top of a double boiler; bring water to a boil. Reduce heat to low; cook, stirring constantly, until chocolate melts. Cool.

Combine eggs and sugar; beat with an electric mixer just until blended. Add chocolate mixture and flour; beat just until smooth. Pour into a greased 9-inch square pan. Bake at 350° for 25 to 30

minutes. Cool completely. Spread with Chocolate-Marshmallow Frosting. Cool and cut into 1½-inch squares. Yield: 3 dozen.

Chocolate-Marshmallow Frosting:

2 (1-ounce) squares unsweetened chocolate
½ cup butter or margarine
1½ cups sifted powdered sugar
1 egg
1 teaspoon vanilla extract
2 cups miniature marshmallows
1 cup chopped pecans or walnuts

Combine chocolate and butter in top of double boiler; bring water to a boil. Reduce heat to low; cook, stirring constantly, until chocolate melts. Cool.

Combine powdered sugar, egg, vanilla, and chocolate mixture in a medium bowl; beat with electric mixer until smooth. Stir in marshmallows and pecans. Yield: enough frosting for one 9-inch square pan of brownies.
Ann Bregman,
West Palm Beach, Florida.

Casseroles Rich With Crabmeat

Begin Elegant Crab Imperial by combining a mixture of egg, mayonnaise, mustard, and Worcestershire sauce; then gently stir in fresh crabmeat and bread cubes. We suggest baking and serving this creation in individual baking dishes. Top each serving with a creamy white sauce and a sprinkling of paprika.

ELEGANT CRAB IMPERIAL

2 slices white bread
2 eggs, beaten
¼ cup mayonnaise
1 teaspoon prepared mustard
½ teaspoon chopped fresh parsley
½ teaspoon salt
⅛ teaspoon pepper
Dash of Worcestershire sauce
1 pound fresh crabmeat, drained and flaked
White sauce (recipe follows)
Paprika
Chopped fresh parsley

Remove crusts from bread slices; cut bread into small cubes. Combine next 7 ingredients; gently fold in bread cubes

and crabmeat. Spoon mixture into four 6-ounce baking dishes; top with 2 tablespoons white sauce. Sprinkle with paprika. Bake, uncovered, at 350° for 15 to 20 minutes. Garnish with parsley. Yield: 4 servings.

White Sauce:

1 tablespoon butter or margarine
1 tablespoon all-purpose flour
½ cup milk
⅛ teaspoon salt
⅛ teaspoon pepper
Dash of Worcestershire sauce

Melt butter in a heavy saucepan over low heat; add flour, stirring until smooth. Cook 1 minute, stirring constantly. Gradually add milk; cook over medium heat, stirring constantly, until thickened and bubbly. Stir in salt, pepper, and Worcestershire sauce. Yield: ½ cup.
Marie Greiner,
Baltimore, Maryland.

Sausage Makes These Dishes

Beckon your family to a meal with the tantalizing aroma of sizzling sausage. And with these recipes, you can serve sausage at any time of the day.

Most of the recipes here call for mild-flavored sausage. But you can always substitute a hot and spicy version.

SAUSAGE SURPRISE

2 pounds smoked sausage, cut into ¾-inch slices
1 large onion, cut into eighths
1 medium cabbage, cut into small chunks
½ cup water
1 pound carrots, cut into ½-inch slices
5 medium potatoes, peeled and cut into ¾-inch cubes

Brown sausage in a Dutch oven; remove and drain on paper towels. Drain off drippings, reserving 1 tablespoon in Dutch oven.

Sauté onion in reserved drippings 3 to 5 minutes; add sausage, cabbage, and water. Cover and cook over low heat 10 minutes. Stir in carrots and potatoes; cover and cook an additional 20 minutes or until the vegetables are tender. Yield: 8 servings.
Sharyl Langley,
Sulphur, Louisiana.

PANCAKE-SAUSAGE ROLLUPS

1 (12-ounce) package blueberry pancake
    mix (canned blueberries included)
1¾ cups milk
¼ cup vegetable oil
1 egg
Vegetable oil
1 pound mild bulk pork sausage
1 (8-ounce) carton commercial sour
    cream
Blueberry syrup

Combine dry ingredients of pancake mix, milk, ¼ cup oil, and egg in a large bowl; stir with a wire whisk until fairly smooth. Rinse blueberries packaged with pancake mix, and drain well on paper towels. Fold into batter.

Brush the bottom of a 10-inch crêpe pan or heavy skillet with vegetable oil; place over medium heat until just hot, not smoking.

Pour ¼ cup batter into pan; quickly tilt pan in all directions so that batter covers pan, making a 7-inch pancake. Turn pancakes when tops are covered with bubbles and edges are slightly dry. Set pancakes aside; keep warm.

Cook sausage in a skillet until browned, stirring to crumble meat; drain well.

Spoon 2 tablespoons sausage and 1 tablespoon sour cream into center of each pancake; roll up and place, seam side down, in a 13- x 9- x 2-inch baking dish. Bake at 400° for 10 minutes. Serve hot with blueberry syrup. Yield: 6 servings.   *Mary Belle Purvis,*
Greeneville, Tennessee.

EGG-AND-SAUSAGE TORTILLAS

8 flour tortillas
½ pound mild bulk pork sausage
½ cup chopped green onion
4 eggs
2 tablespoons whipping cream
½ teaspoon salt
¼ teaspoon pepper
2 tablespoons butter or margarine
½ cup (2 ounces) shredded sharp Cheddar
    cheese
Commercial picante sauce

Wrap tortillas tightly in foil; bake at 350° for 15 minutes.

Combine sausage and green onion in a large skillet; cook until sausage is browned and onion is tender, stirring to crumble meat. Drain well.

Combine eggs, whipping cream, salt, and pepper; beat well. Melt butter in a heavy skillet over medium heat; add egg mixture and cook, stirring often, until

eggs are firm but still moist. Add sausage mixture and cheese, stirring well.

Spoon an equal amount of sausage-egg mixture into center of each warm tortilla. Roll up tortillas; serve immediately with picante sauce. Yield: 8 servings.   *Kathleen Stone,*
Houston, Texas.

Bake A Quick Coffee Cake

You'll find a delicate, sweet flavor in our Cardamom Coffee Cake. The cardamom laces the tender cake layer to make it irresistible.

CARDAMOM COFFEE CAKE

2 eggs, beaten
1⅓ cups milk
½ cup butter or margarine, melted
¼ teaspoon imitation butter flavoring
2 teaspoons vanilla extract
3 cups all-purpose flour
2 teaspoons baking powder
¾ teaspoon salt
1 cup sugar
1 teaspoon ground cardamom
½ cup sugar
½ cup firmly packed brown sugar
½ teaspoon ground cinnamon
Dash of ground nutmeg
2 tablespoons butter or margarine,
    softened

Combine first 5 ingredients; mix well. Combine flour, baking powder, salt, 1 cup sugar, and cardamom in a large bowl; gradually stir in milk mixture, mixing well. Pour into a greased and floured 13- x 9- x 2-inch baking pan.

Combine remaining ingredients, stirring with a fork until crumbly; sprinkle topping over batter. Bake at 375° for 30 minutes or until a wooden pick inserted in center comes out clean. Yield: 15 to 18 servings.   *Mrs. W. C. McGee,*
Raleigh, North Carolina.

Baked Snapper At Its Best

In Stuffed Red Snapper With Lime, each fish is filled with a mixture of green pepper, pimiento, celery, and green onion, then sprinkled with fresh lime juice before baking. To serve, add a garnish of fresh lime slices, green pepper rings, and cherry tomatoes.

STUFFED RED SNAPPER WITH LIME

2 tablespoons sesame or peanut oil
2 (2-pound) dressed red snappers
2 teaspoons lime juice
½ teaspoon salt
½ teaspoon white pepper
¼ cup chopped green pepper
¼ cup diced pimiento
¼ cup diced celery
¼ cup chopped green onion with tops
Juice of 1 lime
¼ teaspoon salt
¼ teaspoon white pepper
Lime slices
1 medium-size green pepper, cut into
    rings
12 cherry tomatoes

Line a shallow baking pan with aluminum foil. Pour sesame oil over foil, spreading to edges of pan. Place fish on foil; sprinkle cavities with 2 teaspoons lime juice, ½ teaspoon salt, and ½ teaspoon white pepper.

Combine ¼ cup green pepper, pimiento, celery, and onion. Stuff cavity of each fish with half of vegetable mixture. Squeeze juice of 1 lime over fish; sprinkle with ¼ teaspoon salt and ¼ teaspoon white pepper. Top fish with lime slices; cover with aluminum foil, leaving a small opening in top. Bake at 425° for 45 to 50 minutes, basting occasionally with pan drippings.

Transfer fish to a serving platter; discard lime slices. Garnish with fresh lime slices, green pepper rings, and cherry tomatoes. Yield: 4 servings.
    Leona Smith,
Jacksonville, Florida.

Tip: Do not thaw fish at room temperature or in warm water; it will lose moisture and flavor. Instead, place in the refrigerator to thaw; allow 18 to 24 hours for thawing a 1-pound package. Do not refreeze thawed fish.

November

Usher in the holiday season in November with plenty of festive party spreads. To help you with seasonal celebrations, our annual *Holiday Dinners* special section appears with recipes for an elegant dinner party, casual menus, and more.

We open the selection with one of the fanciest parties we've ever attended. It's all happening in Little Rock, Arkansas, so come with us as the hostess greets her guests with Hot Mulled Wine and steaming Oyster Bisque. The dinner highlight is a spectacular Ice Cream Yule Log followed by a champagne toast.

Our fabulous entrées will help you dazzle dinner guests with the unusual. Bring on majestic Stuffed Crown Pork Flambé, turn down the lights, and flame it just before serving. Succulent Cider Baked Turkey or Spicy Marinated Beef Tenderloin can also be tasty alternatives.

For dessert, take a look at our double-crust fruit pies with decorated top crusts. On the next few pages you'll find recipes complete with step-by-step instructions for fashioning some fancy crusts.

Roll Out The Double-Crust Pies

Readers shared these tasty pie fillings with us, and our test kitchens home economists dressed the recipes with bright new pastry designs. The result? A striking array of double-crust pies sure to win you compliments.

Each of our crust designs is simple to make, and pastry is easy and fun to work with. But handle this dough as little as possible; excessive handling will toughen the dough and can cause it to shrink during baking.

Pastry will stick to itself easily, allowing the layering effect of some of our designs. To join pieces of pastry, simply moisten the back surface of the top piece, and gently press it to the surface of the lower one.

Any top-crust pastry that sits at room temperature more than 15 minutes during or after shaping should be chilled at least 15 minutes before baking to firm up the shortening in the crust. This promotes pretty and even browning. Our Double-Crust Pastry recipe yields a dough that works well with each of these designs.

Make a Design of Slits

Traditional double-crust pies call for a few slits to allow steam to escape from the filling during baking. Our Peach-Cranberry Pie sports a striking display of diagonal lines, and you can reproduce any other shape with simple designs. You can even monogram your initials. Just use a sharp knife so you can make the cuts cleanly and without tearing or stretching the pastry.

Twirl the Top Crust

Twirling a narrow strip of dough around a top crust is one of the quickest ways you can make a design. Simply roll out the dough to ⅛-inch thickness, and cut it into ½-inch strips with either a plain knife or a fluted pastry cutter. Starting in the center of the pie, wind one strip of pastry in a swirl, twisting the strip as you wind. When the first strip is used, join another strip onto the end of the first strip, moistening and pressing the edges. Be careful not to let the strip touch the pie except where you lay it; where filling gets on the strip, the pastry will become overbrowned.

Decorate With Crust Cutouts

Roll out the top crust, but before you transfer it to the pie, cut designs into the crust using a small canapé cutter. With a circular cutout you can create a rounded design like ours, and with a square cutout you can achieve something that looks like a lattice, without weaving strips. You can also freehand cutout designs in the crust or use cookie cutters. When transferring the crust to the pie, be sure not to stretch the crust, as this can cause it to shrink during baking.

Appliqué With Pastry

With cookie cutters you can make pastry designs to appliqué on top of a plain crust. To make the appliqué adhere, moisten the back, and gently press it to the top crust. Make several slits in the top crust to let steam escape, making them at the seam where the appliqué joins the top crust so as not to interfere with the pastry design.

The Layered Look

We achieved the scalloped design of our Dried Fruit Pie by simply layering small rounded pastry cutouts in concentric circles until the pie was covered. Moisten the back of each cutout before gently pressing it onto existing pastry. Since this crust takes a little longer to make, be sure to refrigerate the pie for at least 15 minutes before baking so it will brown evenly.

DOUBLE-CRUST PASTRY

2 cups all-purpose flour
1 teaspoon salt
⅔ cup plus 2 tablespoons shortening
4 to 5 tablespoons cold water

Combine flour and salt in a bowl; cut in shortening with pastry blender until mixture resembles coarse meal. Sprinkle cold water, 1 tablespoon at a time, evenly over surface; stir with a fork until dry ingredients are moistened. Shape into a ball; chill. Yield: pastry for one double-crust pie.

Vary the placement and length of slits in the crust to create a simple design for Peach-Cranberry Pie. Wooden picks in center of pie help you cut straight lines.

For Holiday Mincemeat Pie, wind strips of pastry in a swirl on top of pie, twisting the strips as you wind.

Use a small canapé cutter to make cutouts in the top crust before transferring the crust to Scrumptious Cherry Pie.

Appliqué designs on pastry by moistening the design on back and gently pressing it onto the pastry. We appliquéd an apple for Apple-Pear Pie.

For Dried Fruit Pie, layer pastry cutouts in concentric circles around the top crust.

APPLE-PEAR PIE

1 recipe Double-Crust Pastry
2 baking apples, peeled, cored, and thinly sliced
¼ cup all-purpose flour
¾ cup sugar
½ teaspoon ground cinnamon
2 medium pears, peeled, cored, and thinly sliced
2 tablespoons lemon juice
2 tablespoons butter or margarine, melted
Buttered Rum Sauce

Roll half of pastry onto a lightly floured surface to ⅛-inch thickness; fit into a 9-inch pieplate. Chill remaining pastry. Arrange apple slices in pastry shell.

Combine flour, sugar, and cinnamon; sprinkle half of mixture over apples. Top with pears, arranging evenly so top crust will lay flat. Sprinkle pears with remaining flour mixture. Pour lemon juice and melted butter over pie.

Roll out remaining pastry to ⅛-inch thickness, and place over filling. Trim edges; then seal and flute. Cut apple and leaf designs as desired out of remaining pastry; moisten backs of cutouts with water, and press onto top crust. Cut several slits in top crust. Bake pie at 375° for 45 to 50 minutes. (Cover edges of pie with aluminum foil to prevent overbrowning, if necessary.) Serve with Buttered Rum Sauce. Yield: one 9-inch pie.

Buttered Rum Sauce:

½ cup firmly packed brown sugar
1 tablespoon cornstarch
1 cup water
½ teaspoon rum flavoring
2 tablespoons butter

Combine first 2 ingredients in a small saucepan; gradually stir in water. Cook over medium heat until mixture is thickened and clear, stirring occasionally. Stir in flavoring and butter. Serve warm. Yield: 1¼ cups.

Mrs. Loren D. Martin,
Knoxville, Tennessee.

PEACH-CRANBERRY PIE

1 recipe Double-Crust Pastry
1 (29-ounce) can sliced peaches, undrained
3 cups fresh cranberries
1½ cups sugar
3 tablespoons cornstarch
¼ cup chopped almonds, toasted
1 tablespoon milk
1½ teaspoons sugar

Roll half of pastry onto a lightly floured surface to ⅛-inch thickness; fit into a 9-inch pieplate. Set aside. Chill remaining pastry.

Drain peaches, reserving 1 cup plus 2 tablespoons liquid. Coarsely chop the peaches; set aside.

Wash cranberries; combine cranberries, sugar, and 1 cup reserved peach liquid in a large saucepan. Cook 7 to 10 minutes or until cranberry skins pop. Combine cornstarch and remaining 2 tablespoons peach liquid, stirring until cornstarch dissolves; add to cranberry mixture. Cook, stirring constantly, until thickened. Stir in peaches and almonds. Spoon mixture evenly into prepared pastry shell.

Roll out remaining pastry to ⅛-inch thickness, and place over filling. Trim edges; then seal and flute. Cut slits in top pastry to allow steam to escape, making a decorative pattern with slits, if desired. Brush top crust (not fluted edge) with milk; sprinkle with sugar. Bake at 400° for 35 to 40 minutes. (Cover edges of pie with aluminum foil to prevent overbrowning, if necessary.) Yield: one 9-inch pie.

Mrs. H. G. Drawdy,
Spindale, North Carolina.

DRIED FRUIT PIE

1½ recipes Double-Crust Pastry
1 cup halved dried apricots
1 cup halved pitted dates
1 cup halved pitted prunes
1½ cups water
½ teaspoon salt
¼ cup sugar
1 (6-ounce) can frozen orange juice concentrate, thawed
1 teaspoon vanilla extract
Sweetened whipped cream or frozen whipped topping, thawed

Roll one-third of pastry onto a lightly floured surface to ⅛-inch thickness; fit into a 9-inch pieplate. Trim edges and flute; set aside. Chill remaining pastry.

Combine fruit, water, and salt in a saucepan; bring to a boil. Cover, reduce heat, and simmer 10 minutes, stirring occasionally. Uncover and cook over medium heat, stirring constantly, 2 minutes or until liquid is absorbed. Stir in sugar, orange juice concentrate, and vanilla. Spoon evenly into pastry shell.

Roll out remaining pastry to ⅛-inch thickness; cut pastry with a 1½-inch fluted cutter. Place cutouts over filling in a ring around edge of pie, first moistening the cutout edges, then overlapping and sealing them to edge of bottom pastry. Continue placing cutouts in rings around pie until top is covered. Bake at 425° for 30 to 35 minutes. (Cover edges of pie with aluminum foil to prevent overbrowning, if necessary.) Serve warm or cool with sweetened whipped cream. Yield: one 9-inch pie.

Mrs. Randall L. Wilson,
Louisville, Kentucky.

Tip: Have your oven thermostat professionally checked at least once a year. Another way to occasionally check oven temperature is to prepare a cake mix according to package directions; the cake should cook the entire recommended time and test done (a wooden pick inserted in the center should come out clean).

SCRUMPTIOUS CHERRY PIE

1 recipe Double-Crust Pastry
2 (16-ounce) cans red tart cherries,
    undrained
1 cup sugar, divided
¼ cup cornstarch
1 tablespoon butter or margarine
Few drops of red food coloring
1 tablespoon grated orange rind
1 teaspoon Grand Marnier or other
    orange-flavored liqueur

Roll half of pastry onto a lightly floured surface to ⅛-inch thickness; fit into a 9-inch pieplate. Set aside. Chill remaining pastry.

Drain cherries, reserving ¾ cup juice; set aside.

Combine ¾ cup sugar and cornstarch in a saucepan; stir mixture to remove lumps. Stir reserved cherry juice into sugar mixture.. Cook over medium heat until smooth, stirring constantly. Add remaining sugar, cherries, butter, food coloring, orange rind, and Grand Marnier; stir until butter melts. Cool and pour into pastry shell.

Roll out remaining pastry to ⅛-inch thickness. Cut pastry with a 1½-inch fluted cutter, making a decorative pattern about 7½ to 8 inches in diameter. Center pastry carefully over the filling. Trim edges; then seal and flute. Bake at 375° for 50 to 55 minutes. (Cover edges of pie with aluminum foil to prevent overbrowning, if necessary.) Yield: one 9-inch pie.
Carin Usry,
Oklahoma City, Oklahoma.

HOLIDAY MINCEMEAT PIE

1 recipe Double-Crust Pastry
1 (28-ounce) jar prepared mincemeat
1½ cups peeled, chopped apples
1 tablespoon dry sherry
Brandied Hard Sauce

Roll half of pastry onto a lightly floured surface to ⅛-inch thickness; carefully fit into a 9-inch pieplate. Trim edges and flute; set aside. Chill remaining pastry.

Combine mincemeat, apples, and sherry; spoon evenly into pastry shell.

Roll out remaining pastry to ⅛-inch thickness; cut pastry into ½-inch strips. Starting in center of pie, twist one strip and wind in a swirl around top of pie. When first strip is used, moisten end of the strip and attach another strip, pinching ends together. Swirl strip around pie. Continue joining and swirling strips until pie is covered.

Bake pie at 400° for 30 to 35 minutes. (Cover edges of pie with aluminum foil

to prevent overbrowning, if necessary.) Serve warm or cool with Brandied Hard Sauce. Yield: one 9-inch pie.

Brandied Hard Sauce:

⅔ cup butter or margarine, softened
2 cups sifted powdered sugar
2 tablespoons brandy

Combine all ingredients; beat at medium speed of an electric mixer until smooth. Yield: 1½ cups.
Mrs. Addis Vestal,
Lexington, Tennessee.

Funnel These Cakes

During a visit to Opryland in Nashville several years ago, Mary Colley of Donelson, Tennessee, first tasted a funnel cake. She liked it so much that she soon came up with her own recipe and has been making them ever since.

Funnel Cakes are good sprinkled with powdered sugar. You can also add a dash of cinnamon or drizzle them with your favorite syrup.

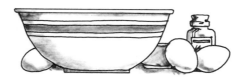

FUNNEL CAKES

2½ cups self-rising flour
¼ cup sugar
1⅓ cups milk
2 eggs, slightly beaten
Vegetable oil
Sifted powdered sugar (optional)

Combine flour, sugar, milk, and eggs in a bowl, beating until smooth. Heat ¼ inch oil to 375° in a skillet. Cover bottom opening of a funnel with finger. (Funnel with a ⅜-inch opening works best.) Pour ¼ cup batter into funnel. Hold funnel over skillet. Remove finger from funnel end to release batter into hot oil; move funnel in a slow, circular motion to form a spiral.

Fry each funnel cake 1 minute or until edges are golden brown; turn and fry until golden. Drain on paper towels. Repeat with remaining batter. Sprinkle with powdered sugar, if desired; serve warm. Yield: about one dozen 5-inch cakes.
Mary Colley,
Donelson, Tennessee.

Fried Cheese With Italian Flair

Make a unique appetizer made with mozzarella cheese: cut it into cubes, coat it with layers of egg, flour, and seasoned breadcrumbs, then fry it until golden brown. When served with spicy tomato sauce, each bite of Italian-Style Fried Cheese is a sheer delight.

ITALIAN-STYLE FRIED CHEESE

1 pound mozzarella cheese, cut into 1-inch
    cubes
3 eggs, well beaten
½ cup all-purpose flour
¾ cup seasoned, dry breadcrumbs
Vegetable oil
Italian-Style Sauce

Dip cheese cubes in egg; dredge in flour, and dip again in egg. Roll cubes in breadcrumbs; place on waxed paper, and chill 1 hour.

Fry chilled cubes in deep hot oil (375°) until golden brown. Drain cubes on paper towels; serve immediately with Italian-Style Sauce. Yield: 1½ dozen appetizer servings.

Italian-Style Sauce:

1 clove garlic, minced
1 tablespoon vegetable oil
1 (28-ounce) can whole tomatoes, chopped
    and undrained
½ teaspoon sugar
¼ teaspoon salt
1 teaspoon dried whole oregano
¼ teaspoon dried whole basil
Dash of pepper

Sauté garlic in oil in a heavy skillet until tender. Stir in remaining ingredients; bring to a boil. Reduce heat and simmer, uncovered, 45 minutes or until mixture is thickened, stirring occasionally. Yield: about 1⅔ cups.
Carolyn Look,
El Paso, Texas.

Tip: Properly canned foods have been sterilized and won't spoil as long as the container remains airtight. However, most canned foods have a "shelf life" of approximately one year—they then may begin to slowly lose flavor and nutrients. If you use large amounts of canned foods, date them at time of purchase and use the oldest first.

Taste The Flavor Of Southern Holidays

The fragrances of cinnamon and cloves linger in the air; there's laughter rippling in the background and wonderful aromas drifting from the kitchen. This could mean only one thing—the holidays are here!

As a holiday gift to you, we are pleased to share this special section of festive recipes, menus, and entertaining ideas to help brighten the season and add to the merriment. We've included a little bit of everything—favorites like Festive Baked Ham and Tart Cranberry Sauce as well as some new ideas for side dishes like Zucchini-and-Corn Soufflé and Easy Asparagus Casserole. We've even included a menu to help you stick to your diet. You'll be surprised to find you've feasted on only 600 calories.

But for those of us who like to do the holiday season up big, we invite you to come along with us to Lenora and Wallace Blaylock's home, Gibb House, in the Quapaw Quarter of Little Rock. The spicy aroma of Hot Mulled Wine drifts through the door as Wallace and Lenora greet their guests.

Lively holiday tunes from the living room piano accompany friendly chatter while the sipping and snacking get underway. Braunschweiger Pâté is one of Lenora's favorite appetizers; she serves it on a silver tray, garnished with cherry tomatoes and sliced party bread.

When the Blaylocks entertain, they make full use of their spacious restored home. "One way to keep a party going is to serve the various food courses in different rooms," explains Lenora. So, after appetizers in the living room, everyone drifts toward the entranceway where Lenora ladles up steaming cups of Oyster Bisque.

Upon entering the dining room, guests find Lenora has saved her best

presentation for last. "I'm a part-time caterer, so I'm always looking for different entrées and interesting ways to present food," says Lenora, as she garnishes the main course, Prairie Wings Mallard. "Wallace hunts each season, so I usually serve duck at least once during the holidays."

Accompanying the ducks are Stuffed Tomatoes, creamy Cucumber Salad Mold, and a perfectly shaped Wild Rice Ring. Lenora also serves Buttered Zucchini and Carrots; she slices the zucchini but leaves the carrots whole to add an interesting look.

As the dinner draws to a close, the spectacular finale is brought from the kitchen—Ice Cream Yule Log. Everyone gets a hefty slice of the log-shaped chocolate cake before ending the evening with a glass of champagne and a toast to a happy holiday season.

Hot Mulled Wine
Braunschweiger Pâté
Oyster Bisque
Easy Bisque Crackers   Herb Sticks
Prairie Wings Mallard
Buttered Zucchini and Carrots
Stuffed Tomatoes   Wild Rice Ring
Cucumber Salad Mold
Ice Cream Yule Log
Wine   Coffee
Champagne

HOT MULLED WINE

2 quarts Burgundy or other dry
   red wine
2 quarts apple juice
3 (3-inch) sticks cinnamon
1½ teaspoons whole cloves
1 teaspoon whole allspice

Combine wine and apple juice in a large container. Tie spices in a cheesecloth; add to wine mixture. Cover and chill wine several hours or overnight.

Pour mixture into a large Dutch oven; bring to a boil. Reduce heat and simmer 3 to 5 minutes. Remove spice bag. Serve hot. Yield: 1 gallon.

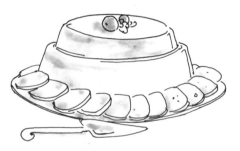

BRAUNSCHWEIGER PATE

1 envelope unflavored gelatin
1 cup boiling water
2 (8-ounce) rolls braunschweiger
1 (8-ounce) package cream cheese,
   softened
1 tablespoon instant minced onion
1 tablespoon chopped fresh parsley
1 tablespoon prepared horseradish
⅛ teaspoon pepper
1 (10½-ounce) can consommé, undiluted
½ teaspoon dry sherry
Party pumpernickel bread
Fresh parsley sprigs
Cherry tomatoes

Dissolve gelatin in boiling water.

Combine the braunschweiger, cream cheese, onion, parsley, horseradish, and pepper, mixing well. Stir in consommé, sherry, and gelatin mixture. Pour into a lightly oiled 6-cup ring mold. Cover and chill several hours or until set. Unmold onto a serving dish. Serve with party pumpernickel bread; garnish with parsley and cherry tomatoes in center of mold. Yield: about 6 cups.

OYSTER BISQUE

2 quarts Standard oysters, undrained
1 cup butter or margarine
1 small clove garlic, minced
8 cups whipping cream
2 tablespoons instant minced onion
1 teaspoon salt
¼ teaspoon white pepper
¼ cup dry sherry

Drain oysters, reserving liquid. Place oysters in container of food processor or electric blender; process just until coarsely chopped. Set aside.

Melt butter in a large Dutch oven; add garlic and sauté until tender. Add whipping cream, reserved oyster liquid, onion, salt, and pepper; heat thoroughly (do not boil).

Add oysters to cream mixture; simmer 5 to 8 minutes or until edges of oysters curl. Stir in sherry. Yield: about 4 quarts.

Note: If serving with Easy Bisque Crackers, salt may be omitted from Oyster Bisque.

EASY BISQUE CRACKERS

3½ tablespoons butter or margarine, softened
3 dozen thin bacon-flavored crackers
2 dozen shredded-whole-wheat crackers
Lemon-pepper seasoning

Spread butter on one side of each cracker; sprinkle each cracker with lemon-pepper seasoning.

Place crackers on cookie sheets, and broil until bubbly and lightly browned. Yield: 5 dozen.

HERB STICKS

1 cup all-purpose flour
½ teaspoon salt
⅓ cup plus 1 tablespoon shortening
2 to 3 tablespoons cold water
2½ tablespoons butter or margarine, softened
1 tablespoon grated Parmesan cheese
1 teaspoon Greek seasoning

Combine flour and salt in a bowl; cut in shortening with pastry blender until mixture resembles coarse meal. Sprinkle cold water, 1 tablespoon at a time, evenly over surface; stir with a fork until all dry ingredients are moistened. Shape into a ball; chill 30 minutes.

Turn dough out onto a lightly floured surface. Roll into a 14- x 8-inch rectangle. Spread with butter; sprinkle with cheese and Greek seasoning. Fold dough in half, forming an 8- x 7-inch rectangle; cut lengthwise into ¼-inch-wide strips. Twist each strip, and place on an ungreased cookie sheet. Bake at 375° for 14 minutes or until twists are golden brown; cool on wire racks. Yield: 2½ dozen.

PRAIRIE WINGS MALLARD

2 cups butter or margarine, divided
12 (1½- to 2-pound) wild ducks, dressed
1½ cooking apples, cored and cut into 12 wedges
1½ oranges, cut into 12 wedges
1½ medium onions, cut into 12 wedges
6 stalks celery, cut in half crosswise
1½ quarts dry sherry
Lemon leaves
Fresh parsley sprigs
Kumquats
Sliced kiwi

Melt ½ cup butter in a large skillet or Dutch oven. Arrange 3 ducks in a skillet; cook over medium heat 5 to 8 minutes on each side or just until golden brown. Remove ducks; repeat procedure with remaining ducks, adding ½ cup butter to skillet each time. Reserve drippings in the skillet.

Place a wedge of apple, orange, onion, and a half stalk of celery in cavity of each duck. Arrange ducks in a single or double layer in an extra-large roaster or two large Dutch ovens; pour sherry and reserved pan drippings over ducks. Add enough water to bring liquid to a depth of 1 inch. Cover and bake at 350° for 3 hours or until ducks are tender, basting occasionally. Uncover and bake an additional 15 to 20 minutes or until ducks are light brown.

Remove ducks from roaster, discarding apple, orange, onion, and celery. Place ducks on a serving platter lined with lemon leaves. Garnish with fresh parsley sprigs, kumquats, and kiwi. Yield: 12 servings.

BUTTERED ZUCCHINI AND CARROTS

2 dozen small carrots
2 teaspoons dried whole dillweed
Dash of pepper
¼ cup butter or margarine, melted and divided
8 medium zucchini, cut into 1-inch slices
¼ teaspoon salt
Dash of pepper
Fresh parsley sprigs

Place carrots in a small amount of boiling salted water in a large saucepan; cook 15 to 20 minutes or just until tender. Drain. Sprinkle with dillweed and a dash of pepper; toss gently. Pour 2 tablespoons melted butter over the carrots.

Arrange zucchini in a steaming rack. Place over boiling water; cover and steam 6 to 8 minutes. Place zucchini in a serving dish. Pour remaining 2 tablespoons melted butter over zucchini; sprinkle with salt and a dash of pepper. Stir gently, and set aside.

Arrange carrots in a spoke pattern around outer edges of a large platter; place serving dish of zucchini in center of platter. Garnish with parsley. Yield: 12 servings.

STUFFED TOMATOES

12 medium tomatoes
½ cup butter or margarine, melted
1 (10¾-ounce) can chicken broth, undiluted
1 (8-ounce) package herb-seasoned stuffing mix
¼ cup chopped fresh parsley
2 tablespoons instant minced onion
1 tablespoon Greek seasoning
¼ cup grated Parmesan cheese

Wash tomatoes. Cut tops from tomatoes; scoop out pulp, leaving shells intact. Reserve pulp for use in other recipes.

Combine butter and next 5 ingredients; mix well. Stuff tomato shells with mixture; sprinkle with Parmesan cheese. Place tomatoes in a 13- x 9- x 2-inch baking dish; cover and bake at 350° for 20 minutes. Uncover and bake an additional 5 minutes or until tops are browned. Yield: 12 servings.

WILD RICE RING

2 (8-ounce) packages wild rice
6 cups water
1 teaspoon salt
½ cup butter or margarine, softened
Lemon wedges (optional)
Fresh parsley sprigs (optional)

Rinse rice under cold running water until water is clear. Combine rice, 6 cups water, and salt in a heavy saucepan; bring to a boil. Cover, reduce heat to low, and cook 1 hour or until rice is tender. Add butter, stirring well.

Pack rice into an 8-cup ovenproof mold. Cover the mold with aluminum foil, and refrigerate overnight.

Bake at 350° for 30 minutes. Unmold onto serving platter. Garnish with lemon and parsley, if desired. Yield: 12 to 14 servings.

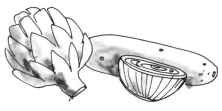

CUCUMBER SALAD MOLD

6 large cucumbers
3 envelopes unflavored gelatin
¾ cup water
1 cup mayonnaise
1 (8-ounce) carton commercial sour cream
1 tablespoon grated onion
1 tablespoon minced fresh parsley
½ cup whipping cream
¼ teaspoon salt
¼ teaspoon white pepper
Cooked fresh artichokes
Cherry tomatoes

Peel cucumbers, and remove seeds; coarsely chop, and place in container of food processor or electric blender; process until smooth.

Sprinkle gelatin over water in a saucepan; cook over low heat, stirring constantly, until gelatin dissolves. Stir gelatin mixture and next 4 ingredients into cucumber puree.

Beat whipping cream until soft peaks form; fold into cucumber mixture. Stir in salt and pepper. Pour into a lightly oiled 6-cup ring mold; chill until firm.

Unmold the salad onto a serving platter. Garnish with artichokes and cherry tomatoes. Yield: 12 servings.

ICE CREAM YULE LOG

1 cup all-purpose flour
⅓ cup cocoa
5 eggs
¾ teaspoon baking powder
¼ teaspoon salt
1 cup sugar
2 teaspoons vanilla extract
Additional cocoa
1 pint vanilla ice cream, softened
1 pint green chocolate mint ice cream, softened
Chocolate frosting (recipe follows)

Grease a 15- x 10- x 1-inch jellyroll pan and line with waxed paper; grease and flour waxed paper. Set aside.

Sift flour and ⅓ cup cocoa together; set mixture aside.

Combine eggs, baking powder, and salt; beat at high speed of electric mixer until foamy. Gradually add sugar, beating until mixture is thick and lemon colored. Fold in flour mixture and vanilla. Spread batter evenly into prepared pan. Bake at 400° for 10 to 12 minutes.

Sift cocoa in a 15- x 10-inch rectangle on a linen towel. When cake is done, immediately loosen from sides of pan and turn out onto cocoa. Peel off waxed paper. Starting at wide end, roll up cake and towel together; cool on a wire rack, seam side down, 25 minutes.

Unroll cake; remove towel. Starting at wide end, spread vanilla ice cream lengthwise over half of cake; spread chocolate mint ice cream over remaining half of cake. Gently roll cake back up; carefully place on a large baking sheet. Freeze until ice cream is firm.

Remove cake from freezer. Diagonally cut a 4-inch piece of cake from the roll. Place rolls on a freezer-proof serving plate, positioning cut edge of short piece against side of longer piece, to resemble a tree branch. Spread chocolate frosting over cake roll. Score frosting with fork tines to resemble bark; make knots with flat side of knife blade. Garnish with holly leaves and red berries. Freeze until serving time. Yield: 12 to 15 servings.

Chocolate Frosting:

3½ cups sifted powdered sugar
½ cup cocoa
¼ cup shortening
¼ teaspoon salt
1½ teaspoons vanilla extract
¼ cup plus 2 tablespoons milk

Combine first 5 ingredients in a large bowl; add ¼ cup milk, and beat until smooth. Add remaining milk, if needed, 1 tablespoon at a time, to make spreading consistency. Yield: enough frosting for one yule log.

Highlight Dinner With Homemade Bread

Whether it's an easy quick bread like Cheese Biscuits or a time-consuming yeast recipe like Poppy Seed Loaf, homemade bread helps make dinner memorable. Here's a collection of favorite bread recipes that you'll want to consider for your holiday menus. Some are easier than others; all yield attractive and delicious results.

CHEESE BISCUITS

2 cups self-rising flour
⅓ cup shortening
½ cup (2 ounces) shredded Cheddar cheese
¾ cup milk

Combine flour and shortening in a medium bowl; cut in shortening with pastry blender until mixture resembles coarse meal. Stir in cheese and milk. Turn dough out onto a floured surface, and knead lightly 3 to 4 times.

Roll dough to ½-inch thickness; cut into rounds with a 2¾-inch biscuit cutter. Place biscuits on an ungreased baking sheet; bake at 450° for 10 to 12 minutes. Yield: about 1 dozen.

*Jacquelyn Christopher,
Asheville, North Carolina.*

REFRIGERATED POTATO ROLLS

1⅓ cups instant mashed potatoes or 2
  cups hot mashed potatoes
4¾ cups all-purpose flour, divided
2 packages dry yeast
1 cup milk
½ cup shortening
½ cup sugar
1 teaspoon salt
2 eggs, slightly beaten

Prepare instant mashed potatoes according to package directions, omitting salt; set aside.

Combine 2 cups flour and yeast in a large mixing bowl; set aside. Combine milk, shortening, sugar, and salt in a saucepan; heat to 115° to 120°, stirring constantly. Stir in potatoes; let cool to 105° to 115°.

Add potato mixture and eggs to yeast mixture; beat 30 seconds on low speed of electric mixer, scraping sides of bowl. Beat 3 minutes on high speed. Stir in remaining 2¾ cups flour (dough will be very sticky).

Place dough in a well-greased bowl, turning to grease top. Cover and refrigerate 8 hours or overnight.

Lightly grease muffin pans. Shape dough into 1-inch balls; place 3 balls in each muffin cup. Cover and let rise in a warm place (85°), free from drafts, 1 hour or until doubled in bulk. Bake at 375° for 20 to 25 minutes or until browned. Yield: about 2½ dozen.

Janice Overman,
Lynchburg, Virginia.

FINGER ROLLS

1 package dry yeast
1 cup warm water (105° to 115°)
1 tablespoon sugar
1 tablespoon vegetable oil
1½ teaspoons salt
3 to 3¼ cups all-purpose flour
½ cup butter or margarine, melted and
  divided

Dissolve yeast in warm water in a large bowl; let stand 5 minutes. Add sugar, oil, salt, and 1½ cups flour; beat at medium speed of electric mixer 2 minutes. Stir in enough remaining flour to make a soft dough.

Turn dough out onto a lightly floured surface, and knead 3 to 4 minutes until smooth and elastic. Place dough in a well-greased bowl, turning to grease top. Cover and let rise in a warm place (85°), free from drafts, 1 hour or until doubled in bulk.

Pour ¼ cup butter into a 13- x 9- x 2-inch baking pan; set aside. Shape dough into twenty 1¼-inch balls; shape each ball into a 4- x ½-inch roll. Place rolls in prepared pan. Cover and let rise 30 minutes.

Lightly brush rolls with remaining ¼ cup butter. Bake at 400° for 18 to 20 minutes or until lightly browned. Yield: 20 rolls.

Deborah Alford,
Independence, Kentucky.

DILLED HONEY-WHEAT ROLLS

1 package dry yeast
½ cup warm water (105° to 115°)
½ cup butter or margarine, melted
1 (12-ounce) carton cream-style cottage
  cheese
3 tablespoons honey
1 tablespoon instant minced onion
2 teaspoons dillseeds
1 teaspoon salt
¼ teaspoon baking soda
1 egg, beaten
2 cups whole wheat flour
2 cups all-purpose flour

Dissolve yeast in warm water; let stand 5 minutes. Combine butter and cottage cheese in a large bowl; stir well. Add yeast mixture and remaining ingredients except flour; beat 1 minute on medium speed of electric mixer. Gradually stir in flour.

Turn dough out onto a lightly floured surface; knead 5 to 7 minutes until smooth and elastic. Place in a well-greased bowl, turning to grease top. Cover and let rise in a warm place (85°), free from drafts, 1 hour or until doubled in bulk.

Punch dough down; shape into twenty-four 1½-inch balls. Arrange in a greased 13- x 9- x 2-inch baking pan; cover and let rise 45 minutes. Bake at 400° for 15 to 18 minutes. Yield: 2 dozen.

Susan Hamilton Clark,
Greenville, South Carolina.

ITALIAN DINNER ROLLS

1 cup milk
3 tablespoons butter or margarine
2 tablespoons sugar
1½ teaspoons dried Italian seasoning
1 teaspoon salt
2 packages dry yeast
½ cup warm water (105° to 115°)
2 eggs
4½ cups all-purpose flour
½ cup grated Parmesan cheese
2 tablespoons butter or margarine,
  melted
Additional grated Parmesan cheese

Combine first 5 ingredients in a small saucepan; cook over medium heat, stirring constantly, until butter melts. Cool to 105° to 115°.

Dissolve yeast in warm water in a large bowl; let stand 5 minutes. Add milk mixture, eggs, and 1½ cups flour; beat at low speed of electric mixer 30 seconds. Beat at high speed 3 minutes; stir in ½ cup Parmesan cheese and enough remaining flour to make a stiff dough.

Turn dough out onto a lightly floured surface; knead 5 to 7 minutes until smooth and elastic. Place in a well-greased bowl, turning to grease top. Cover and let rise in a warm place (85°), free from drafts, 45 minutes or until doubled in bulk.

Punch dough down; let rest 10 minutes. Shape into sixteen 2-inch balls; dip the top of each in melted butter, and coat with Parmesan cheese. Arrange 8 rolls in each of two greased 9-inch cakepans; cover and let rise in a warm place, free from drafts, 15 minutes or until doubled in bulk. Bake at 375° for 20 to 25 minutes. Yield: 16 rolls.

Joy M. Hall,
Lucedale, Mississippi.

POPPY SEED LOAF

1 package dry yeast
1¼ cups warm water (105° to 115°)
2 tablespoons sugar
2 tablespoons poppy seeds
2 tablespoons butter or margarine,
  softened
1 teaspoon salt
3½ to 4 cups unbleached flour

Dissolve yeast in warm water in a large bowl; let stand 5 minutes. Add sugar, poppy seeds, butter, and salt; beat at low speed of electric mixer until smooth. Gradually beat in enough remaining flour to make a soft dough.

Place dough in a greased bowl, turning to grease top. Cover and let rise in a warm place (85°), free from drafts, 40 minutes or until doubled in bulk.

Punch dough down; turn out onto a lightly floured surface, and knead 4 to 5 times. Shape dough into an 8- x 4-inch loaf. Grease a 9- x 5- x 3-inch loafpan; place dough in pan.

Cover and let rise in a warm place (85°), free from drafts, 40 minutes or until doubled in bulk. Bake at 375° for 45 minutes or until bread sounds hollow when tapped. Yield: 1 loaf.

Ella Stivers,
Abilene, Texas.

BACON-AND-CHEESE BREAD

1½ cups all-purpose flour
⅓ cup sugar
2 teaspoons baking powder
½ teaspoon baking soda
½ teaspoon salt
1 cup (4 ounces) shredded sharp Cheddar cheese
¾ cup quick-cooking oats
6 slices bacon, cooked and crumbled
2 eggs, beaten
½ cup milk
¼ cup vegetable oil

Combine first 8 ingredients in a large bowl; set aside. Combine eggs, milk, and oil; add to oat mixture, stirring just enough to moisten dry ingredients.

Spoon batter into a greased and floured 8½- x 4½- x 3-inch loafpan. Bake at 350° for 35 to 40 minutes or until a wooden pick inserted in center comes out clean. Let cool in pan 10 minutes. Yield: 1 loaf.

Polly A. Hughes,
Tarpon Springs, Florida.

Tip: Keep flour in a large shaker for quick and easy flouring of a pan; just shake out the amount needed to cover the pan.

Casseroles Dressed For The Season

Holiday feasts call for vegetable casseroles that are both delicious and colorful. These selections are just that—and they are varied enough to complement just about any entrée.

Don't forget to add an interesting garnish to your casserole. Bits of sliced, colorful vegetables arranged in a pattern will turn an ordinary-looking casserole into a suitable dish for a special menu.

EASY ASPARAGUS CASSEROLE

1 (15-ounce) can cut asparagus, drained
½ teaspoon salt
1 teaspoon white pepper
2 (2-ounce) jars diced pimiento, drained
2 eggs, beaten
1 cup buttery cracker crumbs
1 cup milk
1 cup (4 ounces) shredded Cheddar cheese
¼ cup butter or margarine, melted
Canned asparagus spears (optional)
Pimiento strip (optional)

Combine first 9 ingredients, and spoon into a greased 8-inch square baking dish. Bake, uncovered, at 400° for 30 minutes. Garnish casserole with asparagus spears and a pimiento strip, if desired. Yield: 6 servings.

Anita M. Dail,
Williamsburg, Virginia.

CHEESY BROCCOLI BAKE

2 pounds fresh broccoli
1 cup water
½ teaspoon salt
¼ cup chopped onion
¼ cup chopped celery
¼ pound fresh mushrooms, sliced
2 tablespoons butter or margarine
1 (8-ounce) can sliced water chestnuts, drained
½ pound process American cheese
1 (10¾-ounce) can cream of mushroom soup, undiluted
¼ teaspoon garlic salt
¼ teaspoon pepper
1 cup (4 ounces) shredded Cheddar cheese

Trim off large leaves of broccoli. Remove tough ends of lower stalks, and wash broccoli thoroughly. Cut broccoli into 1-inch pieces. Bring water to a boil; add ½ teaspoon salt and broccoli. Cover, reduce heat, and simmer 5 to 8 minutes or until crisp-tender. Drain.

Sauté onion, celery, and mushrooms in butter until vegetables are tender; drain. Combine mushroom mixture, broccoli, and water chestnuts, stirring gently; set aside.

Combine process cheese and soup; cook over low heat, stirring until cheese melts. Pour over broccoli mixture. Stir in garlic salt and pepper.

Spoon mixture into a greased 2-quart casserole. Bake at 350° for 25 minutes; sprinkle with Cheddar cheese. Bake an additional 5 minutes or until cheese melts. Yield: 8 to 10 servings.

Susan W. Pajcic,
Jacksonville, Florida.

CREAMY CELERY CASSEROLE

2 cups diced celery
1 (8-ounce) can sliced water chestnuts, drained
⅓ cup slivered almonds, toasted
¼ cup butter or margarine
3 tablespoons all-purpose flour
⅔ cup half-and-half
⅔ cup chicken broth
¼ teaspoon salt
1 (4-ounce) can sliced mushrooms, drained
½ cup grated Parmesan cheese

Cook celery in boiling water 5 minutes; drain. Combine celery, water chestnuts, and almonds; spoon into a greased 1½-quart baking dish.

Melt butter in a heavy saucepan over low heat; add flour, stirring until smooth. Cook 1 minute, stirring constantly. Gradually add half-and-half and chicken broth; cook over medium heat, stirring constantly, until thickened and bubbly. Stir in salt. Pour sauce over celery mixture; sprinkle with mushrooms. Bake at 350° for 15 minutes; sprinkle with cheese, and bake an additional 15 minutes. Yield: 6 servings.

Mrs. Robert Boyer,
Summerville, South Carolina.

November 255

CARROT AND ZUCCHINI CASSEROLE

1 pound carrots, cut diagonally into ½-inch slices
3 to 4 small zucchini, cut diagonally into ½-inch slices
½ cup mayonnaise
2 tablespoons grated onion
¾ teaspoon prepared horseradish
½ teaspoon salt
½ teaspoon pepper
½ cup Italian-style breadcrumbs
¼ cup butter or margarine, melted

Cook carrots and zucchini in a small amount of boiling salted water 5 minutes or until tender. Drain vegetables well, reserving ¼ cup of cooking liquid.

Combine reserved liquid, mayonnaise, onion, horseradish, salt, and pepper; add to carrots and zucchini, stirring well. Spoon mixture into a lightly greased 8-inch square baking dish. Combine breadcrumbs and butter; sprinkle over casserole. Bake at 375° for 15 to 20 minutes or until bubbly. Yield: 6 servings.
Shirley Hodge,
Delray Beach, Florida.

JALAPENO-CORN CASSEROLE

1 cup uncooked regular rice
1 medium onion, chopped
1 medium-size green pepper, chopped
1 cup chopped celery
½ cup butter or margarine, melted
1 tablespoon sugar
1 to 2 large jalapeño peppers, finely chopped
2 (17-ounce) cans cream-style corn
1 cup (4 ounces) shredded mild Cheddar cheese
Green pepper rings (optional)
Cherry tomato halves (optional)
Fresh parsley sprigs (optional)

Cook rice according to package directions; set aside.

Sauté onion, green pepper, and celery in butter until vegetables are tender.

Combine rice, sautéed vegetables, and next 4 ingredients, stirring well.

Spoon mixture into a lightly greased 12- x 8- x 2-inch baking dish. Bake at 350° for 40 to 45 minutes. Garnish with green pepper rings, cherry tomatoes, and parsley, if desired. Yield: 10 servings.
Lou Taylor,
Pine Bluff, Arkansas.

MIXED VEGETABLE CASSEROLE

1 (10-ounce) package frozen cauliflower
1 (10-ounce) package frozen cut broccoli spears
1 (8-ounce) package frozen brussels sprouts
1 (16-ounce) jar boiled onions, drained
1 (4-ounce) can sliced mushrooms, undrained
1 (10¾-ounce) can cream of mushroom soup, undiluted
2 (1-ounce) slices process American cheese, cut in half

Cook cauliflower, broccoli, and brussels sprouts according to package directions; drain. Combine all ingredients except cheese; spoon mixture into a lightly greased 12- x 8- x 2-inch baking dish. Bake at 350° for 15 minutes. Arrange cheese across top, and bake an additional 5 minutes or until the cheese melts. Yield: 8 servings.
Mrs. Richard D. Conn,
Kansas City, Missouri.

SWEET BUTTERNUT CASSEROLE

2 pounds butternut squash
1 cup sugar
⅛ teaspoon ground cloves
⅛ teaspoon ground cinnamon
⅛ teaspoon ground nutmeg
⅛ teaspoon pumpkin pie spice
½ cup butter or margarine
3 eggs, slightly beaten
½ teaspoon vanilla extract
Pecan halves

Peel squash, and cut in half lengthwise; remove seeds and membranes. Cook squash in boiling salted water to cover, 25 minutes or until tender. Drain and mash.

Add sugar, spices, and butter to squash; beat on medium speed of electric mixer 1 minute or until smooth. Add eggs and vanilla; beat an additional 30 seconds. Pour into a lightly greased 2-quart shallow baking dish; garnish with pecan halves. Bake at 350° for 35 to 40 minutes or until a knife inserted in center comes out clean. Yield: 8 servings.
Mildred Yenerall,
Doraville, Georgia.

Cookies With Holiday Spirit

A wonderful assortment of homemade cookies is essential for entertaining and gifts during this busy season.

Here is a sampling from our test kitchens that will help keep your cookie jar filled. The spices, fruits, and nuts in these cookies give them a special flavor, making them great for nibbling and for sharing with friends.

FORGET 'EM COOKIES

2 egg whites
Dash of salt
¾ cup sugar
1 teaspoon vanilla extract
1 (6-ounce) package semisweet chocolate morsels
1 cup chopped pecans

Preheat oven to 350°. Beat egg whites (at room temperature) until foamy; add salt. Gradually add sugar, 1 tablespoon at a time, beating mixture until stiff peaks form.

Fold vanilla, chocolate morsels, and pecans into beaten egg whites. Drop by teaspoonfuls onto cookie sheets lined with aluminum foil. Place in oven, and immediately turn off heat. Do not open oven door for at least 8 hours. Carefully remove cookies from aluminum foil. Yield: about 3 dozen.

Catherine Rogers,
Havana, Arkansas.

ENGLISH CHERUBS

1 cup firmly packed brown sugar, divided
½ cup butter or margarine, softened
1⅓ cups all-purpose flour
Dash of salt
2 eggs
½ cup sugar
1 teaspoon vanilla extract
¼ teaspoon salt
½ cup flaked coconut
1 cup chopped pecans

Combine ½ cup brown sugar, butter, flour, and dash of salt in a medium mixing bowl; mix until well combined (mixture will look dry). Press in bottom of a greased 9-inch square pan.

Beat eggs until foamy. Add remaining brown sugar, ½ cup sugar, vanilla, and ¼ teaspoon salt; mix well. Stir in coconut and pecans. Spread over layer in pan. Bake at 350° for 30 minutes or until top is set and lightly browned. Cool; cut into 1½-inch squares. Yield: 3 dozen.
Charlotte Gatton,
Maceo, Kentucky.

HOLIDAY RICHES

2¼ cups all-purpose flour
1 cup sifted powdered sugar
½ teaspoon cream of tartar
½ teaspoon baking soda
¼ teaspoon salt
1 cup butter or margarine, softened
1 egg, slightly beaten
1 tablespoon water
1 teaspoon almond extract
1 teaspoon vanilla extract
Pecan halves

Combine flour, sugar, cream of tartar, soda, and salt in a medium mixing bowl; stir lightly. Cut in butter until mixture resembles coarse meal. Combine egg, water, and flavorings; mix well. Add to dry mixture, stirring until blended; chill dough 1 to 2 hours.

Shape dough into 1-inch balls, and place on ungreased cookie sheets. Press a pecan half in center of each cookie; bake at 350° for 12 to 15 minutes. Yield: about 4 dozen.
Mrs. W. P. Chambers,
Louisville, Kentucky.

OATMEAL-DATE SANDWICH COOKIES

1¾ cups all-purpose flour
3 cups quick-cooking oats, uncooked
1½ cups firmly packed brown sugar
1½ teaspoons baking powder
½ teaspoon salt
½ cup butter or margarine, softened
½ cup shortening
⅓ cup milk
Date Filling

Combine flour, oats, sugar, baking powder, and salt; mix well. Cut in butter and shortening with pastry blender until particles are the size of small peas. Stir in milk. Chill 2 to 3 hours.

Roll dough to ⅛-inch thickness on a lightly floured surface. Cut with a 1½-inch cookie cutter. Place on ungreased cookie sheets; bake at 375° for 8 to 10 minutes. Remove cookies to wire racks. Cool completely.

Spread bottom side of half the cookies with a thin layer of Date Filling. Top with remaining cookies to make a sandwich. Yield: about 3 dozen.

Date Filling:

1½ cups chopped dates
1 cup hot water
3 tablespoons firmly packed brown sugar
1½ tablespoons lemon juice

Combine all ingredients in a saucepan. Cook, stirring constantly, over medium heat until thick and smooth. Cool completely. Yield: about 2 cups.
Linda Heatwole,
Dayton, Virginia.

Fruitcakes Spice Up Your Gift List

Many times you'll want a small item to give as a hostess gift or to surprise a neighbor or schoolteacher. Set up an assembly line, and it won't take long to make and decorate a dozen or more of these little fruitcakes.

We baked each of these recipes in mini-loafpans and small tart pans to make the cakes just the right size for individual gifts. You can use other sizes of pans if you'd like to, but be sure to adjust the baking times accordingly.

Once cooled, decorate the cakes with halved or sliced candied cherries. Brush cherries with corn syrup, and press onto fruitcakes. Then cover the cakes tightly with plastic wrap, and add a bow.

REGAL FRUITCAKE

1 (8-ounce) package candied red cherries, chopped
1 (8-ounce) package candied green cherries, chopped
1 (7-ounce) can flaked coconut
1½ cups coarsely chopped pecans
4¼ cups all-purpose flour, divided
1¼ cups butter or margarine, softened
2 cups sugar
6 eggs
2 teaspoons baking powder
½ teaspoon salt
½ cup orange juice
Candied red and green cherries

Combine first 4 ingredients; dredge with ¼ cup flour, stirring well. Set mixture aside.

Cream butter in a large mixing bowl; gradually add sugar, beating until light and fluffy. Add eggs, one at a time, beating well after each addition.

Combine 4 cups flour, baking powder, and salt; add to creamed mixture alternately with ½ cup orange juice, beginning and ending with the flour mixture. Mix well after each addition. Stir in fruit mixture.

Spoon half of batter into 8 well-greased 4½- x 2½- x 1½-inch loafpans, filling two-thirds full. Spoon remaining batter into 8 well-greased 4¼-inch tart pans, filling two-thirds full. Bake at 350° for 30 minutes or until a wooden pick inserted in center comes out clean. Cool in pans 10 minutes. Remove from pans, and let cool completely. Decorate with candied cherries. Yield: 16 miniature fruitcakes.

APPLESAUCE FRUITCAKE

3 cups applesauce
2 cups sugar
1 cup butter or margarine
1 (16-ounce) package candied red cherries, halved
1 (8-ounce) package candied green pineapple, chopped
1 (8-ounce) package candied yellow pineapple, chopped
1 (8-ounce) package chopped dates
4 cups pecans, coarsely chopped
4½ cups all-purpose flour
1 tablespoon plus 1 teaspoon baking soda
1 teaspoon salt
2½ teaspoons ground cinnamon
1 teaspoon ground nutmeg
½ teaspoon ground cloves
Candied red and green cherries

Combine first 3 ingredients in a saucepan; bring to a boil. Reduce heat and simmer 5 minutes, stirring constantly. Let cool.

Combine fruit and pecans in a large bowl. Combine flour, soda, salt, and spices; add to fruit mixture, stirring well. Add applesauce mixture; mix well.

Spoon half of batter into 10 well-greased 4½- x 2½- x 1½-inch loafpans, filling two-thirds full. Spoon remaining batter into 10 well-greased 4-inch tart pans, filling two-thirds full. Bake at 350° for 25 minutes or until a wooden pick inserted in center comes out clean. Cool in pans 10 minutes. Remove from pans, and let cool completely. Decorate with candied cherries. Yield: about 20 miniature fruitcakes. *Carolyn H. Grover, Anderson, South Carolina.*

LEMON FRUITCAKE

4 cups chopped pecans
1 (15-ounce) package golden raisins
3 cups all-purpose flour, divided
2 cups butter or margarine, softened
2 cups sugar
6 eggs, separated
1 teaspoon baking soda
1 tablespoon water
2 to 4 tablespoons lemon extract
Candied red and green cherries

Combine pecans and raisins; dredge with 1 cup flour, stirring well. Set aside.

Cream butter in a large mixing bowl; gradually add sugar, beating until light and fluffy. Add egg yolks, one at a time, beating well after each addition. Combine baking soda and water; stir into creamed mixture. Add lemon extract and remaining flour; mix well. Stir in pecan-raisin mixture. Beat egg whites (at room temperature) until stiff peaks form; fold into creamed mixture.

Spoon half of batter into 7 greased 4½- x 2½- x 1½-inch loafpans, filling two-thirds full. Spoon remaining batter into 7 greased 4-inch tart pans, filling two-thirds full. Bake at 350° for 25 to 30 minutes or until a wooden pick inserted in center comes out clean. Cool in pans 10 minutes. Remove cakes from pans, and let cool completely. Decorate as desired with candied cherries. Yield: 14 miniature fruitcakes. *Barbie James, Newport, Arkansas.*

Start With A Creative Appetizer

Holiday parties demand special attention to the appetizers. So instead of settling for the usual party fare, impress your guests with Caviar Mousse, Cheese-Filled Phyllo Triangles, or our other unusual appetizers.

MARINATED FLANK STEAK

2 (1-pound) flank steaks
¼ cup plus 2 tablespoons soy sauce
¼ cup sesame seeds
1½ tablespoons oyster sauce
1 tablespoon sesame oil
1 tablespoon peanut oil

Partially freeze steaks, and slice across grain into thin slices; cut slices into 1½-inch pieces. Combine remaining ingredients in a shallow dish; add steak, stirring to coat. Cover and marinate for 6 hours or overnight in the refrigerator, stirring occasionally.

Remove steak from marinade, and place in a single layer in a large shallow baking pan. Broil 3 to 4 minutes, turning once. Yield: 25 appetizer servings.
Susan Kamer-Shinaberry, Charleston, West Virginia.

SEVICHE COCKTAIL

1 cup lime juice
½ cup lemon juice
⅔ cup finely chopped onion
1 jalapeño pepper, minced
1½ pounds fresh red snapper fillets
Shredded lettuce
Lemon slices
Spicy Cocktail Sauce

Combine lime juice, lemon juice, onion, and pepper in a shallow glass dish (do not use metal). Add fish fillets, stirring to coat. Cover and refrigerate 12 hours. Drain fish, and place on a bed of lettuce; garnish with lemon slices. Serve with Spicy Cocktail Sauce and assorted crackers. Yield: 10 to 12 appetizer servings.

Spicy Cocktail Sauce:
⅓ cup catsup
⅓ cup chili sauce
Juice of 1 lemon
¼ teaspoon prepared horseradish
Dash of hot sauce

Combine all ingredients, stirring well. Yield: about ⅔ cup. *Jean Davis, Austin, Texas.*

CAVIAR MOUSSE

2 envelopes unflavored gelatin
2 tablespoons cold water
½ cup boiling water
1 cup whipping cream
2 (2-ounce) jars red or black caviar
¼ cup mayonnaise
1 tablespoon lemon juice
1 tablespoon Worcestershire sauce
Dash of dry mustard
Fresh parsley sprigs

Soften gelatin in cold water; let stand 3 minutes. Add boiling water, stirring until gelatin dissolves. Stir in next 6 ingredients. Pour into a lightly oiled 3-cup mold. Chill until firm. Garnish with parsley; serve with unsalted crackers. Yield: 3 cups. *Heather Riggins, Nashville, Tennessee.*

HOT SWISS CANAPES

3 egg whites
3 slices uncooked bacon, chopped
1½ cups (6 ounces) shredded Swiss
    cheese
¾ cup chopped green pepper
¼ cup chopped green onion
½ teaspoon salt
⅛ teaspoon pepper
24 slices party rye bread

Beat egg whites (at room temperature) until stiff peaks form; fold in next 6 ingredients. Spread about 1 tablespoon mixture on each bread slice. Place on baking sheets, and broil 4 to 5 inches from heat about 5 minutes or until bacon cooks. Serve immediately. Yield: 2 dozen. *Beverly Cotton, Hilton Head Island, South Carolina.*

CHUTNEY ROLL

1 (8-ounce) package cream cheese,
    softened
½ cup chutney, finely chopped
½ cup chopped almonds, toasted
1 tablespoon curry powder
½ teaspoon dry mustard
½ cup finely chopped unsalted dry
    roasted peanuts

Combine first 5 ingredients in a mixing bowl; stir well. Shape into a log; wrap in waxed paper, and chill 1 hour. (Mixture will be soft.) Roll log in peanuts. Chill several hours or overnight. Serve with assorted crackers. Yield: one 6-inch roll. *Carol L. Haggett, Norfolk, Virginia.*

ZESTY PARTY DIP

1 cup mayonnaise
1 tablespoon anchovy paste
½ teaspoon hot sauce
Dash of garlic powder
½ teaspoon dry mustard
2 tablespoons tarragon vinegar

Combine all ingredients, stirring until smooth. Chill several hours or overnight. Serve dip with assorted raw vegetables or boiled shrimp. Yield: 1 cup. *Mrs. E. Lamar McMath, Jacksonville, Florida.*

DATE-FILLED CHEESE PASTRIES

½ cup butter or margarine, softened
1 cup (4 ounces) shredded sharp Cheddar
    cheese
1 cup all-purpose flour
⅛ teaspoon red pepper
Pinch of salt
2 tablespoons cold water
3 dozen pitted dates
3 dozen pecan halves

Beat butter and cheese with an electric mixer until smooth. Combine flour, red pepper, and salt. Add flour mixture and water to cheese mixture, stirring until all the dry ingredients are moistened. Shape into a ball; roll dough to ⅛-inch thickness on a lightly floured surface. Cut into 2-inch squares.

Cut a lengthwise slit in each date; fill each with a pecan half. Place a filled date in center of each pastry square. Fold 2 opposite edges of pastry to center of date, overlapping edges slightly; press gently to seal.

Place seam side down on greased cookie sheets; bake at 400° for 15 minutes or until pastries are lightly browned. Cool on wire racks. Yield: 3 dozen. *Vera Kingsbury, Evansville, Indiana.*

CHEESE-FILLED PHYLLO TRIANGLES

⅓ cup feta cheese, crumbled
⅓ cup cream-style cottage cheese
1 egg, slightly beaten
Dash of salt
Dash of pepper
Dash of ground nutmeg
7 sheets commercial frozen phyllo
    pastry, thawed
⅔ cup butter, melted

Combine feta cheese and cottage cheese. Add egg and seasonings, beating well; set aside.

Cut sheets of phyllo lengthwise into 2-inch strips; keep covered with a damp towel until used. Brush 1 strip of phyllo with melted butter. Place 1 teaspoon cheese mixture at base of phyllo strip; fold the right bottom corner over it into a triangle. Continue folding back and forth into a triangle to end of strip. Repeat process with remaining phyllo.

Place triangles, seam side down, on greased cookie sheets; brush with melted butter. Bake at 350° for 20 minutes. Yield: 3½ dozen. *Marge Biancke, Ann Arbor, Michigan.*

Relishes For Extra Zest

Besides sliced raw vegetables and olives, fill your relish tray with a zesty homemade mixture like our Cabbage Relish or Easy Corn Relish. Tangy, crunchy, and colorful, they'll add that extra special something to your menu.

GARDEN RELISH

½ small head cauliflower, broken into
    flowerets
2 medium carrots, cut into 2-inch
    strips
2 stalks celery, cut into 1-inch strips
1 medium-size green pepper, cut into
    2-inch strips
1 (4-ounce) jar whole pimientos, drained
    and cut into 1-inch strips
1 (3-ounce) jar pitted green olives,
    drained and sliced
¾ cup white wine vinegar
½ cup olive oil or vegetable oil
¼ cup water
2 tablespoons sugar
1 teaspoon salt
½ teaspoon dried whole oregano
¼ teaspoon pepper

Combine first 6 ingredients in a medium saucepan. Combine remaining ingredients in a jar; cover tightly, and shake vigorously. Pour over vegetables; bring to a boil. Reduce heat and simmer, uncovered, 5 minutes. Cool and refrigerate at least 24 hours before serving. Serve the relish with a slotted spoon. Yield: about 1 quart.
Mrs. John Baxley, Augusta, Georgia.

CABBAGE RELISH

4 quarts shredded cabbage
1 large green pepper, shredded
2 small hot red peppers, seeded and finely
　chopped
¼ cup salt
1 quart vinegar (5% acidity)
3½ cups firmly packed brown sugar
2¼ teaspoons mixed pickling spices
1½ teaspoons mustard seeds
1½ teaspoons celery seeds
1½ teaspoons ground turmeric

Combine cabbage, green pepper, and red pepper in a large bowl; stir in salt, and let stand 1 hour. Drain well.

Combine vinegar and sugar in a large Dutch oven; bring to a boil. Add cabbage mixture and remaining ingredients; bring to a boil.

Quickly ladle cabbage mixture into hot sterilized jars, leaving ¼-inch headspace; cover at once with metal lids, and screw bands tight. Process in boiling-water bath 10 minutes. Yield: 6 pints.
Cindy Murphy,
Cleveland, Tennessee.

EASY CORN RELISH

1 (10-ounce) package frozen whole kernel
　corn
3 tablespoons chopped green pepper
3 tablespoons white wine vinegar
2 tablespoons sugar
½ teaspoon salt
⅛ teaspoon coarsely ground black pepper
⅛ teaspoon ground turmeric
1 (2-ounce) jar diced pimiento, drained

Cook corn according to package directions; drain. Stir in next 6 ingredients, and cook over medium heat about 1 minute. Stir in pimiento. Spoon into a bowl; cover and chill at least 8 hours. Yield: about 2 cups.
Mrs. O. V. Elkins,
Chattanooga, Tennessee.

CRANBERRY CHUTNEY

2 cups fresh cranberries
½ cup water
½ cup seedless golden raisins
1 small onion, sliced
1 cup sugar
¼ teaspoon ground ginger
¼ teaspoon ground cinnamon
⅛ teaspoon ground allspice
⅛ teaspoon salt
1 (8-ounce) can pineapple tidbits, drained

Combine first 9 ingredients in a Dutch oven; stir well. Cook over medium heat, uncovered, 10 to 15 minutes or until cranberry skins pop. Stir in the pineapple tidbits.

Reduce heat to low; cook an additional 30 minutes, stirring often. Serve warm or chilled. Yield: about 2½ cups.
Elda Caldwell,
San Antonio, Texas.

Salads Add Sparkle To Holiday Menus

Try these refreshing new salads with your holiday menus. We've included a variety of both fruit and vegetable salad recipes.

CONGEALED ASPARAGUS SALAD

¼ cup sugar
1 cup water
½ cup white wine vinegar
1 envelope unflavored gelatin
½ cup cold water
1 cup chopped celery
1 (4-ounce) can diced pimiento, drained
2 tablespoons grated onion
1 (10½-ounce) can asparagus tips, drained
　and cut into 1-inch pieces
½ cup finely chopped pecans
Juice of ½ lemon
Dash of salt
Lettuce leaves

Combine first 3 ingredients in a saucepan; bring to a boil and cook 5

minutes. Soften gelatin in ½ cup cold water; let stand 5 minutes, and add to vinegar mixture. Stir in next 7 ingredients. Pour mixture into a lightly oiled 4-cup mold; chill until firm. Unmold onto lettuce leaves. Yield: 8 servings.
Ruby Bonelli,
Bastrop, Texas.

BROCCOLI SALAD SUPREME

1 (3-ounce) package cream cheese,
　softened
1 egg
2 tablespoons vinegar
2 tablespoons sugar
2 tablespoons vegetable oil
1 tablespoon prepared mustard
¼ teaspoon salt
⅛ teaspoon garlic salt
Dash of pepper
6 cups chopped fresh broccoli
⅓ cup raisins
2 tablespoons chopped onion
Lettuce leaves
½ pound bacon, cooked and crumbled
Chopped pimiento (optional)

Combine first 9 ingredients in container of an electric blender, and process until smooth.

Combine broccoli, raisins, and onion in a large bowl; add cream cheese mixture and toss gently. Cover and chill at least 3 hours. Place salad in a lettuce-lined bowl; sprinkle with bacon and garnish with chopped pimiento, if desired. Yield: 8 to 10 servings. *Gail Thomas,*
White Hall, Maryland.

MARINATED VEGETABLE SALAD

1 (14-ounce) can artichoke hearts, drained
　and quartered
1½ cups sliced carrots
3 cups cauliflower flowerets
½ cup chopped onion
½ cup sliced celery
½ cup commercial Italian salad dressing
½ cup mayonnaise
2 tablespoons chili sauce
1 tablespoon lemon juice
1 teaspoon dried whole dillweed
Lettuce leaves

Combine first 6 ingredients, tossing well; cover and chill at least 2 hours. Drain vegetables. Combine mayonnaise, chili sauce, lemon juice, and dillweed; pour over vegetables and toss gently. Serve on lettuce leaves. Yield: 6 to 8 servings. *Mrs. James Redd, Smithland, Kentucky.*

CRANBERRY-WHIPPED CREAM SALAD

1 (8-ounce) can crushed pineapple, undrained
1 (3-ounce) package raspberry-flavored gelatin
1 (16-ounce) can whole cranberry sauce
1 teaspoon grated orange rind
1 (11-ounce) can mandarin oranges, drained
1 cup whipping cream, whipped

Drain pineapple, reserving juice; set pineapple aside. Add enough boiling water to juice to measure 1 cup. Combine gelatin and juice mixture, stirring until gelatin dissolves. Stir in cranberry sauce and orange rind. Chill until consistency of unbeaten egg white.

Fold in pineapple, oranges, and whipped cream. Spoon into a 12- x 8- x 2-inch dish; chill until firm. Yield: 10 to 12 servings. *Gail Thompson, Brundidge, Alabama.*

FRUIT SALAD PLATTER

1 medium head lettuce, shredded
2 medium apples, unpeeled, cored, and sliced
2 bananas, sliced
2 tablespoons lemon juice
2 oranges, peeled, seeded, and sectioned
1 (15¼-ounce) can pineapple chunks, drained
3 tablespoons red wine vinegar
¼ cup plus 2 tablespoons olive oil
1 teaspoon sugar
¼ cup chopped unsalted peanuts
¼ cup pomegranate seeds (optional)

Arrange lettuce on a serving platter. Combine apples and bananas in a bowl; add lemon juice and toss gently. Drain. Arrange apples, bananas, oranges, and pineapple on lettuce.

Combine vinegar, oil, and sugar; beat until smooth. Pour over salad; sprinkle with peanuts and pomegranate seeds, if desired. Yield: 8 servings.
Teresa Parker, Laurens, South Carolina.

STRAWBERRY-WINE SALAD MOLD

1 (6-ounce) package strawberry-flavored gelatin
1¼ cups boiling water
1¼ cups rosé
2 (10-ounce) packages frozen sliced strawberries, thawed
1 (8¼-ounce) can crushed pineapple, undrained
1 (8-ounce) carton commercial sour cream
Lettuce leaves
Fresh strawberries (optional)

Dissolve gelatin in boiling water; stir in rosé, strawberries, and pineapple. Chill until consistency of unbeaten egg white.

Spoon about one-third of mixture into a lightly oiled 6-cup mold; chill until partially set. Spread sour cream evenly over gelatin. Add remaining gelatin mixture. Chill until firm. Unmold onto lettuce leaves. Garnish salad with lettuce and fresh strawberries, if desired. Yield: 10 to 12 servings. *Patty Merritt, Jacksonville, North Carolina.*

Serve A Side Dish Of Cooked Fruit

Dress up your table with a spicy side dish of cooked fruit. Cranberries, pineapple, apricots, peaches, pears, and more are mixed with sugar and spices in these easy recipes. Some are served hot, some cold.

ALMOND-CURRIED FRUIT

1 (29-ounce) can sliced peaches, drained
1 (15½-ounce) can pineapple chunks, drained
1 (16-ounce) can pear halves, drained
1 (6-ounce) jar maraschino cherries, drained
½ cup slivered almonds, toasted
⅓ cup butter or margarine, melted
¾ cup firmly packed brown sugar
1 tablespoon curry powder

Place first 4 ingredients in a 13- x 9- x 2-inch baking dish. Sprinkle the fruit with almonds.

Combine butter, brown sugar, and curry powder. Top fruit with brown sugar mixture; bake at 325° for 1 hour. Yield: 8 to 10 servings. *Carolyn Rosen, Nashville, Tennessee.*

BAKED PINEAPPLE

2 (20-ounce) cans pineapple chunks, drained
1 cup firmly packed brown sugar
¾ cup round buttery cracker crumbs
3 tablespoons butter or margarine

Place half of pineapple in a 13- x 9- x 2-inch baking dish. Cover with half of brown sugar and half of cracker crumbs; dot with half of butter. Layer remaining ingredients. Bake at 300° for 45 to 50 minutes. Serve warm. Yield: 6 to 8 servings. *Mary Evelyn Hollaway, Hanceville, Alabama.*

TART CRANBERRY SAUCE

4 cups fresh cranberries
¼ cup water
2 apples, unpeeled and chopped
½ teaspoon ground cloves
1 teaspoon ground cinnamon
½ teaspoon ground ginger
1 cup honey

Cook cranberries in water about 8 minutes until berry skins start to pop. Add apples; cook 5 minutes or until apples are tender. Stir in spices and honey. Serve warm or cold with turkey or ham. Yield: about 3½ cups.
Connie Burgess, Knoxville, Tennessee.

SPICED WINTER FRUIT

1 (17-ounce) can apricot halves, drained
1 (16-ounce) can pear halves, drained
1 (16-ounce) can peach slices, drained
1 (15¼-ounce) can pineapple chunks, drained
1 (15-ounce) jar applesauce
¼ cup sherry
½ teaspoon ground cinnamon
⅛ teaspoon ground nutmeg
2 tablespoons butter or margarine

Arrange the first 4 ingredients in layers in an ungreased 3-quart baking dish; set aside.

Pour applesauce in a small saucepan; cook, uncovered, for 5 minutes. Stir in sherry, cinnamon, and nutmeg; pour over fruit. Dot with butter. Bake at 325° for 1 hour. Yield: 8 servings.

Rebecca Conkling,
Northville, Michigan.

Festive Entrées For Any Size Party

Whether you've invited 4 or 20 for a dinner celebration, you'll want a special entrée just suited for the number of guests you plan to serve. Recipes here vary in the number of servings they offer, so you'll be able to find just the right entrée for your party.

TOURNEDOS MOUTON

2 to 3 large tomatoes
About ¼ cup all-purpose flour
About ¼ cup milk
About ¼ cup dry breadcrumbs
¼ cup vegetable oil
1 cup dry vermouth
1 pound lobster meat, cut into 8 (2-ounce) medallions
3 pounds beef tenderloin, cut into 8 (¾-inch-thick) steaks
¼ teaspoon paprika
Salt and white pepper to taste
Bordelaise Sauce
Creolaise Sauce

Cut tomatoes into eight ½-inch slices. Dredge tomatoes in flour; dip in milk, and roll in breadcrumbs.

Heat oil in a medium skillet over medium heat; add tomatoes, and fry until golden brown, turning once. Drain and set tomatoes aside.

Heat vermouth in skillet over medium heat. Add lobster and simmer about 5 minutes, turning once; drain.

Place steaks over hot coals; grill 4 to 5 minutes on each side or until desired degree of doneness. Sprinkle with paprika, salt, and pepper.

Place a steak on each of the fried tomato slices; top with a lobster medallion. Serve with Bordelaise Sauce and Creolaise Sauce. Yield: 8 servings.

Bordelaise Sauce:

2 tablespoons butter
2 tablespoons all-purpose flour
1 tablespoon minced onion
1 tablespoon minced fresh parsley
1 bay leaf
¼ teaspoon dried whole thyme
¼ teaspoon salt
⅛ teaspoon coarsely ground black pepper
1⅓ cups beef broth
¼ cup dry red wine

Melt butter in a heavy saucepan over low heat; add flour and cook 1 minute until flour is lightly browned, stirring often. Add next 6 ingredients, stirring constantly. Gradually add beef broth and wine, stirring well; cook over medium-high heat, stirring constantly, until thickened and bubbly. Remove bay leaf. Yield: 1⅓ cups.

Creolaise Sauce:

About 1¼ cups butter
8 egg yolks
1 tablespoon water
Juice of 1 lemon
⅓ cup Creole-style mustard
3 dashes of hot sauce

Melt butter over low heat; let stand until milk solids settle to bottom. Skim off white froth on surface. Pour off clear, yellow liquid, leaving sediment in pan. Set aside 1 cup clarified butter.

Combine egg yolks and water in top of a double boiler; beat with a wire whisk until blended. Cook over warm water, stirring constantly, until thick

and opaque. Remove top of double boiler, and set in pan of cold water to stop cooking process. Gradually add clarified butter, stirring constantly; then stir in the lemon juice, mustard, and hot sauce. Yield: about 1½ cups.

SPICY MARINATED BEEF TENDERLOIN

4 cloves garlic, crushed
1 teaspoon salt
1 teaspoon pepper
½ teaspoon hot sauce
1 cup soy sauce
½ cup olive oil
1 cup port wine
1 teaspoon dried whole thyme
1 bay leaf
1 (5- to 6-pound) beef tenderloin, trimmed

Combine first 9 ingredients; mix well. Place tenderloin in a large shallow dish; pour the wine mixture over top, and cover tightly. Refrigerate overnight, turning occasionally.

Uncover tenderloin; drain off marinade, reserving marinade. Place tenderloin on a rack in a baking pan; insert meat thermometer. Bake at 425° for 45 to 60 minutes until meat thermometer registers 140°, basting occasionally with marinade. Yield: 15 to 18 servings.

Note: Bake tenderloin to an internal temperature of 150° for medium-rare and to 160° for medium.

Loy Witherspoon,
Charlotte, North Carolina.

COUNTRY-FRIED VENISON STEAK

2 pounds (½-inch-thick) venison steak
2 teaspoons Worcestershire sauce
1 quart milk
Salt and pepper
¾ cup all-purpose flour
Vegetable oil
1 medium onion, chopped
2 tablespoons all-purpose flour
1 (10¾-ounce) can cream of mushroom soup, undiluted
Hot cooked rice

Trim all fat and remove connective tissues from venison. Cut meat into serving-size pieces, and pound each piece to ¼-inch thickness. Sprinkle with Worcestershire sauce.

Place meat in a shallow 2-quart container. Pour milk over meat; refrigerate for 2 hours.

Remove meat from milk, reserving milk. Salt and pepper meat; dredge in ¾ cup flour.

Cook venison in ½-inch hot oil in an extra large skillet or 2 skillets until it is lightly browned on both sides. Remove from skillet; set aside.

Drain off oil, reserving 2 tablespoons oil in skillet. Add onion to skillet, and sauté until tender. Stir in 2 tablespoons flour, and cook until flour is lightly browned. Add milk to flour mixture, and stir until smooth. Add soup, stirring well. Place venison in soup mixture, and cook over low heat 1 hour. (Water may be added to gravy to prevent scorching, if necessary.) Serve with hot cooked rice. Yield: 6 servings. *Fred Curlin, Statesboro, Georgia.*

STUFFED CROWN PORK FLAMBE

1 (14-rib) crown roast of pork
Salt and pepper
3 green onions and tops, sliced
¼ cup butter or margarine
4 large fresh mushrooms, sliced
2 cooking apples, peeled and diced
3 cups herb-seasoned stuffing mix
1 cup applesauce
3 tablespoons brandy
1 (10-ounce) jar apricot preserves
¼ cup brandy
1 (9-ounce) jar sweet pickled kumquats, drained
¼ cup brandy

Sprinkle roast on all sides with salt and pepper; place, bone ends up, on a rack in a shallow roasting pan. Insert meat thermometer, making sure it does not touch fat or bone.

Sauté onion in butter until tender but not browned. Add mushrooms; cook, stirring constantly, until tender. Add apples; cook, stirring constantly, 1 minute. Stir in stuffing mix, applesauce, and 3 tablespoons brandy; spoon into center

of roast. Cover stuffing and exposed ends of ribs with aluminum foil.

Heat preserves and ¼ cup brandy; set ¼ cup mixture aside. Bake crown roast at 325° for 35 to 40 minutes per pound or until meat thermometer registers 170°, basting every 10 minutes after first hour with brandy mixture.

Remove from oven, and let stand 15 minutes; place on serving platter. Garnish bone tips with kumquats. Heat reserved ¼ cup preserves mixture, pour ¼ cup brandy over heated mixture. Ignite and pour over roast. Yield: 10 servings. *Virginia B. Stalder, Nokesville, Virginia.*

FESTIVE BAKED HAM

1 cup apple cider
½ cup water
1 (5-pound) uncooked ham half
12 whole cloves
1 cup firmly packed brown sugar
1 (21-ounce) can cherry pie filling
½ cup raisins
½ cup orange juice

Combine apple cider and water in a saucepan; bring to a boil. Set aside.

Remove skin from ham. Place ham, fat side up, on a cutting board; score fat in a diamond design, and stud with cloves. Place ham in a shallow baking pan, fat side up; coat top with brown sugar. Insert meat thermometer, making sure it does not touch fat or bone. Bake, uncovered, at 325° about 2 hours (22 to 25 minutes per pound) or until meat thermometer registers 160°, basting every 30 minutes with cider mixture.

Combine remaining ingredients in a saucepan; bring to a boil. Serve sauce with sliced ham. Yield: 10 servings.
Rena Mae Gardner, Dover, North Carolina.

CIDER BAKED TURKEY

1 (5- to 5½-pound) turkey breast
1½ cups apple cider
¼ cup soy sauce
½ cup apple cider
2 tablespoons cornstarch

Place turkey breast skin side up in a large roasting pan; bake at 450° for 30 minutes or until skin is crisp.

Combine 1½ cups cider with soy sauce, and pour over turkey. Insert meat thermometer in meaty portion of breast, making sure it does not touch bone. Cover and bake at 325° about 1½ to 2 hours until meat thermometer registers 185°; baste turkey frequently with the cider mixture.

Combine ½ cup cider and cornstarch, mixing well; stir into pan drippings. Return to oven and bake, uncovered, until sauce is thickened. Transfer turkey to serving platter; serve with sauce. Yield: 12 to 16 servings. *Ella Brown, Proctor, Arkansas.*

COMPANY CORNISH HENS

2 small onions, chopped
2 stalks celery, chopped
1 small green pepper, chopped
4 (1- to 1½-pound) Cornish hens
Salt and pepper
¼ cup bacon drippings
1 (10¾-ounce) can chicken broth, undiluted
¼ cup Burgundy or other dry red wine
¼ cup chopped green onion
¼ cup chopped fresh parsley
1 (4-ounce) can sliced mushrooms, drained
Hot brown rice

Combine onion, celery, and green pepper; set aside.

Remove giblets from hens; reserve for another use. Rinse hens with cold water and pat dry; sprinkle with salt and pepper. Stuff hens lightly with vegetable mixture. Close cavities, truss, and secure with wooden picks.

Heat bacon drippings in a heavy skillet; brown hens on both sides. Remove hens and place, breast side up, in a 13-x 9- x 2-inch baking pan.

Add chicken broth and wine to skillet; simmer 5 minutes. Sprinkle green onion, parsley, and mushrooms over hens. Pour broth and wine mixture into baking pan. Bake at 325° for 1 hour and 30 minutes, basting every 15 minutes with pan drippings. Serve over rice. Yield: 4 servings. *Margaret Paul, Lafayette, Louisiana.*

FRUITED CHICKEN EN CREME

2 tablespoons butter or margarine
6 chicken breast halves
1 (10¾-ounce) can cream of chicken soup, undiluted
1 (15¼-ounce) can pineapple tidbits, drained
1 (6-ounce) can sliced mushrooms, drained
½ cup sliced seedless green grapes
½ cup half-and-half
¼ cup dry sherry

Melt butter in a 13- x 9- x 2-inch baking dish. Place chicken in dish and bake, uncovered, at 350° for 45 minutes. Drain off excess liquid.

Combine remaining ingredients, stirring well. Spoon mixture over chicken; cover baking dish with aluminum foil. Bake 15 to 20 minutes. Yield: 6 servings. *Dorothy Jones, Evergreen, Alabama.*

What Wine To Serve With The Entrée? Some Suggestions

Over the past several years, the South has seen a significant growth of interest in fine wines, and along with that interest come questions about what wine to serve with what food. As wine appreciation has grown in the region, the selection of wine, both domestic and imported, has expanded. It helps to have some sound basis for picking a particular wine for a certain menu.

Much has been written about classic food and wine combinations, but in the final analysis, the "correct" match is one that enhances both the food and the wine. We have taken the entrées presented in "Festive Entrées for Any Size Party" (page 262) and suggested wines to serve with each. Some are very reasonable in price; others are more expensive. Most of these selections, or something equivalent, should be available wherever wine is sold.

Here are the suggestions and the reasons why they suit the dish:

Tournedos Mouton: For such a rich and elegant dish, the cost of the wine should not be a prime consideration. A fine Châteauneuf-du-Pape from France's warm Rhône Valley would have the strength of character to stand up to the richness of the beef/lobster and the spiciness of the paprika. Dig deep into the ole pocketbook and buy a bottle or two of the 1979 Châteauneuf-du-Pape "La Bernadine" from Chapoutier. A much less expensive, but viable, alternative is the good, full-bodied 1977 Inglenook Charbono.

Spicy Marinated Beef Tenderloin: Rich, marinated beef usually overpowers a red Bordeaux and requires a heavier, fruitier wine such as a California Cabernet Sauvignon. A very nice, fairly priced, new entry on the market is Gallo's Cabernet-Limited Release.

Choosing something in a little higher price category, the 1980 Beaulieu Vineyards (BV) Cabernet Beautour would be excellent to counterbalance the spicy richness of this entrée. If the occasion calls for a truly special wine, then you might try the 1980 Robert Mondavi Cabernet Sauvignon.

Country-Fried Venison Steak: The wild taste of the venison needs to be tamed by what wine people call a "big" red wine, i.e. one that has power, deep fruit, and plenty of staying power on the palate. On the less expensive side, the very good, deeply flavored 1980 Almadén Cabernet Sauvignon would work well. Or give the excellent 1978 Charles Krug Cabernet Sauvignon a try. But a very good Rhône would probably be the best choice with this dish. If you don't need to buy too many bottles (it's fairly expensive), choose a luscious, full and peppery 1978/79 Hermitage "La Sizeranne" from the house of Chapoutier.

Stuffed Crown Pork Flambé: When served cool (15 or 20 minutes in the refrigerator), the natural berry-like hint of sweetness of California Zinfandel is always a good complement to the relatively sweet meat of pork. A 1980/81 bottling of Parducci or Martini Zinfandel would be ideal to highlight this pork dish. (For larger get-togethers, you might try Sebastiani's flavorful Country

Zinfandel in the 1.5-liter size, which would be very economical and quite suitable.)

If your taste runs to rosé, you may prefer to try a chilled bottle of the fresh, fruity, and dry 1982 Pedroncelli or Concannon Zinfandel Rosé. (All of the red wines mentioned should be served at about 70°.)

Festive Baked Ham: The classic choice with the sweetness of ham is a dry, full-bodied Alsatian Gewürztraminer. (It is hard to beat chilled 1981 Trimbach Gewürztraminer.) Also appropriate would be the dry, fresh, and nicely made 1982 Sebastiani Chenin Blanc, which, when served well chilled, would bring out the sweetness of the ham. If you really just have to have a red to help warm your bones, then select a blended, lighter styled, simpler one like the 1980/81 Parducci Burgundy.

Cider Baked Turkey: Lighter Zinfandels, French Beaujolais, and especially red Bordeaux wines go well with apple-flavored dishes. And since Bordeaux wine and turkey complement each other so well, this entrée seems to beg for a high quality Bordeaux like the 1978/79 Château Larose-Trintaudon or the 1978/79 Château Greysac.

The most appropriate white wine that comes to mind is California Chardonnay with its characteristic fruity suggestion of sweetness (though the wines are dry). A good value is the dry, but nicely fruity, 1981 Almadén Chardonnay. A French Chardonnay from the Mâconnais region of Burgundy, the 1982 Mâcon-Lugny "Les Charmes," has the creamy richness and apple-like freshness that would enhance the flavors of this Cider Baked Turkey.

Company Cornish Hens: The slightly rich, gamey flavor of Cornish hen seems to require the dry, earthy fruitiness of an excellent French Beaujolais, such as a 1981/82 Beaujolais-Villages from an outstanding producer like Jadot or Louis Latour. But a white might do just as well. Try a deeply fruity California Chardonnay—served not too cold—like the rich, and full-flavored 1981 Robert Mondavi Chardonnay.

Fruited Chicken en Crème: This dish calls for a white wine with just a hint of fruit sweetness to it. The traditionally styled drier 1981/82 Martini Riesling might be just the right wine. Because it is a little bit sweeter than the Martini, the 1982 Beringer Chenin Blanc would perhaps be a better foil for the pineapple in the recipe.

Showy Vegetable Soufflés

Add flair to your holiday dinner by serving the vegetables in a steaming, puffy soufflé. You can make a grand presentation by seating guests at the table before removing your airy creation from the oven. This way the soufflé is sampled at its very best—before it has a chance to shrink or fall.

All of these high risers are baked in straight-sided soufflé dishes. Several of the mixtures will need extra support as they rise, so we've included instructions for adding aluminum foil collars.

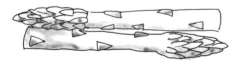

ASPARAGUS SOUFFLE

¼ cup butter or margarine
¼ cup all-purpose flour
1 cup milk
¼ teaspoon salt
¼ teaspoon dry mustard
⅛ teaspoon red pepper
1 cup (4 ounces) shredded sharp Cheddar cheese
1 (10½-ounce) can cut asparagus, drained and chopped
4 eggs, separated

Cut a piece of aluminum foil long enough to fit around a 1½-quart soufflé dish, allowing a 1-inch overlap; fold foil lengthwise into thirds. Lightly oil one side of foil and bottom of dish; wrap foil around dish, oiled side against dish, allowing it to extend 3 inches above rim to form a collar. Secure foil with string.

Melt butter in a heavy saucepan over low heat; add flour, stirring until smooth. Cook 1 minute, stirring constantly. Gradually add milk; cook over medium heat, stirring constantly, until thickened and bubbly. Add salt, dry mustard, red pepper, and cheese; stir until cheese melts. Stir in asparagus, mixing well.

Beat egg yolks until thick and lemon colored. Gradually stir about one-fourth of hot sauce mixture into yolks; add to remaining sauce, stirring well.

Beat egg whites (at room temperature) until stiff but not dry. Gently fold into asparagus mixture. Spoon into prepared soufflé dish. Bake at 350° for 45 minutes or until puffed and golden. Serve immediately. Yield: 6 servings.
Lisa B. Rabon,
Orangeburg, South Carolina.

CARROT SOUFFLE

1 cup mashed, cooked carrot
½ cup firmly packed brown sugar
¾ teaspoon ground ginger
¾ teaspoon ground cinnamon
¼ teaspoon salt
¼ teaspoon mace
1 teaspoon vanilla extract
3 tablespoons butter or margarine
3 tablespoons all-purpose flour
¾ cup milk
4 eggs, separated

Cut a piece of aluminum foil long enough to fit around a 1½-quart soufflé dish, allowing a 1-inch overlap; fold foil lengthwise into thirds. Lightly oil one side of foil and bottom of dish; wrap foil around dish, oiled side against dish, allowing it to extend 3 inches above rim to form a collar. Secure foil with string.

Combine first 7 ingredients; mix well, and set aside.

Melt butter in a heavy saucepan over low heat; add flour, stirring until smooth. Cook 1 minute, stirring constantly. Gradually add milk; cook over medium heat, stirring constantly, until sauce is thickened and bubbly.

Beat egg yolks until thick and lemon colored. Gradually stir about one-fourth of hot white sauce into yolks; add to remaining sauce, stirring constantly. Stir in carrot mixture.

Beat egg whites (at room temperature) until stiff but not dry. Gently fold into carrot mixture. Spoon into prepared soufflé dish. Bake at 350° for 45 to 50 minutes or until puffed and set. Serve immediately. Yield: 6 servings.
Margaret Bishop,
La Grange, Georgia.

ZUCCHINI-AND-CORN SOUFFLE

3 cups shredded zucchini
1 teaspoon salt
¼ cup chopped green onion
¼ cup plus 2 tablespoons butter or margarine, divided
¼ cup plus 2 tablespoons all-purpose flour
1¼ cups milk
1 teaspoon salt
¼ teaspoon pepper
6 eggs, separated
1 (8¾-ounce) can cream-style corn
½ cup (2 ounces) shredded Swiss cheese

Lightly grease bottom of a 2½-quart soufflé dish.

Combine zucchini and 1 teaspoon salt; let stand 5 minutes. Drain zucchini in a colander; place on paper towels and press dry.

Sauté zucchini and onion in 1 tablespoon butter until the onion is tender; set aside.

Melt ¼ cup plus 1 tablespoon butter in a heavy saucepan over low heat; add flour, stirring until smooth. Cook 1 minute, stirring constantly. Gradually add milk; cook over medium heat, stirring constantly, until thickened and bubbly. Stir in salt and pepper.

Beat egg yolks until thick and lemon colored. Gradually stir about one-fourth of hot white sauce into yolks; add to remaining sauce. Stir in zucchini mixture, corn, and cheese.

Beat egg whites (at room temperature) until stiff but not dry. Gently fold into vegetable mixture. Spoon into prepared soufflé dish. Bake at 350° for 55 to 60 minutes or until puffed and golden. Serve immediately. Yield: 8 servings.
Mrs. Robert H. Kirk,
Winchester, Virginia.

BUTTERNUT SOUFFLE

3 eggs, separated
2½ cups mashed, cooked butternut or
  cushaw squash
½ cup milk
¼ cup butter or margarine, melted
½ teaspoon salt
1 teaspoon grated lemon rind
½ cup raisins
3 tablespoons brown sugar

Lightly grease bottom of a 2-quart soufflé dish.

Beat egg yolks until thick and lemon colored. Mix in next 6 ingredients.

Beat egg whites (at room temperature) until foamy; gradually add sugar, one tablespoon at a time, beating until stiff peaks form. Gently fold into squash mixture. Spoon into prepared soufflé dish. Bake at 350° for 1 hour or until puffed and lightly browned. Serve immediately. Yield: 8 servings.
Nelda Albright,
New Caney, Texas.

GOLDEN PARSNIP SOUFFLE

4 cups cubed parsnips
2 tablespoons butter or margarine
1 tablespoon brown sugar
2 tablespoons chopped green onion
¼ teaspoon salt
½ teaspoon grated lemon rind
⅛ teaspoon ground nutmeg
3 large eggs, separated
Paprika (optional)

Lightly grease bottom of a 1½-quart soufflé dish.

Cook parsnips in boiling water to cover 15 to 20 minutes or until tender; drain well. Place parsnips in container of electric blender or food processor; process until smooth. Add next 6 ingredients, and process 15 seconds or until blended.

Beat egg yolks until thick and lemon colored; add to parsnip mixture.

Beat egg whites (at room temperature) until stiff but not dry. Gently fold into parsnip mixture. Spoon into soufflé dish. Bake at 350° for 30 to 35 minutes or until puffed and golden. Sprinkle with paprika, if desired. Serve immediately. Yield: 6 servings. *Clarissa Wells,*
Lancaster, Ohio.

Easy Menus For Casual Parties

Seasonal entertaining doesn't have to be fancy—some of the best meals shared with friends are simple and easy to fix. In our menu featuring Quick Pizza Casserole, you can prepare Sweet-and-Sour Marinated Vegetables ahead of time. While the entrée and bread bake, mix up honey-flavored ambrosia for dessert.

If soup-and-sandwich meals are more your style, you'll enjoy our pita bread sandwiches filled with roast beef and vegetables. They're accompanied by Creamy Tomato Soup made from tomato juice. Garnish each plate with some fresh fruit, such as apple wedges or grapes. Then top off the meal with a slice of Apricot Brandy Pound Cake.

You'll find recipes for our menu suggestions below. Select your favorite, and plan your next casual get-together for this holiday season.

Quick Pizza Casserole
Sweet-and-Sour Marinated Vegetables
Toasted Onion-Herb Bread
Honey Bee Ambrosia
Iced Tea

QUICK PIZZA CASSEROLE

1 pound ground beef
1 (14-ounce) jar pizza sauce
2 cups (8 ounces) shredded mozzarella
  cheese
¾ cup biscuit mix
1½ cups milk
2 eggs

Cook ground beef in a skillet over medium heat until browned, stirring to crumble. Drain off pan drippings. Spoon beef into an 8-inch square baking dish. Top with pizza sauce and cheese.

Combine biscuit mix, milk, and eggs; beat until smooth. Pour mixture over casserole, covering evenly. Bake at 400° for 30 to 35 minutes. Yield: 6 servings. *Sarah T. Helms,*
Lynchburg, Virginia.

SWEET-AND-SOUR MARINATED VEGETABLES

1 (1-pound) bunch fresh broccoli
1½ cups cauliflower flowerets
½ pound fresh mushrooms, cut in half
1 bunch green onions, chopped
½ cup sugar
½ cup vegetable oil
2 tablespoons vinegar
1 teaspoon celery seeds
¾ teaspoon salt
1 teaspoon paprika
2 tablespoons minced green onion
Dash of garlic powder

Trim off large leaves of broccoli. Remove tough ends of lower stalks, and wash broccoli thoroughly. Cut flowerets and stems into bite-size pieces. Combine broccoli and next 3 ingredients in a shallow dish.

Combine remaining ingredients in a jar. Cover tightly, and shake vigorously; pour marinade over vegetables. Cover vegetables and chill at least 3 hours. Yield: 6 servings. *Pat Norton,*
Wexford, Pennsylvania.

TOASTED ONION-HERB BREAD

1 clove garlic, minced
1 teaspoon minced celery
½ cup butter or margarine
1 (14-ounce) loaf unsliced French bread
½ teaspoon dried Italian seasoning
½ teaspoon instant minced onion

Sauté garlic and celery in butter until tender. Cut bread into 1-inch slices; place on a baking sheet. Brush butter mixture over top of bread slices; sprinkle with Italian seasoning and onion.

Cover with aluminum foil; bake at 400° for 10 to 15 minutes or until well heated. Yield: 1 loaf.
Mrs. Guy Curtis Palmer,
Wagoner, Oklahoma.

Tip: Get in the habit of grocery shopping with a list. Watch newspapers for advertised "specials"; then plan a week's menus around bargains in foods the family enjoys.

HONEY BEE AMBROSIA

**4 medium oranges, peeled and sliced
  crosswise
3 bananas, sliced
½ cup orange juice
¼ cup honey
2 tablespoons lemon juice
¼ cup flaked coconut
Maraschino cherry halves (optional)**

Combine fruit in a medium bowl, tossing lightly. Combine orange juice, honey, and lemon juice; pour over fruit, and mix well. Sprinkle with coconut; cover and chill at least 1 hour. Garnish with maraschino cherries, if desired. Yield: 6 servings.   *Carol S. Noble,
Burgaw, North Carolina.*

**Beef Salad Pocket Sandwiches
Creamy Tomato Soup
Fresh Fruit
Apricot Brandy Pound Cake
Iced Tea or Coffee**

BEEF SALAD POCKET SANDWICHES

**1¼ cups shredded lettuce
½ cup (2 ounces) shredded fresh
  spinach
6 Greek olives, pitted and sliced
1 green onion, chopped
1 radish, sliced
3 tablespoons commercial Italian salad
  dressing
1 (3-ounce) package cream cheese,
  softened
3 (6-inch) pita bread rounds, cut
  in half
6 ounces thinly sliced roast beef,
  chopped**

Combine first 6 ingredients; toss gently to coat. Let stand 5 minutes.

Spread about 1½ tablespoons cream cheese inside each bread half; fill each with equal portions of roast beef and salad mixture. Yield: 6 servings.
*Nancy Eisele,
Valrico, Florida.*

CREAMY TOMATO SOUP

**¼ cup minced onion
3 tablespoons butter or margarine
3 tablespoons all-purpose flour
¾ teaspoon salt
¼ teaspoon pepper
1 cup milk
4 cups tomato juice
1 small bay leaf
Minced fresh parsley**

Sauté onion in butter in a large saucepan until tender. Add flour, salt, and pepper, stirring until smooth. Cook 1 minute, stirring constantly. Gradually add milk and tomato juice; cook over medium heat, stirring constantly, until thickened and bubbly. Add bay leaf; simmer 1 minute. Remove bay leaf. Garnish with parsley. Yield: 5½ cups.
*Hazel Slucher,
Taylorsville, Kentucky.*

APRICOT BRANDY POUND CAKE

**1 cup butter or margarine, softened
3 cups sugar
6 eggs
3 cups all-purpose flour
¼ teaspoon baking soda
½ teaspoon salt
1 (8-ounce) carton commercial sour cream
½ cup apricot brandy
1 teaspoon orange extract
1 teaspoon vanilla extract
½ teaspoon lemon extract
½ teaspoon rum extract
¼ teaspoon almond extract**

Cream butter; gradually add sugar, beating until mixture is light and fluffy. Add eggs, one at a time, beating well after each addition.

Combine flour, soda, and salt; mix well. Combine sour cream, brandy, and flavorings. Add to creamed mixture alternately with flour mixture, beginning and ending with flour mixture.

Pour batter into a greased and floured 10-inch tube pan. Bake at 325° for 1 hour and 20 minutes or until cake tests done. Cool in pan 10 to 15 minutes; remove from pan, and cool completely. Yield: one 10-inch cake.
*Gail Thompson,
Brundidge, Alabama.*

Well-Stuffed
Holiday Birds

These moist birds and their flavorful stuffings will rival turkey and cornbread dressing for the most important spot on your holiday menu.

ORANGE-GLAZED
CORNISH HENS

**1 (5-ounce) package brown and wild
  rice mix
1 small onion, chopped
2 stalks celery, chopped
1 tablespoon butter or margarine
⅛ teaspoon poultry seasoning
4 (1¼-pound) Cornish hens
Salt
Melted butter or margarine
Orange glaze (recipe follows)
Hot cooked brown and wild rice
Orange twists**

Prepare brown and wild rice mix according to package directions; set aside. Sauté onion and celery in 1 tablespoon butter until tender. Combine vegetables, rice, and poultry seasoning.

Remove giblets from hens, and reserve for use in another recipe. Rinse hens with cold water, and pat dry; sprinkle cavities with salt. Stuff hens lightly with rice mixture. Close cavities, and secure with wooden picks; truss. Place hens breast side up in a shallow baking pan; brush with melted butter. Bake at 375° for 1½ hours, basting occasionally with butter. Spoon orange glaze over hens, and bake 5 minutes. Serve over rice and garnish with orange twists. Yield: 4 servings.

Orange Glaze:

**¼ cup sugar
½ cup orange juice
½ teaspoon grated orange rind
1 tablespoon butter or margarine
1½ teaspoons lemon juice**

Combine first 3 ingredients in a small saucepan; bring to a boil. Remove from heat; add butter and lemon juice. Yield: ⅔ cup.   *Gwyn Warren,
Clarksville, Texas.*

ROAST CHICKEN AND BROWN RICE

½ cup chopped celery
¼ cup chopped onion
2 tablespoons butter or margarine
½ cup uncooked brown rice, cooked
1 tablespoon commercial blue cheese salad
  dressing mix
1 tablespoon dried parsley flakes
1 (3½-pound) broiler-fryer
¼ teaspoon salt
2 tablespoons butter or margarine,
  melted
¼ teaspoon paprika

Sauté celery and onion in 2 tablespoons melted butter until tender. Combine rice, vegetables, dressing mix, and parsley, stirring well.

Reserve chicken giblets for other use. Rinse chicken with cold water, and pat dry; sprinkle cavity with salt. Fold neck skin over back; secure with a wooden pick. Lift wingtips up and over back, and tuck under chicken. Stuff cavity with rice mixture. Close cavity and secure with wooden picks; truss chicken.

Combine 2 tablespoons melted butter and paprika; brush over chicken. Place chicken in a large oven browning bag; seal bag according to package directions, cutting slits in top of bag. Place bag in a 13- x 9- x 2-inch baking pan; bake at 350° for 1½ hours or until drumsticks are easy to move. Remove to platter. Yield: 4 to 6 servings.

Ada O. Starkey,
Porter, Oklahoma.

Combine first 3 ingredients; let stand 2 minutes. Drain. Add next 9 ingredients; stir well. Stuff cavity of goose with fruit mixture; close cavity with skewers, and fold neck skin over back. Truss goose. Place goose, breast side up, on rack in a shallow roasting pan; insert meat thermometer in breast or meaty part of thigh, making sure it does not touch bone. Bake, uncovered, at 350° for 3 to 3½ hours or until meat thermometer registers 190°. Transfer goose to serving platter. Let stand 15 minutes before carving. Yield: 6 to 8 servings.

Note: Leftover stuffing may be placed in a lightly greased baking dish. Cover and bake at 350° for 25 minutes. Uncover and bake 10 to 15 minutes.

Kathleen Stone,
Houston, Texas.

Sweet Finales—Both Old And New

When it's the season for traditions, many of them take the form of delicious desserts. An old-fashioned Lane Cake is a traditional way to greet your guests. This pretty cake is filled and topped with a fruit-and-nut mixture while the sides are swirled with fluffy white frosting for a holiday touch.

FRUIT- AND PECAN-STUFFED GOOSE

1½ cups chopped prunes
¾ cup chopped dried apricots
2½ cups boiling water
6 cups stale bread cubes
2 cups peeled, diced apple
¾ cup peeled, seeded, and diced orange
½ cup raisins
½ cup chopped pecans
½ cup orange juice
¼ cup butter or margarine, melted
1 teaspoon salt
½ teaspoon poultry seasoning
1 (8- to 10-pound) dressed goose

MARASCHINO NUT CAKE

2 cups plus 2 tablespoons sifted
  all-purpose flour
1⅓ cups sugar
1 tablespoon baking powder
½ teaspoon salt
½ cup shortening
¼ cup maraschino cherry juice
16 maraschino cherries, cut into
  eighths
½ cup milk
4 egg whites
½ cup chopped pecans
White Frosting

Combine first 4 ingredients in a mixing bowl; mix well. Add next 4 ingredients; beat at low speed of electric mixer 2 minutes or until well blended. Add egg whites (at room temperature); beat at medium speed 2 minutes. Stir in chopped pecans.

Pour batter into 2 greased and floured 8-inch round cakepans. Bake at 350° for 35 minutes or until a wooden pick inserted in center comes out clean. Cool in pans 10 minutes; remove from pans, and cool completely on wire racks. Spread White Frosting between layers and on top and sides of cake. Yield: one 2-layer cake.

White Frosting:

1¼ cups light corn syrup
2 egg whites
Dash of salt
1 teaspoon vanilla extract

Bring syrup to a boil.

Combine egg whites and salt in a large mixing bowl. Beat egg whites (at room temperature) until soft peaks form; continue beating, slowly adding syrup. Add vanilla; continue to beat until stiff peaks form and frosting is thick enough to spread. Yield: enough for one 2-layer cake. *Peggy McEwen,*
Columbiana, Alabama.

JAPANESE FRUITCAKE

1 cup butter or margarine, softened
2 cups sugar
5 eggs
3 cups all-purpose flour
2 teaspoons baking powder
¼ teaspoon salt
1 cup milk
1 cup raisins
1 cup chopped pecans
1 teaspoon ground cinnamon
½ teaspoon ground allspice
½ teaspoon ground cloves
Filling (recipe follows)
Pecan halves (optional)
Candied cherries (optional)

Cream butter; gradually add sugar, beating well. Add eggs, one at a time, beating well after each addition.

Combine flour, baking powder, and salt; add to creamed mixture alternately with milk, beginning and ending with flour mixture. Mix well after each addition. Stir in raisins and pecans.

Pour 2 cups plus 2 tablespoons batter into a greased and floured 9-inch round cakepan; set aside.

Stir spices into remaining batter; pour into 2 greased and floured 9-inch round cakepans.

Bake at 375° for 25 minutes or until wooden pick inserted in center comes out clean. Cool in pans 10 minutes; remove from pans, and cool completely.

Spread filling between layers and on top of cake, stacking layers with white layer between spiced layers. Garnish top with pecan halves and candied cherries, if desired. Yield: one 3-layer cake.

Filling:

1 cup sugar
1 tablespoon all-purpose flour
1 cup water
1½ cups flaked coconut
1 (8-ounce) can crushed pineapple, undrained
2 oranges, peeled, sectioned, and finely chopped

Combine sugar and flour in a small saucepan, mixing well; add water. Cook over medium heat 5 minutes, stirring occasionally. Stir in coconut, pineapple, and oranges. Cook over medium heat 5 minutes. Cool mixture completely before spreading on cake. Yield: enough for one 3-layer cake. *Edna Miles, Columbus, Georgia.*

GATEAU PANACHE

6 egg whites
1½ cups sugar
1½ teaspoons vinegar
½ teaspoon vanilla extract
¾ cup ground pecans
2 cups whipping cream, whipped
2 (1-ounce) squares semisweet chocolate, melted
Chocolate curls (optional)

Draw two 9-inch circles on unglazed brown paper. Cut circles out, and place each in the center of a baking sheet. Grease and flour each circle well.

Beat egg whites (at room temperature) in a medium mixing bowl until soft peaks form; gradually add sugar, beating until stiff peaks form. Do not underbeat the mixture. Fold in the vinegar, vanilla, and ground pecans.

Spoon half of meringue mixture onto each paper circle on baking sheets. Using a spatula, shape meringue into circles about 8 inches in diameter. (Meringue will spread out during baking.)

Bake at 275° for 1 hour. Let meringue cool to touch; remove from paper, and allow the layers to cool completely on wire racks.

Place one meringue layer on a serving platter; spread with half of whipped cream. Drizzle with half of chocolate. Top with remaining meringue layer; repeat procedure with remaining whipped cream and chocolate. Garnish top with chocolate curls, if desired. Chill thoroughly. Yield: 10 to 12 servings.

Note: Handle cooled meringue layers carefully to avoid cracking. *Vi Jensen, Grand Prairie, Texas.*

LANE CAKE

1 cup butter or margarine, softened
2 cups sugar
3¼ cups all-purpose flour
1 tablespoon baking powder
¾ teaspoon salt
1 cup milk
1 teaspoon vanilla extract
8 egg whites, stiffly beaten
Filling (recipe follows)
Frosting (recipe follows)
Pecan halves (optional)

Cream butter; gradually add sugar, beating well. Combine dry ingredients; add to creamed mixture alternately with milk, beginning and ending with flour mixture. Mix well after each addition. Stir in vanilla. Fold in egg whites.

Pour batter into 3 greased and floured 9-inch round cakepans. Bake at 325° for 25 minutes or until a wooden pick inserted in center comes out clean. Cool in pans 10 minutes; remove from pans and cool completely.

Spread filling between layers and on top of cake; spread sides with frosting. Garnish with pecan halves, if desired. Yield: one 3-layer cake.

Filling:

8 egg yolks
1½ cups sugar
½ cup butter or margarine
1 cup chopped pecans
1 cup raisins
1 cup flaked coconut
¼ to ½ cup bourbon
½ cup sliced maraschino cherries

Combine egg yolks, sugar, and butter in a 2-quart saucepan. Cook over medium heat, stirring constantly, about 20 minutes until thickened.

Remove from heat, and stir in remaining ingredients. Cool completely. Yield: enough for one 3-layer cake.

Frosting:

¾ cup sugar
2 tablespoons plus 2 teaspoons water
1 egg white
½ tablespoon light corn syrup
Dash of salt
½ teaspoon vanilla extract

Combine the first 5 ingredients in top of a double boiler; beat 30 seconds at low speed of electric mixer or just until blended.

Place over boiling water; beat constantly on high speed 7 minutes or until stiff peaks form. Remove from heat. Add vanilla; beat an additional 1 minute or until the mixture is thick enough to spread. Yield: enough to cover the sides of one 3-layer cake.

Betty Chason, Tallahassee, Florida.

Tip: Use shiny cookie sheets and cakepans for baking rather than darkened ones. Dark pans absorb more heat and cause baked products to overbrown.

RICH CREAM CHEESECAKE

2 cups graham cracker crumbs
2½ tablespoons sugar
1 teaspoon ground cinnamon
¼ teaspoon ground nutmeg
½ cup butter, melted
3 (8-ounce) packages cream cheese,
    softened
1 cup sugar
2 tablespoons all-purpose flour
⅛ teaspoon salt
5 eggs, separated
1 egg
1½ cups commercial sour cream
¼ cup lemon juice
¼ cup sugar

Combine first 5 ingredients; mixing well. Firmly press mixture into a 9-inch springform pan; chill.

Beat cream cheese with electric mixer until light and fluffy; gradually add 1 cup sugar, mixing well. Add flour and salt. Add 5 egg yolks and 1 whole egg, one at a time, beating well after each addition. Stir in the sour cream and lemon juice; mix well.

Beat egg whites (at room temperature) until foamy. Gradually add ¼ cup sugar, 1 tablespoon at a time, beating until stiff peaks form. Fold egg whites into cream cheese mixture; pour into prepared pan.

Bake at 300° for 1½ hours. Turn oven off, and allow cheesecake to cool in oven 3 hours. Chill cake several hours. Yield: 12 servings.
Lynn R. Koenig,
Charleston, South Carolina.

BERRY-CHERRY COBBLER

¼ cup sugar
1½ tablespoons cornstarch
⅛ teaspoon salt
1 (10-ounce) package frozen raspberries,
    thawed and undrained
1 teaspoon lemon juice
1 (16-ounce) can pitted tart cherries,
    drained
¼ cup butter or margarine, softened
¼ cup sugar
½ cup all-purpose flour
⅛ teaspoon salt
Ice cream (optional)

Combine first 3 ingredients in a saucepan. Stir in raspberries and lemon juice; bring to a boil. Cook 1 minute, stirring constantly. Press the raspberry mixture through a sieve or food mill; discard seeds. Stir drained cherries into the raspberry mixture, and spoon into a lightly greased 1-quart baking dish.

Cream butter and ¼ cup sugar; stir in flour and ⅛ teaspoon salt, blending just until mixture resembles coarse meal. Sprinkle flour mixture over fruit.

Bake at 375° for 30 to 35 minutes or until lightly browned. Serve with ice cream, if desired. Yield: 4 servings.
Mrs. Howard B. Vaughn,
Nashville, Tennessee.

PRALINE CHEESECAKE

1½ cups graham cracker crumbs
3 tablespoons sugar
3 tablespoons butter or margarine, melted
3 (8-ounce) packages cream cheese,
    softened
¾ cup firmly packed brown sugar
2 tablespoons all-purpose flour
3 eggs
2 teaspoons vanilla extract
½ cup finely chopped pecans
Whipped cream (optional)
Pecan halves (optional)

Combine first 3 ingredients, mixing well. Press mixture into a 9-inch springform pan. Bake at 350° for 10 minutes.

Beat cream cheese until smooth; gradually add brown sugar and flour, mixing well. Add eggs, one at a time, beating well after each addition. Stir in vanilla and pecans. Pour into prepared pan. Bake at 350° for 40 to 45 minutes. Let cool to room temperature on a wire rack; refrigerate overnight.

Remove sides of springform pan; top cheesecake with whipped cream and pecan halves, if desired. Yield: 10 to 12 servings.
Carol Dicken,
Greenville, Texas.

FROSTED ORANGES

6 large navel oranges
1 quart vanilla ice cream, slightly
    softened
2 tablespoons amaretto or other
    almond-flavored liqueur
4 egg whites
½ cup sugar

Cut a thin slice off bottom of each orange so it will sit flat. Cut a ¾-inch slice from top of each orange. Clip membranes inside orange shells, and carefully remove pulp; reserve pulp for use in other recipes. Spoon ice cream into orange shells. Make an indentation in top of ice cream with back of spoon; carefully pour 1 teaspoon of amaretto into each indentation. Freeze about 4 hours or until ice cream is firm.

Beat egg whites (at room temperature) until foamy. Gradually add sugar, 1 tablespoon at a time, beating until stiff peaks form. Spread meringue over ice cream, sealing to edge of shells. Bake at 450° for 2 to 3 minutes or until lightly browned. Serve immediately. Yield: 6 servings.
Dianne Roberts,
Jacksonville, Florida.

Right: At your next party, offer your guests something different, like this pretty Caviar Mousse (page 258) or Hot Swiss Canapés (page 259).

Page 274: Lane Cake (page 269) is filled and topped with a bourbon-flavored mixture of coconut, pecans, raisins, and maraschino cherries.

Right: *Canned peaches, pears, pineapple, and cherries are sweetened with brown sugar and spiced with curry to make Almond-Curried Fruit (page 261).*

Far right: *Our recipe for Company Cornish Hens (page 263) is an excellent choice for a dinner for four. The hens are basted in a wine mixture and served with brown rice.*

Below: *Holiday menus deserve extra attention, and Italian Dinner Rolls (page 254) can add just the right touch.*

Below right: *Easy Corn Relish and Cabbage Relish are welcome additions to any holiday menu (recipes on page 260).*

Make These Beverages A Tradition

A special occasion is usually celebrated with a special beverage. Our holiday beverages are sure to become traditions in your home.

PINEAPPLE-APRICOT WASSAIL

1 quart pineapple juice
1 quart apple cider
1 (12-ounce) can apricot nectar
1 cup orange juice
2 (3-inch) sticks cinnamon
2 teaspoons whole cloves
1 teaspoon ground nutmeg

Combine all ingredients in a Dutch oven; bring to a boil. Reduce heat and simmer, uncovered, 30 minutes. Strain and discard the spices. Serve hot. Yield: 2½ quarts. *Mrs. Robert H. Kirk, Winchester, Virginia.*

CHRISTMAS FRUIT TEA

2 quarts cranberry juice
1 (46-ounce) can pineapple juice
1 (6-ounce) can frozen lemonade
   concentrate, thawed and undiluted
2 cups apple juice
1 cup orange juice
4 (3-inch) sticks cinnamon
3 whole nutmegs
1½ teaspoons ground ginger

Pour first 5 ingredients into a 30-cup electric percolator. Place cinnamon, nutmeg, and ginger in percolator basket. Perk through complete cycle of percolator; let stand 1 hour. Serve hot. Yield: 1 gallon. *S. Kaye Rousseau, Taylor, Louisiana.*

HOT CITRUS TEA

2 cups water
6 whole cloves
1½ quarts water
8 tea bags
½ cup lemon juice
⅔ cup orange juice
1½ cups sugar

Combine 2 cups water and cloves in a saucepan; bring to a boil. Remove from heat and let stand 2 hours.

Bring 1½ quarts water to a boil in a large saucepan; add tea bags. Remove from heat; cover and let stand 5 minutes. Remove tea bags.

Strain clove mixture; add to tea. Add fruit juice and sugar, stirring until sugar dissolves. Let stand 1 hour. Cook over low heat until thoroughly heated. Serve hot. Yield: 2 quarts. *Sarah Carter, Jesup, Georgia.*

MEXICAN COFFEE

6 cups water
½ cup firmly packed brown sugar
½ cup regular grind coffee
½ ounce unsweetened chocolate
1 small tea bag chamomile tea
1 tablespoon ground cinnamon
2 whole cloves
½ teaspoon vanilla extract

Combine water and sugar in a heavy saucepan; stir until sugar dissolves. Add coffee, chocolate, tea, cinnamon, and cloves; bring to a boil. Reduce heat and simmer, uncovered, 15 minutes, stirring occasionally. Stir in the vanilla. Strain through several thicknesses of cheesecloth. Serve hot. Yield: about 5 cups. *Sheree Garvin, Wilkesboro, North Carolina.*

Tip: Always measure ingredients accurately. For liquids, use a glass measuring cup; this allows you to see that you are measuring correctly. Use metal or plastic dry measuring cups for solids; fill cups to overflowing, and level off with a knife or metal spatula.

COFFEE PUNCH

1 cup sugar
1 cup water
¼ cup plus 2 tablespoons instant coffee
   granules
3 (13-ounce) cans evaporated milk, chilled
1 quart vanilla ice cream, slightly softened
1 (28-ounce) bottle club soda, chilled

Combine sugar, water, and coffee in a small saucepan; cook over medium heat, stirring constantly, until sugar and coffee dissolve. Chill.

Pour coffee mixture into a punch bowl; stir in milk. Add ice cream; stir until partially melted. Add club soda, and stir gently. Yield: 1 gallon. *Marie Harris, Sevierville, Tennessee.*

COCONUT NOG

1 (13-ounce) can evaporated milk
1 (8½-ounce) can cream of coconut
1 cup light rum
1 cup sugar
4 eggs
½ teaspoon vanilla extract
Maraschino cherries (optional)

Combine first 6 ingredients in container of electric blender; process until smooth. Chill. Garnish each serving with a maraschino cherry, if desired. Yield: about 4½ cups. *Susan Kamer-Shinaberry, Charleston, West Virginia.*

CRANBERRY PUNCH

2 quarts cranberry juice cocktail
1 tablespoon grated orange rind
2 cups orange juice
½ cup sugar
5 whole cloves
1 (28-ounce) bottle ginger ale, chilled

Combine first 5 ingredients in a Dutch oven; bring to a boil. Reduce heat and simmer, uncovered, 5 to 10 minutes; remove cloves, and chill. To serve, combine cranberry juice mixture and ginger ale in a punch bowl. Yield: about 3½ quarts.

SPARKLING BURGUNDY BOWL

3 cups grapefruit juice
1 (10-ounce) package frozen raspberries,
  thawed
2 tablespoons lemon juice
½ cup sugar
5 cups Burgundy, chilled

Combine grapefruit juice, raspberries, lemon juice, and sugar in a bowl, stirring until sugar dissolves; chill.

To serve, pour mixture into a punch bowl; add Burgundy, and stir gently. Yield: about 2½ quarts.
Mrs. Richard D. Conn,
Kansas City, Missouri.

Spoon On A Festive Sauce

Ham, pork chops, seafood, turkey, or chicken—they'll all taste better topped with one of these sauces. Each is simple to prepare and adds new interest and flavor to traditional entrées.

CHERRY SAUCE

1 (1-inch) stick cinnamon
1 teaspoon whole cloves
¾ cup sugar
2 tablespoons cornstarch
Dash of salt
1 (16½-ounce) can dark sweet pitted
  cherries, undrained
¾ cup orange juice
1 tablespoon lemon juice

Tie cinnamon and cloves in a cheesecloth bag; set aside.

Combine sugar, cornstarch, and salt in a medium saucepan; mix well. Stir in cherries, orange juice, and lemon juice; add spice bag. Cook over medium heat, stirring constantly, until thickened.

Remove spice bag from sauce; serve sauce warm over pork. Yield: 3 cups.
Lynn Silver,
Wichita Falls, Texas.

Cranberry Wine Sauce will highlight the flavor of pork, turkey, or chicken.

CRANBERRY WINE SAUCE

3 cups fresh cranberries
1½ cups sugar
1¼ cups port wine
¼ cup cold water
1½ tablespoons cornstarch

Wash cranberries and drain. Combine cranberries, sugar, and wine in a large saucepan; bring to a boil, and cook 5 to 7 minutes or until cranberry skins pop.

Combine water and cornstarch; stir into cranberry mixture. Bring to a boil; cook 1 minute, stirring constantly. Serve warm over pork or poultry. Yield: about 3 cups.
Bobbie Vanice,
Kansas City, Missouri.

CURRANT GRAVY

1 cup red currant jelly
1 (6-ounce) can frozen orange juice
  concentrate, thawed and undiluted
¼ cup dry sherry
1 tablespoon Worcestershire sauce
½ teaspoon dry mustard

Combine currant jelly, orange juice concentrate, sherry, Worcestershire sauce, and mustard in a small saucepan; cook over low heat, stirring constantly, until jelly melts and mixture is thoroughly heated. Serve gravy warm over pork or poultry. Yield: about 2 cups.
Lou Kanatgar,
Wilmette, Illinois.

ORANGE SAUCE

½ cup orange juice
¼ cup water
¼ cup catsup
2 tablespoons minced onion
2 tablespoons prepared mustard
2 tablespoons Worcestershire sauce
1 teaspoon sugar
½ teaspoon salt
¼ teaspoon hot sauce

Combine all ingredients in a small saucepan; bring to a boil. Reduce heat and simmer 5 minutes. Serve warm over pork. Yield: 1 cup.   *Linda Reese, Guin, Alabama.*

BECHAMEL SAUCE

2 tablespoons butter or margarine
2 tablespoons all-purpose flour
½ cup milk
½ cup chicken broth
¼ teaspoon salt
⅛ teaspoon white pepper
⅛ teaspoon paprika

Melt butter in a heavy saucepan over low heat; add flour, stirring until smooth. Cook 1 minute, stirring constantly. Gradually add milk and chicken broth; cook over medium heat, stirring constantly, until thickened and bubbly. Stir in seasonings. Serve warm over poultry or seafood. Yield: 1 cup.

Put Knives To Good Use

Kitchens hum with the sounds of busy cooks during the holidays. With all the extra cooking, a good set of knives makes slicing and chopping easier.

On today's market, you'll find knives available in a variety of shapes, lengths, and edges. Here we discuss a basic set of cutlery recommended by our home economists.

A **paring knife** comes in handy for delicate cutting such as peeling and garnishing. We use it when preparing lemon roses, tomato roses, and other garnishes for photography.

A 6-inch **utility knife** is one of the most versatile knives. It's good for dicing celery and potatoes and hand-shredding cabbage and lettuce. But if you've got a lot of chopping and dicing to do, use a **chef's knife**—it gets the job done more quickly.

The serrated edge of a **bread knife** has proven to be best for slicing breads and cakes in our test kitchens. It cuts through cakes easier without mashing them down. It also leaves fewer crumbs. Citrus fruit and tomatoes also slice neater with a serrated cutting edge.

A **boning knife** is good for fine, close work on meats, like removing fat and trimming close to the bone.

Since knives in our kitchens receive a lot of use, we're particularly concerned about durability and how well the blade keeps a sharp edge. In the best quality knives, the tang (part of the blade that extends into the handle) is the same thickness as the blade, the same length as the knife handle, and is attached to the handle with at least three rivets.

The sharpness of the cutting edge is determined by the steel in the blade. Blades made from high-carbon steel sharpen well but tend to rust without proper care. Stainless steel blades won't rust, but they are hard to keep sharpened. A good compromise is knives made from a high-carbon steel alloy like vanadium steel.

Our home economists recommend washing knives by hand rather than in the dishwasher. The high heat of the dishwasher can dull blades and ruin handles. To keep knives sharp, use a sharpening steel regularly.

Proper storage is important, too, it's better to keep them in a knife block or in a special case designed for the knives instead of in a drawer. Stored loose in a drawer, the knives hit each other and nick the blades. If the knives must be kept in a drawer, a protective covering over the blades provides a safety feature as well.

It's important to consider cutting surfaces, also. Cut on wooden cutting boards to protect the knife blades (and your counter tops), as other surfaces will quickly dull sharp edges.

COOKING LIGHT

Let's Celebrate The Light Way

You'll probably be faced with many temptations to overeat during the holiday season. But when planning your own party, you can control calories by preparing this month's "Cooking Light" menu. Complete with appetizer, main course, and dessert, this special meal totals around 530 or 600 calories (depending on which of our two entrées you choose). This is quite a change from the usual holiday fare.

**Tarragon Vegetable Appetizer
Sweet-and-Sour Shrimp
or
Orange Chicken
Wild Rice and Mushrooms
Steamed Broccoli
Honey Wheat Rolls
Light Chocolate Soufflé**

TARRAGON VEGETABLE APPETIZER

2 small carrots, scraped and diagonally sliced
1 (6-ounce) package frozen Chinese pea pods, thawed and drained
6 cherry tomatoes
1 medium cucumber, sliced
⅓ cup Italian reduced-calorie salad dressing
3 tablespoons tarragon vinegar
2 tablespoons water
¼ teaspoon dried whole tarragon
¼ teaspoon freshly ground pepper
¼ teaspoon garlic powder

Cook carrots in a small amount of boiling water 3 to 4 minutes or until crisp-tender; drain.

Combine carrots, pea pods, tomatoes, and cucumber in a large shallow dish. Combine remaining ingredients in a jar; cover tightly and shake vigorously. Pour over vegetables, tossing lightly to coat. Cover and chill overnight. Yield: 6 servings (about 32 calories per serving).

SWEET-AND-SOUR SHRIMP

6 cups water
2 pounds large shrimp, unpeeled
1 (15-ounce) can unsweetened pineapple
    chunks, undrained
Vegetable cooking spray
1 tablespoon reduced-calorie margarine
1 medium onion, thinly sliced
1 small green pepper, cut into 1-inch
    squares
¼ cup vinegar
1 tablespoon cornstarch
1 tablespoon soy sauce
½ teaspoon dry mustard

Bring water to a boil; add shrimp and return to a boil. Reduce heat and simmer 3 to 5 minutes. Drain well; rinse with cold water. Peel and devein shrimp; set aside. Drain pineapple, reserving juice; set aside.

Coat a large skillet with cooking spray; add margarine, and place over medium heat until margarine melts. Add onion and green pepper; sauté until vegetables are crisp-tender.

Combine reserved pineapple juice, vinegar, cornstarch, soy sauce, and mustard, stirring until smooth. Add to vegetable mixture. Cook over low heat, stirring constantly, until thickened and bubbly. Gently stir shrimp and pineapple into sauce; cook until shrimp are thoroughly heated. Yield: 6 servings (about 162 calories per serving).

ORANGE CHICKEN

6 chicken breast halves, skinned and
    boned
2 tablespoons reduced-calorie margarine
1 teaspoon paprika
⅛ teaspoon pepper
1 (6-ounce) can frozen orange juice
    concentrate, thawed and undiluted
1 teaspoon dried whole rosemary
½ teaspoon dried whole thyme

Dot chicken with margarine; place on rack of broiler pan. Broil 3 to 5 minutes on each side or until golden brown.

Remove from oven, and place chicken in a 13- x 9- x 2-inch baking pan. Sprinkle with paprika and pepper. Pour orange juice concentrate over chicken; sprinkle with rosemary and thyme. Bake chicken, uncovered, at 350° for 30 minutes. Yield: 6 servings (about 244 calories per serving).

Doris Clark,
Hurst, Texas.

WILD RICE AND MUSHROOMS

2 cups chicken broth
1 medium onion, chopped
¼ cup wild rice
½ cup uncooked regular rice
1 (2½-ounce) can sliced mushrooms,
    undrained
1 tablespoon chopped fresh parsley

Combine broth and onion in a medium saucepan; bring to a boil, and add wild rice. Reduce heat, cover, and simmer 20 minutes. Add regular rice and mushrooms; bring to a boil. Reduce heat, cover, and simmer 15 to 20 minutes or until the liquid is absorbed. Garnish with parsley. Yield: 6 servings (about 92 calories per serving).

Fran Williamson,
Baton Rouge, Louisiana.

HONEY WHEAT ROLLS

1 package dry yeast
1 cup warm water (105° to 115°)
3 tablespoons honey
3 tablespoons butter or margarine, melted
1 egg
¾ teaspoon salt
2 to 2¼ cups unbleached flour
1¾ cups whole wheat flour
Vegetable cooking spray

Dissolve yeast in warm water in a large bowl. Add honey, butter, egg, salt, and ¾ cup each of unbleached and whole wheat flour; beat at low speed of electric mixer until smooth. Stir in enough of remaining flour to make a soft dough.

Place dough in a greased bowl, turning to grease top. Cover and let rise in a warm place (85°), free from drafts, 1 hour or until doubled in bulk.

Punch dough down; turn out onto a lightly floured surface, and knead about 3 minutes.

Lightly coat muffin pans with cooking spray. Shape dough into 1-inch balls; place 3 balls in each muffin cup. Cover and let rise in a warm place (85°), free from drafts, for 40 minutes or until doubled in bulk. Bake at 400° for 12 to 15 minutes or until golden. Yield: 2 dozen (about 87 calories each).

Linda Houston,
Memphis, Tennessee.

LIGHT CHOCOLATE SOUFFLE

⅓ cup sugar
¼ cup cocoa
1 tablespoon cornstarch
Dash of salt
1 cup skim milk
4 eggs, separated
1 teaspoon vanilla extract
½ teaspoon almond extract
¼ teaspoon cream of tartar

Combine sugar, cocoa, cornstarch, and salt in top of a double boiler; gradually stir in milk. Bring water to a boil. Reduce heat to low; cook, stirring constantly, 8 minutes until thickened.

Beat egg yolks slightly. Gradually stir about one-fourth of hot mixture into yolks; add to remaining hot mixture, stirring constantly. Remove from heat, and stir in vanilla and almond extracts; let cool to room temperature.

Beat egg whites (at room temperature) and cream of tartar until stiff but not dry; gently fold beaten egg whites into chocolate mixture.

Pour into a 1½-quart soufflé dish. Place dish in a 13- x 9- x 2-inch baking pan; pour hot water into pan to a depth of ½ inch. Bake soufflé at 350° for 50 minutes or until puffed. Yield: 6 servings (about 124 calories per serving).

Stir In The Flavor Of Cranberry

Bright, red cranberries can be found on market shelves during November and December—just in time for you to whip up some colorful side dishes and desserts for the holidays.

Cranberries make a beautiful garnish as well. Dip them in beaten egg white, and roll in sugar for frosted cranberries. Fresh berries also add a touch of color when arranged around the turkey.

CRANBERRY-PEAR WILD RICE

1 (6-ounce) package long-grain and
  wild rice
2½ cups water
1 tablespoon butter or margarine
1 teaspoon grated orange rind
1 cup fresh cranberries
¼ cup sugar
3 tablespoons water
1 fresh pear, peeled, cored, and coarsely
  chopped

Combine first 4 ingredients in a medium saucepan; bring to a boil. Cover, reduce heat, and simmer 20 to 25 minutes or until liquid is absorbed.

Combine cranberries, sugar, and 3 tablespoons water in a small saucepan; bring to a boil. Cook over medium-high heat, stirring frequently, 3 to 4 minutes or until cranberry skins pop. Drain.

Combine rice, cranberries, and pear; mix well and serve immediately. Yield: 6 servings. *Carin Usry, Oklahoma City, Oklahoma.*

JELLIED CRANBERRY SALAD

4 cups fresh cranberries, coarsely chopped
1 cup sugar
1 envelope unflavored gelatin
½ cup apple juice
¼ cup finely chopped celery
¼ cup peeled, finely chopped apple
¼ cup chopped pecans

Combine cranberries and sugar in a large mixing bowl; let stand 15 minutes, stirring occasionally.

Sprinkle gelatin over apple juice in a small saucepan. Let gelatin soften for 5 minutes. Cook over low heat, stirring occasionally, until gelatin dissolves.

Add gelatin mixture, celery, apple, and pecans to cranberries; mix well. Pour into an oiled 4-cup mold. Chill. Yield: 8 servings. *Mrs. Bennie Cox, Clinton, Tennessee.*

CRANBERRY HOLIDAY TARTS

¼ cup butter or margarine
½ cup dark corn syrup
1 cup sifted powdered sugar
1 tablespoon cornstarch
2 cups fresh cranberries, coarsely chopped
1 cup chopped pecans
Tart shells (recipe follows)

Combine first 4 ingredients in a medium saucepan; bring to a boil, stirring constantly. Boil 1 minute. Remove from heat; stir in cranberries and pecans. Allow to cool slightly.

Spoon about 2 tablespoons filling into each prepared tart shell; bake at 350° for 12 minutes. Cool in tins 5 minutes; remove from tins and cool completely on wire racks. Yield: 14 tarts.

Tart Shells:

¼ cup butter or margarine, softened
¼ cup sugar
1 egg, beaten
½ teaspoon vanilla extract
1 cup all-purpose flour

Combine butter, sugar, egg, and vanilla in a mixing bowl; beat at medium speed with an electric mixer until well blended. Gradually add flour; mix well. Shape dough into a ball; chill.

Shape dough into 14 (1-inch) balls. Place in ungreased 1¾-inch tart tins, and press flat to cover sides of tins; prick each with a fork. Bake at 400° for 8 minutes or until lightly browned. Yield: 14 tart shells. *Joyce B. Davis, Norfolk, Virginia.*

CRANBERRY CONSERVE

4 cups fresh cranberries
¾ cup water
3 cups sugar
¾ cup water
1 medium orange, peeled, seeded, and
  finely chopped
½ cup chopped pecans or walnuts
⅓ cup raisins

Combine cranberries and ¾ cup water in a Dutch oven; bring to a boil. Cover, reduce heat, and simmer 6 to 8 minutes or until cranberry skins pop. Drain cranberries, and put through a food mill; return to Dutch oven. Add remaining ingredients, and bring to a boil, stirring frequently. Simmer, uncovered, 30 minutes. Quickly spoon into hot sterilized jars, leaving ¼-inch headspace; cover at once with metal lids, and screw bands tight. Process in boiling-water bath 10 minutes. Yield: 4 half pints. *Mrs. R. D. Walker, Garland, Texas.*

Casseroles With Fall Vegetables

There's no denying that Southerners are partial to sweet potatoes and acorn squash. Enjoy these and other favorite fall vegetables in simple casseroles that accent their flavors and bright colors.

COMPANY BROCCOLI BAKE

2 (1-pound) bunches fresh broccoli
2 tablespoons chopped onion
2 hard-cooked eggs, sliced
1 (10¾-ounce) can cream of mushroom
  soup, undiluted
1 cup (4 ounces) shredded Cheddar cheese
½ cup mayonnaise
¼ cup buttered cracker crumbs
1 hard-cooked egg, sliced

Trim off large leaves of broccoli, and remove tough ends of lower stalks. Wash thoroughly; separate into spears.

Cook broccoli, covered, in a small amount of boiling water 10 minutes or until tender. Drain well and arrange in a lightly greased 3-quart baking dish. Sprinkle with onion and 2 sliced eggs.

Combine soup, cheese, and mayonnaise in a small saucepan; cook over low heat, stirring until cheese melts. Pour sauce over broccoli, and sprinkle with cracker crumbs. Bake at 350° for 20 minutes or until bubbly. Garnish with remaining egg slices. Yield: 8 servings. *Marguerite Schemmer, Troy, Missouri.*

CABBAGE AU GRATIN

1 medium cabbage, coarsely shredded
1 (10¾-ounce) can cream of celery soup,
  undiluted
¼ cup milk
1 cup (4 ounces) shredded process
  American cheese
½ teaspoon salt
⅛ teaspoon pepper
½ cup fine, dry breadcrumbs
2 tablespoons butter or margarine, melted

Cook cabbage in boiling water 5 to 7 minutes or until tender; drain well. Place cabbage in a lightly greased 1½-quart baking dish.

Combine soup, milk, cheese, salt, and pepper; mix well. Pour over cabbage.

Combine breadcrumbs and butter, stirring well; sprinkle over cabbage. Bake at 350° for 15 minutes. Yield: 6 servings. *Frances C. Boland, Pomaria, South Carolina.*

EXOTIC CELERY

4 cups diagonally sliced celery
1 (10¾-ounce) can cream of chicken soup, undiluted
1 (2-ounce) jar diced pimiento, undrained
1 (8-ounce) can sliced water chestnuts, drained
1 cup slivered almonds

Cook celery in a small amount of boiling water 8 minutes; drain well.

Combine soup, pimiento, and water chestnuts; mix well. Stir in celery, and pour mixture into a greased 2-quart baking dish; sprinkle with almonds. Bake at 350° for 30 minutes. Yield: 6 servings.
Thelma E. Nordquist,
Lehigh Acres, Florida.

CAULIFLOWER-AND-CARROT CASSEROLE

5 large carrots, scraped and cut into ¼-inch slices
1 medium head cauliflower, broken into flowerets
1 (10¾-ounce) can cream of chicken soup, undiluted
¾ cup milk
1 cup cracker crumbs
2 tablespoons butter or margarine, melted

Cook carrots and cauliflower in boiling water 10 minutes; drain. Place vegetables in a lightly greased 2-quart baking dish.

Combine soup and milk, stirring well; pour over vegetables. Combine cracker crumbs and butter, mixing well; sprinkle over vegetables. Bake at 350° for 30 minutes. Yield: 6 to 8 servings.
Marlene Miller,
Trenton, Florida.

EASY CORN PUDDING

1 (16½-ounce) can cream-style corn
1 (13-ounce) can evaporated milk
5 eggs
¼ cup butter or margarine, melted
¼ teaspoon pepper

Combine all ingredients in container of electric blender; process until smooth. Pour into a lightly greased 12- x 8- x 2-inch baking dish. Bake at 350° for 30 to 40 minutes or until set. Yield: about 8 servings.
Mrs. S. G. Fuzzell, Sr.,
Brent, Alabama.

Tip: For even blending, fill the blender container only three-fourths full for liquids and one-fourth full for solids.

ACORN SQUASH BAKE

2 (1½-pound) acorn squash
Salt to taste
¾ cup maple-flavored syrup
2 tablespoons butter or margarine, melted
⅓ cup chopped pecans

Cut squash into ½-inch-thick slices; remove seeds and membrane. Arrange in a lightly greased 13- x 9- x 2-inch baking dish. Sprinkle with salt. Combine syrup and butter; pour over squash. Sprinkle with pecans. Cover and bake at 350° for 35 to 40 minutes or until tender. Yield: 6 to 8 servings.
Mrs. Richard F. Lamb,
Williamsburg, Indiana.

BUTTERNUT CASSEROLE

3 cups cooked, mashed butternut squash
2 tablespoons butter or margarine, melted
1 tablespoon brown sugar
¼ teaspoon salt
1 tablespoon butter or margarine
6 cups peeled, chopped apple
¼ cup sugar
1½ cups corn flakes, coarsely crushed
½ cup chopped pecans
½ cup firmly packed brown sugar
2 tablespoons butter or margarine, melted

Combine first 4 ingredients, stirring well; set aside. Melt 1 tablespoon butter in a large skillet; add apples and sugar. Cover and simmer 8 to 10 minutes or until tender. Drain off excess liquid.

Stir apples into squash mixture. Spoon into a lightly greased 2-quart casserole. Combine remaining ingredients, stirring well; sprinkle over squash.

Bake at 350° for 20 minutes or until thoroughly heated. Yield: 8 servings.
Mrs. W. H. Colley, Jr.,
Donelson, Tennessee.

ORANGE-GLAZED SWEET POTATOES

8 medium-size sweet potatoes
2 tablespoons grated orange rind
1 cup orange juice
⅓ cup firmly packed brown sugar
⅓ cup sugar
1 tablespoon cornstarch
3 tablespoons butter or margarine, melted
¼ teaspoon salt

Cook sweet potatoes in boiling water 20 to 25 minutes or until tender. Allow potatoes to cool to touch; peel and slice. Arrange slices in a lightly greased 3-quart baking dish.

Combine the remaining ingredients in a small saucepan. Cook, stirring constantly, until thickened.

Pour glaze over sweet potatoes. Bake, uncovered, at 350° for 30 minutes. Yield: 10 to 12 servings.
Mrs. Jack Hampton,
Elizabethton, Tennessee.

COOKING LIGHT

Discover The Secret Of Cooking With Wine

Take away the butter and take away the salt—what's left for a dieter to enjoy? You can experience a whole new world of flavor possibilities when you cook those low-calorie and low-sodium foods with wine. Here's a collection of entrées and side dishes to show you how it's done.

Wine itself contains from 130 to over 300 calories per cup. But at temperatures greater than 172 degrees Fahrenheit, the alcohol calories evaporate. What's more, table wines are almost sodium free. Cooking wine, however, does contain salt and should be avoided if you're on a low-sodium diet.

Savory Veal gets a special touch from a half cup of Chablis, a dry white wine. White wine is also recommended for poultry, seafood, and egg dishes.

The stronger red wines (such as Burgundy) are best with beef, pork, and lamb. Since wine is an excellent meat tenderizer, we suggest marinating less tender cuts of beef in red wine for a few hours before cooking.

Madeira and sherry are both fortified wines (contain more alcohol than regular ones). In Carrots Madeira, the wine is added to unsweetened orange juice to make a tasty, golden glaze.

Enjoy these light recipes, and then try adding wine to your own dishes. When experimenting with wine in cooking, remember that too little is better than too much; you can always add more after tasting. Wine should enhance, not overpower, the taste of food.

BEEF BURGUNDY

1¼ pounds boneless round steak
Vegetable cooking spray
⅔ cup chopped onion
2 cloves garlic, minced
1 cup water
1 cup Burgundy or other dry red wine
2 teaspoons low-sodium beef-flavored bouillon granules
1 teaspoon dried whole thyme, crushed
1 small bay leaf
4 medium carrots, scraped and cut in ½-inch-thick slices
3 tablespoons all-purpose flour
½ cup water
¼ pound fresh mushrooms, quartered
6 small boiling onions
Freshly ground pepper to taste
3 cups hot cooked rice (no added salt)

Trim excess fat from steak; cut into 1-inch pieces.

Coat a large skillet with cooking spray; place over medium heat until hot. Add steak and cook until browned; drain. Place in a 2-quart casserole.

Sauté onion and garlic in skillet 1 minute. Add 1 cup water, wine, bouillon granules, thyme, and bay leaf; bring to a boil, stirring well. Pour mixture over steak; cover casserole and bake at 350° for 1½ hours. Remove from oven, and add carrots; cover and bake for an additional 20 minutes.

Remove steak mixture from oven. Combine flour and ½ cup water in a small bowl; stir into steak mixture. Add mushrooms and onions; cover and bake an additional 15 to 20 minutes until onions are tender. Add pepper and remove bay leaf. Serve over hot rice. Yield: 6 servings (about 259 calories and 70 milligrams sodium per serving).
Patricia Hamby Andrews,
Knoxville, Tennessee.

SAVORY VEAL

1 pound veal cutlets
¼ teaspoon freshly ground pepper
1 clove garlic, crushed
2 teaspoons unsalted margarine, melted
2 small onions, cut into strips
2 green peppers, cut into strips
½ cup Chablis or other dry white wine
½ cup water
1 teaspoon low-sodium beef-flavored bouillon granules·
½ teaspoon dried whole basil
¼ teaspoon dried whole oregano
1½ teaspoons cornstarch
2 tablespoons water
12 cherry tomatoes, halved
3 cups hot cooked corkscrew pasta (no added salt)

Trim excess fat from veal; cut into 1-inch pieces. Sprinkle with pepper.

Sauté garlic in margarine in a large skillet over medium-high heat until tender. Add the veal, and cook until browned. Stir in next 7 ingredients and bring to a boil. Cover, reduce heat, and simmer 5 minutes or until vegetables are crisp-tender.

Combine cornstarch and 2 tablespoons water, stirring until blended; stir into veal mixture. Bring to a boil, and cook 1 minute or until slightly thickened. Stir in tomatoes. Serve over corkscrew pasta. Yield: 6 servings (about 250 calories and 45 milligrams sodium per serving).

SHERRIED SCALLOPS

1 tablespoon unsalted margarine
1 pound fresh scallops
¼ cup dry sherry
½ teaspoon ground coriander
½ teaspoon dried whole basil

Melt margarine in a large skillet over medium heat. Stir in remaining ingredients; cook, uncovered, 5 to 10 minutes. Drain scallops; serve immediately. Yield: 4 servings (about 118 calories and 286 milligrams sodium per serving).
Lynn S. Maitland,
Richmond, Virginia.

CHICKEN IN LEMON AND WINE

1 (3-pound) broiler-fryer, cut up and skinned
2 tablespoons lemon juice
1 clove garlic, crushed
½ teaspoon ground ginger
½ teaspoon dry mustard
¼ teaspoon dried whole thyme, crushed
¼ teaspoon rubbed sage
Vegetable cooking spray
½ cup Chablis or other dry white wine
¼ pound fresh mushrooms, sliced

Sprinkle chicken with lemon juice; rub with crushed garlic. Combine next 4 ingredients and sprinkle over chicken.

Coat a large skillet with cooking spray; place over low heat until hot. Add chicken and cook 10 minutes. Turn chicken pieces over; add wine and mushrooms. Cover and simmer 30 to 40 minutes or until chicken is tender. Yield: 6 servings (about 147 calories and 56 milligrams sodium per serving).
Mrs. R. C. Brown,
Allentown, Pennsylvania.

HOT FRUIT DELIGHT

1 cup Chablis or other dry white wine
2 tablespoons raisins
2 teaspoons butter flavoring
1 (8½-ounce) can unsweetened sliced pears, drained
1 (8½-ounce) can unsweetened sliced peaches, drained
1 (8½-ounce) can unsweetened fruit cocktail, drained

Combine first 3 ingredients in a medium saucepan; cook over medium heat 5 minutes or until raisins are plump.

Combine pears, peaches, and fruit cocktail in a shallow 1-quart casserole; pour wine mixture over fruit. Cover and refrigerate overnight.

Let stand at room temperature 20 minutes. Bake at 350° for 30 minutes. Yield: 4 servings (about 74 calories and 7 milligrams sodium per serving).
Callie P. Harris,
Travelers Rest, South Carolina.

CARROTS MADEIRA

1 pound small carrots, scraped
¼ cup Madeira wine
¼ cup unsweetened orange juice
1 teaspoon cornstarch
2 tablespoons water
2 tablespoons chopped fresh parsley

Place carrots in a small amount of boiling water; bring to a boil. Cover, reduce heat, and simmer 4 minutes; drain. Add wine and orange juice; bring to a boil. Cover, reduce heat, and simmer 4 to 5 minutes or until tender.

Combine cornstarch and water, stirring until blended. Add to carrots; cook over medium heat, stirring constantly, until smooth and thickened. Add chopped parsley, tossing gently. Yield: 4 servings (about 62 calories and 55 milligrams sodium per serving).

Tip: Wine should be stored at an even temperature of 50° to 60°. It is important that bottles of corked table wines be kept on their side so that the corks are kept moist and airtight. Bottles with screw caps may remain upright.

Solve The Leftover Meat Problem

When the company has gone home and the feasting has ended, you may find yourself with extra turkey, ham, or chicken. If you need help disguising the leftovers, try one of these recipes.

TURKEY PARTY SPREAD

2 cups cubed cooked turkey or chicken
2 tablespoons dry sherry
½ cup sliced celery
1½ teaspoons dried parsley flakes
½ teaspoon ground nutmeg
1 teaspoon lemon juice
¼ to ½ teaspoon salt
¼ teaspoon pepper
¼ cup mayonnaise
⅓ cup finely ground toasted almonds

Combine turkey and sherry; cover and refrigerate for at least 1 hour.

Place turkey mixture and next 6 ingredients in bowl of food processor or container of electric blender; process 30 seconds. Scrape sides of container with a rubber spatula. Process an additional 30 seconds. Pour into a mixing bowl; stir in mayonnaise. Cover and refrigerate for 1 hour.

Shape mixture into a ball, and coat with almonds. Serve with crackers. Yield: about 2½ cups. *Lynn Blayney, Charlotte, North Carolina.*

TURKEY MACARONI SALAD

1 (7-ounce) package shell macaroni
4 cups diced cooked turkey
2 cups chopped celery
1 (15¼-ounce) can pineapple tidbits, drained
1 (2-ounce) jar diced pimiento, drained
¼ cup slivered almonds, toasted
1 to 1½ cups mayonnaise
3 tablespoons lemon juice
1½ teaspoons seasoned salt
¼ teaspoon pepper
Paprika

Cook macaroni according to package directions; drain. Rinse with cold water; drain. Combine macaroni and next 5 ingredients in a large bowl.

Combine mayonnaise, lemon juice, salt, and pepper; mix well. Pour over turkey mixture; toss gently. Sprinkle with paprika; cover and chill thoroughly. Yield: 8 servings.
Mrs. M. L. Shannon, Fairfield, Alabama.

ELEGANT TURKEY CREPES

2 (10-ounce) packages frozen broccoli spears
2 cups cubed cooked turkey
1 (10¾-ounce) can cream of mushroom soup, undiluted and divided
3 tablespoons cream sherry, divided
2 tablespoons milk
½ teaspoon Pickapeppa sauce
Crêpes (recipe follows)
1 cup (4 ounces) shredded Cheddar cheese
1 tablespoon grated Parmesan cheese

Cook broccoli according to package directions, omitting salt; drain and set aside. Combine turkey, half the soup, 2 tablespoons sherry, milk, and Pickapeppa sauce; set aside. Combine remainder of soup and remaining sherry in a small saucepan; cook over medium heat until thoroughly heated.

Fill each crêpe with 2 broccoli spears, allowing flowerets to extend at each end. Spoon ¼ cup turkey mixture over broccoli; fold sides of crêpe over filling. Place crêpes, seam side up, in a lightly greased 13- x 9- x 2-inch baking dish. Spoon soup-and-sherry mixture evenly over crêpes; sprinkle with cheese. Cover and bake at 350° for 12 to 15 minutes. Yield: 8 servings.

Crêpes:

3 eggs
1 cup all-purpose flour
1 cup milk
1 tablespoon vegetable oil
Additional vegetable oil

Combine first 4 ingredients in container of electric blender; process 1 minute. Scrape down sides of blender container with rubber spatula; process an additional 15 seconds. Refrigerate 1 hour. (This allows flour particles to swell and soften so crêpes are light in texture.)

Brush the bottom of a 10-inch crêpe pan with oil; place pan over medium heat until oil is just hot, not smoking.

Pour 2 tablespoons batter into pan; quickly tilt pan in all directions so batter covers the pan in a thin film. Cook about 1 minute.

Lift edge of crêpe to test for doneness. Crêpe is ready for flipping when it can be shaken loose from pan. Flip crêpe, and cook about 30 seconds on other side. (This side is rarely more than spotty brown.) Place on a towel to cool. Stack between layers of waxed paper to prevent sticking. Repeat until all batter is used. Yield: 16 crêpes.

Note: Crêpes may be frozen, if desired. Thaw to room temperature, and bake as directed. *Mrs. Jack Different, Harvey, Louisiana.*

TURKEY FRIED RICE

1 tablespoon soy sauce
1 cup diced cooked turkey
¼ cup vegetable oil
1 cup uncooked regular rice
2 cups chicken broth
¼ cup sliced celery
¼ cup finely chopped green pepper
2 tablespoons chopped onion
1 egg, slightly beaten
½ cup shredded lettuce

Pour soy sauce over turkey in a small bowl; set aside. Pour oil into a large skillet; add rice and fry over medium heat, stirring constantly, until rice is browned. Add chicken broth and turkey mixture; cover and simmer 15 minutes or until liquid is absorbed.

Stir in celery, green pepper, and onion; cook, uncovered, 5 minutes. Push rice to side of skillet and add egg, stirring constantly, until set; combine with rice mixture. Stir in lettuce. Serve immediately. Yield: 6 servings.
Mrs. Lester Rolf, Stillwater, Oklahoma.

CHICKEN JEWEL RING SALAD

1 envelope unflavored gelatin
1 cup cranberry juice cocktail
1 (16-ounce) can whole-berry cranberry sauce
2 tablespoons lemon juice
1 envelope unflavored gelatin
¾ cup cold water
1 tablespoon soy sauce
1½ cups chopped cooked chicken
1 cup mayonnaise
½ cup diced celery
¼ cup coarsely chopped almonds, toasted
Lettuce leaves

Sprinkle 1 envelope gelatin over cranberry juice in a saucepan, and let stand 1 minute; cook over medium heat until gelatin dissolves, stirring constantly and scraping sides occasionally. Remove from heat; add cranberry sauce and lemon juice, stirring until combined. Pour mixture into a lightly oiled 6-cup mold. Chill until partially set.

Sprinkle 1 envelope gelatin over ¾ cup water in a saucepan, and let stand 1 minute; cook over medium heat until gelatin dissolves, stirring constantly and scraping sides occasionally. Remove from heat, and stir in soy sauce; cool. Stir in chicken, mayonnaise, celery, and almonds. Spoon over cranberry layer; chill until firm. Unmold onto lettuce. Yield: 8 servings.
Mrs. Marshall M. DeBerry, Franklin, Virginia.

BAKED HAM STRATA

12 slices white bread
1 cup ground cooked ham
6 slices process American cheese
3 eggs, beaten
3 cups milk
½ teaspoon salt
½ teaspoon seasoned salt
½ teaspoon dry mustard
1 cup corn flake crumbs
3 tablespoons butter, melted

Trim crust from bread; arrange 6 slices in a 13- x 9- x 2-inch baking dish. Sprinkle ham over bread; top with cheese slices. Place the remaining bread slices over cheese.

Combine next 5 ingredients, stirring well; pour over bread. Cover casserole and chill overnight.

Combine corn flake crumbs and butter; sprinkle over casserole. Bake at 350° for 45 minutes. Yield: 6 servings.
Mrs. Roy McKnight,
Abbeville, Alabama.

MACARONI-HAM CASSEROLE

2 cups cooked elbow macaroni
1½ cups diced cooked ham
1½ cups diced cooked chicken
1 cup (4 ounces) shredded Swiss cheese
¾ cup sliced green olives
½ cup finely chopped onion
1 (8-ounce) carton commercial sour cream
¾ cup milk
¼ teaspoon dry mustard
¼ teaspoon pepper
¼ cup crushed potato chips

Combine first 6 ingredients; mix well. Combine sour cream, milk, dry mustard, and pepper. Add to macaroni mixture, and mix well. Spoon mixture into a lightly greased 2-quart baking dish. Sprinkle with crushed potato chips. Bake at 350° for 25 minutes or until lightly browned. Yield: 6 servings.
Mrs. David Markoe,
Ijamsville, Maryland.

HAM SPAGHETTI SKILLET

4 slices bacon, diced
½ cup chopped onion
¼ cup chopped green pepper
2 cups chopped cooked ham
1 clove garlic, minced
1 (28-ounce) can whole tomatoes, undrained and chopped
1 (7-ounce) package spaghetti, cooked and drained
1 cup (4 ounces) shredded Cheddar cheese

Cook diced bacon in a large skillet until crisp; remove bacon, reserving 2 tablespoons drippings in the skillet. Drain bacon well and set aside.

Sauté onion and green pepper in reserved drippings until tender. Add ham, and cook until lightly browned. Add garlic and tomatoes; cover, reduce heat, and simmer 30 minutes.

Stir spaghetti into ham mixture, and sprinkle with cheese. Simmer, uncovered, 10 minutes. Sprinkle with bacon before serving. Yield: 4 to 6 servings.
Nell H. Amador,
Guntersville, Alabama.

Give A Gift Of Friendship Tea

Complete your December gift-giving list by making a large quantity of Friendship Tea Mix to share with friends and neighbors. Fill small, attractive jars or tins with the mix and keep them on hand to give as gifts—it makes a welcome remembrance of the holiday season.

FRIENDSHIP TEA MIX

1 (18-ounce) jar orange-flavored instant breakfast drink
1 cup sugar
½ cup pre-sweetened lemonade mix
½ cup instant tea
1 (3-ounce) package apricot-flavored gelatin
2½ teaspoons ground cinnamon
1 teaspoon ground cloves
Boiling water

Combine first 7 ingredients in a large bowl, stirring well. Store mix in an airtight container.

To serve, place 1½ tablespoons mix in a cup. Add 1 cup boiling water, and stir well. Yield: about 50 servings.
Lee Ruth Krieg,
Lubbock, Texas.

New Ways With Chili

When the weather's chilly outside, there's nothing like chili on the inside to satisfy the appetite. We offer several versions that range in cooking time from 45 minutes to 2 hours.

SOUTH-OF-THE-BORDER CHILI

2 pounds round steak, cut into 1-inch cubes
1 clove garlic, minced
2 tablespoons vegetable oil
2 (16-ounce) cans whole tomatoes, undrained and chopped
1 medium onion, sliced
2 teaspoons chili powder
1 teaspoon salt
1 teaspoon dried whole oregano
1 teaspoon red pepper
1 cup water
2 (16-ounce) cans kidney beans, drained

Combine beef and garlic in oil in a Dutch oven; cook over medium heat until beef is browned. Add next 7 ingredients, mixing well; bring to a boil. Cover, reduce heat, and simmer 1½ hours, stirring occasionally. Add kidney beans, and simmer an additional 30 minutes. Yield: about 2 quarts.
Dorothy Campbell,
Mayfield Village, Ohio.

QUICK CHILI

1½ pounds ground beef
1 medium onion, chopped
½ cup chopped green pepper
1 (10¾-ounce) can tomato soup, undiluted
1 (16-ounce) can whole tomatoes, undrained and chopped
1 (16-ounce) can kidney beans, undrained
1 tablespoon chili powder
1 teaspoon salt
½ teaspoon pepper
½ teaspoon garlic powder
2 cups (8 ounces) shredded Cheddar cheese

Combine ground beef, onion, and green pepper in a Dutch oven; cook over medium heat until beef is browned, stirring to crumble meat. Drain off drippings. Add next 7 ingredients, stirring well. Cover, reduce heat, and simmer 1 hour, stirring occasionally. Sprinkle each serving with cheese. Yield: 5 cups.
Pam Sigler,
Lexington, Kentucky.

BEEF AND SAUSAGE CHILI CON CARNE

1½ pounds ground beef
½ pound bulk pork sausage
2 cups chopped onion
2 cloves garlic, minced
2 (16-ounce) cans tomatoes, undrained and chopped
1 (6-ounce) can tomato paste
1 (4-ounce) can chopped green chiles, undrained
¼ cup chopped fresh parsley
2 tablespoons chili powder
1½ tablespoons brown sugar
1 tablespoon vinegar
1 teaspoon cumin seeds
1 teaspoon salt
1 teaspoon pepper
3 whole cloves
1 bay leaf
1 (16-ounce) can kidney beans, undrained

Combine beef, sausage, onion, and garlic in a Dutch oven; cook over medium heat until beef is browned, stirring to crumble meat. Drain off drippings. Stir in next 10 ingredients. Tie cloves and bay leaf in a cheesecloth; add to chili mixture. Cover, reduce heat, and simmer 1½ hours, stirring occasionally. Add beans and simmer 30 minutes. Remove spice bag to serve. Yield: about 2 quarts.
Mrs. Steven Zellner,
Wheeling, West Virginia.

SAVORY POTATO CHILI

1 pound ground beef
½ cup chopped onion
½ cup chopped green pepper
1 tablespoon poppy seeds
½ teaspoon salt
½ teaspoon chili powder
1 (5.25-ounce) package scalloped potato mix
1 cup hot water
1 (16-ounce) can kidney beans, undrained
1 (16-ounce) can whole tomatoes, undrained and chopped
1 (4-ounce) can mushroom stems and pieces, undrained
Grated Parmesan cheese

Combine ground beef, onion, and green pepper in a large skillet; cook over medium heat until beef is browned, stirring to crumble meat. Drain off drippings. Stir in remaining ingredients, except cheese, mixing well. Cover, reduce heat, and simmer 45 minutes or until liquid is absorbed, stirring occasionally. Sprinkle each serving with Parmesan cheese. Yield: 6 servings.
Alice McNamara,
Eucha, Oklahoma.

From Our Kitchen To Yours

Southern cooks will soon be working overtime getting ready for the annual Thanksgiving feast. But we know that it takes more than fine recipes to create a memorable holiday meal; it takes careful planning and scheduling. These tips will help you organize and prepare your meal, leaving you time to relax and enjoy the day.

Plan ahead. Whether you're cooking for a crowd or just for two, decide on your menu at least a week or two before Thanksgiving. That should give you plenty of time to place a special meat order with your butcher. If you want a cut such as a crown pork roast, standing rib roast, etc., your butcher will probably need some notice to get it in stock for you. Remember, this is one of the busiest times of the year for the meat market, so don't wait until the last minute. If you do, you may be disappointed. Plan on buying your turkey ahead of time, too. You'll have plenty of birds to choose from and should be able to get the size you need.

Include in your menu one or more items that can be prepared ahead. Desserts such as pecan pies, pound cakes, chocolate and caramel layer cakes can be made well in advance and frozen. Congealed salads, cranberry sauce, and relishes can be made a day or two in advance. By including some of these "do-ahead" dishes, you'll find the actual cooking on Thanksgiving will take much less time and energy.

Be a list maker. Once you've decided on your menu and selected the recipes to use, then make two grocery lists, one for those items that can be purchased and prepared ahead of time and the other for items like fresh vegetables and produce that need to be picked up later.

Also, list those jobs that can be done a week or so before the holidays. Silver can be polished, and linens can be laundered and pressed ahead of time. And carefully check the serving pieces you'll need. Advance selection of both bakeware and serving pieces can often eliminate a last-minute crisis.

Turkey Talk

Even though some Southern families enjoy serving pork and beef for Thanksgiving, many still want the traditional roast turkey on their table. Here we've assembled a few guidelines on thawing and preparing a turkey that we hope you'll find helpful.

Thaw the bird carefully. You'll probably buy your turkey frozen. It's very important that the turkey be properly thawed before cooking. The best way we know is to let the turkey thaw in the refrigerator. Leave the turkey in its original wrapper, place on a tray (to catch drippings), and refrigerate until the bird thaws. Depending on its size, allow 2 to 4 days for thawing. A 4- to 12-pound turkey will take 1 to 2 days, a 12- to 20-pound will take 2 to 3 days, and a 20- to 24-pound will take as long as 3 to 4 days. Thawing in the refrigerator instead of at room temperature is the safest method to use because it reduces the risk of bacterial growth.

If the bird must be thawed at room temperature due to lack of time, try this method: Leave the bird in its wrapper, and place in a heavy grocery sack, closing the opening. Put the bird on a tray, and let it thaw in a cool room away from heat. Check the turkey frequently. Once thawed, the turkey should be cooked immediately. Remember to allow enough thawing time, since it will take quite a while for the bird to thaw.

Stuffing the turkey. Be sure to remove the giblets from the turkey and use them in making gravy. Rinse the turkey thoroughly before stuffing and pat dry. If desired, lightly salt the cavity; do not salt if bird is to be stuffed.

If the turkey is to be stuffed, do it right before roasting. Never stuff it the night before. For more information on trussing a turkey, see our step-by-step instructions on page 286.

Cooking the turkey. We've found many of our readers prefer roast turkey. To roast the turkey, first place it on a rack in a shallow roasting pan. You'll want to cook it in a 325° oven, uncovered, and without adding any water to the pan. Baste the bird occasionally during cooking with pan drippings or melted butter, if desired.

The most accurate way to determine doneness of the turkey is to use a meat thermometer. The thermometer should be inserted in the thickest part of the thigh muscle, making sure the bulb doesn't touch bone. When the thermometer registers 180° to 185°, the turkey is done. Check for doneness by moving the drumstick up and down—the joint should give easily. Also, press the drumstick with your fingers. The meat will be soft if the turkey is done.

The following timetable can be used if you don't have a thermometer. This chart gives approximate roasting times for stuffed turkeys based on an oven temperature of 325°. Unstuffed turkeys require about 5 minutes less per pound.

Ready-To-Cook Weight	Approximate Roasting Time
4 to 8 pounds	3 to 3¾ hours
8 to 12 pounds	3¾ to 4½ hours
12 to 16 pounds	4½ to 5½ hours
16 to 20 pounds	5½ to 6½ hours

When the turkey is done, let stand 20 to 25 minutes for easier carving.

Refrigerate the dressing quickly. When storing leftover turkey, be sure to remove the dressing and refrigerate in a separate container. Also, don't let the dressing sit at room temperature for very long; refrigerate it as soon as possible after serving.

One More Tip

A final holiday tip—storing fruitcakes. How should I age and store my fruitcakes? That's a question we get repeatedly from our readers during the holidays. We think a good method is to dampen cheesecloth or a linen tea towel with brandy, bourbon, or your favorite spirit and wrap the fruitcake in the cloth. Either place the wrapped cake in a cake tin, or carefully enclose in aluminum foil; then refrigerate the cake. The cake should stay fresh several weeks using this method.

MICROWAVE COOKERY

Fluffy Rice Cooked In The Microwave

There is no reason not to cook rice in your microwave oven; it's a good way to save energy, and the end product is light and fluffy. However, keep in mind that you won't save much time over conventional cooking.

A microwave oven is also a good way to reheat rice. For two cups of cold cooked rice, just add a tablespoon of water, cover, and microwave at MEDIUM HIGH (70% power) for three or four minutes. You end up with rice that tastes and looks freshly cooked.

One word of caution when preparing rice in the microwave oven: Don't try to use a dish that's smaller than what the recipe calls for. If the dish is too small, the water will boil over, causing the rice to dry out and become tough. Also, be

sure to stop and stir the rice as directed in the recipes.

To help decrease the amount of time it takes to cook rice in the microwave, start each recipe by using hot rather than cold water. This way the rice mixture comes to a boil much sooner.

BASIC LONG-GRAIN RICE

1 cup uncooked regular rice
¾ teaspoon salt
1 tablespoon butter or margarine
2 cups hot water

Combine rice, salt, and butter in a deep 2-quart casserole. Stir in hot water. Cover with heavy-duty plastic wrap, and microwave at HIGH for 5 minutes. Stir well. Cover, reduce to MEDIUM (50% power); and microwave 14 to 16 minutes or until liquid is absorbed. Let stand 2 to 4 minutes. Fluff rice with a fork. Yield: 4 servings.

BASIC QUICK-COOKING RICE

2 cups uncooked instant rice
½ teaspoon salt
1 teaspoon butter or margarine
1⅔ cups hot water

Combine rice, salt, and butter in a deep 2-quart casserole; stir in hot water. Cover with heavy-duty plastic wrap, and microwave at HIGH for 8 minutes. Let stand 2 to 4 minutes. Fluff rice with a fork. Yield: 4 to 6 servings.

HERBED RICE

1 large onion, chopped
1 tablespoon butter or margarine
½ teaspoon dried whole basil
¼ teaspoon dried whole thyme
3 cups hot water
1½ cups uncooked regular rice
¾ cup minced fresh parsley
1½ teaspoons onion salt
¼ teaspoon pepper

Combine onion, butter, basil, and thyme in a 3-quart casserole. Cover with heavy-duty plastic wrap, and microwave at HIGH for 3 minutes or until onion is tender. Stir in remaining ingredients. Cover and microwave at HIGH for 5 minutes. Reduce to MEDIUM (50% power) and microwave 20 to 23 minutes, or until liquid is absorbed. Let stand 4 to 5 minutes. Fluff rice with a fork. Yield: 6 servings.

CURRIED RICE WITH ALMONDS

¼ cup chopped onion
2 tablespoons butter or margarine
1 cup uncooked regular rice
1½ teaspoons chicken-flavored bouillon granules
¼ teaspoon ground allspice
¼ teaspoon ground turmeric
¼ teaspoon curry powder
⅛ teaspoon pepper
2 cups hot water
¼ cup slivered almonds

Combine onion and butter in a deep 2-quart casserole. Cover with heavy-duty plastic wrap, and microwave at HIGH for 2 minutes. Stir in next 7 ingredients. Cover and microwave at HIGH for 5 minutes. Stir well. Cover, reduce to MEDIUM (50% power), and microwave 14 to 16 minutes or until liquid is absorbed. Let rice stand for 2 to 4 minutes.

Spread almonds in a pieplate; microwave at HIGH 4 minutes. Add almonds to rice; fluff the rice with a fork. Yield: 4 servings.

Southern Ways With Cornbread

Ask 10 Southerners how to make cornbread, and you'll get 10 different answers. The recipes here reflect the variety of this regional favorite: jalapeño cornbread, deep-fried hush puppies, and old-fashioned spoonbread.

CHEDDAR CORNBREAD

1 cup yellow cornmeal
1 cup all-purpose flour
2 tablespoons sugar
1 tablespoon baking powder
1 teaspoon salt
1 cup milk
2 eggs, beaten
2 cups (8 ounces) shredded Cheddar cheese

Combine first 5 ingredients in a large mixing bowl; set aside. Combine milk, eggs, and cheese; add to dry ingredients, mixing well. Pour batter into a hot, greased 10½-inch cast-iron skillet. Bake at 425° for 15 minutes or until cornbread is golden. Yield: 10 to 12 servings.
Mrs. T. L. Trimble,
Pensacola, Florida.

GOLDEN SPOONBREAD

2 cups water
1 cup yellow cornmeal
¼ cup shortening
2 tablespoons sugar
1 teaspoon salt
2 eggs, beaten
1 cup evaporated milk

Combine first 5 ingredients in a saucepan; cook over medium heat until mixture is thickened, stirring constantly. Remove from heat.

Combine eggs and milk; stir into cornmeal mixture. Pour into a lightly greased 1½-quart casserole.

Bake at 425° for 30 to 35 minutes or until a knife inserted in center comes out clean. Yield: 6 servings.

Kathleen Branson,
Thomasville, North Carolina.

HOT MEXICAN CORNBREAD

1½ cups yellow cornmeal
1 teaspoon salt
1 tablespoon baking powder
2 eggs, beaten
2 tablespoons chopped green pepper
1 (8-ounce) carton commercial sour
  cream
1 cup cream-style corn
¼ cup vegetable oil
1 to 2 jalapeño peppers, chopped
1 cup (4 ounces) shredded Cheddar
  cheese

Combine cornmeal, salt, and baking powder; mix well. Stir in remaining ingredients except cheese. Pour half the batter into a hot, greased 10½-inch cast-iron skillet; sprinkle evenly with half the cheese. Pour the remaining batter over cheese; top with remaining cheese. Bake at 350° for 35 to 40 minutes. Yield: 10 to 12 servings.

Mrs. Glenn Moore, Jr.,
Winchester, Tennessee.

HONEY CORNBREAD

2½ cups yellow cornmeal
1 cup whole wheat flour
2½ teaspoons baking powder
1 teaspoon baking soda
1 teaspoon salt
2½ cups buttermilk
½ cup vegetable oil
2 eggs, beaten
2 tablespoons honey

Combine first 5 ingredients in a large mixing bowl; set aside. Combine buttermilk, oil, eggs, and honey; add to dry

ingredients, mixing well. Pour batter into a greased 13- x 9- x 2-inch baking pan. Bake at 425° for 20 to 25 minutes or until golden brown. Cut cornbread into 2-inch squares to serve. Yield: about 2 dozen.   *Nancy Chaney,*
Tullahoma, Tennessee.

HUSH PUPPIES WITH CORN

1 cup all-purpose flour
1 cup cornmeal
2 teaspoons baking powder
¾ teaspoon salt
¾ cup cream-style corn
½ cup chopped onion
1 egg, beaten
2 tablespoons vegetable oil
Vegetable oil

Combine first 4 ingredients in a large mixing bowl. Add corn, onion, egg, and 2 tablespoons oil; stir well.

Carefully drop batter by level tablespoonfuls into deep hot oil (370°); cook only a few at a time, turning once. Fry 3 to 5 minutes until hush puppies are golden brown. Drain well on paper towels. Yield: about 2½ dozen.

Debbie Baskin,
Shreveport, Louisiana.

Steps To The Perfect Turkey

It's time to bring on the turkey—roasted and stuffed with a savory dressing. Since we want your turkey to be the best ever this year, we're offering step-by-step illustrations for the proper way to stuff it and roast it. For some additional tips about cooking your holiday turkey, see "From Our Kitchen to Yours" on page 284.

Just follow these easy steps to the perfect roast turkey:

—To prepare the turkey for roasting, thaw and remove giblets from the bird. Save the giblets; they're excellent for use in gravy or to add extra flavor to the dressing. After rinsing the turkey with cold water, pat it dry. Since the bird will be stuffed, there's no need to add salt to the cavity.

—Always stuff the turkey just before roasting. To save time, you can mix the dry ingredients for the dressing in advance, then add the liquid ingredients just before time to put the turkey in the

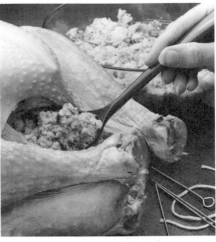

Step 1—*After lightly stuffing the neck cavity with dressing, skewer the neck skin to the back. Then spoon remaining dressing loosely into body cavity.*

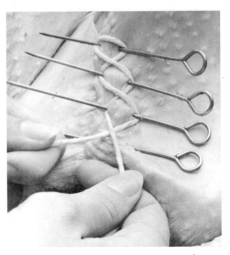

Step 2—*Truss body cavity opening with skewers and heavy cotton cord. Tie turkey legs together with remaining length of cord.*

oven. Stuff the neck and body cavities lightly since the dressing will expand during baking. Figure about ¾ cup of dressing per pound of turkey at thawed, ready-to-cook weight.

—After stuffing, truss the body opening with skewers and heavy cotton cord. Tie the legs together to the tail, or tuck them under the band of skin at the tail. When the turkey is two-thirds done, clip the cord or band of skin.

—Fold the turkey wings across the back so that they will be tucked under the bird when it is breast side up. This keeps the wingtips from overbrowning and makes the turkey easier to carve.

—Place the bird on the rack of a shallow roasting pan and brush with butter, margarine, or vegetable oil. Insert a meat thermometer in the thickest part

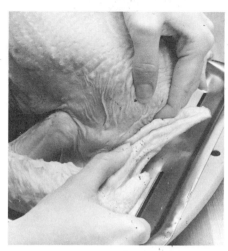

Step 3—Tuck turkey wingtips under the bird. This keeps them from overbrowning and makes the turkey easier to carve.

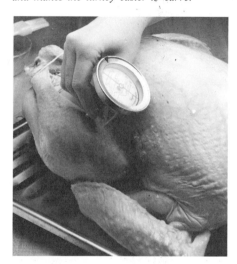

Step 4—Insert a meat thermometer so that the bulb rests in the thickest part of the thigh or breast, making sure thermometer does not touch bone. The turkey is done when it reaches an internal temperature of 180° to 185°.

of the thigh or breast, making sure the bulb doesn't touch the bone.

—Bake at 325° until the meat thermometer registers 180° to 185°. Cooking time depends on the weight of the turkey. Refer to our chart on page 285. If you're preparing a self-basting turkey, check the recommended roasting time on the package, since it usually bakes faster. If you decide not to stuff the turkey, roasting time will be about 30 minutes less than for a stuffed bird.

Using a meat thermometer is the surest way to determine doneness. But, if you don't have one, you can test doneness by pressing the meat at the thickest part of the thigh between your thumb and forefinger. If it feels soft,

then the turkey is done. Also, the drumsticks should move easily at the joints.

If the turkey gets too brown during baking, you can shield the top of the bird with an aluminum foil tent. Don't cover the turkey to roast or add water to the pan since these methods will create a steaming or stewing effect and can give the meat a different flavor.

—Once the turkey is out of the oven, it's best to let it stand 20 to 30 minutes to make carving easier. After dinner, remove any remaining dressing from the turkey, and store both separately in the refrigerator. The dressing will keep well about 3 days.

TURKEY WITH SAUSAGE-CORNBREAD DRESSING

1 (16- to 18-pound) turkey
1 pound bulk pork sausage
1½ cups chopped onion
1½ to 2 teaspoons salt
2 teaspoons dried whole sage, crushed
1 teaspoon dried whole rosemary, crushed
1 teaspoon dried whole thyme, crushed
¼ teaspoon pepper
8 cups cubed cornbread
16 slices white bread, cut in ½-inch cubes
2½ cups turkey or chicken broth
2 eggs, beaten
About ⅓ cup butter or margarine, melted

Remove giblets and neck from turkey; reserve for gravy, if desired. Rinse turkey with cold water; pat dry.

Cook sausage and onion in a medium skillet over low heat until sausage is browned and onion is tender. Drain. Place in a large bowl; add next 9 ingredients, mixing well.

Stuff dressing into neck and body cavities of turkey. Close cavities with skewers and truss. Tie ends of legs to tail with cord; lift wingtips up and over back so they are tucked under bird.

Brush entire bird with butter; place it on a rack in roasting pan, breast side up. Insert meat thermometer in breast or meaty part of thigh, making sure it does not touch bone.

Bake at 325° about 5½ to 6½ hours until meat thermometer reaches 180° to 185°. Baste turkey frequently with pan drippings. If turkey begins to get too brown, cover lightly with aluminum foil. Turkey is done when drumsticks move easily. Remove to serving platter; let stand 20 to 30 minutes before carving. Yield: 20 to 24 servings.

Mrs. R. D. Walker,
Garland, Texas.

Pasta Is Everybody's Favorite

What's your favorite pasta dish? Lasagna, fettuccine, or spaghetti with meat sauce? We've gathered recipes for these and several other popular pasta dishes, deliciously flavored with spices.

When it comes to handling cooked spaghetti, fettuccine, or lasagna noodles, a spoon just doesn't do the trick. Our home economists recommend using kitchen tongs or a wooden pasta utensil to make the job easier.

THICK-AND-SPICY SPAGHETTI

2 large onions, chopped
2 medium-size green peppers, chopped
1 cup chopped celery
2 to 3 cloves garlic, minced
2 tablespoons olive oil
2 pounds ground beef
1 (4-ounce) can sliced mushrooms, undrained
3 (6-ounce) cans tomato paste
1 (16-ounce) can whole tomatoes, undrained and coarsely chopped
3 (8-ounce) cans tomato sauce
2 tablespoons Worcestershire sauce
2 teaspoons chili powder
2 teaspoons dried whole oregano
1 teaspoon dried Italian seasoning
1 teaspoon salt
1 teaspoon ground cinnamon
2 teaspoons vinegar
¼ teaspoon curry powder
3 drops of hot sauce
2 bay leaves
½ cup water
½ cup Burgundy or other dry red wine
Hot cooked spaghetti
Shredded sharp Cheddar cheese
Grated Parmesan cheese

Sauté onion, green pepper, celery, and garlic in hot oil in a large Dutch oven until onion is tender. Add ground beef; cook until browned, stirring to crumble meat. Drain off drippings; stir in next 15 ingredients. Cover, reduce heat, and simmer 1 hour, stirring occasionally. Remove bay leaves, and stir in Burgundy. Spoon sauce over the spaghetti. Sprinkle each serving with cheese. Yield: 10 servings.

Mrs. W. Harold Groce,
Arden, North Carolina.

Tip: Adding 1 or 2 tablespoons of vegetable oil to the cooking water keeps pasta separated.

EASY BEEF AND NOODLES

3 slices bacon
½ cup chopped onion
1 pound ground beef
1 (16-ounce) can whole tomatoes, undrained
½ cup chopped green pepper
¼ cup chili sauce
½ teaspoon salt
½ teaspoon pepper
3 cups egg noodles, uncooked
½ cup water
Shredded Cheddar cheese

Cook bacon in a large skillet until crisp; remove bacon, reserving drippings in skillet. Crumble bacon and set aside.

Sauté onion in drippings until tender; add ground beef, and cook until meat is browned, stirring to crumble. Drain off drippings; stir in tomatoes, green pepper, chili sauce, salt, and pepper. Cover and simmer 10 minutes. Add noodles and water; bring to a boil. Cover, reduce heat, and simmer 30 minutes or until noodles are tender. Stir in bacon; sprinkle with cheese. Yield: 4 to 6 servings.   *Marie Lazelle,*
Grove, Oklahoma.

SAUCY STUFFED MANICOTTI

½ pound bulk Italian sausage
½ pound ground beef
1 clove garlic, minced
¼ teaspoon dried whole basil
¼ teaspoon salt
⅛ teaspoon pepper
2 (6-ounce) cans tomato paste
2 cups water
8 manicotti shells
1 cup ricotta cheese
1 egg, beaten
⅔ cup grated Parmesan cheese
1 cup (4 ounces) shredded mozzarella cheese
4 (1-ounce) slices provolone cheese, halved

Combine first 6 ingredients in a large skillet; cook until meat is browned, stirring to crumble meat. Drain off drippings. Add tomato paste and water; reduce heat and simmer, uncovered, 45 minutes, stirring occasionally.

Cook manicotti shells according to package directions; drain and set aside.

Combine ricotta cheese, egg, Parmesan, and mozzarella cheese; mix well. Stuff manicotti shells with cheese mixture, and arrange in a lightly greased 13- x 9- x 2-inch baking dish. Top with provolone cheese.

Pour meat sauce over manicotti. Cover and bake at 350° for 1 hour. Yield: 4 servings.

SAUSAGE LASAGNA

1 pound bulk Italian sausage
½ cup chopped onion
¼ cup chopped celery
¼ cup chopped carrots
2 (6-ounce) cans tomato paste
1 (16-ounce) can whole tomatoes, undrained and coarsely chopped
½ teaspoon salt
½ teaspoon dried whole oregano
Dash of dried Italian seasoning
1 (8-ounce) package lasagna noodles
3 cups ricotta cheese or cream-style cottage cheese
2 eggs, beaten
½ cup grated Parmesan cheese
2 tablespoons chopped fresh parsley
4 cups (16 ounces) shredded mozzarella cheese

Combine first 4 ingredients in a large skillet; cook until meat is browned, stirring to crumble meat. Drain off drippings. Stir in next 5 ingredients; reduce heat and simmer, uncovered, 30 minutes, stirring occasionally.

Cook lasagna noodles according to package directions; drain.

Combine ricotta cheese, eggs, Parmesan, and parsley; mix well. Spread about ½ cup of meat sauce in a greased 13- x 9- x 2-inch baking dish. Layer half each of noodles, ricotta mixture, meat sauce, and mozzarella cheese. Repeat layers, except mozzarella cheese. Cover and bake at 375° for 25 minutes. Remove cover; sprinkle with the remaining mozzarella cheese, and bake an additional 5 minutes. Let lasagna stand 10 minutes before serving. Yield: 8 servings.   *Anne Reynolds,*
Raleigh, North Carolina.

CHICKEN TETRAZZINI

1 (8-ounce) package spaghetti
1 cup sliced fresh mushrooms
1 small onion, thinly sliced
¼ cup butter or margarine
¼ cup all-purpose flour
1 teaspoon salt
½ teaspoon poultry seasoning
¼ teaspoon pepper
2 cups chicken broth
½ cup whipping cream
3½ cups diced cooked chicken
1 cup (4 ounces) shredded sharp Cheddar cheese

Cook spaghetti according to package directions; drain and set aside.

Sauté mushrooms and onion in butter in a large saucepan until tender. Add flour, salt, poultry seasoning, and pepper; stir well. Cook 1 minute, stirring constantly. Gradually add broth; cook over medium heat, stirring constantly, until thickened and bubbly. Add cream and stir until smooth. Stir in chicken.

Place half of spaghetti in a greased, shallow 2-quart casserole. Spoon half of chicken mixture over spaghetti. Repeat layers. Bake, uncovered, at 350° for 20 minutes. Sprinkle with Cheddar cheese, and bake an additional 5 minutes. Yield: 6 servings.   *Kelly Walters,*
Munfordville, Kentucky.

FETTUCCINE SUPREME

1 (8-ounce) package cream cheese, softened
¼ cup butter or margarine, softened
2 tablespoons dried parsley flakes
1 teaspoon dried whole basil
¼ teaspoon pepper
⅔ cup boiling water
1 (8-ounce) package fettuccine
1 clove garlic, minced
¼ cup butter or margarine
½ cup grated Parmesan or Romano cheese, divided

Beat cream cheese and ¼ cup softened butter on low speed of electric mixer until blended. Add parsley, basil, and pepper; mix well. Add boiling water; beat until mixture is smooth.

Cook fettuccine according to package directions; drain well. Rinse in warm water; drain well and set aside.

Sauté garlic in ¼ cup butter in a small skillet until tender. Combine garlic mixture and warm noodles, tossing gently. Add cream cheese mixture and ¼ cup Parmesan cheese; toss gently. Place in a serving dish; sprinkle with remaining ¼ cup cheese. Yield: 6 to 8 servings.   *Mary Jane Wilson,*
Bovina, Texas.

TASTY MACARONI AND CHEESE

1 (8-ounce) package macaroni
2 cups (8 ounces) shredded Cheddar cheese, divided
1 (5.33-ounce) can evaporated milk
3 tablespoons grated onion
1 teaspoon dry mustard
1 teaspoon Worcestershire sauce
Dash of pepper
2 tablespoons chopped fresh parsley
1 (4-ounce) can sliced mushrooms, drained
1 (2-ounce) jar diced pimiento, drained

Cook macaroni according to package directions; drain and set aside.

Combine 1½ cups cheese and next 6 ingredients in a Dutch oven; cook over low heat, stirring constantly, until cheese melts. Stir in macaroni, mushrooms, and pimiento. Pour mixture into a greased 2-quart casserole. Bake at 350° for 25 minutes. Sprinkle with remaining ½ cup cheese. Bake an additional 5 minutes. Yield: 6 servings.

Evelyn Weisman,
Kingsville, Texas.

Make It Brunch For Two

The next time the two of you have the morning free, why not serve a leisurely brunch? Our tasty and colorful menu will help get your day off to just the right start. And it doesn't take long to prepare.

Zesty Tomato Juice Cocktail
Sunrise Omelet
Sautéed Zucchini and Sausage
Spiced Apple Slices
Easy Breakfast Bread
Coffee

ZESTY TOMATO JUICE COCKTAIL

1 (12-ounce) can tomato juice, chilled
½ teaspoon Worcestershire sauce
½ tablespoon lime juice
3 to 4 drops of onion juice
2 drops of hot sauce

Combine all ingredients, stirring well. Chill. Yield: 1½ cups.

SUNRISE OMELET

2 slices bacon
1 cup peeled, chopped potatoes
4 eggs
2 teaspoons dried parsley flakes
¼ teaspoon seasoned salt
Dash of onion powder
Dash of pepper
1 tablespoon butter or margarine
Cherry tomato slices (optional)
Fresh parsley sprigs (optional)

Cook bacon in a 10-inch omelet pan or heavy skillet until crisp; remove bacon, reserving drippings in skillet. Crumble bacon, and set aside.

Add potatoes to skillet; cook over medium heat until golden brown, stirring frequently. Remove from skillet, and set aside.

Combine eggs, parsley flakes, seasoned salt, onion powder, and pepper; beat well. Melt butter in skillet; rotate pan to coat bottom. Pour egg mixture into skillet. As mixture starts to cook, gently lift edges of omelet with a spatula, and tilt pan so the uncooked portion of egg will flow underneath.

When egg mixture is partially set, spoon bacon and potatoes over eggs; continue to cook until egg mixture is set. Fold right and left sides of omelet over filling. Gently slide omelet onto a serving plate. Garnish with cherry tomato slices and parsley, if desired. Serve immediately. Yield: 2 servings.

Mary V. Kramer,
Nashua, New Hampshire.

SAUTEED ZUCCHINI AND SAUSAGE

¼ pound mild bulk sausage
1 small zucchini, sliced
2 tablespoons chopped onion
3 tablespoons tomato sauce
1 tablespoon grated Parmesan cheese

Cook sausage in a small skillet until browned, stirring to crumble; drain off drippings, reserving 1½ tablespoons in skillet. Add zucchini and onion to sausage in skillet; cook until tender, stirring frequently. Stir in tomato sauce; cook until thoroughly heated. Place mixture in a serving dish and sprinkle with cheese. Yield: 2 servings.

SPICED APPLE SLICES

1 large baking apple, cored, peeled, and thinly sliced
2 tablespoons butter or margarine, melted
1 teaspoon all-purpose flour
1½ tablespoons brown sugar
¼ teaspoon ground cinnamon
1 tablespoon lemon juice

Arrange apple slices in a lightly greased 1-quart baking dish.

Combine remaining ingredients; pour over apple slices. Bake at 350° for 20 minutes. Yield: 2 servings.

Jeane Barnett,
Gastonia, North Carolina.

EASY BREAKFAST BREAD

½ cup self-rising flour
¼ cup milk
1½ tablespoons mayonnaise

Combine all ingredients in a mixing bowl; mix well. Spoon into a greased muffin pan, filling one-half full. Bake at 400° about 18 minutes or until browned. Yield: 2 servings. *Mrs. Ben M. Beasley,*
Orlando, Florida.

Meet A Prize-Winning Cook

Are you willing to compete with 150 other cooks to see who's best? Bill Shealy of Columbia, South Carolina, does that each year at his company picnic. The annual event is judged by professionals—and seven times those judges have named Shealy a winner.

Of course the annual contest isn't the only place Bill displays his cooking talent. "I bring food to the office quite a bit," Bill says.

The most popular dessert with Bill's friends is his recipe for Chocolate Mousse Roll. "They just go crazy at the office when I bring one in," Bill says.

Some of Bill's best recipes are listed below, along with favorites from other Southern men who love to cook.

SCOTCH EGGS

3 cups herb-seasoned stuffing mix, divided
1 pound hot bulk pork sausage
1 tablespoon finely chopped onion
1 teaspoon grated lemon rind
6 hard-cooked eggs, peeled
1 egg, beaten
Vegetable oil
Prepared mustard (optional)

Position knife blade in food processor bowl; add 1½ cups stuffing mix. Process 30 seconds or until crumbs are finely crushed. Stop processor; add sausage, onion, and lemon rind. Process until mixture forms a paste; divide into 6 equal portions, and press mixture around each egg. Dip each coated egg in beaten egg, and roll in remaining stuffing mix.

Deep fry in hot oil (375°) for 4 to 5 minutes or until sausage is done. Drain well. Serve with mustard, if desired. Yield: 6 servings.

LIGHT CLOVERLEAF ROLLS

1 package dry yeast
1½ cups warm milk (105° to 115°)
½ cup sugar
½ cup vegetable oil
1 egg, slightly beaten
1 teaspoon salt
4¾ cups bread flour

Dissolve yeast in ½ cup warm milk in a large bowl; let stand 5 minutes. Add remaining milk, sugar, oil, egg, salt, and half the flour; beat at low speed of electric mixer until smooth. Stir in enough remaining flour to make a soft dough.

Place dough in a greased bowl, turning to grease top. Cover and let rise in a warm place (85°), free from drafts, 1 hour or until doubled in bulk. Let dough rest 15 minutes.

Punch the dough down; turn out onto a lightly floured surface, and knead 10 times.

Lightly grease muffin pans. Shape dough into 1-inch balls; place 3 balls in each muffin cup. Cover and let rise in a warm place (85°), free from drafts, for 1 hour or until doubled in bulk. Bake at 350° for 17 to 20 minutes or until golden brown. Yield: about 2 dozen.

CHOCOLATE MOUSSE ROLL

2 (4-ounce) packages sweet baking
    chocolate
⅓ cup water
1 teaspoon Grand Marnier or other
    orange-flavored liqueur
8 eggs, separated
1 cup sugar
2 tablespoons cocoa
1 cup whipping cream
3 tablespoons powdered sugar
½ teaspoon vanilla extract
Additional powdered sugar
Semisweet chocolate-dipped orange sections

Grease bottom and sides of an 18- x 12- x 1-inch jellyroll pan with vegetable oil; line with waxed paper.

Combine chocolate and water in top of a double boiler; bring water to a boil. Reduce heat to low; cook, stirring occasionally, until chocolate melts. Stir in Grand Marnier; set aside to cool.

Place egg yolks in a large bowl, and beat at high speed of electric mixer until foamy; gradually add 1 cup sugar, beating until mixture is thick and lemon colored. Gradually add the chocolate mixture, mixing well.

Beat egg whites (at room temperature) at high speed of electric mixer until stiff peaks form. Fold egg whites

into chocolate mixture. Pour into jellyroll pan, spreading evenly. Bake at 350° for 20 minutes. Immediately cover top with a damp linen or paper towel; place on a wire rack, and let cool 20 minutes. Carefully remove towel. Loosen edges of the cake with a metal spatula, and sift cocoa over top.

Place 2 lengths of waxed paper (longer than jellyroll pan) over cake. Holding both ends of waxed paper and pan, quickly invert pan. Remove pan and carefully peel paper from cake.

Beat whipping cream until foamy; gradually add 3 tablespoons powdered sugar and vanilla, beating until soft peaks form. Spoon whipped cream mixture evenly over cake. Starting at short side, carefully roll up the cake jellyroll fashion; use the waxed paper to help support the cake as you roll.

Carefully slide roll (on waxed paper) onto a plate, seam side down. Chill. Before serving, sift additional powdered sugar over roll. Garnish with semisweet chocolate-dipped orange sections. Trim away excess paper around sides of roll. Yield: 12 servings.

Note: The chocolate roll is fragile and may crack or break during rolling.

REDFISH COURT BOUILLON

2 cups vegetable oil
4 cups all-purpose flour
2 (15-ounce) cans tomato sauce
3 medium onions, chopped
3 green peppers, chopped
1 stalk celery, chopped
3 (10-pound) redfish
8 quarts water
3 large carrots
3 stalks celery
1½ tablespoons salt
¾ teaspoon pepper
½ teaspoon hot sauce
½ cup chopped green onion tops
½ cup chopped fresh parsley
Hot cooked rice
¾ cup chopped hard-cooked egg
Lemon wedges (optional)

Combine oil and flour in a 4-quart Dutch oven; cook over medium heat about 45 to 50 minutes, stirring frequently, until roux is the color of light peanut butter. Stir in tomato sauce; cook over low heat, stirring occasionally, about 3 hours or until oil begins to

separate around edges of pot. Add next 3 ingredients, and cook until the vegetables are tender.

Fillet the redfish, reserving bones. Cut fish into 1-inch cubes, and set aside in refrigerator. Combine bones and next 3 ingredients in a 20-quart kettle; boil, uncovered, 45 minutes. Strain fish stock through layers of cheesecloth; repeat straining, if necessary.

Return stock to kettle, and bring to a boil. Gradually add tomato sauce mixture, stirring well. Cook over medium heat, uncovered, 1 hour; stir occasionally. Add fish, salt, pepper, and hot sauce; cook 15 minutes, stirring occasionally. Sprinkle with the green onion tops and parsley.

Place rice in individual serving bowls; spoon soup over rice. Top each serving with chopped egg and a lemon wedge, if desired. Yield: about 4 gallons.

Alex Patout,
New Iberia, Louisiana.

SUNDAY CHICKEN CASSEROLE

1 (3-pound) broiler-fryer
1½ cups chopped celery
½ medium onion, chopped
3 tablespoons butter or margarine
2 cups (8 ounces) shredded Cheddar
    cheese
1 (10¾-ounce) can cream of mushroom
    soup, undiluted
3 eggs, slightly beaten
¼ teaspoon lemon pepper seasoning
¼ teaspoon pepper
1 (8-ounce) package herb-seasoned stuffing
    mix

Place chicken in a Dutch oven, and cover with water. Bring to a boil; cover, reduce heat, and simmer 1 hour or until tender. Remove chicken, and let cool, reserving 2 cups broth. Bone chicken, and chop meat; set aside.

Sauté celery and onion in butter in a large skillet until tender. Add reserved broth, cheese, soup, eggs, lemon pepper seasoning, and pepper; mix well. Stir in chicken; spoon mixture into a lightly greased 13- x 9- x 2-inch baking dish. Sprinkle the stuffing mix on top; bake at 350° for 45 minutes. Yield: 8 servings.

Bob Shoffner,
Salisbury, North Carolina.

Tip: The giblets and necks should be removed from whole chickens and turkeys, washed, and cooked within 12 hours.

TARRAGON BRUSSELS SPROUTS

1 pound fresh brussels sprouts or 2
   (10-ounce) packages frozen brussels
   sprouts
2 tablespoons finely chopped onion
1½ tablespoons butter or margarine
1½ tablespoons all-purpose flour
¾ teaspoon dry mustard
¼ teaspoon dried whole tarragon
1 cup chicken broth
1 tablespoon vinegar

Cook brussels sprouts in a small
amount of boiling salted water for 5 to
10 minutes or until tender. (If using frozen brussels sprouts, cook according to
package directions.) Drain and place in
a serving dish.

Sauté onion in butter in a large skillet
2 minutes. Add flour, mustard, and tarragon; cook 1 minute, stirring constantly. Gradually add broth and
vinegar; cook over medium heat, stirring constantly, until mixture is thickened and bubbly. Pour sauce over
brussels sprouts. Yield: 6 servings.
Allan Pollock,
Hendersonville, North Carolina.

SEASONED MUSHROOMS

2 tablespoons butter or margarine
½ cup extra dry vermouth
2 teaspoons beef-flavored bouillon granules
1 medium onion, chopped
2 pounds fresh mushrooms, halved

Melt butter in a Dutch oven. Add
vermouth and bouillon granules, stirring
until granules dissolve. Stir in onion and
mushrooms; cover and simmer 45 minutes. Yield: 6 servings.   *Bill Hines,*
Raleigh, North Carolina.

Warm Up With Soups And Sandwiches

There's nothing like a hot sandwich
or a steaming bowl of soup to take the
chill off a cold November day. Here,
our readers offer recipes for a variety of
soups and sandwiches that are guaran-
teed to do just that.

CORNED BEEF SANDWICHES

1 (12-ounce) can corned beef, shredded
1 cup (4 ounces) shredded sharp Cheddar
   cheese
¼ cup chopped pimiento-stuffed olives
½ cup catsup
1 tablespoon Worcestershire sauce
8 hamburger buns

Combine first 5 ingredients, mixing
well. Spread mixture on bottom half of
each hamburger bun; cover with top of
each bun. Wrap each sandwich in aluminum foil. Bake at 375° for 18 to 20
minutes. Yield: 8 servings.
Gail Thompson,
Brundidge, Alabama.

HOT CHICKEN SANDWICHES

2 cups chopped cooked chicken
1 medium onion, finely chopped
2 hard-cooked eggs, chopped
1 (3-ounce) can sliced mushrooms, drained
½ cup mayonnaise
¼ cup chopped celery
12 slices very thin bread
Butter or margarine, softened
1 (8-ounce) carton commercial sour cream
1 (10¾-ounce) can cream of chicken soup,
   undiluted
About ¼ cup slivered almonds
1 (2-ounce) jar diced pimiento, drained

Combine first 6 ingredients in a small
bowl; mix well. Trim crust from bread.
Lightly butter one side of 6 bread slices
and place, buttered side down, in a 13-
x 9- x 2-inch baking pan. Spread
chicken mixture evenly over bread. Top
with remaining unbuttered bread slices.

Combine sour cream and soup in a
small bowl; mix well. Spoon soup mixture evenly over sandwiches. Sprinkle
with slivered almonds and diced pimiento. Bake at 350° for 15 minutes or
until lightly browned. Yield: 6
servings.   *Evelyn Shaver,*
Mount Olive, North Carolina.

PUFFY CRAB SANDWICHES

2 (6-ounce) packages frozen crabmeat,
   thawed and drained
1½ cups chopped celery
¾ cup mayonnaise
2 tablespoons capers
2 teaspoons prepared mustard
½ teaspoon salt
6 English muffins, split
¼ cup butter or margarine, softened
3 egg whites
3 tablespoons mayonnaise

Combine first 6 ingredients in a medium bowl; mix well and set aside.
Lightly toast muffins; spread each muffin half with 1 teaspoon butter, and set
aside. Beat egg whites (at room temperature) until stiff peaks form; fold in
3 tablespoons mayonnaise.

Spoon about ¼ cup crab mixture
onto each buttered muffin half; top with
beaten egg white mixture, and spread to
cover filling. Bake at 450° about 3 minutes or until golden brown. Serve immediately. Yield: 6 servings.
Lilly B. Smith,
Richmond, Virginia.

CABBAGE SOUP

½ medium cabbage, chopped
4 medium potatoes, peeled and cubed
1 bunch green onions, chopped
5 cups water
1 cup whipping cream
2 tablespoons butter or margarine
1½ teaspoons salt
¼ teaspoon pepper
Grated Parmesan cheese

Combine first 4 ingredients in a large
Dutch oven; bring to a boil. Cover, reduce heat, and simmer 15 to 20 minutes. Stir in whipping cream, butter,
salt, and pepper; cook, stirring constantly, until butter melts and mixture is
thoroughly heated. Spoon into serving
bowls; sprinkle with Parmesan cheese.
Yield: about 3 quarts.   *Larra Andress,*
Birmingham, Alabama.

CHUNKY NAVY BEAN SOUP

1½ cups dried navy beans
1 large ham hock
3 cloves garlic, minced
4 cups water
2 large onions, chopped
3 large potatoes, peeled and cubed
1 (10-ounce) package frozen chopped
   turnip greens, thawed
5 cups water
2 teaspoons salt
½ teaspoon pepper

Sort and wash beans; place in a large
Dutch oven. Cover with water 2 inches
above beans; let soak overnight. Drain
beans; add ham hock, garlic, and 4 cups
water. Bring to a boil; cover, reduce
heat, and simmer 3 hours.

Add remaining ingredients; cover and
simmer an additional 20 minutes, stirring occasionally. Yield: 3 quarts.
Carol Barclay,
Portland, Texas.

LENTIL SOUP

1½ cups dried lentils
6 cups water
1 tablespoon beef-flavored bouillon
   granules
1 (16-ounce) can whole tomatoes,
   undrained and coarsely chopped
2 tablespoons dried parsley flakes
1 large onion, finely chopped
1 medium carrot, thinly sliced
4 medium potatoes, peeled and cubed
1 bay leaf
½ to 1 teaspoon salt
¼ teaspoon pepper
1 clove garlic, crushed
1 cup chopped cooked ham

Combine all ingredients in a large Dutch oven; bring to a boil. Cover, reduce heat, and simmer 1½ hours. Remove bay leaf. Yield: 2½ quarts.

Carole Garner,
Little Rock, Arkansas.

POTATO SOUP

5 medium potatoes, peeled and diced
1 small onion, chopped
1 stalk celery, chopped
2 teaspoons celery salt
1 teaspoon seasoned salt
1 teaspoon dried whole basil
¼ teaspoon pepper
2 tablespoons dried parsley flakes
2 chicken-flavored bouillon cubes
4 cups water
4 slices bacon
2 tablespoons all-purpose flour
1½ cups milk

Combine first 10 ingredients in a large Dutch oven; bring to a boil. Cover, reduce heat, and simmer 20 minutes.

Cook bacon in a large skillet until crisp; remove bacon, reserving 3 tablespoons drippings in skillet. Crumble bacon, and set aside.

Add flour to drippings in skillet; stir until smooth. Cook 1 minute, stirring constantly. Gradually add milk; cook over medium heat, stirring constantly, until thickened and bubbly. Gradually stir milk mixture and bacon into potato mixture. Simmer, uncovered, 15 minutes. Yield: 2 quarts.

Shirley Ann Holbrook,
Paintsville, Kentucky.

Sunny Ideas For Breakfast

For most folks, a good breakfast is the start of a good day. If your family likes to take time to savor a traditional morning meal, get out your apron and try some of these appealing ideas.

FRIED GRITS

4 cups water
½ teaspoon salt
1 cup uncooked quick-cooking grits
2 tablespoons cooked, crumbled bacon
¼ cup plus 1 tablespoon butter or
   margarine, divided

Bring water and salt to a boil; stir in grits. Cook grits until done, following package directions. Remove from heat. Add bacon and 1 tablespoon butter; stir until butter melts.

Pour grits into a greased 8½- x 4½- x 3-inch loafpan. Cool; cover and refrigerate overnight.

Remove grits by inverting pan; cut loaf into ½-inch slices. Melt remaining ¼ cup butter in a large skillet; fry slices over medium heat 5 to 7 minutes or until lightly browned, turning once. Yield: 8 servings. *Dorothy McGinley,*
Wilmington, Delaware.

BAKED CHEESE-AND-GARLIC GRITS

4 cups water
½ teaspoon salt
1 cup uncooked quick-cooking grits
1½ cups (6 ounces) shredded sharp
   Cheddar cheese
½ cup butter or margarine
½ cup milk
1 clove garlic, minced
2 eggs, beaten

Bring water and salt to a boil; stir in grits. Cook grits until done, following package directions. Remove from heat, and add next 4 ingredients; stir until butter and cheese melt.

Add a small amount of hot grits to eggs, stirring well; stir into remaining grits. Pour grits into a lightly greased 2-quart baking dish. Bake at 325° for 1 hour. Yield: 8 servings. *Marian Cox,*
Deming, New Mexico.

Tip: Brush a small amount of oil on a grater before shredding cheese for easier cleaning.

ORANGE FRENCH TOAST

2 eggs
⅔ cup orange juice
3 tablespoons powdered sugar
1 teaspoon ground cinnamon
8 slices white bread
2 tablespoons butter or margarine,
   divided

Combine eggs, orange juice, powdered sugar, and cinnamon in container of electric blender; blend well. Pour egg mixture into a shallow container. Dip each slice of bread in the mixture, coating well on each side.

Melt 1 tablespoon butter in a large skillet; fry 4 bread slices until golden brown on each side. Repeat procedure with remaining butter and bread. Serve hot. Yield: 4 servings.

Audrey Hasenbein,
Gardendale, Alabama.

OPEN-FACE EGG SANDWICHES

1½ tablespoons butter or margarine
1½ tablespoons all-purpose flour
¾ cup milk
¾ cup (3 ounces) shredded Cheddar
   cheese
Salt and pepper
4 eggs
2 tablespoons water
2 tablespoons butter or margarine,
   divided
4 tomato slices, cut ¼-inch thick
4 slices buttered toast
Chopped fresh parsley (optional)

Melt 1½ tablespoons butter in a heavy saucepan over low heat; add flour, stirring until smooth. Cook 1 minute, stirring constantly. Gradually add milk; cook over medium heat, stirring constantly, until thickened and bubbly. Add cheese, ⅛ teaspoon salt, and dash of pepper, stirring until smooth. Set aside.

Combine eggs, water, ¼ teaspoon salt, and dash of pepper; beat well with a fork.

Melt 1 tablespoon butter in a 10-inch skillet. Add egg mixture, and cook over low heat until eggs are partially set; stir occasionally until the eggs are firm but still moist.

Fry tomato slices in remaining 1 tablespoon butter, 1 minute on each side. Place a tomato slice on each piece of toast. Spoon eggs over tomato, and top with cheese sauce.

Garnish sandwiches with parsley, if desired. Yield: 4 servings.

G. C. MacDonald,
Shalimar, Florida.

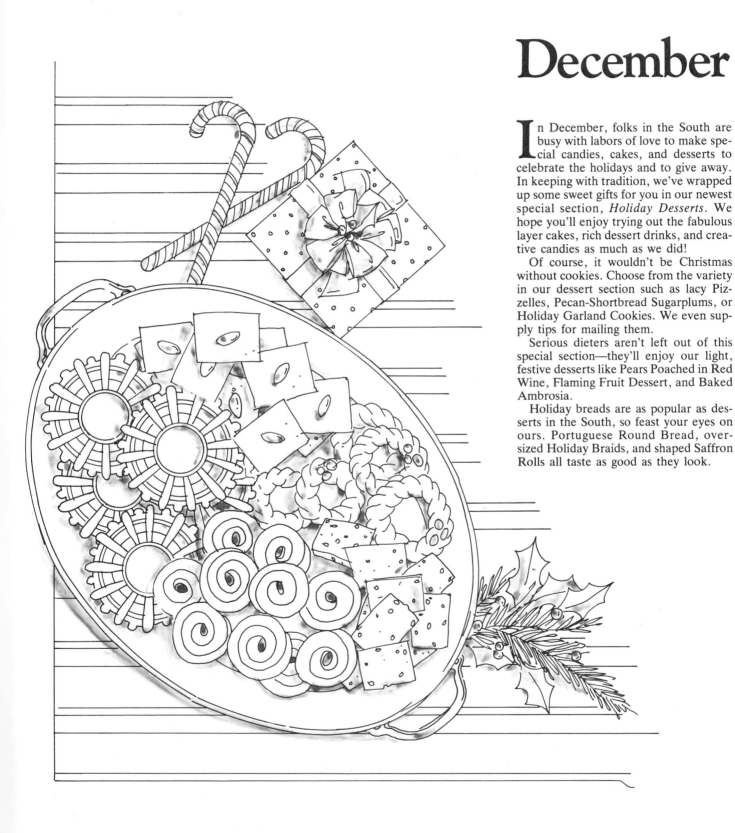

December

I n December, folks in the South are busy with labors of love to make special candies, cakes, and desserts to celebrate the holidays and to give away. In keeping with tradition, we've wrapped up some sweet gifts for you in our newest special section, *Holiday Desserts*. We hope you'll enjoy trying out the fabulous layer cakes, rich dessert drinks, and creative candies as much as we did!

Of course, it wouldn't be Christmas without cookies. Choose from the variety in our dessert section such as lacy Pizzelles, Pecan-Shortbread Sugarplums, or Holiday Garland Cookies. We even supply tips for mailing them.

Serious dieters aren't left out of this special section—they'll enjoy our light, festive desserts like Pears Poached in Red Wine, Flaming Fruit Dessert, and Baked Ambrosia.

Holiday breads are as popular as desserts in the South, so feast your eyes on ours. Portuguese Round Bread, over-sized Holiday Braids, and shaped Saffron Rolls all taste as good as they look.

Holiday Breads Take A Festive Turn

Drizzled with glaze, baked with nuts, or lovingly shaped into loaves, rolls, or braids, breads fill Southern kitchens with Christmas warmth. Their inviting aromas revive memories of holidays in years past.

Like Southerners, people all over the world celebrate the holidays with festive breads. Saffron Rolls, for example, are inspired by the traditions of the Swedes. They usher in the Christmas season with a celebration honoring Lucia, the Queen of Light. It's their custom to serve a breakfast of coffee and saffron bread, beautifully shaped and adorned with raisins.

Austrian Sweet Bread comes to us from Vienna. The rich, cake-like yeast bread is flavored with lemon and almonds and baked in a molded pan. You'll enjoy serving it for a coffee or even for dessert.

Quick breads, such as Pumpkin-Nut Bread or Eggnog Bread, are made without yeast and rely on baking powder to rise. Begin testing for doneness after the bread has baked the minimum time. Insert a wooden pick into the center of each loaf; if it's done, there should be no crumbs clinging to the pick.

Conventional yeast breads need the right conditions to rise properly. Our home economists recommend letting the dough rise in a cold oven with a large pan of hot water underneath. During the first rising, check the dough to see if it's doubled in bulk by lightly pressing two fingertips ½ inch into the dough. If the indentation doesn't disappear, the dough is doubled and ready to be punched down. To check the dough after it's shaped, lightly press it with a finger close to the edge of the pan, and see if the indentation remains.

EGGNOG BREAD

2¼ cups all-purpose flour
2 teaspoons baking powder
1 teaspoon salt
2 eggs
¾ cup sugar
¼ cup butter or margarine, melted
1 cup commercial eggnog
½ cup chopped candied cherries
½ cup raisins
½ cup chopped pecans

Combine flour, baking powder, and salt; set aside.

Combine eggs, sugar, and butter in a large mixing bowl; beat well. Add flour mixture alternately with eggnog, beginning and ending with flour mixture. Stir in remaining ingredients.

Pour batter into a greased and floured 8½- x 4½- x 3-inch loafpan. Bake at 350° for 1 hour and 10 minutes or until a wooden pick inserted in center comes out clean. Cool in pan 10 minutes; remove to wire rack and cool completely. Yield: 1 loaf.

Mary Ann Turk,
Joplin, Missouri.

CITRUS-NUT BREAD

2 cups all-purpose flour
¾ cup sugar
½ teaspoon salt
½ teaspoon baking soda
½ cup chopped pecans or walnuts
1 tablespoon grated orange rind
¼ teaspoon grated lemon rind
1 egg, beaten
¾ cup orange juice
2 tablespoons lemon juice
2 tablespoons vegetable oil
1 teaspoon orange extract

Combine flour, sugar, salt, and baking soda in a large bowl. Stir in pecans, orange rind, and lemon rind. Combine remaining ingredients; add to flour mixture, stirring just until moistened.

Spoon mixture into a greased and floured 8½- x 4½- x 3-inch loafpan. Bake at 350° for 50 to 60 minutes or until a wooden pick inserted in center comes out clean. Cool in pan 10 minutes; remove from pan, and cool completely on a wire rack. Yield: 1 loaf.

Judy Cunningham,
Roanoke, Virginia.

PUMPKIN-NUT BREAD

1 cup butter or margarine, softened
3 cups sugar
3 eggs
3 cups all-purpose flour
1 teaspoon baking powder
1 teaspoon baking soda
1 teaspoon salt
1 teaspoon ground cinnamon
1 teaspoon ground cloves
½ teaspoon ground nutmeg
1 (16-ounce) can pumpkin
1 teaspoon vanilla extract
1 cup raisins
1 cup chopped pecans

Cream butter; gradually add sugar, beating well. Add eggs, one at a time, beating well after each addition.

Combine next 7 ingredients; add to creamed mixture alternately with pumpkin, beginning and ending with flour mixture. Stir in vanilla, raisins, and pecans. Spoon into 4 greased and floured 1-pound coffee cans; bake at 350° for 1 hour or until a wooden pick inserted in center comes out clean. Cool in cans 10 minutes; remove from cans, and cool completely on wire racks. Yield: 4 loaves.

Bobbie Wells,
Ackerman, Mississippi.

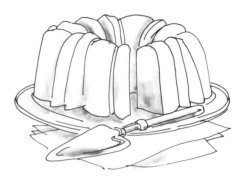

AUSTRIAN SWEET BREAD

2 tablespoons sliced almonds
3 cups all-purpose flour, divided
1 package dry yeast
½ cup sugar
1 teaspoon grated lemon rind
½ teaspoon salt
1¼ cups milk
¼ cup water
½ cup butter or margarine, softened
3 eggs
¾ cup golden raisins
¼ cup finely chopped almonds
Sifted powdered sugar

Arrange sliced almonds in a well-greased and floured Bundt pan or 9-cup baking mold. Set aside.

Combine 2¾ cups flour, yeast, sugar, lemon rind, and salt in a large bowl; stir well. Heat milk and water in a small saucepan to 120° to 130°. Gradually add to flour mixture, stirring well. Add butter and eggs; beat at medium speed of electric mixer 2 minutes. Combine remaining ¼ cup flour, raisins, and chopped almonds; stir into batter (batter will be thin). Carefully pour batter into prepared pan (do not disturb sliced almonds). Cover and let rise in a warm place (85°), free from drafts, 1 hour or until doubled in bulk.

Bake at 375° for 35 to 45 minutes or until golden brown. Cool in pan 10 minutes. Invert onto a serving plate; dust with powdered sugar. Yield: one 10-inch loaf.

ANISE-ORANGE BREAD

2 packages dry yeast
½ cup warm water (105° to 115°)
5 to 5½ cups unbleached flour
¼ cup sugar
2 teaspoons salt
3 tablespoons grated orange rind
1 teaspoon anise seeds, crushed
¼ cup plus 2 tablespoons butter or
   margarine, softened
1⅓ cups orange juice

Dissolve yeast in warm water; let stand 5 minutes.

Combine flour, sugar, salt, orange rind, and anise seeds in a large bowl. Stir in yeast mixture and butter. Gradually add orange juice, stirring until a soft dough is formed.

Turn dough out onto a floured surface, and knead about 8 to 10 minutes until smooth and elastic. Place in a well-greased bowl, turning to grease top. Cover and let rise in a warm place (85°), free from drafts, 1 hour or until doubled in bulk.

Punch dough down; turn out onto a floured surface, and knead 1 minute. Divide dough in half. Shape each half into a loaf, and place in 2 greased 8½- x 4½- x 3-inch loafpans. Cover and let rise in a warm place (85°), free from drafts, 30 minutes or until doubled in bulk. Bake at 375° for 25 to 30 minutes or until loaves sound hollow when tapped. Remove from pans; cool on wire racks. Yield: 2 loaves.

Ella Stivers,
Abilene, Texas.

PORTUGUESE ROUND BREAD

1 cup milk
2 packages dry yeast
¼ cup warm water (105° to 115°)
¾ cup sugar
½ cup butter or margarine, softened
3 eggs
1 teaspoon salt
5½ to 6 cups all-purpose flour
1 egg, slightly beaten
1 teaspoon sugar
½ cup finely chopped pecans

Scald milk; cool to 105° to 115°.

Dissolve yeast in warm water in a large bowl. Add scalded milk, sugar, butter, 3 eggs, salt, and 3 cups flour. Beat 3 to 4 minutes at medium speed of electric mixer until smooth. Stir in enough of remaining flour to make a soft dough.

Turn dough out onto a lightly floured surface, and knead about 5 minutes until smooth and elastic. Place dough in

a greased bowl, turning to grease top. Cover and let rise in a warm place (85°), free from drafts, 1½ hours or until doubled in bulk.

Punch dough down; turn out onto a lightly floured surface. Divide dough in half; roll each half into a 25-inch rope. Place in 2 greased 9-inch round cake-pans, and coil to form a snail shape; pinch ends to seal. Cover and let rise in a warm place (85°), free from drafts, 1 hour or until doubled in bulk.

Gently brush beaten egg over each loaf. Sprinkle each loaf with ½ teaspoon sugar and ¼ cup pecans. Bake at 350° for 35 minutes or until browned. Cool loaves on wire racks. Yield: 2 loaves.

H. Green,
Dallas, Texas.

MORAVIAN FEAST BUNS

5 to 6 cups all-purpose flour, divided
1 cup sugar
2 packages dry yeast
1 teaspoon salt
¾ cup water
½ cup butter or margarine
2 eggs
½ cup cooked mashed potatoes
⅛ teaspoon ground nutmeg
Melted butter or margarine

Combine 1 cup flour, sugar, yeast, and salt in a large mixing bowl; stir well. Heat water and ½ cup butter in a small saucepan to 120° to 130°.

Gradually add hot mixture to flour mixture, beating at low speed of electric mixer until combined. Beat 2 minutes at medium speed. Beat in eggs, potatoes, nutmeg, and ¾ cup flour. Beat an additional 2 minutes. Gradually stir in enough of remaining flour to make a soft dough.

Turn dough out onto a well-floured surface, and knead about 8 to 10 minutes until smooth and elastic. Shape into a ball, and place in a well-greased bowl, turning to grease top. Cover and let rise in a warm place (85°), free from drafts, 1½ hours until doubled in bulk.

Punch dough down; cover and let rise in a warm place (85°), free from drafts, 1 hour or until doubled in bulk.

Divide dough into 12 equal pieces. Roll each piece into a ball, and place on greased baking sheets; press down lightly with fingertips to resemble a bun.

Cover and let rise in a warm place (85°), free from drafts, 1 hour or until doubled in bulk. Cut an "M" in center of each bun with a knife. Brush buns

with melted butter. Bake at 375° for 15 to 20 minutes or until golden brown. Remove from baking sheet immediately. Yield: 1 dozen buns.

Lilly B. Smith,
Richmond, Virginia.

HOLIDAY BRAIDS

6 to 6½ cups all-purpose flour, divided
½ cup sugar
1½ teaspoons salt
1 teaspoon grated lemon rind
2 packages dry yeast
1 cup milk
⅔ cup water
¼ cup butter or margarine
2 eggs
½ cup slivered almonds
½ cup chopped raisins
Vegetable oil
Powdered sugar glaze (recipe follows)

Combine 1½ cups flour, sugar, salt, lemon rind, and yeast in a large mixing bowl; stir well. Set aside.

Heat milk, water, and butter in a small saucepan to 120° to 130°. Gradually add to flour mixture, beating well. Beat 2 minutes at medium speed of electric mixer. Add eggs and ½ cup flour; beat at high speed 2 minutes. Stir in almonds, raisins, and enough of remaining flour to make a stiff dough.

Turn dough out onto a floured surface, and knead about 8 to 10 minutes until smooth and elastic. Cover and let rest 20 minutes.

Divide dough in half; divide each half into thirds. Roll each third into a 14-inch rope. Place 3 ropes, side by side, on a greased baking sheet; braid. Tuck ends under to seal. Repeat with remaining dough.

Brush each braid lightly with vegetable oil; cover and chill 2 hours. Remove from refrigerator; let stand at room temperature 10 minutes. Bake at 375° for 25 to 30 minutes. Remove from baking sheets, and place on wire racks to cool. Drizzle with glaze while warm. Yield: 2 braids.

Powdered Sugar Glaze:

2 cups sifted powdered sugar
3 tablespoons water

Combine sugar and water, stirring until smooth. Yield: about 1 cup.

Tip: Heat a knife blade in hot water; dry off quickly for ease in slicing fresh bread. A wet knife does a smooth job when cutting fresh cake.

HOLIDAY SPARKLE ROLLS

4½ to 5 cups all-purpose flour, divided
2 packages dry yeast
1 teaspoon salt
½ cup water
½ cup milk
½ cup butter or margarine
⅓ cup honey
1 egg
1 cup chopped mixed candied fruit
Additional honey (optional)

Combine 2 cups flour, yeast, and salt in a large mixing bowl; set aside.

Heat water, milk, butter, and ⅓ cup honey in a saucepan to 120° or 130°. Add to yeast mixture, and beat just until moistened. Add egg; beat 3 minutes at medium speed of electric mixer. Stir in candied fruit and enough of remaining flour to make a soft dough.

Turn dough out onto a floured surface; knead about 5 to 8 minutes until smooth and elastic.

Place dough in a greased bowl, turning to grease top. Cover and let rise in a warm place (85°), free from drafts, 1½ hours or until doubled in bulk.

Punch dough down, and divide into 4 parts. Divide each part into 6 pieces. Roll each piece into an 8-inch rope. Place on greased baking sheets, and coil each rope loosely; pinch ends to seal. Cover and let rise in a warm place (85°), free from drafts, 45 minutes or until doubled in bulk. Bake at 350° for 15 to 18 minutes or until browned. Remove from baking sheets while hot; brush with additional honey, if desired. Yield: 2 dozen rolls.

SAFFRON ROLLS

2 packages dry yeast
2¼ cups milk
⅔ cup butter or margarine
½ teaspoon ground saffron
1½ cups sugar
½ teaspoon salt
1 egg
7 to 7½ cups all-purpose flour
Raisins
1 egg, beaten

Place yeast in a large mixing bowl.

Heat milk and butter in a heavy saucepan until butter melts. Remove from heat and cool to lukewarm (105° to 115°). Add to yeast, stirring about 5 minutes until dissolved. Add saffron, sugar, salt, 1 egg, and 3½ cups flour; mix well. Gradually stir in enough of remaining flour to make a soft dough.

Turn dough out onto a floured surface, and knead about 8 to 10 minutes

until smooth and elastic. Place in a well-greased bowl, turning to grease top. Cover and let rise in a warm place (85°), free from drafts, 1 hour or until doubled in bulk.

Punch dough down; turn out onto a floured surface, and knead 1 minute. Divide dough into thirds. Roll each third into a 10-inch rope. Cut each rope into 10 pieces; roll each piece into a 9-inch rope. Place on greased cookie sheets; curl ends in opposite directions, forming "S" shapes. Cover and let rise in a warm place (85°), free from drafts, 30 minutes or until doubled in bulk. Place a raisin in center of each curl, pressing down gently; brush with beaten egg. Bake at 450° for 10 minutes or until browned. Place on wire racks; cool at least 10 minutes before serving. Yield: 2½ dozen rolls.

Do Something Different With Winter Squash

For a change of taste, why not fill an acorn squash with a fruit or meat stuffing, or whip butternut squash into a sweet pie for dessert? During the late fall and winter months, hard-rinded squash are colorful additions to many meals. Try these recipes and sample their rich, warm flavors.

SAUSAGE-STUFFED ACORN SQUASH

2 medium acorn squash
Salt
½ pound bulk pork sausage
1 small onion, chopped
¾ cup breadcrumbs

Cut squash in half lengthwise, and remove seeds. Place cut side down in a shallow baking dish, and add ½ inch boiling water. Bake at 375° for 35 minutes. Turn cut side up and sprinkle with salt; set aside.

Cook sausage and onion in a skillet until browned, stirring to crumble meat; drain. Stir in breadcrumbs; spoon into squash cavities. Bake at 375° for 20 minutes. Yield: 4 servings.

Pat Stratford,
Burlington, North Carolina.

BUTTERNUT SQUASH CHIFFON PIE

1 envelope unflavored gelatin
¼ cup water
3 eggs, separated
1½ cups cooked, mashed butternut squash
¾ cup firmly packed brown sugar
½ teaspoon salt
½ teaspoon ground nutmeg•
1 teaspoon ground cinnamon
½ cup milk
¼ cup sugar
1 baked 9-inch pastry shell
Whipped cream (optional)

Soften gelatin in water; set aside. Beat egg yolks. Combine squash, gelatin, egg yolks, brown sugar, salt, nutmeg, cinnamon, and milk in top of a double boiler. Cook over boiling water, stirring occasionally, about 10 minutes or until mixture is thoroughly heated. Chill until mixture mounds when dropped from a spoon.

Beat egg whites (at room temperature) until foamy. Gradually add sugar, beating until stiff peaks form. Fold into squash mixture; spoon into pastry shell. Chill several hours until firm. Garnish with whipped cream, if desired. Yield: one 9-inch pie.

Dora Farrar,
Gadsden, Alabama.

APPLE-STUFFED ACORN SQUASH

3 medium acorn squash
2 tablespoons butter or margarine, melted
Salt
Ground cinnamon
3 apples, peeled, cored, and chopped
1 tablespoon grated lemon rind
1 tablespoon lemon juice
2 tablespoons butter or margarine, melted
½ cup honey

Cut squash in half lengthwise and remove seeds. Place cut side down in a shallow baking dish, and add ½ inch boiling water. Bake, uncovered, at 375° for 35 minutes. Turn cut side up; brush cut surfaces and cavities with 2 tablespoons butter. Sprinkle lightly with salt and cinnamon.

Combine apples, lemon rind, lemon juice, 2 tablespoons butter, and honey; mix well and spoon into squash cavities. Bake, uncovered, at 350° for 30 minutes. Yield: 6 servings.

Debra S. Petersen,
Slidell, Louisiana.

Holiday Desserts

Holiday Desserts Sweeten The Season

Throughout the month of December you'll hear Southerners talking about the fruitcake they're aging, the divinity they've made, or the beautiful box of homemade confections someone gave them. Everyone loves desserts, and there's no other time of the year more celebrated for its sweets than Christmas.

With this in mind, the Foods Staff is proud to introduce our newest special section—*Holiday Desserts*. The recipes, like our others, were chosen because they were family favorites from across the South.

For starters, take a look at this spectacular array of confections. These cookies and candies include all the ingredients you'd expect to find in a good confection, like nuts, fruit, and chocolate. From old-fashioned Pecan-Shortbread Sugarplums to specially shaped Pizzelles, we're sure you'll find just the right something to please your family or to tuck into a goody box for a neighbor.

APRICOT DIVINITY

3 cups sugar
¾ cup water
¾ cup light corn syrup
1 (3-ounce) package apricot-flavored gelatin
2 egg whites

Combine sugar, water, and corn syrup in a 3-quart saucepan; cook over low heat, stirring constantly, until sugar dissolves. Cook over high heat, without stirring, until mixture reaches hard ball stage (260°).

Combine gelatin and egg whites (at room temperature) in a large mixing bowl; beat until stiff peaks form. Pour hot sugar mixture in a very thin stream over egg whites while beating constantly at high speed of an electric mixer. Continue beating 5 to 10 minutes until mixture holds its shape.

Quickly drop mixture by heaping teaspoonfuls onto waxed paper; cool. Yield: 6 dozen.   *Susie Cole, Lake Charles, Louisiana.*

APRICOT PASTRIES

2 cups dried apricots
2 tablespoons sugar
3 cups all-purpose flour
1 tablespoon sugar
½ teaspoon salt
1 cup shortening
1 package dry yeast
½ cup warm milk (105° to 115°)
1 egg, slightly beaten
½ teaspoon vanilla extract
Sifted powdered sugar

Combine apricots and 2 tablespoons sugar in a medium saucepan. Add enough water to cover apricots, and bring to a boil over high heat. Reduce heat and simmer, uncovered, 15 minutes or until tender. Drain; coarsely chop apricots, and set aside.

Combine next 3 ingredients; cut in shortening with pastry blender until mixture resembles coarse meal. Dissolve yeast in warm milk; stir in egg and vanilla, mixing well. Add to dry ingredients, and stir until blended. Divide dough into fourths; cover and chill at least 1 hour.

Work with 1 portion of dough at a time, keeping remaining dough chilled until ready to use. Roll 1 portion of dough into a 10-inch square on a surface well dusted with powdered sugar. Cut dough into 2½-inch squares; place 1 teaspoon of apricots in center of each. Overlap opposite corners; place pastries 2 inches apart on greased cookie sheets, seam side up. Bake at 350° for 10 to 12 minutes. Immediately remove from pan, and dust with powdered sugar. Yield: about 5 dozen.   *Mae McClaugherty, Marble Falls, Texas.*

BUTTERSCOTCH BARS

½ cup butter or margarine, softened
¾ cup firmly packed brown sugar
1 egg
½ teaspoon vanilla extract
1¼ cups all-purpose flour
½ teaspoon baking soda
½ teaspoon salt
Filling (recipe follows)
1 (6-ounce) package butterscotch morsels
¾ cup mixed candied fruit
½ cup chopped walnuts

Cream butter; gradually add sugar, beating well. Add egg and vanilla, beating until smooth. Combine flour, soda, and salt; stir into butter mixture. Spread evenly in a lightly greased 13- x 9- x 2-inch baking pan. Bake at 350° for 15 minutes.

Spread filling evenly over crust. Combine remaining ingredients; sprinkle over filling. Bake at 350° for 15 minutes. Cool and cut into bars. Yield: about 3 dozen.

Filling:

2 tablespoons brown sugar
2 tablespoons milk
1 tablespoon butter or margarine, melted
1 egg
⅓ cup all-purpose flour
½ teaspoon baking soda
½ teaspoon ground cinnamon
¼ teaspoon salt

Combine brown sugar, milk, butter, and egg; beat at medium speed of an electric mixer until smooth. Combine flour, soda, cinnamon, and salt; add to sugar mixture, beating until smooth. Yield: about ⅔ cup.
Mrs. Randy Throneberry, Shelbyville, Tennessee.

ALMOND TRUFFLES

3 tablespoons butter, softened
½ cup sifted powdered sugar
6 (1-ounce) squares semisweet chocolate, finely grated
1 egg yolk, slightly beaten
2 tablespoons white crème de cacao
24 whole almonds, toasted
½ cup finely chopped almonds

Cream butter; gradually add sugar, beating well. Add chocolate, egg yolk, and crème de cacao; beat until blended. Chill mixture 1 hour.

Shape mixture into 1-inch balls, inserting one whole almond into center of each; roll in chopped almonds. Cover and refrigerate overnight. Yield: about 2 dozen.
Pat Boschen,
Ashland, Virginia.

PIZZELLES

3 eggs
½ cup sugar
¼ cup vegetable oil
½ teaspoon vanilla extract
⅛ to ¼ teaspoon anise oil
1½ cups all-purpose flour
Vegetable oil

Beat eggs at medium speed of an electric mixer until foamy; gradually add sugar, beating until thick and lemon colored. Add next 3 ingredients; mix well. Add flour; beat until smooth.

Brush pizzelle iron lightly with oil; preheat iron over medium heat 2 minutes. Place 1 tablespoon batter in center of iron; close iron and bake 1 minute on each side or until pizzelle is lightly browned. Repeat with remaining batter; cool on wire racks. Yield: about 2 dozen.
Louise Andolina,
Charlotte, North Carolina.

DATE-CREAM CHEESE ROLLUPS

1 cup butter or margarine, softened
1 (8-ounce) package cream cheese, softened
2 cups all-purpose flour
¼ teaspoon salt
2 (8-ounce) packages pitted dates
Sifted powdered sugar

Cream butter and cream cheese; add flour and salt, stirring until blended. Divide dough into fourths; chill at least 2 hours.

Work with 1 portion of dough at a time, keeping remaining dough chilled until ready to use. Roll 1 portion of dough to ⅛-inch thickness on a surface lightly dusted with powdered sugar. Cut dough into 3- x 1-inch strips. Place a date in center of each, and roll up strips jellyroll fashion, starting at short end.

Place rollups on ungreased cookie sheets, seam side down; bake at 375° for 15 minutes or until lightly browned. Repeat with remaining dough. Let rollups cool; sprinkle lightly with powdered sugar, if desired. Yield: 8½ dozen.
Jan Jacobs,
Atlanta, Georgia.

PECAN-SHORTBREAD SUGARPLUMS

½ cup butter, softened
1 cup sifted powdered sugar
3 tablespoons brandy
2 tablespoons light corn syrup
3 cups shortbread cookie crumbs (recipe follows)
1 (8-ounce) package pitted dates, chopped
1 (4-ounce) package chopped candied pineapple
1 (4-ounce) package chopped red candied cherries
1 cup muscat raisins
1 cup finely chopped pecans
¼ cup finely chopped mixed candied fruit

Cream butter; gradually add sugar, beating until light and fluffy. Add brandy and corn syrup; beat well. Stir in remaining ingredients. (Mixture will be stiff.) Shape mixture into 1-inch balls. Chill until firm. Yield: 6 dozen.

Shortbread Cookie Crumbs:

⅔ cup butter, softened
¼ cup plus 1 tablespoon sugar
1½ cups all-purpose flour

Cream butter; gradually add sugar, beating well. Gradually stir in flour. Chill dough several hours or overnight.

Roll dough to ¼-inch thickness on a lightly floured surface. Cut dough with a 1½-inch cutter. Place on lightly greased cookie sheets; bake at 325° for 20 minutes. Cool on a wire rack. Crush enough cookies to yield about 3 cups crumbs. Yield: 6 dozen cookies.
Helen J. Seine,
Austin, Texas.

PISTACHIO FUDGE

4 cups sugar
2 cups milk
½ cup butter or margarine
¼ teaspoon salt
1 teaspoon vanilla extract
¼ cup finely chopped dry roasted pistachios
Candied red and green cherries

Combine first 4 ingredients in a large Dutch oven. Cook over low heat, stirring constantly, until sugar dissolves.

Cook over medium heat, stirring occasionally, until mixture reaches soft ball stage (234°). Remove from heat (do not stir). Cool to lukewarm (110°).

Add vanilla and pistachios; beat with a wooden spoon 2 to 3 minutes until mixture is thick and begins to lose its gloss. Pour into a buttered 8-inch square pan. Mark top of warm fudge into 1⅓-inch squares using a sharp knife. Decorate each square as desired with candied cherries. Cool and cut into squares. Yield: 3 dozen.
Mary Jane Highland,
Carbondale, Illinois.

SPICY HOLIDAY FRUIT COOKIES

3½ cups all-purpose flour
2 teaspoons baking powder
1 teaspoon ground cinnamon
½ teaspoon salt
½ teaspoon ground nutmeg
1 cup shortening
2 cups firmly packed brown sugar
2 eggs
½ cup milk
1 cup chopped pecans
1 cup chopped dates
1 cup chopped candied cherries
½ cup regular oats, uncooked
Red or green whole candied cherries, halved (optional)

Combine first 5 ingredients; set aside.
Cream shortening; gradually add
sugar, beating until light and fluffy. Add
eggs, and beat well. Add dry ingredients alternately with milk, beating
well. Stir in next 4 ingredients.

Drop dough by level tablespoonfuls
onto ungreased cookie sheets. Top each
cookie with a cherry half. Bake at 375°
for 12 to 14 minutes. Cool on wire
racks. Yield: 7 dozen.

Mrs. Billie Taylor,
Afton, Virginia.

HOLIDAY GARLAND COOKIES

1 cup butter, softened
1 cup sifted powdered sugar
2 eggs, separated
½ teaspoon vanilla extract
2¼ cups all-purpose flour
Dash of salt
Red and green candied cherries

Cream butter; gradually add sugar,
beating well. Add egg yolks and vanilla;
mix well. Stir in flour and salt. Cover;
chill at least 1 hour.

Shape 1 tablespoon dough into a 6-
inch rope. Place rope on a lightly
greased cookie sheet, bringing ends of
rope together to form a circle; pinch
ends together to seal. Repeat with remaining dough.

Slightly beat egg whites; carefully
brush each cookie with egg whites. Decorate as desired with red and green candied cherries. Bake at 350° for 10 to 12
minutes or until lightly browned. Yield:
2½ dozen. *M. Wilcox,*
Grand Cane, Louisiana.

Start With A Mix

With so much extra cooking during
the holidays, you'll appreciate these recipes for quick desserts. They all start
with a convenient mix but are dressed
up enough to serve at any occasion.

If you want an elegant dessert in a
hurry, you won't be able to resist our

refreshing Brownie Alaskas. Just bake
brownies from a mix, top with ice
cream, and frost with meringue. Bake
only until the meringue browns, and
serve immediately. Since this dessert requires last-minute preparation, you'll
serve your guests faster if you've
scooped the ice cream in advance (place
the scoops on a cookie sheet, and freeze
until ready to use); the ice cream will
stay firm while the meringue browns.

BROWNIE ALASKAS

1 (15.5-ounce) package fudge brownie
  mix
1½ pints strawberry ice cream
4 egg whites
½ cup sugar
Candied red and green cherry wedges
  (optional)

Prepare brownie mix according to
package directions using a 9-inch square
pan; let cool completely. Cut brownies
into 3-inch squares.

Arrange brownies on a cookie sheet;
top each brownie with a scoop of ice
cream. Freeze at least 1 hour.

Beat egg whites (at room temperature) until foamy. Gradually add sugar,
1 tablespoon at a time, beating until
stiff peaks form.

Remove ice cream-topped brownies
from freezer. Spread meringue over ice
cream, sealing to edge of brownie. Bake
at 500° for 2 to 3 minutes or until lightly
browned. Garnish with cherries, if desired. Yield: 9 servings.

Mrs. Clayton Turner,
DeFuniak Springs, Florida.

REGAL COCONUT CAKE

1 (18.5-ounce) package yellow cake mix
  without pudding
1 (3-ounce) package vanilla pudding mix
1½ cups milk
1 cup whipping cream
2 tablespoons sifted powdered sugar
½ teaspoon vanilla extract
1 (7-ounce) can flaked coconut, divided
Seven-Minute Frosting

Prepare cake mix according to package directions; pour batter into 2
greased and floured 9-inch round cakepans. Bake at 350° for 25 to 30 minutes
or until a wooden pick inserted in the
center comes out clean. Cool in pans 10
minutes; remove from pans, and cool
completely on wire racks.

Combine pudding mix and milk in a
small saucepan; mix well. Cook over
medium heat, stirring constantly, until
thickened and bubbly. Remove from
heat. Cover and chill completely (about
1 hour).

Combine next 3 ingredients in a bowl;
beat until stiff peaks form. Fold
whipped cream mixture and 1½ cups
coconut into chilled pudding.

Split each cake layer horizontally;
place bottom layer of cake on a cake
plate; spread with 1⅓ cups pudding
mixture. Repeat with second and third
layers. Place remaining layer, cut side
down, on top of cake. Cover and chill
cake at least 3 hours. Spread top and
sides of cake with Seven-Minute Frosting; sprinkle top with remaining coconut. Yield: one 4-layer cake.

Seven-Minute Frosting:

3 egg whites
¾ cup sugar
⅓ cup light corn syrup
⅛ teaspoon cream of tartar
Dash of salt

Combine all ingredients in top of a
large double boiler; beat on low speed
of electric mixer for 30 seconds or just
until blended.

Place over boiling water; beat constantly on high speed about 7 minutes
or until stiff peaks form; remove from
heat. If necessary, beat 2 additional
minutes or until frosting is thick enough
to spread. Yield: enough for one 4-layer
cake. *Mrs. Ralph Major,*
Corryton, Tennessee.

*Tip: To test for doneness in baking a
butter or margarine cake, insert a
wooden pick or wire cake tester into
the center of the cake in at least two
places. The tester should come out
clean if the cake is done.*

CHOCOLATE MACAROONS

1 (18.5-ounce) package devil's food cake
   mix with pudding
1 cup flaked coconut, toasted
½ cup regular oats, uncooked and toasted
¾ cup butter or margarine, melted
2 teaspoons vanilla extract
2 eggs, slightly beaten
6 (1.45-ounce) milk chocolate candy bars
¾ cup flaked coconut

Combine first 6 ingredients; chill 30 minutes. Drop dough by heaping teaspoonfuls 2 inches apart on ungreased cookie sheets. Bake at 350° for 10 minutes. Immediately top each cookie with one chocolate square; spread to frost. Sprinkle cookies with coconut. Yield: about 6 dozen.   *Rublelene Singleton, Scotts Hill, Tennessee.*

CHOCOLATE PIE AMANDINE

½ cup milk
1 envelope whipped topping mix
1 (3¾-ounce) package chocolate fudge
   instant pudding mix
⅛ teaspoon salt
½ cup milk
3 to 4 tablespoons amaretto or other
   almond-flavored liqueur
1 baked 8-inch pastry shell
¼ cup slivered almonds, toasted

Combine ½ cup milk and whipped topping mix in a chilled mixing bowl; beat on high speed of electric mixer for 3 minutes or until stiff peaks form. Add pudding mix, salt, ½ cup milk, and amaretto; beat at high speed of electric mixer 2 minutes or until smooth and thickened.

Pour into pastry shell; sprinkle with almonds. Chill 3 to 4 hours. Yield: one 8-inch pie.   *Emily W. Booth, Sandston, Virginia.*

Tip: To determine the size or capacity of a utensil, fill a liquid measure with water, and pour into utensil. Repeat until utensil is full, noting amount of water used. To determine a utensil's dimensions, measure from the inside edges.

Layer Cakes With Lots Of Flavor

If thoughts of your favorite dessert bring visions of layer cakes filled with whipped cream, fruit, or a creamy frosting, then you'll love these recipes. We think they're special enough to serve at your finest Christmas celebrations.

FRESH ORANGE CAKE

2 medium oranges
½ cup raisins
½ cup chopped dates
½ cup pecan pieces
⅓ cup orange juice
½ cup shortening
1¼ cups sugar
2 eggs
1¾ cups all-purpose flour
¾ teaspoon baking soda
¾ teaspoon salt
½ cup buttermilk
Orange Butter Frosting
1 (10-inch) strip orange rind (optional)
Pecan halves (optional)

Remove zest (orange part of peel) from oranges. Position knife blade in food processor bowl. Add orange zest, and cover; process until finely diced. Measure ¼ cup lightly packed zest; reserve remaining zest and orange for other uses.

Combine ¼ cup orange zest, raisins, dates, and ½ cup pecan pieces in processor bowl; cover. Using knife blade, process mixture until diced. Combine fruit mixture and orange juice; set aside.

Cream shortening in a large mixing bowl; gradually add sugar, beating well. Add eggs, one at a time, beating well after each addition.

Combine flour, soda, and salt; add to creamed mixture alternately with buttermilk, beginning and ending with flour mixture. Stir in fruit mixture.

Pour batter into 2 greased and floured 8-inch round cakepans. Bake at 350° for 25 to 30 minutes or until a wooden pick inserted in center comes out clean. Cool in pans 10 minutes; remove from pans, and cool completely on wire racks. Spread frosting between layers and on top and sides of cake. To garnish, tie orange strip into a bow, and place on top of cake; arrange pecan halves around base of cake, if desired. Yield: one 2-layer cake.

Orange Butter Frosting:

¼ cup plus 2 tablespoons butter or
   margarine, softened
3 cups sifted powdered sugar
1½ tablespoons light corn syrup
1½ tablespoons lemon juice
1½ tablespoons orange juice
1½ teaspoons grated orange rind

Cream butter; gradually add sugar, beating well. Add syrup and fruit juice, beating until smooth. Stir in rind. Yield: enough for one 2-layer cake.

Billie Aaron, Gardendale, Alabama.

FRESH APPLE-DATE CAKE

1½ cups peeled, chopped apple
¾ cup chopped dates
1 cup chopped pecans
¼ cup chopped maraschino cherries
3 cups all-purpose flour, divided
⅔ cup shortening
1½ cups sugar
2 eggs
2 teaspoons baking soda
1 cup buttermilk
1 teaspoon salt
1 teaspoon ground cinnamon
1 teaspoon vanilla extract
½ teaspoon almond extract
Apple-Date Filling
Lemon Buttercream Frosting

Combine apple, dates, pecans, and cherries; dredge with ½ cup flour, stirring to coat well. Set mixture aside.

Cream shortening in a large mixing bowl; gradually add sugar, beating well. Add eggs, one at a time, beating well after each addition.

Dissolve soda in buttermilk. Combine 2½ cups flour, salt, and cinnamon; add to creamed mixture alternately with buttermilk mixture, beginning and ending with flour mixture. Stir in fruit mixture and flavorings.

Pour batter into 3 greased and floured 9-inch round cakepans. Bake at 350° for 20 to 25 minutes or until a wooden pick inserted in center comes out clean. Cool in pans 10 minutes; remove from pans, and cool completely on wire racks. Spread Apple-Date Filling between layers; spread Lemon Buttercream Frosting on top and sides of cake. Yield: one 3-layer cake.

Apple-Date Filling:

4 cups peeled, chopped apple
¼ cup water
¾ cup chopped dates
¼ cup sugar
1 tablespoon cornstarch

Combine apple and water in a large saucepan; cover and cook over low heat about 15 minutes or until tender. Drain well. Combine 1½ cups cooked apple and remaining ingredients in saucepan; cook over medium heat, stirring constantly, until thickened. Yield: 2 cups.

Lemon Buttercream Frosting:

¼ cup butter or margarine, softened
1 (16-ounce) package powdered sugar, sifted
4 to 5 tablespoons half-and-half
1 tablespoon grated lemon rind
2 tablespoons lemon juice

Cream butter. Gradually add sugar; beat well. Add remaining ingredients, beating until smooth. Yield: enough for one 3-layer cake. *Aileen Arnold, Searcy, Arkansas.*

LEMON GOLD CAKE

½ cup butter, softened
1 tablespoon grated lemon rind
1¾ cups sugar
6 egg yolks
2½ cups all-purpose flour
2½ teaspoons baking powder
½ teaspoon salt
1 cup plus 3 tablespoons milk
Seven-Minute Frosting
1 (3-ounce) can flaked coconut
Lemon candy slices (optional)

Cream butter in a large mixing bowl; add lemon rind. Gradually add sugar,

beating well. Add egg yolks, one at a time, beating well after each addition.

Combine flour, baking powder, and salt; add to creamed mixture alternately with milk, beginning and ending with flour mixture.

Pour batter into 2 greased and floured 9-inch round cakepans. Bake at 350° for 25 to 30 minutes or until a wooden pick inserted in center comes out clean. Cool in pans 10 minutes; remove from pans, and cool completely on wire racks. Spread Seven-Minute Frosting between layers and on top and sides of cake. Lightly sprinkle top and sides with coconut. Garnish with lemon candy slices, if desired. Yield: one 2-layer cake.

Seven-Minute Frosting:

1½ cups sugar
2 egg whites
1 tablespoon light corn syrup
Dash of salt
⅓ cup cold water
1 teaspoon vanilla extract

Combine first 5 ingredients in top of a large double boiler. Beat at low speed of electric mixer for 30 seconds or until just blended.

Place over boiling water; beat constantly at high speed of electric mixer about 7 minutes or until stiff peaks form. Remove from heat. Add vanilla; beat 2 additional minutes or until frosting is thick enough to spread. Yield: enough for one 2-layer cake.
Gladys Stout, Elizabethton, Tennessee.

BEST FUDGE CAKE

3 (1-ounce) squares unsweetened chocolate
½ cup butter or margarine, softened
2¼ cups firmly packed brown sugar
3 eggs
1½ teaspoons vanilla extract
2¼ cups sifted cake flour
2 teaspoons baking soda
½ teaspoon salt
1 (8-ounce) carton commercial sour cream
1 cup boiling water
Filling (recipe follows)
Mocha Frosting
Chocolate curls (optional)

Melt chocolate; set aside to cool. Cream butter in a large mixing bowl; gradually add sugar, beating well. Add eggs, one at a time, beating well after each addition. Add chocolate and vanilla; mix well.

Combine flour, soda, and salt; add to creamed mixture alternately with sour cream, beginning and ending with flour mixture. Stir in boiling water. (Batter will be thin.)

Pour batter into 2 greased and floured 8-inch round cakepans. Bake at 350° for 30 to 35 minutes or until a wooden pick inserted in center comes out clean. Cool in pans 10 minutes; remove from pans, and cool completely on wire racks. Split cake layers in half horizontally to make 4 layers. Spread filling between layers; spread Mocha Frosting on top and sides of cake. Refrigerate. Garnish with chocolate curls, if desired. Yield: one 4-layer cake.

Filling:

1½ cups whipping cream
1 teaspoon vanilla extract
½ cup sifted powdered sugar

Beat whipping cream and vanilla until foamy; gradually add powdered sugar, beating until soft peaks form. Yield: about 3 cups.

Mocha Frosting:

½ cup butter or margarine, softened
5 cups sifted powdered sugar
¼ cup cocoa
¼ cup strong coffee
2 teaspoons vanilla extract
About 2 tablespoons whipping cream

Combine first 5 ingredients; beat until light and fluffy. Add cream if too stiff, and beat well. Yield: enough for one 4-layer cake. *Pat Campbell, Temple, Texas.*

Tip: Chocolate must be treated delicately. It should always be stored at a temperature under 75°. If a gray color develops, this is a sign that the cocoa butter has risen to the surface. Flavor and quality will not be lessened, and the gray color will disappear when the chocolate is melted.

BLACK FOREST CHERRY CAKE

6 eggs
1 cup sugar
1 teaspoon vanilla extract
½ cup all-purpose flour
½ cup cocoa
⅔ cup butter or margarine, melted
½ cup water
⅓ cup sugar
2 to 3 tablespoons Kirsch
2½ cups whipping cream
½ cup sifted powdered sugar
Cherry Filling
1 (6-ounce) jar maraschino cherries with stems, drained (optional)

Place eggs in a large mixing bowl; beat at high speed of an electric mixer until foamy. Gradually add 1 cup sugar; beat at high speed 10 minutes or until mixture is very thick. Stir in vanilla.

Combine flour and cocoa. Sprinkle about one-fourth of flour mixture over egg mixture; carefully fold in. Repeat with remaining flour, using one-fourth at a time. Gently fold in butter, one-fourth at a time, just until combined.

Pour batter into 3 greased and floured 8-inch round cakepans. Bake at 350° for 15 to 18 minutes or until a wooden pick inserted in center comes out clean. Cool in pans 5 mintues. Remove from pans; cool completely on wire racks. (Layers will be thin).

Combine water and ⅓ cup sugar in a small saucepan. Cook over medium heat, stirring constantly, until sugar dissolves. Bring to a boil; cook, uncovered, 5 minutes, stirring occasionally. Remove saucepan from heat, and let mixture cool. Stir in Kirsch. Sprinkle syrup evenly over cooled cake layers.

Beat whipping cream until foamy; gradually add powdered sugar, beating until soft peaks form. Place 1 cake layer on cake platter; spread with about 1 cup whipped cream, and top with half of Cherry Filling. Top with second layer and repeat procedure; top with third cake layer. Frost top and sides of cake with whipped cream, reserving a small amount for garnish.

Spoon or pipe dollops of whipped cream on top of cake; place maraschino cherries around top edge of cake, if desired. Refrigerate until ready to serve. Yield: one 8-inch cake.

Cherry Filling:

1 (16½-ounce) can pitted dark sweet cherries, undrained
2 tablespoons Kirsch
1 tablespoon cornstarch

Drain cherries, reserving ⅔ cup liquid. Combine cherries and Kirsch in a small bowl; let stand 1 hour.

Combine reserved cherry liquid and cornstarch in a small saucepan, stirring until smooth. Cook over medium heat, stirring occasionally, until mixture is thickened. Cool. Stir in cherry mixture. Yield: 1½ cups.   *Doris Curls,*
Anniston, Alabama.

COOKING LIGHT

Splurge On These Light Desserts

Desserts don't have to be high in calories. Indulge in Flaming Fruit Dessert or Pears Poached in Red Wine, and you'll enjoy a delightfully elegant dessert that adds no more than 180 calories to your menu. These "Cooking Light" desserts are festive enough for the holidays, yet light enough for the serious dieter.

PEARS POACHED IN RED WINE

4 ripe pears
2 tablespoons lemon juice
2 cups Burgundy or other dry red wine
1 cup unsweetened apple juice
4 lemon slices
1 (4-inch) stick cinnamon
Lemon rind strips (optional)

Peel pears, removing core from bottom end but leaving stems intact. Slice about ¼ inch from bottom of each pear to make a flat base. Brush pears with lemon juice to prevent browning.

Combine next 4 ingredients in a Dutch oven; bring to a boil. Place pears in Dutch oven in an upright position; spoon wine mixture over pears. Cover, reduce heat, and simmer 15 to 20 minutes or until tender. Let pears cool in wine mixture; chill, turning pears occasionally. Remove cinnamon. Spoon pears and wine mixture into dessert dishes; garnish with lemon rind strips, if desired. Yield: 4 servings (about 152 calories per serving).

FLAMING FRUIT DESSERT

1 (16-ounce) can unsweetened peaches, undrained
1 cup seedless green grapes, halved
1 cup seedless red grapes, halved
⅓ cup unsweetened white grape juice
½ teaspoon grated orange rind
¼ teaspoon ground cinnamon
¼ teaspoon ground nutmeg
¼ cup rum
3 cups vanilla ice milk

Combine first 7 ingredients in a medium skillet. Bring to a boil; cover, reduce heat, and simmer just until fruit is thoroughly heated.

Place rum in a small, long-handled pan; heat just until warm (do not boil). Ignite rum with a long match, and pour over fruit. Serve sauce over ½-cup portions of ice milk. Yield: 6 servings (about 180 calories per serving).

ORANGE MOLDED DESSERT

2 envelopes unflavored gelatin
2¼ cups water, divided
1 (12-ounce) can frozen orange juice concentrate, undiluted
1 pint orange sherbet, softened
2 medium oranges, peeled, sectioned, and seeded
Vegetable cooking spray
12 whole strawberries or orange twists (optional)

Soften gelatin in ¼ cup water in a mixing bowl; let stand 5 minutes.

Bring remaining 2 cups water to a boil; add gelatin, stirring until dissolved. Add orange juice concentrate; stir until melted. Fold in sherbet; chill until the consistency of unbeaten egg white.

Fold orange sections into gelatin mixture; pour into 12 individual molds coated with cooking spray. Chill until firm; unmold onto serving dishes. Garnish with whole strawberries or orange twists, if desired. Yield: 12 servings (about 112 calories per ½-cup serving). *Beryle Wyatt, Columbia, Missouri.*

BAKED AMBROSIA

3 large seedless oranges
¼ cup pitted dates, chopped
2 tablespoons flaked coconut
¼ cup chopped walnuts or pecans
½ cup plain low-fat yogurt
½ teaspoon vanilla extract
1 tablespoon flaked coconut

Cut oranges in half crosswise. Clip membranes, and carefully remove pulp (do not puncture bottom); set orange shells aside. Chop orange pulp.

Combine orange pulp, dates, 2 tablespoons coconut, and chopped walnuts. Spoon orange mixture into orange shells, and place in a 12- x 8- x 2-inch baking dish. Bake at 350° for 25 minutes. Combine yogurt and vanilla; divide mixture over tops of oranges. Sprinkle with 1 tablespoon coconut. Serve immediately. Yield: 6 servings (about 115 calories per serving).
Mrs. James S. Stanton, Richmond, Virginia.

juice mixture, and beat an additional 3 minutes.

Combine flour, baking powder, and salt; add to egg mixture, mixing well; stir in almond extract.

Beat egg whites (at room temperature) and cream of tartar until soft peaks form. Gradually add ½ cup sugar, 1 tablespoon at a time, beating until stiff peaks form. Gently fold egg white mixture and crushed pineapple into batter.

Spoon batter into an ungreased 10-inch tube pan. Bake at 350° for 50 to 55 minutes or until top of cake springs back when lightly touched. Invert cake; cool 1 hour or until completely cooled before removing from pan. Yield: 16 servings (about 136 calories per serving). *Peggy Blackburn, Winston-Salem, North Carolina.*

Take A Sip Of Dessert

End meals on a deliciously different note by getting out your most elaborate beverage glasses and sipping your way through dessert. These thick and creamy concoctions are filling enough to take the place of a piece of cake or pie.

BANANA FLIP

2 medium-size ripe bananas, cut into 1-inch slices
¼ cup sifted powdered sugar
1 cup vanilla ice cream
½ cup half-and-half
½ cup brandy
¼ cup plus 2 tablespoons créme de cacao
3 cups crushed ice

Combine all ingredients in container of electric blender; process until frothy. Yield: 5 cups.

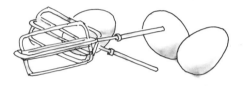

ICE CREAM GINGER FIZZ

2 (16-ounce) cans fruit cocktail, drained
4 eggs
1 pint vanilla ice cream
1 cup ginger ale, chilled
Additional vanilla ice cream (optional)

Combine half of first 3 ingredients in container of electic blender; process until smooth. Pour mixture into a large bowl. Repeat procedure. Gently stir in ginger ale. Pour into individual glasses; top with additional ice cream, if desired. Serve immediately. Yield: 6 cups. *Mrs. Bettina Hambrick, Muskogee, Oklahoma.*

HEAVENLY PINEAPPLE CAKE

1 (8-ounce) can unsweetened crushed pineapple, undrained
6 eggs, separated
½ cup sugar
2 cups sifted cake flour
1 tablespoon baking powder
½ teaspoon salt
1 teaspoon almond extract
½ teaspoon cream of tartar
½ cup sugar

Drain pineapple, reserving juice. Add water to juice to measure ¾ cup, and set aside.

Beat egg yolks at high speed of electric mixer until thick and lemon colored. Add ½ cup sugar and pineapple

SIMPLY SUPER DESSERT DRINK

1 cup whipping cream
1 cup Kalúa or other coffee-flavored liquor
½ cup créme de cacao
½ cup amaretto
1 teaspoon Galliano
2 teaspoons instant coffee granules
8 ice cubes
Shaved chocolate (optional)

Combine first 7 ingredients in container of electric blender; process until smooth. Serve in chilled champagne glasses. Garnish with shaved chocolate, if desired. Yield: 4 cups.
David Edwards, Chapel Hill, North Carolina.

CREAMY EGGNOG

6 eggs, separated
¾ cup sugar, divided
2 cups whipping cream
2 cups milk
¾ to 1 cup brandy or whiskey
Ground nutmeg

Beat egg yolks until thick and lemon colored; gradually add sugar, beating well. Stir in whipping cream, milk, and brandy.

Beat egg whites (at room temperature) until soft peaks form. Fold into brandy mixture. Chill thoroughly. Sprinkle with nutmeg. Yield: 8 cups.
Peggy H. Amos, Martinsville, Virginia.

CHAMPAGNE DELIGHT

1 pint raspberry sherbet, softened
¼ cup plus 2 tablespoons cognac
1 (25.4-ounce) bottle champagne, chilled

Spoon about ⅓ cup sherbet into each of 6 champagne glasses. Add 1 tablespoon cognac to each; stir well. Slowly fill each glass with champagne; stir gently. Serve immediately. Yield: 6 servings.
Maryse H. Rose,
Mary Esther, Florida.

Sweet And Crunchy With Nuts

Whether it's the crunchiness of pecans or the delightful flavor of almonds, nuts are a popular ingredient in holiday desserts.

Grated Apple Pie sports a generous topping of chopped pecans.

ALMOND-CHOCOLATE BARS

1 (8-ounce) package cream cheese, softened
¾ cup butter or margarine, softened
¾ cup sugar
2 cups all-purpose flour
½ teaspoon baking powder
1 teaspoon vanilla extract
1 (6-ounce) package semisweet chocolate morsels
½ cup sliced almonds, toasted

Combine cream cheese and butter in a mixing bowl; beat well. Gradually add sugar, beating until light and fluffy. Combine flour and baking powder; add to creamed mixture, beating well. Stir in vanilla. Spread mixture evenly in an ungreased 13- x 9- x 2-inch baking pan. Bake at 375° for 15 minutes.
Sprinkle chocolate morsels immediately over baked layer; let stand 5 minutes or until chocolate melts. Spread chocolate evenly, to edge of pan. Sprinkle with almonds. Cool, and cut into bars. Yield: about 2½ dozen.
Hattie McNeely,
Archer City, Texas.

GRATED APPLE PIE

1 cup sugar
1 tablespoon all-purpose flour
1 teaspoon ground cinnamon
Dash of salt
4 cups coarsely grated peeled apple
1 egg, beaten
¼ cup plus 2 tablespoons butter, melted
1 unbaked 9-inch pastry shell
1 cup chopped pecans

Combine sugar, flour, cinnamon, and salt in a large bowl; add apple, and toss gently. Stir in egg and butter. Spoon mixture into pastry shell; sprinkle with pecans.
Bake at 400° for 10 minutes; reduce heat to 350°, and bake an additional 50 minutes. Yield: one 9-inch pie.
Charlotte Watkins,
Lakeland, Florida.

Tip: Pans used for pastry never need greasing. The pastry shell or crumb crust will not stick to the sides.

RASPBERRY-NUT STRUDEL

1 cup butter or margarine, softened
1 (8-ounce) package cream cheese, softened
3 cups instant blending flour
Sifted powdered sugar
1 cup raisins
1 cup raspberry preserves
1 cup finely chopped walnuts
1 cup firmly packed brown sugar
1 cup flaked coconut

Cream butter and cream cheese; stir in flour. Divide dough into 4 equal portions. Wrap each in plastic wrap and refrigerate overnight.
Work with 1 portion of dough at a time; keep remaining dough chilled. Sift powdered sugar lightly over working surface. Roll dough into a 12- x 8-inch rectangle. Combine raisins, preserves, walnuts, sugar, and coconut; spread one-fourth of mixture over dough. Roll up jellyroll fashion, starting at short end. Pinch seams and ends together. Place roll, seam side down, on an ungreased baking sheet. Repeat procedure with remaining dough and filling.

Bake at 325° for 55 minutes. Serve warm or at room temperature. Yield: four 12-inch rolls. *Carol L. Haggett, Norfolk, Virginia.*

LAYERED PECAN PIE

1 (8-ounce) package cream cheese, softened
⅓ cup sugar
¼ teaspoon salt
1 egg
1 teaspoon vanilla extract
1 unbaked 9-inch pastry shell
1¼ cups chopped pecans
3 eggs
1 cup light corn syrup
¼ cup sugar
1 teaspoon vanilla extract

Combine first 3 ingredients; beat until smooth. Add 1 egg and 1 teaspoon vanilla, beating until combined; spoon into pastry shell. Sprinkle with pecans.

Combine 3 eggs, corn syrup, ¼ cup sugar, and 1 teaspoon vanilla; beat well and pour over pecans. Bake at 375° for 35 to 40 minutes or until set. Yield: one 9-inch pie. *Mrs. Earl L. Faulkenberry, Lancaster, South Carolina.*

Bake And Send A Tasty Holiday Surprise

Family members who must be away for the holidays always look forward to receiving food packages from home. Preparing food that will hold up and packing it for safe shipment can sometimes be a problem, particularly if it is to go a long distance.

Cookies top the list of snacks most requested. You should carefully select the kind of cookies to be sent and pay special attention to the packaging.

Crisp cookies are best for mailing; soft, moist cookies travel well and are suitable for many areas, but can mold in humid climates. Fragile, lacy-textured cookies will crumble easily.

Packing and Mailing Tips

—Coffee or shortening cans, shoe boxes, or heavy plastic boxes are good containers for shipping baked goods. When packing, make sure freshly baked cookies are completely cool. Then, wrap two cookies, back to back or individually with aluminum foil or plastic wrap. Cushion bottom and sides of container with crumpled foil, plastic wrap, or paper towels. Pack the cookies as tightly as possible, without crushing, and fill spaces with foil or plastic wrap.

—Place the filled cookie container inside a packing box of fiberboard or paperboard with crumpled newspaper, shredded paper, or foamed plastic. Seal the box with tape. If it's necessary to wrap the box, use double layers of heavy brown paper and seal with pressure-sensitive filament tape.

Especially For Children

Most children are experts when it comes to desserts. But their favorites are probably not served in a fancy stemmed glass or on an elegant silver tray. Here's a collection of scrumptious bar cookies that will be special holiday treats for the children in your house.

GRANOLA BARS

4 cups regular oats, uncooked
⅔ cup butter or margarine, melted
½ cup firmly packed brown sugar
⅓ cup honey
1 egg, slightly beaten
½ teaspoon salt
½ teaspoon vanilla extract
1 cup chopped pecans
1 cup raisins

Place oats in ungreased 15- x 10- x 1-inch jellyroll pan. Bake at 350° for 15 minutes, stirring at 5-minute intervals.

Combine remaining ingredients; add oats and mix well. Spread mixture evenly into a lightly greased jellyroll pan. Bake at 350° for 25 minutes. Cool completely and cut into bars. Yield: 5 dozen. *Charlotte Hunt, Medon, Tennessee.*

PEANUT BUTTER 'N' JELLY BARS

3 cups all-purpose flour
1 cup sugar
1½ teaspoons baking powder
½ cup butter or margarine, softened
½ cup peanut butter
2 eggs, slightly beaten
1 cup grape jelly

Combine flour, sugar, and baking powder. Cut in butter and peanut butter until mixture resembles coarse meal. Stir in eggs, mixing well.

Press half of mixture into a greased 13- x 9- x 2-inch baking pan. Spread grape jelly over peanut butter mixture. Crumble remaining dough over jelly. Bake at 375° for 30 to 35 minutes. Cool and cut into bars. Yield: 2 dozen. *Eileen Wehling, Austin, Texas.*

NUTTY CHOCO SNACKS

1¼ cups all-purpose flour
1 cup firmly packed brown sugar
½ teaspoon baking soda
½ teaspoon salt
½ cup butter or margarine, softened
1 teaspoon vanilla extract
1 egg
1 cup quick-cooking oats, uncooked
½ cup flaked coconut
½ cup semisweet chocolate morsels
¼ cup unsalted sunflower kernels

Combine first 7 ingredients in a large bowl, mixing well at medium speed of an electric mixer. Stir in oats and coconut. Press dough into a lightly greased 13- x 9- x 2-inch pan. Sprinkle with chocolate morsels and sunflower kernels. Bake at 375° for 15 to 20 minutes. Cool and cut into bars. Yield: 1½ dozen. *Cindy Zellner, Shorter, Alabama.*

CHEWY MARSHMALLOW BROWNIES

½ cup butterscotch morsels
¼ cup butter or margarine
¾ cup all-purpose flour
⅓ cup firmly packed brown sugar
1 teaspoon baking powder
¼ teaspoon salt
1 egg, slightly beaten
½ teaspoon vanilla extract
1 cup semisweet chocolate morsels
1 cup miniature marshmallows
½ cup chopped pecans

Combine butterscotch morsels and butter in a small saucepan. Cook over medium heat, stirring occasionally, until morsels melt; set aside.

Combine next 4 ingredients; add butterscotch mixture, egg, and vanilla, mixing well. Stir in chocolate morsels, marshmallows, and pecans. Spread mixture in a greased 9-inch square pan. Bake at 350° for 20 to 25 minutes. (Brownies will have a chewy texture.) Cool and cut into squares. Yield: 3 dozen.
Mina DeKraker, Holland, Michigan.

Shape Marzipan Into Colorful Fruit

Colorful marzipan fruit is so versatile that one big batch can serve several functions. You can offer it as a party dessert, or tuck the tiny fruits into decorative paper cups and wrap up as a gift.

To decorate with marzipan, you can stack the fruit around the base of a candle, or secure it with wooden picks onto a craft foam cone or wreath. And don't be surprised if guests pluck off a fruit or two—the almond-flavored candy is an irresistible treat.

Marzipan can be mixed up ahead of time and will keep for several weeks if wrapped in plastic wrap and stored in the refrigerator in an airtight container. Let it come to room temperature before molding fruit.

Tint marzipan with desired colors of liquid food coloring, kneading it until the color is blended. Follow these directions for molding individual shapes.

Leaves: Roll green dough to ⅛-inch thickness on waxed paper. Cut dough into leaves using cookie or canapé cutter. Draw leaf indentations using a wooden pick.

Apples: Shape about 1½ teaspoons red dough into a ball for each apple; gently stretch balls, forming apple shapes. Indent stem ends slightly using a pointed wooden stick. Insert cloves in stem ends. Brush the apples with glaze, if desired.

Strawberries: Shape about 1 teaspoon red dough into a ball for each strawberry. Shape a rounded point at one end; slightly flatten other end. Indent flattened end slightly using a pointed wooden stick.

Combine 2 tablespoons granulated sugar and a few drops of red food coloring, stirring until blended thoroughly and desired color is obtained. Brush strawberries with glaze and roll in red sugar; place strawberries on waxed paper. Shape point on stem end of an equal number of leaves; press point of leaf into each strawberry indention.

Cherries: Shape about ¼ teaspoon red dough into ball for each cherry. Push ¼-inch piece of licorice into each cherry for stem. Brush cherries with glaze, if desired.

Peaches: Shape about 1¼ teaspoons yellow dough into ball for each peach. Push clove into each peach for stem. Press a groove with a wooden pick on one side of each peach. Combine 2 tablespoons water, 2 drops yellow and 2 drops red food coloring, mixing well. Brush mixture on sides of each peach.

Bananas: Shape bananas using about 1 teaspoon yellow dough for each. Push clove into stem end of each banana. Combine 2 tablespoons water, 1 drop green, 4 drops yellow, and 3 drops red food coloring, mixing well. Brush streaks on each banana with mixture.

Oranges: Shape about 1¼ teaspoons orange dough into ball for each orange. Roll each orange over grater to get rough skin. Insert clove in each orange for stem.

Grapes: Shape about 2 teaspoons purple dough into small balls (about ⅛ teaspoon each) for each cluster. Brush balls with slightly beaten egg white and shape balls into cluster. For each cluster, brush egg white on stem end of 2 leaves; attach to back of each cluster, pressing gently to make grapes and leaves adhere to each other. Allow to dry. Brush grapes with glaze, if desired.

MARZIPAN

1 (8-ounce) can almond paste
1½ tablespoons light corn syrup
1⅓ cups sifted powdered sugar
Liquid food coloring
Glaze (recipe follows)

Knead almond paste by hand in a medium bowl. Add corn syrup, and knead into almond paste. Gradually knead in sugar. Cover with plastic wrap, and refrigerate in airtight container until ready to shape.

Tint marzipan by kneading in liquid food coloring, and then shape as desired. Brush with glaze, if desired, to achieve a shinier surface. Let dry overnight on waxed paper; then refrigerate in an airtight container. Yield: about ¾ pound candy or enough to shape approximately 3 dozen small fruits.

Glaze:

2 tablespoons light corn syrup
¼ cup water

Combine corn syrup and water in a saucepan, mixing well. Bring to a boil, stirring until syrup dissolves. Yield: ¼ cup plus 2 tablespoons.

Right: *Nestle colorful fruit marzipan into tiny cups and wrap up as a gift for a friend (recipe above).*

Page 310: *Bake Christmas breads into exciting shapes and flavors. Front to back: Citrus-Nut Bread (page 294), Holiday Sparkle Rolls (page 296), Austrian Sweet Bread (page 294), Portuguese Round Bread (page 295), and Holiday Braid (page 295).*

Above left: *Dress up Almond Truffles (page 298) by serving them in small paper cups; a whole almond hides in the center of each truffle.*

Above center: *Brownie Alaskas (page 299) offer convenience and elegance—just frost an ice cream-topped brownie with meringue and bake. Add holiday color with candied cherry wedges.*

Right: *Snowflake-shaped Pizzelles and pretty Pistachio Fudge are two good reasons to make a batch of Christmas confections (recipes on page 298).*

Far right above: *Clockwise from front: Creamy Eggnog (page 303), Simply Super Dessert Drink (page 303), and Champagne Delight (page 304) make lively dessert drinks for a party.*

Far right below: *Pears Poached in Red Wine (page 302) is a perfect holiday dessert for dieters at only 152 calories per serving.*

Welcome To A Carolina Christmas Brunch

As sure as Christmas comes each year, Kaye and Robert Pendley serve brunch on the Sunday before Christmas Day. It's a tradition for the Gastonia, North Carolina, couple and their special way of entertaining friends and family during the holidays.

Kaye and Robert say they find that a brunch works best for their guests since the time of day doesn't conflict with the multitude of evening parties scheduled for the season.

"We start in the living room with wassail," says Kaye, "then I have the guests go to the dining room and help themselves to brunch, which is set up buffet-style on the dining table." The menu is always popular with the Pendleys' guests—Kaye cooks up a Southern spread of succulent baked ham, eggs, cheese grits, cranberry-apple casserole, homemade biscuits, and a choice of sweet cakes for dessert.

Wassail
Sweet-Sour Glazed Ham
Egg Casserole   Baked Cheese Grits
Cranberry-Apple Casserole
Quick Buttermilk Biscuits
Butter   Jelly
Oatmeal-Coconut Coffee Cake
Apple Cake
Coffee

WASSAIL

2½ cups sugar
1 cup water
1 lemon, sliced
8 (3-inch) sticks cinnamon
1 quart pineapple juice
1 quart orange juice
5 cups Sauterne
½ cup dry sherry
½ cup lemon juice
Pineapple wedges

Combine sugar, water, lemon, and cinnamon sticks in a medium saucepan; bring to a boil and cook 5 minutes, stirring constantly.

Combine next 5 ingredients in a large Dutch oven; bring to a boil, cover, and simmer 10 minutes. Stir in sugar syrup and heat thoroughly. Remove lemon slices and cinnamon sticks. Garnish each serving with a pineapple wedge. Yield: 3½ quarts.

SWEET-SOUR GLAZED HAM

2 cups apple jelly
2 tablespoons prepared mustard
2 tablespoons lemon juice
½ teaspoon ground cloves
1 (5- to 7-pound) fully-cooked ham half
Whole cloves

Combine first 4 ingredients in a saucepan; place over medium heat and bring to a boil, stirring occasionally.

Score fat on ham in a diamond design; stud with cloves. Place ham, fat side up, on rack in a shallow roasting pan. Insert meat thermometer, making sure it does not touch bone. Bake ham, uncovered, at 325° about 1½ to 2 hours until thermometer registers 140°; baste ham every 15 to 20 minutes with sauce. Heat remaining sauce, and serve with ham. Yield: 10 to 14 servings.

EGG CASSEROLE

2 cups seasoned croutons
1½ cups (6 ounces) shredded sharp
    Cheddar cheese
6 eggs, beaten
2 cups milk
½ teaspoon salt
½ teaspoon dry mustard
⅛ teaspoon onion powder
⅛ teaspoon pepper
Hard-cooked egg wedges
Fresh parsley sprigs

Place croutons in a greased 10- x 6- x 2-inch baking dish; sprinkle cheese over croutons. Combine next 6 ingredients; mix well. Pour egg mixture into casserole. Bake at 350° for 25 minutes. Garnish with hard-cooked egg wedges and parsley. Yield: 6 servings.

BAKED CHEESE GRITS

6 cups water
1 teaspoon salt
1½ cups regular grits
½ cup butter or margarine
1 (6-ounce) roll garlic cheese
2 tablespoons sherry
1 to 2 tablespoons Worcestershire sauce
½ teaspoon hot sauce
3 eggs, beaten
Cooked crumbled bacon
Tomato strips
Tomato rose

Bring water and salt to a boil in a large saucepan; gradually add grits, stirring constantly. Reduce heat, cover, and cook 10 minutes. Add butter and cheese, stirring until melted. Add next 4 ingredients, mixing well. Pour into a greased 2½-quart baking dish. Bake at 350° for 45 minutes. Garnish with crumbled bacon, tomato strips, and tomato rose. Yield: 6 to 8 servings.

CRANBERRY-APPLE CASSEROLE

3 cups peeled, chopped apples
2 cups fresh cranberries
2 tablespoons all-purpose flour
1 cup sugar
3 (1⅝-ounce) packages instant oatmeal
    with cinnamon and spice
¾ cup chopped pecans
½ cup all-purpose flour
½ cup firmly packed brown sugar
½ cup butter or margarine, melted
Pecan halves
Additional fresh cranberries

Combine apples, 2 cups cranberries, and 2 tablespoons flour, tossing to coat; add 1 cup sugar, mixing well. Place in a 2-quart casserole.

Combine oatmeal, chopped pecans, ½ cup flour, and brown sugar; add butter, and stir well. Spoon over fruit mixture. Bake, uncovered, at 350° for 45 minutes. Garnish with pecan halves and cranberries. Yield: 6 to 8 servings.

QUICK BUTTERMILK BISCUITS

2 cups self-rising flour
⅓ cup shortening
¾ cup plus 1 tablespoon buttermilk

Combine flour and shortening in a medium-size mixing bowl; cut in shortening with a pastry blender until mixture resembles coarse meal. Stir in buttermilk. Turn dough onto a floured surface and knead lightly 3 or 4 times.

Roll dough to ½-inch thickness; cut with a 2½-inch biscuit cutter. Place biscuits on ungreased baking sheet, and bake at 450° for 10 to 12 minutes. Yield: 10 biscuits.

Tip: Before starting a recipe, make sure you have the equipment needed to prepare it. Be sure to use the correct pan size, especially when preparing cakes, pies, or breads.

OATMEAL-COCONUT COFFEE CAKE

1½ cups boiling water
1 cup regular oats, uncooked
¼ cup butter or margarine, softened
1 cup firmly packed brown sugar
1 cup sugar
2 eggs, slightly beaten
1½ cups all-purpose flour
1 teaspoon baking soda
1 teaspoon salt
1 teaspoon ground cinnamon
1 teaspoon vanilla extract
1 cup flaked coconut
½ cup chopped pecans
½ cup butter or margarine, melted
½ cup firmly packed brown sugar
¼ cup milk
¼ teaspoon vanilla extract

Pour boiling water over oats; let stand 20 minutes.

Cream ¼ cup butter; gradually add 1 cup brown sugar and 1 cup sugar, beating well. Stir in oats mixture. Add next 6 ingredients, and mix well. Spoon into a greased 13- x 9- x 2-inch baking pan; bake at 350° for 40 minutes or until a wooden pick inserted in center comes out clean.

Combine coconut and pecans; sprinkle mixture over cake. Combine remaining ingredients; pour over cake. Return to oven; broil 1 to 2 minutes or until golden brown. Cut into squares to serve. Yield: 15 to 18 servings.

APPLE CAKE

3 eggs
2 cups sugar
1 cup vegetable oil
3 cups all-purpose flour
1 teaspoon baking soda
½ teaspoon salt
1 teaspoon ground cinnamon
3 cups peeled, finely chopped apples
½ cup chopped pecans
Brown Sugar Glaze

Combine eggs, sugar, and oil in a large mixing bowl; beat well. Combine flour, soda, salt, and cinnamon; add to sugar mixture, and beat well. Stir in apples and pecans. (Batter will be stiff.) Spoon batter into a greased and floured 10-inch tube pan. Bake at 350° for 1 hour and 20 minutes or until a wooden pick inserted in center comes out clean. Cool in pan 10 to 15 minutes; remove from pan, and let cool completely. Drizzle Brown Sugar Glaze over cake. Yield: one 10-inch cake.

Brown Sugar Glaze:

¼ cup firmly packed brown sugar
2 tablespoons butter or margarine
1 tablespoon evaporated milk

Combine all ingredients in a heavy saucepan. Bring to a boil and cook, stirring constantly, for 2 minutes. Let cool to lukewarm; drizzle over cake. Yield: about ½ cup.

Main Dishes Don't Always Need Meat

By themselves, pinto beans and corn tortillas aren't considered good sources of protein. But when served together, as in Bean Chalupas, the foods provide high quality protein. Here, we share the secrets of other ways you can serve tasty main dishes without meat.

VEGETABLE FETTUCCINE

2 small zucchini, cut into thin strips
2 carrots, cut into thin strips
1 cup sliced fresh mushrooms
4 green onions, cut into 1-inch pieces
1 clove garlic, minced
¼ cup butter or margarine
1 (15-ounce) can garbanzo beans, drained
½ teaspoon dried whole basil
½ teaspoon salt
¼ teaspoon pepper
1 (8-ounce) package fettuccine
½ (8-ounce) package spinach fettuccine
1 cup grated Parmesan cheese, divided
2 egg yolks
1 cup whipping cream

Sauté zucchini, carrots, mushrooms, green onion, and garlic in butter in a large skillet 5 minutes or until crisp-tender. Stir in beans, basil, salt, and pepper; set aside.

Cook fettuccine separately in two Dutch ovens according to package directions; drain. Combine fettuccine and vegetables in one Dutch oven, and toss gently. Simmer until thoroughly heated, stirring occasionally. Stir in ¾ cup Parmesan cheese.

Beat egg yolks and whipping cream until foamy; add to fettuccini mixture, tossing gently. Cook over medium heat until thickened, stirring gently. Spoon mixture onto a serving platter; sprinkle with remaining ¼ cup Parmesan cheese. Yield: 6 to 8 servings.

CHEESY ZUCCHINI QUICHE

Pastry for 9-inch deep-dish pie
3 eggs
1 cup milk
2 tablespoons all-purpose flour
1 teaspoon dried parsley flakes
2 teaspoons Old Bay seasoning
1 tablespoon mayonnaise
2 cups (8 ounces) shredded Swiss cheese
2 cups shredded, unpeeled zucchini
Zucchini slices (optional)
Fresh parsley sprigs (optional)

Line a 9-inch quiche dish with pastry; trim excess pastry around edges. Prick bottom and sides of pastry with a fork. Bake at 400° for 3 minutes; remove from oven, and gently prick with a fork. Bake an additional 5 minutes. Cool on wire rack.

Beat eggs; add next 5 ingredients and beat well. Stir in cheese and shredded zucchini; pour into pastry shell. Bake at 350° for 35 to 40 minutes or until set. Let stand 10 minutes before serving. Garnish with zucchini slices and parsley, if desired. Yield: one 9-inch quiche.

Doris Pierce,
New Windsor, Maryland.

TOFU LASAGNA

2 (1.5-ounce) packages spaghetti sauce mix
2 tablespoons vegetable oil
1 (8-ounce) package lasagna noodles
½ pound fresh mushrooms, sliced
2 tablespoons vegetable oil
1 pound tofu, crumbled
¼ cup grated Parmesan cheese
1 tablespoon dried parsley flakes
¾ teaspoon garlic salt
2 cups (8 ounces) shredded mozzarella cheese

Prepare spaghetti sauce mix according to package directions, using 2 tablespoons oil instead of butter. Set aside.

Cook lasagna according to package directions; drain and set aside.

Sauté mushrooms in 2 tablespoons hot oil in a skillet for 2 minutes. Set aside.

Combine tofu, Parmesan cheese, parsley flakes, and garlic salt; stir well.

Layer one-third of spaghetti sauce, one-third of noodles, half of tofu mixture, half of mushrooms, and one-third of mozzarella cheese in a lightly greased 13- x 9- x 2-inch baking dish; repeat layers once. Top with remaining noodles and sauce. Bake, uncovered, at 350° for 25 minutes. Sprinkle with remaining cheese, and bake 5 minutes. Yield: 8 servings.   *Betty Marshall,*
Barboursville, Virginia.

BEAN CHALUPAS

2 cups dried pinto beans
5 cups water
2 cloves garlic, minced
1 (4-ounce) can chopped green chiles,
    drained
½ cup chopped onion
2 tablespoons chili powder
2 teaspoons ground cumin
1½ teaspoons salt
1 teaspoon dried whole oregano
Vegetable oil
8 (6-inch) corn tortillas
Shredded lettuce
¾ cup (3 ounces) shredded Monterey Jack
    cheese
¾ cup (3 ounces) shredded Cheddar
    cheese
½ cup sliced ripe olives
½ cup commercial sour cream
4 tomatoes, cut into wedges

Sort and wash beans; place in a large Dutch oven. Cover with water 2 inches above beans; let soak overnight. Drain beans. Add 5 cups water and next 7 ingredients. Bring to a boil; cover, reduce heat, and simmer 1½ hours. Remove 1 cup of beans and place in container of electric blender; process until smooth. Stir pureed beans into bean mixture; cover and simmer 30 minutes. Uncover and simmer an additional 30 minutes.

Heat 2 inches of oil in a large skillet to 350°. Fry one tortilla about 5 seconds to soften; press tortilla into oil with a round, flat potato masher, molding tortilla into a bowl shape. (Use a wooden spoon, if necessary, to shape sides.) Drain well on paper towels. Repeat with remaining tortillas.

Spoon an equal amount of bean mixture into each tortilla; place on a bed of lettuce. Sprinkle with cheese and olives; top with a dollop of sour cream. Arrange tomatoes around chalupas. Yield: 8 servings.

Feature Frozen Vegetable Casseroles

Nothing can compete with the fresh flavor of summer vegetables, but commercially frozen foods are a good alternative when your favorites are out of season. Try combining ground beef, eggs, or canned soups with frozen vegetables; you'll end up with one of these flavorful, color-packed casseroles.

BEEF-AND-VEGETABLE CHOW MEIN CASSEROLE

1¼ pounds ground beef
1 small onion, finely chopped
1 (10¾-ounce) can cream of mushroom
    soup, undiluted
1 (10¾-ounce) can chicken and rice soup,
    undiluted
1 (10-ounce) package frozen mixed
    vegetables
1 cup chopped celery
1 (3-ounce) can chow mein noodles,
    divided

Cook beef and onion in a large skillet until meat is browned, stirring to crumble. Drain well. Stir in remaining ingredients, reserving half of chow mein noodles. Spoon mixture into a lightly greased 2-quart baking dish. Bake at 350° for 30 minutes or until bubbly. Sprinkle remaining noodles over casserole before serving. Yield: 6 servings.
Mrs. W. Paul Jones,
Hopkinsville, Kentucky.

SPINACH-BEEF-MACARONI CASSEROLE

1 pound ground beef
1 large onion, chopped
1 cup diced celery
¾ cup grated carrot
2 (14-ounce) cans Italian-style tomatoes,
    undrained
1 teaspoon salt
1 teaspoon dried whole oregano
½ teaspoon pepper
¼ teaspoon garlic powder
1 (8-ounce) package shell macaroni
1 (10-ounce) package frozen chopped
    spinach, thawed
½ cup grated Parmesan cheese

Combine beef, onion, celery, and carrot in a large skillet; cook until meat is browned, stirring to crumble. Drain off drippings. Add next 5 ingredients. Reduce heat, cover, and simmer 30 minutes, stirring occasionally.

Cook macaroni according to package directions; drain.

Combine meat mixture, macaroni, and spinach; mix well. Pour into a lightly greased 12- x 8- x 2-inch baking dish. Cover and bake at 350° for 25 minutes. Uncover casserole; sprinkle with cheese, and bake an additional 3 minutes. Yield: 6 servings.
Marsha Q. Trott,
Dunkirk, Maryland.

LIMA BEAN CASSEROLE

2 (10-ounce) packages frozen baby lima
    beans
½ cup chopped onion
½ cup chopped green pepper
1 clove garlic, minced
3 tablespoons butter or margarine
1 (10¾-ounce) can tomato puree
¼ cup water
½ teaspoon salt
⅛ teaspoon pepper
½ teaspoon Worcestershire sauce
¼ cup plus 2 tablespoons grated Parmesan
    cheese, divided
⅓ cup soft breadcrumbs
1 tablespoon butter or margarine, melted

Cook lima beans according to package directions, omitting salt; drain well.

Sauté onion, green pepper, and garlic in 3 tablespoons butter in a small skillet until tender. Add lima beans and next 5 ingredients, stirring well. Spoon mixture into a lightly greased 2-quart casserole. Sprinkle ¼ cup cheese over casserole. Combine remaining 2 tablespoons cheese, breadcrumbs, and 1 tablespoon butter; sprinkle over casserole. Bake, uncovered, at 350° for 20 minutes.
Rose E. Londerée,
St. Petersburg, Florida.

BROCCOLI-CORN CASSEROLE

1 (10-ounce) package frozen chopped
    broccoli
1 (10-ounce) package frozen cream-style
    corn
1¼ cups herb-seasoned stuffing mix,
    divided
1 (10¾-ounce) can cream of mushroom
    soup, undiluted
1 egg, beaten
3 tablespoons butter or margarine, melted
1 small onion, finely chopped
½ cup (2 ounces) shredded sharp Cheddar
    cheese

Cook broccoli according to package directions, omitting salt. Drain well.

Cook corn according to package directions. Combine broccoli, corn, 1 cup stuffing mix, soup, egg, butter, and onion; mix well. Spoon mixture into a lightly greased 1½-quart baking dish. Sprinkle with cheese and remaining ¼ cup stuffing mix. Bake at 350° for 30 minutes or until thoroughly heated. Yield: 6 servings. *Jacqueline Dorn,*
Leesville, South Carolina.

Tip: Whenever a recipe calls for a reheating process, the dish can be made in advance up to that point.

BAKED CORN PUDDING

2 (10-ounce) packages frozen cut corn,
    thawed and drained
3 eggs, beaten
¼ cup all-purpose flour
1 tablespoon sugar
1 teaspoon salt
¼ teaspoon white pepper
Dash of ground nutmeg
2 cups half-and-half
1 (4-ounce) jar diced pimiento,
    drained
2 tablespoons butter or margarine,
    melted
1 teaspoon grated onion

Combine all ingredients; mix well. Pour mixture into a greased 2-quart baking dish.

Place baking dish in a larger baking pan; fill pan with 1 inch hot water. Bake, uncovered, at 325° for 1 hour and 15 minutes or until knife inserted in center comes out clean. Yield: 8 servings. *Lillian M. Clendenin, Charleston, West Virginia.*

MICROWAVE COOKERY

Gifts For Microwave Cooks

If you're looking for just the right gift for the microwave cook on your Christmas list, take a look at some of these appliances. We've tried each of the ones listed below in our test kitchens and have come up with a recipe for each piece of equipment so you'll have an idea of the uses for each appliance.

Folks who enjoy cooking meals in a microwave will enjoy a versatile bake oven. Specialty items such as a steam cooker and a popcorn popper make excellent gifts, too. Read the appliance descriptions and recipes to know which is best for the cooks on your gift list.

Popcorn Popper

Popcorn lovers have new options with microwave popcorn poppers. This favorite treat can be prepared without using oil and much quicker than by conventional methods. Models on the market vary in shape, size, and features offered. The self-buttering popper allows butter to melt over the corn as it pops.

After popping, use your imagination to spice up the flavor of the corn. We added garlic salt to corn for crunchy servings of Garlic Popcorn.

Steam Cooker

The microwave steam cooker offers an easy way to steam vegetables, desserts, or one-dish meals in the microwave. The water in the steamer absorbs the microwave energy, the water boils, and steam cooks the food just as in a conventional steamer. Therefore, cooking time is the same as steaming on the range. But the advantage is it takes less energy and doesn't heat up the kitchen.

A metal basket inside the steamer and the metal in the lid reflect microwave energy away from the food so that energy is absorbed only by the water in the steamer. The food is cooked only by steam from the boiling water. The metal used in the steamer is specially designed for microwave use and will not cause arcing inside the oven if used properly.

Bake Oven

Another item is the covered microwave bake oven. It includes a shallow metal pan set in a plastic base with a metal and plastic lid. It's a versatile appliance that is excellent for baking cakes and cornbread, frying potatoes, and stir-frying chicken. Or use it to heat up a frozen pizza. Add your own condiments to the top, and you'll have our Jiffy Jazzed-Up Pizza.

Since metal only reflects microwave energy, a special heat material is attached to the bottom of the pan in the bake oven. It absorbs the energy and heats the metal; therefore, the food in the bake oven is actually cooked on the hot pan and not by microwave energy.

Like the steamer, the metal used in the bake oven is designed for use in the microwave and should not be used in a conventional oven. Also, the metal lid for the bake oven is set atop the oven base so that it never touches the metal baking pan inside the base.

Even with metal designed for microwave use, you should always take certain precautions when cooking with it in the microwave. Make sure the cookware is placed in the center of the oven so that it doesn't touch the sides. The oven sides are metal and when metal is close to or touches metal in the microwave, it can cause arcing. The arcing creates heat, which can cause fire.

EASY STEAMED DINNER

1¼ cups water
2 chicken breast halves, boned and
    skinned
2 small ears fresh corn
1 small zucchini, cut into 1-inch
    pieces
2 carrots, scraped and cut into
    1-inch pieces
1 onion, quartered
1 teaspoon dried whole basil
3 tablespoons butter or margarine,
    softened
¼ teaspoon seasoned salt
¼ teaspoon pepper

Place water in reservoir of a 10- x 8- x 3-inch steam cooker. Replace metal basket and steaming rack. Fill steaming rack with chicken and vegetables; sprinkle with basil. Cover with lid and microwave at HIGH for 20 minutes. Dot with butter, and sprinkle with salt and pepper. Yield: 2 servings.

JIFFY JAZZED-UP PIZZA

Vegetable cooking spray
1 (22-ounce) 12-inch frozen pizza
½ cup sliced fresh mushrooms
½ medium-size green pepper, sliced into
    rings
¼ cup sliced green onion
½ cup (2 ounces) shredded mozzarella
    cheese
¼ cup grated Parmesan cheese

Spray baking pan of a 13-inch round microwave bake oven with vegetable cooking spray. Place pan inside base. Place frozen pizza on pan; set pan and base in center of microwave oven. Microwave, uncovered, at HIGH for 3 minutes. Arrange remaining ingredients over pizza. Cover with lid, and microwave at HIGH for 12 minutes; remove from oven with potholders. Remove lid and place pizza on a pizza plate. Let stand 5 minutes before cutting. Yield: one 12-inch pizza.

Note: Never use baking pan in microwave oven without the bake oven base.

Tip: Need a quick microwave frosting for cakes and cupcakes? Place about 16 mint chocolate patties over a layer cake, or top cupcakes with one patty. The layer cake patties will melt in 2 minutes at HIGH in a microwave and one patty on a cupcake will take 10 to 15 seconds at HIGH in a microwave.

GARLIC POPCORN

½ cup popping corn
1 tablespoon butter or margarine
¼ to ½ teaspoon garlic salt

Place popping corn in base of a microwave self-buttering popcorn popper. Place butter in butter dish, and attach to top of lid. Cover base with lid. Place popper in center of microwave. Microwave at HIGH for 5 minutes or until popping stops. Remove from oven and invert, using lid as a serving dish. Sprinkle with garlic salt, and toss well. Yield: about 2 quarts.

Note: Omit butter, if desired.

Cornbread Dressings With A Difference

Every Southerner has a favorite recipe for cornbread dressing. But if you'd like to try some that are a little different, take a look at the variations our readers have come up with.

Cornbread dressings are an excellent way to keep leftover cornbread muffins and cornsticks from going to waste. Just crumble the bread, and freeze it if you don't plan to use it right away.

HERB-SEASONED CORNBREAD DRESSING

1 cup self-rising cornmeal
1 cup all-purpose flour
1 cup milk
1 egg, beaten
2 tablespoons vegetable oil
4 slices whole wheat bread, crumbled
1½ cups chopped onion
1 cup chopped celery
¾ cup chopped green pepper
¾ cup butter or margarine
4 eggs, beaten
2 (10½-ounce) cans chicken broth, diluted
1 teaspoon ground thyme
1½ teaspoons rubbed sage
1 teaspoon poultry seasoning
1 teaspoon pepper
1 teaspoon salt
1 pint oysters, drained (optional)

Combine cornmeal and flour. Add milk, egg, and vegetable oil; mix well. Pour batter into a well-greased 8-inch square pan. Bake at 400° for 20 to 25 minutes or until lightly browned. Crumble cornbread and combine with breadcrumbs in a large bowl; set aside.

Sauté onion, celery, and green pepper in butter until tender; add to breadcrumb mixture and stir well. Add eggs, chicken broth, and seasonings. Add oysters, if desired. Spoon into a lightly greased 13- x 9- x 2-inch baking dish; bake at 350° for 60 to 70 minutes. Yield: 8 servings.   *Rita Royal,*
Muskogee, Oklahoma.

SQUASH DRESSING

½ cup chopped onion
½ green pepper, chopped
½ cup chopped celery
½ cup butter or margarine
5 cups crumbled cornbread
2 cups milk
1 (10¾-ounce) can cream of chicken soup, undiluted
3 cups chopped, cooked yellow squash, drained
1 teaspoon salt
¼ teaspoon pepper

Sauté onion, pepper, and celery in butter until tender. Add to cornbread, and stir well. Stir in remaining ingredients, mixing well. Pour into a greased 13- x 9- x 2-inch baking dish. Bake at 400° for 50 minutes or until lightly browned. Yield: 8 servings.

Jeanette Mask,
Jacksboro, Texas.

Try These Tempting Chocolate Candies

Rich fudges and chocolate-coated candies fill gift boxes and candy dishes during the holidays. For one of this season's sweetest confections, try Bourbon Balls—roll the sweet filling of powdered sugar, butter, and bourbon-soaked chopped walnuts into balls and dip them in unsweetened melted chocolate.

BOURBON BALLS

1 cup chopped walnuts
¼ cup bourbon
1 (16-ounce) package powdered sugar, sifted
½ cup butter or margarine, melted
1 (8-ounce) package unsweetened chocolate
1 tablespoon shortening

Soak walnuts in bourbon at least 3 hours. Drain. Combine walnuts, sugar, and butter. Shape into ¾-inch balls; chill at least 30 minutes.

Combine chocolate and shortening in top of a double boiler; heat until melted and smooth, stirring occasionally. Using a wooden pick, dip each bourbon ball into chocolate. Place on a waxed paper-lined baking sheet; chill until firm. Store in refrigerator. Yield: about 4 dozen.

Judy Cunningham,
Roanoke, Virginia.

CHERRY NUT FUDGE

3⅔ cups sifted powdered sugar
½ cup cocoa
½ cup butter or margarine
3 tablespoons milk
1 tablespoon vanilla extract
½ cup chopped candied cherries
½ cup chopped pecans

Combine powdered sugar and cocoa; stir well. Set aside.

Combine butter and milk in a medium saucepan over low heat; cook until butter is melted. Remove from heat, and stir in cocoa mixture; stir until smooth. Add vanilla, cherries, and pecans; stir well. Pour mixture into a lightly greased 8-inch square pan; chill until firm. Cut into squares. Yield: about 2½ dozen.   *Pamela Nordyke,*
San Angelo, Texas.

CHOCOLATE BRITTLE

2 cups butter
2 cups sugar
¼ cup plus 2 tablespoons water
12 (1.05-ounce) milk chocolate candy bars
3 cups chopped pecans

Combine butter, sugar, and water in a Dutch oven; cook over low heat until candy reaches hard crack stage (300°). Remove from heat and immediately pour into 2 buttered 12-inch pizza pans, spreading to edges of pans.

Melt chocolate in top of double boiler over hot water. Spread chocolate over brittle; sprinkle pecans evenly on top. Press pecans into chocolate. Let stand until chocolate is firm. Break candy into pieces. Yield: about 4 pounds.

L. K. Simpson,
North Augusta, South Carolina.

Tip: Clean, dry coffee cans make ideal baking containers for gift breads.

QUICK NUT FUDGE

1 (16-ounce) package powdered sugar, sifted
½ cup cocoa
¼ teaspoon salt
¼ cup milk
¼ cup plus 2 tablespoons butter or margarine
1 tablespoon vanilla extract
¾ cup chopped pecans, divided

Combine all ingredients except pecans in top of double boiler; bring water to a boil. Reduce heat and cook, stirring constantly, until mixture is smooth. Remove from heat; stir in ½ cup pecans.

Quickly spread mixture into a lightly greased 9- x 5- x 3-inch loafpan; sprinkle with remaining pecans. Chill until firm; cut into squares. Store in refrigerator. Yield: about 3½ dozen.

Adele S. Cohill,
Nokomis, Florida.

Save time in the kitchen with simple salads. This Grapefruit-Avocado Salad is topped with a delicious Poppy Seed Dressing.

Hurry-Up Salad Ideas

Grapefruit-Avocado Salad helps you cut corners in the kitchen. Make the poppy seed dressing ahead of time; then just before dinner, arrange grapefruit and avocado on lettuce leaves and spoon the dressing on top.

Many people like to serve spinach salad when they need a quick salad idea. Orange-Spinach Salad is a unique variation that calls for tossing wedges of green apple with spinach leaves.

CARROT-TANGERINE SALAD

4 cups shredded carrots
2 tangerines, peeled and sectioned
½ cup raisins
1 teaspoon lemon juice
½ cup mayonnaise
Lettuce leaves

Combine first 4 ingredients; stir well. Chill. Stir in mayonnaise just before serving; serve salad on lettuce leaves. Yield: 8 servings. *Bettye Cortner,*
Cerulean, Kentucky.

GRAPEFRUIT-AVOCADO SALAD

3 grapefruits, peeled, seeded, and sectioned
2 avocados, peeled and sliced
Lettuce leaves
Poppy Seed Dressing

Arrange grapefruit sections and avocado slices on individual lettuce-lined plates. Serve with Poppy Seed Dressing. Yield: 6 servings.

Poppy Seed Dressing:

¾ cup sugar
⅓ cup cider vinegar
1 teaspoon salt
1 teaspoon dry mustard
1 teaspoon finely grated onion
1 cup vegetable oil
1 tablespoon poppy seeds

Combine first 5 ingredients in a small mixing bowl; beat with electric mixer until sugar dissolves. Continue to beat, slowly adding oil. Stir in poppy seeds. Cover and chill; stir before serving. Yield: 1¾ cups. *Joan Sessoms,*
Hope Mills, North Carolina.

Tip: If using only half an avocado, keep the pit in the unused half to prevent browning; wrap and store in the refrigerator.

ORANGE-SPINACH SALAD

1 green apple, cored and cut into wedges
1 tablespoon lemon juice
1 pound fresh spinach, torn into pieces
½ pound fresh mushrooms, sliced
6 slices bacon, cooked and crumbled
1 (6-ounce) can frozen orange juice concentrate, thawed and undiluted
¾ cup mayonnaise

Toss apple wedges in lemon juice; drain. Combine apple wedges and next 3 ingredients in a large bowl; toss well.

Combine orange juice concentrate and mayonnaise; stir until smooth. Serve with salad. Yield: 8 servings.

Mrs. C. Shoemaker,
Boynton Beach, Florida.

EASY VEGETABLE SALAD

1 (1-pound) bunch broccoli
1 (16-ounce) can ripe olives, drained and sliced
1 (8-ounce) can sliced water chestnuts, drained
1 medium-size green pepper, cut into strips
1 medium onion, chopped
4 stalks celery, chopped
½ pound fresh mushrooms, sliced
1 pint cherry tomatoes, halved
1 (8-ounce) bottle commercial Italian dressing

Combine first 8 ingredients in a large bowl. Pour dressing over top; toss gently. Chill 1 to 2 hours. Yield: 10 to 12 servings.   *Mina De Kraker,*
Holland, Michigan.

MIXED VEGETABLE SALAD

2 (10-ounce) packages frozen mixed
   vegetables
1 medium onion, chopped
3 stalks celery, chopped
⅓ cup mayonnaise
1 teaspoon dried whole dillweed
1 tablespoon plus 1 teaspoon lemon juice

Cook mixed vegetables according to package directions; drain and cool. Add onion and celery; set aside.

Combine remaining ingredients; stir until smooth. Pour over vegetables, and toss gently. Cover and chill 2 to 3 hours. Yield: 4 to 6 servings.
Marsha Webb,
Roswell, Georgia.

Soups For The Biggest Of Appetites

A steaming bowl of soup just right for the colder times of year. As the ingredients simmer, they fill the air with an aroma that promises a fitting dish for chilly days.

VEGETABLE-BEAN SOUP

1 cup dried navy beans
2 quarts water
3 carrots, diced
3 medium tomatoes, peeled and chopped
3 small onions, minced
2 stalks celery, chopped
2 cloves garlic, minced
3 tablespoons olive oil
Pinch of ground savory
1 teaspoon salt

Wash beans thoroughly; place in a large Dutch oven. Add water; bring to a boil. Remove from heat; cover and let sit for 1 hour. Return water to a boil; reduce heat and simmer 45 minutes. Add remaining ingredients; simmer, uncovered, about 30 minutes or until beans are tender. Yield: 8 cups.
Betty Collier,
Fern Creek, Kentucky.

HARVEST CHOWDER

4 slices bacon
½ cup chopped celery
½ cup thinly sliced carrots
2 tablespoons sliced green onion
2 cups mashed potatoes
1 (17-ounce) can cream-style corn
½ cup frozen English peas
2 cups milk
½ teaspoon salt
1 cup (4 ounces) shredded Cheddar cheese
1 large tomato, peeled and thinly sliced
Seasoned pepper

Cook bacon in a large saucepan until crisp; drain on paper towels. Crumble bacon, and set aside. Reserve 1 tablespoon drippings in pan.

Sauté celery, carrots, and onion in drippings for 2 minutes. Stir in potatoes, corn, peas, milk, salt, and cheese. Cook over medium heat, stirring constantly, until cheese melts.

Top each serving with a tomato slice, bacon, and a dash of seasoned pepper. Yield: 7 cups.   *Ella Stanley,*
Coeburn, Virginia.

MICROWAVE COOKERY

Speed Dinner With The Microwave

Busy holiday shopping schedules call for meals that are quick and easy. With this in mind, we've adapted several favorite main dishes for simplified preparation in the microwave oven.

When the dinner menu needs something special, you'll want to try our ham slice covered in a pineapple glaze. Or you may prefer Easy Spaghetti; we share instructions for microwaving the pasta, but when you're in a hurry, try cooking the spaghetti conventionally while the sauce microwaves.

FRUITED HAM SLICE

3 tablespoons orange juice
1½ teaspoons cornstarch
1 (8¼-ounce) can crushed pineapple,
   undrained
½ teaspoon ground cloves
½ teaspoon dry mustard
1 (1-inch-thick) slice cooked ham (about
   1½ pounds)

Combine orange juice and cornstarch in a 2-cup glass measure, stirring until smooth. Stir in pineapple, cloves, and mustard. Microwave at HIGH for 2 to 3 minutes or until slightly thickened, stirring at 1-minute intervals. Set aside.

Slash fat along edges of ham to prevent curling. Place ham in a 12- x 8- x 2-inch baking dish, and cover with waxed paper. Microwave at MEDIUM (50% power) for 7 to 8 minutes. Drain if necessary.

Spoon glaze over ham. Cover with waxed paper, and microwave at MEDIUM for 7 to 8 minutes or until hot. Yield: 4 servings.

EASY SPAGHETTI

1 pound lean ground beef
6 cups water
½ teaspoon salt
1 tablespoon olive oil
1 (8-ounce) package thin spaghetti
1 small onion, chopped
¼ teaspoon garlic powder
1 (15-ounce) can tomato sauce
1 (6-ounce) can tomato paste
⅓ cup Burgundy or other dry red wine
1 teaspoon Worcestershire sauce
½ teaspoon dried whole oregano
½ teaspoon dried whole basil
¼ teaspoon dried whole thyme
½ teaspoon salt
¼ teaspoon pepper
Grated Parmesan cheese

Crumble beef in a 2-quart casserole, and cover with waxed paper. Microwave at HIGH for 5 to 6 minutes, stirring twice. Drain well and set aside.

Combine water, ½ teaspoon salt, and olive oil in a 12- x 8- x 2-inch baking dish. Cover with heavy-duty plastic wrap, and microwave at HIGH for 10 minutes. Add spaghetti; cover and microwave at HIGH for 8 minutes, stirring after 4 minutes. Let stand for 1 to 3 minutes; drain well and set aside.

Stir onion and garlic powder into beef. Cover and microwave at HIGH for 2 minutes; stir well. Add next 9 ingredients, mixing well. Cover and microwave at HIGH for 12 minutes, stirring after 6 minutes. Serve over spaghetti and sprinkle with Parmesan cheese. Yield: 4 servings.

JIFFY TACOS

1 pound ground beef
½ cup chopped onion
¼ cup chopped green pepper
1 tablespoon catsup
1 teaspoon chili powder
½ teaspoon salt
½ teaspoon pepper
⅛ teaspoon garlic powder
12 taco shells
2 cups shredded lettuce
2 medium tomatoes, chopped
1½ cups (6 ounces) shredded Cheddar
    cheese
Commercial taco sauce

Crumble ground beef into a 1½-quart casserole. Add next 7 ingredients, mixing well. Cover with heavy-duty plastic wrap. Microwave at HIGH for 5 to 7 minutes or until meat is done, stirring at 2-minute intervals. Drain.

Spoon about 3 tablespoons meat mixture into each taco shell; top with lettuce, tomatoes, and cheese. Serve with taco sauce. Yield: 6 servings.

COOKING LIGHT

Holiday Beverages—Refreshing And Light

It seems that many dieters are more conscious of the calories they eat than of those they drink. However, the calories in holiday beverages can add up quickly. Drink a cup of commercial eggnog, and you've swallowed 280 calories. Or treat yourself to a cup of creamy hot chocolate, and you've increased your daily tally by about 250 calories.

To help you enjoy holiday entertaining, we've come up with reduced-calorie recipes for Festive Eggnog, Mocha Cocoa, and several other special beverages to serve your family or friends.

Enjoy Tart Cranberry Punch when it's cold outside and you want a low-calorie warm-up. Fresh cranberries are very low in calories (only 50 per cup), but are also very tart. We sweetened cranberries with apple cider instead of sugar for Tart Cranberry Punch.

Whenever you're served a beverage other than unsweetened tea or water, sip slowly, so the beverage will last longer and the calories will go further.

You can make a spritzer by adding a little club soda to wine or fruit juice. Since the club soda is calorie-free, your spritzer will have fewer calories per ounce than wine or juice alone.

TOMATO REFRESHER

2 cups tomato juice
1 quart clam and tomato juice cocktail
2 teaspoons Worcestershire sauce
¾ teaspoon celery seeds, crushed
½ to ¾ teaspoon pepper
1½ teaspoons lemon juice
¼ teaspoon hot sauce
Celery sticks (optional)

Combine first 7 ingredients, mixing well. Chill thoroughly. Garnish each serving with a celery stick, if desired. Yield: 6 cups (about 44 calories per ½-cup serving).

BLENDER FRUIT BEVERAGE

1 quart unsweetened orange juice
1 cup unsweetened frozen whole
    strawberries
2 large bananas
6 ice cubes

Combine half of each ingredient in container of electric blender; process until frothy. Pour into glasses; repeat procedure with remaining ingredients. Serve immediately. Yield: 7 cups (about 52 calories per ½-cup serving).

TART CRANBERRY PUNCH

3 (3-inch) sticks cinnamon
24 whole cloves
1 teaspoon whole allspice
1 medium orange, sliced
2 quarts apple cider
2 cups water
3 cups fresh cranberries
Orange rind strips (optional)
Cinnamon sticks (optional)

Place 3 cinnamon sticks, cloves, and allspice in center of a small piece of cheesecloth; tie securely.

Combine spice bag, orange slices, apple cider, water, and cranberries in a large Dutch oven; bring to a boil. Reduce heat, and simmer 5 minutes; remove and discard spice bag and orange slices. For garnish, gently tie orange rind strips around cinnamon sticks and place in individual cups, if desired. Serve warm. Yield: 10 cups (about 46 calories per ½-cup serving).

PEACH FROSTY

1 (8½-ounce) can unsweetened sliced
    peaches, drained
2 cups unsweetened orange juice
1 pint vanilla ice milk
¼ cup plain low-fat yogurt
⅛ teaspoon ground cinnamon
⅛ teaspoon ground nutmeg

Place all ingredients in container of electric blender. Process until smooth. Serve immediately. Yield: 5 cups (about 72 calories per ½-cup serving).

EGGNOG

3 cups skim milk
3 eggs, separated
3 tablespoons sugar
¾ teaspoon vanilla extract
¼ teaspoon brandy flavoring
Ground nutmeg

Combine milk, egg yolks, and sugar in a medium saucepan, mixing well. Cook over medium heat, stirring constantly, 7 to 8 minutes or until mixture thickens slightly. Remove from heat; stir in flavorings. Cover and chill.

To serve, beat egg whites (at room temperature) until soft peaks form; fold egg whites into yolk mixture. Sprinkle each serving with nutmeg, and serve immediately. Yield: 4½ cups (about 73 calories per ½-cup serving).

MOCHA COCOA

3 tablespoons sugar
3 tablespoons cocoa
3 tablespoons instant coffee
    granules
½ cup water
1 (3-inch) stick cinnamon
6½ cups skim milk
1 teaspoon vanilla extract
Additional cinnamon sticks

Combine first 5 ingredients in a large saucepan. Cook over medium heat, stirring constantly, until mixture comes to a boil. Add milk and vanilla; cook until thoroughly heated. Serve each cup with a cinnamon stick. Yield: 7 cups (about 116 calories per 1-cup serving).

Tip: To freshen air throughout the house, boil 1 tablespoon of whole cloves in a pan of water for a few minutes.

Roasts—New Ideas For An Old Favorite

Roast beef for dinner is hard to beat. Maybe it's popular because it's easy to put all the ingredients in the pot and come home to a completed meal. Or maybe it's because of the outstanding flavor of a tender, juicy roast. Whatever the reason, there are lots of ways to dress up this old favorite, and we offer four new ideas.

VEGETABLE-POT ROAST MEDLEY

1 (4-pound) top or bottom round roast
1 (10¾-ounce) can cream of mushroom soup, undiluted
1 cup dry red wine
1 cup chopped onion
2 cloves garlic, minced
1 tablespoon chopped fresh parsley
1 to 1½ teaspoons salt
1½ teaspoons pepper
10 medium potatoes, peeled and quartered
6 carrots, scraped and cut into 2-inch pieces

Place roast in a large Dutch oven or roaster. Combine soup and wine, mixing well; pour over roast. Add onion, garlic, parsley, salt, and pepper; cover and bake at 350° for 1½ hours.

Spoon pan drippings over roast; add vegetables. Reduce heat to 325° and bake 1½ hours or until roast is done and vegetables are tender. Yield: 8 to 10 servings.

Helen K. Smith, Imboden, Arkansas.

BARBECUED POT ROAST

1 (3-pound) beef chuck or shoulder roast
3 tablespoons vegetable oil
1 (8-ounce) can tomato sauce
½ cup water
3 medium onions, thinly sliced
2 cloves garlic, minced
2 teaspoons salt
¼ teaspoon pepper
2 tablespoons brown sugar
½ teaspoon dry mustard
¼ cup lemon juice
¼ cup catsup
¼ cup cider vinegar
1 tablespoon Worcestershire sauce

Brown roast on all sides in oil in a large Dutch oven; combine tomato sauce, water, onion, garlic, salt, and pepper, mixing well. Pour over roast; reduce heat, cover, and simmer 2 hours. Combine remaining ingredients, and pour over roast. Cover and simmer 1 hour or until tender. Yield: 5 to 6 servings.

Mrs. Ted Beckwith, Lebanon, Tennessee.

PEPPERY BRISKET ROAST

1 to 2 teaspoons celery salt
1 to 1½ teaspoons salt
½ to 1 teaspoon onion salt
½ to 1 teaspoon garlic salt
2 teaspoons pepper
1 tablespoon liquid smoke
2 teaspoons Worcestershire sauce
1 (3- to 4-pound) well-trimmed boneless beef brisket
3 tablespoons brown sugar
1 tablespoon dry mustard
Dash of ground nutmeg
½ cup catsup
1 tablespoon soy sauce
1 tablespoon lemon juice
3 drops of hot sauce

Combine first 7 ingredients, mixing well; spread brisket evenly with mixture, and place in a lightly greased 13- x 9- x 2-inch baking dish. Cover and chill 8 to 10 hours or overnight.

Allow brisket to come to room temperature; cover and bake at 300° for 30 minutes. Combine remaining ingredients; mix well and pour over brisket. Cover and bake 1 to 1½ hours or until tender. Yield: 6 to 8 servings.

Lucille Davis, Whitesboro, Texas.

JAVA ROAST

½ small onion
2 cloves garlic
1 (4- to 5-pound) beef chuck or shoulder roast
1 cup vinegar
Vegetable oil
2 cups strong coffee
2 cups water
2 teaspoons salt
½ teaspoon pepper

Cut onion and garlic into small strips; pierce roast at intervals, inserting onion and garlic. Place roast in a large dish, and pour vinegar over top. Cover and refrigerate overnight; drain off vinegar.

Brown roast on all sides in hot oil in a large Dutch oven; add coffee, water, salt, and pepper. Reduce heat, cover, and simmer 3 to 3½ hours. Yield: 8 to 10 servings.

Mrs. Jack Hudgens, Welling, Oklahoma.

Meats Dressed Up For The Holidays

A great holiday meal calls for a very special main dish. Here are some tasty suggestions.

BEEF WELLINGTON

1 tablespoon meat tenderizer
1 (3-pound) boneless eye of round beef roast
3 tablespoons butter or margarine
1 (8-ounce) package liverwurst spread
1 cup chopped fresh mushrooms
2 tablespoons bourbon
2 (10-ounce) packages frozen patty shells, thawed
1 egg yolk
1 tablespoon whipping cream

Sprinkle meat tenderizer on all sides of roast; pierce with a fork. Brown roast on all sides in butter in a large skillet; set aside.

Combine liverwurst spread, mushrooms, and bourbon; beat well, and set aside.

Gently press edges of patty shells together on a lightly floured surface. Roll patty shells into a ⅛-inch-thick rectangle. Spread one-third of liverwurst mixture over top of roast. Place roast lengthwise in middle of pastry, top side down. Spread remaining liverwurst mixture over sides of roast. Bring sides of pastry up to overlap on underside of roast; overlap slightly to form a seam, trimming off excess pastry. Trim ends of pastry to make even; fold over ends of pastry to seal. Invert roast.

Combine egg yolk and whipping cream; brush evenly over pastry. Roll out pastry trimmings; cut into decorative shapes and arrange on top of pastry, as desired. Brush shapes with remaining yolk mixture. Bake, uncovered, in a lightly greased 13- x 9- x 2-inch baking pan at 425° for 1 hour. Transfer to serving platter. Let stand 10 minutes before slicing. Yield: 8 to 10 servings.

Laurie C. Beppler, Norfolk, Virginia.

HONEY-ORANGE GLAZED HAM

1 (5- to 7-pound) uncooked ham
1 (6-ounce) can frozen orange juice
    concentrate, thawed and undiluted
1¾ cups water
¾ cup honey
1½ tablespoons cornstarch

Place ham, fat side up, in a 13- x 9- x 2-inch baking pan; set aside.

Combine remaining ingredients in a medium saucepan, stirring well. Cook over medium heat until thickened, stirring constantly.

Pour half of glaze mixture over ham; bake, uncovered, at 325° for 2 to 2¾ hours (22 to 25 minutes per pound).

Remove ham from oven 30 minutes before cooking time is complete. Score ham in a diamond pattern, making cuts ¼ inch deep in ham fat. Spoon remaining glaze mixture over ham, and return ham to oven. Bake, uncovered, for 30 minutes, basting frequently. Yield: 10 to 12 servings.
Mrs. Parke Cory,
Neosho, Missouri.

FRUIT-STUFFED GOOSE

1 (9- to 10-pound) dressed goose
3½ cups soft breadcrumbs
1½ cups peeled, chopped cooking
    apples
½ cup raisins
½ cup chopped onion
½ cup butter or margarine, melted
2 teaspoons salt
1 teaspoon rubbed sage
1 teaspoon dried whole rosemary
⅛ teaspoon pepper
Fresh parsley sprigs (optional)
Grapes (optional)
Apples (optional)
Oranges (optional)

Remove giblets and neck from goose; reserve for gravy, if desired. Rinse goose thoroughly with water; pat dry.

Combine next 9 ingredients, stirring well. Spoon dressing into cavity of goose; close with skewers. Truss goose, and place breast side up on rack in a roasting pan. Insert meat thermometer in meaty part of thigh or breast, making sure bulb does not touch bone. Bake, uncovered, at 350° for 4 hours or until meat thermometer registers 185° and drumsticks move easily. Baste occasionally with pan drippings. Place goose on a serving platter; garnish with parsley, grapes, apples, and oranges, if desired. Yield: 5 to 7 servings.
Mrs. J. C. Graham,
Athens, Texas.

BAKED PARMESAN CHICKEN

1 egg, beaten
1 tablespoon milk
½ cup grated Parmesan cheese
¼ cup all-purpose flour
1 teaspoon paprika
½ teaspoon salt
Dash of pepper
1 (2½- to 3-pound) broiler-fryer, cut up
    and skinned
¼ cup butter or margarine, melted

Combine egg and milk; stir well and set aside. Combine cheese, flour, paprika, salt, and pepper; mix well.

Rinse chicken, and pat dry. Dip in egg mixture, dredge in flour mixture. Place chicken in a 12- x 8- x 2-inch baking dish; pour butter over chicken. Bake at 350° for 1 hour or until tender. Yield: 4 servings.
Mrs. Alfred L. Stancill,
Bel Air, Maryland.

Stuff A Turkey Breast For Dinner

If you don't want lots of turkey leftovers this year, try a stuffed turkey breast rather than a whole turkey. Our recipe for Turkey Breast With Seasoned Dressing is an excellent entrée for serving 10 to 12 guests.

You can have a butcher bone the breast for you, or do it yourself. Bone it just as you would a whole chicken breast.

STUFFED TURKEY BREAST WITH SEASONED DRESSING

1 medium onion, finely chopped
½ cup butter or margarine
1 cup water
2 chicken-flavored bouillon cubes
2 teaspoons dried green pepper
    flakes
2 teaspoons dried parsley flakes
1 teaspoon dried celery flakes
1 teaspoon poultry seasoning
8 slices day-old bread, cut into
    ½-inch cubes
1 (6-pound) whole turkey breast
¼ teaspoon salt
¼ teaspoon pepper
¼ cup butter or margarine, melted

Sauté onion in ½ cup butter in a large skillet. Add next 6 ingredients and

simmer 5 minutes, stirring to dissolve bouillon cubes. Add bread; stir until mixture is moistened.

Bone turkey breast, leaving skin intact. Cut a pocket two-thirds through each side toward the center; sprinkle each pocket with salt and pepper. Stuff pockets with bread mixture, and secure with wooden picks. Place turkey, skin side up, in a shallow baking pan. Insert meat thermometer making sure bulb rests in meat of turkey. Bake at 325° for 1 hour and 15 minutes or until meat thermometer registers 185°, basting with ¼ cup butter. Yield: 10 to 12 servings.
Mrs. E. T. Williams,
Baton Rouge, Louisiana.

Shrimp Decorate This Tree

This shrimp tree is not only a decorative centerpiece, it's a delicious appetizer, as well. Made of plastic foam covered with endive, it can be assembled quickly and easily.

To completely cover the tree, you'll need about 4 bunches of endive. Wash and separate each bunch, and remove the tough ends of each leaf. Begin by attaching leaves to the bottom of the cone, and move upward; then cover the plastic foam base, and fill in any holes.

After decorating the tree with shrimp, crown it with a bow or Christmas ornament. Place the bowls of Mustard Sauce and Holiday Dip on the endive-covered base, and arrange cherry tomatoes or other raw vegetables between.

SPICY BOILED SHRIMP

10 peppercorns
4 whole cloves
3 bay leaves
½ teaspoon mustard seeds
½ teaspoon dried whole oregano
½ teaspoon dried whole basil
½ teaspoon crushed red pepper
⅛ teaspoon celery seeds
Dash of dried whole thyme
½ teaspoon salt
1 lime, halved
1 lemon, halved
1 clove garlic, crushed
3 pounds fresh large or jumbo shrimp,
    unpeeled

Combine first 9 ingredients in a doubled cheesecloth bag; tie securely with string. Bring 2½ quarts water to a boil in a large Dutch oven. Add salt, lime, lemon, garlic, and herb bag; return to a boil, and cook 2 to 3 minutes. Add shrimp and return to a boil. Reduce heat and simmer, uncovered, 3 to 5 minutes. Drain well; rinse with cold water. Chill. Peel and devein shrimp, leaving tails on, if desired. Yield: 12 appetizer servings.

HOLIDAY DIP

1 cup mayonnaise
⅓ cup minced onion
¼ cup catsup
¼ cup chili sauce
2 cloves garlic, minced
1 teaspoon dry mustard
1 teaspoon pepper
Dash of paprika
Dash of hot sauce

Combine all ingredients; stir well. Cover and chill 2 to 3 hours. Serve with boiled shrimp. Yield: 2 cups.
Mrs. R. L. Bryant,
Franklin, Virginia.

MUSTARD SAUCE

1½ cups mayonnaise
½ cup prepared Creole mustard
1 to 2 tablespoons prepared horseradish
2 tablespoons lemon juice

Combine all ingredients; stir well. Cover and chill 2 to 3 hours. Serve with boiled shrimp. Yield: about 2¼ cups.
Patrick I. Greer,
Meridian, Mississippi.

Our shrimp tree is great for holiday entertaining. Let guests remove Spicy Boiled Shrimp from the endive-covered tree and dip them in Mustard Sauce or Holiday Dip.

With wooden picks, secure a 12-inch plastic foam cone to one corner of a 12- x 12- x 1-inch plastic foam base.

Use florist picks to attach endive to the cone and base, beginning at the bottom and working upward.

Gently spear each shrimp with a wooden pick, and attach to the tree in an appealing pattern.

Save Room For Winter Vegetables

You don't have to give up fresh vegetables just because the weather turns cold. In fact, you'll find some vegetables are plentiful during the winter—cauliflower, carrots, and brussels sprouts are just a few.

For an attractive cauliflower dish, we suggest topping the crisp-tender cooked flowerets with chopped parsley, hard-cooked egg yolks, and breadcrumbs; a sprinkling of lemon juice adds to the flavor.

The key to appealing brussels sprouts is to cook them just until done—no longer. In her Creamed Brussels Sprouts and Celery, Betty Bowles of Charlotte recommends cooking the sprouts 5 to 10 minutes before combining them with a crunchy celery sauce.

Carrots are always available, but winter shoppers will want to try adding hot sauce and sesame seeds to make Deviled Carrots.

BROCCOLI-SWISS CHEESE CASSEROLE

1 (24-ounce) carton cream-style cottage cheese
3 eggs
¼ cup plus 2 tablespoons butter or margarine, melted and divided
⅓ cup all-purpose flour
4 cups chopped, cooked broccoli
2 cups (8 ounces) shredded Swiss cheese
1 (8¾-ounce) can whole kernel corn, drained
¼ cup finely chopped onion
½ teaspoon salt
¼ teaspoon pepper
4 drops of hot sauce
⅓ cup soft breadcrumbs
½ cup cooked, crumbled bacon

Combine cottage cheese, eggs, ¼ cup butter, and flour in container of electric blender; process until smooth. Set mixture aside.

Combine next 7 ingredients, and stir in cottage cheese mixture. Pour into a greased, shallow 2-quart casserole.

Sauté breadcrumbs in remaining 2 tablespoons butter; add bacon, and sprinkle over top of casserole. Bake at 350° for 45 minutes. Yield: 8 to 10 servings.
Mrs. Carl Smith,
Melbourne, Florida.

CREAMED BRUSSELS SPROUTS AND CELERY

1 pound fresh brussels sprouts
2 cups sliced celery
1 medium onion, chopped
3 tablespoons butter or margarine, melted
3 tablespoons all-purpose flour
½ teaspoon celery salt
1 (10¾-ounce) can chicken broth, undiluted

Place brussels sprouts in a small amount of boiling water. Cover, reduce heat, and simmer 5 to 10 minutes or until tender; drain and set aside.

Sauté celery and onion in butter until tender. Add flour and celery salt, stirring until smooth. Cook 1 minute, stirring constantly. Gradually add chicken broth; cook over medium heat, stirring constantly, until mixture is thickened and bubbly. Add brussels sprouts, and stir gently. Cook 1 minute or until thoroughly heated. Yield: 6 servings.
Betty Bowles,
Charlotte, North Carolina.

EASY LEMON CAULIFLOWER

1 tablespoon butter or margarine, melted
⅓ cup soft breadcrumbs
1 medium head cauliflower
1 teaspoon salt
2 tablespoons lemon juice
1 tablespoon chopped fresh parsley
2 hard-cooked egg yolks, finely chopped

Combine butter and breadcrumbs in a small skillet. Cook, stirring constantly, until breadcrumbs are lightly browned. Set aside.

Wash cauliflower, and break into flowerets. Add salt to a small amount of water; bring to a boil. Add cauliflower and cook, covered, 10 minutes or until crisp-tender; drain. Place cauliflower on a serving platter. Sprinkle with lemon juice. Top with breadcrumbs, parsley, and egg yolks. Yield: 6 servings.
Geneva P. Tobias,
Albemarle, North Carolina.

DEVILED CARROTS

6 large carrots, scraped and cut into ¼-inch slices
¼ cup butter or margarine, melted
2 tablespoons brown sugar
1 teaspoon dry mustard
¼ teaspoon salt
3 drops of hot sauce
Pinch of coarsely ground black pepper
1½ teaspoons chopped fresh parsley
1 teaspoon sesame seeds, toasted

Sauté carrots in butter over medium heat 5 minutes, stirring occasionally. Add next 5 ingredients; cook over low heat, 6 to 8 minutes or until carrots are crisp-tender.

Sprinkle carrots with parsley and sesame seeds before serving. Yield: 4 servings.
Mrs. Richard L. Brownell,
Salisbury, North Carolina.

STUFFED BAKED POTATOES

2 large baking potatoes
Vegetable oil
4 slices bacon
¼ cup chopped green onion
½ cup commercial sour cream
2 tablespoons grated Parmesan cheese
½ teaspoon salt
½ teaspoon white pepper
Paprika

Wash potatoes, and rub with oil. Bake at 400° for 1 hour or until done. Allow potatoes to cool to the touch. Cut potatoes in half lengthwise; carefully scoop out pulp, leaving shells intact. Mash pulp.

Cook bacon in a large skillet until crisp; remove bacon, reserving 3 tablespoons drippings in skillet. Crumble bacon, and set aside. Sauté onion in bacon drippings until tender.

Combine potato pulp, bacon, onion, and next 4 ingredients; mix well. Stuff shells with potato mixture, and sprinkle with paprika. Place stuffed potatoes on a baking sheet. Bake at 350° for 15 to 20 minutes. Yield: 4 servings.
Linda Keeton,
Memphis, Tennessee.

Tip: A special topping for cooked vegetables or casseroles can be made by crushing ½ cup herb-seasoned stuffing mix with 2 tablespoons melted butter or margarine; top dish with this mixture and sprinkle with 1 cup shredded cheese.

From Our Kitchen To Yours

Are you tempted to stop by the bakery to pick up dinner rolls for your special holiday meals? If so, just pull out your best yeast roll recipe and create those butter-rich, irresistible, homemade treats yourself. And as you're making them, try some of our test kitchens staff's favorite shapes, glazes, and toppings for dinner rolls. With a few twists, turns, and sprinkles, your rolls will take on a professionally made look—yet have the aroma and goodness of home-baked bread.

We've included directions and illustrations for bowties, butterfans, and other shapes of rolls. The shapes will be easy to adapt for most any yeast roll recipe; just make sure the recipe makes a rather firm dough. If the dough is too soft, the rolls won't hold their shape.

After the rolls are shaped and have risen, very gently but thoroughly brush the rolls with one of the following glazes:

—A whole egg or egg yolk beaten with a little water makes the rolls shiny and golden.

—An egg white-water glaze can be used to hold toppings such as poppy seeds and sesame seeds in place. Try sprinkling some rolls with poppy seeds and others with sesame seeds; this makes for an eye-catching bread basket.

—Melted butter is often brushed on rolls just before baking, but you'll probably want to add more butter after baking for extra flavor and shine.

Crescents

If using a recipe with 3 to 4 cups of flour, you'll need to divide dough in half. Roll one portion of dough into a 12-inch circle on a lightly floured surface. Spread softened butter over dough. Cut into 12 wedges; roll each wedge tightly, beginning at wide end. Seal points, and place rolls on a greased baking sheet, curving into a half-moon shape. Cover and let rise until doubled in bulk. Bake.

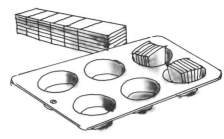

Butterfans

Roll dough into a large rectangle about ¼ inch thick. Spread softened butter over dough. Cut lengthwise into 1-inch strips. Stack 5 or 6 strips, buttered side up, on top of one another. Cut each stack into 1-inch sections. Place each "stacked" section, cut side down, into greased muffin cups. Cover and let rise until doubled in bulk. Bake.

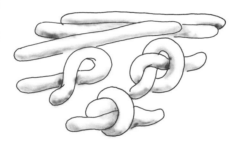

Bow Ties

Roll dough into several long ropes about ½ inch in diameter. Cut ropes into 8-inch strips. Carefully tie each dough strip in a knot. Place bow ties on a lightly greased baking sheet. Cover and let rise until doubled in bulk. Bake.

Easy Pan Rolls

Lightly grease one or two 9-inch cakepans. Shape dough into 1½-inch balls. Place balls in pans, leaving about ½ inch space between them. Cover and let rise until doubled in bulk. Bake.

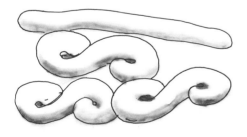

"S" Rolls

Divide dough into several small portions. Roll each portion into a 9-inch rope about ¾ to 1 inch thick. Place on greased baking sheets; curl ends in opposite directions in an "S" shape. Cover and let rise until doubled in bulk. Bake.

Hurry-Up Cloverleaf Rolls

Lightly grease muffin pans. Shape dough into 2-inch balls; place one ball in each muffin cup. Using scissors, make one X-shaped cut in each. Cover and let rise until doubled in bulk. Bake.

Traditional Cloverleaf Rolls

Lightly grease muffin pans. Shape dough into 1-inch balls; place 3 dough balls in each muffin cup. Cover and let rise until doubled in bulk. Bake.

Appendices

EQUIVALENT WEIGHTS AND MEASURES

Food	Weight or Count	Measure or Yield
Apples	1 pound (3 medium)	3 cups sliced
Bacon	8 slices cooked	½ cup crumbled
Bananas	1 pound (3 medium)	2½ cups sliced, or about 2 cups mashed
Bread	1 pound	12 to 16 slices
	About 1½ slices	1 cup soft crumbs
Butter or margarine	1 pound	2 cups
	¼-pound stick	½ cup
Cabbage	1 pound head	4½ cups shredded
Candied fruit or peels	½ pound	1¼ cups cut
Carrots	1 pound	3 cups shredded
Cheese, American or Cheddar	1 pound	About 4 cups shredded
cottage	1 pound	2 cups
cream	3-ounce package	6 tablespoons
Chocolate morsels	6-ounce package	1 cup
Cocoa	1 pound	4 cups
Coconut, flaked or shredded	1 pound	5 cups
Coffee	1 pound	80 tablespoons (40 cups perked)
Corn	2 medium ears	1 cup kernels
Cornmeal	1 pound	3 cups
Crab, in shell	1 pound	¾ to 1 cup flaked
Crackers, chocolate wafers	19 wafers	1 cup crumbs
graham crackers	14 squares	1 cup fine crumbs
saltine crackers	28 crackers	1 cup finely crushed
vanilla wafers	22 wafers	1 cup finely crushed
Cream, whipping	1 cup (½ pint)	2 cups whipped
Dates, pitted	1 pound	3 cups chopped
	8-ounce package	1½ cups chopped
Eggs	5 large	1 cup
whites	8 to 11	1 cup
yolks	12 to 14	1 cup
Flour, all-purpose	1 pound	3½ cups
cake	1 pound	4¾ to 5 cups sifted
whole wheat	1 pound	3½ cups unsifted
Green pepper	1 large	1 cup diced
Lemon	1 medium	2 to 3 tablespoons juice; 2 teaspoons grated rind
Lettuce	1 pound head	6¼ cups torn
Lime	1 medium	1½ to 2 tablespoons juice
Macaroni	4 ounces (1 cup)	2¼ cups cooked
Marshmallows	11 large	1 cup
	10 miniature	1 large marshmallow
Marshmallows, miniature	½ pound	4½ cups
Milk		
evaporated	5.33-ounce can	⅔ cup
evaporated	13-ounce can	1⅝ cups
sweetened condensed	14-ounce can	1¼ cups
Mushrooms	3 cups raw (8 ounces)	1 cup sliced cooked
Nuts		
almonds	1 pound	1 to 1¾ cups nutmeats
	1 pound shelled	3½ cups nutmeats
peanuts	1 pound	2¼ cups nutmeats
	1 pound shelled	3 cups
pecans	1 pound	2¼ cups nutmeats
	1 pound shelled	4 cups
walnuts	1 pound	1⅔ cups nutmeats
	1 pound shelled	4 cups

Food	Weight or Count	Measure or Yield
Oats, quick-cooking	1 cup	1¾ cups cooked
Onion	1 medium	½ cup chopped
Orange	1 medium	⅓ cup juice and 2 tablespoons grated rind
Peaches	4 medium	2 cups sliced
Pears	4 medium	2 cups sliced
Potatoes, white	3 medium	2 cups cubed cooked or 1¾ cups mashed
sweet	3 medium	3 cups sliced
Raisins, seedless	1 pound	3 cups
Rice, long-grain	1 cup	3 to 4 cups cooked
pre-cooked	1 cup	2 cups cooked
Shrimp, raw in shell	1½ pounds	2 cups (¾ pound) cleaned, cooked
Spaghetti	7 ounces	About 4 cups cooked
Strawberries	1 quart	4 cups sliced
Sugar, brown	1 pound	2⅓ cups firmly packed
powdered	1 pound	3½ cups unsifted
granulated	1 pound	2 cups

EQUIVALENT MEASUREMENTS

3 teaspoons	1 tablespoon		2 cups	1 pint (16 fluid ounces)
4 tablespoons...............	¼ cup		4 cups	1 quart
5⅓ tablespoons...............	⅓ cup		4 quarts	1 gallon
8 tablespoons...............	½ cup		⅛ cup.....................	2 tablespoons
16 tablespoons...............	1 cup		⅓ cup.....................	5 tablespoons plus 1 teaspoon
2 tablespoons (liquid) ...	1 ounce		⅔ cup.....................	10 tablespoons plus 2 teaspoons
1 cup........................	8 fluid ounces		¾ cup.....................	12 tablespoons

HANDY SUBSTITUTIONS

Ingredient Called For	Substitution
1 cup self-rising flour	1 cup all-purpose flour plus 1 teaspoon baking powder and ½ teaspoon salt
1 cup cake flour	1 cup sifted all-purpose flour minus 2 tablespoons
1 cup all-purpose flour	1 cup cake flour plus 2 tablespoons
1 teaspoon baking powder	½ teaspoon cream of tartar plus ¼ teaspoon soda
1 tablespoon cornstarch or arrowroot	2 tablespoons all-purpose flour
1 tablespoon tapioca	1½ tablespoons all-purpose flour
2 large eggs	3 small eggs
1 egg	2 egg yolks (for custard)
1 egg	2 egg yolks plus 1 tablespoon water (for cookies)
1 cup commercial sour cream	1 tablespoon lemon juice plus evaporated milk to equal 1 cup; or 3 tablespoons butter plus ⅞ cup sour milk
1 cup yogurt	1 cup buttermilk or sour milk
1 cup sour milk or buttermilk	1 tablespoon vinegar or lemon juice plus sweet milk to equal 1 cup
1 cup fresh milk	½ cup evaporated milk plus ½ cup water
1 cup fresh milk	3 to 5 tablespoons nonfat dry milk solids in 1 cup water
1 cup honey	1¼ cups sugar plus ¼ cup liquid
1 (1-ounce) square unsweetened chocolate	3 tablespoons cocoa plus 1 tablespoon butter or margarine
1 tablespoon fresh herbs	1 teaspoon dried herbs or ¼ teaspoon powdered herbs
¼ cup chopped fresh parsley	1 tablespoon dehydrated parsley
1 teaspoon dry mustard	1 tablespoon prepared mustard
1 pound fresh mushrooms	6 ounces canned mushrooms

Recipe Title Index

An alphabetical listing of every recipe by exact title
All microwave recipe page numbers are preceded by an "M"

Cabbage and Tomatoes, 104
Cabbage au Gratin, 279
Cabbage Medley, 104
Cabbage Relish, 260
Cabbage Rolls, 104
Cabbage Soup, 291
Cabbage Supreme, 206
Cabbage with Polish Sausage, 104
Cajun Red Beans and Rice, 26
Candied Bananas, 179
Candied Carrots, 225
Cantaloupe Soup, 120
Caramel Frosting, 43
Cardamom Coffee Cake, 246
Cardamom White Bread, 41
Carrot and Zucchini Casserole, 256
Carrot-and-Zucchini Salad, 240
Carrot-Nut Loaf, 117
Carrot-Orange Cookies, 149
Carrot Pie, 117
Carrot Pudding Cake, 24
Carrot-Raisin Salad, 117
Carrots in Brandy Sauce, 86
Carrots Madeira, 281
Carrots Marsala, 56
Carrot Soufflé, 265
Carrot-Tangerine Salad, 316
Cashew Chicken, 21
Cashew Shrimp Supreme, 29
Cauliflower-and-Carrot Casserole, 280
Cauliflower-Brussels Sprouts Salad, 240
Cauliflower Quiche, 86
Caviar Crown, 78
Caviar Mousse, 258
Celery-and-Cauliflower Salad, 39
Celery au Gratin, 38
Celery Oriental, 206
Chafing Dish Franks, 143
Champagne Delight, 304
Chantilly Cream, 91
Cheddar Cornbread, 285
Cheddar-Vegetable Omelet, 205
Cheese-and-Chile Dip, 31
Cheese-and-Mushroom Pizza, 226
Cheese Biscuits, 253
Cheese Blintzes, 71
Cheese Bread, 208
Cheese-Filled Phyllo Triangles, 259
Cheese 'n' Beef Ball, 230
Cheese Sauce, 49, 138, 188
Cheese Toast Treats, 100
Cheese Wontons with Hot Sauce, 74
Cheesy Anytime Soup, 66
Cheesy Asparagus Casserole, 32
Cheesy Beef Burgers, 217
Cheesy Beef-Stuffed Shells, 217
Cheesy Bread Pudding, 68
Cheesy Broccoli Bake, 255
Cheesy Broccoli Dip, 92
Cheesy Cherry Tomatoes, 135
Cheesy Chicken Tetrazzini, M87
Cheesy English Pea Casserole, 216
Cheesy Frank-Topped Potatoes, 3
Cheesy Green Onion Quiche, 194
Cheesy Hominy Casserole, 170
Cheesy Italian Broccoli Bake, 5
Cheesy Manicotti, 216
Cheesy Onion Dip, 145
Cheesy Parmesan Noodles, M7
Cheesy Pork Chops, 102
Cheesy Potato Casserole, 53
Cheesy Sausage Crêpes, 71
Cheesy Scalloped Potatoes, 82

Cheesy Spinach Lasagna, 204
Cheesy Vegetable Chowder, 20
Cheesy Zucchini Quiche, 312
Chef's Garden Salad, 146
Cherries Jubilee, 139
Cherry and Blackberry Tart, 225
Cherry Compote, 139
Cherry Filling, 302
Cherry Glaze, 143
Cherry Nut Fudge, 315
Cherry Salad with Honey-Lime
  Dressing, 139
Cherry Sauce, 276
Cherry Slump, 139
Cherry Tomatoes with Rum, 192
Chervil Butter, 129
Chervil Sauce, 128
Chewy Marshmallow Brownies, 306
Chicken à la King, 137
Chicken alla Romano, M58
Chicken-Almond Pocket Sandwiches, 69
Chicken-and-Spinach Tossed Salad, 157
Chicken-Asparagus Casserole, 76
Chicken-Avocado Kabobs, 68
Chicken-Avocado Salad Platter, 2
Chicken Cacciatore, 118
Chicken Chowder, 20
Chicken in Lemon and Wine, 281
Chicken in Orange Sauce, 8
Chicken Jewel Ring Salad, 282
Chicken Liver Pâté, 108
Chicken Livers in Italian Sauce, 117
Chicken Marsala, 137
Chicken Parmesan, 184
Chicken Pasquale, 67
Chicken-Pea Salad, 218
Chicken Piccata, 35
Chicken Rollups in Gravy, 184
Chicken Salad Mold, 80
Chicken Spaghetti, 105
Chicken Stack-Up Salad, 80
Chicken Tetrazzini, 288
Chicken-Tomato Bake, 35
Chicken-Vegetable Crêpes, 70
Chicken-Vegetable Stir-Fry, 151
Chicken with Snow Peas, 137
Chiles Rellenos, 150
Chili con Carne, 30
Chili Meat Sauce, 4
Chili-Tamale Pie, 68
Chili-Topped Potatoes, 3
Chilled Chocolate Dessert, 177
Chilled Coconut Dessert, 116
Chilled Fruit Compote, 123
Chinese Beef Stir-Fry, 151
Chinese Fruit Medley, 22
Chinese Meatballs, 116
Chinese Spinach Sauté, 208
Chocolate-Almond Frosting, 241
Chocolate Brittle, 315
Chocolate-Caramel-Nut Cake, 23
Chocolate Chip Coffee Cake, 231
Chocolate Chip Squares, 170
Chocolate-Coconut Cake, 23
Chocolate-Coconut Pie Shell, 100
Chocolate Cream Pie, 192
Chocolate Doughnuts, 95
Chocolate Dream Dessert, 198
Chocolate Frosting, 79, 99, M233, 253
Chocolate Fudge Frosting, 105
Chocolate Glaze, 220
Chocolate Macaroons, 300
Chocolate-Marshmallow Frosting, 245

Chocolate Mayonnaise Cake, 99
Chocolate Meringue Pie, 158
Chocolate Mint Snaps, 103
Chocolate Mousse Roll, 290
Chocolate-Peanut Cookies, 223
Chocolate Pecan Pie, 12
Chocolate Pie Amandine, 300
Chocolate Sauce, 189
Chocolate-Sour Cream Pound Cake, 239
Chocolate Tea Brownies, 79
Christmas Fruit Tea, 275
Chunky Navy Bean Soup, 291
Chutney Roll, 259
Cider Baked Turkey, 263
Cider Ice, 162
Cinnamon Coffee Cake, M203
Cinnamon Sticky Buns, 244
Cinnamon Twists, 53
Citrus-Nut Bread, 294
Citrus Party Punch, 141
Clam Quiche, 215
Cocktail Cheese Ball, 174
Cocoa-Coffee, 55
Cocoa-Kahlúa Sundaes, M58
Coconut Bread, 140
Coconut Fruit Bowl, 111
Coconut Nog, 275
Coconut-Pecan Frosting, M233
Coconut-Pineapple Drink, 172
Coffee Punch, 275
Coffee Sponge Cake, 229
Coleslaw with Grapes and Almonds, 59
Company Beef Stew, 85
Company Broccoli Bake, 279
Company Chicken, 125
Company Chili, 30
Company Cornish Hens, 263
Congealed Asparagus Salad, 260
Cool Gazpacho, 140
Coquilles St. Jacques Crêpes, 13
Corkscrew Macaroni Toss, 163
Corn-and-Ham Skillet Dinner, 190
Corn and Zucchini, 190
Cornbread-and-Sausage Dressing, 213
Cornbread Skillet Casserole, 243
Corn Burger Pie, 156
Corn Chowder, 20
Corned Beef and Cabbage, 104
Corned Beef and Cabbage au Gratin, 16
Corned Beef-Cauliflower Salad, 16
Corned Beef Sandwiches, 291
Corned Beef Soup, 16
Cornish Hens with Tarragon, 143
Corn Relish, 189
Cottage Cheese-Dill Bread, 154
Country-Fried Venison Steak, 262
Country Grits and Sausage, 54
Country Pecan Muffins, 222
Country Pie, 155
Country-Style Coleslaw, 59
Crab and Shrimp Sauce Piquante, 92
Crabmeat Imperial, 72
Crabmeat-Topped Potatoes, 3
Crab Snacks, 93
Cracked Pepper Steak, 109
Cranapple Punch, 142
Cranberry-Apple Casserole, 311
Cranberry Chutney, 260
Cranberry Conserve, 279
Cranberry Holiday Tarts, 279
Cranberry-Pear Crisp, 207
Cranberry-Pear Wild Rice, 279
Cranberry Punch, 275

Month-by-Month Index

An alphabetical listing within the month of every food article and accompanying recipes
All microwave recipe page numbers are preceded by an "M"

Month-by-Month Index   339

General Recipe Index

A listing of every recipe by food category and/or major ingredient
All microwave recipe page numbers are preceded by an "M"

General Recipe Index   357

THE Magazine For You
if You Share Our Interest
in the South.

SOUTHERN LIVING
features articles to help make
life for you and your
family more comfortable,
more stimulating, more fun...

SOUTHERN LIVING is about your home and how to make a more attractive, more convenient, more comfortable place to live. Each issue brings you dozens of decorating and remodeling ideas you can adapt to your own surroundings.

SOUTHERN LIVING is about gardening and landscaping and how to make the outside of your home just as attractive as the inside. In addition to gardening features, you'll find a monthly garden calendar pinpointing what to plant and when, plus a "Letters to our Garden Editor" section to answer your own particular questions.

SOUTHERN LIVING is about good food and entertaining, with recipes and menu ideas that are sure to delight your family and friends. You'll discover recipes with a Southern accent from some of the South's superlative cooks.

SOUTHERN LIVING is about travel and just plain fun. Every new issue offers an information-packed monthly calendar of special events and happenings throughout the South, plus features on the many fascinating places of interest the South has to offer.

To find out how you can receive SOUTHERN LIVING every month, simply write to: SOUTHERN LIVING, P. O. Box C-119, Birmingham, AL 35283.